How to Make Profits In Commodities

W. D. Gann

MORE PROFITS IN COMMODITIES THAN STOCKS

FOREWORD:

I am writing this book to supply a universal demand: and give rules that will forecast the trend of commodities. Conditions have changed rapidly during the last few years and will change more rapidly after this great war is over than ever before in history. Men will return to the soil of Mother Nature to make a living. Investors and speculators will have to look for new ways to make money in the future and will find it more difficult in the stock market; therefore, the necessities of life, the basic commodities, will offer greater opportunities than investments in stocks and bonds, providing the trader knows the rules to follow.

My object is to write something that will be helpful to people in trade lines and to those who have long years of experience in the commodity market, as well as the inexperienced trader who wants knowledge and needs to learn the ways to start right, and to protect his capital and make profits. Life affords no greater pleasure than that of helping others who are trying to help themselves.

I am going to give the best of my forty years of experience in this book, and I hope to show others the way to help themselves and follow mathematical rules in the commodity market, which will result in profits. I do not believe in gambling or reckless speculation, but am firmly convinced, after years of experience, that if traders will follow rules and trade on definite indications, that speculation can be made a profitable profession. Trading in commodities is not a gambling business, as some people think, but a practical, safe business when conducted on business principles.

I offer this book to the public with a sincere conviction that if they put in the time studying, they will derive great benefits.

W. D. GANN

INDEX

CHAPTER I

CHAPTER II

CHAPTER III

CHAPTER IV

NEW RULES FOR TRADING IN COMMODITIES

HOW TO MAKE PROFITS IN COMMODITIES
CAN MONEY BE MADE IN COMMODITY FUTURES?

If I were not thoroughly convinced by actual experience, that money can be made trading in commodity futures, I would not write this book. I have made a success in the business, and I know that anyone else can make a success, if they follow rules.

WHY YOU CAN MAKE MORE PROFITS TRADING IN COMMODITIES THAN STOCKS

1. Commodities follow a seasonal trend and are much easier to forecast. They move with supply and demand.

2. It requires much less work to keep up charts and calculations on Commodities. There are 1200 stocks listed on the New York Stock Exchange and you must keep a separate chart on as many of them as you wish to forecast the trend. With Cotton, you need one to three charts, and the same with Grain and other Commodities.

3. When you have a forecast made up for Cotton or Grain, if you are right, you are sure to make money because all options follow the same trend. There are no cross-currents, as in stocks, with some stocks declining to new low levels and others making new highs.

4. In dealing in Futures, there are no heavy interest charges as there are when long of stocks and no dividends to pay as when short of stocks.

5. Dividends can be suddenly passed or declared which will affect stock prices. This cannot happen to commodities.

6. Pools cannot manipulate a commodity as they can a stock.

7. Facts about commodities are generally known while many stocks are mystery stocks all the time and some stocks are subject to false rumors.

8. The stages of the business cycle tell more about the prices of the commodities than they do about stocks.

9. Commodities are governed only by demand and supply. This is not always true of stocks.

10. Speculation in commodities is more legitimate than speculation in stocks because you are dealing in necessities.

11. Commodities are consumed. Stocks are not. This has a bearing upon the ease of forecasting commodity prices.

12. You can forecast tops and bottoms of commodities with greater certainty than of stocks.

13. Stock prices tend to move by groups of stocks, while commodities move independently.

14. Notable speculators like Armour, Patton, Livermore and Dr. E. A. Crawford, have discovered after long experience that they can make money with greater certainty in commodities.

15. Stocks go into receivers' hands and go out of business. Commodities go on forever. Crops are planted and harvested each year.

16. There is always a demand by consumers for commodities, which is not the case with stocks.

17. Since the Securities Exchange Law was passed, marginal requirements are much higher on stocks than on Commodities. Therefore, you can make more money on the same capital by trading in Cotton, Wheat, Corn, Rubber or other Commodities, than you can by trading in Stocks.

18. When you learn the rules for forecasting and trading in Commodities, you will see that they never change, because there will always be wheat, corn, and cotton crops each year. These crops will be consumed, while stocks change and you have to study new stocks to keep up with changed conditions.

KNOWLEDGE IS POWER

Webster said, "The man who can teach me something is the man I want to know." King Solomon, credited with being one of the wisest men that ever lived, chose knowledge and understanding above everything else. "Wisdom is the principal thing: Therefore, get wisdom and with all thy getting, get understanding."—Proverbs 4-7.

The difference between success and failure in trading in Commodities is the difference between one man knowing and following fixed rules and the other man guessing. The man who guesses usually loses. Therefore, if you want to make a success and make profits, your object must be to know more; study all the time; *never* think that you know it all. I have been studying Stocks and Commodities for forty years, and I do not know it all yet. I expect to continue to learn something every year as long as I live. Observations, and keen comparisons of past market movements, will reveal what Commodities are going to do in the future, because the future is but a repetition of the past. Time spent in gaining knowledge is money in the bank. You can lose all of the money you may accumulate or that you may inherit—that is if you have no knowledge of how to take care of it—but with knowledge you can take a small amount of money and make more after time spent in gaining knowledge. A study of Commodities will return rich rewards.

CHAPTER I

FOUNDATION FOR SUCCESSFUL TRADING IN COMMODITIES

To those of you who have traded in Wheat, Corn, Cotton, or any other Commodity and have lost money, I ask you this question—"Did you ever stop and consider WHY you have lost money?" If you have, you must answer honestly that you have lost money because you were guessing, following brokers' opinions, or following someone's advice who thought he knew more about it than you did. You probably bought when good news had been discounted and sold when bad news had been discounted. You did not follow any well-defined plan, or fixed rule, and after you had made a mistake and made a loss, you did not make any change when you made the next trade, but continued in the same old rut, and the result was that most of the time you were loser on balance.

Another reason for your failure to make profits was because you did not admit to yourself that you could be wrong and did not protect yourself when you made the trade. However, you made the mistake or however you made the loss, the fault was your own, because you had no definite rule to know just when to buy and when to sell.

You should learn to trade on knowledge and eliminate fear and hope. When you are no longer influenced by hope or fear, and are guided by knowledge you will have the nerve to trade and make profits. When you learn the past history of a Commodity, learn the way it is running, what cycle it is in, and then make a trade on definite knowledge, your chances for success are 100% greater. You must learn to trade on facts and to eliminate hope and fear. Learn to protect your capital and profits by use of STOP LOSS ORDERS. Then you will make real profit. When you make a trade and you are wrong, and realize your mistake, there is only one way to correct that mistake, and that is to get out of the market or protect with a STOP LOSS ORDER, limiting your loss to a small percentage of your capital. Your STOP LOSS ORDER protects you in many ways. When you buy a Commodity and protect it with a STOP LOSS ORDER, 1, 2, 3 or 5 cents away, you have limited your loss and know that you cannot lose any more. If you buy or sell Cotton, Hide, Rubber, or any Commodities traded in cents per pound or bushel, protected with stop loss order 20, or 40 points away, risking $100.00 or $200.00 on a contract, you know how much you can lose, and you should be able to take this loss and still have capital to trade with again. A safe plan is to follow rules and that is the only way in which you can hope to make a success in the future.

Nothing will help you more than going over the past history for Commodities, studying its actions under different periods and applying the rules that I will give you later. If you know what a Commodity has done in the past, you have a better chance to determine what it will do in the future. Supply and demand govern the prices of Commodities and all of the buying and selling is recorded in the prices.

If you study price movements correctly, they will tell you more about what the market is going to do than any broker, newspaper, or so-called inside information. The time period is the most essential, because time tells what prices are going to do.

LEARN TO BE INDEPENDENT: The greatest help that I can give you is to show you how to help yourself. If a man or woman depends upon others for advice, or for inside information and follows what others think about Commodities, he will never make a success in speculation—or anything else. You must learn to be independent. Learn to do by doing, and to know by study and application. When you are following something that you KNOW, you will have the confidence and courage to be successful.

An intelligent man will not follow blindly the opinion of others, without knowing the basis of their opinion. When he himself sees, understands and knows the rules that forecast the trends of Commodities, he will become a successful man, and knowledge will give him the nerve to carry out his conviction. Then he will no longer say, "If I knew that the information I received on wheat was right, I would buy 100,000 bushels, or sell 100,000 bushels." When he knows, based on study, that the indication on Wheat is definite, then he will buy, not with fear or hope, but with confidence and courage.

No matter what business you are interested in, learn all you can about it. The most important thing outside of your health for you to protect is your money. Therefore, take time to study. Prepare yourself to handle your money yourself and do not depend forever and entirely upon others.

A DEFINITE PLAN: Make up your mind to have a definite plan or aim in the future. Decide to follow rules when you buy or sell Commodities.

First, prove to yourself that the rules that I give you are good. They have worked in the past and they will work in the future. The rules given in this book are practical rules. They have cost me forty years of experience and hundreds of thousands of dollars to learn. I KNOW they will work. Don't take my word for it. Prove to yourself that they are good. You will have to put in time for study. You will have to make sacrifices. But, if you are not willing to work and make sacrifices, you will not make a success at anything. I have studied and improved my methods every year for the past forty years. I am still learning. I hope to make greater discoveries in the future.

After long years of study and research, I have simplified and perfected my rules so that they are practical for others to use and apply. I have eliminated unnecessary details, and have cut down the work so you can get results quicker. You can make profits by strictly adhering to rules. Make up your mind. If you are *not* going to follow rules, don't start speculating or trading in Commodities—or anything else for you will lose in the end.

KNOWLEDGE BRINGS SUCCESS. There is only one key which unlocks the door to big profits and that key is KNOWLEDGE. You cannot get knowledge without work. I have made a success by hard work and you, too, can make plenty of profits out of the Commodity market, if you study and work hard enough. Work is the only way to find the ROYAL ROAD TO RICHES in Commodity trading or speculating. Money always comes to knowledge. Without knowledge, money is worthless. You can increase your capital and make wise investments when you have acquired the proper knowledge.

QUALIFICATIONS FOR SUCCESS

1. KNOWLEDGE. I cannot say too much about the gaining of knowledge. You cannot get knowledge without spending time in study. You must not look for a quick and easy way to make money in the Commodity market. When you have paid in advance with time and study, and gained the knowledge, then you will find it easy to make money. The more time you put in gaining knowledge, the more money you will make later. Knowledge is not enough. You must put into use what you learn in order to benefit. You will learn by doing. Action and execution at the proper time bring profits.

2. PATIENCE. This is one of the very important qualifications for success in trading in commodities. First, you must have the patience to wait for an opportunity to determine a definite buying or selling point. When you make a trade, you must have the patience to wait for opportunities to get out right, or to make the profit. You must determine a definite change in trend before you close a trade to take profits. This only results from study of past market movement, and from acquiring the proper knowledge.

3. NERVE. A man can have the finest gun in the world, but if he hasn't the nerve to pull the trigger he will never kill any game. You can have all the knowledge in the world, but if you haven't the nerve to buy and sell you cannot make profit. Knowledge gives a man nerve, makes him bold and enables him to act at the right time. When a man fails to buy or sell at the right time, the result is that he becomes afraid. Fear is a detrimental influence. When he has too much nerve and buys on hope at the top, he is guessing. When influenced by hope alone, he cannot expect profits.

4. GOOD HEALTH. No man makes a great success in any business, unless his health is good, because a brilliant mind cannot work successfully with a weakened body. You will not have the proper patience or enough nerve, if your health is impaired. When you are in bad health, you become despondent, you lose hope, you have too much fear, and you will be unable to act at the right time.

I have been through the game through all of these years. Anything that could happen in the future in trading has happened to me. I have learned through experience. I have tried to trade when I was in bad health, always resulting in failure, but when I am in good physical condition, I act at the right time, making a success. If your health gives away, the most important thing is to work to get your health back in perfect shape, for HEALTH is WEALTH.

5. CAPITAL. When you have acquired all other qualifications for making a success trading in Commodities, you must, of course, have capital, but if you have KNOWLEDGE and PATIENCE, you can start with small capital and make large profits, provided you use STOP LOSS ORDERS; take small losses and do not OVERTRADE.

Remember, NEVER BUCK THE TREND. After you determine the trend of the market, go with it and regardless of what you think, hope, or fear, you will make a success. Follow rules to determine the trend and do not work on hope or guess work.

FACTS YOU SHOULD KNOW ABOUT
TRADING IN COMMODITIES

HOW TO READ THE GRAIN OR COTTON TAPE. Many people outside of New York and Chicago have the opinion that they could make a great success if they could go to Chicago and read the grain tape there, or if they could go to New York and read the Cotton tape, or the tape on any other Commodity. To stand in a brokerage office or sit in a brokerage office and try to beat the market by reading the ticker and watching every quotation that comes out, is the most foolish thing a man could do, and the greatest waste of time, and the man who thinks that is the way to make money trading in Commodities is making the mistake of his life. Those of us who have tried it, know. Expert tape readers are few and far between. It is a study of a lifetime, and while the tape does show the trend of the market, there are so many minor changes and quick reversals that the average man cannot tell whether the main trend has turned or whether it is only a minor change that will last a few hours, a few days, or a few weeks before the main trend is resumed again.

Ask any honest broker what percentage of traders who stay in the broker's office all the time and watch the tape make a success. If he is frank, he will tell you that 98% of them lose their money over a period of years. This is no fault of the broker, and no fault of the business. The trader invites the misfortune upon himself by trying to make a success by trading in the wrong way and not following rules. While, in a brokerage office you hear too many rumors, you get too many opinions, and there is no human being with a mind so strong that he cannot be influenced at times. You get too much gossip; you hear too much about large traders who are buying and selling and you do not always know whether these large traders are buying for long account or covering shorts, or just what the buying or selling means. If beating the Commodity market or making profits by trading were this easy, everybody would be rich.

Remember, you must pay in advance for what you get by time and study, and the time you spend in a brokerage office is wasted in most cases. There are too many disturbances, too many cross currents, in a brokerage office or around a ticker—too many ways to get you wrong.

You make a greater success when you sit at home or in your office, quietly follow your charts and trade on definite indications.

I am not guessing or giving you a wild theory. I have gone through the mills. I have had every ticker in my office for years. I have thought I could not get along without them, and lost plenty of money by having them in the office and getting in wrong because the ticker showed some minor trend and threw me off the main trend which I had figured. I made a greater success when I took all of the tickers out of my office and have not had a ticker in my office for the past ten years.

Therefore, my advice to you is not to try to learn to read the tape in a brokerage office, or to stand in the office and watch the tape. You can't make money that way. Follow the rules that I shall give you later. Study the charts and then you will know how to read the tape in a mathematical, scientific way and you will make profits instead of losses.

How the Tape Fools You. The tape does not fool traders. The traders fool themselves, because when the market is moving very fast and Wheat, Corn, Cotton or any other Commodity is moving up very fast, it increases the imagination of the man who is watching the market too closely. It causes him to become too optimistic and have too much hope, and he buys often right on top of a particular move, then a reaction follows, and after the reaction runs for several hours or several days, the market starts moving fast from the down side and the man's hope changes to fear, and he sells out at the market, often at the bottom.

When you get too close to anything, especially to the ticker tape, it warps your judgment, and causes you not to follow rules or act on a well-defined plan, but to trade on hope or fear. A man cannot watch the tape and not be influenced by hope or fear.

Suppose that a trader has been watching the grain tape or the cotton tape all day and the market has been constantly advancing. Then around 2:00 P. M. the market suddenly starts to decline rapidly and gets weaker near the close. The man who is watching the tape thinks the market looks very weak and he sells out, maybe goes short. The result of this decline in the last half hour or the last fifteen minutes was floor traders evening up. They often do not carry anything over night, because they do not have to pay any commission. Therefore, the selling or buying of floor-traders in the last fifteen to thirty minutes may cause the market to appear to have a change in trend, while on the other hand, there has been no change in the main trend. The next morning when buying orders come in, the main trend moves right on up, and the man who sold out because he was scared the night before has lost his position and may not get in again until the market is very much higher.

The same thing happens when a market has been declining all day. In the last fifteen minutes or last half hour, floor traders even up. Other traders do not want to carry an increased amount of commodities over night, so they are reluctant to sell. The result is that the market becomes thin or the offering small, the market rushes up fast in the last fifteen to thirty minutes, so the man who is short of the market, and right with the main trend, covers his shorts and buys for long account. The next morning the market resumes its normal course and continues on down. The trader, by watching too closely, has made a mistake, is out of the market and has missed his opportunity.

Another great mistake that the man who watches the ticker all the time makes is that he trades too often. He gets in and out several times a day and each time he pays a commission. If he buys or sells higher each time—which he often does—he decreases his chances of making profits. There are about 300 trading days in a year. Suppose a man made a trade every day during the year, which would be 300 trades, and considering that his commission and the getting in and out of the market cost him one-half point on grain, or $1/2$c. Then he would pay 150 points in commission and expenses during the year. Or, trading in the same way in Cotton, if it cost him 10 points to get in and out, he would pay out about the same amount of money in the year in commissions. On the other hand, suppose that a man follows the rules, follows the trend, makes one trade each month, and that trade is successful. Then he would pay 12 commissions a year instead of 300, thus cutting his expenses down to about 6 points against the scalper's expense of 150. To succeed in any business, you must consider the expenses. The losses in speculation are a part of the expenses, as well as the commission. If your losses or expenses are greater than your profits, then it is not a profitable business, and the result is a net loss.

Another fact that traders often overlook is that the more times a man gets in or out of the market, the more times he changes his mind. Therefore, the percentage of his being wrong increases. In either big Bull or Bear markets, there are often reverse moves opposite to the main trend where some big profits can be made and often made quickly, but you can't catch these profits by jumping in and out every day, or staying too close to the ticker.

You have to trade on good reasons, on basic facts and rules that have proved successful in the past. Trading on hope or fear will never help you to make a success. If every man and every woman that puts in days, weeks, and months in a brokerage office would put in that same amount of time staying at home, or in their office, studying the past action of the market, they would make a success and would find that time would turn into profits in the future.

Make it a rule to quit wasting your time, because time is money. Put in your time studying and you will be well repaid for it.

FALSE HOPES. When a man is long or short of the market and has a loss, it is but human nature to hope that it will go his way and that the trend will change. This is a great mistake. When the market starts to go against you, you should face the facts. Find out if you are wrong and WHY you are wrong and leave all hope or fear out. If you are in doubt and don't know that the market is in a definite trend, get out. STOP YOUR LOSS quickly. To hold on and hope when a trade is going against you will never result in anything but losses. When the market is going against you, delays are dangerous. It is much better to take action now than to trust to uncertain future. The time to hold on is when the market is moving in your favor.

The professional floor traders who have no commission to pay often buy and sell many times during the day and take small profit, but they also take quick losses and never let them run far.

Learn to *face* the *facts* and to *eliminate hope* and *fear.* Suppose that a man is wrong in the market and has been called for margin the early part of the day. As a rule, the first thing he should do would be to get out of the trade and not put up more margin, because the chances are that he is wrong. But he doesn't do that. He holds on and hopes that the market will rally before the day is over. He tells the broker that he will either put up more margin or get out before the close. The result is that he waits all day and the market fails to rally. The last hour comes and hope gives away to despair and he sells out at the close. He is not the only trader doing that. The result is that the market closes weak and near the bottom. He finds that he would have been much better off if he had sold out early in the day when he first got the margin call.

the market starts to advance in the early part of the day, the trader does not admit to himself that he is wrong on Wheat or Cotton and get out immediately. He waits for a reaction to get out better and to cover his shorts. The reaction fails to come by noon, fails to come by one o'clock and two o'clock. Finally, in the last hour there are a lot of others short who get scared and start to cover and the market advances very fast. The result is that near the close, when all the shorts are frightened, the trader who has been waiting for a reaction to get out, has to cover his shorts on top. This, in many cases, leaves the market in a weak technical position. The next day a reaction comes, but it does not help the man who traded on hope or fear.

A successful trader studies human nature and does the opposite of what the general public does. The average trader does not worry the first day of a decline in Grain, Cotton, or any other Commodity. He considers it is just a reaction and the market will rally the next day. But, if it continues to decline the second and third day, then he thinks that it is a sure thing that it has gone far enough and that a rally will take place. If it is in a real Bear market and the main trend is down, the rally doesn't come. It may continue for seven to ten days. Then, the human mind can stand the strain no longer, and the trader gives up the idea that the market is ever going to rally, so he sells out, probably right on the bottom of a 7 or 10-day decline. This same man would not sell the first day the market started to decline and gave an indication that something was wrong. Neither would he sell on the second or third day. Therefore, after it had gone down 7 to 10 days, he becomes convinced that the trend had changed, gets scared and sells out. Again, he is trading on fear, rather than on facts or by following definite rules.

The longer the market advances or declines, especially when the main trend is up for weeks or months, the stronger it gets and the smaller the reaction in the last stage, because in these last stages, hope gives away to despair. When a market is advancing, hope and optimism increase to the limit and people buy, not using sound judgment, but buying on hope. This is the way the public trades. To make success you must follow rules and trade opposite to the general public.

COMMODITY MARKETS DISCOUNT FUTURE EVENTS.

As a general rule, crop reports or important events are usually discounted, except when there is something very sudden and unexpected. Therefore, the man who trades on the events instead of the cause is nearly always wrong.

After a very Bullish crop report comes out, the market is often TOP, and often when a very Bearish report comes out the market is Bottom.

You can determine all of this and the position of the trend by keeping charts and studying them. In this way you will know when a definite trend is due and when to buy on good news and when to sell on bad news. As a general rule, you make more money buying when bad news is out and more money selling when good news is out. However, in a wild run-away market, when the trend is strongly up, it will continue up and continue to advance on good news until everybody gets loaded up. Then good news will no longer help to put the market up. The first time the market fails to advance on good news, *something is wrong* and you should *get out*. Always follow your charts for a definite indication. The same applies when a market has been declining for a long time. When a very Bearish crop report comes out, or very unfavorable Bearish news comes out, and prices refuse to decline, something is wrong. Somebody on the inside knows that prices are low enough and they are buying and supporting the market. After all, it is a question of supply and demand that determines when the market it top or bottom. Let your motto be to trade on a rule and to follow a well-defined plan and not jump to conclusions or get in or out of the market on good or bad news, unless the rules tell you that it is time for a change in trend.

HUMAN ELEMENT THE GREATEST WEAKNESS

When a trader makes a profit, he gives himself credit and feels that his judgment is good and that he did it all himself. When he makes losses, he takes a different attitude and seldom ever blames himself or tries to find the cause within himself for the losses. He finds excuses; he reasons with himself that the unexpected happened, and that if he had not listened to someone's else advice, he would have made a profit. He finds a lot of ifs, ands and buts, which he imagines were no fault of him. This is why he makes mistakes and losses the second time.

The investor and trader must work out his own salvation and should blame himself and no one else for his losses, for unless he does, he will never be able to correct his weaknesses. After all, it is his own acts that cause his losses, because he did the buying and the selling. You must look for the trouble within and correct it. Then you will make a success, and not before.

One of the main reasons why traders make losses is because they do not think for themselves. They allow others whose advice and judgment is no better than their own to think for them and advise them. To make a success, you must study and investigate for yourself. Unless you change from a "lamb" to a thinker and seek knowledge, you will go the way of all lambs, — to slaughter under the margin caller's axe. Others can only help you when you help yourself.

I can give you the best rules in the world and the best methods for determining the position of a Commodity, and then you can lose money on account of the human element, which is your greatest weakness. You will fail to follow rules. You will work on hope or fear instead of facts. You will delay. You will become impatient. You will act too quickly or you will delay too long in acting, thus beating yourself on account of your human weakness, then blaming it on the market. Remember that it is your mistake that causes losses and not the action of the market or the manipulators. Therefore, strive to follow rules, or keep out of speculation, for you are doomed to failure.

If you will only study the weakness of human nature and see what fools these mortals be, you will find it easy to make profits by understanding the weakness of human nature and going against the public and doing opposite of what other people do. In other words, you buy near the bottom on knowledge and sell near the top on knowledge, while other people who just guess do the opposite. Time spent in study of price, time and past market movements, will give you a rich reward.

WHY KEEP A RECORD OF PRICES

You should keep charts and records of past market movements because your memory is too short.

By studying past history and knowing that the future is but a repetition of the past, you can determine the cause according to the time and conditions. Sometimes it is necessary to go a long way back to determine the cause, because you must study war, its effect, the conditions before war and what follows.

The average man's memory is too short. He only remembers what he wants to remember or what suits his hopes and fears. He depends too much on others and does not think for himself. Therefore, he should keep a record, graph or picture of past market movements to remind him that what has happened in the past can and will happen in the future. He should not allow his enthusiasm to get the better of his judgment and buy on hope, thinking that there will never be another panic. Panics will come and bull markets will follow just as long as the world stands and they are just as sure as the ebb and flow of the tides, because it is the nature of man to overdo everything. He goes to the extreme when he gets hopeful and optimistic. When fear takes hold of him, he goes to the extreme in the other direction.

Traders made the mistake of selling too soon and buying too late in 1929. These mistakes could have been avoided if the traders had kept up charts on individual Commodities, because they could have seen that they were making higher *bottoms* and higher *tops* all the time, especially those Commodities which were in strong position and they should not have sold them short. However, the charts, when properly interpreted, showed the uptrend on each different Commodity right along and the trader would have make no mistake if he had interpreted the charts properly and had followed the trend. Buying and selling on hope or fear is poor business. Every man who makes a trade should make it with a good sound reason and then he must figure that he COULD BE WRONG and should place a STOP LOSS ORDER for his PROTECTION in case he finds he has made a mistake.

Always look up the Commodity that you are going to trade in and get its record before you make a trade. If it has had a big move previously or a few years before and seems to be in a narrow, trading range, or what I call a sideways move, leave it alone until it shows some definite move. If the Commodity has been a leader in a previous bull campaign or a leader in a previous bear campaign, the chances are that it may not be a leader in the next campaign, unless the chart distinctly shows that it is going to lead in an advance or decline.

Study each Commodity and watch how it acts on rallies and how it acts on reactions, so you can determine whether it is in a section of a bull campaign, which will be resumed later, or whether it is in a bear campaign, which must run out 3 to 5 sections before the bottom is reached. Look over your chart and you will find that each Commodity, when it starts on the down trend runs out 3 to 4 sections.

First, it has a sharp decline. Second, it rallies and is distributed. Third, it has another decline, ending the second section of the decline. Fourth, it rallies and meets selling. Fifth, it has another decline, ending the third section down. Sixth, it rallies and hesitates. Seventh, it has a final big break or what we call the clean-out, when investors, traders and everybody got scared and decided that Commodities are never going up again and sell out everything. When this final clean-out comes, that is the time to buy for the long pull for another bull campaign.

Profits made over a long period of years can be lost in a decline which will run from 5 to 7 weeks, like the decline in July, 1933, when Dr. E. A. Crawford failed. Accumulated profits over a long period of time are lost because traders have not protected themselves with STOP LOSS ORDERS. A STOP LOSS ORDER is much better protection for traders because it works automatically. A man may have a mental stop, yet when the price reaches there, he does not sell out. Traders get used to normal markets, which have normal reactions of 5 to 12 points, or cents per bushel. They think when the big decline comes and Wheat has gone down 10 to 20 cents, it has gone low enough and they are not worried. Then the decline continues, as it did in 1929, during the panic, when Commodities went down 50 to 100 cents per bushel. What chance has a trader to get out with profits or with his capital unless he uses a STOP LOSS ORDER or sells at the market as soon as he sees a decline start?

KEEP UP TO DATE: A man can get into a rut in trading just the same as he can get into a rut in anything else. By keeping up-to-date, I mean to study charts and past records to know whether it is a normal or abnormal market. When you are in a war period, by studying past war periods, you know about how Commodities will act. When it is a normal market, after peace, you know about how Commodities will act. Be progressive. Do not consider that after the war is over there will be the same range of prices that there were before the war. When there is a large supply of any Commodities, do not consider that it will mean a big Bull market. When there is a very small supply of any Commodities, even if prices are at comparatively high levels, if your chart shows the trend is up, follow it that way and figure that it is going to be a Bull market.

Always be progressive. Do not cling to old ideas or theories. Learn to follow the trend, regardless of what you hope or think or what statistics say. Then you will make money because you will be going with the market trend and not against it.

THE BEST WAY TO TRADE: The most money is made by swing trading, or in long pull trades, that is following a definite trend as long as the trend is up or down, but you must learn by rules to wait until the market gets out of a rut or a trading range. Wait for definite indications that it is going higher or lower, before you take a position for a long pull trade. Always figure that YOU CAN BE WRONG and that the market could reverse. Therefore, follow your profits up with a STOP LOSS ORDER, or get out when you get a definite indication that the market has reached a turning point and that the trend is changing.

TIME TO STAY OUT OF THE MARKET: This is something important for everyone to know. You cannot make money by trading in the market every day or by getting in and out every day. There comes a time when you should stay out, WATCH and WAIT until you determine a DEFINITE CHANGE IN TREND. Long periods of rest and relaxation protect your health and help your judgment which will result in profits later. A study of market movements will convince you that the market has its periods of rest. Often the market has a resting period when it is a Bull market and does not react much, but it consumes considerable time before the upward move is resumed. The same thing applies in a Bear market. Often a Commodity will decline and stop, move up and down in a comparatively narrow range and not have much advance, but it is simply holding, hesitating, resting, and getting ready for another downward move. In these periods of narrow trading markets, you will make money by staying out of the market and waiting for a definite indication of trend. Once you are out of the market, you can judge it from an unbiased standpoint and form a clear picture of its future course, but when you are in the market, you are often influenced by your hopes and fears because you want to see the market go your way. When you are out you see the market as it is and it makes no difference which way it goes because you are ready to go with the trend when it changes.

WHAT TO DO WHEN COMMODITIES ARE GOING AGAINST YOU: When you make a trade and it starts to go against you, you should immediately find out what is wrong and stop it. If you find that you made a mistake and that you bought or sold against the trend, then there is no use holding on and hoping. The correct thing to do is to get out. STOP YOUR LOSS. Then your judgment will clear and you can make a new trade in a better way and have more chance of being right. Holding on to a losing trade will never help you.

WHAT TO DO WHEN YOU HAVE A SERIES OF LOSSES: When you make one to three trades that show losses, whether they be large or small, something is wrong with you and not with the market. Your trend may have changed. My rule is to get out and wait. Study the reason for your losses. Remember you will never lose any money being out of the market. Holding on to a losing trade is the worst thing you can do, and as a rule it continues to go against you, and the quicker you take a loss, the better. Trade with the main trend. It never pays to sell short in a Bull market because you are bucking the trend and may miss the top. It never pays to buy in a Bear market, because you are bucking the trend and may miss the bottom and have losses. As a rule, when you buy or sell Grain, and it goes against you 3 to 5c, you are wrong, and you may just as well get out. If you can't get within 3 to 5c of the top or bottom, you are wrong and it might go against you 15 or 20c. The same thing with Cotton. If you can't get within 40 to 50 points from the top or bottom of the cotton market, you are wrong and you may just as well take the loss and get out. Remember that markets often run into abnormal run-away markets, without your knowing it and radical change in the trend may take place. How can you expect to come out of a deal with profits if you are bucking the trend and get into one of these wild runs up or down. Rapid advances and declines in Wheat and Cotton, or other Commodities, often run from 6 to 7 weeks and sometimes for several months without much of a reverse move. Therefore, when you get into one of these abnormal moves and buck the trend, you are doomed to failure and will lose all the margin you can put up.

Study the charts and convince yourself that I am telling you the truth. Go over the indications and the rules that I have given you. See how far advancing markets have run and how small the reactions have been. See how far they have declined and how small the rallies have been. Then ask yourself the question, "If I get into one of these wild, run-away moves and the market starts going against me, how much money can I lose?" Answer yourself honestly and you will say, "I can lose all I put up." The proper thing to do is to go with the trend in these moves. When you see you are wrong, *double* up and *buy,* if you are short. If you are long, and the trend reverses, double up and go short. The money is made by going with the trend and not by bucking it.

How Much Profit To Expect: Many traders make the mistake of expecting too much profit in a normal market. They hope for more than they get. The idea is to follow the trend and to determine whether you are in a war market, an abnormal market or just a normal trading market. Do not expect too much profits but follow up if you are right and protect your profits and get out when the trend changes, not before. The average man or woman who goes into trading or speculation of Commodities expects too much gain on their money. They expect to double their money in a few days, a few weeks, or a few months. This can be done at times, but these opportunities are rare and far between. The man or woman who expects big profits the first time a trade is made usually lose all the money they put up.

The way to succeed is to have a rule, so that when you start trading with a certain amount of capital, you will never lose the capital and over a period years you will make better than the average return on the money. Did you ever stop to figure what a gain of 25% per year means, over a period of 20 years? Suppose you start with a capital of $1,000.00 and increase it 25% a year for 10 years, it amounts to $9,313.25. $10,000 increased at the rate of 25% a year, amounts to $93,132.17 in ten years. You can see how easy it is to accumulate a moderate fortune in a reasonable length of time, if you are conservative and do not expect too much. Most traders are too greedy. They want to get rich in too short a period of time. They OVER TRADE. The result is that they lose their capital and then blame the Chicago Board of Trade, Wall Street, or someone else. The trouble was that they fooled themselves and gambled instead of making a conservative investment or speculative trade.

Learn to LIMIT YOUR RISKS. Do not expect abnormal profits in normal markets. By doing this, your chances for success are greatly increased.

How To Answer Margin Calls: When you buy or sell a Commodity and put up a certain amount of money, which is the amount required by your broker as margin, and later you are called on for additional margin, it is evidence that you are wrong and that the market is going against you. If you put up 10c per bushel and the market has gone against you 6 or 7c, you are wrong for that much and the chances are that you will be wrong for 6, 7, or 20c more. Why hold on to a losing trade? The way to answer the margin call is to sell out. Find out what is wrong and make the next trade according to a well-defined rule and you will not have to put up additional margin.

Joint Account: Never have a joint account or trade in partnership with others if you can possibly avoid it. When two men start an account together, they may agree upon the right time to buy, but when it comes time to sell, they will seldom agree. One will be willing to take a certain amount of profits and sell out and the other one will refuse to sell. This is where the hitch comes when it comes to closing a trade. The result will be that one will hold on against his better judgment, because his partner wants to hold on, and finally the trend goes against them, the partner will decide that it is time to sell out because he is scared and the other man agrees and they get out and take a loss.

You must learn to work independently and not be influenced by the opinions of others. When you get ready to act, be in a position where no one can tell you or influence you from TAKING ACTION when you think it is the RIGHT TIME. My opinion is that the only way two people can make a success by trading in a joint account is for one man to do the buying and selling, and the other man to put in the STOP LOSS ORDERS. If the other man is wrong, STOPS will protect him and the losses will be small. When once he gets right and lets the profits run, he will make money, but the other partner makes it his business to protect the profits by following up with STOP LOSS ORDERS. I have seen two men work successfully this way, because one man will buy or sell a Commodity and will not place the STOP LOSS ORDERS, but the other man who knows the danger of the risks is protecting them. He puts on the *stops* and they are protected. The other man who naturally has the large profits will not follow it up with a STOP LOSS ORDER. The partner who is watching the trade and knows that they can count only on the amount of profits they have protected with stop losses, places the stop loss order.

TIME LIMIT TO HOLD FOR PROFIT: When you make a trade, it must be on a good rule and for a good reason. There must be the possibility of a reasonable profit within a reasonable length of time. Remember one thing, *you can be wrong when you make the trade* and *it can go against you*. Therefore, *your loss must be stopped.* You can be wrong when the Commodity does not go against you. That is, it can remain in a narrow trading range for a long time. Therefore, you should be prepared to get out when the Commodities show they are not going to move.

The best rule that I can give you is to always determine, before you make the trade, that you have a definite indication that the move is on. Then, you can expect to make profits within a reasonable length of time. If the market is in a long Bull campaign or a long Bear campaign, the idea is to follow up as long as the market shows the trend is moving in your favor. When you get into a market that is dead and inactive, you lose patience, as well as lose interest on your money, which is equal to an actual loss. If you are out of the market with that same amount of money, you can grasp a new opportunity when there is a fast move coming and can make more money in a short period of time.

Remember you often make money by staying out of the market and waiting for an opportunity. The time limit to hold a Commodity depends upon the position you are in and the indication on your chart.

FACTS YOU NEVER HEAR ABOUT SHORT SELLING: Many people are born Bulls. They always want to buy something before they sell it. When you tell them that they should sell a Commodity short, they begin to tell you how the market may be cornered. If they looked up the records, they would find that there is not a corner in a Commodity on an average of more than once every 15 to 20 years. Therefore, the chances of getting in a Commodity, it being cornered and losing a whole fortune is very small. If you keep up with the market and study it and follow the rules you are WITH THE TREND.

When a Commodity is cornered, you are on the buying side and not on the selling side.

Always learn the facts by studying past history, and don't be afraid to sell short. There is just as much profit and in fact, quicker money made on the short side than there is on the long side, after the trend turns down. Most of newspaper writers discourage short selling, and the Government often discriminates against short selling. Why should this be? The trouble is that politicians who want to influence the public to follow them and vote for them, always have to condemn something and work against it. Therefore, the politician is always talking against Wall Street, the Chicago Board of Trade, etc., trying to make the public believe that the Stock Exchange and the Board of Trade do everything against the trader, instead of telling the trader the truth that he makes the mistake himself and that stock exchanges and commodity exchanges are in no way to blame for his losses.

There is no business on earth in any place in the world where there is a set of more honorable men than the members of the commodity exchanges in this country. The trader gets a square deal. The men who govern the Board of Trade do not run the market and should not be blamed for the mistakes that traders make on account of their ignorance, but the politician has to cover up his own mistakes and blame somebody else for something all the time. In fact, he is always against something.

Follow the trend of the market. Be as willing to sell short in a Bear market as you are to buy in a Bull Market. Be neither a chronic Bull nor a chronic Bear. When you go into the Commodity business, let your object be to make money and have no choice as to which side you make it on. Learn to **FOLLOW THE TREND** and you will make a success.

WHAT CAUSES BOOMS AND WARS

History proves that wars break out every 20 to 25 years. It also proves that there is a great wave of SPECULATION and a BOOM of some kind in nearly every country every 20 to 25 years. Why do these WAR PERIODS and BOOM TIMES come at such regular cycles or intervals? The main cause of these is that HUMAN NATURE NEVER CHANGES. Every 20 years a new generation comes along. They are full of hope, optimistic and are progressive and up-to-date. They are inexperienced. They know nothing of war or of the bitterness of war, because they have never been in a fight. They are anxious to get into a fight. It is easy for the politicians to induce the young men to go to war, but it is hard to get the old fellows who have had the bitter experience and the suffering, to go to war. They want no more of it. The young buck is wild and always ready to run and to fight.

It is the same with the Commodity market. The young generations either have inherited money or they make money, and they want to take a chance. It is the nature of youth to gamble, to take chances, and to be fearless of danger. Therefore, the young generation are anxious and eager to try their hands at SPECULATION. When they get into a RUN AWAY BULL MARKET, they have no more sense than to keep on BUYING. They throw caution to the wind. This increased BUYING power causes Commodities to go to HEIGHTS UNWARRANTED BY SUPPLY AND DEMAND. The result is that when this BOOM is over, the young generation suffer severe LOSSES, get some valuable experience and are not so anxious to try it again.

Just as sure as young generations come along from time to time, we will continue to have BOOMS in business, BOOMS in the STOCK MARKETS and COMMODITIES, LAND BOOMS and other wild WAVES of speculation. Youth has to be served and young nature has to have its fling. That is why HISTORY REPEATS, because HUMAN NATURE DOES NOT CHANGE and each coming generation have to go through the same EXPERIENCE as the former GENERATION did.

BUYING OR SELLING TOO LATE OR TOO SOON: You can be *right* on the *trend* and still *buy* too *late* or *sell* too soon, and lose money. You can wait to buy until after a market has had a sharp advance and you know that the trend is up. If the market has had enough advance, a reaction is due. When the reaction comes right after you buy, if you lose courage, lose your nerve, become pessimistic and sell out you are out of the market. After that, the upward movement is resumed.

You often sell out longs too soon or sell short too soon, because the market has had a good advance and it looks as though it is high enough. You hope it is, but HOPE will never make profits. You must FACE the FACTS. Wait for a definite CHANGE in TREND. If you sell too soon and the market goes against you, or if you sell out longs too soon, you will often make the mistake of then buying back just about the time the market reaches TOP and get caught with a loss.

FOLLOW the TREND. Trade when the indications show that the market is up or down trend. Don't wait too long. Remember, DELAYS are DANGEROUS. Too long a delay in getting out causes greater losses. Too long a delay in getting in causes you to miss profit. Learn to ACT and ACT QUICKLY at the RIGHT TIME, so long as you are acting WITH THE MAIN TREND.

WHAT TRADERS DON'T WANT TO KNOW: With all due respect to my readers, many traders when they are in the market don't want to know the facts or don't want to know the truth. They hope the market will go their way. They want it to go their way and they want to be told that it will. When you are in the market, you should be unbiased and try to determine whether you are in right or wrong. When you find you are in wrong, admit it quickly and get out. Our old rule is, *when in doubt, always get out.* When you have nothing to hold on for but hope, sell out at the market quickly. Don't look for the man who will advise you that your position is *right* and that the market will soon start going your way. Look for the *man that will tell you the truth and prove it to you. Better still, learn how to prove it to yourself* whether you are *right* or *wrong. Face the facts.*

Admit it. Change your position. Change your mind. Change with the trend and you will make profits.

WHEN A MAN'S TREND CHANGES: When you are trading and have had a long period of success, that is, have been making trades right and making profits for several weeks, months, or years, there will come a time when your luck (if you want to call it luck), will change, or your trend will change, the same as the market. When your trend changes it may run against you for weeks or months. The way to determine when your trend changes is if you make a trade and it shows a loss get out of the market. Then if you make a second or third trade and it shows a loss, something is wrong. Your trend has changed. You had better get out. Watch, wait, and study. When you think you have a definite indication, make another trade. If this trade moves in your favor and it shows profit, your trend is again running in your favor and you should continue to trade. When you make the fourth or fifth trade and it shows a loss, small or large, something is wrong and you better get out. Take care of your health and watch for another opportunity. It is possible that you may be tired or that you may have some troubles or worries that are making you act wrong. Your judgment is bad. You are not able to see correctly what the market will do. In this case, there is only one thing to do—get out, wait and rest.

HOPE AND FEAR: I have written about this often in all my books, and I feel that I cannot repeat it too often. The average man or woman buys Commodities because they *hope* they will go up or because somebody advises them they will go up. This is the most *dangerous* thing to do. *Never trade on hope.* Hope wrecks more people than anything else. Study the market and determine the trend. *Face the facts,* and when you trade, trade on *facts,* eliminating hope.

Fear causes many losses. People sell out because they fear commodities are going lower, but they often wait until the decline has run its course and they sell near the bottom. Often when they have been out of the market for some time, they get in because they fear it is going higher. Never make a trade on fear. The Bible says, "Ye shall know the truth and the truth shall make you free." *Know* the *facts* and *know* the *truth.* When you do this, you will have no hope or no fear, and you will trade on well-defined rules and go with the trend and will make profits.

NORMAL AND ABNORMAL MARKETS: By studying past history and studying war periods, you will learn when markets are moving in a normal zone and when they are moving in an abnormal zone. As a general rule, markets move in the abnormal zone during war times. However, up to this writing, October 1, 1941, this war has been an exception, because Wheat and some other Commodities have not had an abnormal move during this present war.

The reason for this is, that all foreign countries had prepared for war by laying in a large supply of grain and production has been increased. England has bought most of her supplies from Canada. The United

States' supply of wheat has been increasing, and our price, due to Government control, has kept 40c to 50c above world prices, with the result that we have lost most of our foreign trade.

Soy beans have had an *abnormal move,* or regular war move which has resulted from the increased use of Soy beans. The fact is that the major supply of Soy beans comes from the United States. Don't overlook the fact that when any commodity gets high enough where everybody can make money in it, production will increase and the price will go down again. The time will come when the Government will no longer be able to control the production of crops, and prices will decline not only to normal levels but below normal levels. They have always declined when there is over-production. There is likely to be many years of lower prices in Commodities after the war is over, regardless of any mild boom or spurt that may come after peace.

Study the movements after war in the past, and you will be able to tell more about whether the moves will be normal or abnormal in the future. Apply all the rules that I give you. They will help you in different kinds of markets.

HEDGING: Many traders have the idea that when they are in a Commodity, in wrong and it starts declining, they can hedge and protect themselves, that is, sell short some other Commodity to make up the loss on the one they have bought. There is no greater mistake than this. It often turns out that the trader loses on both trades. If you are in the market WRONG and don't know what to do, there is but one thing to do. Get out and wait until you know there is a *definite trend.*

A trader may sell short May Wheat and it goes against him. He decides to buy December Wheat for a hedge. Often he makes another serious mistake. When he is short of May Wheat and long of December, it is but natural that when the market declines, he has a profit on December Wheat, he will cover the short and take a profit, holding on to his long position in May Wheat. The trend may be definitely down and continue down. The result is, that getting in the hedge only increased his loss. *Hedging is never advisable,* that is, to buy one Commodity and to sell another of the same Commodity. It does not pay and you must avoid it. Get out of the market and wait until you can *determine* the *trend,* and then *buy* or *sell* and do not do any *hedging.*

NORMAL OR AVERAGE ADVANCES OR DECLINES: Normal or average moves depend upon the price at which a Commodity is selling and the time period it is in. Wheat, Corn, or other Commodities in the grain line may advance for some time, having only normal reactions of 5c or 6c a bushel. When they get higher, they will react 10c to 12c a bushel. Later on, they will react 15c or 20c a bushel Still the main trend may be up if in a long Bull market. The same applies when a market is declining. Wheat may have rallies of 5c to 6c a bushel. When several sections have run out, rallies of 10c to 12c a bushel may occur. Later a rally of 15c to 20c a bushel occurs. When greater than 15c to 20c advances or declines occur, it is a sign that the market is changing from *normal* to *abnormal* moves and you should watch your charts and go with the trend.

Apply the same rules to Cotton, or to any other Commodity. Watch for the reaction point. We will give examples and rules for this later in the book.

CREEPING MARKET: In the early stages of a Bull market, Wheat, Cotton, or any other Commodity will often move up very slowly, having small reactions and small rallies, but gradually working higher. After a long period of time, a creeping market will start a *final run-away* move, or what we call a *grand rush,* moving up very fast and having very small reactions. People often get fooled and sell a creeping market short, because it keeps having reactions and they expect a profit. Finally when it gets into a *run-away* move, they are short and hold on and hope, thinking it is only going to have a normal run. The result is that they have big losses. The same applies when a market is in a narrow range and declining. It will work down very slowly, having moderate rallies for quite a long while. Finally, it *breaks wide open.* Then the trader who has not watched his position gets caught, because when a market changes from a *creeping Bear market* to a *run-away* move, he runs into heavy losses.

POPULAR TRADING PRICES

The human mind works in the same way most of the time, because human beings do not change. People get used to certain figures and they trade at these prices more than at others. The average man thinks in multiples of 5 and 10. The popular trading prices are 25, 50, 60, 75, 100, 150, 175, etc. The public nearly always use these even figures in buying or selling, and that is why Cotton, Wheat, Corn, or any other Commodity, will often advance or decline to near these even figures and then turn. For example, if the traders all have a lot of selling orders at 75c a bushel for Wheat, the market may advance to 74¾, or 74⅞. Then, these heavy offerings being above the market, the market does not advance to 75c. The traders fail to sell at the even figure and the market declines. Later, they sell out at lower levels. It is the same way about buying and fixing prices. Traders want to buy at 100, 75, 50, or at 125, 150, or at some even figure like 56, 58, 60, 62, 82, or 86, and these prices are often missed by an eighth or three-eighths.   By having a fixed buying point, the trader misses getting in near TOP or BOTTOM and misses an opportunity to make money.

When buying or selling you should never fix a price, that is, never set a buying or selling price. When the market reaches a point where your charts and rules indicate it should be bought, place a buying order at the market. Limiting orders has cost many men thousands of dollars. The same applies when the market reaches the level where your charts indicate *time to sell. Sell at the market.* Remember, delays are dangerous. When you want to sell, sell out. When you want to buy or sell do so at the market and you will save a lot of time, trouble, and losses, and will increase your profits.

Study of the extreme high and low prices in the past will convince you how Commodities often miss these popular trading prices in these even figures. There is another thing that is well to *know* and to *remember*. It is human nature to want to buy things cheap, and trade at low levels. If Wheat, or any other Commodity, has been selling below $1.00 per bushel for a long time, when it first reaches $1.00, people think it is too high and they often sell. Later, when the price gets to 112 or 120 or higher, they become convinced that it is going to $2.00 per bushel. They buy when it is too high and this results in losses. The trouble is they *do not know* when the *trend has changed* and whether it is in a *normal* or an *abnormal* market. By going over past records, you will find in most cases that when any Commodity advances above $1.00, it usually goes considerably higher. As a rule, when Wheat gets above $1.00 per bushel and holds this level, it will advance to $1.15, $1.20, $1.25, or some other price at much higher level. The same applies when Wheat breaks below $1.00 per bushel and stays under this level, as it often goes very much lower.

COTTON: People will get used to prices of Cotton at 8 to 10c per pound. After a long period of years, when conditions change and Cotton crosses 10c per pound, they will all sell out and go short, and will buck the trend. When it advances to 12c a pound, they will think it is a sure sale and is going to react. Finally, when it gets up around 15c a pound, they all start buying and rush the market up around 17 or 18c a pound. Then comes the first sharp reaction of 200 to 300 points, they all get wiped out and have losses. This is because they would not recognize changed conditions and go *with the trend*.

Remember that supply and demand govern prices. When prices move up to new high levels, there is somebody buying and it is useless to buck the trend. The same applies when a market is declining. When a market works down to lower levels than it has been for a long time, the selling pressure is greater than the buying pressure and you should go *with the trend* and not against it.

HOW TO SELECT THE COMMODITY THAT WILL LEAD A DECLINE OR AN ADVANCE

By keeping up a monthly high and low chart, or a quarterly chart on any Commodity, and by keeping up charts on most of the active Commodities, you will be able to determine which Commodity is going to lead in a Bull market or which Commodity is getting ready to lead in a Bear market. By following the rules given later, determining whether a Commodity is making higher TOPS and higher BOTTOMS, whether it has crossed Resistance Levels for a long period of time, or whether it has broken BOTTOMS or Resistance Levels over a long period of time, you can determine which Commodity will lead the first advance or decline. By reviewing past records, you will find that some Commodity always advances first. Other Commodities come along later and at the end of any Bull campaign, some Commodity that has led first will be the first to decline. The idea is to follow the trend of each Commodity individually. Do not figure because Lard is declining Soy Beans are going to decline at the same time. Do not figure because Cotton is declining that Wheat is ready to go down, unless the chart shows it.   Select the Commodity that you will buy according to its individual position on the chart, when it gives definite indication that it is going to make a move.   Remember that it requires time to buy a large amount of any Commodity and time to sell it.   After buying or selling is completed and the supply has been absorbed, or the demand has been filled, the *trend changes* and an opposite move starts, which lasts for a considerable period of time.   You can understand all of this by the study of past movements and by following the rules.

BEST COMMODITIES TO TRADE IN: Under normal conditions and as a rule, you can make the most money by trading in Wheat, Corn and Soy Beans, because these Commodities make the greatest range and it is just as easy to forecast them as it is Oats, which move in a smaller range.   There are exceptional years when the Oat crop might be extremely short or Rye crop extremely large.   Then Rye or Oats would make a considerable range.   The basic Commodities are the ones that return the most profit over a long period of years. Cotton is one of the best Commodities to trade in because trade lines keep it active by hedging and buying.   Changing prices will increase or decrease production and increase of supply or demand.   By studying charts of the other Commodities, you can determine the time when they indicate an abnormal move one way or the other.   It pays to trade in them, but the public does most of the trading in Wheat, Corn, and Soy Beans, and are educated how to trade in Cotton more than they are in Cocoa, Coffee, Sugar, or other Commodities.   The result is, the range of fluctuations are wider, and you have a better opportunity for making profit by trading in the leading commodities.

FORMATIONS AT TOP OR BOTTOM

In studying the past record of market movements, if you study the formation on a weekly chart or on a monthly chart, at extreme low levels or extreme high levels, you will get a picture that will be valuable to you in future movements, because you will note the different formations before any big advance takes place.   Remember that one good picture is worth a thousand words.   That is why we make up charts and study past records for market movements.   By a study of these different formations you will find it helpful in determining the trend. All of this will be covered later under RULES and different kinds of TOPS and BOTTOMS.

SUDDEN UNEXPECTED NEWS: Many traders often write and ask me, "How can you tell what the market will do or what to do when some sudden, unexpected news happens over-night, such as war breaking out, the death of the President, a storm damaging Cotton seriously, the failure of a large trader or brokerage house, or something of that order?" My answer is that coming events cast their shadows before, and the market is nearly always prepared for these events and gives some indication of change in trend before these events take place.   For example:

1917—February 2, when Germany declared unrestricted U-boat war,
    Cotton and Wheat had a sharp decline.

WHEAT:

1916—November, high 195. The market had a big advance and indicated that a reaction was due.

December, low 154. This was a sharp, quick decline in a short time and a rally was indicated.

1917—January, high 191, failing by 4 cents per bushel to reach the old TOP at 195, indicated down trend and you should have sold short. February 2, on the U-boat scare, Wheat broke wide open, declining to 154½. You should have previously sold short because the trend was down. The fact that it failed to break the low of December of 154, indicated that it was making BOTTOM, and you should have bought on bad news, because all indications pointed to the fact that the United States would enter the war and that war would continue, which is Bullish on Wheat.

COTTON:

1916—November, high 21.50. The market had advanced from 13.80 in August, which was a big advance, and a reaction was due.

December, low 16.50. This was a decline of 400 points, and a rally was due.

1917—January, high 19.10, failing by 240 points to reach the old high, showed that the main trend was down and you should have sold short. Therefore, you would have been short when the big break occurred after the unexpected U-boat news.

February 2, on this news, Cotton opened down 300 to 400 points, declining to around 13.75, you should have been short and should have covered on bad news on this wide open break. We will show under rules later why Cotton was a buy around this level. Many people sold both Wheat and Cotton on this bad news and sold near the bottom. These were the lowest levels reached for several years. This again proves that the market had already given indications that it was going down before bad news came out.

1933—March, low for Wheat, 46c per bushel. After President Roosevelt came into office and we went off the gold standard, Wheat had a rapid advance. In fact, a regular war move in peace times. July 18, high $1.28. Up 72c per bushel in 4 months. The last advance was from June 19, low 97½. This is an advance of 30½c per bushel in 19 days. Before the failure of Dr. E. A. Crawford, the market had already given signals of TOP and you should have been out and short. Therefore, when the wide open break occurred on the failure of Dr. Crawford, you should have been short and the adverse news, or unexpected news, would not have affected you. After Dr. Crawford's failure, Wheat declined 30c per bushel in 3 days.

As a rule, these unexpected events are not unexpected to someone on the inside, because someone knows something about news of this kind in advance, and anticipates it, and the market also gives an indication of the change of trend.   When bad news is out it is time to buy.   When good news is out it is time to sell.   The market will always show by the position on the chart how great a decline or advance will occur when news of importance comes out.

BUYING POWER GREATER THAN SELLING POWER: When a market advances, it advances on buying and increased demand. When the buying power is greater than the selling power, the market makes higher TOPS and higher BOTTOMS and continues to move up until selling power becomes greater than buying power. Then the trend reverses. You must study your charts and follow all the rules to determine when this change takes place.

SELLING POWER GREATER THAN BUYING POWER: When the supply exceeds the demand, and selling power is greater than buying power, it is but natural that prices must decline to a level where support or buying power will come in and over-balance selling power.   Then the trend changes, temporarily at least, and a rally takes place.   Study all of my rules and charts to determine when this change in trend takes place.

WHY REACTIONS ARE SMALLER AT HIGH LEVELS: In a Bull market reactions get smaller as prices go higher, because optimism and hope increase after a prolonged advance.   When the buying power is greater than the selling power, traders are bidding for Commodities and the price continues to work higher.   Reactions are small because they are buying orders under the market, as people are waiting for reactions to buy.

Therefore, do not expect large reactions at high levels until final TOP has been reached.   When the first reaction exceeds the last reaction in a Bull market, you can figure that the trend has reversed temporarily.

WHY RALLIES ARE SMALLER AT LOW LEVELS: After a market has been declining for a long time, people have been holding on, hoping, and gradually selling out all the way down.   The buying power decreases.   People have lost confidence.   After Wheat has declined 50c a bushel, there will be less buying power than there is after Wheat has advanced 50c a bushel, because people have lost confidence because they have lost money.   They buy less because they have less money.   On the other hand, after a market has had a prolonged advance and traders have made large profits, their buying power is increased because they have more margin or capital to buy with.   For this reason, it is always safer to sell after prices are down a considerable way from the TOP or when they get to lower levels, because *rallies* will be *smaller* and your *risks* will be *less*.

BUYING AND SELLING BALANCED: After Wheat, Cotton, or any other Commodity, has had a prolonged advance, it finally reaches a level where buying and selling power becomes balanced or about equal. Then, the market may move in a narrow trading range for a few days or a few weeks until selling power over-balances buying power and then the trend changes again.

Buying and selling is often more evenly balanced at low levels than at high levels, because the market, when it advances very fast, reacts very fast. After a market has been declining for a long time, it reaches a resting level or a balanced period when trade interests sell on rallies and buy on reaction, and·traders find a ceiling, TOP or Resistance Level where they sell. Then, a few cents per bushel lower, they buy because they are taking a scalping position. The markct may remain in this trading range for several weeks or months because buying and selling are about balanced. When it reaches a stage of this kind, you have to watch the charts, study them and apply all of my rules. Wait for the market to show when one opposing force overcomes the other. When buying power over-balances selling power, the market breaks out of the trading range and advances. When selling power over-balances buying power and the market becomes over-sold, it breaks out of the trading range and declines to lower levels. Later in the book we will give examples of all of these positions, so that you can study the market when it is in trading range where buying and selling are about balanced.

GOVERNMENT CONTROL OF COMMODITIES

Since the New Deal started and the Government has attempted to regulate production and control prices, they have interfered with the natural law of supply and demand. This, in my opinion, does more harm than good, and my opinion is shared by many able business men and grain dealers throughout the country. We believe that this Government control of production and prices will end after the war, because ine Government cannot go on subsidizing and paying out money tv farmers to stop producing crops, and at the same time, place the burden of taxation on the business man and other taxpayers to stop production. The Government gives the farmer something for nothing. When this Government interference in Commodity prices is over, prices will follow the law of supply and demand, and seek a proper level of prices based on supply and demand. Nature balances everything. Weather conditions and weather cycles change from time to time. After a series of favorable years of weather conditions and good crops comes unfavorable weather conditions and short crops. The Government cannot control the weather and cannot control natural law. Therefore, it is the best for all concerned for the Government to let the control of production and prices alone and let the law of supply and demand take its course. Then, people in trade lines, investors and speculators will know that they can figure on a natural, normal trend.

DULL AND NARROW AT HIGH LEVELS: Wheat and other Commodities often become very dull and narrow when they reach extremely high levels and the volume gets small. As long as they are in a trading range at these high levels, the SAFEST THING to do is to STAY OUT and watch until they BREAK THE RESISTANCE LEVELS and show they are GOING LOWER.

VOLUME OF SALES

When Commodities break bottoms or Resistance Levels, volumes will increase, or if the movement reverses and starts up, volume will increase and COMMODITIES or Cotton will cross previous high Levels, become more active and work higher. It always pays to wait until a dead, inactive market shows which way activity is going to start.

Grain or other Commodities often get into an extremely WEAK POSITION where there cannot be anything but very SMALL RALLIES, after there has been a prolonged advance. Traders and investors gain confidence in Grain and buy it on every little reaction, until finally the market is well distributed and over-bought. When a decline starts, there are no buying or supporting orders ON THE WAY DOWN. When INVESTORS and TRADERS, who have bought at HIGHER LEVELS, start SELLING OUT, the Grain market gets weaker ALL THE TIME and rallies GET SMALLER.

Don't be afraid to SELL Grain SHORT after it has had BIG DECLINES because it is in a WEAKER POSITION and SAFER SHORT SALES than when it is at higher levels.

WHEN THE MARKET IS IN STRONGEST POSITION OR IN WEAKEST POSITION

Wheat or other Commodities are in the strongest position after there has been a prolonged decline, and the market starts making higher BOTTOMS, especially after a sharp, fast decline, when rallies have been small. After the 2nd or 3rd higher BOTTOM has been made and TOP of a previous rally has been crossed, the market is in the strongest position. Advancing BOTTOMS always indicate strength, and an advance usually starts from the 3rd or 4th higher BOTTOM, that is, the big advance which runs for a long time with only small reactions. You make money quickest when you get in on a move of this kind.

Reverse this rule in a Bear Market. A market is weakest when it is making lower TOPS. The 3rd or 4th lower TOP, after it breaks the last low or previous BOTTOM, the market is in the weakest position and it indicates that the main trend is down and declines will be faster.

COMMODITY EXCHANGES SERVE A USEFUL PURPOSE

From time to time political leaders and agitators, who want to fool the people all the time, criticize and condemn the Commodity Exchanges and talk about closing them up and putting them out of business.

The Commodity Exchanges throughout the country are just as much a necessity as the grocery store or the dry goods store, because they serve to keep the public informed on the price of commodities. The Commodity Exchanges benefit the farmer, because he always knows how supply and demand govern prices and can look at his newspaper and see what prices are on wheat, corn or oats in Chicago or other market centers and he knows what he should get for his products and commodities.

A farmer who has a very large acreage of wheat, corn or oats, can benefit through the use of the Commodity Exchanges. Suppose in the Spring of the year or in the Summer he sees that he has a large crop and, before it becomes time to harvest, prices are very high. Suppose that wheat was selling at $1 a bushel. The farmer knows that he will be able to harvest 2,000 bushels and he has reason to believe that, when harvest time comes, he cannot sell his wheat at $1 a bushel, but in the month of May it is selling at $1 a bushel on the Chicago Board of Trade and the Kansas City Board of Trade. He gives his broker an order to sell 2,000 bushels of wheat for July, September or December delivery at $1 per bushel. This is a hedge against the wheat which he expects to deliver later. Wheat declines to 80c per bushel. When the farmer harvests his wheat, 80c is all he can sell it for. He sells for 80c a bushel, buys in the short contract which he sold at $1, and has 20c a bushel profit. Or he can make the actual delivery on the Chicago Board of Trade or any other Commodity Exchange and he will have received $1 per bushel for his wheat.

The political agitators never tell the farmers of the benefits the Exchanges give him, but they always criticize and find the faults.

Business men could not do business without the Commodity Exchange. Suppose a large cotton mill expected to use 100,000 bales of cotton. They cannot buy this cotton at high levels and take chances on its declining 2c, 3c, or 5c a pound before it is used up and have a loss on it, but they can buy a large amount of cotton and then sell futures to hedge it, so that if cotton declines there will be no loss. On the other hand, suppose a cotton mill needs 100,000 bales of cotton in the next year, but they do not have the cash to buy it with. They can put up $5 or $7 a bale margin and buy futures for delivery six months later and have ample protection. Then, if the market advances, they have their requirements covered and they can buy their cotton from time to time as they need it and not worry about the price.

It is the same with the flour mills. If they have a large supply of wheat on hand, and prices start to decline, they can sell futures against it, and then, no matter how low wheat goes, they are insured and protected.

Suppose wheat is selling at a very low level, as it was in 1932 and 1933, around 44c per bushel. The flour mill has every reason to believe that wheat will again sell at $1 per bushel, or higher. But, they do not have the cash to buy millions of bushels of wheat to supply his needs for a year or more, but he can go into the future market and buy wheat for delivery six or nine months advance, put up margin, and then buy his wheat as he requires it, and when wheat reaches $1 per bushel, or higher, he has made the profit on his future contracts and in doing this is able to sell flour for less money to the public and then the public can buy bread from the bakers without a great advance because wheat has advanced.

The proof of the value of the Commodity Exchanges is that in many foreign countries they have been in existence hundreds of years and are fulfilling an economic need.

The Chicago Board of Trade was organized in 1848 and has been in existence nearly 100 years, and has served a useful purpose to the country.

The New York Cotton Exchange was organized in 1870 and has been of great benefit to the producer and the consumer.

No matter what kind of business a man is in, there will be a certain number of people who will make fools of themselves, gamble and lose their money. Just because a few people act unwisely—over-trade— buy when they should sell—or sell when they should buy—lose their money—and then blame the Cotton Exchange and the Commodity Exchange, it is no reason why the general public or the politicians should condemn the Commodity Exchange because a few men act unwisely. When any man loses money buying and selling commodities, stocks, or loses money in business, it is his own fault, and the blame should not be laid on others. The man who makes progress and makes a success finds the cause for his mistakes was within himself and blames no one but himself and in the future profits by his mistakes and tries to avoid making the same mistake again.

No man or woman will ever make a success in life or find happiness by blaming their misfortunes upon others.

HOW TRADES ARE MADE AND CLOSED

Now, supposing that in January "A" orders his commission merchant to buy 5,000 bushels Wheat for May delivery at 85 cents per bushel and deposits required margin to secure commission merchant against loss. If it advances to 95 cents per bushel, even if it be within a short time, he can order his commission merchant to sell it, and may immediately withdraw his profits, less commission, and funds previously deposited as security, although the commission merchant may have to wait till May before he can settle the contract he entered into on behalf of his customer. Then the Wheat bought by the commission merchant is delivered at the purchased price and he, in turn, delivers it to the person it was sold to when his customer closed out his trade.

On the other hand, if "A" orders his commission merchant to sell 5,000 bushels Wheat for May delivery at 85 cents per bushel, after depositing required margin to secure commission merchant against loss, and it advances, he has to maintain the minimum margins and at 95 cents, he can order his commission merchant to buy it in and the merchant will render an account of the trade, showing its losses. In the latter case, had "A" not ordered the Wheat bought in at 95 cents after ordering it sold at 85 cents, the commission merchant would have been compelled to call for maintenance margins to secure the open contracts, as 10 cents, plus commission, had already been exhausted by the market advancing that much above prices originally sold at.

In like manner Soy Beans, Corn and all other Grains, Provisions, Cotton, Cottonseed Oil are bought and sold, likewise settled.

In Board of Trade parlance parties who have sold for future delivery are called "shorts" and those who have bought for future delivery are called "longs". Hence the term frequently used on an advancing market, "shorts", are covering or buying in, and on a declining market, "longs", are unloading, selling out or realizing.

SELECTING YOUR BROKER: When you start to open an account, the first thought must be the safety of your capital and the reliability of your broker. Always open your account and trade with a broker who is a member of some of the leading Commodity Exchanges.

The Chicago Board of Trade, the Winnipeg Grain Exchange, Kansas City Board of Trade, New Orleans Cotton Exchange, New York Cotton Exchange, Commodity Exchange, Inc., of New York, Coffee and Sugar Exchange of New York, Cocoa Exchange of New York, Mercantile Exchange in Chicago and Produce Exchange in New York are regularly organized institutions and are conducted by the most honorable, fair men in the world, and when you open an account with members of any of these leading exchanges, your money will be safe and you will be assured of honesty in the execution of your orders, and reliability in every way.

Do not trade with bucket shops where the man who sells to you when you buy only profits by your losing.

In this day and time there are very few bucket shops in existence, but once in a while one does spring up and, for your own protection, be sure that when you open your account, it is with a regular broker who is a member of one of the leading exchanges. It will be easy for you to find out who a reliable broker is and who is a member of the exchange. Banks always know about this and every broker is required to publish a list of the exchanges of which he is a member.

CHAPTER II

FORM READING

RULES FOR DETERMINING THE TREND OF COMMODITIES

STUDY: A man who will not work hard and STUDY and pay in advance for success will never get it. If you will put in the time, study and go over the records of Wheat, Soy Beans, Cotton and other Commodities for many years back, you will be convinced that the rules work and that you can make money by following the main trend of the Commodity market.

FORM READING: Eighty-five per cent of what any of us learn is from what we see. It has been well said, "One good picture is worth a thousand words." That is why FORM READING, or the reading of various formations at different periods of time, is so valuable. The future is but a repetition of the past. The same formation at TOPS or BOTTOMS or intermediate points at different times indicates the trend of the market. Therefore, when you see the same picture or formation in the market the second and third time, you know what it means and can determine the trend.

You do not have to accept my word that the rules I give you will work in the future as they have in the past, but you owe it to yourself to prove by past records that these rules work; then you will have the faith to follow them and make money.

You can never make a success of anything, if you just guess, follow inside information so-called, tips, or trade on hope. You must not trade on what you think, but on what you know. You must follow proven rules that have proved to be accurate by past history.

CAPITAL REQUIRED

The first point to consider in operating any method on the Commodity market is the amount of capital required, with which you can trade and never lose your capital over a period of 5, 10 or 15 years, and be able to make profits. A method that will make profits and never lose your capital is the kind of a method that every man should follow to make a success.

As a general rule, I have always considered it advisable to use at least $3,000 capital for every 10,000 bushels of Wheat or other Commodity traded in, and to limit STOP LOSS ORDERS to not more than 3 cents on every 10,000 bushels. In this way you will be able to make 10 trades on your capital and the market would have to beat you 10 consecutive times to wipe out your capital, which it will not do if you follow the rules. Whatever amount of capital you use to trade with, follow this rule: Divide your capital into 10 equal parts and never risk more than 10 per cent of your capital on any one trade. Should you lose for three consecutive times, then reduce your trading unit and only risk 10 per cent of your remaining capital. If you follow this rule, your success is almost sure.

When Wheat, Corn, Oats, Rye, or Soy Beans are selling at low levels from 40 to 60c per bushel, you can start with a capital of $1,000.00 and trade in 5,000 bushel lots. The first trade should be made at a time when you can place a *stop loss order* not more than 2 cents away and you should try to start when your risk will only be 1 cent, if possible. In other words, with a capital of $1,500 you must figure that you would be able to make at least 7 to 10 trades and the market would have to beat you 7 to 10 consecutive times to wipe out your trading capital. With this method it is almost impossible for that to happen, provided you follow the rules and trade on definite indications.

This method will make the most money trading when Commodities are selling at high levels. When Wheat or Soy Beans are selling at $1.75 to $2.50 per bushel, you should use $2,000 capital for each 5,000 bushels you trade in.

If you want to start trading in small units or job lots of 1,000 bushels, use a capital of $300 for each 1,000 bushels and never risk more than 3 cents on the initial trade. Try to make the first trade, if possible, where your *stop loss order* will not be more than 1 or 2 cents from buying or selling point. *Never risk more than one-tenth of your capital on any one trade.*

KIND OF CHARTS TO USE

A busy man or specialist should keep a weekly high and low chart on Wheat, Corn, Soy Beans, Cotton, or any Commodity he is interested in. He should also keep up monthly high and low charts on several Commodities and watch them for indications of activity. Watch these different Commodities when they indicate a change in trend and when they show activity. By crossing old TOPS and showing activity, it is a good time to buy, or when they break old BOTTOMS or Resistance Levels, it is a good time to sell short.

QUARTERLY CHART: The more time period used in a chart, the more important it is for determining a change in trend. By a quarterly chart, or a seasonal chart, we mean a chart using the four time periods or seasons of the year. We use the first three months of the year—January, February and March. Then we use the high and low prices of Wheat, Soy Beans or other Commodities for these three months, the Winter quarter. Next we use April, May and June to complete the Spring quarter. After that, July, August and September for the Summer quarter. Last October, November and December, for the Fall quarter. This makes four periods of three months each in each year. Study a quarterly chart carefully and you will see how these quarterly periods show when an important change in trend takes place. Observe how many times after a prolonged advance or decline the first time prices break the BOTTOM of a previous quarter it indicates a change in trend and a Bear market starts. The first time the prices of one quarter exceed the high levels of the previous quarter, it nearly always indicates a change in trend and a Bull market follows. If you will study any quarterly chart carefully and note the position of Wheat or any other Commodity in connection with the monthly high and low chart, and the weekly high and low chart, you will find it very helpful in determining a change in the main trend. I advise keeping up a quarterly chart on each individual Commodity that you trade in.

WHEN TO USE DAILY HIGH AND LOW CHART: When the markets are very active and fluctuating over a wide range, especially in the last stages of a Bull market or the last fast decline in a Bear market, you should keep up a Daily high and low Chart on Wheat, Soy Beans or other Commodities, and the Resistance Levels, applying the same rules as used for the Weekly Chart, because the Daily Chart will give you the first change in the minor trend, which may later be confirmed by the Weekly Chart as a change of the main trend. Full instructions will follow under "Resistance Levels."

MAJOR AND MINOR TRENDS

You will always make the most money by following the main trend of the market, although to say that you must never trade against the trend means that you will miss a lot of intermediate moves which will made big profits. Your rule must be: When you are trading against the trend, wait until one of the rules gives you a definite indication of a buying or selling point at BOTTOM or TOP, where you can place *close stop loss orders.*

There are always two trends—a major trend and a minor trend. The minor trend is a reversal of the main trend, which lasts for a short period of time. When the main trend is down, it is much safer to sell Wheat or other Commodities short on rallies at a point where the rules indicate that they are TOP than it is to buy on a reaction.

In a Bull campaign or advancing market, it is much safer to wait for minor reactions and buy when the rules indicate that it is time to buy than it is to sell short on rallies. You will always make the most money by waiting for a definite indication of the trend before *buying* and *selling.*

PRICE TELLS THE TREND

Because history does repeat, the price of Wheat or other Commodities *tells* the *story* of the *future,* because it records the consensus of opinion throughout the country. Commodities do not go up unless there is *increased buying.* They do not *go down* unless there is *increased selling.* The price of Wheat or any Commodity tells what everybody is thinking and what the majority of people are doing. The price registers *Supply* and *Demand.*

Greed, and desire for large gains, do not change. They are inherent elements of human nature, and it is the *human element* that *beats* the *average man* and causes *losses* in business investment or speculation. The *human element* prevents a man from taking *paper profits* when he has them. He hopes and *wants too much.* When a man has a *loss,* he *hopes* and *refuses* to sell because he expects a *rally* that *does not* come. The trouble is, he does not *face facts.* When the market goes against him, the *quicker* he *acts, the better.* He *hopes* for *rallies* and finally when *hope* gives *way* to *despair,* he *sells out,* and often at the *BOTTOM. Never trade* when you are *scared,* and *never trade* just on *hope. Do not guess.* Follow my rules. Success can only be attained by following *definite rules. Change* when *conditions change* and when the *trend changes,* but have a *rule* and a *reason,* so that you will not guess that the *trend is changing,* but will *know.* Too much *hope* is more *dangerous* than *fear* and will leave man in *greater disaster.*

PERCENTAGE OF HIGHEST SELLING PRICE, LOWEST SELLING PRICE AND RANGE

Mathematics is the one *exact* science. All nations agree on the accuracy of the science of mathematics and use it, regardless of what language they speak. In all other lines, scientists disagree, but when it comes to using mathematics, the chemists, the astronomer, the economist and the accountant all rely upon mathematics and agree upon its accuracy. They all agree that 2 and 2 make 4. Any method or system to make money trading in Commodities must be based upon the exact law of mathematics. Each TOP or BOTTOM in Wheat, or other Commodities comes out in accordance with an exact mathematical proportion to some other TOP or BOTTOM.

BOTTOMS FORECAST FUTURE TOPS

RULE: From any extreme low level of Wheat, Soy Beans, Cotton, or other Commodities, use the low level as a base and use the percentage of this base to determine the Resistance points from TOPS to BOTTOMS on the way up.

The basis of our money is 100 cents to the dollar, or $1.00 as a unit. The correct way to figure percentages is to divide the low price by 8, getting 12½ percent, 25 percent, 33 1/3 percent, 37½ percent, 50 percent, 62½ percent, 66 2/3 percent, 75 percent, 87½ percent, and 100 percent. These are the most important percentages. *Fifty percent, or one-half of the lowest selling point is the most important point, for Resistance or for TOPS or BOTTOMS.* The next or most important point, is three-fourths, or 75 percent, DOUBLING THE LOW PRICE or 100 percent is the next most *important point.*

Remember this rule, that a *100 percent advance* from any BOTTOM, or a *50 percent advance* from any BOTTOM, are the two most *important points* to watch for determining Resistance points, *high or low levels.* You must apply *time cycles* and *time rules* in connection with figuring percentages on the BOTTOM.

EVEN PERCENTAGE OF HIGH AND LOW PRICES

We have given the rules for percentages of high and low prices of 12½ percent and multiples of 12½ percent and 33 1/3 percent and 66 2/3 percent. But for COTTON, LARD, HIDES, RUBBER and other commodities that fluctuate in points of one hundredths of a cent, the RESISTANCE LEVELS will often come out around 10 percent, 20 percent, 30 percent, 40 percent, 60 percent, 70 percent and 80 percent of these important TOPS and BOTTOMS.

Sometimes when a market is very strong, a decline will only run 10 percent of the last high instead of 12½ percent. At other times, if the market is very weak, a rally will only run 10 percent instead of 12½ percent. At other times the reactions and rallies will come out around 20 percent instead of 25 percent.

You can also apply 10 percent and multiples of 10 percent to advances or declines or percentages of high and low prices of WHEAT, CORN and other commodities that sell at cents per bushel.

After the market makes FINAL BOTTOM and has the first SECONDARY REACTION of importance, figure the percentage of that secondary reaction. Then watch for other reactions to run about the same. This is your yard, or measuring stick, for future movements.

For instance, suppose a decline runs 20 percent on the first reaction. Then watch 20 percent reaction and when the market exceeds 20 percent, figure that the trend is changing.

Suppose that the first rally was 20 percent, 25 percent or 50 percent, of the first sharp decline. Then watch the market on the way down and see if the same rallies or the same percentages run, and then when the market has run out enough time, watch for the first time that the market rallies a greater percentage than the last or first percentage, then it indicates the trend is changing.

But remember that the most important thing is the TIME PERIOD and when time overbalances or shows a change in trend, it is much more important than a percentage of prices. For example, after a prolonged advance, if a commodity has never reacted more than two months or one month, the first time that it exceeds this time period, it indicates a change in trend. Apply the same rule on the DOWN side. The first time the time period exceeds the greatest time period on the way down, consider the trend has changed, at least temporarily.

TOPS FORECAST FUTURE BOTTOMS OR LOW LEVELS

By using the percentage of the TOPS, you can determine Resistance points or BOTTOMS on the way down. Follow this rule. You must also use the range between extreme high and extreme low, 50% of this range is a very important resistance point; 75% next important and 100% most important. You must never overlook using the lowest BOTTOM, as well as other BOTTOMS, and must never fail to use the highest TOP, or the extreme highest level, as well as minor TOPS. Always consider extreme high and low levels as most important.

WHEAT: Going back to 1852 and using the base, or BOTTOM, of 28½, 100% advance equals 57. 200% advance equals 85½. 250% advance equals 99¾. My rule is that a 50% advance on the lowest selling price or 150% advance, 250 or 300 are the most important points. Of these the most important points to watch are the 50% and the 100% advances.

RESISTANCE LEVELS

If we wish to avert failure in speculation, we must deal with causes. Everything in existence is based on exact proportion and perfect relation. There is no chance in nature, because mathematical principles of the highest order are at the foundation of all things. Faraday said: "There is nothing in the Universe but mathematical points of force."

Every Commodity makes a TOP or BOTTOM on some exact mathematical point in proportion to some previous high or low level.

The movement of Wheat, or any Commodity between extreme high and extreme low, either in a major or minor move, is very important and by a proper division of this range of fluctuation, we determine the points where Resistance or support will be met on a reverse move, either up or down.

By carefully watching these Resistance Levels in connection with time periods, you can make a greater success and trade with closer *stop loss orders*. You can tell by the Resistance Points why Wheat or other Commodities should receive support or meet selling at old TOPS or BOTTOMS.

RANGE OF FLUCTUATIONS

12½ OR 1/8: Take the extreme low and extreme high of any important move. Subtract the low from the high to get the range. Then divide the range of fluctuation by 8 to get the 1/8 points, or 12½, 25%, etc., which are Resistance Levels or buying and selling points. When Wheat, or other Commodity, stops around these levels and makes BOTTOM or TOP on or near them it shows a change on the time period. This is the place to buy or sell. Sometimes Wheat, Soy Beans, or other Commodities will hold for 3 to 7 days, or longer, making BOTTOM or TOP around these important Resistance Levels, and at other times may hold for several weeks around them, proving that buying or selling takes place around these points.

33 1/3% AND 66 2/3% OR 1/3 AND 2/3 POINTS: After dividing a Commodity by 8 to get the 1/8 points, the next important thing to do is to divide the range of fluctuation by 3 to get 1/3 and 2/3 points. These 1/3 and 2/3 points are very strong, especially if they fall near other Resistance Points of previous moves or when they are divisions of a very wide range. The 1/3 point equals 33 1/3 percent, and 2/3 equals 66 2/3 percent.

HIGHEST SELLING PRICE

Next in importance is the division of the highest price at which a Commodity has ever sold and each lower top.

Divide the highest selling price by 8 to get the 1/8 points and also divide by 3 to get the 1/3 and 2/3 points.

This is very important, as a Commodity after breaking the half-way point or 50% of the fluctuating range, will often decline to the half-way point of the highest selling price, and will also work on the other Resistance Points in the same way.

When Wheat or other Commodities are advancing, they will often cross the half-way point or 50% of the highest selling point and then advance to the half-way point of the fluctuation range and meet Resistance.

MOST IMPORTANT COMMODITY MOVEMENTS TO CONSIDER: The first and most important point: Consider the Resistance Levels between the extreme high and extreme low in the history of Wheat, Soy Beans, Cotton, or other Commodities.

Next important point to consider: Resistance Points or divisions of the highest price at which the Commodity has ever sold.

Then consider the fluctuation of each campaign which runs one year or more, the longer the time period, the more important. Figure the range between extreme high and extreme low and divide into 8 equal parts to get the Resistance Points.

Then figure a third or fourth lower TOP and divide it by 8 to get the Resistance Points.

SECONDARY BOTTOMS AND TOPS: After the market has made final *bottom* in a Bear Campaign and the first rally takes place, then follows a *secondary reaction,* making a *higher bottom.* The half-way or 50% point between the high of the first rally and the low on secondary decline is very important from which to figure Resistance Levels. The half-way point between the TOP of the first rally and the BOTTOM of the secondary reaction is a strong support point.

After final TOP in a Bull Campaign has been reached and the first sharp decline takes place, a *secondary rally* follows, making a *lower* TOP. This *lower top* is an important point from which to figure Resistance Levels. The half-way point between the BOTTOM of the first reaction and the secondary TOP is a strong Resistance Level.

STRENGTH OF RESISTANCE LEVELS: When a Commodity is advancing and crosses the 1/4 or 25% point, the next most important point to watch is the half-way point or gravity center, or 50% of the Average of the range of fluctuations.

Second, the next point above the half-way point is the 5/8 point, or $62\frac{1}{2}$%.

Third, the next and strongest point after the half-way point is crossed is the 3/4 point, or 75%.

Fourth, if the range is very wide, it is important to watch the 7/8 point, or $87\frac{1}{2}$%, of the move. This will often mark the TOP of an advance.

But in watching these Resistance Points, always watch the time period and old TOPS and BOTTOMS on the weekly chart and follow rules given on Formations. If Wheat, or other Commodities, start making TOPS or BOTTOMS around these Resistance levels, it is safe to sell or buy.

THE 50% OR HALF-WAY POINT

Always remember that the 50% reaction or half-way point of the range of fluctuation of the extreme highest point is a point for support on the down side or for meeting selling and Resistance on the way up. This is the balancing point because it divides the range of fluctuation into two equal parts.

When Wheat advances or declines to this half-way point, you should sell or buy with a *stop loss order* 1, 2, or 3 cents, according to whether Wheat is selling at very high or very low levels.

The wider the range and the longer the time period, the more important is this half-way point when it is reached.

You can make a fortune by following this one rule alone. A careful study and review of past movements in any Commodity will prove to you beyond doubt that this rule works and that you can make profits following it.

A minor half-way point would be the $\frac{1}{2}$ point between a minor TOP and a minor BOTTOM. Reactions usually run half of the last move or to the half-way point.

When the range between the $\frac{1}{2}$ or 50% point, and the $\frac{5}{8}$ or $62\frac{1}{2}$% point is 8 to 12 cents or more, and the Commodity crosses the half-way point, it will go to the $\frac{5}{8}$ point and meet Resistance and then react or decline. The $\frac{5}{8}$ point is a very important point to watch for TOP or reaction. Wheat will often react from the $\frac{5}{8}$ point back to the half-way point and be a buy again.

The same rule applies when Wheat, or a Commodity, is declining. If the range is 15 to 20 cents or more between the $\frac{1}{2}$ point and the $\frac{3}{8}$ point, then Wheat breaks the half-way point; it will decline to the $\frac{3}{8}$ point and make BOTTOM and rally to the $\frac{1}{2}$ or 50% point or higher.

When Wheat is in a narrow trading range, it will often fluctuate between the $\frac{5}{8}$ point on the up side and the $\frac{3}{8}$ point below the half-way point, making BOTTOMS and TOPS around the half-way point and at the $\frac{5}{8}$ and $\frac{3}{8}$ points, moving in $\frac{1}{4}$ of the full range of fluctuation. See examples later in the book.

When Wheat or any Commodity advances to a half-way point and reacts several points from this level, then finally goes through it, you can expect it to make the next Resistance point indicated on your Resistance Level Card or the next old TOP.

The same applies when Wheat or any other Commodity declines and receives support several times at a half-way point, then breaks through it. It indicates the next Resistance point on your Resistance Level Card or the next important BOTTOM.

STRONGEST POINTS: The greatest indication   strength is when a commodity holds one or more points above the half-way point, which shows that buying or support orders were placed above this important *Resistance Level.*

WEAKEST POINTS: A sign of *weakness* is when a Commodity *advances* and fails to reach the half-way point by one or more points, or by 1 or 2c per bushel, then declines and breaks the last BOTTOM or other Resistance points.

NEXT RESISTANCE LEVELS

AFTER THE MAIN HALF-WAY POINT HAS BEEN BROKEN: The next Resistance Level to watch after the main half-way point has been broken is the next half-way point of some previous move. By Main half-way point, I mean the half-way or 50% point of the extreme fluctuating range of the life of Wheat, or any Commodity.

Another very important Resistance Level after the main half-way point is crossed is the half-way point or ½ of the highest selling price. This is a stronger support level than the half-way point of minor fluctuating moves because it cuts the highest selling price in half, and is a strong buying or selling point until it is crossed by 3 cents. It is important when Wheat, or any other Commodity, is selling at very high levels, medium or low prices.

RESISTANCE POINTS NEAR SAME LEVELS: When two half-way points or any other two Resistance Points, either in the range of fluctuation or the division of the highest selling price, occur near the same level, you should add these two points together and divide by 2, as the half-way point between these two points will often be a support point on a decline or a selling point on a rally.

HOW TO LOOK UP RESISTANCE LEVELS: When you find an important Resistance Level or the strongest one—the half-way or 50% point—at a certain level, look to see if there are any other Resistance Levels around this price, whether it be ⅛, ¼, ⅜, ⅝, or 2/3 point. You may find 3 or 4 Resistance Levels around the same price. The more you find, the stronger Resistance the market will meet when it reaches this level. Take the highest Resistance Level around this same price and the lowest, and add them together to get the average point of Resistance.

Watch the activity of Wheat or other Commodity, when it reaches these Resistance Levels. If it is advancing very fast or declining very fast on large volume of sales, do not consider that it is going to stop around these Resistance Levels unless it stops or holds one or two days around these prices. Then sell or buy with *stop loss orders.* Also consider whether the market is in 3rd or 4th section from BOTTOM or in 3rd or 4th section from TOP down, as time is very important.

Use all the rules and figure that the important TOPS and BOTTOMS will come out on the strongest points, like the 1/3, 2/3, ¼, ⅜, ½, ⅝ and ¾ points.

Do not overlook the fact that it requires time for a market to get ready at the BOTTOM before it advances and requires time to distribute at the TOP. The longer a market has been running, the more time it will require to complete accumulation or distribution, except rapid advances which make sharp single TOPS, then break back fast.

WHEN WHEAT OR COMMODITIES DECLINE UNDER OLD TOPS. When Wheat breaks back under old TOPS of previous campaigns the Resistance Levels between old BOTTOMS and these old TOPS will be important points for support and Resistance. Examples follow later in the book.

SMALL GAINS IN LAST STAGE OF BULL OR BEAR MARKET. When a bull or advancing market is nearing the end of a campaign, the gains or runs will often get smaller, which is a sign that Wheat or other Commodities are meeting with greater selling pressure.

Example: Suppose Wheat is moving up and crosses a previous TOP and advances 20 cents, then reacts 10 cents; later crosses the last TOP and advances 15 cents and reacts 5 to 7½ cents; again advances above the last TOP, but only goes 10 cents above it and reacts 5 cents or more, this would be a sign of weakness or that the TOP was near, because each move was making a smaller gain. In very active fast markets, when volumes of sales are large, the last run may be a greater number of points or cents. Reverse this rule in a declining market.

If Wheat has made several moves down of 10, 15, or 20 points or cents, and each one gets shorter or when Wheat breaks BOTTOM and the declines get smaller, it is a sign that the selling pressure is decreasing and that a change in trend is near. In fast panicky markets the last decline may be a larger number of points with very small rallies. This is a final wave of liquidation.

In the last stages of BULL or BEAR campaigns, use only the half-way or 50% points of short or minor moves. It is most important to watch the Resistance Levels of the final move, which may have run several weeks or months, particularly the half-way point. When it is exceeded by 3 full cents, the trend usually reverses.

LOST MOTION: There is lost motion in every kind of machinery. There is also lost motion in the Grain market or any other Commodity due to momentum, which drives Wheat or other Commodities slightly above or below a Resistance Level. The average lost motion is 1⅞ cents. That is why a 3 cent *stop loss order* is best and is caught the least number of times.

When Wheat or Soy Beans are very active and advance or decline fast on heavy volume, they will often go 1⅞ cents above a half-way point or other strong Resistance Level but will not go 3 cents beyond it. The same rule applies on a decline. It will often pass an important Resistance Point by 1⅞ cents, but not go 3 full points or cents beyond it.

This is the same rule that applies to a gravity center in anything. If we could bore a hole through the earth and then drop a ball, momentum would carry it beyond the gravity center, but when it slowed down, it would finally settle on the exact center. This is the way Wheat or Commodities act around these important centers.

A study of the Resistance Levels between BOTTOMS and TOPS of different Commodities will prove how accurately the market works out to these important points.

RULES TO DETERMINE BUYING LEVELS

BUYING POINTS

1. BUY at OLD BOTTOMS or OLD TOPS. When a commodity declines to an OLD BOTTOM or to an OLD TOP, it is always a buying point with a STOP LOSS ORDER. In fact, you should never buy unless you can figure where to place a STOP LOSS ORDER 1c to 3c away and when commodities are selling at high prices, never more than 5c away.

For cotton, place stops 20 to 40 points—never more than 60 points when prices are at very high levels. Remember, it is safe to buy when a commodity reacts to OLD TOPS the first, second, or third time, but when it declines to the same level the fourth time, it is dangerous to buy, as it nearly always goes lower.

BUY when wheat or any commodity declines 1c to 3c under old tops or old bottoms. However, wheat or any commodity is always strongest if it holds just around the OLD TOPS or OLD BOTTOMS and does not break 1c to 3c under. Holding slightly higher than these old levels is a still stronger indication.

When wheat is selling at $1.00 or higher and crosses OLD TOPS, it can react 5c but is stronger if it stops at OLD TOPS or only goes 1c to 2c under OLD TOPS. After prices cross OLD TOPS they can react 5 points under the OLD TOPS but not more. If the market is really strong, it should not go as much as 5c under $1.00, except in very rare cases when the market is in a wide trading range and very active.

2. SAFER BUYING POINT. Buy when wheat, cotton or any commodity crosses a series of tops of previous weeks, showing that the minor or the main trend has turned up as indicated by charts on individual commodities.

3. SAFEST BUYING POINT. Buy on a secondary reaction after wheat, cotton or any commodity has crossed previous weekly tops and the advance exceeds the greatest rally on the way down from the top.

4. BUY when the first rally from the extreme bottom exceeds in time the greatest rally in the preceding Bear Campaign.

5. BUY when the period of time exceeds the last rally before extreme lows were reached. If the last rally was 3 or 4 weeks, when the advance from the bottom is more than 3 or 4 weeks, consider the trend has turned up and commodities are a safer buy on a secondary reaction. Examples later in the book will prove this rule.

6. BUY AFTER BREAKAWAY POINTS ARE CROSSED ON INDIVIDUAL COMMODITIES. The market will then be in the runaway move where you can make large profits in a short period of time.

7. BUY when wheat, corn, cotton or any commodity declines to 50% of highest selling prices, or to ½ or 50% range between extreme high or extreme low prices. This is one of the safe buying points as we will prove later by examples of past market movements. When there is a 50% reaction of the last move up, it becomes a buying point so long as

the main trend is up. Watch the action of wheat, soy beans, cotton or other commodities when they react to ⅞, ¾, ⅝, ⅜, ¼ and ⅛ points of previous moves. If the commodity holds for several days or weeks around one of these points it is a place to buy, protected with a STOP LOSS ORDER. Remember that ¼, ½ and ¾ are the strongest resistance points and as a rule are the best buying points, especially as long as the main trend is up.

8. BUY against double or triple bottoms, or buy on first, second or third higher bottom and buy a second lot after wheat, soy beans or cotton makes second or third higher bottom, then crosses previous top. Always use STOP LOSS ORDERS for protection in case the market reverses. REMEMBER YOU CAN'T BE RIGHT ALL THE TIME. The STOP LOSS ORDER gets you out if you are wrong. Try to take small losses and large profits. That is the way to keep ahead of the market.

9. BUYING RULE FOR RAPID ADVANCES AT HIGH LEVELS. In the last stages of a Bull Market in wheat, soy beans, cotton or any other commodity, reactions are small. Buy on 2 day reactions and follow up with STOP LOSS ORDER 1c to 2c under each day's low level. Then when the low of a previous day is broken you will be out. Markets sometimes run 10 to 30 days without breaking low of previous day.

Examples will be shown later in the book.

RULES TO DETERMINE SELLING LEVELS

When we refer to selling points we mean to either sell out long commodities or sell short.

1. SELL at OLD TOPS or OLD BOTTOMS. An important point to sell out longs and sell short is at OLD TOPS or when wheat or commodities rally to OLD BOTTOMS the first, second or third time. As a rule, it is risky to sell the fourth time that wheat or any commodity advances to the same level because it nearly always goes higher. When you sell short, place STOP LOSS ORDERS 1c, 2c or 3c above OLD TOPS or OLD BOTTOMS. For cotton, place stops 20, 40 and not more than 60 points above OLD TOPS or under OLD BOTTOMS. When prices are at high levels above $1.00, the prices can advance 5 points above old tops or 5 points above old bottoms without changing the main trend.

When wheat, soy beans and corn are selling at $1.25, $1.50 or $2.00 per bushel, prices can go 5c above OLD TOPS or 5c under OLD BOTTOMS. But this seldom happens, as a study of previous tops and bottoms will prove. When the market is weak and the main trend down, the rallies stop right under OLD BOTTOMS and should not go more than 2 points above them. If prices go 3 points above, it is an indication that the market is strong and likely to go higher. If prices decline 5c under these levels, this indicates that the market is very weak.

2. SAFER SELLING POINT. Sell when wheat, soy beans, cotton, or any commodity breaks the low of a previous week or a series of bottoms of previous weeks as indicated by the trend and rules.

3. *SAFEST SELLING POINT*. Sell on a *secondary rally* after wheat, soy beans, cotton, or any commodity has broken the previous bottoms of several weeks or has broken the bottom of the last reaction, turning trend down. This *secondary rally* nearly always comes after the first sharp decline in the first section of a Bear Campaign.

4. SELL after the first decline exceeds the greatest reaction in the preceding Bull Campaign or the last reaction before final top.

5. SELL after BREAKAWAY POINT is crossed.

6. SELL when the period of time of the first decline exceeds the last reaction before final top of the Bull Campaign. Example: If wheat or any commodity has advanced for several months or for one year, or more, and the greatest reaction has been four weeks, which is an average reaction in a Bull Market, then after top is reached and the first decline runs more than 4 weeks, it is an indication of a change in the minor trend or the main trend. The commodity will be a safer short sale on any rally because you will be trading with the trend after it has been definitely defined.

7. SELL at 50% or ½ point of last high to low of sharp decline or sell at 50% of highest selling point or 50% of greatest range. Sell when wheat, soy beans, cotton, or any commodity rallies 50% of a previous move down. Examples will be given later in the book to prove this rule.

8. SELL against Double Tops or Triple Tops, or SELL when the market makes lower tops or lower bottoms. It is safe to sell when wheat, soy beans, or cotton, makes a second, third, or fourth, lower top, also safe to sell after *double* and *triple bottoms* are broken. Remember to always place a *stop loss order* and trade with the main trend.

9. SELL in last stages of Bear Market or when there is rapid decline and only 2 days rallies and follow down with *stop loss order* 1 cent above the high of the previous day. When wheat or any commodity rallies 1 cent or more above the high of the previous day you will be out on *stop*. Fast declining markets will often run 10 to 30 days without crossing high of the previous day. Examples will be given later in the book.

WHAT IS MEANT BY TOPS AND BOTTOMS

In order that you may not be confused, I will define what is meant by a bottom. A bottom does not mean the low of any day, week or month. A top does not mean the high of any day, week or month. Of course, the low of any day, week or month is the bottom of that particular day. The top of any particular month or week is the top of that day, week or month, but this does not refer to a *buying* or *selling* point.

When I refer to a SINGLE TOP, DOUBLE TOP, or TRIPLE TOP, I mean a price at which wheat, soy beans or cotton has advanced and reacted below some previous bottom on the daily or weekly chart, making a swing down and then a swing up. The bottom is the low of that particular swing. The last extreme low level is called a FINAL BOTTOM. The last extreme high level is called a FINAL TOP. Examples will be given later in the book to prove this rule.

SINGLE TOPS AND BOTTOMS. A SINGLE TOP is where wheat, soy beans, corn or cotton advances to a high level and does not reach the same level a second time, days, weeks or months apart. A SINGLE BOTTOM is where wheat or other commodities decline to a low level, making a bottom, and does not reach this same level again days, weeks, or months later. From SINGLE TOPS, LOWER TOPS are made. From SINGLE BOTTOMS, higher BOTTOMS are made.

DOUBLE TOPS AND BOTTOMS. A DOUBLE TOP IS WHEN THE PRICE ADVANCES TO A HIGH LEVEL, then reacts and advances again to the same level a second time. These DOUBLE TOPS are more important if they occur weeks, months or years apart. The more time between the top and bottom, the more important it is.

For example: If wheat made a top one year and then one year later made the same top, failing to cross it would indicate a greater decline, and a Bear market to follow. Apply the same rules to bottoms which occur several years apart. The farther apart they are, when they make a double bottom and hold, the greater advance to follow. DOUBLE TOPS are the safest to SELL against protected with *stop loss orders*. DOUBLE BOTTOMS are SAFEST TO BUY against protected with *stop loss orders*. STOP LOSS ORDERS, as a rule are 2 to 3 cents below the BOTTOMS. The SAFEST STOP LOSS ORDER IS 3 cents above or below any old top or bottom, as these are caught the least number of times.

TRIPLE TOPS AND BOTTOMS. TRIPLE TOPS and BOTTOMS are the MOST IMPORTANT. By going over past records you will find that the greatest advances and declines, or those that last the longest, start from TRIPLE TOPS or TRIPLE BOTTOMS. TRIPLE BOTTOMS occurring several weeks apart are more important than several days apart. TRIPLE TOPS occurring several months apart are more important than several weeks apart, and the most important campaigns start when TRIPLE TOPS or BOTTOMS occur several YEARS APART.

For example: The same low level occurring in THREE CONSECUTIVE YEARS at different times, or the same high level occurring in THREE CONSECUTIVE YEARS at different times, indicates THE GREATEST REVERSAL and the GREATEST ADVANCE or DECLINE. Therefore, it is IMPORTANT to WATCH for these TRIPLE TOPS OR TRIPLE BOTTOMS, because they are very significant of changes in trend, and very important to trade against. Example later of Triple Tops and Bottoms.

FOURTH TOP SAME LEVEL. This is something that very seldom occurs, but when a top is made around the same level for the FOURTH TIME and wheat, cotton or soy beans fail to go through this level, it means a big REVERSAL AND RAPID DECLINE. Our rule says that when wheat, soy beans, or cotton advance to the same level a fourth time, the trend nearly always reverses and it goes through to HIGHER LEVELS. When they reach the same level the fourth time watch prices very closely for a MAJOR CHANGE IN TREND.

FOURTH TIME NEAR SAME LOW LEVEL. When wheat, soy beans, or cotton decline to the same low level or bottom the FOURTH TIME and fail to go through, then reverse and turn the trend up, it is a sure indication of MUCH HIGHER PRICES, because in most cases, when the decline occurs and the prices reach the same level the FOURTH TIME, they usually go through to much lower prices. Always follow the rule when prices break through BOTTOMS THE FOURTH TIME. You can expect much lower prices and only small rallies.

Remember that commodities remain much longer at low levels than they do at high levels. After a long decline it takes time for accumulation to take place, confidence to be established and for the public to start buying again on a large scale.

TWENTY-EIGHT VALUABLE RULES

In order to make a success trading in the commodity market, the trader must have definite rules and follow them. The rules given below are based upon my personal experience and anyone who follows them will make a success.

1. Amount of capital to use: Divide your capital into 10 equal parts and never risk more than one-tenth of your capital on any one trade.

2. Use *stop loss orders*. Always protect a trade when you make it with a *stop loss order* 1 to 3 cents, never more than 5 cents away, cotton 20 to 40, never more than 60 points away.

3. Never overtrade. This would be violating your capital rules.

4. Never let a profit run into a loss. After you once have a profit of 3 cents or more, raise your *stop loss order* so that you will have no loss of capital. For cotton when the profits are 60 points or more place *stop* where there will be no loss.

5. Do not buck the trend. Never buy or sell if you are not sure of the trend according to your charts and rules.

6. When in doubt, get out, and don't get in when in doubt.

7. Trade only in active markets. Keep out of slow, dead ones.

8. Equal distribution of risk. Trade in 2 or 3 different commodities, if possible. Avoid tying up all your capital in any one commodity.

9. Never limit your orders or fix a buying or selling price. Trade at the market.

10. Don't close your trades without a good reason. Follow up with a *stop loss order* to protect your profits.

11. Accumulate a surplus. After you have made a series of successful trades, put some money into a surplus account to be used only in emergency or in times of panic.

12. Never buy or sell just to get a scalping profit.

13. Never average a loss. This is one of the worst mistakes a trader can make.

14. Never get out of the market just because you have lost patience or get into the market because you are anxious from waiting.

15. Avoid taking small profits and big losses.

16. Never cancel a *stop loss order* after you have placed it at the time you make a trade.

17. Avoid getting in and out of the market too often.

18. Be just as willing to sell short as you are to buy. Let your object be to keep with the trend and make money.

19. Never buy just because the price of a commodity is low or sell short just because the price is high.

20. Be careful about pyramiding at the wrong time. Wait until the commodity is very active and has crossed Resistance Levels before buying more and until it has broken out of the zone of distribution before selling more.

21. Select the commodities that show strong uptrend to pyramid on the buying side and the ones that show definite downtrend to sell short.

22. Never hedge. If you are long of one commodity and it starts to go down, do not sell another commodity short to hedge it. Get out at the market; take your loss and wait for another opportunity.

23. Never change your position in the market without a good reason. When you make a trade, let it be for some good reason or according to some definite rule; then do not get out without a definite indication of a change in trend.

24. Avoid increasing your trading after a long period of success or a period of profitable trades.

25. Don't guess when the market is top. Let the market prove it is top. Don't guess when the market is bottom. Let the market prove it is bottom. By following definite rules, you can do this.

26. Do not follow another man's advice unless you know that he knows more than you do.

27. Reduce trading after first loss; never increase.

28. Avoid getting in wrong and out wrong; getting in right and out wrong; this is making double mistakes.

When you decide to make a trade be sure that you are not violating any of these 28 rules which are vital and important to your success. When you close a trade with a loss, go over these rules and see which rule you have violated; then do not make the same mistake the second time. Experience and investigation will convince you of the value of these rules, and observation and study will lead you to a correct and practical theory for successful Trading in Commodities.

TOPS AND BOTTOMS

HIGHER BOTTOMS AND HIGHER TOPS. Supply and demand govern market movements and it requires a greater buying power than a selling power to force commodities to higher levels. When the selling pressure is greater than the buying pressure, wheat, soy beans, cotton, and other commodities work lower. After commodities make bottom and start to advance, if they continue to make higher bottoms and higher tops, the trend is up. They must make higher bottoms and higher tops in order to show a strong Bull market. Therefore, it is very important to watch THE FIRST, SECOND, THIRD and FOURTH HIGHER BOTTOMS, and remember to always use the rule of three in everything. The THIRD HIGHER bottom is just as important as THREE BOTTOMS at the SAME LEVEL, because it shows the market is gaining strength and is receiving good support. After it makes a THIRD higher BOTTOM on a swing and goes through to a new high level, or crosses the last top resistance level, it is indication of much higher prices.

HIGHER TOPS AND HIGHER BOTTOMS. For a market to continue to advance and SHOW A BULL MARKET, it must RAISE its BOTTOM and RAISE its TOP; however, a market may stay in a trading range for a long time without ever LOWERING A PREVIOUS TOP, but when it does BREAK OUT into a NEW HIGH or NEW LOW, then it indicates much GREATER RANGE OF PRICES. A DECLINING MARKET must LOWER the TOPS and LOWER the BOTTOMS because this SHOWS when pressure is WORKING AGAINST the MARKET or when SUPPORT is greater than SELLING PRESSURE.

LOWER TOPS AND LOWER BOTTOMS. After a market makes the FINAL TOP and selling pressure is greater than the buying pressure, it must naturally decline and make lower bottoms and lower tops, because the trend has changed to the down side.

CROSSING OLD TOPS OR BREAKING OLD BOTTOMS. When wheat, soy beans, or any other commodity crosses old tops or advances above the highs of previous campaigns, whether it be a weekly or monthly top, it is an indication of stronger buying power and a change of trend. After these old tops are crossed, the market often advances 3 to 5 cents and then declines to the old top levels, sometimes declining 2 cents under them, but seldom declining 3 cents. Therefore, it is a safe place to buy when the market reacts to the old top, or buy 1 or 2 cents under the old top, protected with *stop loss order* 3 cents away.

When a Commodity breaks old bottoms or previous bottoms on a weekly, monthly or swing chart, it indicates that the trend has turned down. The market may go 5 or more cents lower and then rally back to these old bottoms. That is why it is a safe short sale of wheat or any commodity with stop 2 or 3 cents away. Sometimes the market will rally 1 to 2 cents above these old bottoms, but seldom goes 3 cents. The rule is, old bottoms become tops and old tops become bottoms. What was at one time the *ceiling* later becomes the base, bottom or buying point. What was at one time the base or bottom, after it is broken and the market rallies, becomes the *ceiling,* top or selling point.

SECONDARY RALLY OR LOWER TOP. After a prolonged advance when wheat or any commodity reaches final high and the Bull campaign is over, there is usually a sharp severe decline, lasting anywhere from 1 to 2 and possibly 3 weeks or months. After the first sharp decline, the market may remain in narrow trading range for 10 days or 2 or 3 weeks, or in some cases even longer.

After that, there is a SECONDARY RALLY, sometimes getting up near the OLD TOP and sometimes not reaching it by many points. Going over past records you will find that a market seldom fails to have this SECONDARY RALLY. When this SECONDARY RALLY comes, especially after the TREND has TURNED DOWN, it is the safest rally on which to SELL SHORT, because the decline is faster from that time on and rallies are smaller. Examples will be given later in the book.

By knowing that these SECONDARY RALLIES usually take place, you should always cover shorts on the first sharp break and then BUY for the SECOND RALLY. Never buy until the market has given an indication that it is TURNING the TREND UP again. The safest place to SELL SHORT, especially the second lot, is after the TOP of the SECONDARY RALLY when the market breaks the bottom of a previous day or week of a swing movement, showing that the main trend is again down.

SECONDARY DECLINE OR HIGHER BOTTOM. After a Bear campaign ends, whether it ends with a sharp severe decline, or declines slowly, making FINAL BOTTOM, there is usually a quick rally lasting anywhere from a few weeks to two months. Then the SECONDARY REACTION takes place, making a HIGHER BOTTOM, and this BOTTOM is the SAFEST PLACE to BUY, although you should always try to BUY near the LOW LEVELS, but waiting until the trend shows a definite indication of change. Never guess. If you guess, you are likely to miss the BOTTOMS and TOPS by many points. If you wait for definite indication, follow rules, you will get in near TOP and BOTTOM.

Watch the FIRST, SECOND and THIRD lower TOPS, because they are important, and the THIRD LOWER TOP is just as important as THREE TOPS AT THE SAME LEVEL and is one of the SAFE PLACES TO SELL SHORT for a greater decline. Remember the market often makes TWO OR THREE SWINGS up while distribution is taking place, and makes TWO or THREE LOWER TOPS before the big break starts or the long Bear campaign gets under way.

HIGHER BOTTOMS AND LOWER TOPS. This is something that often occurs, when the market is in a trading range. The BOTTOMS WORK UP, continue to make slightly HIGHER BOTTOMS but LOWER TOPS. This happens when the market is COMING TO A BALANCE and getting ready to break out one way or the other. After making a SERIES of HIGHER BOTTOMS and slightly LOWER TOPS, when the market CROSSES TOPS, it is an indication of much higher levels. On the other hand, the FIRST TIME IT BREAKS AN IMPORTANT BOTTOM, it is an indication support has been withdrawn and that the decline will continue.

COMMODITIES THAT FAIL TO CROSS FORMER TOPS IN A BULL MARKET. Many commodities do not follow a Bull campaign. If wheat or some other commodity has been advancing for some time and fail to cross the former tops, it is an indication that they are not in a strong position and YOU SHOULD NOT BUY THEM. Always BUY the commodities that show they are in the STRONGER POSITION by applying all the rules. If they cannot cross OLD TOPS, the time period has not run out and while they may cross them later, it is better to wait until they show a definite indication before buying. Some of these commodities are usually the best to sell short when a Bear market starts.

COMMODITIES THAT FAIL TO BREAK OLD BOTTOMS IN A BEAR MARKET. There are often a few commodities in a Bear market that are strong. While they may not advance against the trend, however, in time some of them go exactly opposite the trend. They fail to break old bottoms. These are not the kinds of commodities to SELL SHORT, because they are in a stronger position. Always select the commodities to SELL SHORT that are going with the trend in a Bear market. Our rule is that you can make the most money trading with the trend. Sometimes the corn crop may be very short and wheat crop very large. Then corn will have a big advance while wheat declines or holds in a narrow range.

PERIOD OF ACTIVITY OF COMMODITIES. Study the action of each individual commodity and you will be able to determine its trend and period of activity. Therefore, it is very important to have a record years back on wheat and on the individual commodities and to locate these OLD TOPS and BOTTOMS so that you will know when they are crossed or broken.

Remember this; GIVE THE MARKET TIME TO SHOW THE TREND. It takes time to accumulate commodities after a prolonged decline. It takes time to sell or distribute commodities after a prolonged advance. By studying the record of past movements, you can tell about the time required at the top or bottom before a big change in trend should take place. When OLD BOTTOMS are BROKEN that have been made years previous it means the market is in a very WEAK POSITION and going MUCH LOWER. On the other hand, when

tops that are made years previous are crossed, it means BUYING
POWER IS INCREASING and that wheat or other commodities are
going MUCH HIGHER.

FLAT BOTTOMS AND TOPS. The market often spreads out over quite
a period of time, making a flat top lower than the extreme high of the
move, and at the same time, making a flat bottom, moving in a narrow
trading range. When a commodity reaches this stage, you just have
to watch it and wait for it to break over the previous top or to break
under the previous bottom. When a market reaches extreme low, it
often makes a long narrow range or what we call flat bottom. You
must not judge the trend has definitely changed until it moves out of
this flat range, crossing the tops to show up trend or breaking the bottoms
to show a reversal and lower prices.

WITHIN MOVES. By within moves, I mean wheat, corn, soy beans, or
cotton, holding within a range over many days, weeks, or months. This
is a resting period, when the market is getting ready or waiting for
something important to happen before a trend changes. The wheat market may make a range of 15 or 20 cents in one week, one month, or in
several months. Then several months or weeks may pass without breaking the bottom of this period, or crossing the top. This, we call "within
moves," because the moves are within the range of the last high and
the low. As long as it is in the within range it does not indicate any
definite trend until it breaks out, crossing the top or breaking the
bottom. Study past records and you will find some of these periods.

TOP AND BOTTOM FORMATIONS

SINGLE TOPS AND BOTTOMS. This top can be a sharp, fast decline,
followed by a fast advance, or even a slow decline followed by a quick
rally from the bottom with no secondary reaction until it advances
to higher levels. A single bottom is a sharp decline, followed by a rally,
reaching the same level only once. Examples later in the book.

"U" BOTTOM OR FLAT BOTTOM. This "U" bottom is a formation where
wheat or other commodity remains for 3 to 10 weeks or more in a narrow trading range, making about the same top and bottom levels several times; then when it crosses the intermediate tops it has formed a
"U" or flat bottom and is at the *breakaway point* — the safest place to
buy.

BREAKAWAY POINTS. This point is where the real fast moves start
after time has run out, and the main trend changes. It is a safe point to
buy or sell for quick profits, as the run is on. Study the examples of
these Breakaway Points given later in the book and you will see the
great value of them and can prove to yourself that the largest profits
are made in the shortest period of time by buying or selling after the
Breakaway Points.

After accumulation or distribution at bottom or top has been completed, with considerable time consumed, there is a BREAKAWAY
POINT. When you buy or sell Commodities at this point, you make
money very quickly.

Study the volume of sales, the space and price movements, and the last and most important time period. Similar action of the market usually occurs around the same month years apart.

Study the different types of bottom formations — sharp, double, triple, flat and ascending bottoms.

"W" Bottom or Double Bottom. When wheat or other commodities decline and make bottom, then rallies for 2 to 3 weeks or more, declines and makes a bottom around the same level the second time, then advances and crosses the previous top, it has formed a "W" or double bottom. It is safe to buy when it crosses the top or middle of the "W", which is the BREAKAWAY POINT.

"W V" Bottom or Triple Bottom. This is a third higher bottom after a double bottom or three bottoms near the same level. It is safe to buy when wheat or other commodities has formed a "W" and a "V" on the side and crosses the second top of the "W".

"W W" Bottom or 4-Bottom Formation. This formation shows first, second, third and fourth bottoms. The safest point to buy is at the BREAKAWAY POINT or when wheat or other commodities crosses the middle point of the second "W".

You should study the various types of tops — sharp, flat, double, triple, and descending tops.

Single "A" or Sharp Top. After a prolonged advance or at the end of a Bull Campaign, wheat or other commodities often make a single sharp top, advancing 17 to 26 weeks or more with only small reactions lasting sometimes 10 days to 2 weeks, then follows a sharp, quick decline. It is safe to sell on a subsequent or secondary rally and safer to sell when it breaks the last leg of the "A" or when it breaks the bottoms of the first sharp decline.

"U" Top or Flat Top. When the wheat market makes several tops near the same level and the bottoms on reactions are near the same level, holding in a narrow trading range, it forms a "U" top or flat top. It is safe to sell short when it breaks under the series of weekly bottoms.

"M" Top or Double Top. When wheat or other commodities reach top after a substantial advance, then react 3 to 7 weeks or more and rally again to around the same top, an "M" or double top is formed. Then when wheat declines and breaks under the low of the last reaction or under the middle of the "M", it is safe to sell short.

"M A" Top or Triple Top. This formation occurs when wheat, soy beans, or cotton make 3 tops near the same level and the 2nd and 3rd tops are slightly lower. When these formations are made at tops after a long advance, they are signals for a major decline. The more time between tops, the stronger the indications for a big decline. It is safe to sell when wheat breaks the last bottom or breaks the end of the "M" and safer to sell when it breaks the bottom of the "A", which is the BREAKAWAY POINT.

"M M" or 4-Top Formation. This formation occurs when wheat or other commodities make 4 tops at the same level or slightly lower. It is safest to sell short when wheat breaks the second point of the second "M" or the low of the last reaction.

SECTIONS OF MARKET CAMPAIGNS

A Bull or Bear Campaign in wheat or other commodities runs out in 3 to 4 sections.

BULL MARKET

1st Section   Advance after final bottom, then a secondary reaction.

2nd Section   Advance to higher levels, above the highs of previous weeks and of the first advance, then a reaction.

3rd Section   Advance to new high for the move. In many cases this means the end of the campaign, but you must watch for a definite indication before deciding that the third run up means a change in the main trend.

4th Section   Often four sections are run out and this 4th move or run-up is the most important to watch for the end of a Bull Campaign and a change in trend.

Minor Bull Campaigns of short duration, running one year or less, often run out in two sections, especially if the first section is from a sharp bottom. Always watch the action of the market after the second advance to see if it is forming a top and gives indications of a change in trend.

BEAR MARKET.   A Bear Campaign runs opposite to a Bull Campaign.

1st Section   There is a sharp, severe decline which changes the main trend, then a *secondary rally* on which Commodities are safer short sales. That marks the end of the 1st section.

2nd Section   There is a second decline to lower prices, followed by a moderate rally.

3rd Section   A third decline or move to still lower prices, which may be the end of the campaign.

4th Section   There is often a 4th move, which you must watch closely for bottom. In determining whether it is final bottom you use all of the other rules, watching old tops and old bottoms and resistance levels for definite indication that the main trend is ready to change.

Minor Bear Campaigns of short duration, running one year or less, often run out in two sections, especially if the 1st Section is from a sharp top. Therefore, always watch the action of the market after the 2nd decline to see if it is forming a bottom and gives indication of a change in trend.

In extreme cases, like 1915 to 1920, and the Bear Campaign which followed from 1920 to 1921 and the Bull Market from 1923 to 1925, there are as many as 7 sections up or down, but this is abnormal and unusual and only occurs many years apart. Go back over all of the campaigns we have worked out and you will see how these sections or moves work out.

HOW TO DETERMINE CHANGE IN THE MAIN TREND
BY SPACE MOVEMENTS

When a decline in cents exceeds the greatest decline of a previous reaction by one or more cents, it is an indication of a change in trend.

When the market has run out 3 or more sections in a Bull Campaign, go back over the record and find out what the greatest reaction has been in any section, whether 10, 15, 20, 30 cents, or more. Suppose wheat has been advancing for a long time and the greatest reaction in the Bull Market has been 10 cents and the market has reached the 3rd or 4th section of the campaign. The first time wheat or other commodities breaks more than 10 points, or more than the greatest reaction, it is an indication that the main trend has changed or will change soon.

This does not mean that a rally cannot take place after this definite signal of reversal has been given, as usually after the first signal of a change in trend is given there is a *secondary rally* in a Bull Market. Time has to be allowed at top for distribution to take place. Therefore, just because you get a definite indication that the main trend has changed do not jump to the conclusion that you can sell short right at that time and that there will be no rally. Always sell on rallies, if possible. However, there are times that you can sell at new low levels when bottoms are broken. Judge this by applying all of my rules.

TIME PERIOD. Another way to tell when the main trend is changing. RULE. When a campaign has run only 3 or 4 sections and the TIME period on a reaction exceeds the greatest time of a previous reaction consider that the main trend has changed.

Go over the records and find the greatest time period from any minor top or the duration of a reaction in previous sections of the Bull Market. If you find that the greatest reaction has been about 4 weeks, the first time the market declines consecutively for 5 weeks or more it is an indication that the main trend has changed and that wheat or commodities will be short sales on a secondary rally.

Apply the same rules in a Bear Market. When the SPACE movement or number of points that wheat or the other commodities have rallied during a Bear Campaign is exceeded, then the main trend is changing and a Bull Campaign is starting.

A reversal in SPACE movement after the second run or 2nd Section in a Bull or a Bear Market, would not mean as important a change in trend as if it came after the 3rd or 4th Section had run out, either up or down.

Examples of all these rules will be referred to in the working out of each Bull and Bear Campaign from 1841 to 1941 on wheat, so that you will know just how to apply the rules in future market movements.

MANY WEEKS IN NARROW RANGE. When wheat or other commodities hold for 2 to 6 weeks or 10 to 13 weeks in a narrow range, then cross tops or break bottoms of previous weeks, the trend has changed and you should go with it. The longer the period of time in a narrow range, the greater the advance or the decline when wheat breaks out of the range, either up or down. Examples later in the book.

SIDEWAY MOVEMENTS. You often hear traders say wheat can only go two ways, up or down, and that it should be easy to keep right on the market. This statement is not exactly correct. If wheat or other commodities always moved straight up or straight down, it would be easy to make money, but wheat often has sideway moves. While it is in a movement of this kind, it holds in a narrow trading range sometimes weeks or months getting neither higher nor lower than a previous top or bottom. Moves of this kind fool traders many times and cause losses. Wheat starts up and they think it is going higher, but stops, reacts, gets back around the old bottom, and goes up again. When wheat or other commodities is in a position of this kind, the only thing to do is to leave it alone until it breaks out of the trading range one way or the other. After it gets out of the sideway movement, which is always accumulation or distribution, and breaks into new high or new low territory, then you can trade in it with some certainty of having determined the correct trend. Examples to follow later in the book.

Following this rule will save you many months and weeks of waiting and will prevent losses, because if you wait until the market gets into new territory before you get in you certainly will have a better chance to place a close *stop loss order,* which will protect you or get you out in case the market is not going to move. If you make a trade when it is in a sideway movement between two points, your chances for making profits are much smaller. These sideway moves are periods of rest and preparation for a new move one way or the other way.

ACCUMULATION OR DISTRIBUTION ON SIDE. After a market has advanced to the 3rd or 4th Section, then has a sharp decline and rallies, it will often remain for a long period of time in a range while DISTRIBUTION is taking place ON THE SIDE. The top of the range may be several points below the extreme high. In FORM READING it is very important to note the range from high to low in this zone of distribution. Wheat is a short sale at the top of this range of distribution on the side and a safer sale when it breaks the low point of this range, which is the BREAKAWAY POINT.

At the end of a Bear Campaign, after the first sharp advance, there is a secondary reaction, then a long period of ACCUMULATION ON THE SIDE, with several moves up to the top of the range and back to the bottom of the range of accumulation. The market is a buy at the bottom of this range and a safer buy when the tops of this range are crossed, as that is the BREAKAWAY POINT and a signal for a fast advance. Examples of these sideway accumulation and sideway distribution will be shown in the different campaigns worked out later in the book.

LAST STAGE OF BULL OR BEAR MARKET. In fast advancing markets in the last stage of the campaign reactions get smaller as prices work to higher levels, until the final section or run has ended. Then comes a sharp, quick reaction and a reversal in trend.

In the last stage of a Bear Market, after all old bottoms and resistance levels have been broken, rallies get less or smaller as prices work lower. Therefore, people who buy have no chance to sell on rallies until the final bottom has been reached and the first rally takes place.

This is why it never pays to buck the trend in the last stage of a Bull Market or the last stage of a Bear Market.

ACCUMULATION ABOVE LOW LEVELS. This is accumulation or good buying on the side. The market declines, making the sharp bottom, rallies, reacts and stays well above the old bottom and accumulates on the side, showing strength because it is moving up and down in a narrow range above the bottom. Somebody is BUYING and not waiting for it to go back to OLD LEVELS, because they know that liquidation has run its course and that wheat, soy beans, or other commodities are not going back to these OLD low LEVELS. After ACCUMULATION takes place ON THE SIDE at HIGHER LEVELS, watch when the UPPER LEVELS are CROSSED and the trend TURNS UP and go with it.

RANGE OF BOTTOMS. Never consider that a major or a minor trend has reversed or changed until the bottoms of previous weeks have been broken or the tops of previous weeks have been crossed. The number of points that wheat or other commodities should deline below a bottom to indicate a change in trend to lower levels varies according to the price at which wheat or other commodities are selling. We consider a range within 1 to 3 cents a double or triple bottom or a double or triple top. In a strong market wheat will break only 1 cent under a bottom and then rally. In extreme cases, not more than 2 cents. As a rule when bottoms are broken by 3 full cents it is an indication for lower prices before any rally of importance.

RANGE OF TOPS. The range at the top — the range for double tops is about 3 cents. These tops can be in a range of 1 to 3 cents and still be considered double and triple tops. Advancing 1 to 2 cents above an old top does not always indicate that the main trend has changed and that commodities are going up immediately but advancing 3 cents above old tops is nearly always a definite indication that higher prices will follow before much reaction. At the end of Bull or Bear Markets some false moves are often made and quick reversals follow.

HOW FAR SHOULD COMMODITIES DECLINE BELOW OLD TOPS AFTER ADVANCING ABOVE THEM?

In order to still show uptrend, after wheat or the other commodities have advanced above old tops, then reacted, when in strong position they will stop right around the old tops or sometimes go 1 to 2 cents below the old tops but seldom more than 3 cents. Regardless of how high wheat is selling, a decline of more than 5 cents below the old tops would indicate that the trend had reversed and at that immediate time wheat would not go higher but would go lower for a while. It can decline 5 cents under old tops and still be in a Bull Market, all depending on what section the market is in. A signal in the last section is most important according to rules.

WHY COMMODITIES MOVE FASTER AT HIGH LEVELS
AND SLOWER AT LOW LEVELS

The HIGHER wheat goes, the FASTER the move and the GREAT-ER the opportunities for profits. The reason for this is that most of the public's BUYING and SELLING is at low levels. After wheat has been at a LOW LEVEL, say 75 cents or lower, for a long number of years and the public has bought a large amount of it, it advances to around 90 cents and the public BUY MORE. When it reaches 100 or around this figure, they either all SELL OUT or the public gets over-confident and comes in and BUY so much wheat that it has a big decline. When the public takes profits, the insiders BUY because they believe that it is WORTH MORE and going to SELL HIGHER later. When the public SELLING is all ABSORBED, it is easier for the buyers to mark wheat up fast, because they do not encounter heavy selling. When wheat gets around 180 to 200, there is always a lot of SHORT COVERING, and the people who bought wheat at LOWER LEVELS, sell out and take PROFITS. The general public does not trade much in wheat above $2.00. Therefore, after wheat or soy beans crosses this level, it is a FIGHT between the PROFESSIONAL SHORT SELLERS and the strong financial INTERESTS who are backing it. Wheat or soy beans can move from $2.00 to $3.00 in less time than it takes to move from 50c to $1.00, because the people who are trading in it are large traders and BUY OR SELL large amounts. Every commodity must reach a level where the insiders will sell enough to check the advance and turn the main trend down. Then comes the big opportunity for the man who will sell HIGH PRICED wheat SHORT, but he must wait until the charts and rules show that the main trend has turned down.

HOW FAR WHEAT CAN DECLINE UNDER OLD BOTTOMS
IN BEAR MARKETS

Reverse the rule we have just given you in a Bear Market. When wheat or other commodities advance to old bottoms they are short sales because *bottoms* become *tops* and *tops* become *bottoms*. They should not go more than 1 to 2 cents above the old bottoms and on an extreme should not go more than 3 cents. When wheat or beans are at high levels, if they advance more than 5 cents above an old bottom, it is an indication that they are going higher and are not going to work lower immediately with the main trend.

FAST MOVES UP OR DOWN OVER A RANGE OF
5 TO 7 OF 10 TO 12 CENTS

Whether the market is very active or in trading range, all indications are more accurate and more valuable when the market is quite active.

After wheat or other commodities have been advancing for some time and have run out 3 or 4 sections, if there are several moves of 10 to 12 cents up or down in a range, making several bottoms and several tops in this range, it indicates either accumulation or distribution. When the bottoms in a range of this kind are broken it is an indication of lower prices. When the tops in a range of this kind are crossed, it is an indication of higher prices. Study the range on sideway accumulation and the range on sideway distribution.

An advancing market may have several reactions of 10 to 12 cents, then have a reaction of 20 to 24 cents. After an advance, if it declines from any top more than 20 cents, it will usually run 30 to 40 cents. Go over the records of the commodities when they have been selling at very high levels and prove to yourself the value of this rule.

HOW TO MAKE THE GREATEST PROFIT

You will always make the most profit by following the main trend and playing the long swing. You can never make much money jumping in and out of the market trying to scalp it. If you will put in time and study to determine the main trend, and then follow it the length of time that it should run and not get out until you get a definite indication of change in trend, you will make big profits. It is much better to make 3 or 4 trades each year and make large profits, than it is to try to make 100 to 200 trades a years and be wrong half the time, and finally wind up with a net loss.

Let your rule be to GO WITH THE MAIN TREND, AND NEVER BUCK IT. If you don't know what the trend it, don't get in the market. If you will study the rules I give you and go back over the records far enough, you will convince yourself that profits can be made by following rules and that you can't miss making money if you go with the main trend. You will learn that there are times when it will pay you to stay out of the market and wait for a definite indication and a real opportunity, which is sure to come if you wait.

CHAPTER III

FORECASTING COMMODITY MOVES

IMPORTANT TIME PERIODS

TIME is the most important factor of all and not until sufficient time has expired does any big move start up or down. The TIME factor will overbalance both Space and Volume. When TIME is up, space movement will start and large volume will begin, either up or down. At the end of any important movement — monthly, weekly or daily — TIME must be allowed for accumulation or distribution or for buying and selling to be completed.

Never decide that the main trend has changed one way or the other without consulting the RESISTANCE LEVELS from TOP to BOTTOM and without considering the position of the market and the CYCLE of each individual Commodity.

Always consider whether the main TIME limit has run out or not before judging a reverse move. Do not fail to consider the indications on TIME, both from main TOPS and BOTTOMS.

YEARLY BOTTOMS AND TOPS: It is important to note whether a Commodity is making higher or lower BOTTOMS each year. For instance, if a Commodity has made a higher BOTTOM each year for 5 years, then makes a lower BOTTOM than the previous year, it is a sign of reversal and may indicate a long down cycle. The same rule applies when Grain or other Commodities are making lower TOPS for a number of years in a Bear Market.

FORECASTING COMMODITY MOVES Monthly moves can be determined by the same rules as yearly.

Add 3 months to an important BOTTOM, then add 4, making 7, to get minor BOTTOMS and reaction points.

In big upswings a reaction will often not last over 2 months, the third month being up, the same rule as in yearly cycle — 2 down and the third up.

In extreme markets, a reaction sometimes only lasts 2 or 3 weeks, then the advance is resumed. In this way a market may continue up for 12 months without breaking a monthly BOTTOM.

In a Bull market the minor trend may reverse and run down 3 to 4 months; then turn up and follow the main trend again.

In a Bear market, the minor trend may advance 3 to 4 months, then reverse and follow the main trend. As a general rule, Grains never rally more than 2 months in a Bear market; then start to break in the 3rd month and follow the main trend down.

FORECASTING WEEKLY MOVES. The weekly movement gives the next important minor change in trend, which may turn out to be a major change in trend.

In a Bull market, Grain will often run down 2 to 3 weeks, and possibly 4 weeks, then reverse and follow the main trend again. Usually the trend will turn up in the middle of the third week and close higher at the end of the third week, the market only moving 3 weeks against the main trend. In some cases the change in trend will not occur until the fourth week; then the reversal will come and Grain closes higher at the end of the fourth week. Reverse this rule in a Bear market.

In rapid advances with big volume, a move will often run 6 to 7 weeks before a minor reversal in trend, and in some cases, like 1916-1917-1924-1925-1933-1937-1941, these fast moves last 13 to 15 weeks or $\frac{1}{4}$ of a year, and in extreme cases, longer. These are culmination moves up or down.

IMPORTANT TIME PERIODS. As there are 7 days in a week and seven times seven equals 49 days, seven weeks, often mark an important turning point. Therefore, you should watch for TOP or BOTTOM around the 49th to 52nd day, although at times a change will start on the 42nd to 45th day, because a period of 45 days is $\frac{1}{8}$ of a year. Also watch for culminations at the end of 90 to 98 days, and 120 to 135 days from any important TOP OR BOTTOM from which a fast move starts.

After wheat or any other commodity has declined 7 weeks, it may have 2 or 3 narrow weeks on the side and then turn up, which agrees with the monthly rule for a change in the third month.

Always watch the annual and seasonal trend of a Commodity and consider whether it is in a Bull or Bear year. In a Bull year, with the monthly chart showing up, there are many times that Grain will react 2 or 3 weeks, then rest 3 or 4 weeks, then it advances, then goes into new territory, advancing 6 to 7 weeks more. Watch these resting periods in a trading range.

After a Commodity makes TOP and reacts 2 to 3 weeks, it may then have a rally of 2 to 3 weeks without getting above the first TOP, then hold in a trading range for several weeks without crossing the highest TOP or breaking the lowest level of that range. In markets of this kind, you can buy near the low point or sell near the high point of the range and protect with a *stop loss order* 1 to 3 cents away. A better plan would be to wait until the Commodity shows a definite trend before buying or selling. Then buy the Wheat or other Commodity when it crosses the highest point, or sell when it breaks the lowest point of the trading range.

FORECASTING DAILY MOVES. The daily movement gives the first minor change and conforms to the same rules as the weekly and monthly cycles, although it is only a minor part of them.

2-DAY MOVES. In fast markets there will only be a 2-day move in the opposite direction to the main trend and on the third day the upward or downward course will be resumed in harmony with the main trend. See chart and examples of Soy Beans, 1941.

A daily movement may reverse trend and only run 7 to 10 days, then follow the main trend again.

MONTHLY CHANGES IN TREND. During the month, natural changes in trend occur around 6th to 7th, 9th to 10th, 14th to 15th, 19th to 20th, 23rd to 24th, 29th to 31st. These minor moves occur in accordance with TOPS and BOTTOMS of individual Commodities.

It is very important to watch for a change in trend 30 days from the last TOP or BOTTOM. Next watch for changes 60, 90, 120 days from TOPS or BOTTOMS. 180 days or six months — most important and often marks changes for greater moves. You should watch for important minor and often major changes also around the 270th and 330th day from important TOPS or BOTTOMS.

IMPORTANT DATES TO WATCH FOR TREND CHANGES

January 2nd to 7th and 15th to 21st: Watch these periods each year and note the high and low prices made. Until these high prices are crossed or low prices broken, consider the trend up or down.

Many times when Commodities make low in the early part of January, this low will not be broken until the following July or August and sometimes not during the entire year. This same rule applies in Bear Markets or when the main trend is down. High prices made in the early part of January are often high for the entire year. Examples later in the book.

ANNIVERSARY DATES AND SEASONAL CHANGES. It is very important to watch the date when an individual Commodity makes extreme high or low. One year, two years and three years from this anniversary date will often indicate another TOP or BOTTOM. At the end of any year it is an important time period to watch for a change in trend.

The first important time period to watch from any anniversary date, is in the third or fourth month, then around the sixth or seventh month, where many important tops and bottoms are reached. Sometimes important changes occur around the tenth or eleventh month. The most important changes occur around one year, 18 months, 24 months, 30 months, 36 months, 42 months or 48 months. To prove to yourself the value of these anniversary dates, all you have to do is to study and watch how the trend changes on any individual Commodity around these periods. The most important to watch of these anniversary dates, are the ones when a final TOP or final BOTTOM is made.

HOW TO DIVIDE THE YEARLY TIME PERIOD

Divide the year by 2 to get $\frac{1}{2}$ or 6 months, which equals 26 weeks.

Divide the year by 4 to get the 3 months' period or 90 days, which is $\frac{1}{4}$ of a year or 13 weeks.

Divide the year by 3 to get the 4 months' period, which is 1/3 of a year or 17 1/3 weeks.

Divide the year by 8, which gives $1\frac{1}{2}$ months or 45 days. This is also $6\frac{1}{2}$ weeks, which shows why the 7th week is always so important

Divide the year by 16, which gives $22\frac{1}{2}$ days or approximately 3 weeks. This accounts for market movements that only run 3 weeks up or down and then reverse. As a general rule. when Wheat or any Commodity closes higher the 4th consecutive week, it will continue higher. The 5th week is also very important for a change in trend and for fast moves up or down. The 5th is the day, week, month, or year of Ascension and always marks fast moves up or down, according to the major cycle that is running.

How to Determine Change in Minor Trend. Minor Advance. When the wheat market is advancing and makes a TOP around the same level for 2 or more weeks, especially when the range is very narrow near TOP levels, prices breaking under the BOTTOM of 2 weeks or more, the minor trend has turned down and you should follow it until there is another definite indication of a change in trend.

Minor Reaction. After Wheat or other Commodity has been declining for several weeks or several months and prices make BOTTOM 2 weeks or more around the same level and hold in a narrow trading range for 2 weeks or more and then cross the TOPS of the past 2 or 3 weeks on the up side, the minor trend has changed, at least temporarily, and you should go with it.

Dull Market. A dull market, in a narrow trading range at any point, indicates that it is getting ready for some kind of a change and you should follow it which ever way it breaks out, up or down, after these narrow, dull periods.

Duration of Minor Moves. Rule for Minor Time Periods in Bull Markets. In an advancing market or Bull Campaign, when indications are given for a minor reaction, prices will react 3 to 4 weeks, but as a rule in the 4th week they will rally and close higher. In some cases there will only be a sharp, quick reaction of 2 weeks and then the main trend will be resumed. After a decline of 3 to 4 weeks should the market have a minor rally, then break back under the BOTTOM of the 3rd or 4th week, it will be an indication of a greater change in the trend and probably a change in the main trend.

In extreme cases, after a *secondary rally* in a Bull Market, prices will decline as much as 6 to 7 weeks, seldom more, before the main trend is resumed.

Rule for Time of Minor Rallies in Bear Markets. These rules are reversed in a Bear Market. Rallies in a Bear Market last 2 to 4 weeks. Should a rally hold into the 5th week, it is likely to run into the 6th or 7th week; then you can watch for an important change in trend.

After a rally of 3 to 4 weeks and a *secondary reaction* in a Bear Market, should the market advance and cross the levels made at the end of the 3 or 4 weeks' rally, then the trend is changing, at least temporarily and higher prices — even in a Bear Market — are indicated.

ACCUMULATION AND DISTRIBUTION
TIME REQUIRED

By going over past history of the Grains and other Commodities, or ʋɪ any individual Commodity, and *studying the past record,* you can see the TIME REQUIRED TO ACCUMULATE AT THE BOTTOM and the TIME REQUIRED TO DISTRIBUTE AT THE TOP. You can judge the future of the Commodity by the TIME REQUIRED IN THE PAST. To make a success you must continue to STUDY PAST RECORDS, because the market in the FUTURE will be a REPETITION OF THE PAST.

THE FINAL TOP OR BOTTOM. When the market reaches final top, if it is a very active market, as a rule the volume of sales are quite heavy, and Grains advance rapidly. A signal top or sign of a final top is indicated on the daily chart by the market opening high or low, then advancing rapidly to a new high and the same day breaking under the opening and closing near the low of the day. For a market to advance, it must show a gain on the day and if it has made a gain on the day and if it has had a big advance and fails to hold it, it shows that it has reached the level where selling pressure is greater than buying pressure. This same rule holds true on a weekly chart. Suppose the market opens strong on Monday morning and closes above the high of that week. It is an indication that the trend has changed. The wider the range on a daily or weekly and closing at a top or bottom, the more important is the indication for a change in trend.

HOW TO DETERMINE FIRST CHANGE IN TREND BY OPENING AND CLOSING PRICES

The weekly high and low chart with the opening and closing prices on it is one of the best charts to use for determining trend of Wheat or other Commodities. That is why we have often used the Weekly Chart on Commodities and get all the indications according to it.

The closing price at the end of the week or at the end of any day is most important because, regardless of how high or how low Wheat has been during the week or during the day, the closing price shows exactly what it has lost or gained at the end of the time period.

After Wheat or other Commodities have been advancing for a considerable period of time and have reached an old TOP or a section of the campaign which indicates that a change in trend could take place, it is very important in active markets to watch the opening price on Monday morning. Should Wheat or a Commodity not sell more than one point above the opening price on Monday morning and then decline and close at or near the low levels of the week on Saturday, this is the first indication of a change in trend on the Weekly Chart. Don't fail to use my other rules and wait for the proper declines in TIME or SPACE or until previous weekly BOTTOMS have been broken before deciding that there is a definite change in trend.

Reverse this rule at the BOTTOM of a decline or after there has been a sharp, fast decline in a very active market. Watch the opening price on Monday morning. Should Wheat decline rapidly around the middle or latter part of the week, then after making BOTTOM, reverse and rally quickly and on Saturday close above the opening on Monday morning it is a strong indication that the trend is reversing and that prices are going higher temporarily. Use all of my other rules, the crossing of previous weekly tops, the reversal of the SPACE movement in points, also reversal in TIME, before deciding that a definite change in trend is indicated.

It is also very important to know at the end of the week if prices close under *old bottoms* or under *bottoms of previous weeks* or close above *old tops* or above tops of previous *weeks* as it is an indication of *weakness* or *strength.*

DETERMINING RIGHT TIME TO SELL. Many traders get in the Grain Market right, but get out wrong. They may have bought right, but they do not know when to sell, or what rules to follow to determine when Wheat or a Commodity has reached top. Suppose you get in Wheat after it has gone through a long period of accumulation, like some of the periods which show on the yearly charts. You want to get the maximum profits once you get in right and there are certain signs that you must watch in order to know when it is time to sell. Wheat in the early stages of a bull market, nearly always creeps, or moves up slowly, having many reactions, but when it comes to the finish or final grand rush and reaches the boilng point, there is a fast move up. My rule is, wait to sell your Wheat until it boils, as long as it is moving in your favor and you can follow it up with a stop loss order. Most Grains that are very active finish a bull campaign with a fast advance, lasting 6 to 7 weeks, sometimes as much as 10 weeks, moving very fast. At these times the volume is usually extra large, which indicates that there is big buying and selling going on and that Wheat is reaching a level for final top and distribution. Most of the time a fast advance of 6 to 7 weeks marks the culmination of an upward swing, just as a fast decline of 6 to 7 weeks especially on heavy volume, when there is a panicky decline, marks the end of a bear campaign, when you should cover shorts and wait. Examples later in the book.

Remember that *sharp reactions* follow from TOPS where there is a *final grand rush* after a fast move up and the same way in most cases where Wheat is very active after a *fast move down.* The first rally is very swift and runs a considerable number of points before a *secondary reaction* and a settling period takes place. Watch for these fast moves both up and down to sell out long wheat and **sell** short. Remember, *don't buck the trend.* Place a *stop loss order.* Get out quickly if a Commodity starts moving against you. These fast moves up and down, show how foolish it is for a trader to buy or sell against the trend and expect to put up margin and hold on. These fast moves are the moves to pyramid on and not to be bucked and held on against the trend.

WHEN GRAINS ADVANCE INTO NEW RECORD HIGH AND LOW PRICES.

When Grains or other Commodities advance to higher levels than they have been for many years, or decline to lower levels than they have sold before in several years, they are in new high or new low ground and you must have a rule to follow when Commodities reach new high or new low record prices.

First, apply all of your other rules and do not *buy* or *sell* until there is a *definite indication* of a change in the main trend.

When Wheat or other Commodities advance to a new high level where they have never sold for years, it is an advance of some percentage of last TOP or BOTTOM, especially if it is in the first or second Section of the Bull Campaign. Should new highs be made in the third or fourth Section, then the advance into new high ground may not be very many points before *final high* is reached and the *trend changes.*

When a Commodity advances or DECLINES into NEW TERRI-TORY or to PRICES which it has not REACHED FOR MONTHS OR YEARS, it shows that the force or DRIVING POWER is work-ing in that DIRECTION. It is the same principle as any other force which has been RESTRAINED and BREAKS out. WATER may be held back by a dam, but if it breaks through the dam, you would know that it would continue downward until it reached another dam, or some obstruction or resistance which would stop it. Therefore, it is very important to watch OLD LEVELS of Grain. The longer the time that elapses between the BREAKING into NEW TERRITORY, the greater the move you can expect, because the accumulated energy over a long period naturally will produce a larger movement than if it only accumulated during a short period of time.

You should watch the action of the market when it has advanced 7 cents into new high territory, watch 10 to 12 cents, watch 25 to 36 cents and on an extreme advance watch around 40 to 45 cents, where there is likely to be resistance and TOP made. These are Average moves and it depends upon the activity and the price of a Commodity whether it will stop on any of these points. By following the trend indications and rules, you will be able to determine when the first move into new high territory has run out and the trend has changed.

Reverse the above rules in a Bear Campaign.

When the Grains or other Commodities are selling between 50c and $1.25 advance into new high ground, these average movements of 7, 10, 15, 20 and 24 points or cents work out quite accurately. After Wheat advances above $1.25, it moves faster to higher levels than it does below $1.25. Above $2.00, the movement increases and the range is much wider. The same when Wheat or the other Commodities get above $2.00 per bushel — they have a still greater range and faster moves. This depends upon how long the campaign has been running, how many moves or sections the campaign has run out and how much prices are up from the last BOTTOM or how far down from the last TOP.

VOLUME OF SALES OF COMMODITIES

After considering the three important factors ... FORMATIONS, TIME, and RESISTANCE LEVELS ... the fourth and next very im-portant factor is the VOLUME OF SALES AT TOPS AND BOT-TOMS.

The VOLUME OF SALES is the real driving power behind the

market and shows whether SUPPLY or DEMAND is increasing or decreasing. Large buying or selling orders from professional traders, the public or any other source of supply and demand, are bound to be registered on the tape and shown in the volume of sales on WHEAT, SOY BEANS, COTTON, or any other COMMODITY.

Therefore, a careful study of the VOLUME OF SALES will enable you to determine very closely a change in trend, especially if you apply all of the other rules for judging position according to the Formations, Resistance Levels and Time.

RULES FOR DETERMINING CULMINATION BY VOLUME OF SALES

1 — At the end of any prolonged Bull Campaign or rapid advance in any Commodity, there is usually a large increase in the volume of sales, which marks the end of the campaign, at least temporarily. Then, after a sharp decline on heavy volume of sales, when a secondary rally takes place, and the volume of sales decreases, it is an indication that Wheat or any other Commodity has made final top, and that the main trend will turn down.

2 — If Wheat, Soy Beans, Cotton or other Commodities hold after making a second lower top and get dull and narrow for some time, holding in a *sideways movement,* and then break out on increased volume, it is a sign of a further decline.

3 — After a prolonged decline of several weeks, months, or several years, at the time Wheat or other Commodities are reaching bottom, the volume of trading should decrease and the range in fluctuation should narrow down. This is one of the sure signs that liquidation is running its course and that the Commodity is getting ready to show a change in trend.

4 — After the first sharp advance, when the trend is changing from a Bear Market to a Bull Market, the Commodity will have a *secondary* reaction and make *bottom,* just the same as it had a *secondary* rally after the first sharp decline. If the volume of sales decreases on the reaction and then the Commodity moves up, advancing on heavier volume, it will be an indication of an advance to higher levels.

These rules apply to the general market, and to individual Commodities and sales of Commodities traded in on the Chicago Board of Trade and the New York Cotton Exchange. Keep a record of Daily Volume of Sales also Weekly and Monthly Total Sales.

SUMMARY: Sales increase near the top and decrease near the bottom, except in abnormal markets, like October and November 1929, when there was a panicky decline in everything, when a large volume of sales occur at the bottom, making a sharp bottom from which a swift rally follows.

After the first sharp rally there is nearly always a SECONDARY decline when the volume decreases, as shown under *Rule 4.*

Study the volume of sales in July 1933 and in March 1937, May and June 1940, and August and September 1941.

OPEN INTEREST. Study the past record of open interest, when extreme high or extreme low is reached, and see if the highest open interest occurs several days or several weeks before extreme high prices are reached. When this occurs, it indicates that wise buyers, who bought when prices were low, sell out when prices are high and everybody is optimistic and buying more. And yet the market advances to higher levels and the volume of sales daily increases, while the open interest decreases. This is an indication that the final Top is near.

When the market has had a prolonged decline, and before final low is reached, the open interest starts increasing. This is an indication that good buying is taking place.

The total volume of sales daily indicate the culmination at different stages of the market.

For example: From October 1938 to April 1939, the highest total sales of all Wheat daily on the Chicago Board of Trade, did not exceed 22,000,000 Bushels, and total sales were as low as 5,000,000 Bushels per day.

1939

May 2 — Total Volume of sales on Wheat was 69,000,000 Bushels. This was a great increase in volume, and showed a change in trend in the Wheat market.

Aug. 24 — Total sales of Wheat 50,000,000 Bushels.

Sept. 7 — Total Sales 58,000,000 Bushels. This was another culminating point and indicated change in trend. This heavy volume of sales was due to buying by speculators after the outbreak of the War. The volume of sales of Oats, Corn and Rye were exceptionally large at this time, because the public were heavy buyers.

December — The volume of Wheat was very large this month.

Dec. 7 — Sales 50,000,000 Bushels.

Dec. 13 — Sales 53,000,000 Bushels.

Dec. 19 — Total sales 71,000,000 Bushels. Wheat reached top in December and this enormous volume of sales indicated that the public were heavy buyers at high levels, and the volume of trading was the greatest around this top that it had been for several years. When the market declined in January and February, 1940, volume of trading dropped down to 10,000,000 bushels per day, and only a few times as much as 35,000,000.

1940 Apr. 9 — Total sales 60,000,000 Bushels. The volume of trading had again reached the stage where it gave indication of Top for Wheat.

April 17-18 — Total Sales 45,000,000 Bushels.

May 1 — Total Sales 50,000,000 Bushels.

May 4 — Total Sales 15,000,000 Bushels.

May 10 — Total Sales 45,000,000 Bushels.

Wheat reached final high in the early part of May.

May 10 — Hitler started the drive against France and Belgium, and all Commodities declined fast, Wheat having a wide open break and declining the limit every day for several days. Volume of sales increased rapidly.

May 15 — Total sales 80,000,000 Bushels of Wheat. This was a record on the decline and indicated heavy liquidation by the public, but it did not mean Wheat was final bottom. The volume of sales was large for several days, running 65,000,000, and 45,000,000 and finally May 24, sales were down to 10,000,000 Bushels per day, indicating that liquidation had run its course temporarily.

1940

Aug. 16 — Total Sales 33,000,000 Bushels. This was the first time since May that sales were this high. The Wheat market was declining and reached final low Aug. 16 to 20th, and the advance started.

Prices continued to advance until November 1940.

Nov. 7 — Total Sales of Wheat 29,000,000 Bushels. The first time sales had been this high since August. Wheat had a big advance. The public as usual, were heavy buyers at the top, as indicated by a large volume of sales.

The market declined for three months.

1941

Feb. 17-18 — Final Low on Wheat. The volume of sales had dropped down to as low as 5,000,000 bushels per day, and had not been higher than 15,000,000 bushels per day since Dec. 1940.

Wheat started to advance and the volume of sales increased running as high as 20,000,000 bushels per day in March.

May 14 — Total sales 32,000,000 bushels.

May 19-22 — Sales 25,000,000 Bushels. Wheat reached top in May and declined to June 2nd, when volume of sales were down to 10,000,000 bushels per day, indicating that the public was not buying much when prices were at low levels.

July 31 — Total sales reached 10,000,000 Bushels.

Aug. 2 — Total sales reached 20,000,000 Bushels.

Aug. 13 — Last Low, sales 41,000,000 Bushels. This was the largest volume since Aug. 1940. After this date Wheat advanced to a new high level, shorts covered and the public bought heavily. The advance continued to Sept. 12, when final high was reached.

Aug. 27 — Sales 22,000,000.

Sept. 3 — Sales 20,000,000.

Sept. 4 — Sales 20,000,000.

Sept. 5 — Sales 24,000,000.

Sept. 9 — Sales 25,000,000. This was three days before final top was reached and indicated the public was still buying heavily.

Sept. 10-11-12 — Sales around 22,000,000 bushels per day. Sales decreased on the day extreme high was reached. This was an indication that the public was loaded up and that the wise boys were selling.

Sept. 20 — A sharp decline and bottom for a moderate rally. Sales 20,000,000 bushels.

Sept. 30 — Top of rally. Sales 11,000,000 bushels. This was a secondary rally, with a volume of sales 50% less than they were at the top which indicated that the public was loaded and could not buy more, making Wheat a safe short sale on decreasing volume of sales.
A rapid decline followed.

Oct. 16 — This was a panic day. Wheat declined 10c per bushel. The limit permitted for one day. Total volume of sales on Wheat 32,-000,000 bushels. This was the largest volume of sales since Aug. 4th, and indicated bottom for a rally.

Oct. 17 — Prices went slightly lower then rallied. Total sales 28,000,-000 bushels.

Oct. 23 — Top of rally. Sales 17,000,000 bushels. A Secondary decline followed.

Oct. 28 — Low of reaction. Sales 13,000,000 bushels. Smaller volume on the secondary decline, indicating that liquidation had run its course for the present and that heavy selling pressure was over, at least temporarily. A rally followed.

Nov. 5 — Sales 14,600,000 bushels.

Nov. 6 — 9,700,000 bushels.

Nov. 7 — 10,685,000 bushels. The market slowed down on this rally and the volume of sales indicated that there was not enough buying power to bring about a rapid advance at that time.
Study the volume of sales on Corn, Oats and Rye at extreme high levels, in order to determine when they are reaching top and bottom. All grains follow the same general trend and as a rule, when the volume of Wheat is large or extremely small, the volume of other grains runs proportionately the same.

OPEN INTEREST ON WHEAT. In the Spring of 1940, the open interest on Wheat was around 130,000,000 bushels, and from that time, gradually declined until 1941.

Jan. 21 — The open interest was 47,000,000 bushels, and never got above 50,000,000 bushels again, and continued to decline after Wheat started to advance from the low of Feb. 1941.

Apr. 9-12 — Open interest in Wheat was down to 41,000,000 bushels, which was the lowest in many years. Wheat and other grains advanced in April and May, and the open interest increased.

May 10-13 — Open interest 47,000,000 bushels.
Then the open interest started to decrease again.

May 22 — Extreme low, 39,000,000 bushels. This was at the time that Wheat and other grains were reaching the highest levels for the move.

May 28 — The open interest was just above 42,000,000 bushels.

June 9 — Open interest 38,000,000 bushels. This was the extreme low for open interest.

June 19 — Open interest again around 42,000,000 bushels.

June 30 — Open interest just under 40,000,000 bushels. From this last low level, the open interest started to increase.

Aug. 1 — Open interest 53,000,000 bushels.

Aug. 14 — Open interest 49,000,000 bushels. This is the last low and Wheat and Soy Beans started advancing at this time.

Sept. 12 — The day that Wheat reached extreme high, the open interest on Wheat was 53,000,000 bushels, and while Wheat declined, the open interest increased.

Oct. 6 — Open interest 59,500,000 bushels. The open interest remained around this high level until Oct. 11th, making no further gain, an indication that the public was still buying and that someone who knew Wheat was too high was selling. From Oct. 11th, open interest started to decline.

Oct. 17 — The day Wheat reached extreme low, the open interest was down to around 51,000,000 bushels, the lowest it had been since Sept. 5th, but with the price of Wheat 15c per bushel lower than it was on Sept. 5th .

The sharp decrease in the open interest of over 8,000,000 bushels in less than one week's time, indicated heavy liquidation, and that the public had sold out on the break.

Since Oct. 17, there has been very little change in open interest figures.

Oct. 22 — Open interest 53,000,000. From that time until Nov. 8th the open interest held around 52,000,000 and slightly under.

The reason why the open interest does not run up to 100,000,000 bushels or more, as it did years past, is because of Government regulations. This causes big traders not to carry a large amount of Wheat over night. The open interest under present conditions represents mostly the Trade interest and the public, as big speculators no longer carry a large line of Wheat.

May 1940 — When Wheat was $1.13 per bushel, the open interest was around 130,000,000 bushels.

Sept. 1941 — When Wheat was 15c per bushel higher than May 1940, the open interest was less than half as much as it was in May 1940. Another reason why the open interest is not so large in Wheat is because there has been a lot of trading in Soy Beans and other grains, also, many Grain traders have gone into the cotton market during 1941 because there were big opportunities for profits in cotton. This has increased the volume in cotton trading and decreased the volume of trading in Wheat, which is reflected in a smaller open interest.

Study the open interest in any option of any grain that you trade in, and also study the daily sales of each individual option of grain. You will find it helpful if you will keep up the weekly volume of sales on the most active option and apply the rules for Volume of Sales. This will help you to determine when extreme high or low prices should be reached.

CHAPTER IV

TIME PERIODS, RESISTANCE LEVELS AND
TRADING EXAMPLES ON GRAIN

WHEAT. Wheat is traded in on the Chicago Board of Trade, Winnipeg Grain Exchange, Kansas City Board of Trade and the Minneapolis Chamber of Commerce.

The largest grain center in the United States is in Chicago and the largest volume of future trading is on the Chicago Board of Trade. All of the records of future prices on wheat and other grains in this book are based on prices of the Chicago Board of Trade.

A contract for wheat on the Chicago Board of Trade is 5,000 bushels. It is quoted in cents per bushel. The minimum fluctuation is ⅛c per bushel, or $12.50 on a contract of 5,000 bushels.

The commission for buying and selling a contract of 5,000 bushels is $15.00.

The margin requirements on wheat vary with the price of wheat, running from $300 to $1,000, or more when wheat is at a very high level.

Job lots are traded in on the Chicago Board of Trade. A job lot is 1,000 bushels and the margin requirements are the same proportion as on a regular contract. You can buy or sell 1,000, 2,000, 3,000 or 4,000 job lots of wheat, or any other grain, on the Chicago Board of Trade.

NATURAL PERCENTAGE RESISTANCE POINTS

The basis of our money is 100 cents to a dollar. Long years ago we had the dollar divided into bits. People talked about one bit, two bits, four bits, six bits, and one dollar. They have become used to dividing the dollar into eighths, and they want to buy and sell on this basis. This makes these natural resistance points for prices in Wheat, Corn, and other Grain. Dividing the dollar by eight, we get:

⅛	12½c	⅝	62½c
¼	25c	¾	75c
⅜	37½	⅞	87½c
½	50c	1	1.00

which are Resistance Levels, or buying and selling points for Wheat, Corn, Soy Beans, or Oats. By going over the past records, you will see how often BOTTOMS and TOPS come out at these natural points. After the price gets above $1.00 per bushel, the natural Resistance Points are 112½, 125, 137½, 150; 162½, 175, 187½, 200; 212½, 225, 237½, 250; 262½, 275, 300; 312½, 325, 337½, and 350. The dollar can also be divided into sixteen equal points, or 100 can be divided into rts. This gives a point of 6¼c, and would make:

18¾	143¼	243¾
43¾	156¼	256¼
56¼	168¾	268¾

68¾	181¼	281¼
81¼	193¾	306¼
93¾	206¼	318¾
118¾	218¾	331¼
131¼	231¼	343¾

Also Resistance Points of some importance, and many times BOTTOMS and TOPS come out on these points.

In addition to the division of the dollar into eighths and sixteenths, people buy and sell at other even figures. These even figures are important to watch for BOTTOMS and TOPS on grain. For example:

30	65	95
40	70	105
45	80	110
55	85	115
60	90	120

PERCENTAGE OF HIGH AND LOW PRICES DETERMINE FUTURE RESISTANCE LEVELS.

TREND OF WHEAT OR OTHER COMMODITY ABOVE $1.00 PER BUSHEL

This analysis will cover the price of Wheat and show you where Resistance Levels are crossed and broken, and what happens when Wheat, or any other Commodity gets above $1.00 per bushel. It shows how we are able to forecast future TOPS by percentage of the last extreme high and future BOTTOMS by the percentage of the extreme low price or minor TOPS and BOTTOMS.

1841—Wheat crossed $1.00 and reached high at 110, just 2½c under the natural point of 112½, and at the exact even figure of 110.

1850—Wheat crossed $1.00 for the first time in several years, advanced to 103. Failing to get more than 3c above $1.00 indicated weakness.

1853—Wheat crossed $1.00, advanced to 110, the old TOP of 1841, making this a DOUBLE TOP and a selling level.

1854—Low 92c, later crossed $1.00 and advanced to 130, the highest level for many years. We divide the highest price by 8 to get the percentage of Resistance Point. ⅛ gives 113¾ and ¼, or 25%, off 130, gives 97½, and ⅜, or 37½%, off gives 81¼, and 50% off gives 65, which is the one-half point, or the most important resistance point. We divide 130 by 3 to get the one-third and two-thirds point. This gives 43½, as one-third of 130, and 87 as two-thirds of 130.

1854—After the high of 130 in 1854, Wheat declined to 90, which is 30% of the highest selling price and holding 3c above 87, the one-third point, indicating it was still in a strong position.

1855—Wheat again crossed $1.00 per bushel.

June, high 170, and 40c per bushel above the TOP in 1854. Failing by 5c to reach 175, the important 175% point. When Wheat reached this level, it was again important to divide 170 by 8 to get the Resistance Points on the way down. 25% of 170 would equal 42½; and 85 would equal 50%, and 21¼ would equal one-eighth, which would make 148¾ a very important point, or a decline of 12½%, breaking this level indicated lower. Divide 170 by 3 to get the one-third and two-thirds points, which gives 56⅝ as the one-third point, and 113¼ as the two-thirds point.

1856—Wheat again broke under $1.00 per bushel.

1856—Low 77, holding 2c above the natural Resistance Point at 75c, or ¾ of a dollar, and declining 8 points under 50%, or one-half of 170. When the price again advanced above 85, which is one-half of 170, it indicated a stronger position and prices advanced.

1857—Wheat crossed $1.00 again.

May, high 128, and 3c above a natural point at 125.

Wheat again broke under $1.00 and declined to 50c per bushel. 45¾ was seven-eights, or 87½% of the range from 28c to 170. 28c was the extreme low of Wheat reached in 1852, and also a basis from which to figure prices. 50c, or half of $1.00, is always an important Resistance Level. 53⅛ was eleven-sixteenths of 170, making this a natural support point, or buying level. The range between 128 and 170 was 42. The 50%, or half-way point between 28 and 170, was 99, making it important when Wheat crossed $1.00 again. It is important to always watch percentages of the base, or lowest point. 28c being the extreme low; 56c would be 100% advance; 84c a 200% advance; 112 a 300% advance; 140 a 400% advance, and 168 a 500% advance; 196 a 600% advance; 224 a 700% advance on the base. Also, one-half of 28, or 14c, added to any TOP or BOTTOM is important, and one-fourth of 28, or 7c, is important. Therefore, 84 would be a 200% advance on the base or BOTTOM, and 85 would be 50% of 170, the highest selling point up to this time, therefore, making 84 and 85 important Resistance Levels, and when Wheat crossed these levels it indicated higher.

1859—Wheat crossed 84 and 85, and later crossed $1.00.

May, high 130, same high as 1854, and only 2c above the high of May, 1857, making this a natural selling point against old TOPS. Wheat again broke back under $1.00 and broke the Resistance Points at 84 and 85.

August, low 50c, back to the old BOTTOMS of 1857 and 1858, and a natural buying level where there were double BOTTOMS and one-half of 100; the half-way point between 130 and 50 would be 90, making 50c a natural support point. 56c was 100% advance on the base or low point of 28c. The last high was 130, and the last low 50c, making the 50%, or half-way point, 90c per bushel; therefore, when Wheat crossed this level again, it indicated higher. Also, crossing 99, one-half between 170 and 28c, put it in a much stronger position.

1860—Wheat again crossed these Resistance Levels and crossed $1.00 per bushel. Made high, 114; a natural Resistance Point, 300% up from 112, and 100 was 100% advance on the low of 50. Wheat later broke back under $1.00, placing it in a weaker position.

1861—Last low in June, 55c; holding 5c above the double BOTTOMS, indicating strength and getting support just under 56c. The 100% advance on the base of 28 was an important buying point.

1862—After the Civil War broke out, Wheat held in a narrow trading range, and failed to reach $1.00 per bushel this year.

1863—Wheat crossed $1.00 per bushel, made high at 112, and later in the year broke back under $1.00 again. Declined to 80c, which was the last low before the big advance started. This was 5c under the half-way point of 170.

1864—Wheat crossed $1.00 per bushel; later crossed the old TOPS at 128 and 130, which indicated much higher prices. Late in the year 1864 Wheat crossed 170, the high of 1855, which indicated a big Bull market and much higher prices.

September, high $2.20 per bushel. 700% advance on the base of 28 was 224, and there were TOPS around 110. A 100% advance on 110 would give 220. 50% on 130 TOP would give 195. From this extreme high we would figure the Resistance Levels between the extreme low of 28c and $2.20, making the half-way point 124, and one-half, or 50% of 220, would be 110. The total range from 28c to $2.20 was $1.92 per bushel. ⅛ of this range would be 21½ and one-fourth, 43, and one-half was 86c. 25% from 220 would be 198⅛. Breaking back under this level was the first indication of weakness and lower prices.

1865—April, low 102. The price held above $1.00, the base level, and only went 8c per bushel under 110, the half of 220. Then prices crossed 110 again and 124, the other Resistance Point. indicating higher. Late in 1865 prices crossed 110.

September, high 151. The half-way point from 220 to 102 was 156. The fact that prices could not reach this important half-way point and stopped on the natural Resistance Point of 150 indicated good selling and a place to sell short.

1866—February, low 116. Note that the two Resistance Points were 110 and 124. Half of these points would give 117. This was a higher BOTTOM and a big advance followed. Later, prices crossed all former Resistance Points and TOPS, and later crossed the extreme high of 220.

1867—April, high $3.00 per bushel. From September, 1865, high, 151, if we add 100% to this TOP, we get 302, and we know that 300, or 3 times 100, is an important selling point, and these even figures are always Resistance Points. Again we figure the Resistance between the extreme low and the extreme high, or between 28c per bushel and $3.00 per bushel, also the BOTTOM at 50c per bushel to $3.00 per bushel, and the last low of 102 to 300. Dividing the highest selling price by 8, one-eighth gives 37½, and one-fourth gives 75, and one-half gives 150. The one-half, or 50% point, between extreme low of 28 and 300 was 164. From 50c per bushel to $3.00 per bushel, the one-half point was 175, and from 102 to $3.00 per bushel the half-way point was

$2.01 per bushel. The first important indication of weakness and change in trend was when prices broke back to 262½, or one-eighth of the highest selling price.

1867—August and September, low, 170; back to the old TOPS of June, 1855, and a point to buy for rally. Failing to decline to 164, one-half of 300 to 28c per bushel, was an indication of strength.

1868—May, high, 221; at the same TOPS as 1864. This was an advance of 51c per bushel. A sharp decline followed from this level. Later, all support levels were broken; prices continued to make lower TOPS and lower BOTTOMS.

1869—April, low, 103; same low as April, 1865, and still holding above $1.00 per bushel; $1.00 being two-thirds of 300, an important support point. Also note 1865 low, 102, making this a strong support or buying point.

August, high, 145; failed to reach 150, which was one-half of $3.00 per bushel.

October, broke back under $1.00 per bushel for the first time since 1863, which indicated extreme weakness, being under all-important 50%, or one-half points, and breaking under $1.00 per bushel after such a long period of time indicated much lower prices.

1870—March, low, 74c per bushel; back to the old TOP levels of 1862.

Note November, 1862, last low of 75c, making this natural support point a buying point.

In the Summer of 1870 prices again crossed $1.00.

July, high, 120. This was an advance of 45c per bushel.

1870—November, low, 95; just 5c under $1.00, indicating strength and a buying point again.

1871—Prices again crossed $1.00 per bushel.

1871—April, high, 134. Note lower TOPS than previous TOPS.

1871—August, low, 99; back to the old support point, just 1c under $1.00.

1872—August, high, 156, or 6 points above one-half of $3.00 per bushel, and 156 was a natural Resistance Point.

1872—November, low, 102; again holding above $1.00 per bushel and indicating strength; there being several BOTTOMS around this level. A rally followed.

1873—August, high, 146; this time failing to rally under one-half of $3.00 per bushel; making lower TOPS than 1872, showed weakness. From this level the market declined fast and broke support levels.

1873—September, low, 89c per bushel; down to a natural support level. Later in the year prices again crossed $1.00 per bushel.

1874—April, high, 128; just 3 points above 125, the natural Resistance level, and making lower TOPS right along. Later in the year prices broke $1.00 again.

1874—October, low, 81c. Breaking the low of 1872, but holding above the lows of 1870 indicated support and a rally followed.

1875—The advance started in February and prices again crossed $1.00 per bushel.

August, high, 130; just 2c above the high of 1874, a selling level and a double TOP. Later in the year prices again broke $1.00 per bushel.

December, low, 94c per bushel, again receiving support under $1.00, and a moderate rally followed.

1876—May, high, 108. Prices again broke back under $1.00 per bushel.

July, low, 83c; higher than the BOTTOM of 1874; also 2c higher than the low of March, 1870, making this a buying level for a rally.

1876—October. Prices again crossed $1.00 per bushel, showing strength and indicating higher.

1877—May, high, 176. A natural Resistance Level was 175, and a selling level. From 300 was down 225 points; 150 was one-half of 300; 164 was one-half from 28 to 300, and when prices broke back under 164, and later under 150, they were in a very weak position and declined fast.

August, low, $1.00 per bushel; a strong support level and buying point. From 1870 low, 74, to 176, high, would make the half-way point 125; and 88, one-half of 176, the last high selling point. Prices later broke 125 and a fast decline followed.

1878—February, low, 101. Still holding above $1.00 per bushel, and a rally followed.

1878—April, high, 114. Note 112½ was the natural selling point.

1878—June, low, 88. One-half of 176, a natural buying point for rally. Later, prices crossed $1.00 again.

August, high, $1.08 per bushel, then prices broke back under $1.00.

October, low, 77. Note 1874 low was 76; prices were still 3c above the 1870 low, making these triple BOTTOMS a place to buy for rally.

1879—Prices crossed 88, the half-way point of 176, and later crossed TOPS at 114.

1879—December, high, 133.

1880—January, high, 132; a decline followed and prices broke 125, one-half of 74 to 176, and later broke back under $1.00.

1880—September, low, 86c; just 2c under one-half of 176, and above the lows of 84 in August, 1879; an advance followed and prices again crossed $1.00 per bushel, and later crossed 125.

1881—October, high, 143; under the highs of July, 1877, and failing to reach one-half of $3.00 per bushel was a sign of weakness.

1882—February, low, 120; making lower TOPS and failing to reach 125 was a sign of weakness; a reaction followed, then another advance.

1882—April, high, 140. Note that this was lower than the 1881 TOP, making this a double TOP and a selling level. A fast decline followed; prices broke 125 and 120; a resistance point, turning the main trend down and later broke back under $1.00 per bushel.

1882—December, low, 91c; held above 88, the one-half of 176, and above the 1880 lows, making this a support point to buy for rally.

1883—May, high, 113. Note that the high in February was 111, and that 112½ was a natural Resistance Point. Failing to go 3c over the old TOP showed weakness. Later in the year prices again broke back under $1.00 per bushel.

1884—Prices worked lower, making lower TOPS and lower BOTTOMS, later breaking 88, the half of 176.

December, low, 70; just 4c under 1870 lows and a rally followed.

1885—April, high, 92; just 4c above one-half of 176; a decline followed.

1886—July, September and October, lows, 71 and 72; held above December, 1884, low; a buying point and a rally followed.

1887—June, high, 95; up to the last high of 1884 and staying under $1.00 showed weakness. Later prices broke 88, the half of 176, and late in June, low, 65; back to the low of 1862; a place to buy for rally because 67½ was a natural Resistance Point. A rally followed and prices crossed 88, the half of 176. One-half of 176 to 65 was 120½. Prices had not sold at $1.00 since 1883, therefore, when they crossed $1.00 again, they indicated higher prices; the next point being 113, the high of 1883, which price was crossed and later prices crossed 120½, the half-way point between 176 and 65.

1888—Prices advanced fast and crossed 143, the high of 1881. Later they crossed 176, the high of May, 1887; an indication of very much higher prices.

September, high, $2.00 per bushel; two-thirds of $3.00, the highest selling level, and prices had not sold at $2.00 per bushel since 1868. The range from 65c to $2.00 was $1.35 per bushel. Divide this by 8 to get important Resistance Point. One-eighth of this range would be 16⅞; therefore, when prices broke back under 183, they indicated lower. One-eighth of $2.00 per bushel, or 12½%, would be 175. Breaking this level showed weakness. 50% of 65 to 200 would be 132½. The Resistance Points would be 183⅛; 166¼; 149⅜; 132½; 115⅝; 98¾; 71⅞; the seven-eighths point, or 87½% from 65 to $2.00; the important percentage points of $2.00 were 175, 150, 125, $1.00, 75, etc., and the other natural Resistance Points. The high price of $2.00 per bushel, September, 1888, was the result of a corner. Prices always break back quickly from a corner, because a corner is a squeeze due to shortage, and when Wheat begins to move to the market, as it always does in the Fall of the year, prices decline. From $2.00 per bushel, prices broke wide open, breaking back under 150, the half of $3.00 per bushel, and later breaking under 132½, the half point between 65 and $2.00. After prices broke $1.00 per bushel, which was 50% decline from $2.00, the market was in a very weak position.

1889—June, low, 75c; holding above the lows of 1888 and above 87½% of 65 to $2.00, making this a buying point, and a rally followed. October, high, 96½; still holding under $1.00 per bushel, showing weakness.

1890—January, low, 74; only 1c under the lows of June, 1889, and still above 1888 low, indicating a support for rally.

1890—May, high, $1.00 per bushel; a natural selling level, and one-half of 200, the highest selling price.

1890—July, low, 85; a natural support point. Later crossed $1.00 per bushel.

1890—August, high, 108. Later broke back under $1.00 again.

1891—January, low, 87; above July, 1890, lows, and the three-eighths point of $2.00 per bushel, and at five-eighths of 65 to $2.00, making this a natural buying point. Prices again crossed $1.00 per bushel.

1891—April, high, 115; still lower than October, 1888, prices. From 74 low to 115 high, the one-half point would be 94½; a decline followed and prices broke $1.00 per bushel again. Later broke 94½, one-half of 74 to 115.

1892—December, low, 67c, and 2c above the lows of 1887, making this an old BOTTOM. A natural place to buy.

1893—April, high, 85. This was five-eighths of 65 to 200 and a natural selling point. A decline followed and, later in the year, prices broke the old lows of 1870, putting the market in a very weak position.

1894—July, low, 50c per bushel, back to the old lows and one-half of 100, and a decline of 75% from $2.00 per bushel. Note 50c per bushel was the last low in April, 1853, making this half-way point of $1.00 per bushel a safe buying point. When prices reach extreme low levels they have to hold in a narrow trading range for some time before big advances take place.

1894—December, high, 57. This was only a small rally.

1895—January, final low, 49c per bushel; only 1c under previous low level. Here we would again figure Resistance Levels between $3.00, the 1867 high, and $2.00, the 1888 high, to 49c, the extreme low, and still use the old base of 28c per bushel. The range between $3.00 per bushel and 49c would be $2.51. One-eighth of this would be 31⅜. This would give the following Resistance Points:

12½	80⅜	67½	205⅞
25	111¾	75	237¼
37½	143⅛	87½	268⅝
50	174½	100	300

After the decline to 49c per bushel, prices held in a narrow trading range for six months.

April, prices crossed the highs from the last two quarters, which turned the main trend up and indicated higher prices.

May, high, 81. Note the last high in April, 1891, was 115. Figuring to 49c low to 115, the half-way point would be 82%. This makes 81 a selling level. A decline followed.

December, low, 54; the same low as April, 1895, and a buying level; 5c above the extreme low of 49c per bushel.

1896—February, high, 67c; near 25% advance on base of 49c.

June and July, low, 54; same low as December, 1895, a double BOTTOM and a buying level. A rally followed and prices crossed 67, the high of February, 1896, a signal for still higher prices.

1896—November, high, 86. Note 85¾ is 87½% advance on 49c. Also note April, 1893, high, 85, making this old TOP a selling level for reaction.

1897—April, low, 64, Note 87½% of 49 to $2.00 was 64¾. Prices held 10c higher than 1896 lows. Later, prices crossed the highs of 1887 and 1888, indicating higher prices.

August, high, $1.00 per bushel; one-half of $2.00; one-third of $3.00 per bushel, and two-thirds from $2.50 per bushel. A decline followed.

October, low, 88; back to old TOPS and BOTTOMS, and at one-fourth of 49 to $2.00; a buying point, and a rally followed. Prices crossed $1.00 per bushel and later crossed 115, the old TOP, and later crossed 125, the half of $2.00 per bushel to 49, indicating higher prices. A rapid advance followed.

1898—May, high, 185. This was the Leiter corner. Note that 182 was ⅞ of 200 to 49. Armour brought about the collapse of the market and failure of Leiter by shipping wheat into Chicago by express trains. The decline was rapid, as all of these declines are when the market is cornered, and the man who tries to corner it goes broke, and cannot get out. Here again we figure from the extreme low of 49c per bushel to 185, which gives $1.17 per bushel as the one-half point. One-half of 185 would be 92½; one-eighth of 185 is 23⅛, which gives the following points for Resistance: 161⅞, 138¾, and 115⅜, which is the three-eighths or 37½% point; 92½ or 50% decline, or the half-way point; 69⅜ gives 62½% decline or five-eighths point. It is always important to figure percentage of the lowest price.

50% advance on 49c would give 73½%
100% advance on 49c would give 98c
150% advance on 49c would give 122½
200% advance on 49c would give 147
225% advance on 49c would give 169¼

1898—September, low, 62c; just 2c under the low of April, 1897; a support level and buying point.

1899—January, high, 79c. This was one-eighth of 49 to $3.00, which was 80⅜. A small reaction followed.

July, high, 79c; same high as January, 1899; a double TOP and selling level.

1900—May, 63, low; just 1c above the low of September, 1898, a double BOTTOM and a place to buy.

October, high, 81; just 2c above the old TOPS of 1899, and a 25% point of 49 to 185; a selling level.

1901—September, low, 63⅛. This was the last low; the same as May, 1900; a double BOTTOM and a buying point.

1902—January, high, 85c; just 2c above 25% of 49 to 185, and up against old TOPS and a place to sell.

August, low, 68½c; higher than the previous lows. Note that 66 was one-eighth of 49 to 185, and 69⅜ was three-eighths decline from 185, making this a buying point, and 67½ was a natural buying point or Resistance point and the market held 1c above it.

1903—August, high, 85¾; just ¾ of a cent above the TOP of May, 1902, and still under 92½, or one-half of 185.

1903—November, low, 76. Note that 75 is three-fourths of a hundred, and that 50% added to the low of 49 gives 77½, making this a natural support or buying point.

1904—January; prices crossed old TOPS of 85 and 86, showing great strength and indicating an up trend. Later crossed 98 and $1.00 per bushel, which was a 50% advance on the base or BOTTOM of 49. Going above $1.00 indicated higher prices.

February, high, 109. Note 108 was seven-sixteenth of 185 to 49, and there were many old TOPS and BOTTOMS around 108 to 110.

June, low, 81c. Note 80⅜ was one-eighth of 49 to 300 and 50% on 49 gives 78½. Note old TOPS at 79 and 81, making this a natural support point and buying level. A rally followed and prices crossed 92½, one-half of 185, and later crossed $1.00. 50% of 49 to 185 was 117.

September, high, $1.19; just 2c above one-half of 49c to $1.85. A selling level.

October, low, 108. Note TOP of February, 1904, was 109, making this a buying level against old TOPS.

1905—February, high, 121½; just 2½c above the TOP of September, 1904; a double TOP and selling level. Later when prices broke back under 117, the half-way point of 185 to 119, and then prices broke 108, the old BOTTOMS, they were very weak and breaking under two previous quarters indicated lower prices. 1901 low, 63, to 1905 high, 121½, the one-half point being 91½. The following points are important between 63 and 121½:

70½	⅞ point	95⅞	⅜ point
78¾	¾ point	107	¼ point
85	⅜ point	114½	⅛ point
92¼	½ point		

1905—June, low, 82.   Low in 1904 was 81 and TOP around this level makes this a natural support level and buying point.

October, high, 93.   Note one-half of 63 to 121½ is 92¼, and one-half of 185 is 92½, making this a safe selling level.

1906—September, low, 75½.   Note 77¾ was three-fourths of 63c to 121½, and that 75c is a natural support point.   Also, March, 1906, low, 76½, makes this a double BOTTOM and a safe buying point.

1907—Low, 75; the third time at this same level, where there were old TOPS and BOTTOMS; again a safe point to buy.

1907—April prices crossed the high of two previous quarters, indicating higher prices.   Note 121½ to 75 low was 98¼, the half-way point.   Later, prices crossed 98¼, and crossed $1.00, getting into a very strong position.

1907—October, high, 112½.   Note 114¼ was seven-eighths of 63c to 121½, and 75 to 112½ was 37½% or three-eighths of one hundred, making this a natural point at 112½, a selling level for reaction.   Later, the trend turned down and prices broke back under $1.00.

1908—April, low, 89c; just under the one-half point, and a rally followed.   Prices crossed 92½, the half point, and later crossed $1.00.

1908—May, high, 111; a lower TOP than October, 1907.

1908—July, low, 92; at the half-way point and higher than April, 1908. This was a buying point.

1908—December, high, 111.   This made three times around this level, and it was a selling level.   A small reaction followed.

1909—January, low, 104; failing to get back to $1.00 per bushel was a sign of strength.   Later, prices crossed the old TOPS at 111 and 112, and crossed 114¼; and seven-eighths of 63 to 121½, and then crossed 117, one-half of 49 to 185, placing the market in a very strong position.

May, high, 135.   Note 134 was five-eighths of 49 to 185 and that 138¾ was three-fourths of 185, making this a strong selling level.   137½ is a natural Resistance Level.   Here we figure 1907,

March, low, 75c to 135 high; an advance of 60c per bushel makes one-eighth of the range 7½c, giving the following points:

Seven-eighths equals 82½.
Three-fourths equals 90¾.
Five-eighths equals 97½.
One-half equals 105, or 50% decline.
Three-eighths equals 112½.
One-fourth equals 120.
One-eighth equals 127½.

Then, dividing the high selling price by 8, we get the following important points:

One-sixteenth equals 8.43.
One-eighth equals 16⅞.
One-fourth equals 33¾.
One-half equals 67½.

This would give 118⅛; 101¼; 84⅜, and 67½ as very important points or Resistance Levels.

1909—August, low, 97. Note 97½ was five-eighths of 75 to 135. Later, prices crossed $1.00 again.

1910—February and May, high, 116 and 117. Note 118⅛ was one-eighth of 135 and 120 was one-fourth of 75 to 135, making this a selling level.

1910—July, low, 92; note 90 was three-fourths of 75 to 135; down to old BOTTOM and TOP levels of 1908, making this a buying point. A rally followed.

July, high, 115; the third time around this level, making this a sure, safe, selling level. Later prices broke one dollar, and when they broke 105, half of 75 to 135, it was in a very weak position.

1911—March and April, low, 85. Note that three-eighths of 135 was 84⅜, and 82½ was seven-eighths of 75 to 135, making this a buying level. A rally followed. Later, prices crossed 97½, the five-eighths of 75 to 135, and later crossed $1.00.

October, high, 107; the market held around these levels for four quarters, making TOPS, making this a selling level.

1912—January, low, 98c. Note 97½ was five-eighths of 75 to 135, and $1.00 was the natural support level, and a rally followed.

May, high, 119; note one-eighth of 135 was 118⅛, and 120 was one-fourth of 75 to 135, making this a natural selling point. 135 to 185 gives 110 as the 50%, or half-way, point. 85 to 119 gives 102 as the half-way point. From May, 1912, a decline followed and, when prices broke 110, the half-way point from 85 to 135, they indicated lower and, later, prices broke 102, the half-way point from 85 to 119, and when they broke $1.00 they showed real weakness and a rapid decline followed.

1913—March, low, 88; holding 3c above 1911 lows showed strength; a small rally followed.

1913—July, high, 99; failed to make 100, or 102, the half of 85 to 119. There were two quarters with TOPS around this level, making it a safe selling level. Later, when the decline got under way, prices broke the BOTTOMS around 88.

1914—June, low, 76¾; holding above 1906 and 1907 BOTTOM prices, making this a buying level.

July; war broke out and prices advanced rapidly. War is always Bullish on Wheat, especially if prices are at very low levels when war breaks out. The last range was 76¾ to 135.

September, high, 132; just 3c under 1909 TOPS of 135. Prices had advanced 55c within a very short period of time. 62½%

of 49 to 185 was 134, making this a selling level, especially with prices under the 1909 TOPS.

October, low, 111; back to old TOPS and old BOTTOMS. 112½ was a natural support, or Resistance Level, and 110 was the 50% point from 85 to 135 and 112½ was three eighths of 75 to 135; the advance was resumed and prices crossed 119 and later crossed TOPS of 1909 at 135, indicating much higher prices.

1915—February, high, 167. Note 168 was seven-eighths of 49 to 185; the range from 76¾ to 167 was 90¼, giving one-eighth points of 11¼, giving the following points:

$$97................\textstyle\frac{7}{8}\text{ point}$$
$$107................\textstyle\frac{3}{4}\text{ point}$$
$$117................\textstyle\frac{5}{8}\text{ point}$$
$$127................\textstyle\frac{1}{2}\text{ point}$$
$$137................\textstyle\frac{3}{8}\text{ point}$$
$$147................\textstyle\frac{1}{4}\text{ point}$$
$$167................\textstyle\frac{1}{8}\text{ or }12\textstyle\frac{1}{2}\%$$

One-eighth of 167, the highest selling point, would be 20⅞, and one-sixteenth would be 10⅜, making prices at these points important. From 167 a sharp decline followed, breaking 155¾, the 25% point of 76 to 167, an indication of weakness, and then broke 150, the half of $3.00 per bushel. Later broke 144½; 25% of 76¾ to 167. When it broke 121⅞, which was 50% of 76¾, to 167, it was in a very weak position.

1915—September, low, 93. Note 88⅛ was seven-eighths of 76¾ to 167, and 94 was nine-sixteenths of 167; this was a decline of 74c. 100% advance on 49, the last extreme low level, was 98. Then figure 63, the low level, 50% on this, would give 94½; making 93 an important support level. Later, prices crossed $1.00, which is three-fourths of 167, and later crossed 111¼; 25% of 167 to 93. December, high, 127. Note 130 was one-half of 167 to 93; a natural point for reaction. A moderate reaction followed from this level.

1916—January, high, 138. Note 133¼ was three-eighths of 167 and 139¼ was five-eighths of 167 to 93 low, making 138 a selling level. May, low, $1.04. Note five-eighths of 167 was 104⅜, making this a support level and a buying point. Holding above $1.00 per bushel was an indication of strength, and holding 11c above the low of 93 also showed strength. From 138 to 104, the half-way point was 121. When prices crossed this level they were in strong position and advanced fast.

August; prices crossed the TOPS of 138 and later crossed 167, indicating higher prices. Prices did not stop at the old TOP of 185 made in 1898; the advance continued and prices crossed $2.00, the TOP of 1888, and also crossed important Resistance Levels.

November, high, 195; a selling level as prices were just under 200, the old TOP level.

1917—February, low, 154½. Note October, 1916, low 154, making this a double BOTTOM and a buying level. Prices holding above 150, a natural Resistance point, which is one-half of $3.00 per bushel, made this a strong point.

April; prices crossed $2.00 per bushel, the highest since 1867 of $3.00. The advance was rapid.

May, high, $3.25 per bushel, the highest price in history. When the prices reached these levels, the Government stopped future trading.

From the high of $3.25 we figure Resistance Levels from the extreme low of 28c per bushel, and then figure 49c per bushel to $3.25, and from 63c per bushel and 75c per bushel and 93c per bushel, the last low levels, to get improtant Resistance Points on the way down.

Cash Wheat Prices

After future trading was stopped, there was some cash trading.

1918—September, low, 222.

1919—April, high, 292.

August, low 224.

December, high, 350; the highest in history. This was a natural selling point , because it was at the half-way point between 300 and 400. From the low of 220, reached in April, 1919, to the high of 350, makes a 50% reaction point 285. Breaking this would be the first indication of very much lower prices. Future trading was resumed in July, 1920, and the first sales of the July option were around 275, which was 10 points under the half-way point of the last move, showing the main trend down.

1919—A sharp, severe decline followed. You would refer to the Resistance Levels from the extreme low of 28 to 350 and from the low of 1895 of 49c to $3.50, and from the low in June, 1914, of 76¾ to $3.50; also the percentage point of $3.50, the highest selling price. Note that 262½ was 75% of 350, and when prices broke under this level they were in a weak position, and later, when they broke the last low at 220 they were in a very weak position and indicated 175, which was 50% of the highest selling price. 189 was 50%, or the half-way point, between 28 and 350.

All of these important Resistance Points and 50% reaction points were broken, and prices declined rapidly. You should have sold short all the way down.

1920—December, low, 152; note that 149.33 was 33-1/3 % of 49 to 350, making this a natural support point, and 150 was one-half, or 50%, of 300, and 150 is always a natural buying or selling point. Also, 148¾ was three-eighths, or 37½%, between 28 and 350. From this level a rally followed.

1921—January, high, 175, one-half of 350; a natural selling point. A further decline followed.

March, low, 137; note 135⅜ was the 33-1/3% point between 228 and 350, and 135 was down to old TOP levels and back to two TOPS in 1916, also a TOP at 135 in 1909, making this a buying point at these old TOP levels and Resistance Points. Of course, when you buy around any of these points you should always place a *stop loss order* for protection in case the market reverses. A moderate rally followed. Prices later broke 137 and 135.

1921—April, low, 119. There were a series of old BOTTOMS and TOPS around this level. 124 was 25% between 49c and 350, and 116⅝ was one-third of 350. After such a drastic decline in such a short period of time, a natural rally was in order, and the advance was sharp and swift.

May, high, 184; just under the half-way point between 28 and 350, which was 189, and nine points above one-half of 350.

Adding the 2 points together gives 182, and there were many old TOPS around this level, making 184 a natural selling point to sell out longs and sell short, because the main trend of the market was still down. This was an advance of 65c in a very short period of time.

Taking the high of 275 when future trading started again, to this low of 119, would make the half-way point 197. The fact that the market failed to reach this level showed weakness. A decline of 350 to 119 is 231 points. One-third of this would be 77 points. The market failing to get anywhere near one-third of the decline indicated weakness. One-fourth of 231 would be 57¾ added to 119, the low point, would give 176¾, making this a Resistance Level, and when the price broke back under this level it indicated weakness. It is important to watch the half-way point from 119 to 184, which was 151½. When prices broke back under this level they declined fast. Later breaking the low of 119.

November, low, 98c; holding just 2c under $1.00 per bushel, and above the last low levels of 1915 was an indication of strength.

The last low in 1916 was 104. Looking over the Resistance Levels, you find that there were many old BOTTOMS and TOPS around this level in previous campaigns. There is always support the first time around $1.00 per bushel, anyway, making this a buying point for rally. A sharp, quick advance followed.

1922—February and April, high, 150 and 148; note that 149.33 was one-third point between 350 and 149, and that 148¾ was the three-eighths point between 28c per bushel and $3.50, and 151½ was the half-way point between 119 and 184, and from the last high of 184 to 198, the half-way point, or 50% rally, was 141.

You should have gone short around 150, protected with *stop loss order*. When prices broke back under half of the last range, or under 141, you should have sold more. The market declined fast

August, low, 105; holding above the previous low levels and holding above $1.00 per bushel indicated a point for rally again.

$108\frac{5}{8}$ was 25% between 28c and 350, and the last low in May, 1916, was 104. A rally followed.

September, high, 126; a moderate reaction followed from this high.

1923—April, high, 127; making a double TOP at this level. Note that $124\frac{1}{4}$ was one-fourth of 49c to 350, and that from 98 to 150, the half-way point was 124. In view of the fact that, for several months, prices could not advance 5 points above this half-way point, made it important to sell just as soon as prices broke back under 124. When they broke below the two previous quarters they were in a weaker position.

July, low, 96; back to the old low level of October, 1915, and only two points under November, 1921, making this a buying level. Failing to go 5c under $1.00 per bushel was an indication of strength. This was a triple BOTTOM years apart around this level, and when prices crossed $1.00 per bushel again, they were in a stronger position. For three quarters the market remained in comparatively narrow range, making three TOPS around 112 to 114.

1924—March and April, low, 103; making a higher BOTTOM and holding above $1.00 per bushel indicated support and a place to buy, especially as the market was dull and narrow around these low levels. The advance was resumed. Prices crossed 112, where there were three TOPS, indicating the market in a very strong position, and later crossed 128, a series of TOPS, indicating great strength. The last low was 96 and the high was 150, making the half-way point 123. Figuring 184, the last TOP of May, 1921, to the low of 96 in July, 1923, made the half-way point 140. After prices crossed 123 and 138 they were in a much stronger position and the market advanced rapidly.

Crossed 175, which was one-half of 350, and later crossed 189, which was one-half of 28 to 350.

1925—January, final high, $205\frac{7}{8}$ for May Wheat. You naturally expect TOPS around 200 because there is always selling around these even figures. Looking back over the old charts you would find 350 high to 49 low, the half-way point was $199\frac{1}{2}$. Momentum, public optimism, and big buying carried the market beyond this half-way point, but it did not remain there long. When prices broke back under $2.00 per bushel, it was an indication of lower prices and you should have sold out all long Wheat and sold short. A rapid decline followed. From this level the important point to figure was from 96 low up to $205\frac{7}{8}$. Also, you should not overlook the fact to figure the important point from 325, the high of May Wheat in 1917, to the low of 49c. This gave the 50% or half-way point at 186. Breaking back under this level indicated weakness. Figuring the high on May Wheat in 1917, from 326 to 96 gave a half-way point of $210\frac{1}{2}$. That May Wheat failed to advance to this half-way point was an indication of weakness. The fact that it hesitated around $2.00 per bushel, or a little higher, was an indication of a selling level. From 96 to 205⅞ would give a half-way point of 151½; 25% of the advance from 96 to 206⅞ indicated 178½. When prices broke back under this level they were in a weaker position and indicated lower. You should have sold short all the way down.

1925—April, low, 137. Note that the three-eighths point between 96 and 205⅞ is 137¼, making this a strong support or buying level, after the 50% or half-way point had been broken, which was 151. There were old TOPS and BOTTOMS around this level. 137½ was a natural support level, being 137½% from zero, or 37½% on the second $1.00 per bushel. A rally followed. July, high, 164; note from 205⅞ to 137, the half-way point is 171½. The fact that prices failed to reach this level was an indication of weakness and a further decline followed.

October, low, 135; down to old BOTTOM levels. Failed to decline 3c under the previous BOTTOMS. You should again have covered shorts and bought. A rapid advance followed.

December, high, 185. There were three TOPS around this level. 182 was the half-way point between 350, and was also half-way point between 350 and 28, making this a natural selling level.

1925—A decline followed. Next, you figure from 135 to 185; that is, using the 50% reaction point as important, making 160 the half-way point of this last move; breaking back under this level was an indication of weakness. When it broke 150, where there were important Resistance Points, it was in still weaker position and indicated lower prices. Note that 114¾ was three-eighths or 37½% between 28c per bushel and 350. Prices declined rapidly during 1926.

1927—March, low, 131. Note that 131¼ was 37½% decline from 350 and there were many old TOPS and BOTTOMS around this level in previous campaigns, making this a natural point to buy for rally.

May, high, 158. Note that three-eighths of 49c to 350 was 161⅞. Prices failing to reach this level indicated weakness, and falling far below the half-way point of 350 was another indication of weakness. 25% from 96 to 350 gives 159½. Another indication why this would be a Resistance Level and a place to sell out and sell short, especially if prices held at this level. When prices broke back under the important points around 150 and later broke the half-way point between 131 and 158, which was 145, they indicated lower, and you should have sold short.

November, low, 126; down to a series of old TOPS and BOTTOM levels, only 5 points under the low of March and April, 1927, 124¼ was 25% between 49 and 350, and 127¾ was 12½% between 96 to 350. Prices were very dull and narrow at this level and remained in a narrow range for several months. Therefore, you should have covered all shorts and bought. When prices crossed 137, the high of the last quarter, they indicated higher and you should have bought more. A rapid advance followed.

1928—May, high, 171. Note that 175 is one-half of 350, and 165-3/8 was 3/8 of 96 and 205-7/8, making this a selling point. But the fact that it failed to rally to one-half of 350, showed weakness, staying below one-half of the highest selling point. Also note that May 1926, the last high was 171 and from that level, the main trend turned down. Therefore, around 170 to 171 was a point to sell out longs and sell short, especially as this was a fast run up in the month of May when the trend so often changes and turns down. A rapid decline followed. From the last low to the last high; 126 to 171; 50% reaction or the half-way point, would be 148½. When prices broke back under this level they were in a very weak position. In fact, breaking 150 always indicates weakness and lower prices. A rapid decline followed; prices finally breaking the low of 126, with only small rallies from time to time.

1929—May, low, 93c per bushel. This was one year from the time that May Wheat sold at 171, and this was the lowest level since September, 1915, when May Wheat sold exactly at 93c, making this again a support point against an old BOTTOM and a buying level, protected with *stop loss order* 3c away. Note that 103 was 50% decline, or one-half of 205-7/8. Prices went 10c under this important half-way point to the last old BOTTOM. The fact that prices only declined 3c under the low of July, 1925, was an indication of strength, and when prices again crossed $1.00 per bushel, it was a place to buy as higher prices were indicated. Crossing 103 the last half-way point was very important for higher prices.

A rapid advance followed.

August, high, 164. 3/8 of 49c to 350 was 161-7/8. This was an advance of 71c per bushel in a short period of time. 162½ was one-half of 325, the highest price that May Wheat ever sold in May, 1917. Makes this important half-way point a selling level, as prices hesitated and showed good selling. This was a place to sell out and sell short. Another important point to consider was that each TOP was lower.

REVIEW:

1925—January, high, 205-7/8.

    December, high, 185.

1926—January, high, 180.

1928—May, high, 171.

1929—August, high, 164.

All lower TOPS, showing that the main trend was down. The next important point to figure was the Resistance Point between 93 and 164. 25% decline would be 146¼. Of course, breaking 150, and important points around this level indicated lower, but breaking back 25% of the last advance, indicated weakness and lower prices. From this last high, the decline was rapid, because the panic in the stock market started in September, 1929, and later prices broke under 138½ which was the half-way point, or 50% decline between 93c and $1.64, placing the market again in a very weak position. The decline was rapid. All the attempts by the Government to support the market failed, and the prices continued to work lower. Rallies were small and all important support levels were broken. In 1930, prices broke under 93c per bushel, breaking under all lows since the war began; later breaking 76-¾, the low of June, 1914.

1930—November, low, 73c per bushel. Look back on your old records and you will find in 1901, 1902 and 1903, a series of BOTTOMS at this level, making this a point for at least a moderate rally. 68¼ was ⅛ point between 28c and 350, and 87½ was ¼, or 25% between the low and $3.50 per bushel. 81¼ was ¼ of $3.25 per bushel, the highest level that May Wheat ever sold.

1931—May, high, 86½; just under the ¼ point, or 25% of $3.50 per bushel. Failing to get back under the old BOTTOM level of 93c was a sign of weakness, and lower prices followed. November, low, 59c; back to the low of January, 1895, and at 50c, one-half of a dollar, always a point for some support and a rally. Prices held in a narrow range and a moderate rally followed.

1932—September, high, 65c. This was still under the ⅛ point between 28c per bushel and $3.50, and a weak rally because it was only 10 months from the BOTTOM. Prices failed to hold. They even failed to get to 67½; a natural selling point. At this point the important point to watch would be between 49 and 65, 57 being the half-way point. When this point was broken it was also under the BOTTOM of previous quarter and indicated lower prices. December, final low, 43¼ for the May option, and December Wheat declined to the extreme low of 41½c per bushel. 43-¾ was ⅞, or 87½% decline from 350, the highest selling point.
40⅝ was 87½% decline from the highest price of May Wheat of 325, making these levels natural support points and buying points. These low prices in December, 1932, were the lowest prices Wheat had sold for 80 years. The last time that prices were at these low levels was in 1852. It was only natural after such a drastic decline in such a short period of time, that prices should make BOTTOM and a Bull Campaign start. Wheat under 50c a bushel was certainly far below the cost of production. Therefore, Wheat was a buy at this time as a long pull investment. The last point on May Wheat to watch was from 65 to 43-⅝; the 50% or half-way point would be 54¼. When May Wheat crossed this level it indicated higher.

1933—March, high, 66½.

April, low, 45; making a higher BOTTOM and holding above the half-way point indicated strength. Then, when prices crossed 57, or getting above the high of the past quarter, it indicated higher and you should have bought more.
You would now figure the important Resistance Points from

205-⅞ to 43¼; also 325 to 43¼, and, of course, $3.50 per bushel to 43¼, the extreme low on May Wheat, but you should consider 325; 205-⅞; 185; 171½; 164; the last highs on May down to 43¼ the important Resistance Points. When May Wheat crossed 63-⅝, it was above the ⅛ point between 43¼ and 205-⅞. When it crossed 61, it was above the ⅛ point between 43¼ and 185, and when it crossed 64-⅜, it was above the ⅜ point of 71½. When it crossed 61½, it was above the ⅜ point of 164. The important 50% Reactions or half-way points are as follows:

½ of 205⅞ is 103	½ of 174⅞ is 85¾
½ of 185 is 92½	½ of 164 is 82

The half-way point between 164 and 43¼ was 103-⅝. Therefore, when Wheat advanced and crossed $1.00 per bushel, it was in a very strong position and indicated higher prices.

July, high, 128. Note 131¼ was ⅜ of $3.50, and 128⅝ was ⅝ of 205⅞, making this a very important Resistance Point. Also, 124⅝ was one-half between 43¼ and 205⅞, and 128¾ was 2/3 from 171½ to 43¼; 123 was ¾ of 164, making this an important selling point, especially as this advance had been very rapid. Again we must not overlook the fact that volume of sales was large. The percentage on the lowest selling price would be: 100% on 43¼ would be 86½; a 200% advance on the base or lowest selling price would be 129-¾, making 128 a natural point to sell out longs and go short. This was an advance of 85c per bushel, or nearly ⅞ of a dollar, in a very short period of time; the advance had been too rapid. Everybody had gotten too bullish; Dr. E. A. Crawford had bought Wheat and was overloaded with other commodities. His failure caused the sharp decline, as the public was overloaded, too. Prices broke 30c per bushel in three days. The decline was so drastic that the Government had to peg prices and this almost stopped trading on the Chicago Board of Trade. The important point to figure after prices reached 128¼ was the price between 43¼ and 128¼. This would make 117⅝, a 12½% decline. 107 a 25% decline. 96⅝, a 37½% decline; Half of the total advance would be 35-¾. Prices declined rapidly and rallies were small.

1934—April, low, 73; note that November, 1930, the low was 73, and October, 1931, high was 73, and May, 1932, high, 74: making these old BOTTOMS and TOPS a natural buying point. 75-⅛ was 62½%, making this a safe, sure buying point for rally, because the selling had been overdone, just the same as the buying had been overdone at the TOP. 75% of one dollar is always a natural support point, and there were many other Resistance Levels around this price to indicate that BOTTOMS should be reached there. The important point between 128¼ and 73, was the half-way point of 100½. Always when prices cross $1.00, it is important to watch for higher prices anyway. The first indication was a rally of 25% of the decline. When prices advanced above 86¾, they were in strong position and indicated higher. Then,

crossing the TOPS of the previous quarter around 97 and crossing
$1.00 they were in strong position and the market moved up fast.
The lowest reaction was 88, in July, 1934. After that the market
advanced rapidly.

1934—August, high, 117. Note that ⅝ of 73 to 128 was 114¼, and that
1/3 of $3.50 per bushel was 1.16⅝ and that ¼ or 25% between
49 and 325 was 117-⅞, and ⅝ of 185 was 115-⅝; one-half of
43¼ to 185 was 114⅛, and 2/3 of 171½ was 114⅜ and ⅝ of
43½ to 164 was 118-¾, making 117 a natural, strong Resistance
Point; a place to sell out and sell short, especially as a change in
trend nearly always takes place in the month of August. This
was opposite the seasonal trend. Prices are nearly always lower
in August, and when there is a rapid advance in August, a change
in trend takes place and a quick reversal follows. A quick decline
followed from this high in August. One of the important points
to watch was the 50% decline from 73 to 117 which was 95c. The
important Resistance Levels around $1.00 are always important.
When prices broke $1.00 they indicated lower and breaking 95c
showed they were in a very weak position. Rallies were small.
Prices continued to work lower.

1935—July, low, 81c. Note that 81⅝ was ⅛ between 43¼ and $3.50
per bushel and that 81¼ was 25% of 325. There were old TOPS
and BOTTOMS around this level, making it a natural support
level. Prices became dull and narrow on this decline and this was
a place to buy protected with *close stop loss order.* From 117 to
81, the half-way point was 99. Therefore, when prices advanced
above $1.00 per bushel again, they were in a stronger position
and indicated higher.

October, high, 107; this was 75% advance from 81 to 117. Prices
became dull and narrow on this rally and indicated TOPS. Therefore, it was a place to sell out and sell short with a *close stop loss
order,* then watch the important half-way point, 94c from 81
to 107.

1936—May, low, 90c. There were many Resistance Points to indicate
support around this level. 92½ was one-half of 185; 90½ was
1/3 between 185 and 43¼; 91⅜ was 37½% or ⅜ of 43¼ to
171½; 88½ was 37½% from 43¼ to 164. The market had been
making progressive BOTTOMS, that is, making higher BOT-
TOMS right along on the quarterly charts since the low of

December, 1932. After the high of July, 1933, BOTTOMS had
been lower, that is lower BOTTOMS in August, 1934 and a lower
BOTTOM in October, 1935. Therefore, when prices crossed 94,
the important half-way point, and still better, when they could
cross $1.00 per bushel, they indicated higher. Finally, when they
crossed a series of quarterly TOPS around 103 to 105 and crossed
the high of 107 of October, 1935, they were in a very strong
position and indicated much higher. July, high, 117; back to the

old TOP of August, 1934. From this TOP only a moderate reaction took place, prices declining to 110 in October, holding
above the previous TOP levels and above important Resistance
Levels. When prices crossed 117, the double TOP, they indicated
much higher and crossing 128, the TOP of July, 1933, indicated
much higher prices. You should have continued to buy Wheat
and followed it up with *close stop loss orders.*

1937—April, high, 145-⅛ for May Wheat. This was the final high and
the end of the Bull Campaign which started in December, 1932.
Prices advancing $1.02 per bushel for the May option from the
extreme low. From $3.50 per bushel to 43¼ the 1-3 point was
145½. From 49 to 325, the 1/3 point was 140⅞. From 325 to
43¼, the ⅝ or 37½% point was 148-⅞. From 205-⅞ to 43¼,
the ⅝ point was 144-⅞. 75% of 185 was 138-¾. From 185 to
43¼, 75% was 149-⅝. From 171½, 87½% was 150. From 164,
87½% was 143½. From 164 to 43¼, 87½% was 148-⅞. All of
these important Resistance Levels, just under 150, a natural selling point, made this an important point to sell out and sell short.
The safest place to sell would be after it had given an indication
of lower prices by breaking daily BOTTOMS or swing moves or
breaking back under weekly BOTTOMS, or by declining 25%
of the last move up, which was from 90c per bushel to 145, or 55c
per bushel. The 25% decline would be 131¼; 250% added on to
the extreme low of 43¼ would give 151-⅜; the fact that prices
failed to reach this level indicated 145 as the selling level. Declining 25% or breaking 131¼ indicated lower, but breaking back
under 120-¾ which was 200% advance on the low selling price
of 43¼, also breaking back under 128, the TOP of July, 1933,
indicated weakness and lower prices to follow. You would now
figure the percentage of 145-⅛ and the range and percentage
between 145-⅛ and 43¼. Note 72½ was one-half of 145-⅛ and
94⅛ was half-way between 43¼ and 145⅛. The market declined
rapidly and during the summer of 1937 and in the fall a panicky
decline took place in the stock market which also influenced
selling in wheat and other Commodities. Prices broke 94½, the
half-way point between 43¼ and 145 which indicated extreme
weakness.

1937—November, low, 87c. Breaking the low of May, 1936, by 3c per
bushel, 90¾ was ⅝ of 145⅛. A moderate rally followed.

1938—January, high, 99c. Failing to get back to $1.00 per bushel was
an indication of weakness. Again breaking back under 94-⅛
half-way point between 43¼ to 145⅛ indicated weakness and
lower prices to follow. You should have sold short. The decline
continued and all support levels were broken; rallies were very
small.

1938—September, low, 63c per bushel.
63-⅝ was ⅛ of 205-⅞ to 43¼.
61 was ⅛ of 185 to 43¼.
61½ was ⅜ of 164.
50% on the lowest selling price of 43¼ was 63-⅞. Making this a

natural support point and a buying point. Also notice that in 1932, there was one TOP at 65 and two TOPS at 63. Therefore, this was back to an old BOTTOM or buying level. Markets remained in a very narrow trading range for 6 months.

1939—January, high, 71. Failing to get back to 72½, one-half of 145 showed the market was not yet ready to advance. A moderate reaction took place, prices declining to 67. Later, prices crossed 72½.

1939—May, high, 80. Note that 81⅜ was ⅝ between 145⅛ and 43¼. 83-⅜ was ¼ of 145-⅛ to 63.

The market was dull and narrow around this level, made TOPS and broke back under 72½, indicating lower.

1939—August, low, 64. Down to the old Resistance Levels and making a double BOTTOM and holding one cent above the previous BOTTOMS indicated good support and a buying level. When prices crossed 72½, the half-way point of 145⅛, they indicated higher.

September 1st, war broke out and there was a rapid advance, prices reaching 91 in September, but failed to reach the half-way point or 50% rally between 43¼ and 185, and 1-3 between 63 and 145⅛ was 90⅛. There were old BOTTOMS around these levels. A moderate reaction followed.

October, low, 79¼. Failing to reach 76½, the half-way point between 63 and 90 was an indication of strength and a place to buy, especially as prices became dull and narrow around this level. A rally followed and prices crossed 90. Later they crossed 94, the half-way point between 145-⅛ and 43¼, placing the market in a very strong position and indicated higher prices. War is always Bullish on Wheat and the public buys on war news.

1939—December, high, 111. Note the last high in October, 1937, was 110, making this a selling level around the old TOPS; a reaction followed.

1940—February, low, 95½. Failing to reach 94⅛, the half-way point between 43¼ and 145⅛ was an indication of strength and higher prices followed.

May, high, 113. May is always a month for a change in trend and higher prices often occur in this month.
114¼ was ⅝ between 63 and 145-⅛.
111⅛ was 2/3 between 43¼ and 145⅛.
108⅞ was 75% of 145⅛.

Making this a selling level. Prices remained in a narrow trading range for several weeks and on May 10, when Hitler started his drive against France and Belgium, Wheat broke wide open, breaking all support levels, and declining fast, breaking as much as 8c per day for 2 or 3 days, going the limit permitted in one day. It is important here to figure the half-way point and other important points between 63 and 113. Note that 106¾ was 87½% between 62¾ and 113, and that 100⅜ was 75% or ¾ between

62-3/4 and 113. When Wheat broke under $1.00 per bushel, it was in a very weak position. When it broke under 94-1/8, the half-way point between 145-1/8 to 43 1/4, it was still in a weaker position and indicated lower prices. Prices declined rapidly after they broke 94. There were practically no rallies at all, until prices declined to around 77c per bushel. After that there was a quick rally of 6 or 7c per bushel. Then the decline continued.

1940—August, low, 70. This was final bottom, and a natural support or buying point because there were a series of old TOPS and BOTTOMS around this level.

69 was 12 1/2% between 62-3/4 and 113
70 was 12 1/2% between 64 and 113
64 being the last BOTTOM in 1939.
68-3/4 was 25% of 145-1/8 to 43 1/4
69-3/8 was 37 1/2% of 185
Note 72 1/2 was 1/2 of 145-1/8.

Prices failed to decline 3c per bushel under this level, making this a buying point, especially as the seasonal trend nearly always changes in August, and when prices are low in August, it is time to buy for rally. The market started to advance, wheat crossed 72 1/2, the important point, and continued to work higher. November, high, 90, still under the half-way point of 145 1/8 to 43 1/4 and up to old TOP and BOTTOM levels, a natural Resistance Point for reaction. A moderate reaction took place.

1941—February, low, 78. From the low of 70 to 90, the half-way point was 80. The market failing to decline 3c per bushel under this half-way point made it a natural support point and a buying point, protected with *stop loss orders*. The advance was resumed and prices crossed the TOP of November at 90, placing the market in a very strong position. The advance continued and there were nothing but moderate reactions of 5 or 6c per bushel. The May option advanced to 102 before the end of May, advancing above $1.00 per bushel. We know that after Wheat advances to $1.00 it indicates much higher levels before any important reaction takes place. After all options advanced above $1.00 per bushel, they held up and never reacted much. In July and August prices were strong, crossed important resistance levels, crossed 113, the high of 1940, placing Wheat in a very strong position and indicating much higher prices.

September, high, for May Wheat 129-5/8. Note that:

127 was 75% of 145 1/8.
124 1/2 was 75% of 62-3/4 to 145-1/8.
131-1/4 was 37 1/2% of 350.
128 5/8 was 5/8 or 62 1/2 % of 205 7/8.
124-5/8 was 50% or half-way point between 43 1/4 and 205-7/8.
128-5/8 was 75% of 171 1/2, making this a most important Resistance Level and selling level. Prices advancing less than 2c above the high of July, 1933, indicated weakness. By going back over past records, you can see how many important TOPS and

BOTTOMS occurred around 126 to 130. Prices held in a narrow trading range for several weeks, and the first indication of weakness was when prices broke under 25% between 70 and 129⅝, which was 122-⅛ and 25% between 78 and 129-⅝, which was 123-⅛, breaking under these levels indicated weakness and lower prices. You should have sold out longs and sold short.

September 22, May Wheat declined to 122½. This was a natural support level around 25% above $1.00. Then an advance followed.

October 2, high 128¼, making a lower TOP and getting dull on the rally. When the decline got under way, and May Wheat broke under 124, you should have put out a heavy line of shorts. When it broke 122, you should have sold more. A wide open break followed.

1941—October 17, low, 109½.

Note that 106-⅞ was 87½% of 64 to 113.

106-¾ was 37½% between 62-¾ and 113.

107-⅝ was 87½% between 70 and 113.

109¾ was 2/3 between 70 and 129⅝.

110¼ was ⅝ between 78 and 129-⅝, making this a natural support level and a buying point, especially as it was a sharp severe decline on very heavy volume of trading. On October 16, prices declined the full limit of 10c per bushel permitted in one day.

October 17, prices opened down about ½c per bushel, May Wheat declining to 109½. Rallied 7c per bushel the same day. This was a decline of 30c per bushel from the TOP and you should figure that it would rally 50%, or to around 119-⅝. Up to this writing, October 21, 1941, May Wheat rallied to 121-¾, and should it rally to around 122 to 124, it would meet heavy selling against old Resistance Levels, breaking back half of the last rally, or especially breaking under 115½ would indicate a further decline.

Watch all important Resistance Levels between important TOPS and BOTTOMS. Study the position on the weekly high and low chart; the monthly chart and the quarterly chart in order to determine when change in trend in Wheat should take place. Always give the market time when it is slow and narrow around important Resistance Levels to show whether it is going to hold or whether it is going to cross this Resistance Level and go higher. If it is declining, determine whether it should break the Resistance Level and go lower. When the market has rapid sharp declines, then you should not wait too long.

When the market reaches Resistance Levels, you should cover and buy, or at least cover shorts and wait. The same applies when a market has a rapid advance, reaching extreme high levels. It often does not remain there long and you have to sell on sharp TOPS without waiting long.

Follow all the rules for signal days, signal weeks and signal months, and the rules for important changes in trends. Never overlook the fact that volume and open interest play an important part in determining when extreme high or extreme lows will be reached.

Keep up charts. Keep all the rules before you. Memorize the rules. Have them written down where you can see them. Failing to follow some important rule may cause you to miss an important TOP or BOTTOM and to miss the opportunity for making big profits.

WHEAT — SEASONAL TREND FROM 1841 TO 1941

By going over past records you will see that during the period of 101 years, wheat has reached extreme low prices the following numbers of times during each calendar month of the year:

January, only 2 times, these were 1895 and 1881.

February, 7 times.	August, 16 times.
March, 12 times.	September, 8 times.
April, 14 times.	October, 13 times.
May, 5 times.	November, 10 times.
June, 9 times.	December, 12 times.
July, 6 times.	

From the above you can see that, during the months of March and April, the most lows have been made, but in the month of August there were the greatest low levels made, in this period. However, October and December together show a greater percentage of low levels. This gives you an idea how to follow the seasonal trends. You would expect very few extreme low levels to be made in the month of January, and very few extreme low levels to be made in the months of May and July. Then February and September next. Therefore, when the market should reach low levels in March or April, you should buy for rally because most tops come out in May. Then when prices are high in May or early June you should sell short figuring it would follow the seasonal trend and make low levels in August.

When prices are advancing and reach high in August or September, then you would expect low levels in October, November and December. Always judge the position according to the trend shown on the chart and apply all the rules to get the main trend.

HIGH LEVELS FROM 1841 TO 1941. Below you will see the number of times in each month of the calendar year that wheat has reached extreme high prices or top levels for this year:

January, 15 times.	July, 7 times.
February, 6 times.	August, 10 times.
March, 1 time.	September, 9 times.
April, 11 times.	October, 11 times.
May, 19 times.	November, 2 times.
June, 2 times.	December, 11 times.

From these figures you can see that when prices reach high in January you can expect the top for reaction because of the large number of times that it makes tops. June and November and March are the months that fewest highs were made. During March only one important top was reached. In June and November only two highs were made. The next smallest number of tops was in February and July.

You will see that there were nineteen important tops made in the month of May; therefore, May is always the important month to sell out long and sell short for a decline into August. There were eleven tops made in April. Tops often come in April instead of May. When prices advance during the summer against the seasonal trend you will see that ten tops have come out in August, and eleven in October. Therefore, August, September and October, as long as the trend is working up, would be the most important months to watch for a change in trend.

Suppose that the market had made low in October, or in August, and was advancing. December would be the next important month to watch for a change in trend. In fact, December and January are always important months to watch for a change in trend and for tops. When prices are advancing the next important time to watch for change in trend is April and May. Most of the highest levels in history and the biggest advances have come in the month of May and most corners have come in the month of May, although a few have come in July and September. A study of all these important points, time periods and seasonal changes in connection with the other rules and indications will help you in determining the main change in the trend of wheat, or of any other commodity.

TOP FORMATION FOR WHEAT

These examples are to show when single, double, triple and other important tops and bottoms occur and why resistance is met at certain levels and support at other levels. This review of the past action of the market will help you to study and determine future prices of wheat.

1841—September, high, 110, a single sharp top.

1842—February and March, a double top.

1842—July, second top, lower, showing weakness and a decline followed.

1842—December, first bottom, a single bottom.

1843—February and March, double bottom, third bottom, only one cent under December 1842, a buying point.

1844—July. A single sharp top. A fast decline followed.

1845—October, a single sharp bottom. An advance followed.

1845—December, a single sharp top. A decline followed.

1846—March and April. A double top.

1846—June and July. A double bottom. A rally followed.

1846—November. A triple bottom. Safe place to buy. A big advance followed.

1847—August. A single bottom.

1847—November and December. A double bottom.

1848—September. A single sharp top. A fast decline followed.

1847—1848—1849—1850. These series of low levels at 50c per bushel, 50% or one-half of one dollar, making this a sure safe buying point after prices had received support for so many times.

1850—Marked the last low of 50c, price advances followed.

1850—May, high, $1.03, a single sharp top.

1850—June, a lower top, $1.00. An important selling level. A decline followed.

1850—October and November, low, 35c, same low as 1846 and 1847, a triple bottom. A safe place to buy for a rally.

1851—January, high 60c per bushel. Wheat up around the same level. A safe place to sell out and sell short.

1851—August, September and October, low, 30c per bushel.
November, low, 28c per bushel. A double bottom and a buying point.

1852—April and May, last low and extreme low, 28c per bushel, a triple bottom. At this low level only 3c above 25c, or 25% of one dollar, making wheat a safe investment. A great upswing followed which lasted until June 1855, when wheat sold at $1.70 per bushel.
Using the low point of 28c per bushel as base, a 500% advance added to 28c gives 1.68, showing why top was made at 1.70.

1853—January, high, 80c, a sharp top.

1853—April, low, 50c. A sharp bottom but down to old bottom level, and a safe, sure buying point.

1853—March, low 52c, a higher bottom and a safer buying level. A fast advance followed and previous tops were crossed. Advanced to the highest level since September, 1841.

1853—October, high, 1.10, this was a double top against September, 1841, selling level and a sharp decline followed.

WHEAT SWINGS FROM TOP, DECEMBER 1919 TO LOW, DECEMBER 1930

1919—December. High. 350.

1920—July. High. 275½.

1920—September. High. 249½.

1920—November. High. 209½. This last high has never been reached since.

1925—January. High. 205⅞. Again failing to reach the high of November, 1920.

1925—December. High. 180.

1926—April. High. 171½.

1928—April. High. 171.

1929—August. High. 164.

1933—July. High. 128.

1937—April. High. 145-⅛.

1940—April and May. High. 112 and 113.

1941—September. High. 129-5/8. It is well to keep in mind, or to keep on your records, important tops and to note when they are crossed, because crossing these high levels indicates the next resistance point or the next important top.

After wheat reached low in December, 1932, it had been making lower tops and lower bottoms. When the trend changed you would expect the market to make higher tops and higher bottoms, and work higher right along. Therefore, we should go back for two or three years and see important rally points, or tops, on the way down. With these records before you, you would know that when May wheat crossed 65, it would indicate higher. The next top was at 73, the next top at 86, the next one at 114, the next at 117, next at 130 and the last, of December, 1929, of 143½. You would also watch old bottoms as they became tops. I have not called attention to these but you can see them on the records in the back of the book and on the chart. The reason you should keep up with all of these old tops and bottoms is because history does repeat and old tops become bottoms and bottoms become tops, and resistance on the way up against these old tops and bottoms is at the important resistance levels between tops and bottoms.

Remember, always to give the market a little time when it reaches old tops and old bottoms to see whether it is going through or whether the trend is going to change. Do not fail to place *stop loss orders* when you make a trade, for your protection, in case you are wrong or the market reverses. Always remember the fact that you *can be wrong* and that *stop loss orders* are to *limit* your *loss,* and to *protect* your *capital.*

After the bottom was reached in December, 1932, you should work out all the important 50% points from the top all the way down. For example: 147½, half-way point 71-3/4; 130 High, half-way point 65; 115, half-way point 57½; high 114, half-way point 57; 86, half-way point 43, this being the last high in January 1931, and a 50% decline gave 43. The market made low at 43¼, a safe buying level. When the market started to advance first indication of higher prices would be when it crossed 50c per bushel. The next when it crossed 57 and 58½ important resistance levels. The next, 65, because it was top at 65, and 65 is one-half of 130. The next important point, 71½, half of the last high of 143, and 73 was important, because this was a top and bottom level. Watch the important percentage points, especially the percentage on the low of 43¼; 50% on 43¼ would give 65; 100 % would give 86½; 150% would give 108¼; 200% would give 120-3/4; 212% would give 140-7/8. You would figure these same percentages on December option low of 41½. With all of these important tops and bottoms in mind, and the resistance points, you are in a position to watch the market as it works up and you can tell the point where it should hesitate and react and these points where, when crossed, would indicate higher prices. Study and analyze any grain option, Corn, Oats, Rye, Lard, or any other Commodities in the same way that we have analyzed wheat and you will be able to determine the future course of prices, and important changes in trend.

GREAT SWINGS IN WHEAT

These great swings from extreme low to extreme high, covering a long period of years are very important to study, because it will help you to determine time periods in the future.

1841—September, high, 110.

1852—April, extreme low, 28c; range, 82c; time, 128 months; the greatest rally during this period was 26 months, and the advance was 60c per bushel.

1852—April, low, 28c per bushel.

1867—April, high, $3.00 per bushel; a total advance of $2.72 per bushel; time, exactly 15 years or 180 months. During this long advance, which was subject to rallies and reactions in minor Bull and Bear campaigns, the greatest decline was from January, 1856, $1.35 per bushel, to November, 1856, 77c per bushel; a decline of 58c per bushel; time, 10 months. Using this same period and adding it to April, 1867 — 15 years added gives April, 1882.

1882—May, high, 140. Previous to this, extreme high was reached in October, 1881. From this extreme high of 140 in May, 1882, prices never sold higher until they declined to 69c per bushel in December, 1884. This shows the importance of a change in trend at the time these major time periods run out, balancing previous time periods.

1867—April, final high, $3.00 per bushel.

1884—December, low, 69c per bushel; a total decline of $2.31 per bushel; time, 214 months.

1887—June, low, 65c per bushel; a total decline of $2.35 per bushel; time, 242 months or 20 years and 2 months. If we apply this time period to the future it will give August, 1907.

1907—August, low, 94⅜.

1907—October, high, 112⅝.

1908—February, low, 90¾.

1908—May, high, 111; a slightly lower TOP than October, 1907, making this a selling level.

1888—September, high, $2.00 per bushel.

1895—January, low, 49c per bushel to $2.00, decline of $1.51 per bushel; time, 76 months.

1901—Adding 76 months to January, 1895, gives May, 1901. May, low, 63⅝, and last Extreme Low.

1901—July, low, 64½; a Higher Bottom. This was the last low before a big advance took place, running out this important time period very close to the previous time period.

1895—January, low, 49c to

1898—May, high, $1.85 per bushel; total advance, $1.36 per bushel. Time, 40 months. Adding this period to May, 1898, gives September, 1901.

1901—October, low, 72, from which an advance started.

1898—May, high, $1.85.

1898—September, low, 62⅝.

1900—May, low, 63⅝; double bottom against September, 1898, a decline of $1.21⅜ per bushel from 1898; time, 24 months. If we add this time of 24 months to May, 1900, it gives May, 1902.

1902—May, high, 76½; from which a reaction followed to August, low, 68½, which was the last low before prices advanced to very much higher levels.

1909—May, high $1.35¼. This was the highest price of wheat since 1895.

1895—January, 49c per bushel; an advance of 86¼c per bushel. Time, 14 years and 4 months, or 172 months. Add this time period to May, 1909, gives September, 1923.

1923—October, high, $1.14⅝. This was the last high before it started to decline.

1901—May, low, 63⅝, to

1909—May, high, $1.35 per bushel; advance of 61⅜c. Time, 108 months or 9 years. Adding this time period of nine years to 1909 gives

1918—May.
The Government stopped trading in futures in 1918, so there is no accurate comparison of prices for this period.

1914—June, low, 76½c; from 1909 May high, $1.35, gives 58½c decline. Time, 61 months, or 5 years and 1 month. Add this time to 1914, June, low, gives July, 1919, when prices were at a high level, but no future trading had started up to this time.

1919—December, high, $3.50 per bushel; from 1914 June low, 76½, an advance of $2.73½ per bushel. Time, 66 months.

1914—June, low, 76½ to

1917—May, high, $3.25 per bushel. An advance of $2.48½ per bushel. Time, 36 months. Add this time to May, 1917, gives May, 1920, when all commodities as well as Wheat started declining in April, 1920. Future trading in Wheat started again in July, 1920.

1895—January, low, 49c, to

1919—December, high, $3.50; an advance of $3.01 per bushel. Time, 300 months or 25 years.

1919—December, high, $3.50, to

1921—November, low, $1.03¼; decline, $2.46¾, in 23 months.

1917—May, $3.25, to

1921—November, $1.03¼; a decline of $2.21¾ per bushel in 54 months.

1923—June, low, $1.01½; a decline of $2.48 per bushel from December, 1919. Time, 42 months.

1922—March, low, $1.00¼ per bushel; from 1917 $3.25 low, a decline of $2.24¾. Time, 82 months.

1919—December, to

1924—March; from the high to $1.00¼ low; range, $2.49¾. Time, 51 months. One of the fastest advances in history started in 1924, in March.

1925—January, high, $2.05⅞; an advance of $1.05⅝ per bushel. Time, 10 months. This was 30 years from the low in 1895, when wheat sold at 49c.

1923—June, low, $1.01½, to

1925—January, high, $2.05⅞; an advance of $1.04⅜ per bushel. Time, 18 months. Using percentages, 100% advance from $1.00¼ would give $2.00½ per bushel. Again applying percentages to the low of 1923, June, of $1.01½ per bushel, would give $2.03 per bushel, making this an important resistance and selling level.

1914—June, low, to

1919—December, high; time, 66 months. Add this to December, 1919, gives June, 1925. There was no important bottom in June, 1925, but in April, 1925, low, $1.36½, and August, 1925, high, $1.68. A sharp decline followed. From the high of January, 1925, prices continued to work lower, making lower tops and lower bottoms. Prices broke under $1.03 and later broke under $1.00 per bushel, under the half-way point, or 50% decline from the highest selling point, $2.05⅞. They were in a very weak position and continued to work lower with nothing but minor rallies. Using the time period, from 1895 to December, 1919, a period of 300 months or 25 years, and adding this to get the percentage gives 50% of the time period, which is an important period for a change in trend; this gives 1932, June.

1932—June, low, 49⅜. This was the lowest wheat had sold up to this time. In September, 1932 ,prices advanced to 68c. Later, prices declined to December. Adding 75 months more to June, 1932, to get three-fourths or 75% of the time period, gives September, 1938. Wheat sold at 62¾ in September, 1938, and never sold lower until it advanced to $1.45⅛ in April, 1937.

1938—September, low, 62¾; adding 36 months to September, 1938, gives September, 1941. May wheat sold at $1.29⅝ September 12, 1941, which proves how accurately these percentages of time periods work out the same as percentages of the price at tops and bottoms. Add 37 months to September, 1938, which gives October, 1941. May wheat broke from $1.28 in the early part of October, 1941, to $1.09½ to October 17, 1941, again showing how these important time periods work out. Adding 25 years, or the complete time period, to December, 1919, gives December, 1944, which will be a very important month to watch for tops or bottoms or changes in trend on wheat.

ADVANCES OR DECLINES FROM TOP TO BOTTOM

All moves in wheat, or other grains, obey a natural mathematical law, and come out in accordance with some previous top or bottom or resistance level.

A normal reaction on wheat runs 5c to 7c per bushel, and 11c to 12c per bushel; then 24, 36 and 48c per bushel in abnormal or major moves.

From any important low level or high level, resistance levels work out well in even 12c moves and multiples of 12. You will find it helpful if you add the percentage point to any bottom to get resistance on the way up and subtract the resistance point from any top. That is, the natural resistance points, which are as follows: 12½c—25c; 37½c—50c; 62½c—75; 87½c—$1.00; $1.12½—$1.25; $1.37½—$1.50; $1.62½—$1.75; $1.87½—$2.00, etc., which are the 12½%, 25%, 37½% 50%, 62½%, 75%, 87½% and 100% moves. It is also important to watch for major and minor tops and bottoms and change in trend when prices are one-third or 33 1/3% up, or two-thirds or 66 2/3% up, from any bottom or down from any top.

The moves of one-sixteenth of a dollar, or 6¼ points, added to any of these other points, or subtracted from them, also are important to watch.

EXAMPLES OF WHEAT CAMPAIGN

1938—December wheat, low, 62½c.

1941—High, $1.25, an advance of 62½c per bushel, also an advance of 100% on the lowest selling price.

1938—May wheat, 64c per bushel.

1941—High, $1.29⅝, an advance of 65⅝c per bushel; again, from the low of 62¾c for May wheat to $1.29⅝ advance was 66⅞c, or nearly 67½c. From May wheat low at 70c per bushel to $1.29⅝, an advance of 69⅝c per bushel, which was almost five times 12, and just under 62½c per bushel, a natural point.

1941—September, high for May wheat, $1.29⅝.

1941—October, low, $1.09½; a decline of 20c per bushel, which was one-third or 33-1/3% from 70c to $1.29⅝. A rally in October from $1.09½ to $1.22¾ was two-thirds of the decline from $1.29⅝ to $1.09½.

ALL GRAIN FOLLOWS GENERAL TREND. In most cases, when the trend of Wheat is up, Corn, Rye, Oats, all follow the trend of Wheat, the same with Soy Beans. Most of the time they make tops and bottoms on the same basis. There are exceptional cases, however, and these you have to watch. Corn crops do not mature nor are harvested at the same time as Wheat. In a year when the Corn crop is extremely short and the Wheat crop is good, Corn will advance faster than Wheat. A few times in history Corn has sold at higher prices than Wheat.

COMPARISON OF WHEAT AND CORN PRICES

By watching the chart formation at bottoms and the time when Corn is up from the bottom you will be able to tell the change in trend when Corn starts gaining on Wheat. During these periods, it is safer to buy Corn and you will make larger profits in Corn than you will in Wheat. During these abnormal years, when the Corn crop is very short, Corn has made a greater range in prices than Wheat.

When Corn is selling near the same level as Wheat, or slightly higher than Wheat, it is a better short sale. But never sell it short for a big decline until it shows definitely that the main trend has turned.

1932—December. Low on May Wheat. 43¼c per bushel.

1933—February. Low on May Corn. 23½c per bushel. From this you will see that at the bottom Wheat was selling 20c per bushel higher than Corn.

1934—The Corn crop was very short. Only 1,146,684,000 bushels.

1935—The corn crop was still below normal. 2,015,017,000 bushels.

1936—The corn crop was again extremely short. 1,253,763,000 bushels. This caused an enormous advance in Corn in 1935-1936. Corn finally sold higher than Wheat. A comparison of the Wheat and Corn prices for 1935 and 1936 will show you how the Corn gained on Wheat until it finally sold higher.

CORN

1933—February, May; Corn low, 23½c. July, high, 83c. September, low, 44c. October, high, 50c.

1934—April, low, 40c. May, 59c. August, 88½c. October, 95c. December, 93c.

1935—March, low, 76c. April, high, 92c. August, high, 56c. October, low, 62c. November, low, 57c.

1936—January, high, 63c. March, low, 68½c. April, high, 65½c. July, option, low, 85c. August, high, 99c. September, low, 87½c.

1937—January, high, $1.13. February, low, $1.04. May, high, $1.40.

WHEAT HIGH AND LOW PRICES

1935—March 90c. (Note at this time Wheat was 14c higher than Corn.) April, high, $1.03. June, low, 78c. July, high, 96c. August, low, 85¼c. October, high, $1.09½. (At this time Corn was 52c, or 57c per bushel under Wheat.) November, low, 93c. January Wheat, high, $1.04. Corn, 85c, or 41½c under. May Wheat, 83c.

1936—July Wheat $1.10½. Corn 85c. Wheat only 25½c higher than Corn. August Wheat, high, $1.16½. Corn, 99c. Wheat only 17½c per bushel under corn. Corn gaining on Wheat. September Wheat, high, $1.17¼. Corn, 87½c; 30c a bushel under Wheat.

1937—January Wheat, 113½c per bushel; Corn, 113c, Wheat only one-half cent per bushel above corn. February Wheat, $1.29. Corn, $1.04. Corn 25c under Wheat. May Wheat, $1.10. Corn, $1.40 per bushel, or 30c above Wheat. During the Summer after the July option went out in 1937, Corn was higher than some of the Wheat options. The main trend in Wheat turned down before Corn. Later in 1937 Corn showed down trend and it was a better short sale than Wheat and moved down faster into 1938.

You should also study and watch the comparisons between Wheat and Corn at extreme high and low levels and note when Corn shows stronger up trend than Wheat, or stronger down trend. In this way you will be able to catch some of the important moves and make larger profits trading in Corn at certain times and in Wheat at others. Always trade with the main trend.

WHEAT MONTHLY MOVES UP AND DOWN

These moves up cover the number of months that prices advance or move up without breaking under the low of the previous month. The moves down cover the time from Top or High prices of an advance, to the low of reaction, until the market reverses and crosses the high of a previous month.

Note during one hundred years of the record of Wheat prices that only two times during this period did a move last ten months on the up side without breaking the low of a previous month and reacting.

EXCEPTIONAL YEARS: 1881-1924. These were the exceptional years when the market advanced ten months without reversing the trend or breaking the low of the previous month. Therefore, when prices have advanced as much as nine to ten months without any reaction lasting over one month, you can expect top for a reaction, and probably a final top or bottom, as the case may be.

NINE MONTHS: Moves have lasted nine months four times, up or down, during the last one hundred years.

SEVEN TO EIGHT MONTHS: Twenty-two times during the past hundred years, movements have lasted as much as seven to eight months before a culmination or a change in trend.

FIVE TO SIX MONTHS: Forty-seven times, the movements have lasted five to six months before a change in trend, making it important for you to watch for a reversal or a change in trend, when Wheat has *advanced or declined* FIVE TO SIX MONTHS from any important top or Bottom, and the greater the advance or decline and the more rapid the movement in the last month the surer the indication of a change in trend.

THREE TO FOUR MONTHS: During the past hundred years 106 times advances or declines have lasted three to four months, which shows that there were two times as many moves culminating three to four months as there were in FIVE TO SIX MONTHS, which proves the importance of the seasonal trend or a change for some kind of a reaction or rally at the end of THREE TO FOUR months. These moves are more important when the range in prices has been abnormal or above the average, and when the last move during the last month has a wide range of fluctuation, as when Wheat is very active, it makes it more important for a change in trend.

TWO-MONTH MOVES: During the past hundred years there were 107 moves that lasted TWO MONTHS, almost the same as the THREE TO FOUR MONTH move. One of our rules is that a Bull Market will only react TWO MONTHS, before the main trend is resumed, and that a Bear Market or declining market will often run for many months, or for one year or more, and never rally more than two months against the main trend.

SHORT TIME MOVES: Natural reactions often run 28 to 36 days, then the main trend is resumed. In a Bull market, when there is a reaction or decline, 28 to 36 days, it is usually safe to buy. In a Bear market, or declining market when there is a rally or an advance, lasting 28 to 36 days, it is usually safe to sell short.

During the past one hundred years there were 120 times that a movement lasted only one month. If you will study past records you can see the position from top or bottom, when Wheat or any other commodity advances or declines one month from any previous top or bottom. The number of months that the market has already advanced or declined from any main top or bottom will determine whether a a one-month reverse move indicates any change in the main trend.

Apply all of the other rules, percentage and resistance points, as well as time periods, to determine when culminations are taking place. Remember to wait for definite indication of a change in trend, according to rules. Do not guess or trade on hope or fear. FACE FACTS, and follow the rules, always placing STOP LOSS ORDERS for your protection in case you are wrong or the market reverses.

The following moves Up or Down do not necessarily all occur under the year listed. For example: At the end of one year an upward movement may have already run Two Months, and in the following year it continues to advance for three months more. The record would show a five months' advance or five months up in that year, although it had moved up two months from bottom in the previous year.

1841-42—Five months	Up.		1851—Eight months	Down.	
1842-43—Eight months	Down.		One month	Up.	
Five months	Up.		Two months	Down.	
1844—Eight months	Up.		1852—Three months	Up.	
Five months	Down.		Two months	Down.	
1845—Seven months	Up.		Nine months	Up.	
Four months	Down.		1853—Three months	Down.	
Two months	Up.		Six months	Up.	
1846—Six months	Down.		Two months	Down.	
Two months	Up.		1854—Five months	Up.	
Two months	Down.		Three months	Down.	
1847—Six months	Up.		Two months	Up.	
Three months	Down.		One month	Down.	
Two months	Up.		1855—Seven months	Up.	
1847—One month	Down.		Two months	Down.	
1848—Six months	Up.		Four months	Up.	
Two months	Down.		1856—Three months	Down.	
Two months	Up.		Two months	Up.	
Three months	Down.		Six months	Down.	
1849—Two months	Up.		1857—Seven months	Up.	
Four months	Down.		1858—Seven months	Down.	
Two months	Up.		Six months	Up.	
Four months	Down.		Three months	Down.	
1850—Six months	Up.		1859—Five months	Up.	
Five months	Down.		Three months	Down.	
One month	Up.		1860—Nine months	Up.	

Three months	Down.
One month	Up.
Three months	Down.
1861—Five months	Up.
Two months	Down.
Three months	Up.
One month	Down.
1862—Eight months	Up.
One month	Down.
One month	Up.
One month	Down.
1863—Three months	Up.
Six months	Down.
Five months	Up.
1864—One month	Down.
Four months	Up.
Three months	Down.
One month	Up.
1865—Five months	Down
Two months	Up.
One month	Down.
Three months	Up.
1866—Five months	Down.
Five months	Up.
One month	Down.
Three months	Up.
One month	Down.
1867—Five months	Up.
One month	Down.
One month	Up.
One month	Down.
One month	Up.
One month	Down.
1868—Five months	Up.
Eight months	Down.
1869—Two months	Up.
Three months	Down.
1870—Four months	Up.
Seven months	Down.
1870—Four months	Up.
One month	Down.
Two months	Up.
One month	Down.
1871—Five months	Up.
Four months	Down.
One month	Up.
Two months	Down.
1872—Two months	Up.

One month	Down.
Two months	Up.
Two months	Down.
One month	Up.
Four months	Down.
1873—Two months	Up.
Two months	Down.
One month	Up.
Two months	Down.
One month	Up.
One month	Down.
1874—Seven months	Up.
Six months	Down.
Two months	Up.
1875—Two months	Down.
Three months	Up.
One month	Down.
Three months	Up.
Four months	Down.
1876—Five months	Up.
One month	Down.
Seven months	Up.
One month	Down.
1877—Two months	Up.
Four months	Down.
One month	Up.
1878—Six months	Down.
Two months	Up.
Two months	Down.
Two months	Up.
Two months	Down.
1879—Five months	Up.
One month	Down.
Three months	Up.
Two months	Down.
Four months	Up.
1880—Four months	Down.
One month	Up.
Three months	Down.
Three months	Up.
One month	Down.
1881—Ten months	Up.
Two months	Down.
1882—One month	Up.
One month	Down.
Two months	Up.
One month	Down.
1882—One month	Up.
Four months	Down.

1883—Five months	Up.
Five months	Down.
Two months	Up.
1884—One month	Down.
One month	Up.
Two months	Down.
One month	Up.
Eight months	Down.
1885—One month	Up.
Two months	Down.
One month	Up.
Five months	Down.
One month	Up.
1886—Seven months	Down.
Two months	Up.
Three months	Down.
Three months	Up.
1887—One month	Down.
Four months	Up.
One month	Down.
Four months	Up.
1888—Three months	Down.
Two months	Up.
One month	Down.
Three months	Up.
1889—Four months	Down.
One month	Up.
Four months	Down.
One month	Up.
One month	Down.
Two months	Up.
Two months	Down.
1890—Five months	Up.
One month	Down.
Two months	Up.
Four months	Down.
1891—Four months	Up.
Three months	Down.
One month	Up.
1892—Seven months	Down.
Two months	Up.
Six months	Down.
1893—Four months	Up.
Three months	Down.
Two months	Up.
Two months	Down.
1894—One month	Up.
Two months	Down.
Two months	Up.

	Three months	Down.
	One month	Up.
	One month	Down.
	Two months	Up.
1895—One months	Down.
	Four months	Up.
	Four months	Down.
	One month	Up.
	Two months	Down.
1896—Four months	Up.
	Two months	Down.
	Five months	Up.
1897—Four months	Down.
	Four months	Up.
	One month	Down.
1898—Nine months	Up.
	Five months	Down.
	One month	Up.
	One month	Down.
1899—Two months	Up.
	Two months	Down.
	Four months	Up.
1900—Nine months	Down.
	Five months	Up.
	Two months	Down.
1901—One month	Up.
	Three months	Down.
	Four months	Up.
	Two months	Down.
1902—Two months	Up.
	Three months	Down.
	Two months	Up.
	Two months	Down.
1903—Five months	Up.
	Two months	Down.
	Five months	Up.
	Three months	Down.
1904—Three months	Up.
	Two months	Down.
	One month	Up.
	One month	Down.
	Three months	Up.
	Two months	Down.
1905—Four months	Up.
	Four months	Down.
	One month	Up.
	One month	Down.
	Three months	Up.
1906—Five months	Down.
	Three months	Up.

Three months	Down.	
One month	Up.	
1907—One month	Down.	
One month	Up.	
One month	Down.	
Four months	Up.	
One month	Down.	
Two months	Up.	
One month	Down.	
1907—One month	Up.	
1908—Two months	Down.	
One month	Up.	
One month	Down.	
One month	Up.	
One month	Down.	
Six months	Up.	
1909—One month	Down.	
Four months	Up.	
Three months	Down.	
1910—Seven months	Up.	
Two months	Down.	
One month	Up.	
Four months	Down.	
1911—Two months	Up.	
Three months	Down.	
Two months	Up.	
Two months	Down.	
Three months	Up.	
Two months	Down.	
1912—Five months	Up.	
Four months	Down.	
One month	Up.	
Two months	Down.	
1913—One month	Up.	
Two months	Down.	
One month	Up.	
One month	Down.	
Three months	Up.	
Two months	Down.	
1914—Two months	Up.	
Two months	Down.	
One month	Up.	
One month	Down.	
Three months	Up.	
One month	Down.	
1915—Four months	Up.	
One month	Down.	
One month	Up.	

Five months	Down.
1916—Four months	Up.
Two months	Down.
One month	Up.
One month	Down.
Seven months	Up.
1917—One month	Down.
One month	Up.
One month	Down.
Three months	Up.
Two months	Down.
One month	Up.
1918—Three months	Down.
Three months	Up.
1919—One month	Down.
Three months	Up.
Two months	Down.
One month	Up.
One month	Down.
Five months	Up.
1920—Eight months	Down.
One month	Up.
Two months	Down.
1921—Two months	Up.
Three months	Down.
One month	Up.
Three months	Down.
One month	Up.
Two months	Down.
1922—One month	Up.
One month	Down.
Three months	Up.
Four months	Down.
1923—Eight months	Up.
Three months	Down.
Three months	Up.
Two months	Down.
1924—Two months	Up.
One month	Down.
Ten months	Up.
1925—Three months	Down.
One month	Up.
Six months	Down.
Two months	Up.
1926—Three months	Down.
Two months	Up.
Four months	Down.
One months	Up.
One month	Down.

1927—One month	Up.	
Two months	Down.	
One month	Up.	
Six months	Down.	
1928—Five months	Up.	
Four months	Down.	
Two months	Up.	
Three months	Down.	
1929—Two months	Up.	
Three months	Down.	
Three months	Up.	
Three months	Down.	
One month	Up.	
1930—Five months	Down.	
Two months	Up.	
Four months	Down.	
1931—Two months	Up.	
Two months	Down.	
Two months	Up.	
Five months	Down.	
Two months	Up.	
One month	Down.	
1932—Two months	Up.	
One month	Down.	
One month	Up.	
Two months	Down.	
Three months	Up.	
Four months	Down.	
1933—Six months	Up.	
Three months	Down.	
One month	Up	
One month	Down.	
1934—Two months	Up.	
Two months	Down.	

Four months	Up.	
Two months	Down.	
Two months	Up.	
1935—Three months	Down.	
One month	Up.	
One month	Down.	
Six months	Up.	
One month	Down.	
1936—Two months	Up.	
Four months	Down.	
Four months	Up.	
One month	Down.	
1937—Seven months	Up.	
Two months	Down.	
One month	Up.	
Four months	Down.	
1938—Two months	Up.	
Eight months	Down.	
1939—Four months	Up.	
Two months	Down.	
Two months	Up.	
Two months	Down.	
Four months	Up.	
1940—Two months	Down.	
Two months	Up.	
One month	Down.	
One month	Up.	
Two months	Down.	
Three months	Up	
1941—Two months	Down.	
Seven months	Up.	
One month	Down to Oct.	

EXTREME LOW PRICES OF WHEAT
AND FUTURE TIME PERIODS TO WATCH

1932—December, low, 43¼, for May wheat; December wheat at this time sold at 41½. This was a decline of May wheat of 3.06¾ per bushel from the high of $3.50 in December, 1919; time, 156 months. Add this time to December, 1932, and it will balance in December, 1945, making this important. December, 1945, will also come out against other important time periods.

1917—May, high, $3.25; December, low, 43¼c; a decline of $2.81¾; time, 187 months. Adding this time to the bottom gives July, 1947, as another very important time period when a change in trend is due.

1937—April 10. High, $1.45¼, from December, 1932, low of 43¼c;

advance, $1.02 per bushel; time, 51½ months. Add this to 1937 to balance time gives July 25, 1941. Wheat advanced rapidly from July 25, 1941, and reached high in September, 1941.

1938—September, low, 62¾c, from April, 1937; a decline of 87⅞c; time, 18 months.

1940—April, high, $1.13; an advance of 50¾c per bushel in 19 months, just one month over the previous time period. April, 1937, to April, 1940, is exactly 36 months or three years.

1940—August, low, 70c, for May wheat; a decline of 43c per bushel in four months.

1941—September 12, high, $1.29⅝, from September, 1938, low, 62¾c; advanced 66¾c in 36 months, same time period as April, 1937, to April, 1940. Go back over past records and you will find many important tops and bottoms coming out 36 months apart.

TIME FROM MAIN TOP TO MAIN TOP
AND
TIME FROM MAIN BOTTOM TO MAIN BOTTOM

1841, September, to August and December, 1843; 24 to 27 months.

1845, December, to 1848, September; 45 months.

1848, September, to 1850, May; 20 months.

1850, May, to 1855, June; 60 months.

The major extreme high tops were:

1841, September, to 1885, June; 165 months.

1855, June, to July, 1857; 24 months.

1857, June, to 1859, May; 24 months.

1859, May, to 1861, May; 24 months.

1861, May, to 1864, September; 40 months.

1864, September, to 1867, April; 31 months.

1855, June, to 1865, April; 122 months.

1855, June, to 1864, September; 111 months.

1867, April, to 1872, June and August; 62 to 64 months.

1872, August, to 1873, August; 12 months.

1873, August, to 1877, May; 45 months.

1867, April, to 1877, May; 121 months.

1877, May, to 1879, December; 31 months.

1879, December, to 1881, October; 22 months.

1881, October, to 1888, September; 83 months.

1867, April, to 1888, September; 257 months.

1877, May, to 1888, September; 135 months.

1888, September, to 1891, April; 31 months.

1891, April, to 1898, May; 85 months.

1888, September, to 1898, May; 115 months.

1898, May, to 1905, February; 81 months.

1905, February, to 1909, May; 51 months.

1898, May, to 1909, May; 132 months.

1909, May, to 1915, September; 76 months.

1915, September, to 1917, May; 20 months.

1898, May, to 1917, May; 228 months.

1909, May, to May, 1917; 96 months.

1917, May, to 1919, December; 31 months.

1898, May, to 1919, December; 247 months.

This was closest to the time period from April, 1867, to September, 1888, which was 257 months.

1919, December, to 1925, January; 49 months.

1925, January, to 1926, January; 12 months.

1926, January, to 1928, May; 26 months.

1928, May, to 1929, August; 15 months.

1929, August to 1933, July; 47 months.

1933, July, to 1934, August; 13 months.

1933, July, to 1937, April; 47 months.

1937, April, to 1940, May; 37 months.

1940, May, to 1941, September; 16 months.

1925, January, to 1937, April; 147 months.

By adding 147 months to April, 1937, we get July, 1949, as an important time period when there should be an important change in trend.

WHEAT SWINGS 1841 TO 1941

		High	Low	Advance or Decline	Time in Months
1841	Sept. to	110			
1843	Feb. and Mar. to		30	90	18
1845	Dec. to	90		60	34
1846	June and July		35	55	6
1848	Sept. to	95		60	26
1849	June		50	45	9
1850	May to	103		53	12
1852	Apr.		28	75	23
1854	June to	130		102	26
1854	Oct.		90	40	4
1855	July to	170		80	8
1855	Aug.		100	70	1
1855	Nov. to	146		46	3
1855	Dec.		125	11	1
1856	Jan. to	135		10	1
1856	Nov.		77	69	12
1857	July to	127		50	8
1858	Feb.		52	75	7
1858	Aug. to	100		48	6
1858	Nov.		54	46	3.
1859	May to	130		76	6
1859	Aug.		50	80	3
1860	May to	114		64	9
1860	Dec.		66	48	7
1861	May to	125		59	5
1861	July		55	70	2
1861	Oct. to	75		20	3
1862	Jan.		64	11	3
1862	Aug. to	92		28	6
1862	Nov.		75	17	3
1863	Aug.	112		37	4
1863	Mar. to		80	42	5

WHEAT SWINGS 1841 TO 1941—*Continued*

		High	Low	Advance or Decline	Time in Months
1863	Oct. to	115		35	2
1863	Dec.		105	10	2
1864	Aug. to	226		121	8
1864	Oct. to		150	76	2
1864	Nov.	192		42	1
1865	March to		102	90	4
1865	Sept.	151		49	6
1866	Feb. to		78	73	5
1867	May	300		222	15
1867	Apr. to	300			
1867	Aug.		155	145	4
1867	Oct. to	203		48	2
1867	Dec.		180	23	2
1868	May to	221		41	6
1868	Nov.		105	116	6
1868	Dec. to	133		28	1
1869	Apr.		103	30	5
1869	Aug. to	147		44	4
1869	Dec.		76½	70½	4
1870	Feb. to	82		5	2
1870	Apr.		73¼	8¾	2
1870	July to	131½		58¼	3
1870	Nov.		103	28½	4
1871	Apr. to	134		31	5
1871	Aug.		99	35	4
1871	Sept. to	132		33	1
1871	Dec.		117	15	3
1872	Aug. to	161		44	8
1872	Nov.		101	60	3
1873	Aug. to	146		45	10
1873	Sept.		89	57	1
1874	Apr. to	128		39	7

WHEAT SWINGS 1841 TO 1941—*Continued*

		High	Low	Advance or Decline	Time in Months
1874	Oct.		81	47	6
1874	Dec. to	93		12	2
1875	Feb.		83	10	3
1875	Aug. to	130		47	6
1875	Dec.		94	36	4
1876	May to	108		14	5
1876	July to		83	25	2
1877	May	176		93	10
1877	Aug. to		100	76	3
1877	Sept.	118		18	1
1878	Feby. to		101	17	5
1878	Apr.	114		13	2
1878	Oct. to		77	37	6
1879	July	110		33	9
1879	Sept. to		85	25	2
1879	Dec.	133		48	3
1880	Aug. to		86	47	8
1880	Nov.	112		26	3
1881	Jan. to		95	17	2
1881	Oct.	143		48	9
1882	Feb. to		120	23	4
1882	May	140		20	3
1882	Nov. to		91	49	6
1883	May	113		22	6
1883	Oct. to		90	23	5
1883	Dec.	99		9	2
1884	Apr. to		76	23	4
1884	May to	95		19	1
1884	Dec.		69	26	7
1885	Jan. to	81		12	1
1885	March		73	8	2
1885	Apr. to	92		19	1

WHEAT SWINGS 1841 To 1941—*Continued*

		High	Low	Advance or Decline	Time in Months
1885	Sept. to		76	16	5
1885	Nov.	91		15	2
1886	June to		71	20	7
1886	Aug.	79		8	2
1886	Oct. to		69¾	9⅝	2
1887	Apr. to	84		14⅝	6
1887	June		65	19	2
1887	Dec. to	79		14	6
1888	Apr.		71	8	4
1888	Sept. to	200		129	5
1889	Jan.		94	106	4
1889	Feb. to	108		14	1
1889	June		75	33	4
1889	July to	85		10	1
1889	Aug. to		75	10	1
1889	Oct.	83		8	2
1890	Feb. to		74	9	4
1890	May	100		26	3
1890	July to		85	15	2
1890	Aug.	108		23	1
1891	Jan. to		87	21	5
1891	Apr.	116		29	3
1891	July to		84¾	31¼	3
1891	Sept.	100		15¼	2
1892	Jan. to	84		16	4
1892	Feb. to		92	8	1
1892	Oct.		69	23	8
1893	Apr. to	85		16	6
1893	July to		54½	30¾	3
1893	Sept.	69		14¾	2
1894	Feb. to		54	15	5
1894	Apr. to	64		10	2

Wheat Swings 1841 To 1941—*Continued*

		High	Low	Advance or Decline	Time in Months
1894	July to		50	14	3
1894	Dec. to	57		7	5
1895	Jan.		49	8	1
1895	May to	81		32	4
1895	Dec.		54	27	7
1896	Apr. to	67		13	4
1896	July to		54	13	3
1896	Nov.	85⅞		31⅞	4
1897	Apr. to		64⅛	21¾	5
1897	Aug. to	100½		36⅜	4
1897	Oct.		87½	13	2
1898	May to	185		97½	7
1898	Sept.		62⅝	122⅜	4
1899	Jan. to	79½		17	4
1899	March to		66⅜	13⅛	2
1899	May	79½		13½	2
1900	May to		63⅝	16	12
1900	July to	83		19⅜	2
1901	July to		64½	18½	12
1901	Aug.	80½		16	1
1901	Oct. to		72	8½	2
1902	Jan.	84¾		12¾	3
	Apr.		70⅝	14⅛	3
	May	76½		5⅛	1
	Aug. to		68½	7¾	3
1903	Jan.	82¾		14¼	5
	Feb.		71½	11¼	1
	Oct. to	89¼		18¼	7
1904	Feb.	109		19¾	4
	June		79¼	29¾	4
	Sept.	118¾		39½	3
	Nov. to		108	10¾	2

WHEAT SWINGS 1841 TO 1941—*Continued*

		High	Low	Advance or Decline	Time in Months
1905	Feb.	121½		13½	3
	June		80½	41	4
	Oct.	92⅞		12⅜	4
	Dec. to		86½	6⅜	2
1906	Jan.	89⅛		3⅜	1
	July		73⅞	15½	6
	Oct. to	80⅜		6½	3
1907	Mar.		74⅝	5¾	5
	June	101		26⅝	3
	Aug.		94⅜	6⅝	2
	Oct.	112⅝		18¼	2
1908	Feb.		90¾	22	4
	May	111		21¼	3
	June		83½	27½	1
	Dec.	111		27½	6
1909	May	135¼		24¼	5
	Aug.		96¾	38½	3
1910	May	116¼		19½	9
	June		88⅜	28	1
	Aug.	111		22⅝	2
	Dec.		95	16	4
1911	Jan.	102⅝		7⅝	1
	Apr.		84⅜	18¼	3
	May	104¾		20⅜	1
	July		86	18¾	2
	Oct. to	107¼		21¼	3
1912	Jan.		98	9	3
	May	119		21	4
	Dec. to		88½	30½	7
1913	Feb.	94⅝		6	2
	July		85½	9⅛	5
	Aug. to	98¼		13	1

WHEAT SWINGS 1841 TO 1941—*Continued*

		High	Low	Advance or Decline	Time in Months
1914	July		76½	21¾	11
	Sept.	132		55½	2
	Oct. to		111¼	21¾	1
1915	Feb.	167		55¾	4
	Sept. to		93	74	7
1916	Feb.	136		43	5
	June		102½	33½	4
	Nov. to	195¾		93¼	5
1917	Feb.		154½	41¼	3
	May	325		170½	3
	Aug.		199¾	125¼	3
	Aug. to	260		60¼	1
1918	June		217	43	10
	Dec. to	242		25	6
1919	May	280		38	5
	Aug.		260	60	3
	Dec. to	350		90	4
1920	Feb.		235	115	2
	May to	345		110	3
1921	Mar.		137½	207½	10
	May	187		49	2
	July		114	73	2
	Sept.	142¾		28¾	2
	Nov. to		103	39½	2
1922	Feb.	149⅞		46¼	3
	Sept.		104½	45⅜	7
	Dec. to	126¾		22¼	3
1923	Jan.		115¼	11½	1
	Apr.	127¼		12	3
	June		101½	25¾	2
	Oct.	114⅝		13⅛	4
1924	Mar. to		100¼	14⅜	5

WHEAT SWINGS 1841 TO 1941—*Continued*

		High	Low	Advance or Decline	Time in Months
1925	Jan.	205⅞		105⅝	10
	Apr.		136½	69⅜	3
	Aug.	168		31½	4
	Oct.		133	35	2
	Dec. to	185		52	2
1926	June		130¾	54¼	6
	July	155		25¼	1
	Sept.		138	17	2
	Oct. to	150⅝		12⅝	1
1927	Jan.		136¼	14⅜	3
	Feb.	143		7¼	1
	Apr.		130¼	13¼	2
	May	156		26½	1
	Oct. to		126¾	30	5
1928	Apr. to	171½		44¾	6
1929	Jan.		115¾	55¾	9
	Feb.	133⅝		18	1
	May		93¼	40⅜	3
	July	164		71	2
	Nov.		121¾	42¼	4
	Dec. to	143¼		21½	1
1930	June		91¼	52	6
	Aug.	114		22¾	2
	Nov. to		73	41	3
1931	Jan.	86⅛		13⅛	2
	Apr.		81½	5	3
	May	86¼		5⅛	1
	Oct.		48¾	37½	5
	Nov. to	73		24¼	1
1932	March		52	21	4
	May	60⅜		8⅜	2
	June		49⅜	11	1

WHEAT SWINGS 1841 TO 1941—*Continued*

		High	Low	Advance or Decline	Time in Months
	Sept.	65		15⅝	3
	Dec. to		43¼	21¾	3
1933	Jan.	51¾		8½	1
	March		46⅛	5⅝	2
	July	128⅛		82	4
	Oct.		75	52⅝	3
	Nov. to	96⅞		21⅞	1
1934	Jan.		83	13⅞	2
	Feb.	93⅝		10⅝	1
	Apr.		72⅞	20¾	2
	Aug.	117		40	4
	Oct.		93⅜	23⅝	2
	Dec.	105⅛		11¾	2
1935	Mar.		90½	14⅝	3
	Apr.	102⅝		12⅛	1
	June		78⅞	23¾	2
	Oct.	107		28⅛	4
	Dec. to		94⅜	12⅝	2
1936	Jan.	104⅛		9¾	1
	June		83⅝	20½	5
	Dec. to	137¾		54⅛	6
1937	Jan.		125¾	12	1
	Apr.	145⅛		19⅜	3
	June		105	40⅛	2
	July	132⅛		27⅛	1
	Nov. to		85⅛	47	4
1938	Jan.	99¼		14⅛	3
	Sept. to		62¼	37	9
1939	May	81¼		19	8
	July		63⅞	17⅜	2
	Sept.	90⅝		26¾	2
	Oct.		79½	11⅛	1

WHEAT SWINGS 1841 To 1941—*Continued*

		High	Low	Advance or Decline	Time in Months
	Dec. to	109¾		30¼	2
1940	Jan.		96⅛	13⅝	1
	Apr.	113		16⅞	3
	May		76¾	36¾	1
	June	86½		9¾	1
	Aug.		70	16½	2
	Nov.	89¾		19¾	3
1941	Feb.		78	11¾	3
	Sept. 12	129⅝		51⅝	7 months
	Oct. 17		109½	21⅛	35 days
	Oct. 24	122¾		13¼	7 days
	Oct. 28		116¼	6½	4 days
	Nov. 7	122¾		6½	10 days
	Nov. 12		116½	6¼	5 days

MAY WHEAT SWINGS AND TIME PERIODS

		Time in Months			Time in Months			Time in Months
1895			1904			July	99	4
Jan.	49		Feb.	109	3	Oct.	87	3
May	81	4	June	81	4	1914		
Dec.	55	7	1905			May	100	7
1896			Feb.	121½	8	June	77	1
Feb.	67	2	June	82	4	Sept.	132	3
June	54	4	Oct.	93	4	Oct.	111	1
Nov.	86	5	1906			1915		
1897			Mar.	77	5	Feb.	167	4
Apr.	64	5	June	89	3	Sept.	93	7
1898			1907			1916		
May	185	13	Mar.	75	9	Jan.	138	4
1898			Oct.	112	7	May	104	4
Sept.	62	4	1908			1917		
1899			Apr.	89	6	May	325	12
Jan.	87	4	May	111	1	July	210	3
July	87	10	July	92	2	1918		
1900			1909			Dec.	242	18
May	63	10	May	135	10	1919		
Oct.	89	5	Aug	97	3	Feb.	223	2
1901			1910			Apr.	222	4
Apr.	70	6	May	117	9	Aug.	220	6
Aug.	89	4	June	92	1	Dec.	350	4
Sept.	63	1	July	115	1	1920		
1902			1911			Feb.	236	2
Jan.	85	4	Mar.	85	8	May	345	3
Aug.	69	7	Oct.	107	7	1921		
1903			1912			Apr.	119	11
Jan.	82	5	Jan.	98	3	May	184	1
Mar.	71	3	May	119	4	Nov.	98	6
Aug.	86	5	1913			1922		
Nov.	76	3	Mar.	88	10	Feb.	150	3

MAY WHEAT SWINGS AND TIME PERIODS—*Continued*

		Time in Months			Time in Months			Time in Months
Aug.	105	6	Nov.	73	10	Nov.	85	7
Sept.	126	1	1931			1938		
1923			May	86	6	Jan.	99	2
Jan.	115	4	Sept.	50	4	Sept.	63	9
Apr.	127	3	Oct.	73	1	1939		
July	96	3	Nov.	49	1	May	80	8
Oct.	114	3	1932			Aug.	64	3
1924			Feb.	63	3	Dec.	109	4
Mar.	101	5	Mar.	52	1	1940		
1925			Apr.	63	1	Feb.	95	2
Jan.	205⅞	10	May	52	1	May	113	3
Apr.	137	3	Sept.	65	4	Aug.	70	3
July	164	3	Dec.	44	3	Nov.	90	3
Oct.	135	3	1933			1941		
Dec.	185	2	July	128	7	Feb.	78	3
1926			Dec.	80	5	Sept.	129⅝	7
Mar.	154	3	1934			Oct.	109½	1
May	171	2	Feb.	94	2			
1927			Apr.	73	2			
Mar.	131	10	Aug.	117	6			
May	158	2	Dec.	94	4			
Nov.	126	6	1935					
1928			Mar.	91	3			
May	171	6	Apr.	103	1			
1929			July	81	3			
Jan.	115	9	Oct.	107	3			
Feb.	133	1	1936					
May	93	3	Mar.	95	5			
Aug.	164	3	Apr.	105	1			
Nov.	120	3	May	90	1			
1930			1937					
Jan.	138	2	Apr.	145	11			

HARVEST TIME OF THE WORLD

The following shows the month of the Wheat harvest in the Wheat growing sections of the world:

JANUARY—Australia, New Zealand and Chili.

FEBRUARY, MARCH—East India, Upper Egypt.

APRIL—Lower Egypt, Syria, Cyprus, Persia, Asia Minor, India, Mexico Cuba.

MAY—Algeria, Central Asia, China, Japan, Morocco, Texas and Florida.

JUNE—Turkey, Greece, Italy, Spain, Portugal, South of France, California. Louisianna, Mississippi, Alabama, Georgia, Carolinas, Tennessee, Virginia, Kentucky, Kansas, Arkansas, Utah, Missouri.

JULY—Roumania, Bulgaria, Austria Hungary, South of Russia, Germany, Switzerland, France, South of England, Oregon, Nebraska, Minnesota, Wisconsin, Colorado, Washington, Iowa, Illinois, Indiana, Michigan, Ohio, New York, New England and Ontario, Canada.

AUGUST—Belgium, Holland, Great Britain, Denmark, Poland, Quebec, Canada, Columbia, Western Canada, North and South Dakota.

SEPTEMBER AND OCTOBER—Scotland, Sweden, Norway and North of Russia.

NOVEMBER—Peru, South Africa and Argentine.

DECEMBER—Burmah and Argentine.

CORN HARVEST TIME

JANUARY—New South Wales.

MARCH AND APRIL—Argentine.

SEPTEMBER, OCTOBER—All European countries.

OCTOBER—The crop of the United States is harvested principally in this month.

WHAT MONTHLY CROP REPORTS REFER TO

The monthly crop reports of the Department of Agriculture give the following information in the months named:

JANUARY AND FEBRUARY—Number and value of farm animals in the United States; general miscellaneous crop reports; farm animals of the world.

MARCH—Supplies of Wheat, Corn and Oats in farmer's hands, and the quantities of the crops. Also, an estimate of the Wheat crop of the world.

APRIL—Condition of Winter Wheat and Rye. Number of farm animals and losses from disease.

MAY—Condition of Winter Wheat and Rye; condition of meadows and Spring pastures; Cotton area and planting; Spring plowing.

JUNE—Acreage and condition of Winter Wheat, Spring Wheat, Rye, Barley, Oats, Clover, Cotton and Rice, and average condition of Spring pastures.

JULY—Acreage and condition of Corn; average condition of Winter Wheat and Spring Wheat; quantity of Wheat in farmer's hands; average condition of Winter and Spring Rye; average condition of Oats and Barley; acreage and condition of Potatoes and Tobacco; average condition of Cotton, Clover, Timothy and Pastures.

AUGUST—Average condition of Spring Corn, Spring Wheat, Spring Rye, Oats, Barley, Tobacco, Pastures, Cotton; acreage and condition of Buckwheat, Potatoes and Hay; quantity of Oats in farmers' hands.

SEPTEMBER—Average condition of Spring Wheat, Corn, Buckwheat, Potatoes, Tobacco, Cotton; acreage and condition of Clover; average condition of Winter Wheat, Winter Rye, Oats and Barley when harvested; number and condition of Stock Hogs.

OCTOBER—Average yield per acre of Wheat, Rye, Oats and Barley; average condition of Buckwheat, Corn, Potatoes, Tobacco and Cotton.

NOVEMBER—Average yields of Corn, Potatoes, Hay, Tobacco, Buckwheat, Cotton, compared with the year previous.

DECEMBER—Area and product of Wheat, Corn, Oats, Rye, Barley, Potatoes, Hay, Tobacco for the year; farm prices of the principal Agricultural products on December 1. Acreage of Winter Wheat and Winter Rye sown and condition of growing crop.

EXTREME FLUCTUATIONS OR CORNERS — WHEAT

1867—On May 18 prices were forced to $2.85 but closed at $2.16.

1871—August of this year, prices were advanced to $1.30 but closed at $1.10½.

1872—During August Wheat sold to $1.61 but closed at $1.19.

1881—August of this year prices advanced from $1.19 to $1.38 and closed at $1.38.

1887—In June the memorable Cincinnati combination to corner Wheat developed. Prices were advanced from 80⅝c, but market collapsed and declined to 68c.

1888—It was in September when a successful corner was run, Wheat selling from 89¾c to $2.00—top prices reached the closing day.

1898—In May Wheat sold to $1.85, but did not hold, and closed at $1.25.

1902—In September a successful corner was run, Wheat selling up to 95c, and closed at that figure.

1909—In May a corner was run and the closing price was $1.34.

1915—In September the market closed $1.15¼, prices advancing about 6c just before the close of the session.

1921—In May prices advanced from $1.32 to $1.87, and closed at $1.87.

1922—In May Wheat sold to $1.47½, and closed at $1.16.

WHEAT PRICES TO BOTTOMS, OR EXTREME LOW TO EXTREME LOW

				Advance or Decline	Time Months
1841	August to	low,	56	—	
1843	March	low,	30	D. 26	31
1844	December to	low,	38	U. 8	21
1845	November	low,	37	D. 1	11
1846	July to	low,	35	D. 2	8
1846	November	low,	35	—	4
1847	August to	low,	40	U. 5	9
1848	August	low,	50	U. 10	12
1849	December to	low,	50	—	16
1850	March	low,	50	—	3
1850	March to	low	35	D. 15	8
1846	December	low,	35	—	—
1850	November to	low,	35	—	47
1851	November	low,	28	D. 7	12
1852	April to	low,	28	—	5
1846	June	low,	35	U. 7	2
1852	April to	low,	28	D. 7	70
1854	October	low,	90	U. 62	30
1855	August	low,	100	U. 10	8
1856	April	low,	100	—	8
1856	October	low,	77	D. 23	6
1856	October to	low,	77	—	
1858	February	low,	52	D. 25	16
1859	August	low,	52	—	18
1860	December to	low,	67	U. 15	16
1861	October to	low,	55	D. 12	10
1863	August	low,	80	U. 25	22
1865	April to	low,	102	U. 22	20
	July	low,	104	U. 2	3
1866	February to	low,	116	U. 12	10
1867	February	low,	170	U. 54	12
1869	December to	low,	78	D. 92	34
1870	March	low,	74	D. 4	3
1871	August	low,	99	U. 25	17
1872	November to	low,	101	U. 2	15
1873	September	low,	89	D. 12	10
1874	October to	low,	81	D. 8	11
1875	February	low,	83	U. 2	4
1876	July to	low,	83	—	6
1877	August	low,	100	U. 17	11
1878	October to	low,	78	D. 22	16
1879	April	low,	84	U. 6	8

WHEAT PRICES TO BOTTOMS, OR EXTREME LOW
TO EXTREME LOW *continued*

				Advance or Decline	Time Months
1879	August to	low,	84	⸺	4
1880	September	low,	86	U. 2	13
1882	December to	low,	91	U. 5	27
1883	October	low,	90	D. 1	10
1884	December to	low,	70	D. 20	14
1885	March	low,	73	U. 3	4
1885	September to	low,	76	U. 3	6
1886	October	low,	74	D. 2	13
1887	June	low,	65	D. 9	8
1888	April	low,	71	U. 6	10
1889	June	low,	75	U. 4	14
1889	August	low,	75	⸺	2
1890	February	low,	74	D. 1	6
1891	July	low,	85	U. 11	17
1892	October	low,	69	D. 16	15
1892	December	low,	69	⸺	2
1893	June	low,	55	D. 14	6
1894	July	low,	50	D. 5	13
1895	January	low,	49	D. 1	6
1895	December	low,	54	U. 5	11
1896	June	low,	54	⸺	6
1897	April	low,	64	U. 10	10
1898	September to	low,	62	D. 2	17
1899	March	low,	67	U. 4	6
1900	May to	low,	64	D. 3	14
1901	April	low,	70	U. 6	11
1902	August to	low,	69	D. 1	16
1903	March	low,	71	U. 2	7
1904	June to	low,	81	U. 10	15
1905	June	low,	82	U. 1	12
1906	March to	low,	77	D. 5	9
1906	September	low,	75½	D. 1½	6
1907	March to	low,	75	D. ½	6
1908	April	low,	91	U. 16	13
1909	August to	low,	97	U. 6	16
1910	June	low,	91	D. 6	10
1911	April to	low,	84½	D. 6½	10
1912	December	low,	89	U. 4½	20
1913	March to	low,	88	D. 1	3
1913	May	low,	88	⸺	2
1913	October	low,	86	D. 2	5

WHEAT PRICES TO BOTTOMS, OR EXTREME LOW
TO EXTREME LOW *continued*

			Advance or Decline	Time Months
1914	June	low, 84½	D. 1½	8
1911	April to	low, 84½	———	—
1914	June	low, 84½	——	38
1915	September to	low, 93	U. 8½	15
1916	May	low, 104	U. 11	8
1917	February to	low, 154½	U. 50½	10
1918	September	low, 222	U. 77½	19
1919	August to	low, 220	D. 2	11
1920	November	low, 152	D. 68	15
1921	April to	low, 119	D. 33	5
1921	November	low, 104	D. 15	7
1922	August to	low 105	U. 1	10
1923	July	low, 104	D. 1	11
1924	March to	low, 101	D. 3	8
1925	April	low, 137	U. 36	13
1925	October to	low, 135	D. 2	6
1926	November	low, 137	U. 2	13
1927	April to	low, 131½	D. 5½	5
1927	November	low, 127½	D. 4	7
1928	December to	low, 117	D. 10½	13
1929	May	low, 93½	D. 23½	6
1930	November to	low, 73	D. 20½	18
1931	October	low, 49	D. 24	11
1932	December to	low, 43¼	D. 6¾	14
1933	February	low, 46	U. 2¾	4
1934	April to	low, 73	U. 27	14
1935	May	low, 82½	U. 9½	13
1936	May to	low, 90	U. 7½	12
1937	November	low, 85½	D. 4½	18
1938	September to	low, 62¾	D. 22½	11
1939	August	low, 64	U. 1¼	11
1940	August to	low, 70	U. 6	12
1941	February	low, 78	U. 8	6

SOY BEANS

MONEY-MAKING MOVES. Long years ago, Cotton was King and more trading was done in Cotton than any of the other commodities, because there were wide swings and great opportunities for making money. Cotton is no longer King. The Soy Bean is King, as far as money-making moves are concerned. There have been some of the widest swings on Soy Beans of any commodity, giving the greatest opportunities for making profits provided you know how to follow the trend.

Soy Bean production in the United States was very small up until after the World War. Since that time production has increased every year, and the uses for Soy Beans have increased. There are a hundred different uses for Soy Beans besides being used for oil, food and different kinds of bread. They contain a high protein value, are the basis for glue, are used for fertilizer, also in the making and manufacture of soap, and in many ways take the place of cottonseed oil and lard. There is a great future for Soy Beans for manufacturing purposes. Henry Ford has already developed uses for Soy Beans to take the place of steel and wood in the making of automobiles. Soy Beans have been grown in China for hundreds of years.

In 1924 the total Soy Bean crop was 4,947,000 bushels, and in 1925 4,875,000 bushels, and since that production has never been this low. In 1931 the total production was 10,733,000 bushels. This was a record crop to this time. In 1932, 14,975,000 bushels. In 1933 the crop was 13,149,000 Two years of shorter crops after the record. The 1933 crop was the last crop that was that small. The 1935 crop, 44,878,000 bushels, a record up to that time. The 1936 crop, 29,943,000 bushels. This caused a big advance in Soy Beans to $1.82½ a bushel in April, 1937. 1940 crop, 79,837,000 bushels. 1941 crop estimated at 111,000,000 bushels. From this you can see how demand for Soy Beans has increased. The increased uses and the high prices have caused farmers to plant them in the place of Corn and other commodities. As the demand increases for Soy Beans, the production will increase, because the prices of Soy Beans are so much higher than Corn and Wheat and farmers can raise them for the same cost, and naturally will plant more Soy Beans and less Corn and Wheat. Soy Beans can be grown almost anywhere that Corn is grown, and also can be grown in the Southern States where Cotton is grown.

When any commodity reaches a price where there is a great profit in growing it, there is sure to be over-production and, with the enormous amount of land in the United States to produce Soy Beans, production will no doubt be increased until there is such a great over-production that it will be more than enough to supply the demand and the Soy Beans will seek very much lower levels.

Soy Beans should follow about the same seasonal trend as Corn, because they are harvested about the same time of the year, and Corn is harvested in the Fall of the year.

Future trading in Soy Beans was started on the Chicago Board of Trade October 6, 1936. There has only been five years of future trading.

Before that time accurate records of High and Low prices were not kept. However, from what records we can gather from the Government from 1913 to date we give the months in which the most Highs and Lows have been made in order to help you to determine when the seasonal trend should change.

Soy Beans—Months When Most High and Low Prices Have Been Reached

This covers the period from 1913 to 1941, or 28 years.

During this period: January High 4 times—Low 7 times.
February High 3 times—Low 7 times.
March High 2 times—No Lows.
April High 1 time—No Lows.
May High 3 times—No Lows.
June High 3 times—No Lows.
July High 3 times—Low 2 times.
August High 1 time—Low 2 times.
September High 1 time—Low 1 time.
October High 3 times—Low 11 times.
November High 1 time—Low 5 times.
December High 2 times—Low 5 times.

From the above you can see that most Highs have been reached in January, the month when seasonal Lows are usually reached in Corn and Wheat. Soy Beans have made High 3 times during May, June and July and 3 times during October and 3 times in February. The months when the least number of Highs have been made are April, August and September; also November. In each of these months only one High has been reached during the 28-year period. From this record you would expect seasonal Highs in January and February at certain times when the market was running opposite the seasonal trend. If Lows were reached in January and February, according to the seasonal trend, then you would watch the Highs in May, June and July and, if the crop was very short and the market running against seasonal trend, you would expect Highs in October.

You will note that seven Lows were made in January and February; therefore, the early part of the year you would expect the most Lows to be made, but from March to June there had been no extreme Lows for the year made; therefore, during this period you should be careful of being short, and expect the market to advance to seasonal Highs in May, June or July.

October is the record month for Lows, 11 Lows having been made in October. This is due to the fact that receipts are very heavy and this is the first delivery month. During the months of November and December, 5 Lows have been made. Therefore, you should expect Soy Beans to follow the same seasonal trend as Corn, making Lows from October to January, and some years as late as February. When they follow the seasonal trend they advance from February to May, and possibly from June to July. During the Summer, if it looks like a large crop, prices may work lower during August and September, but if there was a crop scare during these months an advance would take place.   To determine the trend of the Soy Bean, apply all of the rules that we apply to other commodities, using the seasonal trend, resistance levels, time periods from BOTTOMS to TOPS and from TOPS to BOTTOMS, always watching the time from any extreme High or Low. Do not overlook anniversary dates to watch for TOPS and BOTTOMS in the same month that previous TOPS and BOTTOMS have been made.

Soy Bean Swings From High to Low Levels—1913 to 1941

1913—October High 196. November Low 157,

1915—January High 235. October Low 188.

1918—February High 382.

1919—February Low 300.

1920—February High 405.   This was the record High and from this we figure resistance levels to 44, the extreme Low.

1921—December Low 208.

1922—February High 260.

1923—February 213. October 209.

1924—February 226. November 260.

1925—February 264. December 217.

1926—January 238. December 180.

1927—February 220. December 161.

1928—February 169. June 213. November 169.

1929—January 182. July High 246. November Low 170.

1930—June High 216.   This was the last time Soy Beans sold at this High Level.

1931—November Low 52c

1932—March High 67. December Low 44c. This was the final Low on Soy Beans.

1933—July High $1.04. October Low 68c.

1934—July High 154. November Low 88c.

1935—February High 126. October Low 68.

1936—August High 119. September Low 110. October 6 — Future trading started on the Chicago Board of Trade. October-May Soy Beans Low 120.

1937—January High 170. February Low 151. April High 182½. July beans at this time sold at 177. This was the final High and big decline followed. August Low 93c. September High 105. October Low 93c. A DOUBLE BOTTOM, same low as August 1937. A rally followed.

1938—February High 107. October Low 68c. Making a TRIPLE BOTTOM. Same Low as October, 1933, and 1935. October is the month when most seasonal Lows are made. This TRIPLE

BOTTOM would have been a safe, sure place to buy for a big advance.

1939—May High 98¾. July Low 67c, the fourth time at the same level. This was still a safe place to buy Soy Beans protected by the *stop loss orders*. December High 131.

1940—February Low 102. March High 117½. August Low 69c for May Soy Beans. This was the fifth time at the same level and this time holding 2c above the last Low and 1c above previous Low, making TRIPLE BOTTOMS around the same levels for three successive years. Our rule says that the greatest advances come from TRIPLE BOTTOMS three years apart. These TOPS and BOTTOMS were as follows:

1939—October Low   68c

July Low   67

1940—August Low   69

and the greatest advance since futures were traded in on the Board of Trade followed this last BOTTOM of August, 1940.

1940—November High $1.05

December Low 85½. The last Low and a safe buying level.

1941—January High 101

February Low 89¼. A higher BOTTOM than December. Good support and a place to buy. When Soy Beans crossed 105, the TOP of November, 1940, you should have bought. This was the Breakaway Point. When prices crossed the High of 1940 at 117½ they would have been a safe buy, even at high prices.

1941—May High 143⅞ for May Soy Beans, 1941 delivery.

The May Option for Delivery in 1942 opened in July, 1941, at 139¾, advanced quickly and crossed the High of 143⅞, indicating higher prices. When prices crossed 154, the last High of July, 1934, it was a sure indication of very much higher prices. The next TOP was 182½, made in April, 1937. This TOP was crossed and the next High was 216, the High of 1930.

1941—June 27, October Beans, 1941 Delivery. High 148¾ for October Beans, the last two days advance was 11c a bushel. From 98c Low this was 50¾c advance and a 50% advance on 98 would give 147 as a Resistance Level. From 44 to 182½, the 75% Resistance Level was 148 and 233% on 44 was 146⅝, making this a Selling Level. Also 125% advance on 66 is 147⅝. Note 150 is the natural Selling Level. At this same date December beans sold at 150¼. This was the place to sell out and go short. A sharp, quick decline followed, lasting four market days.

July 2 Low 133½. Note from 121 to 148¾ that 134½ was the half-way point and buying level. Our rule says buy at OLD TOPS because OLD TOPS become BOTTOMS and OLD BOTTOMS become TOPS.

The fact that the market held just above 133 indicated good buying.

This was a 15c decline, the greatest after prices started up from 89¼ for the May option. 15c is a normal decline. The market had only declined four days, not enough time to show any change in the main trend.

Our rule says after the first sharp decline a *secondary rally* follows. You should have bought for this *secondary rally*.

July 8 High 146½. A five-day rally and a lower TOP. Time to sell out and go short, protected with *stop loss order* above the OLD TOP at 148¾.

July 11 Low 137½ was a four-day decline.

July 12 High 145½, a one-day rally and a third lower TOP. A place to sell.

July 17 Low 137. Only half cent under the previous bottom. A sign of strength.

July 21 High 142, a three-day rally and lower TOPS. A place to sell.

July 23 Low 135. A swift decline, holding 2c above the Lows of July 2. A higher BOTTOM above the half-way point. This was an indication of change in trend and time to cover shorts and buy.

July 26 High 143. Above the previous TOP and a four-day rally. First time since July 8. A sign of better buying and a change in trend. Time to buy on a reaction.

July 30 Low 137½, a two-day reaction and a higher BOTTOM, an indication of good buying. You should have bought, protected with *stop loss orders*.

October beans advanced and crossed TOPS of the previous rally.

August 9 High 147½ over previous TOPS but still under the TOPS at 148¾.

August 12 Last Low 142. Above the half-way point between 148¾ and 133½, showing strength and closing the day at the high price, indicating prices were going higher.

August 20, October Beans crossed 148¾, the OLD TOP, a sure sign of higher prices. A place to buy more. The sharpest advance in years followed, with no reaction lasting more than two days and no reaction of over 5c per bushel from any High Level. This was a *fortune-making move* in a *short period of time*.

September 12 Final High October Beans High 194¾.

December Beans High 197½. May Beans Extreme High 202.

The average price for the three options was 1.9808, just under $2.00 a bushel, the natural Selling Level. Why should May Beans be top at $2.02? Because 202½ was one-half or 50% of 405, the Extreme High, and 50% advance of the highest Selling price is a safe Selling Level, especially after a market has advanced for a long time. Note that 200% advance on 65¾, the Extreme Low of December Beans, was 197¼, and the High of December Beans was 197½. This was a safe, sure Selling Level, protected with a *Stop Loss Order* about 3c away.

Another reason that this was a selling Level was that September was the month for a Seasonal High and a change in trend was due. Beans were up from the Low in August, 1940, into the thirteenth month, and from the Low in February, 1941, had advanced for seven months, and our rule says watch for change in trend in the sixth or seventh month and at the end of each year. October would be three years from the OLD BOTTOM in October, 1938, and as October is a month when there are nearly always low prices, you would expect a decline in October. You should also look up the greatest reaction since the Low of August, 1940. The greatest reaction on May Beans was from 105 to 85½, or 19½c, and the greatest reaction from any High on October and December Beans was 15½c. Therefore, when December beans declined over 15c a bushel the space movement was over-balanced and indicated Lower prices.

At this high level it is interesting to figure why May Soy Beans made Top at 202. 1920 February extreme high $4.05 per bushel. Fifty per cent of this price was $2.02½. This was the most important and strongest resistance level and it is one of the reasons why Soy Beans made Tops at $2.02. Another reason was using the percentage of the base 44, the extreme low price 350% added to this low of 44 would give $1.98. Next extreme low of May Soy Beans, 67c per bushel. Add 200%, or three times the lowest selling price, and we get $2.01, which shows how accurate prices work out to these important percentages. Another reason why Soy Beans made Tops just above $2.00 per bushel is that $2.00 is always a selling level, especially after there has been a great advance.

From 67c per bushel to $2.02, the advance was 135, and 37½% on $1.00 would give $1.37½. This is another reason Soy Beans reached the selling zone. From the extreme low in December, 1932, of 44c to the extreme high was an advance of $1.58 per bushel, and when any option advances $1.50 per bushel or more around this level there is always resistance and a reaction.

Further reasons for expecting Tops in August and September was that the last Low was in August, 1940. We always expect a change in trends one year, two years, and three years from any important top or bottom. In view of the fact that the month of October had recorded the most lows in Soy Beans, we figure that they would be a short sale in the month of September for a big decline in October. The reason to expect this decline in October was that low price of 68 was made in October, 1933, and again in 1935. October Low 68, 1937 October Low 93c, 1938 October Low 68c. 1939 July Low 67 and 1940 August Low 69. Last Low of the reaction in February, 1941, was 89¾c. Our rule says to always watch for a change in trend in the sixth to seventh month from Bottoms. Soy Beans had advanced into the seventh month from the last Low. From 89¼ to 202 was 112¾ advance. This is an actual resistance or selling point, as it is 12½% on $1.00. All of these indications and the fact that the time had run into the seventh month of the last Low, and had run into the thirteenth month from the last extreme Low, was an indication to watch for Tops when Soys Beans reached $2.02 per bushel. December Soy Beans sold at $1.97½. The writer sold Soy Beans short at $1.95⅞, and sold short all the way down following the big decline, covering shorts and buying on October 16,

1941, when May Soy Beans, Wheat, Rye, Corn, and all the other grains, declined to limits of 8 and 10c per bushel.

Prices opened slightly lower on the morning of the 17th, then rallied 8c per bushel. October 17 Low on May Soy Beans was 154½, a decline of 47½ per bushel from the high of September 12. One-third of the total advance of $1.35 would be 45c. Subtracting 45c from $2.02 would give $1.57 as the support level or buying point. 25% of the highest selling price would be 50½c, or 151½.

REVIEW:

1940—November High for May Soy Beans 105. Figuring the half-way point from the Top at 105 to the extreme high of 202 gives 153½ as the support level. Soy Beans declined on October 17, 1941, to 154½. Figuring 250% advance from the extreme low at 44 gives $1.54, also a selling level. Another reason for the low of October 17, 1941, was that there were old TOPS around this level. 1934 July High for July option 154. Our rule says that old Bottoms become Tops and old Tops become Bottoms. After May beans had declined to 154½, a total decline of 47c, and having declined one-third of the total advance from 67c to 202, we would figure a rally of one-third of the decline from 202 to 154½. This would give 170⅛. October 22, May Soy Beans advanced to 169¾. This was also around old Bottom and Top levels, and other resistance points, and the writer sold Soy Beans short on this rally, figuring that it would come back, anyway, to make a double bottom or have a secondary decline to around the bottom of October 16. October 28, May Soy Beans declined to 155½, making a higher bottom by 1c and making this a buying level. The writer covered shorts on this decline. A rapid advance followed, and on October 31, 1941, May Soy Beans have again advanced to 169½.

1941—November 7, High 178. This was 50% or half of the move from 202 to 154½. A safe, sure selling level. The writer sold Soy Beans short at this time and advised his clients to sell short, some of them selling short at 177¾. A quick decline followed and on November 13, May Soy Beans declined to 164¾. Note that 166¼ is the 50% or half-way point between 154½ to 178, making around this level a point for a rally. From November 13 LOW 164¾, the market rallied. November 14 HIGH 170⅜. Note from the extreme low of the option, 139¾, to the extreme high of 202, the 50% or half-way point was 170⅞, making Soy Beans again a short sale around 170. The writer sold Soy Beans short at 169½. November 15 LOW 163½. The market closed weak at this low, with the main trend DOWN.

For Soy Beans to show strong UP trend again, they will have to cross 171 and to show a real bullish indication they will have to cross the high of 178, the half-way point between 154½ and 202. Breaking 161¼, which is the half-way point between 154½ and 178, would indicate lower.

Breaking 154½ would indicate 140, or lower.

Note that 151½ is 25% decline from the top of 202, the extreme high. Under this level would mean that the market was in a very weak position.

The next important date to watch for a change in trend on Soy Beans will be December 12, 1941, three months from the high. Also January 12, 1942, four months from the high in September. December and January are important for a change in trend in Soy Beans. If they are low and at resistance levels around this time, it will be the time to buy for a rally.

Apply all of the rules and do not buy until there is a definite indication of bottom and a change in trend.

Trading Examples—Soy Beans—August 20, 1940, to October 16, 1941.
    See chart in back of book covering one to three-day moves
        and volume of sales and open interest.

These are example of what could have been done by trading according to the rules. It is not my intention to lead anyone to believe that any average human being would get results of this kind, regardless of how well they understood the rules. The reason why they would not buy and sell and make large profits of this kind is the HUMAN ELEMENT, which causes a man to act too often on hope and fear, instead of facing facts and following rules.

1940—August 20—May Soy Beans, LOW 69c. The reason for buying
    was a triple bottom.
    We start with a capital of $1,000, which will margin 5,000 bushels
    of Soy Beans at 20c per bushel.
    Bought 5,000 May Soy Beans at 70c, placed stop loss order at 66.
    Risk limited to $200 and commission.

October 8—Raised STOP LOSS ORDER to 74.

October 29—Raised STOP LOSS ORDER to 81¼. Keeping Stop Loss
    Orders 1c to 3c under bottoms.

November—After prices crossed tops, bought 5,000 at 89c.
    Placed Stop on 10,000 at 86c.

November 18, HIGH $1.05. The greatest reaction had been 5c.
    Raised STOP LOSS ORDER TO 99c.
    Sold 10,000 at 99c on stop.
    PROFIT—$2,500, less commission of $25. This was made on an
    initial risk of $200. From this time on you could trade on
    profits and never risk any more of your original capital.
    Sold short 5,000 bushels at 99c.
    Placed Stop at $1.06, 1c above November 18 high.

November 22, LOW 91¾.

November 25, HIGH $1.00.
    Reduced stop to $1.01.
    Sold short 5,000 more at 90¾.

December 18, LOW 85½.
    Bought 10,000 bushels at 87c to cover shorts because 87c was
      one-half of 69 to 105.
    At this time you would have TOTAL PROFIT of $3,287.50.

Bought 5,000 at 87 for long account.   Placed stop at 84.

1941—January 7, HIGH 1.01½.

January 21, LOW 95¼.

January 25, HIGH 98½. A second lower top. Sell out longs or raise
stops to 94¼.
Sold 5,000 at 94¼.
PROFIT on this deal, $362.50.
Total profit to this date, less commission, $3,650.
Sold short, 5,000 at 94¼.

February 18, LOW 89¼.

February 21, HIGH 92.

February 24, LOW 89¼. A double bottom and higher than Decem-
ber lows and also above the half-way point.
Time to cover shorts and buy.
Bought 10,000 bushels at 92c for long account, stop at 86c.
PROFIT TO DATE—$3,762.50.

March 19, HIGH $1.09. When prices crossed $1.05, bought 5,000 more
at $1.06. Stopped 15,000 at $1.02, 3c under the top of $1.05.

March 23, LOW $1.04.
Bought 5,000 more at $1.10.
Raised stop on 20,000 to $1.06, or 3c under $1.09 top.

April 17, HIGH 124½.

April 24, LOW 117⅝.
Raised stop on 20,000 to 114⅝.
Bought 5,000 more at 125½.
Raised stop on 25,000 to 122½.
The market was then in the runaway move and you should have
followed up, protected with stop loss orders 1c under the low
of each day.

May 21, HIGH 143⅞.

May 22, LOW 136.
Stop was raised to 136⅞.
Sold 25,000 on stop at 136⅞.
PROFIT TO DATE—$11,706.25, less commission.

We now use October beans for trading examples.

May 31, LOW 121.

June 4, HIGH 126⅞.

June 6, LOW 121. A double bottom. We wait for 3c rally to see
that the bottom is going to hold, and then buy.
Bought 20,000 at 124, stop at 120.
Bought 10,000 at 134.
Stopped 30,000 at 131.

The reason for buying at 134 was because prices had crossed
133, the high of May, 1941.

A rapid advance followed.

June 27, HIGH 148-¾

Raised stop on 30,000 to 142-3/4, 1c under previous day's low.
Sold 30,000 at 142-3/4.
PROFIT TO DATE—$15,931.25.
Sold short, 20,000 at 142-3/4.

July 2, LOW 133-1/2. Down to old bottoms and at the 50%, or half-way
point of 121 to 148-3/4.
Bought 20,000 at 134-1/2.
Bought 20,000 for long account at 134-1/2, stop 131.
PROFIT TO DATE—$17,581.25.

July 27, LOW 135. A higher bottom.
Raised stop to 132-1/2.

July 30, LOW 137½.
Raised stop to 134-1/2.

August 23—Bought 20,000 at 150.
Placed stop on 40,000 at 145-3/4.

September 22—Bought 10,000 at 162.
Raised stop on 50,000 to 155. This was 1c under the low of August 29.

September 6—Bought 5,000 at 172.
Made stop on 60,000 at 169.

This was a runaway market and reactions were not lasting more than one day and more than 5c a bushel. As shown by the chart in the back of the book, with volume of sales and open interest on soy beans.

The plan was to do no guessing—to follow definite rules—and we have proved in other examples why October beans should have been sold out on September 12, and you should have sold short. But we followed this advance, raising stop loss orders 1c under the low of the previous day.

September 12—Final HIGH, 194-3/4.
Raised stop to 185, 1c under previous day.

September 14—Sold 60,000 bushels at $1.85.

TOTAL PROFIT TO DATE—$44,481.25.

With this amount of capital you could have traded in 50,000 or even 100,000 bushels and have plenty of margin. But we must follow the rules and never risk more than 10% of the capital on any one trade.

September 14—Sold 20,000 October beans at 185.
Sold 10,000 at 175.

September 22—Bought 30,000 at 172.

TOTAL PROFIT TO DATE—$47,381.25.

September 27—Bought 20,000 at 172.
Followed up with stop loss orders 1c under previous day's low.

September 30—Sold 20,000 at 177.

TOTAL PROFIT TO DATE $48,381.25.

September 30—Sold short 20,000 at 177.

October 7—Sold short 20,000 at 165½.

October 16—Bought 40,000 at 149 because 148-¾ was the old high of June 27.

TOTAL PROFIT TO DATE $57,281.25.

Trading over a period of fourteen months, starting with $1,000 capital and a risk of $200., strictly following rules and doing no guessing, the above profits were possible and I have good reason to believe that there are men in Chicago who did make trades that showed profits somewhere near these examples of profits made trading on paper.

The question arises—if such opportunities occur every few years and these enormous profits are possible, why don't more people quit guessing, follow rules, and make more money. There are dozens of reasons that I could give you, but the important one is the HUMAN ELEMENT. People reason that the market is too high or too low and trade on fear or hope. How many men, after soy beans had advanced from 69c a bushel to $1.50 a bushel, could, or would believe, that they were going to advance to $1.95 and $2.02 per bushel from August 13 to September 12, a period of 30 days? Yet it happened and the rule showed uptrend and all you had to do was to keep on buying and follow rules and forget about the price, or what you thought about it.

April, 1937—May soy beans high, 182½.

How many people would believe at that time that six months later, or in October, 1937, soy beans would sell at 93c or that in October, 1938, eighteen months later, they would sell at 67 and 68c a bushel.

Never trade on what you hope or what you fear, but trade on facts and what you know. FOLLOW THE RULES and FOLLOW THE TREND up or down and you will make profits provided you use STOP LOSS ORDERS and do not try to get rich too quick by risking all your capital on one trade. Remember, you may be wrong and then when another opportunity comes, you would have no capital with which to take advantage of it.

My final advice is when you start to trade, make up your mind to follow definite rules, or keep out of the market. You are sure to lose if you follow guesswork and act on hope or fear.

SOY BEANS. In 1936, October 6, trading in futures began on the Chicago Board. May Soy Beans started at $1.20 per bushel and never sold lower. It is important here to figure why this was the bottom. Note 121 on May Soy Beans was 187% of 44, the extreme low, and crossing 121 indicated higher. In 1936, October 16, high for this week was 129. Note that 130 was one-half of 216 to 44, making 129 to 130 a strong resistance level. Also, 132 was 200% on 44.

1936—October 24. The week ending at this time, low on May Soy Beans, 121¼, a secondary reaction and a higher bottom. A safer buying level.

October 31, High 127¼. A lower Top.

November 14, Low 123½. Note that 124½ was one-half of 120 to 129, and 123½ was the third higher bottom. A sign of strength and good support, making this a buying level.

BREAKAWAY POINT—

November 23, prices crossed 129, the OLD TOP and later crossed 132, which was 200% on 44, the base low price, making 133 a safer buying level, because after the breakaway to new high prices, the runaway move always follows. The Runaway move did follow and the advance was swift, with very small reaction.

1937—January 16. High 162. Note 162 was $\frac{3}{4}$ of 216 the high of 1930 and 164-$\frac{3}{8}$ was one-third of 405 to 44, and 158-$\frac{3}{4}$ was 2-3 of 216 to 44, making this a safe selling level for a reaction. This was really the second Top, as there was one Top in December 1936 at 160$\frac{1}{2}$. This was really a double Top. A reaction followed.

1937—February 27, Low 151$\frac{1}{4}$. A 12$\frac{1}{2}$% reaction, a normal reaction in price and a normal reaction in time, as our rule says reactions run from 3 to 6 weeks and then the normal or main trend is resumed.

151$\frac{7}{8}$ is $\frac{3}{8}$ of 405 and 151$\frac{1}{2}$ is $\frac{5}{8}$ of 44 to 216, making this a support and buying level, especially as February is the month for seasonal lows. The reaction was only normal reaction in a Bull market. The advance was resumed.

1937—March 27. Safest BUYING POINT. When prices crossed the three weeks High of 156, which was the half-way point of the last move, it was the safest buying point and when they crossed 162, the last high, it was still safe to buy, protected with *stop loss order*. A rapid advance followed.

1937—April 10th. Final High 182$\frac{1}{2}$. Note that $\frac{3}{8}$ of 405 to 44 was 179$\frac{3}{8}$, making this a selling level, but you should wait for a definite change in trend.

April 17. Low 173$\frac{1}{2}$.

April 24. High 181$\frac{1}{2}$. A lower Top and double top. This was the place to sell short, protecting with *Stop loss order* 3c over the first Tops or at 184$\frac{1}{2}$.

1937—May 1. Low 170$\frac{1}{2}$. Breaking the Lows of the three previous weeks showed down trend and made it a safe short sale.

After the first of May you would trade in the July or December options, as our rule is that one should never trade in the current options in the month of delivery. So, the July and December options would be the ones in which to trade.

August 7. May Soy Beans Low 97. Note that one-half of 182$\frac{1}{2}$ is 91$\frac{1}{4}$ and 44c to 182$\frac{1}{2}$ the 50% or the half-way point was 113$\frac{1}{4}$. Note that 95$\frac{3}{4}$ was $\frac{3}{8}$ of 44 to 182$\frac{1}{2}$, making 97 a support level for a rally. There is usually support after an option declines to around $1.00 or just below. It is the same when an option advances to around $1.00 there is selling.

Also note that 99 was 112% on 44.

1937—August 14. High 110$\frac{3}{4}$. This was only one week's rally. Note that 110 was 125% on 44 and 108 was half of 216, also 108$\frac{1}{2}$ was $\frac{3}{8}$ of 44 to 216 and being under 113$\frac{1}{4}$, the half-way point between 44 to 182$\frac{1}{2}$, was in a weak position and made this a selling level.

1937—September 4. Low 94. Note that ⅜ of 44 to 182½ was 95¾ resistance levels, and a rally followed.

1937—September 11. High 105. One week's rally — a normal rally and a 13% advance — a normal advance. 105 was ⅛ or 12½% of 120, the low in 1936.

1937—September 25. Low 93.
October 16. Lows around 92. Note 90¼ was 25% of 120 and 90⅛ was one-third of 44 to 182. May Beans held for several weeks in a narrow range, making bottoms just above 90.

1937—Week ending December 25. Prices crossed the Tops of the Previous five weeks showing up-trend and making it safer to buy.

1938 — January 29 to February 12. There were three tops, 106 to 106½, just above the Old Tops of 105 and still under 108, the half-way point of 216, making this a selling level.

1938—February 19. Prices broke under the Lows of the three previous weeks, indicating a short sale. A decline followed, prices broke 92, the low of the option, showing the main trend down.

1938—April 30. Low 89½. At this point you would start trading in July or December Beans and follow the trend which was already down.

1938—August 6. May Beans started at 83½ and in a weak position, because it was under old Bottoms.

1938—September 10. Low 76.

1938—September 17. High 82¾. Only one week's rally and selling level.

1938—October 22. Low 68½. Remember that October is the month when most seasonal lows have been made, and consider this a buying level. It was a double and triple bottom.
1932 March Low 67c.
1933 October Low 68c.
1935 October Low 68c.
making this a triple Bottom and a safe buying level. A rally followed.
From the High in August, 83¾, to the low of 68½, the half-way point is 76⅛. Crossing this high level was a signal for higher prices.

1938—October 29. High 75½.

1938—November 5th. Low 72c. A secondary decline and Higher Bottom and a buying level.

1938—December 3rd. Prices crossed the Tops of six previous weeks which were made around 77. This was the *breakaway point* and a safe buying level after previous Tops were crossed.

1939—January 14. High 84¾. One cent over the August Highs. The market held in a dull narrow range and a reaction followed.

1939—February 11. Low 79c. A normal four weeks' reaction and down only 5¾. A very small, normal reaction in a bull market, making this a safe buying level.

1939—March. Prices crossed the Old Tops and continued to advance.

1939—May 20 to 29. High 99c. Under $1.00 and a selling level. At the time of the year when Seasonal Highs are often made. At this time you would start trading in July or December Beans.

1939—May 27. December Beans opened at $83\frac{1}{2}$ under Old Bottoms and in a weak position, with the trend down. You should have sold short. Prices continued to move lower and rallies were very small; therefore, you would have stayed short. From 99c to 68c the half-way point was $83\frac{1}{2}$; therefore, when December Beans were under $83\frac{1}{2}$ they were in a weak position.

1939—August. May Beans Low 67c. December Beans Low $65\frac{3}{4}$. Down at Old Bottoms which was Double and Triple Bottoms. A buying level protected by *stop loss orders* about 3c under these Old Bottoms. 66 was 50% advance on 44c, the extreme Low, thus making 66 to 68 strong support level. December Beans were very dull and narrow, holding four weeks below $68\frac{3}{4}$ and not breaking $65\frac{3}{4}$.

SAFE BUYING LEVELS

BREAKAWAY POINTS

1939—August 26th. December Beans crossed 69. This was the breakaway and a safe buying point. The last High 83 to $65\frac{3}{4}$ made $74\frac{1}{2}$ the half-way point.

1939—September 2. Prices crossed $74\frac{1}{2}$ and advanced to $75\frac{3}{4}$, showing strong uptrend.

1939—September 9. High 90c. Under Old Bottoms and selling levels. Note $90\frac{1}{8}$ was one-third of $182\frac{1}{2}$ to 44 and 88 was a 100% advance on 44. This was a very sharp advance in three weeks and time for a reaction.

1939—October 14. Low 78c. A 12c decline. A normal decline in a bull market. Five weeks was a normal time reaction. From 66 to 90. Note 78 was the 50% reaction point and a safe place to buy.

As October is the month when most seasonal lows have been made, this was still a safer time to buy.

The advance was resumed, prices crossed 90, showing strong uptrend. The market worked up with no reaction, breaking the Lows of previous weeks.

1939—December 23. High $129\frac{1}{2}$. Note $124\frac{3}{4}$ was one-half of 182 to 67c, making this a selling level and 130 was one-third of 216 to 44, making this a resistance level. Also, the market had advanced for four months which is the normal time period for an advance. We start trading again in May Beans for 1940 delivery. For example:

1939—December 23. May Beans High $131\frac{1}{2}$. This was a single sharp Top and a quick decline followed.

1940—January 6. Low 116. Rallied to 119, then broke 116 where there were several weeks Bottoms. Note from 67 to 131½, a 12½% decline, would give 120¾, making this level the first indication for lower. Later breaking 115, which was a 25% decline of this range, put the market in a very weak position and indicated short sale.

1940—February 3. Low 102. Here was a buy, as one-half of 67 to 131½ was 99¼, and holding above 100 was a buy for a rally.

1940—March 16. High 117¾. Just under the last two Tops and one-half of 131½ to 102 was 116¼, making this a safe place to sell out longs and sell short on a five weeks normal rally.

1940—April 13. Low 106. A small rally followed.

1940—April 27. High 111¾. A selling level. After this it broke all supports showing the main trend down.

1940—May 18. Low 91¼. Trend still down. At this time you would be trading in July or December Beans.
December Beans started in June and we continue the examples of trading in December Beans.

1940—June 29. December Beans Low 71½. One-third of 216 was 72, making this a point for a rally.

1940—August 3rd. High 77. A weak rally for five weeks. A selling point.

1940—Weeks ending August 10th, 17 and 24. During all these weeks Lows were 67½ to 70, down to Old Bottoms and Triple Bottoms. A safe buying point because August was the month for a Seasonal Change in trend and for seasonal low. The fact that for all of these years prices stopped every time they declined to around 67 or 68 made this a buying point every time, protected with *stop loss orders* 3c under. The market held for two weeks in a 2c range, then the trend turned up.

1940—September 7 to October 12. There were six weeks Tops at 76 to 77½. During the week ending October 19th, the *Breakaway movement* started. Prices advanced fast.

1940—November 23. High 107. Note 108 was one-half of 216, making this a selling level.
From this point we use May Beans for a trading example.

1940—November 23. May Beans High 105. Under Old Bottoms and 105⅝ was one-third of 182½ to 67, and 103½ was 50% advance on 69, which was the Low of August 1940, making 105 a selling level for a reaction, especially after an advance which had lasted 13 weeks, one-fourth of the year. The market was moving opposite the Seasonal Trend, and should run down from January to February.
From 69 to 105, the half-way point was 87.

1940—December 21st. Low 85½. The natural resistance point and the fact that 87 was one-half of 69 to 105 made this a logical buying level.

1941—January 11. High 101½. A three weeks rally. Note that 101¼ was ¼ of 405 and 103½ was a 50% advance on 69. A reaction followed.

1941—February 22. Low 89¼. A higher Bottom than December and this time holding above 87, the half-way point from 69 to 105, showed greater strength and made it a better buy. February is also a month for seasonal lows. A rally followed, prices crossed 101¼, and later crossed 105, the last Top, showing strong up-trend, and indicating Soy Beans a good buy even at these higher levels. As a rule, when Wheat or Soy Beans advance above $1.00 per bushel, react below $1.00 per bushel, and later cross $1.00 the second or third time, prices always move very much higher and hold up for a long time. 113½ was one-half of 44 to 182½. Prices crossed this level, showing a strong up-trend and you should have bought more Beans. The market continued to work higher.

Reactions were very small.

1941—May 21. High 143⅞. Note 144 was 2/3 of 67 to 182½. From this time on we use October Beans for 1941 delivery for an example.

1941—May 21st. October Beans High 133. They had advanced from 98c, the low of March 31, and were up 35c per bushel. Note that

135 was 1/3 of 405
130 was ½ of 44 to 216
135 was ⅝ of 216
134¼ was ¼ of 44 to 405
130¾ was ⅝ of 44 to 182½

132 was 100% advance on 66 Low, making 133 a safe selling level for a reaction, especially after such a fast run up and a sharp Top. A fast decline followed.

1941—May 31. Low 121. A 12% reaction, a normal reaction, and 10 days is a normal time period for a reaction.

1941—June 4. High 126⅞. June 6 Low 121. A double Bottom. Note 121 was 187 % on 44 and 120¾ was 75% on 69 Low. This was only a two weeks reaction and a normal decline in cents per bushel, making this a buying level. Prices crossed 127, the half-way point of 133 to 121, indicating higher prices. Later when they crossed 133 they showed strong uptrend and you should have bought more. Note that no reaction lasted more than 2 days. This was an indication of the strongest kind of a bull market. You could have bought all the way up and followed up with *stop loss orders* under the lows of the previous day.

CORN

Corn is traded in on the Chicago Board of Trade, the Kansas City Board of Trade and the Winnipeg Grain Exchange.

The greatest volume of trading in corn is on the Chicago Board of Trade.

A contract for corn is 5,000 bushels.

The minimum fluctuation is ⅛c per bushel, which is $12.50 on a contract.

The commission for a round turn of 5,000 bushels is $12.50.

The margin requirements vary according to price running from $300 up to $1,000.

CORN SEASONAL CHANGES 1859 TO 1941 — 82 YEARS

	High	Low
January	5	37
February	3	17
March	17	5
April	5	11
May	2 0	4
June	1 5	2
July	5	9
August	17	1
September	12	2
October	6	11
November	10	2
December	9	20

From the above you can see that corn has made high in the month of May 20 times during the above period and high in August 17 times, and in June 15 times. Therefore, May and August are most important months for tops and a change in trend.

June is the next important month for high levels and this is usually when prices run over into the early part of June after making highs in May. The next important months for high levels are March and September, and November and December next in importance.

MONTHS WHEN LEAST NUMBER OF TOPS HAVE BEEN REACHED:

February, only three tops have been reached in this month. This is the smallest of any month. The next months are April, July and October, when high levels have been reached about the same number of times.

When corn is following the seasonal trend you would watch the month of May and August as most important for tops and a place to sell out and go short. The reason why most tops are reached in August is that more crop scares occur in July and August than any other months. Then later in the Fall around September and October crop scares occur on account of killing frosts. Knowing these records of the past, if the trend had turned up in December or January you would not sell out in February but would wait for the month of March to see if top was made and if the trend still showed up you would wait for the month of May. If there was a sharp advance sell out long corn and wait for reaction to buy again, or until a double top was made or the trend turned down, then sell short.

If the advance in corn started late in the year and there was no indication of a top in the latter part of May or early June you would wait for the month of August when tops should be made according to seasonal trend, but never sell out and go short until all the rules indicate a definite change in trend.

MONTHS WHEN LOWEST PRICES HAVE BEEN REACHED: You will note from the above record that prices have been low during January 37 times and during December 20 times, making a total of 57 times out of 82 years lows have been reached in December and January. Therefore, these are the months to watch for seasonal lows. This is due to the fact that the heaviest receipts of corn usually run from November to January, depressing the price.

February is the next month when most lows have been made, having made low 17 times in this month. You would watch for buying opportunities and low prices on corn in January and February, and hold if the trend was up until May or early June, and if the market was in a very strong position and main trend up you could hold until August, which would be 6 months from February low. Our rule says always watch for change in trend in the sixth or seventh month from any extreme low or high point.

The next months in importance for low prices are April, July and October. The most important is October, because receipts of new corn are usually heavy in October.

MONTHS WHEN LEAST NUMBER OF LOWS HAVE BEEN REACHED: June, September and November, during 82 years lows have been reached only 2 times in each of these months. In September extreme lows were reached in 1861 and 1896.

August is the real exception, and only 1 time during 82 years has corn reached low for the year in the month of August. This exception was in 1909. This is certainly a warning to anyone not to expect corn to reach low levels in August and not to go short expecting lows in August, because the seasonal trend proves that August is the second month of the year when most tops are reached.

During 82 years there has only been five lows in the month of March and four lows in the month of May. Therefore, these are dangerous months to be short expecting lows during these periods.

During extremely short crop years prices will move opposite the seasonal trend and make highs in the months when seasonal trends usually indicate lows. Follow the rule that there is seldom ever more than 3 times during the normal seasonal trend months before there is a change or reversal. This does not mean that if the high for 3 years is in May or in August that the lows the following year will come out in May or August, but they will come out in some of the other months where there is a smaller number of tops.

Always apply the rules and don't overlook the fact of how many years or months corn has advanced or declined from a previous extreme high or low. Watch the cycles on crops and this will help you to determine when extreme high or low prices should be reached.

GREAT SWINGS ON CORN

If you will study the swings on Corn from extreme High to extreme

Low, keeping this record before you, and knowing the important resistance points between extreme High and extreme Low, you will be able to determine resistance levels in th future and when Tops and Bottoms should come out.

1859—October High 81 cents.

1861—October Low 20 cents per bushel. This was the last Low on Corn and the main trend turned up as Corn got scarcer during the Civil War time and prices continued to work higher.

1864—November Extreme High 140. From this Level figure the percentage from the extreme Low to the extreme High and from the extreme High back to the extreme Low. Subtract the extreme low price from the extreme High price. Note that 140 was 600% advance on the low of 20 cents per bushel. The important points between 20 cents per bushel and 140 would be as follows:

$\frac{1}{8}$	125	$\frac{3}{8}$	95	$\frac{5}{8}$	65
$\frac{1}{4}$	110	$\frac{1}{2}$	80	$\frac{3}{4}$	50
1/3	100	2/3	60	$\frac{7}{8}$	35

Taking 1/3 of 1.40, the High Selling price is 46⅝ and 2/3 of 140 is 92¼. Then taking the percentage of the highest Selling Price, ⅛ would be 17½ points, or 122½, and ½ of the Highest Selling Price 70, and ¼ of the Highest Selling Price would be 35. Subtracting this from the Top would give 105. All of these Resistance Levels would indicate that when prices broke back under $1.00 they were in very weak position and indicated lower. After the war was over in 1865 the prices of all commodities declined.

1866—February Low 33¾ cents for Corn. In looking at the Resistance Level you will find that this is the ⅞ point down from 1.40, making this a natural resistance point for Rally.

1867—October High 1.12 per bushel. Note that 1.10 was ¼ point between 20 cents per bushel and 1.40 and 1.12½ is a natural Selling Level, being 12½% on 1.00 per bushel. Here the percentage between 33¾ and 1.12 should be figured as Resistance Points on the way down, but you would still use Resistance Points between 20 cents per bushel and 1.40, because these were the extreme points. The first indication of lower prices after 1.12 would be when prices broke under 1.00 per bushel or 25% from 33¾ to 1.12. After prices decline below 1.00 per bushel, they decline fast, with very small Rallies.

1869—January Low 44 cents. Down near the 1/3 point of 1.40 per bushel. Bottom was made here and this was a Buying Level. The market was stronger when Corn crossed 50 cents per bushel.

1869—August High 97½ cents per bushel. Failing to reach 1.00 per bushel was an indication of weakness and made this a Selling Level. August is the seasonal month for change in trend when most Tops are reached. Therefore, this would have been the place to sell out and sell short.

1873—April Low 27 cents per bushel, within 7 cents per bushel of the

1861 Low. A 75% decline from 1.12 would give 28 cents per bushel, making this a support buying level. With prices holding above 25 cents per bushel, ¼ of a dollar was important and indicated a Rally.

1874—September High 86 cents. Note that a 200% advance on 27 cents would give 81 cents and this price was under the 2/3 point of 1.40 per bushel, making it a Selling Level.

1879—January Low 29½ cents per bushel, 2½ cents above the Low of April 1873, making this a Double Bottom and a Higher Bottom and a place to buy.

1882—September High 81½ cents. This was a seasonal month for Tops and a place to sell out and sell short, especially as 80 was ½ of 20 cents to 1.40.

1883—October Low 76 cents. Low in a month when seasonal trends indicate Lows come out.

1884—September High 87 cents. A Double Top against 1874 High and again in a seasonal month for Tops, making this a place to sell out longs and go short.

1884—October Low 34½ cents, making the Third Higher Bottom since 1873 Low and, as 35 cents was ⅞ of 20 cents to 1.40, this was a natural support level for Rally and a moderate Rally followed.

1885—April High 49 cents per bushel. Just under the 50-cents Level and at the ¾ point, making this a Selling Level for reaction.

1886—October Low 33 cents, only 1½ cents lower than October 1884 and two years apart indicated a change in trend in a month when seasonal lows are made. A Rally followed.

1888—December High 61 cents. 60 cents was 2/3 of 20 cents to 1.40, making this a Selling Level and 100% on 33 Low would give 66. Failing to make 100% advance showed weakness.

1889—February Low 27½ cents, the lowest since 1873 and a Double Bottom against this old Low. making this a Buying Level for Rally.

1889—September High 48 cents, the month for a seasonal High, and at the same High 1 cent under April 1885, and under 50 cents per bushel made this a Selling Level.

1890—January Low 27½ cents. A Double Bottom and a Buying Level. Double Bottoms coming several years apart, according to our rules, is more significant of a rapid advance. A rapid advance followed this Double Bottom.

1891—June High 75½ cents per bushel. This was 75% of 1.00 and a natural normal Selling Level. Also 5 cents under the halfway point between 20 cents and 1.40. In view of the fact that the Low came out in January, where the most extreme Lows are made according to seasonal trends, and the market had advanced over five months, made this a point to watch for change in trend and Selling Level.

1892—January Low 36½ cents. A Higher Bottom and at a month for seasonal Lows. Time to buy for Rally. The fact that there had been a Double Bottom at 27½ cents, this secondary decline was 9½ cents higher, which would indicate strength and a safer place to buy, especially after the market advanced and crossed Tops over the previous months. A rapid advance followed this Third Higher Bottom.

1892—May High 1.00 per bushel. The first time since 1867 and 1869 High was 97½ cents per bushel, making this a Double Top. Corn was high enough at $1.00 per bushel at that time but prices did not stay up long. At this High you would take the last extreme low of 27 cents per bushel and figure the important Resistance Point, but always remembering that the extreme High was 1.40 and the extreme Low 20 cents per bushel. These points and the percentage of these Tops and Bottoms were important. Note that 1.00 was 400% advance from the extreme Low of 20 cents and was a little over 250% advance on the Low of 27 cents per bushel, making this a Selling Level. 50% of 27 cents to 1.00 per bushel is 63½. When Corn broke back ⅛ and 25% of the range or declining under 95 was the first indication of lower prices.

1894—January Low 34 cents per bushel. A time for seasonal change and for seasonal Lows and 2½ cents per bushel under the Low of January 1892 — two years later. Not going 3 cents per bushel lower indicated strength and a point to buy for Rally.

1894—August High 59½ cents per bushel. Note that 60½ was ½ between 20 cents and 1.00, and failing to reach 63½ cents, the halfway point between 27 and 1.00, was a sign of weakness. In fact, the market stayed under this 50% point once it declined under it for many years. After the High of 59½ cents per bushel from the Low of 34, the market broke back under 50 cents per bushel and broke under 47 cents, a weaker position, and later broke the Low at 34 cents per bushel, indicating extreme weakness.

1896—July Low 19½ cents per bushel. This was the extreme Low and note that it was down to the Low of October 1861, making a Double Bottom. You would know that Corn was down below the cost of production at this time and it was a safe buy around these Levels. This was an 80% decline from 1.00 per bushel and about 87½% of 1.40, the High Level reached in 1864.
The market was dull and narrow around these Low Levels for several months. Study the monthly High and Low chart at this Bottom and also study the quarterly chart.

1897—The first quarter was higher and in March crossed the high of the previous quarter of 1896. You should have bought more Corn and then followed the main trend until it showed an important change. Here again you would still use your base figures of 20 cents per bushel to 1.40 and use 20 cents per bushel to the High at 1.12 and 20 cents per bushel to the last High at 1.00 per bushel, figuring percentage points on the way up.

1897—August High 38 cents per bushel. A 100% advance on 19½c

would give 39c. August was the month when more seasonal
tops came out than any other except May. Therefore, you
would expect top at this time, October low 28c per bushel.
Around the half-way point from 19½c to 38c making this the
buying level, as this was the secondary reaction after the main
trend turned up, having crossed the Tops of 1896 where there
were three-quarterly Tops.

1898—December High 39½c. This was opposite the seasonal trend
and making Tops in the month that should have been the Bottom month; therefore, important to sell out and sell short, especially as the price failed to cross 40c.

1899—July Low 29c. Again opposite the seasonal trend and making
Low in a month that is usually high. Making a Higher Bottom
than October 1897 was an indication of strength and a place to
buy, holding above the 50% level, was also an indication of
strength and a buying level.

1900—May High 42c in the month for a seasonal High and a time to
sell out and sell short, especially as the price did not advance
3c per bushel over the High of December, 1898.

1900—August Low 34½c. Holding the half way point at 29c to 42c
was an indication of strength and a buying level. The safest
place to buy was in January 1901 when prices crossed 38c
the high of the previous quarter showing Up Trend. The market
moved up fast advancing to new High Levels crossing the Top
of 42c. When this Top was crossed you should buy more and
hold for Higher Prices. Advance was rapid in 1901.

1901—December High 69c. This was nearly 150% advance on the
Low of 19½ and note that 70 was one-half of 140 the last High
and a selling price. This was opposite the seasonal trend making TOPS in a month when usually most Bottoms are reached;
therefore, a safe place to sell out and sell short. A large crop had
been discounted. At this level you would figure the importance of
the resistance points between 19½ and 69, breaking back 25%
was the first indication of lower prices. Also consider the last
Low of 34½, the resistance points between this Low Level and
the Tops. This was an indication of great weakness when prices
declined under 57½, two quarterly Bottoms.

1902—July Low 38½c per bushel. 50 percent decline from 69c would
be 34½c per bushel, holding above this important point 100%
advance on the base of 19½c was an indication of strength
and a buying level. The market was still making progressively
Higher Bottoms with each year's campaign. From each year's
Lows, as you can see on the quarterly chart, prices moved up.

1903—September High 53c. Note that 50% or one-half from 69c to
38½c was 53¾, making this a selling level, for at least a reaction.

1903—October Low 41c. This was running according to seasonal Lows.
A Higher Bottom than 1902. The market was dull and narrow

and you had plenty of time to see it was making double Bottom and buy.

1904—February High 58c per bushel, under Old Bottoms and at resistance levels, and a safe place to buy.

1904—April Low 42c. A higher bottom and a buying level. Note old Bottoms and Tops around this level.

1904—August High 55c. A third lower Tops, and a selling level.

1904—October Low 44c.

1905—January Low 44c. Still making higher Bottoms and moving in a narrow trading range.

1905—March and May High 49½. Failing to reach 50c per bushel was an indication of weakness and the fact that the last High came in May, the month of seasonal Highs, was an indication to sell out and sell short.

1905—July Low 42½.

1905—October Low 42½c.

1906—January Low 42½. Three quarters at the same low level and still higher than the previous months, making double and triple Bottoms, which was an indication of higher prices.

1906—June High 53½c. Higher than the previous months, but failed to reach the Top of August, 1904, was a sign for selling and a reaction.

1906—July Low 42c. This was three years with Bottoms made around this Low Level and each level had been higher since 1902. Indication of increased buying power and a support point to buy for rally. When there are triple Tops and triple Bottoms greater advance in prices is indicated. At this low level you would figure the last range from 69c to 38½c, and when the half-way point was crossed at 53¾ you would figure it was going very much higher. There was a top in June, 1906, at 53½, near this half-way point. Crossing this after such a long period of time indicated very much higher prices. The market advanced and crossed other resistance levels and continued to work higher with very small reactions.

1908—March High 68c. A double Tops against December, 1901, and a selling level for a reaction.

1908—May Low 55c. Holding above the half-way point and above old Tops and Bottoms, a buying level for rally. A rapid advance followed.

1908—September High 83c. First time prices have been this high since 1892. Note resistance levels around this price and 82½c was important because 80c was one-half between 20c a bushel and 140, and 80c was 300% advance on the base or Low of 19½c, making this selling Level for a reaction. A sharp reaction followed.

1908—October Low 59½c. Important resistance point and a Higher Bottom. Rally followed.

1909—March High 59c. An old Top Level and a selling point.

1909—May Low 58c. Double Bottom not getting 3c under previous Bottoms, a point for rally.

1909—June High 75½c. One year from previous High and at a selling level.

1909—August Low 52½c. At the half-way point and the support point, and the only time in history that prices of corn up to this time made Low in August, running opposite to the seasonal trend making this the place to buy, expecting higher prices in December opposite the seasonal trend.

1910—March High 70½c. Lower than previous Tops, but was one-half of 140, making this a selling level.

1910—July Low 52½c. Double Bottom again and buying level. A quick rally followed.

1910—August High 56c. A lower Top and selling level.

1910—October Low 47c.

1911—January and April Low 46½c. This was triple Bottom at the one-third point of 140 and above 125% on the base of 19½. Making this a buying level, especially as prices held for nine months; when prices crossed 52½ again you should buy more.

1911—August High 68c. Note old Tops and Bottoms around 68 and 69c, and August is the month for a Tops on corn for change in seasonal trend, sell out and sell short for a reaction.

1912—January Low 62c and 200% advance on the Bottoms of 19½c and 60c being two-thirds between 70c and $1.40, making this an important support level. A rally followed.

1912—June High 83c. A Double Bottom against June, 1908, and a selling level. When a double Bottom of this kind occurs it is safe to sell short and you should then figure the percentage point between 19½c and 83c. The half-way point would be 51¼c, and half of 83 or 50% decline would be 41½c. From the Top at 83, a 25% reaction from the last Low of 46½c would be the first indication of lower prices. A decline followed.

1912—October Low 47c per bushel. Back to the old Bottoms, making this double and triple Bottoms, prices held in a narrow trading range for several weeks, in fact for more than two months, this would be the place to buy for a rally.

1913—January Low 48c. Still near Low Levels. January is the seasonal month to expect a change in trends and Bottoms, therefore this would be a safe buying level. Advance was rapid and reaction small.

1913—September High 75½. An old Top Level and selling level. Because September is the month for seasonal change in trends, especially as most Tops come out in August. A reaction followed.

1914—April Low 64c. Note that one-half of 47 to 83 was 65c and there were other important resistance levels around 65c, making this a buying level. War broke out in July and a rapid advance followed.

1914—September High 79½c. Under the old Tops of 83. Reaction followed.

1914—October Low 68½c. The Higher Bottom indicated higher prices.

1915—February High 83c. The third time at this level. February opposite the month for seasonal change, showed High at a time when prices should have been low. Therefore, you would watch for an indication for Tops, sell out and sell short. Prices broke back under the half-way point of a previous move, indicating weakness. Sharp decline followed.

1915—October Low 55c per bushel. Holding above 50c a bushel was a sign of strength and making Tops in October, the month for seasonal Lows, was important and you should have bought because war has a bullish effect on prices of corn and everything else. Advance followed.

1916—March High 81½. A still lower Tops than February, 1915. A selling level. A reaction followed.

1916—May Low 63c per bushel. After a series of Bottoms and Tops around this level. This was a natural half-way point or support level and a place to buy, especially as prices were running opposite seasonal trends, making lows in the month of May when most Highs are made.

Prices holding above the Lows of 1915, indicated strength. Half-way point from the last High at 83 and 63 was 72. This point was crossed and prices indicated higher. For the fourth time prices crossed the 83c level. Our rule says that when they reach the same Tops the fourth time they nearly always go through and they did go through with a rapid move upwards. Prices crossed all levels since the Civil War, crossing $1.00 per bushel. and the next point was Tops at $1.12, then the old Tops of $1.40, but none of these stopped the market for anything except a moderate reaction.

1917—June High $1.62 for May corn. From the Old Tops of 83 add 100%, which gives $1.66. To the last high of March, 1916, of 81½c add 100% on this tops, which would give $1.63, a possible Top and selling level. A rapid decline followed from this extreme high. The Government stopped trading in wheat, but trading in corn continued.

1917—July Low 103. From 20c per bushel to $1.62 would make a 50c decline 91c. Holding above $1.00 per bushel was an indication of strength and higher prices. Advance followed and prices continued to work higher.

1918—October Low $1.08 per bushel. Higher Bottom than 1917. An

1918—August High 166½. This was the month for seasonal change in trend and the month for Tops. Prices failed to get 5c per bushel higher than Tops of June, 1917, an indication of weakness and sign of a reaction. Sharp reaction followed.

indication of support. Advance was resumed and prices advanced 25% over the last extreme High and later crossed the extreme High of $1.67, indicating higher prices. After crossing this level the next important point would be around $2.00 per bushel, a 100% advance on the price of $1.00 per bushel.

1919—September High $1.99. Failing to reach the price of $2.00 per bushel showed that there was good selling. When prices reached this level, you would figure the resistance points from the last Low point of $1.08 and then figure the resistance point from 19½c per bushel to 199. From 47c per bushel, and also from 41c per bushel, where there was a series of Bottoms. All of these indicated important resistance levels on the way down.

1919—January Low $1.15, still making Higher Bottoms and showing that the main trend was still up, that corn was good to buy for another advance. Prices worked higher, crossing 25% of the last High and later to 50%.

1920—May High $1.97. Final Tops and a Double Top, under the Previous Tops, making this a safe place to sell short, because May is the month for a seasonal trend change, and where most Tops are made. Figure from $1.50 to $1.99, first using the 25% of this and then 50%. Fifty per cent level was broken, indicating much lower prices. Later prices broke lower than $1.15 and then broke the lows of $1.03 and $1.08, and broke $1.00 per bushel, breaking back 50% under the High selling price, indicating weakness and lower prices.

After years of high prices in corn, and increase in production, and with speculators loaded up because they had gotten used to higher prices in corn, it was but natural that a drastic decline would follow. Prices of all commodities declined fast under heavy liquidation. The demand for cash corn was small and the lower prices declined the more the selling increased.

Prices continued to decline in 1921, with nothing but small rallies, October low of 50¼c per bushel, breaking all low levels with the exception of the lows in 1911 and 1912, when 50c was a natural support and buying level, and a 75% decline from $1.99 would give 49¾, making this a natural support level or buying point after such a drastic decline. 49¾ was one-fourth of $1.99. The last High of March 1921 was 76¾. This would make 63 the half-way point of the last move, and a rally was indicated,

1921—with still another Top in 1921, June, at 67. This would make 58 the half-way point of this move and crossing this indicated higher.

1922—February High 70. Note 68⅝ was one-eighth of $1.99 to 50 and 66⅜ was one-third of $1.99, making this a selling level for reaction. 50% advance on 50 would give 75, making this an important point to sell for reaction.

1922—April Low 55½. Down to Old Bottoms.

1922—August High 64½. Under important resistance level and at one-fourth of 19½ to $1.99. A reaction followed.

1922—November Low 55½. Making a Double Bottom and a strong
buying level. This was the secondary reaction, making it safer
to buy. From 50 to 70 the half-way point was 60. There was
one Top at 64½ and one Top at 65½. Crossing these levels
indicated higher. The advance continued, prices crossed 70, the
old High, and later crossed 76¾, the High of March, 1921, indicating higher prices.

1923—June High 84½. This was an Old Top and Bottom level.
Natural resistance point. 75% advance on 50 would give 87½.
Market reaching High in the month of June, the month of the
seasonal change in trend for Tops. You should have sold out
and gone short.

1923—July Low 54½. The same low as January, 1923. A buying
point because it was down to resistance levels. From 64½ to
84½ would make 74½ the half-way point. Crossing this level
indicated stronger position and, when it advanced above it, it
stayed above it. Should have bought more at this level. Later
prices crossed the Tops of 84½, showing strong uptrend.

1924—June High 99½ was one-half of 199, the high selling price, making
this a resistance level.
July Low 84. Down to OLD TOPS levels and resistance points
and a buying level. The advance was resumed and prices advanced, crossing $1.00 and later crossing $1.09¼, the 50% point
between 19½ and 199.

1924—August High 122. Note 124½ was the half-way point between
199 and 50c, making this a selling level.
October Low 101. Holding above $1.00 was a strong indication
for buying. Note that 105⅞ was three-eighths of 50 to 199,
making this the buying level. Advance was resumed.

1924—December High 133. December was the month for BOTTOMS
but at this time the market was running opposite seasonal trends
due to a very short crop. When prices were high in December,
a reaction was indicated. Note that:

> 132⅝ was two-thirds of 199,
> 131⅝ was five-eighths between 199 and 19½,

making this a selling level for reaction.

1925—January Low 103½, a DOUBLE BOTTOM, the place to buy for
another rally.

1925—March High 137, not 5c above the TOP of December. Note that
139½ was two-thirds of 19½ to 199, making this a selling level.
and 137 was the natural resistance level as 37½% on $1.00 gives
137½ as the selling level. Here you figure the last low 1.03½ to
137. The first time the market broke back 25% of this indicated
lower and breaking back one-half of this move or breaking 120
indicating lower Corn prices broke back under this level and later
broke the DOUBLE BOTTOM at 104, indicating a further decline.

1925—April Low 92c. This was under 99½, which was one-half of 199 and one-third of 50 to 199 was 99⅝. Prices crossed these resistance levels and crossed 100, indicating higher prices.

1925—June High 120. Failing to make 124½, the 50% point between 50c and 199, was an indication of weakness, also five-eighths of 199 was 124⅜ and 114½ was the half-way point between 92 and 137. After prices made TOP in June time to sell out and sell short. Market declined fast. Rallies were very small. A larger crop following a year of very short crop helped to depress prices.

1926—January Low 71½ down to OLD TOP and BOTTOM levels for a rally.

1926—March High 88. Note 87¼ is an important point between 50c and 199, making this a selling level. Reaction followed.

1926—May Low 67c. Higher than January and July, 1923, when last Bottoms were made. There were several resistance levels around this point, making this a buying point for a rally. From 88 to 67 the half-way point was 78. This point was crossed and higher prices were indicated. The advance followed.

1926—August High 87½ failing to reach $1.00 was a sign of weakness and this was OLD TOPS AND BOTTOMS levels anyway, 99½ being one-half of 199, making this a selling level. The fact that August was the month for tops and seasonal trends was a definite indication to sell out and sell short. Prices continued to work lower, subject to normal rallies.

1927—April Low 69. A double BOTTOM and a higher BOTTOM on a secondary reaction and a safer place to buy. The last high was 97½, the last extreme low 67, making the half-way point 82½ and one-fourth point 74½. The market crossed both of these resistance levels and moved up fast, later crossing the top at 97½ and crossing $1.00, putting the market in a very strong position.

1927—September High 120. Just under one-half of 50c to 199, also five-eighths of 199 was 124⅜. There were other OLD TOP levels and one at exactly the same point in August, 1924, making this a double TOP and selling level. The indication was stronger because it came out in September, a month for seasonal trend. A sharp, quick decline followed.

1927—October Low 87. Back to OLD TOP and BOTTOM and support levels according to resistance points, 87¼ being one-fourth of 50c to 199. A rally followed.

1928—June High 122. Same high as June, 1927, and a natural selling level. Also note that 109¼ was one-half of 19½c to $1.99, making this a selling point and also because it came out in a month for Tops according to seasonal trend was another indication to sell out and sell short. A sharp, quick decline followed.

1928—July Low 76½. Down to OLD BOTTOM and TOP resistance levels and a natural resistance level. Time to buy for rally.

1929—March High 103½. Lower than previous TOP and at OLD TOP AND BOTTOM level, a selling level. Decline followed.

1929—April Low 78. Higher BOTTOMS than July, 1928. Buy for rally. The advance was resumed.

1929—September Final High 109½, a third lower TOP and exactly at the half-way point between the two great extremes 199 High and 19½ Low. This was a safe, sure selling level, especially as this was the month for a seasonal high and change in trend.

1930—April Low 72c. This was a natural support and buying level and higher than previous buying level. Rally followed.

1930—June High 88c. Natural resistance level, old TOP and BOTTOM levels, and a selling level. A reaction followed.

1930—July Low 72c. There was a rapid advance in the month of July, prices advancing to 103½ up to OLD selling levels coming out in a month for a TOP according to change in trend. Note 105⅞ is three-eighths of 50 to 199 and this TOP was lower than the last High of November, 1929, making a selling level. The main trend was down because all tops from 1929 were lower, and 1919 High 199, May 1920 High 197, September 1920 High 170, March 1925 High 136, September 1927 High 122, June 1928 High 112, December 1929 High 110, July 1930 High 103½. All lower Tops, showing this was a bear market. Commodity prices were gradually working lower. Stocks were declining rapidly and conditions were panicky in 1930.

1930—October Low 66c, down to DOUBLE BOTTOMS and just above the lows of 1923. This was a buying point for rally. Especially since October was one of the months for seasonal changes.

1930—December High 89½. Opposite the seasonal trend making TOPS in a month that most BOTTOMS are made in, and at a resistance point and selling level where many OLD TOPS AND BOTTOMS have been made. This was a point to sell out and sell short. A decline followed. 50% of the last move was broken, later the BOTTOM of 72c was broken. Prices declined faster.

1931—Conditions throughout the country were getting worse. Stocks were declining, everything was on the toboggan. Corn had very small rallies from time to time, breaking the old support levels of 64, later breaking the support levels at 65.

1931—April Low 51½ or 2c above 1921. Holding above 50c a bushel was a natural point for rally.

1931—September High 61½c at OLD BOTTOM and TOP levels and a selling point. Main trend was down and prices continued to decline. Broke through low level of 51½c and then broke the bottoms at 50c, indicating weakness and lower prices.

1932—April Low 27½c. Back to the lows of 1897. A natural point for at least a rally.

1932—August High 40½c, a 100% advance on the low of 19½, August being the month for TOPS according to seasonal trend, the market still showed main trend down. Therefore, you should have sold out and sold short.

1933—February Low 27½c for May corn.

Extreme low for corn was reached December, 1932. Low 20¾ for the December option. 1¼c higher than the extreme Low of 19½c made in 1896 and 20c Low in September, 1861, making DOUBLE BOTTOMS many long years apart. Corn at these low levels was below the cost of production and was a safe, sure investment, to buy and hold for several years to come until conditions became normal and prices advanced again to normal level. A study of the quarterly chart, the monthly chart and the weekly chart at these low levels gave a definite indication that prices were making final BOTTOMS. First definite indication of the rapid advance after the market became over-sold was when prices crossed 30c per bushel or advanced above the high of previous BOTTOMS around 27½ and 28. Here you should have bought more corn.

President Roosevelt was inaugurated in March, 1933. In April the country went off the Gold Standard. This caused a rapid advance in all commodities.

When this Low level was reached, you should have made up resistance charts from the following secondary TOP to the extreme low level: 137½, 122, 112, 104 and the last High December 1930, 89½, also the first point to watch was the last High March 1932 at 43, and from August 1932 40½ to the extreme High crossing 50% of these last ranges.

1933—August High 82½. This was the month to sell out and sell short because it was the month for tops according to seasonal trend. The market had had a big advance, and was at resistance levels at all of these Tops. You should consider the 50% reaction from 137, which would give 68½, 122 would give 60, 112 would give 56c, 104 would give 52c. At 82½ the market had advanced 300% on the base or low level, which was a big advance in a short period of time. One-half of the high of 82½ would give 41¾, one-half between 23¾ and 82½, the high and low on May corn, would give 53⅛ as the half-way point. A 100% advance on 23¼, the low level, would be 46½. Still using the old base of 19½, extreme low, 50% advance would be 39½. All of these points should be kept in mind and watched as the market moved between High and Low Levels.

1933—October Low 44c. Note 43 was one-eighth between 19½ and 1.99, making this a natural support point for rally after such a drastic decline.

1933—November High 56 at Old Bottom and Top Levels. Reaction followed. The main trend was still down, the market holding under the important half-way point.

1934—April Low 40c. Over a 50% decline from August High at 82½ and down to natural support levels. This was big *secondary decline* from the first sharp advance, making it a safe buying level. When prices crossed 50c per bushel they were in a stronger position. Later crossed 50% of the last advance and indicated a stronger position.

1934—June High 63. A moderate reaction followed July Low of 56½, old Tops and Bottom levels and natural support level. Prices crossed the half-way point at 61 and later crossed the Tops at 63, indicating much higher prices.

1934—December High 93½. Making Tops opposite the seasonal trend. the place to sell short for a reaction.

1935—January Low 76¼. This was the month for Bottoms, according to seasonal trends, and a rally followed.

1935—March High 92½. A lower Top and a Selling place.

1935—April High 92. Making the third Lower Top. Nearer the time for seasonal Tops, which was the place to sell out long corn and sell short. Watch the half-way point between 76 and 93½. When this was broken it indicated lower prices. A fast decline followed.

1935—July Low 56½. Down to an old Bottom and Top Level. Note that 58½ was the half-way point with a 50% reaction point between 93½ and 23¼, making this a safe, sure buying level. The market remained in a narrow trading range for several months, making slightly higher Bottoms and receiving better support. This was the year of dust storms and a severe drought. Corn crops were the smallest for many years. A rapid advance followed. Prices crossed the half-way point between 93½ and 56, indicated higher, and later crossed Tops of 93, advancing rapidly.

1937—May Final High 140. A double Top against March, 1925, when prices were 137. Note that 139½ was two-thirds of 19½c to $1.99 and 133⅛ was five-eighths between 50c and $1.99, making this a safe place to sell out long and sell short. Top was reached in the month of May, the month when most seasonal trend Tops are made. You would sell September or December corn at this time when the prices of these options were high. You would know the trend was down, even though these options were at much lower levels, and they were a short sale. From this Top, 140, you would figure your future resistance levels and percentages. One-half of this being 70, one-fourth being 35c and one-eighth being 17½c. Also figure from 20¾, extreme low in December, 1932, to 140 to get important resistance levels.

1937—October Low 56½. Down to Old Bottom Levels and the fact that there was a double Bottom, it was a natural resistance point. Three-eighths of 140 was 52½, and one-fourth of 140 to 20¾ was 50¾. Holding above these levels was an indication of strength, and a rally was indicated, but October was the month for a seasonal change in trend.

1938—March High 63. Note 63¾ was one-third between 140 and 20¾ and there were many old Bottoms and Top levels around this price. A reaction followed and rallies were very small.

1939—January Low 47c.   Just under 50, a natural support and resistance level.

1939—March High 54.   Under old Bottoms and at old Tops.   Sell short.

1939—April Low 47.   The market held for several months at these low levels.

1939—May High 51¾.   Very small rally and at resistance levels, and under previous tops.   Showing weakness.

1939—July Final Low 42c.   Two cents above the lowest of April, 1934. One-eighth between 19c and 199 is 43, and 46⅝ was one-third of 140, the extreme high level.   A 50% advance on extreme low of 20¾ would be 41½, making this a strong support level and buying level, especially as prices came out opposite the seasonal trend.

1939—September High 63¾.   Again an old Top and Bottom level and at the last top of December and March, 1938.   Note 63¾ was one-third between 20¾ and 104, making this a selling level for reaction and especially when September was the month for Tops according to seasonal trends.

1939—October Low 51c.   Down to Old Top Levels and a resistance point.   From 42 to 63½, and 53 was a natural resistance or the 50% point, and a buying level.   Holding above 50c per bushel was a sign of strength and indicated higher prices.

1939—December High 61¼.   A lower Top.   Running opposite to seasonal trends, and a sale for reaction.

1940—May High 69c.   An old Top and Bottom Level, and note that 70 was one-half of 140, the highest selling point, making this a resistance level.   May is the month for Tops according to seasonal trend.   Therefore, you would sell out and sell short.

1940—July Low 55c.   Higher Bottom than the previous bottoms in May. After the High in the early part of May a sharp decline followed. Before the May option expired prices declined to 54.   Note that 61 was the halfway point between 69 and 50.   When prices crossed this 50% reaction point, they indicated higher.

1941—March High 68¾.   This was a double Top and a moderate reaction followed.   Down to 63c, then prices advanced, crossed the Tops of 64, later crossing the Tops of August, 1937 at 74, indicating higher.

1941—September 12 High 91½ for May Corn.   Note that 93¼ was two-thirds of 140, and that 95⅜ was five-eighths from 140 to 20¾.   Also note 1934 Tops, 93½ and 92½ and 92.   The market became dull and narrow and moved up and down around this Top level, indicating it was making Top, giving you plenty of time to sell out long and go short.

1941—October 16 Low 72¾.   This day corn broke the limit.   A wide open break.   Prices were down to old tops and bottoms and support levels.   Note that 70 was one-half of 140 and 74 was three-eighths of 199; and from the last low of 42 to 93½ note that 67 was one-half point or 50% reaction. Holding above this indicated higher. From the last Low in 1940 of 54 to 91¾ the half-way point was 73, making this a natural support point and buying level for rally. The advance was resumed and, up to this writing, Ocotber 30, 1941, May corn has rallied to 83c, or about half of the last decline.

It is important at this time to check resistance levels, and keep up all important resistance levels from extreme low to extreme high, 140, for May corn, and then from 42 up to 91½, and from 23½ on May corn to 91¾.

Should May corn break below 67, one-half between 42 and 91½, it would indicate weakness and lower prices. The upper resistance levels are 87¼, one-fourth of 50c to 199. Also, 87½ is five-eighths of 140, the last extreme high. May corn should meet selling around 83 to 84, and react again in December, 1941, or January, 1942 when prices should be lower according to seasonal trends.

If prices are lower around this time, then expect them to work higher in April and May, 1942, to the month when seasonal change in trend is indicated.

The last high was May, 1937, and the five years will be May, 1942. This will be very important for a change in trend. May was extreme high and extreme low, both in the same month. Watch for important changes in trends in the months seasonal trend has been made in the past, or when top Bottoms have been reached. The fact that extreme lows were reached in October, December, 1932, and February, 1933, will make January and February, 1942, important for a change in trend.

As long as May corn can hold above 70c per bushel, or one-half the extreme high of 140, it is in a stronger position. Breaking back under 70⅜, one-half of 20¾ and 140 would be the first indication of weakness.

Keep up the weekly high and low charts, the monthly and also the daily high and low charts, when corn is very active; it will help you to determine the change in trends. Do not fail to always keep up a quarterly high and low chart on corn and study this in connection with other charts, as it will give you the most important change in trend, because the quarterly gives the seasonal changes each year, as it runs three months covering the four seasonal periods of the year. Remember to follow my rule: "NEVER GUESS." Apply my rules and determine tops and bottoms. Do not trade on hope or fear, but face facts and follow the rules and you will make profits.

RYE

Rye is traded in on the Chicago Board of Trade. The fluctuations are in cents per bushel. A contract for rye is 5,000 bushels. The minimum fluctuation is ⅛c, which is $12.50 on a contract. An advance

or decline of 1c would make a profit or loss of $50 on each contract.
The commission for buying and selling rye is $12.50 per contract.
The margin requirements on rye run from $300 per contract up, depending on the price of rye.

SEASONAL CHANGES

MONTHS WHEN EXTREME HIGH AND LOW HAVE BEEN REACHED:

	Highs	Lows			*Highs*	Lows
January	17	7	July		10	6
February	7	8	August		7	19
March	4	10	September		10	6
April	6	10	October		8	7
May	15	5	November		10	16
June	7	10	December		8	10

From the above you will see that the greatest number of high levels on Rye have been reached in the months of January and May, and if you will go over the records you will find that the most rapid advances and most of the extreme high prices were reached in the month of May. Therefore, you should watch the months of January and May for tops in the change in trend, especially if Rye has been advancing for three months or more.

The next important months to watch for tops or high levels are July, September and November.   From 1896 to 1941, during each of these months, high levels were reached ten times, making these months average the same number of tops.

The next months in importance for tops are October and December. Tops have been reached eight times in these months during the past 45 years.

The next months in importance for tops are February, June and August.   Tops have been reached in these months seven times during the past 45 years.   April next, six times.

March is the month when Highs have been reached only four times during the past 45 years.

From this you can see that if the market is advancing in March, and the main trend is up, it is not likely to reach top until May.   Then when it is advancing during the Summer most tops are reached in the month of July.

When low is reached in August, then you can expect tops to come in September or October and as late as November.

The seasonal trend runs up from January or February to May, then down to August and up until October or November, then down until January or February.   This is the natural seasonal trend.

Suppose that Rye or any other commodity follows the seasonal change and makes high in May for three consecutive years.   You can then expect the fourth year to be low in May or prices to run opposite the seasonal changes.   The same with the month of August.   If prices are low for three consecutive years in August you can expect the next year or fourth year that prices will be high or run opposite to the seasonal trend.   In some cases prices will only make top according to the seasonal trend for two years, then be opposite in the third year.

SEASONAL LOWS.   During the past 45 years the months when extreme low prices have been reached are listed above.

You will see that the most lows have been reached in August.   Therefore, when Rye has been declining for several months and reaches low in the month of August, it is safe to buy for a rally.

November is the next most important month for lows on Rye. Sixteen lows have been reached in this month.   If the market has been declining for several months and is low in November you can buy for a rally that should last until January anyway.

In March, April, June and December, Lows have been reached 10 times each during the past 45 years.

February and October are next in importance.

You will notice that during the past 45 years lows have been reached in the month of May only five times.   This is because May is the month for tops, and bottoms do not come out very often opposite to the seasonal trend.

The next months when the smallest amount of lows have been reached are July and September.   Only six lows have been reached in these months.

January is the month that shows the greatest number of high prices. Therefore, January shows only seven lows during the 45 years.   However, when prices have reached high in September, October or November and declined in January or February, you should watch the market closely for a change in trend.

Remember to study all the rules and watch all of the indications.   If you overlook one rule or one important point, it may cause you to miss the top or bottom and a big opportunity for making profits.

HOW TO FORECAST RYE BY PERCENTAGE OF LOWEST PRICES AND HIGHEST PRICES

Rye follows the general trend of wheat and other grains, but the high and low prices on Rye are made in accordance with previous tops and bottoms of Rye.   Check the time period from each extreme low and extreme high to get the time factors on Rye, using all the rules that we apply to wheat or any other commodity to forecast the trend of Rye. Never judge that the trend has changed until you get a definite indication by crossing of resistance levels or changes, according to time periods. Do not overlook the seasonal changes in Rye and the months when the most highs have been made and the most lows have been made.   Rye seasonal changes run very close to wheat seasonal changes, as you will find by going over past records.

1896—August Low 28c per bushel.   This was the extreme low for Rye and the lowest prices reached since the Civil War days.

1897—April Low 30c.   A higher bottom and a higher support level, indicating higher prices. We take 28c per bushel as the base to figure future prices on and future buying and selling levels (refer to tables showing the different percentages on the low price of 28c per bushel). For example, 56c is 100% advance on 28. 84c is 200% advance on 28. 112 is 300% advance on 28 and 140 is 400% advance. 168 is 500% advance. 196 is 600% advance and 224 is 700% advance. These even 100% advances on the base are of course the most important resistance levels and important for buying and selling points. The next important percentage is 14c or the 50% advance on 28c.

50% advance on 28c would be 42, the next would be 70c, 98c, 126, 154, 184 and 210. All of these points are 50% or 150%, 250%, etc. However, watch the market around any of these important resistance levels, especially around the one-third and two-thirds and around the three-fourths point or 75% on the base of 28c. The 75% point is 49c, 77c, 105, 133, 161, 189 and 217.

After the double bottom in 1896 and 1897, Rye prices started to advance and make higher bottoms.

1898—June Low 41c.

1898—May High 75c. Note that 74.66 was two-thirds point on the base, and 77 was three-fourths point on the 200 percentage line and 75 is ¾ of 1.00, a natural selling level, as we referred to before. After the Top was made at 75, one-half of this high selling price would be 37½, and a 50% decline between 75 and 28c would give 51½.

1898—August Low 41c, a double Bottom against the June Low. Note that 42 is 50% on 28, making this a Resistance Level and a Buying Level.

1899—March Low 50, July Low 51, November Low 49. The market was making progressive Higher Bottoms.

1899—May High 62. Note that 63 is 125% on 28c, making this a Resistance Level.

1899—November Low 49c. 49c is 75% on 28c and 50c is always a Resistance Level, being one-half of $1.00.

1900—August Low 48c. Still holding around the same Low Levels of 1899 and getting support indicated a rally.

1900—January High 67c. Note that 66½ was the Resistance Level, or three-eighths on the 200 or 300% base, and 66 2/3 of 1.00 is always a natural Buying or Selling Level or Resistance Level.

1903—January Low 48, April Low 48, December Low 50½. The market getting support around the 50c Level and holding these Levels for a period of years indicated higher prices.

1903—September High 60c. This was just under the Top at 62 and under the Top at 67, making this a Selling Level.

1904—April Low 66, a Higher Bottom and Higher Support Level, indicating higher prices.

1904—February High 77, May High 78, November High 81c, making three Tops during the year in a range of 4c per bushel. After the first Top in February at 77, you should watch prices around these Levels, especially because 77 is 175% on 28c, making this a Resistance Level and a Selling Level.

1905—March High 78½. Again up around old Top Levels and a sale for reaction. The market had a moderate reaction then went higher.

1905—May High 84c. 84c is 200% on the base of 28, making this a Resistance Level and a Selling Level, and from 28c the price was up 56c per bushel. At the last Low of 50 cents prices were up 34c. From the last Low at 48c was 36c advance, all of which advances are Resistance Points.

After the High in May, 1905, which was seasonal High, the seasonal reaction followed.

1905—August Low 57½. Note the following points: From 78 to 28 the 50%, or the half-way point was 53, from 28 to 81 the half-way point was 54½, and from 28 to 84 the half-way point was 58c, making 57½c around this Level a logical Buying point for rally.

1906—August Low 55½. Still holding the old Bottom and not breaking 3c lower, making it a Buy around this Level.

1906—December High 65. Up around Old Top and Bottom Levels.

1907—January Low 60. A Higher Bottom and at old Tops Levels, making this a natural support point.

1907—September High 91c. This was the Highest Level for years and when prices crossed 65 and later crossed the High Levels around 80, you would expect a further advance. Note that 91 is 225% on 28, and 50% on the last low at 60 would give 90.

1907—October Low 72c, a 19c reaction. 70c is a natural support and Resistance Point because it is one of the half-way points or 150% on 28c.

1908—January 87c, making a lower Bottom just 3c above the Top of 1905, and 87½ being a Natural Resistance Level, or 225% on 28c.

1908—April 74c, making a Higher Bottom than 1907 and showing support.

1908—May High 86, a Double Top and a Selling Level.

1908—November 73, a Double Bottom against April Low. A Buying Level for rally. Note the Highs in 1908 were January, 87; May, 86; and July, 80, Double Tops and then a Lower Top.

1909—June High 91, a double Top against September 1908 and a Selling Level. 1/3 of 91c, the High Point, would give 60 as an important support point.

From November Low 67 a rally followed.

1910—January High 82c. Note that 79c is ½ between 91c and 67c, and there have been several old Tops around this Level, making this a natural Selling Level for a reaction.

1910—May Low 74c. An old support Level and one of the series of Bottoms and Tops. A Rally followed.

1910—May Low 74c. An old support Level and one of the series of Bottoms and Tops. A Rally followed.

1910—July High 80c. A Lower Top and an indication of Lower prices, and at a natural Selling Level.

1910—August Low 72c. This was ½ between 55c and 91, or 73 was the ½ point. By looking over the chart you will see a series of old Tops and Bottoms around the 72c level, making this a buying level.

    Here it is well to not overlook the fact that after the Low in August 1906 the market had been making Higher Bottom. The Low in August 1907 was 69 cents, and the Low in August 1909 was 67c, the Low in August 1910 was 72c, over a period of three years time, making a Double Bottom and then in the third year making a Higher Bottom, indicating higher prices. The advance started and when prices crossed the Tops at 80 and 82 it was an indication of much Higher Prices and you should have bought more Rye. Later prices crossed the Double Tops at 91c, an indication of much higher prices. If we take the percentages of the last low at 72 and add 50% to this, we get 108 as a possible Top.

1911—May High 113. Note that 112 was a 300% advance on 28 cents per bushel, making this a natural Selling Level. Also 12½% on 1.00 is 112½. At this Top you would figure all of the percentage points, from 28c, the base Low to 113, from the Lows at 48c, the Low at 55c, the Low at 60c, and from the Low at 67c and the last Low at 72c, the last half-way point would be between 72c and 113. A 25% decline from the last Low to High would be the first indication of lower prices. The range from 72c to 1.13 was 41c. 10¼c would be a 25% reaction. This would give 102¾. Breaking this Level indicated Lower Prices and a sharp decline followed.

1911—July Low 81c. Down to a series of Old Top Levels. Old Bottoms becoming Tops made this a buy for reaction and especially as this was a natural support point, being 187½% on 28c per bushel. A Rally followed.

1911—November High $1.00. Natural Selling Level. Note that 101½ was 262½% on the base of 28c and 97c was a 50% Rally or ½ between 113 and 81, making this a logical Selling Level. Then you would consider the half-way point of the 50% reaction between 81 and 1.00. This would be 90½c. When prices broke 90½c, they indicated lower and a rapid decline followed, later breaking Low at 81c indicated the main trend strongly down and the market in a very weak position.

1912—February Low 93. A very weak Rally to April at 96½c. After this when the market broke 90c per bushel it declined fast.

1912—December Low 58c per bushel. Note that a 50% decline from 113, the high point, would give 56½ as an actual support Level.

In going back over the records you can find a series of Tops and Bottoms around 58c, making this Bottom for Rally.

1913—January High 65½c. February Low 58. A Double Bottom and a place to buy for Rally. The fact that the market held above 56½, the half of the high selling point, showed strength.

1914—August High 70c. Failed to reach the old Bottom Level at 72, a sign of weakness, and 70 was a natural selling point, being 150% on the base of 28c per bushel. A decline followed.

1914—January Low 60c, February Low 64c, March Low 59c.

1914—May High 67c per bushel, under old Tops and Bottoms and lower than the previous Tops, making this a Selling Level. 66½ was 137½% on the base of 28 cents.

1914—July Low 55c. This was a final drive just before the war started and the market got support just 1½c under the half-way point or 50% down from 113. Note also in August 1906, the last low was 55c, making this a Double Bottom and a Buying Level. The war broke out and war is always bullish on Rye, as well as everything else, and an advance followed. You would here figure the percentage point between 55 and 113, 12½% would give 62¼ and 25% was 69½. Prices advanced rapidly and when they crossed 69½ were above the Top of May 1914, and when they crossed 70 cents were above the Top of August 1913, showing a strong uptrend and the advance was fast.

1914—August High 101, a Double Top against November 1911 and $1.00 is always a Selling Level for a reaction at least.

1914—October Low 88, a natural reaction of 13c per bushel and 87½ was the natural support point, being 212½% on the basis of 28c per bushel. 50% on the Bottom of 55 would give 82½. The fact that the market held so far above this level was an indication of great strength and ½ between 113 and 55 cents was 84c and after once getting above the half-way point and holding above it indicated higher prices and that prices were going back to the old Tops or higher.

1915—February High 131. Note 129½ and 133.66 were percentage points on the base that were important for resistance and Selling Level. The market had advanced 76c per bushel and 75c or ¾ of a dollar is a natural Resistance point. From the last low of 88c, if you add 50% to the base it gives 132 as an actual Resistance point or Selling Level. Never overlook the fact to watch 50% advance on any Tops or Bottoms or 50% decline from any Tops. These are always important points to buy or sell against. After the Top was reached at 131 the first important point to watch would be a 25% decline of the last run from 88c to 131. This would give 120½, breaking this would indicate lower. The next important point would be a 50% reaction of 109½ and we always watch old Tops and old Bottoms for Resistance and never overlook the fact that after the first sharp decline there must be a *secondary* Rally.

1915—March Low 112, down to the old Top of May 1911, and a buying point. A secondary Rally followed.

1915—May High 122. This was a 50% Rally of the first decline and a natural point to sell short. Prices declined fast and when they broke 112 and 109 indicated lower prices.

1915—September Low 91c. Down to old Top Levels and holding above the last Low Level with a natural support and buying point.

1915—October High 107. From 122, the last High, to the Low of 91c, gives a half-way point of 106½.

1915—November Low 94, a Higher Bottom and a natural support point. A buy for Rally.

1916—January High 105, a Lower Top and a short sale.

1916—February Low 90, a Double Bottom, in fact a triple bottom, because October 1915 last Low was 88c per bushel. Remember that fast advances follow triple Bottoms or triple Tops. Prices crossed 1.00, indicated much higher, and later crossed the Top at 105 and 107, which indicated great strength. Crossed the half-way point from 90 and 131, which was 110½, indicating much higher, and later crossed 131, showing a strong uptrend.

1916—November High 153.

1916—December Low 130, back to the old Top. A Buying Level. A rapid advance followed, prices crossed the High of 153, and a runaway advance followed.

1916—May High 245. Note 250 is a natural selling price or 2½ times $1.00 per bushel and 700% on 28c, Bottom, gave 250. A sharp decline followed lasting three months.

1916—August Low 165. Note that 164½ is 487% on the base of 28c per bushel and 162½ is ⅝ of the second hundred and is also a natural Resistance point. This was a decline of 80c per bushel. The last Low in October 1914 of 88c per bushel to the high of 245 would give a half-way point of 166½, making 165 a safe buying point with a stop loss order.

September High 192, November Low 176, reacting about half the advance. Later prices crossed the TOP at 192 and crossed $2.00, indicating much higher, and later crossed 245.

1918—March Final High 295. Note $3.00 is always a natural selling level. You would watch for selling around this price. The last low was 152 and adding 100% on this would give 304. From this extreme High Level the decline was rapid.

1918—August Low 155. Almost a 50% decline from the High Selling Point.

1918—November High 175. Back under old BOTTOM LEVELS of November 1917 and a natural SELLING LEVEL. A Rapid Decline followed. Prices broke the Bottom at 155 and broke the half-way point of 295.

1919—February Low 124. Note that 126 is 350% on the base of 28c per bushel and at 125 is always a natural support point or 25% on $1.00.

1919—April High 181, just above old TOP and BOTTOM LEVELS and a natural SELLING LEVEL, 182 being 550% on a 28c base.

1919—June Low 138. Note that 140 is 400% on the base of 28c per bushel.

1919—July High 169. A Lower TOP and around old Bottom Levels. A reaction followed.

1919—November Low 133. Around Old TOP and BOTTOM LEVELS and a natural support Level, as you will see on the Resistance Table. Another rapid advance.

1920—January High 185½, just above the Top of April 1919 and a natural Resistance Point or Selling Level. A Sharp Decline followed.

1920—February Low 144. Note that ½ of 295 is 147½, making this a Support Point and Buying Level. From this Low Level the last rapid advance took place.

1920—June High 241. Note that June 1917 High was 245, making this a Selling Level as Resistance Points on the base were around this Level.

1920—August. First sharp decline to 170, down to old Top Level and just above 50% from 88 to 245, making this a buying level.

1920—September High 210. Note from 241 to 170 the half-way point is 205½, making this a selling level. Prices broke under $2.00 per bushel and indicated lower.

1920—November Low 141, a Double Bottom against February and at a natural support and percentage point.

1921—January Last High 173. Note series of Old Top and Bottom Levels around this point and just above the half-way point from 88 to 245 and 28c to 295 gives a half-way point or 50% reaction of 161½. Breaking back under this Level indicated lower.

1921—April Low 124, a Double Bottom against February 1919, a buying point for Rally.

1921—May High 167. This was the last Rally and the last High. Note old Tops and Bottoms Levels around this Level, making it a selling Level. The important half-way points at this Level, 88 to 245 being 166½, and ½ of 295 is 147½. Breaking back under this Level showed weakness and indicated Lower Prices and a Rapid Decline followed with small rallies.

1921—November Low 73c. After first breaking the Lows at 124 and later breaking the Lows around 88 to 90c per bushel, the market was in a very weak position. 75 was an actual Support Level and you will notice several Tops and Bottoms around 70 to 65, making this a point for rally. Also note that 70 is 150% on the base of 28c.

1921—December High 90. Under a series of old Bottoms and a natural Selling Level.

1922—January Low 77, a higher Bottom than previous Bottoms and a Secondary Reaction. The market became dull and narrow and this was the place to buy for another Rally.

The last High September 1921 was 109 to 73 which made the halfway point at 90½. When prices crossed this Level they indicated Higher.

1922—May High 111, a Double Top just 2 points above the High of September 1921, a Selling Level, as this is a natural Resistance Point. A sharp Decline followed and the first indication of Lower Prices was when prices broke under 25% from 73 to 111, which was 101¼. Later broke the halfway point of the last move 92½. These Levels were broken and prices continued to decline fast.

1922—August Low 69, down to Old Tops and Bottoms Levels. Note that 70 is 150% advance on the base of 28c. This was the first time that prices had been this Low since 1914.

1922—November High 93, under old Bottom Levels and a natural Selling Level. This was a Resistance Point.

1922—December Low 83.

1923—February High 89.

1923—March Low 81.

1923—April High 88. A Lower Top and a safe place to sell Short. When prices broke the last Bottom at 81 they indicated Lower and breaking back under the halfway point were still in a weaker position.

1923—June Low 63½c. Note that 63 is 125% advance on the base and there was a series of old Tops and Bottoms around this Level, making this a buy for Rally. The market moved up and down in a narrow range with many fluctuations around this Level.

1923—September High 74½.

1923—November Low 65½, a second Higher Bottom.

1924—January High 74, a double Top and a Selling Level.

1924—March Low 65, a Third Higher Bottom, making this a Triple Bottom and a sure indication to buy for much Higher Prices. You should have bought here with a Stop Loss Order at 63. The first definite indication of higher prices and change in trend was when prices crossed the Double Tops at 74. After crossing this Level you should have bought more, expecting considerably Higher Prices. The crop of Rye and Corn was short this year and a rapid advance followed. From these Levels you should figure Resistance Points from the Extreme High and Secondary Tops all the way down. From the extreme High of 295 to 64 gives 179½ as the 50% Rally or Halfway Point, and 245 Tops to 64 gives 154½, a 50% point. The last Top was January 1921, 176, making 118½ as the 50% or Halfway Point. The advance got under way in the spring of 1924 and was rapid and the prices at 88 and 92 were crossed and later the Tops at 112 were crossed, indicating the next Tops around 167 to 173.

1925—January High 173, the same High as January 1921, four years later, and note the series of Old Tops and Bottoms around this Level and 175 was the natural Resistance Point or Selling Level. Note that 175 was 525% on the base of 28c, and you should always sell short placing a Stop Loss Order 3 or 4c away against the Double Tops or against Old Tops or Old Bottoms. This was a safe place to sell short as the market had had an advance of 10 months which is an abnormal run and a change in trend was due. The first indication of a change in trend would be breaking back 12½% of the advance or 64 to 173. This would be 159⅜. Prices declined fast, breaking back 12½%, later 25%, and finally broke back under 118½, which was the 50% point between 64 and 173.

1925—April Low 108. Note old Tops and Bottoms around this Level and 108 being a natural Resistance Point on the base, makes this a Buying Point for Rally.

1925—May High 127, a normal Rally of 19c, from which you will note 126 was 350% on the base of 28c per bushel, and 125 is a natural Resistance Point. Prices broke back under 118½, the Halfway Point between 64 to 173, and indicated Lower and a Fast Decline followed.

1925—July Low 95c. Under $1.00 per bushel and at a natural Buying Point for Rally. Note that 94½ is 250% advance on the base, making this a natural support point.

1925—August High 115. Note that from 127 High to 95 Low gave 111 as the Halfway Point. Prices broke back under this, indicated Lower, and later breaking the Bottom at 95 were in a very weak position.

1925—September Low 79. Again down to old Bottom and Top Levels and to a natural support Level against the base. A sharp Rally followed.

1925—December High 111, an old Top and Bottom Level and a natural Selling Level and a lower Top than previous Tops.

1926—March Low 82. A Higher Bottom and an indication of better support.

1926—April High 93.

1926—May Low 82. A Double Bottom and a Third Higher Bottom and a natural support Level making this a buying point. When prices crossed the Tops at 93 they indicated still higher.

1926—July High 110½. A Double Top slightly lower than the previous Tops. A decline followed.

1926—September Low 93. Down to old Top Levels and a Buying Point for Rally.

1926—October High 103. Just a little more than 50% Rally. A decline followed.

1926—November Low 91. A Double Bottom and down to old Top Levels. A Buying Level, especially as the market had a Triple Bottom in 1924 and again a Triple Bottom in September, March and May 1925 and 1926.

1927—January High 109½, a fourth lower Top and three Tops near this Level made this a Selling Level for a reaction.

1927—March Low 96. This was a Higher Bottom and a Higher Support Level and indicated a buy for Rally.

1927—May High 121½. Just under 125, a natural Selling Level and Old Top and Bottom Level, making this a selling point for reaction. A sharp reaction followed.

1927—August Low 94. A Double Bottom against a series of Bottoms and Tops and a Buying Point for Rally. The market was dull and narrow and moved in a narrow range for a while, then the important point to watch was High at 121½ to 94 Low. 25% of the last move would be 101 and 50% would be 107¾. The market crossed the 25% and later crossed the halfway point indicating Higher.

1928—May High 139½. Note old Tops and Bottoms around this Level. 140 was 400% advance on the base of 28c per bushel. 100% advance on the last Low of 64 would give 128, and from the last High of September 1920 of 210 to 64, would give 137 as a halfway point, making this a natural Selling Level. The last point to watch was from the Low in August 1927 at 94. 25% of this move would be 133. The market broke this Level indicating lower and later broke 117, the halfway point of last move.

1928—September Low 93. Down to a series of old Bottom and Top Levels and a Double Top against August 1927, making this a Buying Level for Rally. No secondary Rally had taken place, therefore a *secondary Rally* was due. Figure the last move from 93 to 140 which would give the halfway point at 116½.

1928—October High 112½. Failing to reach the halfway point which was a natural selling point indicated a reaction.

1928—December low 99. $1.00 is always a support Level and a selling point. A Rally followed.

1929—February High 115. Just under the ½ point of the last move and a natural Selling Level. A sharp decline followed and the market broke back under the ½ of the last move and later broke to the last Bottom, indicating lower.

1929—May Low 85c. This was above the last two Bottoms of 82c in March and May 1926 and when Bottoms come out in May a Rally follows as this is the month for seasonal trend and Tops. When a market runs opposite the seasonal trend, then it runs opposite the next seasonal trend. Note that in previous years High Levels had been reached in May and this was one year from the last Top in May 1928 and a place to watch for a change in trend and a Buying Point. A rapid advance followed.

1929—August High 118. A Double Top and around the half-way point, being a 3 months Rally and August the month for a change in seasonal trend. The market was running opposite the seasonal trend and you should expect High and sell Short. The first sharp decline carried prices down to November Low of 96½, down to a natural support point and old Bottom and Top Levels.

1929—December High 110½. Note the series of Tops and Bottoms Levels. This was the place to sell and when prices broke back under the half-way point of the last move they indicated Lower.

Later when prices broke   Lows of 97 it was in a weak position as prices had been making Lower Tops and Lower Bottoms. When the Lows were broken at 85 and at 80, the market was in a still weaker position.

1930—March Low 58c per bushel. Back to the old Levels of 1914 having broken the Low Levels of 1923 and 1924, indicating weakness, but this was a natural Rally Point and a Rally followed.

1930—April High 70½. A natural Selling Point. A Decline followed.

1930—June Low 52. Down to old Low Levels of 1903 and holding above 50c was a natural point to buy for Rally. A Rally followed.

1930—August High 71½. A Double Top and under a series of old Bottom and Top Levels making this a natural Selling Level for lower prices.

1930—November Low 45. Down to the Low of November 1900. The main trend was still down which was the natural point to buy for Rally.

1930—December High 56. Under old Bottoms and a Selling Level. Failing to Rally halfway of 71 to 45 indicated weakness and a sharp decline followed.

1931—April Low 35. This was the first time since 1897 that prices had been this low. The market had been making lower Tops and lower Bottoms right along, showing that the main trend was still down and the selling pressure was greater than the buying pressure. A moderate Rally followed.

1931—May High 45. Under the last old Bottom and a selling point.

1931—July Low 36. A Higher Bottom and a Higher Support Level. This was the safer place to buy on a *Secondary Decline*. The market rallied and when prices crossed 45 they indicated higher and you should have bought more.

1931—November High 64. Under old Bottom Levels and a natural Resistance Point. Prices broke back under the Halfway Point from 35 to 64.

1931—December Low 35. Down to old Bottoms and a third Higher Bottom, a Buying Level for Rally.

1932—April High 51. A Lower Top and a Selling Level.

1932—May Low 34½. A Double Bottom and Buying Level. A Rally followed.

1932—June High 45½. Old Top Levels and a Selling Level.

1932—August Low 33. Just under the Low of 1932 but the main trend was down. A moderate Rally followed.

1932—September High 38. Three Tops at this Level. A Selling Level.

1932—November *Final Low* 26c for the December Option. Just under the old Lows of 1896, a Buying Level for a long-pull investment. A safer buying point would be after the trend turned up by crossing previous Tops or the ¼ point of the last move down which was 45½ to 26. The upward move started in 1933.

1933—January High 39. This was above the halfway point at 36 on the last move and had crossed three previous Tops by 1c, a signal that the main trend had turned up and that Rye would be a safe buy on any reaction.

1933—February Low 32½. Note that from 26 to 39 this was the half-way point and this was a *secondary* reaction after the main trend turned up. Prices moved up faster during April and in May crossed the Highs of 1931 indicating that the main trend had turned up and that prices had moved up out of the valley of depression and were making back for old mountain peaks or old Tops of previous years.

Review Double Bottoms

Study the Double Bottom formation in 1931 and 1932, Bottoms were made at 31½ and 31.

May, 1931, First Low 31½, and in November rallied to 63, Selling Point.

November, 1932, 1 year later, Low 31, a Double Bottom and Buying Level. 63 High to 31 Low made the half-way point 47. The market held for several months making Lows around 38, a Higher Support Level. 25% advance on 31 would be 39. The market crossed this Level, indicating higher prices, and later crossed the Tops at 40, showing an upward trend and continued to advance, and later crossed the Tops at 63. Note that ½ of 128½, the 1928 high, was 70. Crossing this Level indicated very much higher prices. All commodities advanced in the spring of 1933 and Rye moved up fast. Reactions were very small and you should have bought Rye all the way up but you would have had to have sold out quickly before Dr. E. A. Crawford failed, as the decline was very rapid.

1933—July High 111. A Double Top same as April 1927 and a selling Level. From 31 to 111 makes the half-way point at 71. The first indication of lower prices was a break of 12½%, or breaking 101 and breaking $1.00 indicated lower prices. Later prices broke 71½, the half-way point.

1933—August Low 64. This was an old Bottom Level and a Buying Level for Rally.

1933—September High 78. A normal Rally in a bear market and at Resistance Levels where it should have been sold short.

1933—October Low 44. Down to old Bottom and Top Levels. Note that 26 was the extreme low and a 50% advance gives 49 and from the Low at 30 a 50% advance gives 45, making 44 the Support Level and a Buying Level. 12½% of the decline from 111 to 44 gives 52⅜ and 25% gives 60¾.

1934—January High 65. Under old Bottoms and a Selling Level. Note that 63½ was the halfway point from 26 to 111, making this a Selling Level for a reaction.

1934—April Low 49. The Low of a *secondary reaction and* a Higher Bottom, making this a better Buying Level. From 65 to 49, the halfway point was 57. The market crossed this level and indicated higher. Later crossed the Tops of 65, indicating still higher prices. 44 to 111 the ½ point was 87½ and from 111 to 26 the halfway point was 63½.

1934—August High 91. Up to old Bottom Levels and a Selling Level. 44 to 91 gives the halfway point of 67½. Breaking back 25% from 44 to 91 indicated lower prices.

1934—October Low 66. Note 67½ was ½ of 44 to 91, making this a Support Level and a Buying Level.

1934—December High 82½. The fact that the market could not Rally to the halfway point between 66 to 91 showed weakness and made this a better Selling Level. The market continued to decline and Rallies were small.

1935—May Low 42. Note that from the last High of 82½ a 50% Reaction of 82½ to 41¾ makes this a Buying Level and it was Higher Bottoms than the Lows of previous campaigns and only 2 cents under 44, the Low of October 1933. May, being opposite to the seasonal trend, in other words making Bottoms in May when as a rule most Tops are made, indicated that a change in trend should take place. A Rally followed.

1935—October High 57. A Resistance Level and Selling Point.

1935—December Low 47, a 3 months' Bottom around this Level, a Higher Support Level and a good place to buy.

1936—February High 59. A Double Top and Selling Level.

1936—May Low 50. A Third Higher Bottom and a safe Buying Level. Because this was the second year that prices had made Low in the month of May opposite the seasonal trend. This indicated that they should advance and one year later make higher prices in the month of May. We always watch for a change in trend one, two and three years from any important Top and Bottom. In view of the fact that in April 1934 prices were lower, it was almost a sure thing that prices would be very much higher later.

1936—December High 121. This was the Top of a rapid advance and under old Top Levels of 1928—July 1928 High 122—200% advance on 42, the Low, would give 126.

1937—February Low 102. Holding above $1.00, showed strength and a Rally followed.

1937—May High 123½. Making High in a month for seasonal change in trend against the old Top Levels makes this a Triple Top and a Selling Level. 113 was ½ of 102 to 123½. Breaking this level was the first indication of lower prices. Breaking $1.00 indicated lower prices. From 42 to 123½, the halfway point was 87¾. This Level was eventually broken.

1937—June Low 76. A natural Support Level at 75 and old Bottom Levels around this point made this a Buying Point for Rally.

1937—July High 95. Under ½ or the half-way point of the last move and failed to reach $1.00. Later prices broke under 86, the half-way point of 76 to 95, and a further decline followed.

1937—November Low 64. Note ½ of 26 to 123½ was 74¾ and ½ of 140 was 70, and 150% of 90 to 26 is 65, making 64 a Buying Level for Rally.

1938—January High 73¾. Old Top Levels. From 95 to 64 the half-way point was 79½. Failing to reach this point indicated weakness and made a good short sale at this price. 64 to 77¾ gives the half-way point at 70¾. Breaking this Level indicated lower and great weakness and the market continued to decline.

1938—September Low 39½. Just 2½c under the Low of 42 and down to the Lows of 1935, three years from the last Bottom. The market held for three months, making Lows around 39½, making this a Buying Level. Note that 50% advance on 26, the extreme Low, is 39 as a Support Level.

1939—January High 49. Under old Bottom Levels. A reaction followed.

1939—March and April Low 40¾. A Higher Bottom indicating better support and a place to buy. A Rally followed and prices crossed 49, indicating higher prices.

1939—October High 57½. Note that 50% added to 39½, the Bottom, gives 59¼, making 57½ the Selling Level, as old Bottoms and Tops were also around this Level. After the High of 57½ in October 1939, a reaction followed.

November Low 40½, a Triple Bottom, and higher than previous Bottoms, making this a safe Buying Level. Prices crossed 49, indicating higher, and later crossed the Top of 50c, indicating a strong upturn. Note that from 123½ to 39½ the half-way point was 81½.

1940—January High 77½. A Double Top against January 1938 and a safe Selling Level, under the half-way point at 79¾.

1940—March Low 63½. An old Bottom Level and a place to buy for Rally.

1940—April High 73½. A lower Top and Selling Level, breaking 63½ Bottom later indicated lower prices. Note 39½ to 77½ the half-way point is 58½ and breaking this point again indicated extreme weakness.

1940—August Low 39½. A Buying level.

1940—October High 57½. Note that 50% added to 39½, the Bottom, gives 59¼, making 57½ the Selling Level, as old Bottoms and Tops were also around this Level. After the High of 57½ in October 1939, and 1939 November Low 40½, this was a Triple Bottom, and higher than previous Bottoms, making this a safe buy. Prices crossed 49, indicating higher, and later crossed the Top of 57½, showing uptrend. Note from 123½ to 39½ the half-way point was 81½.

1940—November High 49½c. A reaction followed.

1940—December Low 42. A higher Bottom showing better support and a safer place to buy.

1941—January High 49½. A Double Top and a reaction followed.

1941—February Last Low 40½. A Triple Bottom and a series of Higher Bottoms, making this a safe Buying Level. Later prices crossed the Double Top at 49½ indicating a strong uptrend and you should have bought more. From 39 to 77½ the half-way point is 58½. When prices crossed this Level you should have bought more and followed up with Stop Loss Orders as reactions were small. Note that the last low was in February 1941; therefore you would watch the rule for Tops six and seven months from Bottoms and September is one of the important months for top when the market is running against the seasonal trend. A change in trend was due.

1941—September High 80¾. Back to old Top Levels. Note that 123½ to 49 gives 81¼ as the half-way point, making this a Selling Level. Note also in 1938 and 1940 the Top Level was 77½, indicating that the market would reach peak selling around this Level.

Look up weekly High and Low and Daily High and Low and you will see that the market was meeting resistance and that this was the place to sell out all longs and sell short. First indication of the change in trend was breaking 12½% or breaking 75. Later the market broke 70 or 25% of the last advance from Low to High. This indicated greater weakness. A rapid decline followed and on October 16th Rye declined the limit of 10c per bushel. October 17 Low 57 at old Top Levels. Note 59¾ was ½ of 39 to 80¾, making this a safe Buying Level, protected with a Stop Loss Order in case the market should reverse. From 80¾ to 57 the half-way point is 68¾. A sharp Rally followed and prices advanced to 70, where they were selling at the time of this writing, October 29, 1941. Should May Rye later cross 80¾, the high of September 1941, it would indicate Higher, probably the next Tops around 95, and then getting above $1.00 would indicate Tops around 116 to 118 or 121 to 123. Should May Rye break under the half-way point from 39 to 80¾, that is break 59¾ again, that would indicate greater weakness and lower prices and probably decline to around 50 to 48, a support level.

Study the Bottom formations in 1931 and 1932 and again the Bottoms in 1935 and 1938 and 1941. Note the long number of months that the market stayed in the narrow trading range, making slightly Higher Bottoms.

1942—April or May, may mean higher prices and final Tops because that is five years from April, 1937 High and two years from May, 1940 when bottoms were made and a fast decline followed. Study the weekly and monthly charts on Rye and watch resistance levels, follow all the rules and you will be able to determine the changes in trend.

OATS

Oats are traded in on the Chicago Board of Trade. A contract for oats is 5,000 bushels. The fluctuations are in cents per bushel. The minimum fluctuation is ⅛c, or $12.50 on a contract.

The commission for buying and selling oats is $12.50 per contract.

The margin requirements on oats run from $250 up, depending on price.

SEASONAL CHANGES IN TREND 1861 TO 1941

	Low	High
January	7	10
February	6	8
March	8	6
April	6	8
May	5	14
June	1	7
July	4	13
August	19	2
September	8	6
October	15	2
November	4	4
December	8	13

YEARLY HIGH AND LOW AND SEASONAL CHANGES

From the above you can see that from 1861 to 1941, a period of 80 years, Oats made Lows in the month of August 19 times and in October 15 times. Therefore, August and October are the most important months to watch for Lows according to the seasonal trends, when the market is running true to form. This is due to the fact that the receipts of oats are heavy in August of each year, and again in October.

The next months when the greatest number of lows have been reached are March, December, and September eight times each. Therefore, on the basis of averages you would expect the months of March, September and December Lows to run out about the same number of times. January is next, having made lows 7 times; February and April 6 times; May 5 times, because May is the month each year for seasonal highs. November only 4 times and July only 4 times.

June Lows for the year have only been made one time in the month of June in 80 years. This proves that June is not the month to expect seasonal lows on Oats, and if the trend is running down in June you would not expect lows until the month of August.

Later in the year, if prices were running down in September, having started down late in the summer, you would watch October for extreme lows and change in trends. The next important months would be December and January where a change in trend is due and where most bottoms are made.

You will see that for the month of May highs have been made 14 times and in December, May and July 13 times each. Therefore, May, July and December are the most important months to watch for a change in trend, or for higher prices. When high prices occur at this time, if the market has been advancing for some time, you should sell out and sell short. Apply all of the other rules to determine a change of trend. February, April and January are the next months when the most highs have been made, January being 10 times during the period and February and April 8 times, making January the next in importance to watch after December. February and April next. Highs have been made 6 times in September, and 6 times in March, 7 times in June. These are the months of next importance to watch for a change in seasonal trend.

August and October. Highs have been made the least number of times in these months. Only 3 highs have been made in August and 2 in October because these are the months that show the greatest number of bottoms. These are the months for seasonal bottoms and not for seasonal tops. When Tops are made in August and October the market is running opposite to seasonal trends, which it does at times. November is next. Only 4 tops having been made in November. Therefore, when oats are advancing in November you would not expect them to make Tops this month, but would watch for Tops in December or in January when the greatest number of seasonal Highs have been made.

When the market is advancing in any of these months and extreme Highs have been reached, you should judge how many months the market has been advancing from low levels, and how far the market is up from extreme low levels, then judge whether Tops will be reached in the first seasonal change month like May, or whether the prices will run on to July or in extreme cases whether the prices will run until September.

EXTREME HIGH AND
LOW PRICES

1861—April and July Low 13c. Future contracts of oats have not sold
    lower than this level since.

1896—September Low 14¾.

1933—February Low 16c for the May option of Oats. Therefore, the basis for figuring Low prices would be 13c and 15c and the percentage of these prices. Using the lowest Base, 13c, a

50% advance would be	19½c
100% " " "	26c
150% " " "	32½c
200% " " "	39c
250% " " "	45½c
300% " " "	52c
350% " " "	58½c
400% " " "	65c
450% " " "	71½c
500% " " "	78c
550% " " "	84½c
600% " " "	91c
650% " " "	97½c
700% " " "	104
750% " " "	110½

For the present time, 1941, you could use the base of 1933, 16c per bushel, 100% would be 32c, 200% would be 48c, 300% would be 64c, 400% would be 80c, and 500% advance on the base would be 96c.

HIGH LEVELS FROM WHICH TO
FIGURE PERCENTAGE

1867—High 97c. You will note after that the Highs were 74, 71, 72½. 62, 53½, 38, and 35. These were in 1887. The low in 1886 was 35. All yearly tops have been lower since 1867; therefore, in 1887, in May, when prices reached 38, they were higher than the top in 1886 and indicated higher prices and that oats should be bought on a reaction.

1891—April High 56½. This was the last high before lower prices. After the lows in 1896, Tops were gradually working higher and bottoms working higher, indicating a slow Bull market.

1909—May 62½c. Tops were lower.

1910—February 49c.

1912—April 58½c.

1915 March 60½c. During the World War, when prices crossed 62c, which was the last high in 1882, it indicated the next high around 71 and 72, 74 and 90.

1916—November High 57.

1917—June High 85.

1918—February High 93. Higher than June 1867. An indication that prices were going higher.

1919—December High 89c. A slightly lower Top, but on a reaction the market made a higher bottom, showing that the main trend was still up.

1920—May $1.09 per bushel. This was the final high for oats, and a record high. This would be the basis for figuring percentage to get resistance levels on the way down.

$\frac{1}{8}$ or   12$\frac{1}{2}$%   of 109 is 13$\frac{5}{8}$

$\frac{1}{4}$ or   25%   of 109 is 27$\frac{1}{4}$

$\frac{1}{2}$ or   50%   of 109 is 54$\frac{1}{2}$

1/3 or 33-1/3   of 109 is 36$\frac{3}{8}$

2/3 or 66-2/3   of 109 is 72$\frac{5}{8}$

Note oats declined from $1.09 and the following would be the resistance points, on the way down. One-eighth, or 12$\frac{1}{2}$%, off would give 95$\frac{3}{8}$, making this point an indication of lower. 25% decline would give 81$\frac{3}{4}$. Of course, the 50% decline would be 54$\frac{1}{2}$. From this high level, at 109, you could take the last low in 1896, 14$\frac{3}{4}$, for even figures use 15c as low, and then get the important resistance points from extreme low, which would be as follows:

$\frac{1}{8}$	26$\frac{3}{4}$	$\frac{5}{8}$	73$\frac{3}{4}$
$\frac{1}{4}$	38$\frac{1}{2}$	1/3	77$\frac{3}{4}$
1/3	46$\frac{3}{8}$	$\frac{3}{4}$	85$\frac{1}{2}$
$\frac{3}{8}$	50$\frac{1}{4}$	$\frac{7}{8}$	97$\frac{1}{4}$
$\frac{1}{2}$	62	100	109

These would be the percentage points and resistance levels to watch on the way down.

1917 High was 85c

1918 High was 93c

1919 High was 89c

These Tops are all important to figure resistance levels from. In 1924 the High was 66$\frac{3}{4}$, the last extreme high, and 1928 May was 68$\frac{1}{4}$. Figure 25% — 50% and the other important points.

Watch these percentage points on the way down for buying levels and selling levels on rallies. 90c is an important top level for oats. The percentage of 90 to 13 the extreme low level is quite important as you can see by going over past records.

$\frac{1}{8}$ of 90 is 11$\frac{1}{4}$		$\frac{5}{8}$ of 90 is 56$\frac{1}{4}$
$\frac{1}{4}$ of 90 is 22$\frac{1}{2}$		$\frac{3}{4}$ of 90 is 67$\frac{1}{2}$
1/3 of 90 is 30		$\frac{7}{8}$ of 90 is 78$\frac{3}{4}$
$\frac{3}{8}$ of 90 is 37$\frac{1}{2}$		100 of 90 is 90
$\frac{1}{2}$ of 90 is 45		

Then from the extreme low of 19c to 90c, figure the $\frac{1}{8}$ points for resistance levels. The resistance levels between the extreme high of 109 to 13c are important. Watch the 50% reactions and 50% rallies on any important TOPS and BOTTOMS. Do not overlook the fact that when bottoms are ascending and tops are higher the main trend is still up. When tops are lower and bottoms are lower, the trend is down. Apply all of the rules, watch the months when seasonal trends are indicated and you will be able to determine the change in trend in oats.

Remember, you learn the future by a study of the past, because history does repeat itself.

IMPORTANT BOTTOMS
ON OATS

Study the Bottom formations in 1896 and 1897. Notice how the market remained for a long time in a narrow trading range. When it crossed the Tops or upper levels, the main trend turned up and prices worked higher.

Study 1900 and 1901. 1905 and 1906. 1910 and 1911. 1914 Bottoms before the War broke out. Notice how oats, like other commodities and grains had been making progressive higher bottoms and had remained in a narrow trading range for many months before the War broke out in July, 1914. Then the main trend turned up, indicating much higher prices by crossing Tops of the previous years.

Study 1921 Bottoms.

Study 1932 and 1933. Note the long period and narrow trading range.

The market holding well after the first bottom was reached and not going much lower, showing it was receiving support, laying the foundation for higher prices later. The fact that oats did not decline below the lows of 1896 in 1932 and 1933 was an indication of strength, because wheat, corn and other commodities did go below the 1896 levels. Later in 1933 Oats had a greater advance on percentage from the low levels than wheat.

Next study 1938 and 1939 Bottom formations and note that the price in August 1938 was about 50% higher than the low in February 1933 on May oats. In 1939, July, price was 2c higher and in 1940 August the price was 2c higher than 1939, and 4c above the 1938 Bottom, showing that there had been three years of good support or buying around these low levels. Oats was laying the foundation for higher prices.

1941—February Last Low 54c. A 50% advance on 1938 low would give 37½c. In 1941 the low was slightly under this. 100% advance on 25c would give 50c. 100% advance on 29c would give 58c.

1941—September High 57½c per bushel for May oats, making this a selling level. Look back to Tops in 1937 of 56½, Tops in 1934 of 59½, Tops in 1933 of 56¾, making this a double Top and selling level for a reaction at least. A sharp decline followed in October 1941.

BARLEY FUTURES

Barley is traded in on the Chicago Board of Trade, the Duluth Board of Trade, the Minneapolis Chamber of Commerce, and the Winnipeg Grain Exchange. On all of these exchanges, the contract is 5,000 bushels and fluctuations are in $\frac{1}{8}$ of a cent per bushel and the minimum fluctuation of $\frac{1}{8}$ on 5,000 bushels is $6.25 per contract. The commission rate is the same on all of the exchanges — $12.50 per contract regardless of the price at which barley is selling.

In order to forecast the future trend of barley, apply all rules that we apply to other commodities, look up the extreme high and the extreme low prices, figure the resistance levels and percentage of extreme low and percentage of extreme high and the percentage of the range between extreme high and extreme low and you will be able to determine the trend and buying and selling points.

Barley follows very close to the trend in wheat and other grains, as you can see by looking up the extreme high and extreme low prices. However, the high and low prices on barley at extremes sometimes vary a month or two from wheat and corn and other commodities.

We are giving some swings and some high and low prices on barley based on prices on the Minneapolis Exchange. These will serve as a guide for resistance levels. You can see by these prices when extreme high and extreme low have been reached and when extreme lows have been reached in the same month around the same prices, making double bottoms and double tops.

LARD

Lard is traded in on the Chicago Board of Trade. A contract is 50,000 pounds. The fluctuation of lard is $2\frac{1}{2}/100c$. The minimum fluctuation is $12.50 per contract.

The commission for buying and selling lard is $20 per contract.

The margin requirements vary, according to the price at which lard is selling, running from $300 to $1,000 per contract.

LARD SEASONAL CHANGES—1869 TO 1941:

SHOWING NUMBER OF TIMES HIGH AND LOW
HAVE BEEN MADE IN EACH MONTH

	High		Low
January	Times	24	Times	13
February		13		8
March		9		4
April		7		6
May		6		7
June		4		6
July		5		4
August		7		6
September		9		4
October		8		9
November		6		7
December		5		21

LARD SEASONAL CHANGES:

Lard, like all other commodities, makes tops and bottoms and the highs and lows at regular seasonal changes. From the above table you can see that from 1869 to 1941, a period of 72 years, lard has made highs 24 times in the month of January and 13 times in the month of February. The next months of importance for tops are March and September, each showing highs 9 times. Then April August and October, showing highs 7, 8 and 9 times. July and December show only 5 tops.

June shows the least number of tops — only 4 in this period of time, therefore, if Lard was advancing in the latter part of the year you would watch for a seasonal change in trend, with tops in January, February or not later than March especially if the trend had been up for several months. If Lard started an advance in the summer you would watch for a change in trend and Tops in September and October as the records show that most Tops are reached between these months.

MONTHS WHEN MOST LOWS HAVE BEEN REACHED. The Month of December shows 21 Lows in the period of 72 years and January shows 13 lows, therefore, when Lard was declining in the latter part of the year, and the corn crop was large, corn was cheap, hogs plentiful, lard would make Low in December or January and then the trend would turn up and run until March and April before the seasonal trend changed. The next important months for Lows are February, May and October. These months showing 7, 8 and 9 times that lows were made. June and August show 6 lows. March, July and September show 4 lows. These are the months when the least lows have been made. Each of these months show a greater number of seasonal Tops. You should always be careful about going short of Lard just before these months when so few seasonal lows have been reached, as the chances are against making low prices in these months. Again, if the trend is up, you should be careful about buying in January or February, for most Highs are reached in these months. Buy in the months when the most lows are indicated — when the market comes out low at these times, and sell in the months where most highs are indicated, if there is an indication that the trend is changing. Apply all of the rules — determine when tops and bottoms will be reached.

SWINGS ON LARD. You will find it valuable to study these swings and note when the important bottoms have been made in the past and use them as a guide for the tops and bottoms of the future. These old tops and old bottoms are landmarks to warn you that when prices reach these levels there is likely to be tops or bottoms, all depending upon how long the trend of Lard has run upward or downward from previous tops or bottoms.

1869 February High $20.75.

1873 November Low $6.50.

1875 April High $16.75.

1879 August Low $5.25.

1882 October High $13.10.

1891 February Low $5.37.

1893 March High $13.25.

1896 July Low $3.25. This was the final Low and Lard has never been as low as this level since. Therefore, $3.25 is the basis on which to figure percentage from the Bottom, and $20.75, the high price, would be the basis for figuring percentage and resistance levels. Take the difference between $20.75 and $3.25 and get the important point. Also use the other Tops which were lower Tops to get the important resistance points, and watch as the market advances.

The trend turned up after the low in 1896, and prices worked higher for several years. In 1902, September High $11.60, was still lower than the Highs in 1892 and 1896. Note that the half-way point of the 50% rally between $3.25 and $20.75 was 12c. Therefore, as long as the market is under this level it would be a short sale for a reaction.

LARD AND HOG PRICES—COMPARISON:

1898 TO 1941. It is helpful in determining the price of Lard to compare the price of Hogs, especially at extreme High and extreme Low prices. Price of Hogs determines the cost of Lard and Hog prices are determined by the cost of Corn to feed the Hogs. Lard prices are quoted in cents per pound and Hog prices are quoted in cents per pound, or at $2.00, $4.00 or $3.00 for 100 pounds at Chicago.

1898 — Lard	Low	450
Hogs	Low	325
1902 — Lard	High	1025
Hogs	High	825
1904 — Lard	Low	625
Hogs	Low	390 to 425
1910 — Lard		1415
Hogs		1125
1914 — Lard		750
Hogs		750

Although in 1912 and 1913 Hogs had sold as low as 550.

1915 — Lard		750
Hogs		675
1917 — Lard	High	2850
Hogs		20c or $20 per 100 lbs.
1919 — Lard		36c per lb.
Hogs		2360
1922 — Lard		790
Hogs		5c per pound
1925 — Lard	High	1750
Hogs		1475
1926 — Lard	High	1710
Hogs		1525

1932-1933 — Lard	Low	375 — This was extreme low.
1932-1933 — Hogs	Low	$2.00 per hundred or 2c per lb. This was extreme Low on Hogs and the Lowest since Civil War.
1935 — Lard	High	1750

This was an abnormal runaway market in Lard, reaching high in August and prices collapsed. A sharp decline followed.

1935 — Hogs	High	1225	1939 — Lard	Low	5c
1936 — Lard	Low	10c	1939 — Hogs	Low	4c
1936 — Hogs	Low	1225	1940 — Lard	Low	410
1937 — Lard	High	1415	1940 — Hogs	Low	410
1937 — Hogs	High	14c	1941 — Lard	High	1160
		1941 — Hogs	High	1240	

From the above figures you can see at some times the price of Hogs per pound was higher than the price of Lard. At other times the price of Lard was very much higher than the price of Hogs. Going back over past history, we find that when the price of Hogs was down as low as the price of Lard or Lower, it was time to buy Lard for a substantial advance. Then at times like 1917 and 1919, the price of Lard was 8 to 13c above the price of Hogs, time to sell Lard and sell short. Again in 1939 and 1940, Lard was down around the same Levels with Hogs and at times Hogs slightly under the price of Lard. This was an indication that Lard was a purchase for an investment because prices were too low. Hog prices were too low compared with the price of Corn.

However, if you keep up all of the indications on the Chart for Lard, consider the Resistance Levels, the Percentage on High and Low prices, the time periods between Extreme Low and Extreme High, you will be able to forecast the trend of Lard without considering the price of Hogs. The *price and the time tell the trend changes* and the more you study past records and the movement of Lard, the firmer you will be convinced the price does show the Supply and Demand and in the end the Supply and Demand is what determines the price. When there are more buyers than sellers, prices advance and when there are more sellers than buyers, prices decline and the price of Lard or any commodity shows what the majority of people think and what the majority of people are doing. The market goes down when more people sell and when the selling is better than the buying. It is simply a question of the balancing of buying and selling power. When one side over-balances the other prices reverse and move the other way until Levels are reached where a change in sentiment and a change in buying or selling power takes place and again the trend changes.

The higher prices go the greater the selling pressure and the smaller demand. People buy less Lard at 20c a pound than they do at 10. They buy less at 36c a pound than they do at 20 or 25, because poor people cannot afford to pay these prices. On the other hand, the lower prices get the more the demand increases. When Lard gets down to three or four cents a pound, as it has under extreme panicky conditions, the demand increases until the supply is absorbed. Large users of Lard will lay in a large supply at these low Levels. Gradually all of the offerings are absorbed. Then the trend changes and when the market starts to advance people who have missed buying at low prices start stocking up and the result is a run in the market.

Prices never get so high but what speculators and some people think that they are going higher. That is why you can always sell at high prices. On the other hand, prices never go so low but that people get pessimistic and some of them think they are going lower. If this were not the case, Lard would not have sold at 36c a pound in 1919 because someone had to buy it and someone believed it would go higher. On the other hand, in 1932 and 1933 Lard would not have sold at 3.75 per pound unless some of the people believed that Lard would go lower. Otherwise, they would not have sold it at that time. Neither would Hogs have declined to 2c a pound and sold at that level unless people believed that hogs would go lower.

Of course some of them were forced to sell, but if people had the faith and the confidence in 1932 and 1933 that Hogs would be worth 12c a pound in 1935, they would not have sold at 2 or 3c a pound but would at least have held back part of the supply for higher prices.

Human nature never changes and that is why prices swing from the one extreme level to the other. People get too hopeful and optimistic when prices are high. Then when prices reach extreme low, they get too blue, too pessimistic and over-sell. After the proper period of time of low prices has expired the trend turns up with a long upward swing. These ranges and fluctuations will continue until human nature changes and that has not happened in thousands of years or is not likely to happen in the future, because each new generation makes the same mistakes and does the same fool things as the past generations. The reason for this is that most of the people act either on hope or fear and fail to face facts. As long as they do this, they will do wrong most of the time. Therefore, the big profits in the commodity market are made by those who have the wisdom to buy when they have every indication of the prices being too low and then have the nerve and knowledge to sell when they have definite indications that prices are too high. Remember one thing. Prices are never so low but what they can go lower as long as the trend is down and prices are never so high but what they can go higher as long as the trend is up.

My rule is to go with the trend and only change when the trend changes. In this way you will make profits instead of losses. Let me again impress on you the fact that you can be wrong, that you can interpret the market wrong and if you do, then the way to protect yourself is always to place the STOP LOSS ORDER, limiting your risks, knowing that if you get out with a small loss you will still have capital to get in when there is another opportunity to buy or sell.

Protection of your capital must always be your first thought. You cannot afford to enter the market without a definite idea of just exactly how much loss you are going to take. The profits can take care of themselves. However, when you have profits on paper you should follow up and protect these profits with STOP LOSS ORDERS in case the trend should reverse. You must remember that you can make a mistake when the market is TOP or BOTTOM. Once you are in the market, if you do get wrong, get right by getting out quickly and taking a small loss.

LARD—BOTTOMS AND TOPS, AND RESISTANCE LEVELS

1904—October Low 620.

1905—May low 620. A BOUBLE BOTTOM. Note that 650 was 100% in advance of the base of 325, making this DOUBLE BOTTOM 620 a safe buying level. The main trend was up and prices worked higher.

1907—February high 990. Note that a 200% advance on the base of 325 would give 975, making this the selling level and around 10c per pound or at any of the even figures, lard always meets selling anyway.

1908—February Low 700 or 7c per pound, making a higher BOTTOM than 1904 and 1905, holding 50 points above 650 natural resistance level was an indication of strength and a place to buy.

1910—March High 1460. Note 100% advance on 7c, last Low would make 14c. This was the first time prices had been this high since 1882 and 1893. Note there were TOPS at that time at 1310 and 1325. March was the month for seasonal TOPS. When the market reached this level, you should have sold out and gone short.

1911—April Low 850. This is another month when seasonal Lows are made, and the price was higher than the previous BOTTOM by 150 points and a natural resistance level.

1912—October High 1190. Thirty points above the TOP of September and June 1160, making this a DOUBLE TOP and selling level and holding under 12c the 50% rally point between 325 and 2075 was also an indication of a selling level.

1913—January Low 950. Note that a 200% advance on the basis of 325 is 975, making this the support level and the buying level and the market was making higher BOTTOMS right along showing main trend was still up.

1913—July high 1190. A DOUBLE TOP against October 1912 and a selling Level.

1914—August Low 850. A DOUBLE BOTTOM against April 1911, DOUBLE BOTTOM is always a safe place to buy protected with *stop loss orders*. When buying lard you should always use a stop loss order 30 to 50 points under each BOTTOM where you buy, or 30 points above resistance points when you sell. The war broke out the early part of August 1914 and prices advanced rapidly.

1914—November high 1150. Under the DOUBLE TOPS 1190. The resistance points are as follows: 1915 July Low 750, which was

100 points under the DOUBLE BOTTOMS or 850, holding 50 points above the Low of February 1908. This is the natural buying Level as all even figures 5c, 750, 10c 1250, 15c 1750, 20c, 2250, 25c, etc., are points and prices where the public buys and sells.

At this time the market gave every indication of making BOTTOMS. The trend turned up and the prices crossed 950, which was ½ of 750 to 1150, and an indication of higher prices. Showed strong uptrend. Later prices crossed the TRIPLE TOP 1150 to 1190, indicating very much higher prices. Getting above the 12c Level was over the half-way point between 2075, and 325. Later prices crossed 15c and 16c Levels, the highest since 1875. Being in a war period indicated much higher prices, finally crossing 2075, the high of 1869. If you take the highs and add 100% to the TOPS, the extreme high level of 2075 would give 4150 as a possible TOP. Adding 100% to 1575 would give 3150. Figuring the last Low of 750, 100% would give 15c, 200% 2250, 300% 30c and 400% 3750.

1919—June high 36c per pound. When this TOP was reached you should figure resistance points and percentage from previous low.

1919—February last Low 2225. This would make a 25% decline 3255. Breaking this level would indicate lower. Then take the extreme Low to the extreme High and this gives 50% or 1987. Also note that 1000% advance of 325 gives 3575, figuring the TOP of 2075 and the TOP of 36c, the half-way point between these TOPS was 2837. Breaking this Level was a sign of weakness and indicated much lower. From the Top of 1750 to 36c, the 50% or half-way point was 2675. Figure the percentages on 36c. One-half of this would be 1800, and ¼ would be 9c, and ⅛ would be 450, and 1/16 would be 225. When the market broke back 225, or 1/16 of 3600, it was an indication of lower price.

The last Low at 8c a pound to 36 would give the half-way point at 22c per pound.

In 1930 prices declined fast and all commodities broke rapidly. You should have sold Lard short and sold short all the way down, because even if the supply was short, after prices broke 25c per pound, then broke 20c, time to sell short. After it broke 18c per pound, breaking 50% of the High selling price, it was in a weaker position. Prices worked lower in 1920 and 1921 and rallies were very small.

1922—January Low 790. Down to OLD BOTTOMS and TOP LEVELS and 50 points above the low of July 1915 the last extreme low. This was a buying Level. Later when prices crossed 9c a pound, 25% of 36c, they indicated higher.

1924—December High 1750. Just 50 points under 18c, ½ of 36c, making this a safe selling level for reaction.

1925—February Low 1460. 13c per pound decline and down to a buying Level for rally. A rally followed.

1925—High 1775, a DOUBLE TOP against December 1924 and still under 18c per pound made this a safe selling Level because there were four TOPS around 1700 to 1775. From this Level you would figure the half-way point between 1460 to 1775. This would give 1615. When it broke this Level it indicated lower prices. Later breaking 1460 indicating main trend down and a very weak market. After the 1925 High the real Bear market started on wheat, corn and all commodities, and there was a fast decline. Rallies were small and lard as well as other commodities was a good short sale all the way down.

Remember the rule. The lower prices get the smaller the rally until the market finally gets over-sold and main trend turns up. The higher prices get, the smaller the reaction of the market until it gets over-bought and finally reverses and changes trends.

Prices continued to work lower during 1928 and 1929. There was a panicky decline in all commodities in 1930 and 1931, as prices declined lower and rallies were small.

1932—April Low 420. A rally followed.

August High 540.

October Low 410.

November High 540. A TRIPLE TOP having made this same high in January 1932, August and November. From November High a decline followed.

December Low 390. Down to the lowest Level since 1896. The market showed that it was receiving support.

1933—January High 460.

February Low 375. Final Low. Note four BOTTOMS in a range of 50 points and holding 50 points above the Low 325 showed strength and a good buy. This was a place where you could have bought Lard as an investment, but it would have been safer to buy after the main trend turned up when prices crossed the TOPS at 540.

1933—March High 490.

April Low 410. This was the last reaction and a third higher BOTTOM, a safe sure buying Level. Then when prices crossed 5c and 540 you should have bought more.

May High 690. Under OLD BOTTOMS and selling Level.

1933—December Low 450. Well above the DOUBLE and TRIPLE BOTTOMS making this a buying Level, and the safest buying Level yet because it was the Low of a *secondary reaction* after the main trend had turned up.

1934—February High 650.

May Low 585. A safe buy on this reaction. Then when prices advanced and crossed 7c the high of May 1933, it was a safe sure buying Level.

If you look at the two resistance levels, you will see that from 1775, the last High in August 1925 to 375, the resistance levels are as follows: ⅛, or 12½%, 560, and 25% is 725, 37½% is 9c, and 50% is 1075, and 62½ is 1250, and 75% is 1425, and 87½% is 16c, and 100% is 1775. All of these resistance points are important to watch on the way up. After prices got above 7c per pound there was no reaction of more than 1c per pound until August 1935.

1935—August Final High 1740. Up to OLD TOPS Level 1924, 1925 and 1926, making this a DOUBLE and TRIPLE TOP and a selling Level in view of the fact that the price was still under 50% of 36c or 18c per pound made it a selling Level. On 375 to 1740 the 50% reaction point would be 1057, the first indication of lower prices would be when prices broke back 175 points or when prices broke lowest, selling point of 375, or when the time period exceeded the time period of the last reaction. From this sharp TOP the market collapsed and prices declined the limits for three consecutive days. Buyers went on a strike. Lard was too high for people to use and the decline was rapid.

1936—June Low 10c per pound. This was the half-way point or just under the half-way point between 375 and 1740, making this a buying level for at least a rally.

1936—December High 1410. Note that from 1740 to 10c the 50% rally point was 1370.

1937—January High 1410. A DOUBLE TOP against December 1933 and a selling Level because it was not 50 points over the half-way point. A 50% rally. 1425 was also ¾ of 1775. From this Level the main trend turned down and prices worked lower and rallies were very small. Later breaking the minor support levels around 1125.

1937—August Low 10c per pound. A moderate rally followed.
September High 1160. Again the trend turned down and when the prices broke 10c per pound they were safe short sale because they indicated much lower and showed great weakness. Prices continued to work lower.

1939—August Low 5c per pound. The 50% decline from the Lows of 10c a pound, made in June 1936 and August 1937.

1939—September High 825. Up to OLD BOTTOMS and TOP levels and selling levels. Later prices broke 650 which was ½ of 5c to 825 and the decline continued.

1940—December Low 410. Down to the old Lows of 1932 and 1933 a support Level and a buying Level. Note this was a sharp decline. Prices rallied quicker than they had from any time since August 1939, showing this a good buy.

1941—January High 7c. Around OLD TOP AND BOTTOM Levels and a natural point for a moderate reaction.
February Low 612. Buying Level down to OLD TOP Levels. Advance followed.

1941—June High 1160. A selling Level or DOUBLE TOP against the last high of Sept. 1937. Note that 12c was 1/3 of 3600 and as long as prices were under 12c they indicated lower. Also note that 2/3 of 1740 was 1160 making this a selling Level.

August Low 990. At OLD BOTTOM Levels and buy for a
rally. September High 1150. A DOUBLE TOP and Selling
Level. In fact a TRIPLE TOP because the last High in September 1937 was 1160. This was the place to sell out all long
Lard and sell short, and when prices broke 1070, or half of the
last move, they indicated weakness and lower prices and breaking
10c per pound was still weaker.

October 16 Low 862. This was BOTTOM of a panicky decline,
when everybody was scared and selling regardless of price.

This was down to OLD BOTTOM and TOP Levels and a Support Level. Also note that ½ of 1750 TOP was 875, making this
a safe level to cover shorts and buy for rally. The next selling
level on the rally would be around 10c per pound under the OLD
BOTTOMS Levels or half of the decline from 1160 to 862.

Study all BOTTOM formations of 1896, 1905, 1914, 1916, 1921,
1926, 1932 to 1933, and 1939, and 1940, you will learn how to determine the trend of Lard. Study the TOP formations at extreme high
and note in most cases that prices do not remain long at extreme High
Levels. Sharp TOPS are made and quick sharp reactions follow, but
when prices get to extreme Low Levels, they remain for a long period
of time, because everybody is afraid, depressed, have lost money, and
have no confidence to buy. Later if prices advance, people get more
confidence and continue to buy until they get over-optimistic and
overloaded. That is why sharp declines follow these last final grand
rushes to extreme high prices. Continue to study the past action of
the markets and you will learn how to determine the future action of
Lard or any other commodity.

COTTON TRADING

Cotton is traded in on the New York Cotton Exchange, New Orleans
Cotton Exchange, Memphis Cotton Exchange, and in foreign countries on the Liverpool Cotton Exchange. A contract on the New York
Cotton Exchange is for 50,000 pounds or 100 bales. Minimum fluctuations are 1.01 of a cent per pound. This is $5.00 per point on a con-
tract. If cotton advances 100 points, or 1c per pound, you would make
$500.00 on a contract, less commission. The commission for buying
and selling cotton is from $25.00 up, according to the price at which
it is selling. The marginal requirements run from $500.00 on each 100
bale contract up to $1,000 or more per contract, based on the selling
price. A contract on the New Orleans Cotton Exchange is 50 bales,
or a job, and there is a regular job lot market for trading in cotton
in New Orleans on the Exchange. Fluctuation on 50 bale lots is the
same as on 100 bale lots, except that the gain or loss on 50 bales is
$2.50 per point, instead of $5.00 on 100 bales at the regular contract.

COTTON — SEASONAL TREND

1816 to 1941

Below we give the month in which the greatest number of TOPS
and BOTTOMS were reached during this period, in order for you to

see how the seasonal trend runs and know how to determine changes in trends in the future, and what month to watch for the most important changes.

During this period of one hundred and twenty-five years, we have listed the number of times during each month when HIGHS and LOWS have been reached.

January	LOW, 27 times	HIGH, 19 times
February	LOW, 12 times	HIGH, 5 times
March	LOW, 9 times	HIGH, 14 times
April	LOW, 6 times	HIGH, 11 times
May	LOW, 8 times	HIGH, 11 times
June	LOW, 5 times	HIGH, 7 times
July	LOW, 4 times	HIGH, 5 times
August	LOW, 4 times	HIGH, 11 times
September	LOW, 11 times	HIGH, 15 times
October	LOW, 11 times	HIGH, 14 times
November	LOW, 8 times	HIGH, 8 times
December	LOW, 31 times	HIGH, 19 times

From the above you can see that during the months of December and January 58 LOWS have occurred and if we include February, which is the next highest month, we get 70 times out of 125 years that the extreme LOW has occurred in December, January or February. The reason for so many LOWS occurring in these months is that the weight of the crop, the greatest amount of selling and the final government estimate of the crop comes out in December and this establishes low prices which come out in December but sometimes run into January and February before EXTREME LOWS are reached. When the crop is extremely short, the market often runs opposite the seasonal trend and makes TOPS in December or January.

The next important months for extreme lows are September and October, lows being made eleven times during these two months. The next months which are important for LOW prices are March, May and November, eight and nine lows being made in these months. The smallest number of lows has been made in the months of June, July and August, five lows in June and only four in July and August. These months are the months when high prices are reached. Therefore, very few lows are reached at the end of the old crop year.

Crop scares occur mostly in July, August and September.

You will note that nineteen HIGH were reached in January, fourteen in March, fifteen in September and fourteen in October. Therefore, January and March are important for HIGHS and for a change in trend. SEPTEMBER IS THE MOST IMPORTANT MONTH IN THE YEAR FOR A CHANGE IN TREND, because when the government crop report is issued in September each year, it is generally known whether the crop will be large or small and a change in trend takes place in September. When prices have advanced, September is the time to sell. You will note that during August, September and October a total of 40 HIGHS have been reached, making these months important for TOPS and CHANGES IN TREND. In the months of December and January a total of 38 HIGHS were reached. This is when the market is running opposite the seasonal trend. Therefore, when prices have been advancing for several months and have reached HIGHS in December and January, it is usually safe to sell out.

In the months of September and October, 29 HIGHS have been reached during this period, so when the market starts to advance early in the summer, you should watch for a change in trend in September or October.

March is the next month in importance, 14 HIGHS being made in this month. Therefore, if the market is low in October and December and advanced up to March, you would watch for a TOP to sell out.

April, May and August are each the same, — 11 HIGHS being reached in these months, making them next in importance to watch for a change in trend.

February and July — HIGHS have been reached only 5 times in each of these months during the 125 years. Therefore, these months are the least important to expect HIGHS under normal conditions.

A study of the charts and of the time periods from HIGHS to LOWS as well as the resistance levels in connection with the seasonal changes will help you to determine the important changes in trend. Use and apply all of the rules.

TIME PERIODS TO WATCH. Our rule is to watch for an important change in trend in the third or fourth month, up or down from any important BOTTOM, and the faster the advance, the surer that the change will come in the third or fourth month. The next important time period to watch for change in trend is the sixth or seventh month. Always watch for a change in trend twelve months, twenty-four months, thirty-six months, and in fact, at the end of any year, or series of years, from any important top or bottom. Watch for a change in trend in a year and a quarter, or fifteen months, a year and a half, or eighteen months, a year and three quarters, or in the twenty-first month, and apply the same percentage of time to greater time periods and if the market comes out exactly HIGH or LOW in the seasonal months where most of the TOPS or BOTTOMS are made, then watch for the next change in trend at the next important month where seasonal changes take place.

EXTREME LOW LEVEL OR BASE FOR COTTON. In 1844 cotton sold at 5c per pound. Again in 1894 and 1898 cotton sold at 5c. Therefore, we take this as a base or EXTREME LOW POINT to figure percentage and to get resistance LEVELS for buying and selling. 25% of 5c added to 5c gives 6.25c. 50% is 7.50c and 75% is 8.75c and 100% is 10c. The RESISTANCE LEVELS above 10c as follows: 11.25, 12.50, 13.75, 15c, 16.25, 17.50, 18.75 and 20c. Above 20c RESISTANCE LEVELS are: 21.25, 22.50, 23.75, and 25c, which is 400% advance on the base, and 26.25, 27.50, 28.75 and 30c, which is 500% advance on the base. Above 30c would be 31.25, 32.50, 33.75, 35c, 36.25, 37.50, 38.75 and 40c. Above 40c would be 41.25, 42.50, 43.75 and 45c. By going back over past records, seeing how many times TOPS and BOTTOMS are made around these RESISTANCE LEVELS, at certain percentage points, you will see how valuable they are from any HIGHER BOTTOM or from any important TOP or BOTTOM, calculating the percentage point in the same way, figuring that 50% advance on any bottom or any top is the most important point and then 100% advance on any bottom is most important for RESISTANCE, and 100% advance on any top is the next most important RESISTANCE LEVEL and for another top. Refer to the percentage tables in the back of the book and you will find most of these important PERCENTAGE POINTS calculated so that you can easily refer to them when the market has reached a point where resistance LEVELS are indicated. Never overlook the fact to apply all of my time rules. Time over-balances price and DECLINES or ADVANCES do not start until time is up or the market reaches the month for a change in trend according to the time from TOP to BOTTOM, or in the month where seasonal change is up or down.

COTTON — SINGLE DOUBLE, AND TRIPLE TOPS AND BOTTOMS. The only way that we can know and forecast the future is by a careful study and review of past history. That is the reason for going back so far, to prove to you how the market has acted in the past, in order that you may determine what it is likely to do in the future.

1828—May LOW, 1310.

1830—October HIGH, 1325. A DOUBLE TOP.

1832—November HIGH, 1290. A TRIPLE TOP.

1835—June HIGH, 20c.

1836—June HIGH, 20c. A DOUBLE TOP, and SELLING LEVEL.

1839—April HIGII, 17c. A SINGLE TOP.

1841—January and May, 1140. A DOUBLE TOP and SELLING LEVEL.

1844—December LOW, 5c . An EXTREME LOW.

1845—January, LOW, 5c. A DOUBLE BOTTOM.

1847—July, HIGH, 13.25.

1847—May, HIGH, 13.50. A DOUBLE TOP and SELLING LEVEL.

1848—November, LOW, 6c. The first higher BOTTOM showing strength and a safer buying level.

1850—October, HIGH, 15c. A SINGLE TOP.

1852—January, LOW, 825. A SECOND HIGHER BOTTOM, showing strength and indicating higher.

1853—March, April and August, HIGH, 1160. A TRIPLE TOP and selling level.

1855—January, 840. A DOUBLE BOTTOM and BUYING LEVEL.

1855—May, HIGH, 13c. A SINGLE TOP and SELLING LEVEL.

1855—December, LOW, 9c. A SECOND HIGHER BOTTOM, and a safe buying point.

1857—September and October, HIGH, 1570. A DOUBLE TOP.

1858—January LOW, 925. A THIRD HIGHER BOTTOM and safer BUYING LEVEL.

1858—September and October, HIGH 1375. A DOUBLE TOP and SELLING LEVEL.

1859—December, 740. A FOURTH HIGHER BOTTOM and a safer place to buy.

1860—December, 725. A DOUBLE BOTTOM one year later. Notice that from 1844 to 1860, a period of 16 years, the market has been making HIGHER BOTTOMS and HIGHER TOPS. The trend was UP. The war broke out in 1861 and war is always bullish on cotton. The market had already laid the foundation for higher prices and had given definite signals for making HIGHER BOTTOMS right along.

1863—February HIGH, 91c. A SINGLE TOP and the highest in history up to that time.
June, LOW, 53c. A SINGLE BOTTOM.
October, HIGH, 92c. A DOUBLE TOP   against February and a SELLING LEVEL.

1864—April, LOW 71c. A SINGLE BOTTOM, much higher than the previous.
September, EXTREME HIGH $1.89 per pound, a SINGLE SHARP TOP, from which it rapidly declined.

1865—April, LOW 37c. A SINGLE sharp BOTTOM.
October, HIGH 59c. A SINGLE TOP.

1866—May, 33c. A SINGLE sharp BOTTOM, 4c under the low of April, 1865.
You can see from the above record that before the war ended the market started to discount it. That is what cotton and the other commodities often do when important events occur. That is why, as a rule, you can buy on bad news and sell on good news. There are exceptions to this, but as a rule, the position of prices on charts and the time will tell you whether good or bad news is going to act on the market opposite to the general trend or whether it will reverse.

1866—October HIGH 37c. Under the old BOTTOM of 1865 and a SELLING LEVEL. A SINGLE sharp BOTTOM. The market broke fast from this high.

1867—December, 1570. A SINGLE sharp BOTTOM.

1868—May and July HIGH 3250. A DOUBLE TOP and SELLING LEVEL.

1869—August, HIGH 35c. A SINGLE TOP and the LAST HIGH before a big DECLINE.

1871—March and April, LOW 1350. A DOUBLE BOTTOM and the lowest since 1860.

1872—June, HIGH 2740. A SINGLE sharp TOP, from which a fast decline followed. Note that 100% advance on the last low of 1350 gave 27c, making this a SELLING LEVEL.

1872—September, LOW 1770. A SINGLE sharp TOP.

1873—February, HIGH 2250. A natural SELLING LEVEL on the basis of 5c for LOW LEVEL.

1873—April, LOW 18c. A SINGLE BOTTOM.

1873—June, LOW 18c. A DOUBLE BOTTOM and BUYING LEVEL. July, HIGH 2190. A SECOND LOWER top and a SAFE SELLING LEVEL.

1873—November and December, LOW 1380. A DOUBLE BOTTOM and the same as 1871.

1874—May, HIGH 19c. A SINGLE TOP and SELLING LEVEL. October, LOW 1440. December, LOW 1410. A DOUBLE BOTTOM and higher than 1873, making this a buying level.

1875—March and April, 1740. A DOUBLE TOP lower than 1874 and a SELLING LEVEL.

1875—October, 1270. A SINGLE BOTTOM.

1875—December, HIGH 1470.

1876—March, HIGH 1470. A DOUBLE TOP the same as December, 1875.

1876—May, June and July, 1140 LOW. A TRIPLE BOTTOM and BUYING LEVEL.

1877—January, HIGH 1770. A TRIPLE TOP against 1875 and 1876, a safe SELLING LEVEL, as it was just under old BOTTOMS.

1878—November and December, 960 and 950 LOWS. A DOUBLE BOTTOM. Note the last EXTREME HIGH in October, 1866, was 37c and in 1869 August HIGH was 35c. Note 75% of 37c is 925 and holding above this level indicates strength. The 1874, May HIGH was 19c, a 100% advance on 950, would give 19c a selling level and the last HIGH in May, 1874 was 19c, making this a DOUBLE TOP.

1879—May, HIGH, 1420. A SINGLE TOP, but a DOUBLE TOP and TRIPLE TOP against 1875, 1876 and slightly lower than these tops.

1879—August, LOW 10c. A SINGLE BOTTOM and higher than 1878, showing strength.

1879—December, HIGH 1490. A SINGLE TOP and a SELLING LEVEL.

1880—September, LOW 1050. A SINGLE BOTTOM, but the SECOND HIGHER BOTTOM from 1878, indicating strength and higher prices.

1880—December, HIGH 1355. A SINGLE TOP and a LOWER TOP, a SELLING LEVEL.

1881—May, LOW 1035. A DOUBLE BOTTOM AND A THIRD HIGHER BOTTOM.

1881—August, HIGH 13c. A DOUBLE TOP and a THIRD LOWER TOP, showing weakness. Main trend down. Market continued to decline with only small rallies.

1883—April and July, LOW 980 and 970. A DOUBLE BOTTOM the same as 1878. Buy for a rally.

1884—April and July, HIGH 1140. A TRIPLE TOP AND SELLING LEVEL.

1884—October, LOW 965. A DOUBLE BOTTOM against 1883.

1885—February, HIGH 1150. A DOUBLE TOP AGAINST 1884 and a SELLING LEVEL.

1886—February, LOW 870. A SINGLE BOTTOM.

1887—June, HIGH 1050. A LOWER TOP and a SELLING LEVEL.

1887—July to October, 920. A DOUBLE BOTTOM.

1887—December, HIGH 1090. A DOUBLE TOP and SELLING LEVEL.

1888—October, LOW 920. A DOUBLE BOTTOM AGAINST 1887. A slow advance followed.

1890—March, HIGH 1140. A DOUBLE TOP against 1885, a SELLING LEVEL.

1892—March, LOW 630. A SINGLE BOTTOM but a support LEVEL and a buy for rally.

1893—July, HIGH 1020. A SINGLE TOP and selling LEVEL.

1894—November, LOW 510. This was an EXTREME LOW, but cotton sold at 5c per pound at this time. These are the lowest prices since 1844 down to the base of 5c per pound and a buy for an investment, as cotton was below the cost of production. The market held for five months in a narrow trading range, showing that there was enough buying to absorb all the selling and the market could not go lower.

1895—October, HIGH 925. A SINGLE TOP and lower than 1893.

1896—July, LOW 620. A HIGHER BOTTOM than 1894 and a SAFER BUYING LEVEL.

1896—September, HIGH 870. A DOUBLE TOP and a LOWER TOP. A SELLING LEVEL.

1898—October and November, LOW 515. A DOUBLE BOTTOM against 1894 and a safe BUYING LEVEL. July option, 540, a double bottom against 1894. After nearly two years in a hundred point range, the main trend turned up in 1899, showing strong uptrend.

1900—July, 10c. A RESISTANCE LEVEL. A 100% advance on 5c. September, LOW 875. A RESISTANCE LEVEL and a HIGHER BOTTOM. A BUYING POINT.

1900—October, HIGH 10c. A DOUBLE TOP and a SELLING LEVEL.

1901—July, LOW 720. A DOUBLE BOTTOM and higher than December, 1899. A buying level.

1901—November, 720. A DOUBLE BOTTOM against July, making this a safer buying point, as this was in a month for seasonal LOW.

1902—May, HIGH 960. A LOWER TOP and SELLING POINT. September and December, LOW 830 and 820. HIGHER BOTTOMS than 1901, showing main trend UPWARD.

1903—July, HIGH 1380. This was the year of the bad crop, due to boll weevil damage. Daniel J. Sulley made a fortune by buying cotton and the whole South followed him, which brought about a rapid advance. Note that 1380 was the highest since 1881. This was a natural SELLING LEVEL. A sharp decline followed.

1903—October, LOW 930. A DOUBLE BOTTOM and back to old TOP and BOTTOM LEVELS. A rapid advance followed, the crop being very short.

1904—February, HIGH 1755, for the July option — the highest since August, 1869, when prices were 35c. Note that 50% of 35c is 1750, making this a SELLING LEVEL, and 1750 was 250% advance on the base of 5c.

1904—March, — Daniel J. Sulley failed and a big decline followed.

1904—December, LOW 685 for the July option, back to 1899 and 1900 bottom levels. Cotton held for five months in a 150 point range, showing it was extremely inactive. No one believed it would go up again. Farmers were burning up cotton in Texas.

1905—March, LOW 7c. A THIRD HIGHER BOTTOM and a BUYING LEVEL. These low prices in the Spring of the year caused farmers to plant less cotton and was the seasonal month to buy.

1905—August, HIGH 1260. Over 5c advance from the low in March and in a month for seasonal HIGH. Back under old bottoms of 1904. A SELLING LEVEL. From 510 to 1755, the half-way point is 1185 and 1250 is a natural SELLING LEVEL, being 150% on the 5c base. A decline followed.

1906—August, LOW 9c. One year from the top, running opposite the seasonal trend and time to watch for bottom.
October, HIGH 1165. A LOWER TOP than 1905.

1907—January to April LOW 930. A DOUBLE BOTTOM against August, 1906, a safe buying point. A rally followed. 1907 was the year of crop scares and damage by floods occurred.

1907—July HIGH 1295. A DOUBLE TOP against 1905 and a SELLING LEVEL. The market held and made a LOWER TOP in August and September. In September, the month for seasonal change in trend, the main trend was DOWNWARD, and the market declined.

1907—December, LOW 10c. A RESISTANCE LEVEL and down to the lows of 1908.

1908—January, HIGH 1150. AN OLD TOP AND BOTTOM LEVEL. A SELLING LEVEL.

1908—April and May, LOW 850. AN OLD BOTTOM LEVEL AND A BUYING LEVEL. A sharp rally followed in May, making HIGH 1140, a DOUBLE TOP against January, 1908, a SELLING POINT. This was the time that Livermore cornered the cotton market and made a vast fortune.

1908—October, LOW 830. A DOUBLE BOTTOM and higher than in 1908. A safe BUYING LEVEL. Cotton was slow for several months.

1909—April—THE BREAKAWAY POINT. Prices reached the old tops at 960, showing strong UPTREND and a fast move followed. This was the breakaway point and the run where big money is always made in a short period of time. Crossing 1065, half of 1290 to 815, showed strong uptrend. Eugene Scales was the Bull leader this year and the whole South followed him on the Up-side the same as they followed Sulley. Whenever there is someone trying to bull the market, if they have a leader, they all buy. The market advanced rapidly and reactions were small.

1909—December, HIGH 1650. Under the top of 1904, the Sulley year. The advance had run over fourteen months. The change in trend was due because December was the month for LOWS. The market was running opposite the seasonal trend and the reaction was overdue. A sharp decline followed.

1910—January, LOW 1340. Old TOP and old BOTTOM LEVELS. Note 1375 is a natural buying level. A rally followed.

February, HIGH 15c. Only one month's rally and a selling point. April, LOW 14c. A HIGHER BOTTOM and a BUYING LEVEL.

1910—July, HIGH 1655. A DOUBLE TOP and a SELLING POINT.

1910—September, LOW 1290. September is the month for a seasonal change in trend. This was the time to buy.

1910—December, HIGH 1545. A LOWER TOP and a three months' rally. Change in trend due. This was one year from the high in December, 1909 and the market seldom makes more than two tops opposite the seasonal trend. A decline followed.

1911—February LOW 1375. AN OLD BOTTOM and a BUYING LEVEL. May, HIGH 1615. A THIRD TOP and slightly lower. Triple tops three years apart. Our rule says that the greatest decline comes from triple tops or triple bottoms. The 1911 crop for the year turned out to be a very large crop and the market was a safe short sale in May because it was a month for seasonal change in trend. From 1290 to 1650, the 50% or half way point is 1470. Crossing this level indicated much lower prices and a selling point. The market declined fast and rallies were very small.

1911—December LOW 880. Down to 1908 and 1909 BOTTOMS. December was the month for change in trend. In the two previous years the market had gone opposite the seasonal trend and made TOPS in December. This was a fast move down. Our rule says watch for change in trend in the sixth to seventh month. There had been no important rallies since the market went down in May. This was the place to BUY.

1912—January—the trend turned UP and prices crossed highs of previous months, making a safer buy.

1912—July, HIGH 13c. Under old bottoms. Seven months' rally. Time for a change in trend. Sell out long and sell short. September, LOW 1065. This was the month to watch for important change in trend. Note from 880 to 13c, 1090 was the half-way point and the market had declined for three months. When it crossed 1090 again it indicated much higher.

1912—December, HIGH 13c. A DOUBLE TOP and SELLING LEVEL. Again running opposite the seasonal trend and one year from the previous BOTTOM, making it important for change, according to our rules.

1913—April, LOW 1125. Held three months around this level. A BUYING LEVEL.

September HIGH 1385. Under OLD BOTTOMS of five months and again September is the month to watch for seasonal change in trend. Time to sell out and sell short.

1914—March, LOW 1150. A DOUBLE BOTTOM and higher than 1913. A BUYING LEVEL.

1914—June, HIGH 1340. A LOWER TOP and a three months' rally and a month for change in trend. A decline started and when war news came at the end of July, the market broke wide open.

July 30, LOW 10c for July cotton. The Exchange was closed on account of heavy selling and remained closed until November, 1914, when it re-opened.

December, LOW 750 for the July options. A RESISTANCE LEVEL and higher than 1904 and 1905 lows. Note that one-half of 1650 was 825. Under this price was a safe buying level, but when it crossed 825 again, it was a safer buy because it showed stronger uptrend. War has always been bullish on cotton.

1915—April, HIGH 1050. Under the old bottom and a SELLING POINT. July, LOW 840. A HIGHER BOTTOM and a three months' DECLINE. 750 to 10c made 9c the half-way point and crossing this level it was a safer buy. Later when it crossed 1050, you should have bought more.

1915—October, HIGH 1360. A TRIPLE TOP against 1913 and 1914. A SELLING LEVEL, as October was running opposite the seasonal trend and the advance had lasted three months. Time for a change. Sell out and sell short.

November, LOW 1180. One month's normal reaction. Rally followed.

December, HIGH 1325. A LOWER TOP, and December running opposite the seasonal trend and one year from the EXTREME LOW. A change in trend was due. This was the time to sell short protected with close STOP LOSS ORDER.

1916—February, LOW 1140. A LOWER BOTTOM LEVEL and only two months' normal reaction. February is one of the months for LOWS and for a change in trend.

In May the trend turned up.

June, HIGH 1350. An old TOP LEVEL for the fourth time. Our rule says when prices reach the same level the fourth time they nearly always go higher.   There was only a small reaction in August and prices crossed the old top, the highest since 1904, indicating higher prices.

In October prices crossed 1755 and crossed the TOPS of all moves since 1872 and 1874, indicating much higher prices.

1916—November, high 2150. Back to the OLD TOPS of 1872 and 1873, and 2125 was the RESISTANCE LEVEL from the base of 5c.   November running opposite the seasonal trend and this last move had lasted four months and the market was up two years from the EXTREME LOW.   A CHANGE IN TREND was due. When markets are very fast and active, as they were at this time, you should use daily and weekly high and low charts, applying all of the same rules to the daily charts.   Watching when the time is overbalanced and when the last reaction point is broken, also watch the 25 and 50% points of the last high.   Do not overlook the fact to watch for change in trend in the third and four months and knowing that in normal markets small reactions often only run 30 to 36 days.

If you are in position where you can keep up close moves on the market when the market is very active, keep a chart of every 30 point move, watch the bottoms and tops made on the 30 point chart.   The first time it breaks back under a bottom, the 30 point move would indicate the change in trend, and crossing the tops of the 30 point moves indicates higher.   This is an exception to the general rule and you should use the daily chart to apply all of these rules, which will catch these fast moves.   Watch the market as it moves up to see whether the reaction is two or three days and if it has a long run, which it often does, never reacting more than two days.   The first time it breaks back three days or closes lower the second day, it is an indication of change in trend and you should reverse sell out and sell short.   Apply the same rule on a fast declining market.   If rallies only last two days, then after a sharp quick decline, the first time there is a rally of two days or more, cover shorts and buy, or buy on the first and secondary reactions, after the first sharp advance.   You should use the daily high and low charts in very rapid moving markets.

Note that 200% advance on 750, the last low, gave 2250 as a possible resistance level.

1917—February 2, LOW 1375. Down to old top levels.   This sharp decline of 300 to 400 points in one day was caused by the German U-Boat scare when Germans declared unrestricted U-Boat warfare and it was generally known that we would enter the war.

Note that 33 1/3% of 2160 was 1440.   The market was three months down and this was a panicky decline and our rule says to always BUY on panicky declines and sell on rapid advances. 1375 was 175% on 5c, the base, a BUYING LEVEL, and was a buy anywhere from 1440 down.   Crossing 1440 again showed strong uptrend and from 2160 to 1375, the half-way point or 50% point was 1762.   Crossing this level later showed strong uptrend and later crossing 2160 was a very strong uptrend.

1917—July, HIGH 2750. Note June 1872 high 2750 and then applying the rule, adding 100% advance to the bottom of 1375 gives 2750. This proves the value of these rules and proves the value of keeping the old records, because these rules give 2750 as the SELLING LEVEL and it was the fifth month up and a fast advance, and was three years from the time the war started. A change in trend was due and this was the time to sell out and go short.

1917—LOW 2005. Note from 1375 to 2750 the half-way point is 2062. This was only a two months reaction, a normal reaction, and the market was down to a BUYING LEVEL. 20c per pound is 300% on the base of 5c, making this a BUYING LEVEL and we always watch for a change in trend in September and as the market has had a sharp decline, we expect the trend to be up. Therefore, buy and protect with STOP LOSS ORDERS about 50 points down.

1917—December, the price crossed 2750, the old HIGH, and back into new high territory, the highest level since the Civil War. The World War was creating a great demand for cotton, causing higher prices.

1918—January, HIGH 31c.
February, LOW 2880. A one month's normal reaction in a bull market. Buy for a rally.

1918—April, HIGH 3390. OLD BOTTOM. Note August, 1866, high 33c—the market had advanced for seven months and had been a fast move up from February, making fourteen months up and a change in trend was due. No reaction had lasted for more than two months. From the last LOW 2880 to 3390 the 25% reaction point was 32.65. Breaking 3060 the LOW of March indicated much lower prices. From 3390 to the LOW of 1375 gives 2387 as the half-way point.

1918—May, LOW 2310. A decline of 1070 points in two months. The market then rallied and held for two months, June and July, above 24c, making it then a safer BUYING POINT, after the market had settled and made HIGHER BOTTOM. Higher prices continued and a fast move followed.

1918—September and July option, HIGH 3550.
The October option at this time sold for 3725, which was a record for that option. Refer to August, 1869 high of 35c, which made this a selling level, and the 1904 high of 1755, 100% advance gave 3510 as a SELLING LEVEL. These old landmarks or peak prices of high mountain ranges are valuable guides for the future.

1919—January, LOW 1920. From 3550 to 1920 there was a decline of 1630 points in four months. Our rule says fast moves seldom last longer than four months. January was the month for seasonal LOW and this was the time to BUY.
September, 1917, last low 2005 and April, 1917, last low 1920, making 1920 a place to watch for BOTTOM and to BUY protected by CLOSE STOP LOSS ORDERS.

1919—July, HIGH 36c. A DOUBLE TOP as against 1918 and a SELLING LEVEL.

1919—September, LOW 2850. AN OLD TOP AND BOTTOM LEVEL. Only a two months' reaction and a normal reaction. September is a month for seasonal change in trend and one year from 1918 TOP. Time to watch for a change in trend.

1919—October option sold at this time for 3725 a second time, making a DOUBLE TOP and making this a SELLING LEVEL.

1919—November. July cotton sold at 3630, a DOUBLE TOP against July, 1919.

1919—December, LOW 2910. A HIGHER BOTTOM.

1920—January, HIGH 34c. A LOWER TOP.

1920—February, LOW 2940. A THIRD HIGHER BOTTOM AND BUYING LEVEL.

1920—April for July cotton, HIGH 4030.
October option HIGH 3725 for the third time at exactly the same price. Our rules are that the greatest decline comes from triple tops, especially where there are three tops three years apart, or three consecutive years. April was the high month for all options, some options selling as high as 4320.
In the month of July the July options sold at 4375, the highest of any option, but as far as time periods are concerned, the real TOP must be figured for April and the high prices for April are the bases for figuring TOPS and BOTTOMS. You will find it will work out accurately if you take 4320 for the TOP BASE and figure from 4320 to 5c per pound.
Refer to 1866 October HIGH of 44c. These highs in April, 1920 and July, 1920, were close to this level.
The October option high of 3725 to 515 gives the half-way point at 1862, and that is half of 3725, and half of 515 to 3725 gives 2120 as an important, half-way point.
The last low of October option in December, 1919, was 21c and 12½% of the range from 3725 would give 3520. Breaking this level showed downtrend and indicated lower levels.

1920—April, Low 3375. High 3525 for October option.

1920—May for October option High 3680, Low 3420. This gives 35c as the half-way point and breaking this point indicated weakness and showed this was the time to SELL more. When the market broke 3420, the LOW of May, it was in a still weaker position and a rapid decline followed. Later prices broke 2920, the low of February, 1920, and a wide open break followed.
From the 1919 January LOW 1810 to 3725 gave 2767 as 50% point. When prices broke under this level, it was a wide open break. This was the year when cotton should have been sold short all the way down and a great fortune could have been made in one year. Opportunities of this kind come many years apart and when they do come, either on the UP or DOWN side, if you play the trend as long as it runs one way, you can make a very large amount of money.

1920—December, LOW 1360 for October cotton. Down to the 1917 LOW. December is the month for seasonal lows and time to BUY for rally, especially after such a drastic decline.

1921—January, HIGH 1660, a 300 point rally in one month, a normal rally and the time to sell out and go short as the main trend was still downward. As long as the market held under 1867, one-half of 3725, it was still in a weak position.

1921—March, LOW 1210. Down to 1916 lows and at SUPPORT LEVELS. A rally followed. Remember after every sharp decline there comes first a sharp rally and then a *secondary decline*, when it is *safer to buy*. Always remember to apply this rule for TOPS and BOTTOMS where there are fast moves.

May, HIGH 1520. From this level to 1210 gives 320 points, about the same number of points as the rally from December, 1920 to January, 1921, which was 300 points. This was a level to SELL. A decline followed.

1921—June, LOW 1125. Down to the lows of February, 1916, and a SECONDARY RALLY, and only 60 points under March, 1921. and fourteen months from April, 1920, time for a change. From 1520 to 1150, note 1335 is the half-way point. Crossing this level indicated strength and higher prices and later when prices crossed 1520, they showed strong UPTREND and it was time to BUY more. A rapid advance followed.

1921—September, HIGH 2180. Note that 2120 was one-half of 515 to 3725, the extreme high and low on October cotton, making 2160 a SELLING LEVEL. 2160 was one-half of 4320, the highest any option sold in April, 1920. This was the month for a seasonal change in trend and as a big advance had taken place and it lasted for three months, this was the time to sell out LONG COTTON and go short. A decline followed. October, LOW 1585. Figuring from 1050 to 2210, the 50% point was 1630 and 3/8 of 4375 was 1541, making 1585 a BUYING LEVEL for a rally.

December, HIGH 1820. A two months' normal rally, making DOUBLE TOP, a SELLING LEVEL, as the market was running opposite the seasonal trend and a change was due.

1922—January, LOW 1550. A DOUBLE BOTTOM against October low and January was a month for seasonal change. Buy for a rally. The market held for several months in a narrow trading range, with prices under 18c. In May crossed six months TOP around the 18c level, showing strong uptrend. This was the place to BUY more.

From 1550 LOW to 2210 HIGH, the 50%, or half-way point was 1880. When prices crossed this level, they showed strong uptrend.

June, HIGH 2310. Under old BOTTOMS and a SELLING LEVEL. 2270 was one-half of 515 to 4030. The market was up six months from the LOW and this was the time to watch for a change in trend and a reaction.

August and September, LOW 2110. A DOUBLE BOTTOM
and a BUYING LEVEL, as 2015 was 50% or ½ of 4030, the
high in April, 1920. September was the important month for a
change in trend. Prices moved up and crossed 2160, half-way of
4320, showing strong uptrend, and later crossed the TOP at 2310.
This was the third section of the bull market. Note that a 200%
advance on 1050 is 3150, or the RESISTANCE LEVEL.

1923—March, HIGH 3070. Failing to reach 3150 was a sign of weakness. From the LOW in January of 1550, a 100% advance would
be 3100, making this a strong RESISTANCE LEVEL and a
SELLING LEVEL under 31c. This was six months of a fast
advance and our rule says to watch for the change in trend in the
sixth or seventh month. This was 21 months from the 1921 LOW
and 15 months from December, 1921 LOW.

When markets are very active and making a wide range as
they were at this time, you should use the daily and weekly high
and low charts for the first indication of a change in trend. The
daily and weekly charts showed that the market was meeting
selling around 3070. The advance from 2110 to 3070 was 1060
points and 50% on 2010 was 3015, making this the SELLING
LEVEL. The first decline of 12½% from this level or breaking
2930, was a SELLING LEVEL, and when prices broke below
the previous month, it is an indication of lower prices.

1923—May, LOW 2350. AN OLD TOP and BOTTOM. This was a
two months' normal reaction and was followed by a quick rally.

June, HIGH 29c. A one month's rally and a LOWER TOP. A
sharp decline followed.

August, LOW 22c. The old TOP and BOTTOM LEVELS of
September, 1921 and note that 2188 was 50% of 4375, the extreme
HIGH. August was a month for a change in the seasonal trend,
with the market down five months from the extreme high, or
from the TOP in March.

During the month of August crop reports were very bad and
the government crop report on the 8th was very bullish, showing
a short crop. This was the year when there was too much rain
and floods and the boll weevil did serious damage. From the 1st
of August, one of the fastest declines in history followed, prices
crossing all RESISTANCE LEVELS. September. The crop report this month was extremely bullish. Prices crossed the 50%
resistance level of the last move, and later crossed the old TOP
of 3070 showing strong UPTREND. This was the kind of a market where you could have bought all the way up and made a
fortune in four months' time.

1923—November 30th. Final High. HIGH 3650 for March cotton.

December HIGH 3770. Note that 250% advance on 1050 LOW
gives 3675. November was running opposite to the seasonal
trend, due to very short crop year. This was a four months' fast
advance and our rule says to watch for a change in trend as these
fast advances seldom run more than four months. The market

was 30 months, or two and a half years, from extreme LOW. Also 24 months up from December, 1921 LOW of 1550 and was in the fourth, or final section, of a bull market. The fourth month marked the end and a change in trend. This was the time to sell out all LONG COTTON and sell short, regardless of how bullish the news was. Everything was discounted and a sharp decline followed.

SECTIONS OF THE BULL MARKET.

First section, 1050 to 2210, an advance of 1160 points.
Second section, 1550 to 2310, an advance of 860 points.
Third section, 22c to 3650 for July cotton, an advance of 1450 points.

> Note that in 1918 and 1919 there were old
> TOPS around 3550 to 3630, making tops in
> November RESISTANCE LEVELS.

The total advance from 1050 to 3650 for July cotton was 26c or 2600 points. $12\frac{1}{2}\%$ is 1375. 25% is 1700. 33 1/3% is 1916. $\frac{3}{8}$, or $37\frac{1}{2}\%$ was 2025. 50%, or $\frac{1}{2}$, equals 2350. $\frac{5}{8}$ equals 2675. 2/3 equals 2882. 75% equals 30c. $\frac{7}{8}$ equals 3325 and 100% equals 3650.

Therefore, when the market broke back under 3325, the $12\frac{1}{2}\%$ point, it indicated lower. Study of the daily high, low and weekly charts at this time would have given the first indication of the important change.

At 3650 the extreme high levels on July cotton, the percentages are as follows:

> $12\frac{1}{2}\%$ is 456. 25% is 912. 33 1/3% is 1216.
> $37\frac{1}{2}\%$ is 1368. 50% is 1825. 66 2/3% is 2432.
> 75% is 2737. $87\frac{1}{2}\%$ is 3300. 100% is 3650.

From the last LOW, 1550 to 3650, the 50% or half-way point is 26c.

In November, 1923, when extreme highs had been reached, prices had been advancing for several days at 200 points per day, which was the limit of fluctuation allowed in one day. The market had become heavily over-bought. The public were bullish and talked 50c per pound for cotton. When these conditions exist, it is time to go against the crowd and against the public and sell short.

1924—March, LOW 2590. Total decline of 1060 points, or 100% on the base of 5c per pound. 25% of 2650 was 912 points off of 3650. 150% advance on the LOW of 1050 gives 2625, making this a SUPPORT LEVEL and a BUYING LEVEL. The market was twelve months from March, 1923. A change in trend was due. The time period was four months' decline against the four months' advance. Time had balanced. From 3650 to 2590, gives a 50%, or half-way point at 3120. One-eighth of the range is 2723. Crossing 2723 at $12\frac{1}{2}\%$ between 3650 and 2590 indicated higher prices.

1924—April, HIGH 3050. Old TOP and old BOTTOM LEVELS. From 1050 to 3650, a 75% advance gives 30c, making a TOP of 3050 a SELLING LEVEL. A sharp decline followed.

May, LOW 2760. This was 62½% of 4375 and 2675 was 62½% of 1050 to 3650 and 75% of 3650 was 2737, making this a BUYING LEVEL for a RALLY.

1924—July. Prices crossed 3050, the old high, indicating higher, and the July options reached a high of 3540 in the month of July.

This was under old TOP LEVELS and around the 1918 TOPS. It was a four months advance, the same period as two previous moves and twelve months from July, 1923. A change in trend was due. Time to sell out and go short.

OCTOBER OPTIONS, weekly.

From this time on we will use the October options for examples of changes in trend and BUYING and SELLING LEVELS. In 1923, December, the October option was 30c.

1924—August, HIGH 2990. A DOUBLE TOP and SELLING LEVEL.

Also, 2996 was 75% of 3725, the TRIPLE TOP on the October option. In 1923, July 30, October option LOW 2090.

In 1923, October option HIGH in the month of October, 3030, making 2610 the important 50% or half-way point on the October option.

RESISTANCE LEVELS. October option 3130 to 2090.

12½	% equals	30c
25	% "	2870
33 1/3%	"	2784
37½	% "	2740
50	% "	2610
62½	% "	2580
66 2/3%	"	2430
75	% "	2350
87½	% "	2020
100	% "	2090

Therefore, the October option at 30c was an exact percentage point and SELLING LEVEL. Then breaking under 2870 was the first indication of lower prices.

1924—SEPTEMBER 20th—October option LOW 2150. A HIGHER BOTTOM than 1923. It was very important to find out the reason why the option met support at 2150. From 515, the LOW of 1898, to the EXTREME HIGH of 3725 for October option,— the 50% or half-way point was 2120 and the EXTREME HIGH LEVEL in April, 1920, of any option was 4320. 50% of this was 2160, making 2150 a BUYING LEVEL, protected with a STOP LOSS ORDER

OCTOBER 6th, HIGH 2660. A two weeks' rally. A normal rally. Again, 2610 was the half-way point from 2090 to 3130, making this a SELLING LEVEL.

NOVEMBER 1st—October option LOW 2150. A DOUBLE BOTTOM and back to the 50%, or half-way point. A SAFE BUYING LEVEL.

NOVEMBER 15th—HIGH 2415. UNDER OLD BOTTOM. A one week's rally. A SAFER PLACE TO BUY. The last HIGH on October cotton in October was 2660. The last LOW was 2150. 50% of this was 2405, making 2415 a SAFE SELLING LEVEL.

DECEMBER 6th, LOW 2255. A 50% reaction of the last move, making this a BUYING LEVEL. Prices moved up and crossed 2415, indicating higher points.

1925—MARCH 7th, 14th and 21st. Each week made a high of 2560, A TRIPLE TOP. Another reason why this was a SELLING LEVEL was that from 515 to 3725, note 62½% was 2520, and the market was four months from the last LOW. March is the month for seasonal trend, making this a SELLING LEVEL.

APRIL 4th, LOW 2385. A rally followed.

APRIL 25th, HIGH 2515. A LOWER TOP and a RESISTANCE LEVEL. A SELLING LEVEL. A decline followed. The market made three weeks BOTTOMS under 24c, then turned the trend down.

MAY 16th, LOW 2155. The third time this important half-way point was reached. A TRIPLE BOTTOM and a BUYING POINT, with STOP LOSS ORDER around 21c. A rally followed.

1925—JULY 30th, HIGH 2560. A DOUBLE TOP and the same as March and four months later. A change in trend due. SELL short, protected with STOP LOSS ORDER at 2590. A decline followed.

SEPTEMBER 5th, LOW 2175. The FOURTH HIGHER BOTTOM, holding above 2160, half of 4320 and 2120 is 50% of 515 to 3725. A two weeks' rally followed.

SEPTEMBER 19th, HIGH 2475. A FOURTH LOWER TOP. A sign of weakness. This rally was only a normal rally and September is a month for seasonal change in trend, making this the time to sell and sell short.

For the week ending October 10th, the LOW for the October option was 2120, at the 50% point between 515 and 3725. The market rallied to 2180.

The May option and July option had made THREE BOTTOMS around 2160 in 1924 and 1925, proving how important this 50% point, or one-half of the HIGH SELLING PRICE, is.

MAY AND JULY OPTIONS:

1925—October. In this month, both the May and July options broke under 2160 for the first time since 1923 and a wide open break followed because, like water breaking over or under a dam, the upward pressure forces prices lower fast and once the half-way point or gravity center was broken, the next important point was 1862 to 1800, or one-half of 1923 HIGH, and of the October option one-half of 3725. An important SUPPORT POINT and was indicated after breaking the other important points.

1925—October. May cotton declined to 1850, the next important half-way point of resistance, and down to old top of 1922, making this a BUYING LEVEL.

1925—November, HIGH 2040. Under old bottoms and one-half of 2160 to 1840. Only a one month's normal rally. November is a month for change in trend.

1925—December, LOW 1835. A DOUBLE BOTTOM at the half-way point. A SAFE BUY, protected with STOP LOSS ORDERS. December is the month for seasonal LOWS.

1926—January, HIGH 20c. Under OLD BOTTOMS and RESIST-ANCE LEVEL.

March, LOW 1830. The THIRD BOTTOM made at the same level. A BUYING LEVEL for rally.

May, HIGH 19c. A small rally. A DOUBLE TOP and SELL-ING LEVEL.

HERE WE GIVE EXAMPLES IN OCTOBER OPTION:

1926—March. The October option LOW 1725, had broken 1862, 50% of 3725 and 37½% of 515 to 3725 was 1717, making 1725 a BUY-ING LEVEL for a rally.

1926—April, HIGH 1810. A SELLING LEVEL as long as the market was under 1862.

1926—June. October option broke 1725.

June 19th,—LOW 1620.

1926—July 10th, LOW 1610. A DOUBLE BOTTOM and BUYING LEVEL.

July 30th, HIGH 1810. A DOUBLE TOP against April. A three weeks' normal rally and a SELLING LEVEL.

1926—August 14th, LOW 1810. The third time at this low level. A BUYING LEVEL, but be sure to protect with STOP LOSS ORDER around 1890.

August 20th, HIGH 1815. A TRIPLE TOP and SELLING LEVEL. Still under the important half-way point. A one week's reaction followed, to 1750.

1926—September 11th, HIGH 1805. The fourth time at this same level, but slightly lower. Time to sell short, as September is the month for seasonal change in trend. In view of the fact that the market had held below 1860, the half-way point, for 9 months, it showed it was a very weak position. On September 8th, the government showed the largest crop for many years,—in fact, a record crop.

A big decline followed, but the market had already forecast big crop by declining under the important 50% point of HIGH SELLING LEVEL and staying there for many months. This again proves that *time and price* tell the story and forecast the trend often long before the news comes out.

OCTOBER 9th, LOW 1260. A RESISTANCE LEVEL, one-third, or 33 1/3% of 3725, was 1242. A rally followed.

OCTOBER 13th, HIGH 1375. A one week's rally.

DECEMBER 4th, LOW 1250. Again at the RESISTANCE POINT, a DOUBLE BOTTOM. A big crop had been discounted and December a seasonal month for LOWS made this a BUYING LEVEL. In 1923 the October option HIGH was 3130 to 1250 LOW made 2190 the 50% point. A total decline of 1880, made 235 points, 12½% of the range, and 117 points 6¼% of the range. The first rally of 117 points would indicate higher and an advance of 235 points on 1250 or crossing 1585, would be a signal for higher prices. The bad news was out and the worst had been discounted. The demand for cotton was the largest it had been for many years. Therefore, this was the time to BUY.

October cotton crept up slowly and crossed 1367, the first indication of higher prices.

1927—January 15th—crossed the top of 13 weeks, or one-fourth of a year—showing strong uptrend.

March 5th, HIGH 1490. Just under the 15c level, which is always a selling level or a buying level when prices react around this level. However, the main trend was UP and only a two weeks' reaction followed to 1390. A 100 point decline was a normal decline in a normal period of time and, failing to react 50% from the last move, showed strong uptrend.

1927—July. The government report showed a short crop. Prices moved up fast and crossed 1862, the half-way point.

JULY 30th, HIGH 1915. Back to the OLD TOP and a sale for a reaction. The market was seven months UP from the bottom. Watch for change in trend in the sixth and seventh months.

AUGUST 6th, LOW 17c. A one week's sharp decline down to old bottom levels of 1718 which was 37½% of 515 to 3725, making this a BUYING LEVEL. From the bottom of 1250 we will figure percentages on this. 50% advance on 1250 would be 1875.

AUGUST 8th, Government report bullish, showing short crop. A rapid advance followed, prices crossing 1862, the important point, and later crossed the TOP at 1915 showing strong uptrend.

SEPTEMBER 8th, HIGH 2440. An advance of 740 points in one month's time. This was the final grand rush and the market was up nine months from the December, 1926 LOW, and no reaction lasted more than two weeks. September is the month for seasonal change in trend and when TOPS come out in September, it is an important reversal. This was one year from 1926 TOP.

This was the time to sell long cotton and sell short. The last TOP in September, 1925, was 2475 and 2477 was 75% of 515 to 3725. This was a SAFE SELLING LEVEL. The market was the safest short sale when prices broke back for three weeks because time had then exceeded the greatest reaction on the way up. Also when prices broke over 100 points was an indication of lower prices.

1927—SEPTEMBER 24th, LOW 1980. A two weeks' sharp decline of 460 points. A point to BUY FOR RALLY. Remember that a *secondary rally* always follows the first sharp decline and usually a secondary rally is at least 50% of the first decline. Figuring 2440 to 1980 would give the 50% point at 2210.

OCTOBER, HIGH 2190. Under the 50% resistance point. A SELLING POINT and only a one week's rally. A fast decline followed breaking 1980, showing the market in a very weak position and later breaking 1862, the important 50% point, and showed the main trend down.

DECEMBER 17th, LOW 1800. A rally due.

DECEMBER 24th AND 31st, HIGH 1910. Under old bottoms and a SELLING LEVEL and only a two weeks' rally.

1928—February 4th, LOW 17c. A DOUBLE BOTTOM against August, 1927, and a buying level. Down 740 points and February a month for a change in trend. The market was down five months and eleven months from the last low, March, 1927. A rally followed and prices crossed 1862, the important point, showing uptrend.

From 2440 to 17c, the 50% point was 2070, and 2258 was 33 1/3% of 3130 to 515.

1928—June 30th, LAST HIGH 2280.
The market held for two weeks above 2200, then broke 2200, showing downtrend and greater weakness. The greatest reaction had been from 2155 to 2015, or 160 points. Breaking more than this and breaking 2120 was the first sign of weakness and a decline followed.

SEPTEMBER 15th, LOW 1730. The third time at this level and a HIGHER BOTTOM. September is the month for seasonal change in trend and one year from the 1927 TOP made this a BUYING LEVEL for rally. The advance followed and prices crossed 1862, showing uptrend.

1929—MARCH 16th, HIGH 2060. A SELLING LEVEL, because 1730 to 2280 made 2005 the 50% point. Under 2120 it was in a weak position. This was nine months from the June high, and was 75% of a year. The market became dull and narrow at the top, indicating that the advance had run out.
MARCH 30th, LOW 1940. This showed that the main trend was DOWN. The market rallied one week, then declined.
JULY AND AUGUST, LOW 18c and 1785. A DOUBLE BOTTOM. A rally due.

SEPTEMBER 14th, HIGH 1950. A DOUBLE TOP and selling level.

September the month for a seasonal change in trend. The crop report by the government this month was bearish and the market slowly worked lower. There was a panicky decline in stocks and this helped to force cotton prices lower. Rallies were very small.

1930—MARCH 8th, LOW 1440. The bottom of the sharp decline and one year from March, 1929, indicated a rally due.

APRIL 5th, HIGH 1625. A four weeks normal rally of 185 points which is a normal rally according to our rules. 1585 was 33 1/3% of 515 to 3725, making this a SELLING LEVEL. A long, slow decline followed.

1930—OCTOBER 11th, LOW 975. A natural RESISTANCE LEVEL, as 100% advance on 5c, the 1894 and 1898 low, is 10c. The market was down 66 2/3% of 3130, the 1923 high. October was the month for a change in trend. A rally was due.

NOVEMBER 15th, HIGH 1235. One-third of 3725, a SELLING LEVEL on a five weeks' normal rally.

DECEMBER 20th, LOW 1010. A HIGHER BOTTOM and a safe BUYING LEVEL, as December was the month for seasonal LOWS.

1931—FEBRUARY 28th, HIGH 1228. A DOUBLE TOP against November, 1930, a SELLING LEVEL.

A decline followed. Prices broke 980, showing weakness. JUNE 6th, LOW 850. Down to OLD BOTTOM LEVEL, 50% decline from 17c, the important bottom, gave 850 as the RESISTANCE LEVEL. 33 1/3% decline from the last top of 1240 gave this as a RESISTANCE, or BUYING POINT for rally.

1931—JUNE 27th, HIGH 1075. A three weeks normal rally. Under old bottom and a normal rally of 225 points. This was a SELLING LEVEL, because the market could not advance into the fourth week. The supply of cotton was large and the demand was small. Business conditions were bad and stocks were declining. All of this worked against the price of cotton, as the main trend was DOWN.

1931—OCTOBER 10th, LOW 535. The lowest since 1898 and down to old bottom levels and a place to BUY. Remember that after the market reached the extreme LOW LEVEL, past study and experience proves that it will remain at LOW LEVEL for a long time, working up and down in a narrow range. October was one year from the low of 1930 and almost a 50% decline from the 10c bottom.

NOVEMBER, HIGH 770. Not quite a 50% advance from the low of 535. Could not rally over five weeks, showing not ready to go up and stay up. A slow, narrow market followed.

1932—FEBRUARY 20th, last HIGH 760. A DOUBLE TOP and SELLING LEVEL.

1932—June 11th, Final LOW 520. A DOUBLE BOTTOM against October, 1931 and down to the old lows of 1894 and 1898. This was the time to BUY cotton for an investment, as it was far below the cost of production.

1932—August 13th,—prices crossed the tops of fifteen weeks previous, getting above 650, showed strong UPTREND. This was the time to buy more as it was the Breakaway Point.

1932—September 3rd, HIGH 945. Under old bottoms and almost a 100% advance on the extreme low of 520. Prices held for four weeks after a fast advance, showing the market was meeting selling. September is the most important month for seasonal change in trend. A decline followed.

1932—October, LOW 605.
November, HIGH 710.
December 10th, LOW 600. Down to old top levels and a big SECONDARY DECLINE, making this a SAFER BUYING LEVEL. This price was 75% from 520 to 945. The market was slow and narrow until March, 1933.

President Roosevelt was inaugurated March 4, 1933 and immediately issued a proclamation closing all of the banks. This forced the stock exchange and all of the commodity exchanges to close for a short time. The closing of the banks and the exchanges scared traders and the people throughout the country, but the worst had been discounted and when the exchanges opened, prices had a quick, sharp advance instead of a decline.

1933—March 18th. October cotton HIGH 755. These prices were above all highs since November, 1932 and turned the main trend definitely UP, making the market a safe BUY on a reaction. This quick, sharp advance caused people who had been scared to sell out their long cotton whether they had a profit or a loss, and this caused a sharp reaction.

1933—April 1st, LOW 650. A two weeks normal reaction and 105 point decline was normal. This was another good SECONDARY REACTION and holding 50 points above the low level of December 10th showed strength and made it a SAFE BUY.

1933—April 22nd,—prices crossed 750.

BREAKAWAY POINT—BUY MORE:

When prices crossed the high of March 18th, the market was still a safer buy, because it was a definite indication that the buying was better than the selling. President Roosevelt issued a proclamation and the country went off of the gold standard. This was bullish on cotton and all commodities and a rapid advance followed.

1933—July 17th, HIGH 12c. This was 33 1/3% of 3725 and 1169 was 25% on 515 to 530. This had been one of the fastest advances in history. Prices reached the selling level almost 150% on 520, the low, and exactly 100% advance on the low of 6c, the low of December, 1932.

In July Dr. E. A. Crawford failed. He was heavily long on cotton, as well as all other commodities.

1933—August 19th, LOW 850. A four weeks decline, and a normal decline. Down 350 points. Note that 842 was 12½% of 515 to 3725, making this a BUYING LEVEL. August is the month for seasonal change in trend. The market was one year up from the EXTREME LOW PRICES or from the LOW of the SECONDARY BOTTOM.

September, LOW again 850. A DOUBLE BOTTOM and a safer BUYING LEVEL, as September is the month for seasonal change in trend.

September 30th, HIGH 1005. A SELLING LEVEL. 100% advance on 5c.

1933—October 18th, LOW 855. A TRIPLE BOTTOM at this level and a BUY FOR RALLY. A rally followed. Prices crossed 1040, which was a 100% advance on 520 and showed strong uptrend. The market continued up and the reaction was small.

1934—August 11th, HIGH 1390. Why should the market make top at this level? 1387 was 33 1/3% of 520 to 3130, a selling level, an l August is the month for a change in trend. Prices broke back under weekly bottoms.

1935—March 23rd, LOW 1005. Down to old bottom and top levels. 50% decline from 600 to 1390, making this a BUYING LEVEL.

1935—August, LOW 1035. A DOUBLE BOTTOM and a HIGHER LEVEL. A safer buying level. The crops were smaller and the reports bad and the trend turned upward. The market was running opposite the seasonal trend.

1935—December, HIGH 1160. A TRIPLE TOP and SELLING LEVEL. Under old bottom.

1936—January 11th, LOW 985. The third time at this same level, a TRIPLE BOTTOM and a safe BUYING LEVEL.

1936—February 29th, LOW 985. A DOUBLE BOTTOM at this time and a SAFER BUYING LEVEL.

1936—May 2nd, HIGH, 1015: A HIGHER BOTTOM and still safer to buy, as the trend was UP.

June 6th,—prices crossed 1050 over a twenty-week line of TOPS. This was the BREAKAWAY POINT and a safer buying level because the main trend had turned up.

1936—July 11th, HIGH 1280. A DOUBLE TOP against 1935 TOP, the selling level, and one year from the top at the same level.

1936—October 31st, LOW 1115.
November 14th and 21st, LOW 1105. A DOUBLE BOTTOM and buying level, as 1140 was 50% of 985 to 1295.

1936—December 5th, HIGH, 1115. A HIGHER BOTTOM and a SAFER BUYING LEVEL, as December is the month for seasonal lows. Here October cotton should have been BOUGHT, protected with STOP LOSS ORDER at 1090.

1937—February 27th—prices crossed the tops of the past six months around 12c. This was the BREAKAWAY POINT and a safer place to BUY.

1937—April 10th, HIGH 14c. This was FINAL HIGH, a DOUBLE TOP against August, 1934 and one year from July and August tops at 1280 and 1387 was 25% of 520 to 3725, which made this a SELLING LEVEL, protected with STOP at 1430. Our rule says that the further away in time old tops and bottoms are, the more important they are. All commodities have had a big advance and everybody was bullish and the market was over-bought. This was the time to sell out cotton and go short.

1937—April 17th—prices broke the LOW of the previous four weeks, showing downtrend and no rally after that lasted over two weeks, showing a real bear market.

1937—October 9th—LOW 785. A BUYING LEVEL, as 756 was 12½% of 2440 to 520 and 737 was 12½% of 2290 to 520 and 810 was 12½% of 1400 to 726, the last low. 50% of 515 made 772 a BUYING LEVEL, or SUPPORTING LEVEL.

1937—November 6th, LOW 790. A DOUBLE BOTTOM, and a SAFER PLACE TO BUY.

1938—February 26th, HIGH 945. Under 10c, the old bottom, and a four months slow rally. The market was slow, dead and narrow at the top, meaning that there was very little buying power. This was the time to SELL.

1938—June 4th, LOW 760. A THIRD BOTTOM and a SAFER BUY-ING LEVEL.

1938—July 9th, HIGH 810. A small five weeks gain.

1938—December 10th, LOW 726. This was the month for seasonal lows and prices were back to old 1933 tops, making this a BUY-ING POINT.

1939—April 15th, LOW 735. A HIGHER BOTTOM. Our rule says that when the market starts making higher bottoms and higher tops, it is in a stronger position. Therefore, it was a safer buy at this time.

1939—May 27th—the prices crossed the eight months top around 8c. A BETTER BUY, as this showed the BREAKAWAY POINT and UPTREND.

1939—September 9th, HIGH 1015. Under old bottom and a 100% advance on the 515 base. This was the one week's rush up on war news, and when the market did not continue on up, it was a short sale, as September is the month for a change in trend and the government report was Bearish. Time to SELL OUT LONG and GO SHORT.

1939—November, LOW 825. A DOUBLE BOTTOM, the same as August, 1939 and a buying level. A slow move upward started.

1940—January 6th, HIGH 1015. ANOTHER DOUBLE TOP, against September, 1939.

1940—January 27th, LOW 915. A three weeks normal decline and a 100 point reaction, which was normal at these levels.

1940—April 20th, HIGH 1025. A THIRD TOP. The market got very dull and narrow and could not go through these old tops. This was the time to SELL OUT and GO SHORT.

1940—May 10th—the Hitler Drive started against France and Belgium. Stocks broke wide open and wheat and all other commodities declined. On May 10th cotton started declining fast.

1940—May 18th, LOW 840. A THIRD BOTTOM at this same level and a BUYING LEVEL.

1940—June 8th—again LOW 840. The fourth time—did not go lower, making this a safer buying point, as 842 was 25% of 515 to 3130.

1940—July, HIGH 965.

1940—September 21st, HIGH 965. A DOUBLE TOP and SELLING LEVEL under old bottoms.

1940—October 26th, LOW 870. A FOURTH HIGHER BOTTOM and a BUYING LEVEL. A slow upward move followed.

1941—January, HIGH 1005. Just under a series of old tops.

1941—February 22nd, LAST LOW 950. A HIGHER BOTTOM and a sign of strength.

1941—March 8th—prices crossed 1015 for the first time since August, 1937, a sure sign of very much higher prices, because after such a long period of time, when prices advanced over 10c, which is 100% on the extreme low of 5c, it was an indication that it would go another 100% to around 15c per pound anyway.

Looking back over the records, you will find that in 1934 and 1937, TOPS were made around 14c. After the advance started in March, 1941, the reactions were small, not more than fifty to sixty points.

1941—June, HIGH 1525. Prices had crossed the 14c level without a reaction, indicating that it was a very strong bull market. A one week's reaction followed, with prices down to 1448. Failing to react to the old top levels of 14c showed great strength. This was the time to BUY MORE.

1941—July 28th, HIGH 1746. The first time prices had reached this level since December, 1929. Prices were under a series of old tops and bottoms.

250% advance on 5c would be 1715. Another reason why 1746 was high and a selling level was that the low of the option in October, 1940, was 870. 100% advance on this is 1740, making this a SAFE SELLING LEVEL, after such a prolonged advance with such small reaction. The daily chart gives the first indication of a change in trend by over-balancing the time.

From the last low on June 28th of 1455 to the top, no reaction was more than two days and no reaction in points of more than 60 points. Therefore, when the market broke back for more than two days and over 60 points, it indicated a change in trend.

1941—August 13th, LOW 1582 for the December option. This was a sixteen day decline and 180 points, which was a normal decline. The trend again turned up.

1941—September 12th, FINAL HIGH, December cotton, 1848. The October option HIGH was 1860. This had reached the important selling level, the half-way point, or 50% of the highest selling price on October of 3725. September is the month for a change in trend and this was a safe **SELLING LEVEL**.

December cotton at this time would have been the best option to trade in. Again you would watch for definite indication of change in trend by an over-balancing of time with the last move up.

December cotton from the last low August 13th from 1582 to 1848—the greatest reaction was three days and the greatest number of points in reaction was 60 points. Therefore, when the market broke back more than three days and the break was more than 60 points, this indicated the trend had turned down.

SIGNAL DAY

September 12th **HIGH** for December cotton, 1848, **LOW** the same day 1802. The price opened at 1818 and closed at the bottom. This was a **SIGNAL DAY** and an indication that the selling was better than the buying because the market closed weak and at the low level. The volume of sales had been running for several days around 300,000 bales per day, which was a heavy volume.

On September 13th there was practically no rally. Prices broke the lows of previous days, but on the third day down had declined over 60 points, indicating the main trend had turned, both on time and points. Only one day's rally followed and prices broke wide open.

September 16th **LOW** was 1765. This showed that the trend was **DOWN**.

September 27th **LOW** was 1655. Down to old bottom level and a normal decline. After the first sharp decline, our rule says a **SECONDARY RALLY** follows and it is usually about 50% of the first decline.

1941—October 2nd, **HIGH** 1757. A **SELLING LEVEL**, because 50% of 1848 to 1655 was 1751 and this was only a four day rally and a safe **SELLING LEVEL** on this 50% advance. A rapid decline followed with nothing but small rallies.

1941—October 16th—prices broke below 1665 and declined nearly 200 points. **EXTREME LOW** 1557 for the December option. This was a real panicky day. The volume of sales on the New York Cotton Exchange for cotton broke the records for one day, being a total of 549,000 bales. This was the day to cover all shorts and **BUY**. Prices were down to old top levels and 1585 was 33 1/3% of 515 to 3725 and 200% advance on 515 was 1545. A 34 day decline, or about five weeks. This was a normal decline and after such a drastic decline on such heavy volume, a rally was due.

1941—October 24th, **HIGH** 1680. Eight days' rally, or a little over one week, of 133 points advance. From 1780 to 1557, a 50% rally was 1670, making the market again a safe short sale.

1941—October 27th, **LOW** 1596. Same level as October 20th. A small rally followed.

1941—November 3rd, HIGH 1631. The main trend was still down, and prices closed at the LOW around 1606 at this writing, November 16, 1941. The present position of the market, with the main trend down, with prices back to 16c level, with indications lower, and breaking 1557, the low of October 16th, indicates still lower. The next important top point is the old top level of 14c made in 1934 and 1937.

December is the next important month for a change in trend and if prices are low at that time, the trend should change either in December, 1941, or January, 1942, because these are the months for seasonal lows. December would be three months from September HIGH and January would be four months. Therefore, you should watch for a change in trend around these times— around December 12th and January 12th. If the prices come out LOW, this would mean the time to BUY .

Later, if prices cross 1860, the top of September, 1941, and the important half-way point, it will indicate the next important 50%, or half-way point, around 2160.

Looking back over the records you will find that the last low for December cotton was around 11c April 23, 1941. Therefore, April and May, 1942, will be important months to watch for a change in trend and if prices have advanced around that time, watch for an indication to sell out and go short.

If the war continues until the Spring of 1942, it is possible that a greater wave of inflation may get under way and that cotton may have another rapid move UP.

The proper thing for a trader to do is to have no hopes or fears, or no pre-conceived ideas or notions about what the market is going to do, but keep up the charts, watch for a change in trend and go with the trend, without hoping or fearing anything. Then he will be able to make profits, provided he always protects the trades with STOP LOSS ORDERS in case he is wrong or that the market reverses.

LONG SWING AND SECTIONS OF BULL MARKET

You must not overlook the fact that the EXTREME LOW of cotton was reached in October, 1931 and June, 1932 and that SECONDARY, or HIGHER BOTTOMS were made in November and December, 1932 and the last bottom in March, 1933—that the main trend has been UP since 1932 and that BOTTOMS have been HIGHER and TOPS have been HIGHER. Sections of the market have been as follows.

The first small section was June, 1932 to September, 1932.

The second section ended July 17, 1933, the 12c level.

The third section was in August, 1934 at the 14c level.

The fourth section was in April, 1937, at the 14c level.

Then the final low of the minor bear campaign which started in April, 1937 ended in December, 1938, with prices at 725. Again in April, 1939, prices were at 735. From that time on, BOTTOMS were HIGHER and TOPS were higher.

The first section of this bull campaign ended at 1015 in September, 1939.

The second section, or DOUBLE TOP, ended in April, 1940, at 1025 for the October option. The third section ended September 12, 1941. This may be the final section, but there is a possibility of a fourth section in 1942. In watching the future for a change in trend, do not overlook the fact to watch all of the months for TOPS and BOTTOMS when the market is one year, two years, three years, four years, five years, or one and one-half years, two and one-half years, or three and one-half years from any important TOP or BOTTOM.

For example, December, 1941 will be three years from the last low in December, 1938.

April, 1942, will be three years from the last low in April, 1939.

September, 1942, will be three years from the high in September, 1939.

April and May, 1942, will be two years from the tops in April, 1940.

October and November, 1942, will be two years from the last low in 1940 and therefore important for a change in trend.

February, 1942, will be one year from the last low in February, 1941, making February an important month to watch for a change in trend.

Watch all important RESISTANCE LEVELS and figure the resistance points from 726 to 1848 and from 515 to 1848. Then take the last low of April 23, 1941, December cotton low 11c to September 12, 1941 high of 1848, and figure to $12\frac{1}{2}\%$, to 25%, $37\frac{1}{2}\%$ and 50% points. The levels of this last low are very important.

For example, 25% of 1848 would give 1660 and a 50% decline would be 1474. A 25% decline off the high selling price 1848 would give 1386. This would agree with the old tops around 14c as SUPPORT LEVEL.

COTTON MOVES AND TIME PERIODS
1894 TO 1941

Reviewing past records is the only way you will be able to determine and judge the trend of cotton in the future. It is always important to know what has happened in the past and for how many months important moves have run before there was a reaction lasting one to two months, or longer.

The cotton market does not go straight up or straight down. Most of the moves are in minor time periods of one to two months, as you can see by going over the records.

During the last forty-seven years, there have been 102 moves in cotton lasting one month or less. There have been 52 moves lasting two months. There have been 27 moves lasting three months. There have been 16 moves lasting four months. There have been 12 moves lasting five months. There have been 7 moves lasting six months. There were no moves lasting seven months. There have been 2 moves lasting eight months. There have been 3 moves lasting nine months. There have been 2 moves lasting ten months.

From this data you can see that after the market moves up fast for as much as two months, you have to watch for a possible change that will last one month, or longer. After a market has moved up or down for three months, the chances are greater for a move running two to three months in the opposite direction. When a market has moved up for four consecutive months, the chances are still increased for a greater reaction. Most of the fast, rapid advances or declines have never lasted more than four months before a reaction of one or more months took place.

Therefore, when a market is very active and advancing or declining fast, the most important time periods to watch are three to four months from top or bottom.

During this period, moves lasting six months have occurred seven times. Our rule says that it is important to watch for a change in trend in the sixth or seventh month, or around one-half of a year from any bottom or top.

It is also important to watch for a change in trend one year, two years and three years from an important top or bottom, but cotton does not advance or decline without rallies and reactions for twelve months, twenty-four months, or any other long period of time.

During the last forty-seven years, moves lasting ten months have only occurred two times. These were in 1909, when high prices were reached in the month of October and in 1941, when high prices were reached in the month of September. Both of these were BULL markets and knowing that the last low was November, 1940, and when prices reached high in September, 1941, and had run ten months, the record, without ever reacting a full month, this would be proof, from past records, that a big reaction was in order, which would last one month or more. In October, 1941, a sharp decline followed.

After the cotton market breaks out over a period of months, or a series of yearly tops and starts to advance fast, you can figure that when it runs three to four months, a change in trend is due, with a reaction to run one or two months.

Apply the same rule on a declining market. After a market has held for a series of months or a series of years and then breaks into new low levels, you can expect a fast decline lasting three to four months. Then watch for a change in trend and a rally which may last as much as two months.

The long swings in cotton, that is, making higher bottoms and higher tops, seldom last more than three years before there is a reaction running around twelve months. The same applies in a declining market. When a market is declining into the third year, it seldom goes beyond thirty-six months before an advance which lasts nine to twelve months.

LAST SEASONAL HIGHS OR LOWS. In considering when or where cotton will reach extreme high or low, do not overlook the fact to keep your records up on the last moves, whether it made top or bottom in a month where most seasonal tops and bottoms are made, or whether it was running opposite the seasonal trend. For example, suppose that cotton made high in October or November, which are seasonal months for low prices. Then you would expect the next low to come out, according to the seasonal trend, around December.

On the other hand, suppose that cotton made lows for two or three years in the month of December, which is one of the important months for lows according to the seasonal trend. After that, if the trend turned up, you would watch for highs, opposite the seasonal trend, in October, November and December.

Do not overlook the fact that when a crop is very short, prices run opposite the seasonal trend and make highs in October, November and December. For example, the last extreme short crop was 1923 and prices advanced rapidly for four months and reached high on November 30th.

Keeping up with all past records will help you to determine the trend in the future.

VOLUME OF SALES ON COTTON

FEBRUARY, 1941 TO NOVEMBER 10, 1941

The daily volume of sales on cotton is very important when the market is very active. You will find it of great help if you will study the volume of sales daily and extreme high and extreme low prices. You should keep up the total volume for each week and at the end of each month you should figure up the total volume. This will help you in determining when extreme highs and extreme lows take place.

1941—February 1, for October cotton, LOW 990. Sales were small, running 50,000 to 60,000 bales per day.

February 17—LAST LOW 950. Sales 75,000 bales per day. An increase of sales at the low level, showing good buying.

February 26—HIGH 10c. Sales 40,000 bales.

March 10—HIGH 1070. Sales 260,000 bales. This was large for one day and the largest for any day in this month.

March 13—Low 1050. Sales 100,000 bales. This showed that the selling pressure was not great when the market reacted.

March 17—HIGH 1090. Sales 200,000 bales. An indication that the selling was poor and the buying good and that traders were bidding for cotton.

March 22—LOW 1055. A small reaction. Sales 35,000 bales, the smallest for several months and on a reaction, showed there still was not any great selling pressure.

March 29—A NEW HIGH, 1125. Sales 220,000 bales. At this time the largest sales took place before the tops.

April 3—HIGH 1145. Sales 175,000 bales.

April 8—LOW 1090. Sales 125,000 bales. Sales still decreasing on reaction.

April 19—LOW 1105. Sales 50,000 bales. Small sales, the market going dead on the reaction.

April 23—LAST LOW 1110. Sales 110,000 bales. Good buying took place. The advance started.

April 26—LOW 1110. Sales 45,000 bales. A slow advance with the sales starting to increase.

May 12—HIGH 1270. Sales 175,000 bales.

May 13—Sales 310,000 bales. Market still working higher. This was the largest volume of sales for more than a year.

May 14—HIGH 1325. Sales 295,000 bales. Slightly under the previous day's sales. A small reaction followed.

May 19—LOW 1295. Sales 95,000 bales. Sales decreasing on the decline. Still good to buy.

June 2—LOW 1315. Sales 35,000 bales. An advance started as the volume of sales started to increase. The market moved up faster from this level.

June 23—HIGH 15c . Sales 295,000 bales.

June 27—HIGH 1525. Sales 190,000 bales. Sales were smaller the day the market reached the extreme high, having been larger the day before.

June 30—LOW on the reaction, 1448. Sales 175,000 bales. The volume of sales was smaller on a decline.

July 5—HIGH 1480. Sales 20,000 bales. Small sales on a rally. The market was starting to work up.

July 23—HIGH 1682. Sales 305,000 bales. Up to the record high of May 13th. A moderate reaction followed.

July 24—LOW 1625. Sales 175,000 bales. Sales again smaller at the bottom.

July 25—HIGH 1710. Sales 295,000 bales. Almost up to the record.

July 28—HIGH 1746. Sales 200,000 bales. Again the largest sales were a few days before the top. From this top a sharp, swift decline followed.

July 31—LOW 1600. Sales 375,000 bales. The largest for several years. This sharp decline indicated the market was making bottom for a rally as the traders had gotten scared and had sold out.

August 4—HIGH 1715. Sales 150,000 bales. Smaller on the rally. A selling level.

August 13—LOW 1565. Note that before this low was reached, sales were larger—August 12, sales 305,000 bales and August 13, sales 215,000 bales. This was a sharp decline and indicated the market was making bottom.

August 16—LOW 16c. Sales 37,000 bales. The market became very narrow and sales were the smallest for many months. This was an indication to buy for another rally, as prices were above bottom levels.

September 12—FINAL HIGH 1848 for December cotton. Note that the largest sales occurred this time before the market reached top.

September 8, sales 305,000 bales, close to the record.

September   9—Sales 250,000 bales.

September 10—Sales 210,000 bales.

September 11—Sales 175,000 bales.

September 12—Sales 265,000 bales.

The largest sales occurred four days before the top, indicating that the public had gotten loaded up with cotton and that the buying power was decreasing.

From this top a rapid decline followed. All commodities declined from around this time.

September 27—LOW 1655. Sales 140,000 bales.

September 22—Sales 260,000 bales. Sales smaller at low level.

October 2nd—HIGH 1755. This was the top of a SECONDARY RALLY. Sales 265,000 bales. Smaller than at the extreme high. A fast decline followed and all commodities declined during this period.

October 16—LOW 1557. Down nearly 300 points from the extreme high on September 12th. Sales 540,000 bales. A record for one day on the New York Cotton Exchange. This was a panicky decline and a time to cover shorts and buy. From this low a sharp, quick rally followed.

October 24—HIGH 1675. Sales 215,000 bales. Smaller sales on a rally. Note that October 23, the day before this high, sales were 245,000 bales.

October 25—LOW 1605. Sales 95,000 bales. Smaller on a reaction.

After that the market held in a narrow trading range of 30 to 40 points and with sales running as low as 100,000 bales per day and not at any time running more than 140,000 bales per day. This indicated that traders had evened up after the market had reacted 75 points from the last high and were waiting for some important development or for the market to show activity before an increase of buying power or selling power would start, which would show an increase in the volume of sales per day.

By studying the volume during the important periods when cotton crosses important resistance levels on the UP side and breaks important resistance levels on the DOWN side, you will be able to determine when a change in trend takes place.

Apply the rules to volume of sales of cotton and it will help you in determining the changes in trend.

COTTON RECORD CROPS

Two record crops have occurred in only two consecutive years, 1898-99 and 1925-26.

Three record crops 2 years apart, 1904-1906-1908. The total for 3 years 39,600,00 bales.

The time from the new record crop to the next record:

1891 to 1894   3 years

1894 to 1898   4 years

        1898 to 1904 6 years
        1904 to 1911 7 years
        1911 to 1914 3 years
        1914 to 1926 12 years
        1926 to 1937 11 years
        1926 to 1931 5 years   A 17,000,000-bale crop.
        1931 to 1937 6 years
Short Crops—time from record crop to smallest crop:
        1859 to 1864 5 years
        1891 to 1892 1 year
        1894 to 1895 1 year
        1898 to 1899 1 year
Although 4 years of small crops followed the record crop of 1898.
        1904 to 1905 1 year
        1904 to 1909 5 years
1909 was the smallest crop after 1904 until record crops were produced again:
        1911 to 1912 1 year
        1911 to 1921 10 years. The 1921 crop was about one-half the size of the 1911 crop.
        1921 to 1926, for five years the crops were larger each year following the extreme short crop of 1921.
        1926 to 1927 1 year
        1927 to 1931 4 years   Larger crops but 1931 not a new record.
        1926 to 1934 8 years   1934 was 9 million bales less than 1926.
        1931 to 1934 3 years   From 17 million bales to a crop of less than 10 million bales
        1934 to 1937 3 years   From smallest crop to a record
        1937 to 1938-39 1 and 2 years ‚2 crops under 12,000,000 bales
        1939 to 1940 1 year   1940 under 13 million bales.
1941 crop, according to the Government Estimate of September 8th, will be around 11 million bales, the shortest since 1937, and 4 years smaller crops.
        From 1895 last crop around 7 million bales
        To 1921 last crop around 8 million bales—26 years
        From 1921 to 1934 last 10-million bale crop—13 years
        From 1921 to 1941—20 years
        From 1934 to 1941— 7 years.
According to all past cycles and records, crops should be larger in 1942, and probably much larger by 1944. If war should last to 1944, as Government leaders think, and cotton prices remain at high levels, the cotton production is sure to increase, no matter what the Government does to curtail it. If the farmer can sell cotton at 16 to 18 cents. he will produce enough to force prices down to 8 cents, or probably 5 cents again.

From my study of past cycles I believe we are in a long down trend of commodity prices, and that the period from 1841 to 1850 is likely to be repeated in 1941 to 1950, with some years of very low prices for cotton, wheat, corn and other commodities. But you must study all charts and apply all the rules and follow the trend as it develops and be ready to change when the charts show a change in trend.

COTTON CROPS OF THE UNITED STATES

Cotton growing started in a small way in 1790.

1790 crop	6,600 bales	
1802 crop	231,000 bales	
1808 crop	334,000 bales	
1819 crop	632,000 bales	
1826 crop	1,057,000 bales	First time over 1 million bales
1839 crop	2,064,000 bales	First time over 2 million bales
1842 crop	2,379,000 bales	Record crop to that date
1846 crop	1,779,000 bales	
1852 crop	3,416,000 bales	First time over 3 million bales
1859 crop	5,387,000 bales	First time over 5 million bales
1860 crop	3,849,000 bales	
1861 crop	4,500,000 bales	Then Civil War broke out and production ceased
1864 crop	300,000 bales	Smallest crop since 1818
1866 crop	2,100,000 bales	September prices highest in history, $1.89 per pound. After civil war was over production increased each year. From 1859 to 1866 small crops.
1870 crop	4,300,000 bales	Sixth year, larger crop.
1871 crop	2,780,000 bales	First year small crop, then increased each year.
1880 crop	6,606,000 bales	First crop over six million to that date.
1881 crop	5,470,000 bales	Only one year smaller crop.
1882 crop	6,950,000 bales	Record to date.
1883 crop	5,600,000 bales)	Two smaller crops, then production
1884 crop	5,600,000 bales)	increased each year.
1891 crop	9,035,000 bales	First crop over nine million bales.
1892 crop	6,680,000 bales	Only one year smaller crop.
1894 crop	9,901,000 bales	A record to that date, then record crop brought price of cotton to 5c per pound, the lowest since 1844-48.
1895 crop	7,150,000 bales	One year smaller crop.
1898 crop	11,187,000 bales	First time over 11 million bales. This caused the price of cotton to decline to 5c per pound. Then followed five years of smaller crops. This was the first time since 1864 that there had been more than two years smaller crops.

1899 crop 9,500,000 bales	This was smallest crop after the record. Then followed four years with crops from 9,600,000 to 10,600,000 bales.
1903 crop	Under 10 million. This was the first serious boll weevil year and was known as the "Sulley" year. Daniel J. Sulley figured that the boll weevil would continue to destroy crops for many years to come and he made a fortune buying cotton. Following prices prevailed in 1903: January low 810; 1904 February high 1755; September high 1060. Sulley failed in March 1904 and the price of cotton declined fast, reaching low in January, 1905, when farmers burned cotton to try and get prices up. When the price of cotton reached 17½c per pound in the Spring of 1904, farmers, believing prices were up to stay, planted the largest acreage up to that time, and a record crop caused extremely low prices.
1904 crop 13,451,000 bales	The first crop over 12 and 13 million up to that time. Low prices caused farmers to plant less.
1905 crop 10,400,000 bales	In January, 1905, the October option sold at 700. In July the October option sold at 1130.
1906 crop 12,800,000 bales	September 1906 low 810.
1907 crop 11,100,000 bales	1907 high 1260.
1908 crop 13,150,000 bales	Prices were low in the early part of 1908, and Livermore ran a successful corner in the Spring of that year. High prices in the Spring induced the farmers to plant a large crop. 1908 May, Sept. and Dec. lows 825. This was the second crop over 13 million bales and the third crop in five years around 13 million bales. This caused low prices in the Summer and early Fall of 1909. A new Bull leader, Eugene Scales, started with $500 and ran it into a fortune of several million dollars. Nature helped Scales with a small crop and boll weevil damages.
1909 crop 10,100,000 bales	The smallest since 1903. The January low was 840.
1910 crop 11,600,000 bales	In 1910 Scales and W. P. Brown, of New Orleans, cornered the market and forced prices to 20c in August. Later Scales went broke and Brown got badly bent. 1910

October cotton high 1500. Again the greed for gold caused farmers to plant larger acreage, and prices declined.

1911 crop 15,550,000 bales The first crop over 15 million bales, and prices broke wide open in the Fall of the year, because the supply of cotton was greatly in excess of the demand. 1911 high (June) 1380, October low 885.

1912 crop 13,500,000 bales Much smaller crop, and prices recovered. 1912 July high 1320. A sharp decline followed. October low 1000.

1913 crop 13,900,000 bales Still there was over-production. May and June low 1080, September high 1420.

1914 crop 16,738,000 bales The first crop over 16,000,000 bales. Again a Bull Pool had been buying cotton. John Hill and S. H. Pell & Co. were buying on a large scale and the public followed and were loaded up with cotton. At the end of July, 1914, when it was plain that war would start in Europe, there was heavy selling of stocks from Europe, and all over the United States. This resulted in a wide open break in cotton. S. H. Pell & Co. failed and many other brokers and their customers were hard hit. The New York and New Orleans Cotton Exchanges closed on July 30, 1914, and remained closed until November, 1914. The large crops of cotton forced prices to below 6c to the farmers. The "Buy a Bale" and "Save the South" movement started, and bales of cotton were displayed in hotel lobbies in New York City. Some people paid $50.00 per bale for cotton, when it was only worth $30.00 on the farms. For October cotton, July high 1300; July low 940; Dec. low 775.

After low levels for cotton were reached in December, 1914, prices slowly worked higher, due to war demands, even though there were very large supplies.

1915—January, low, 840.

1915—April, high, 1090.

1915—July, low, 880.

1915 crop, 11,191,000 bales; 1916 crop, 11,415,000 bales; 1917 crop, 11,302,000 bales; 1918 crop, 12,141,000 bales; 1919 crop, 11,421,000 bales. This was five years of smaller crops, or five years between record crops to the lowest crops. This was the same period of time that crops decreased each year during the Civil War. These years of extremely small crops caused extreme high prices and the visible supply of cotton was greatly reduced.

1916 cotton reached the highest prices of any time since 1872.

1916—October, high, 1950. From this high level a reaction followed.

1917—February, last low, 1375. This low was caused by selling when everybody became scared when Germany declared unrestricted U-boat war and it was feared that the United States would enter the war. As usual, on bad news on February 2, when cotton opened down four to five hundred points, or 4c to 5c a pound, it was bottom, and this was the time to buy.

1918—September, October cotton sold at 3725.

1919—January, low, 1810.

1919—October, high, 3725. Second time at same level.

1919—December, low, 2700.

1920—April, high, 3725. This was the third time in three consecutive years that October cotton sold at exactly the same high price, 3725, making this a triple top and a sure indication for a big decline to follow. The extreme high of all cotton options was reached in April, 1920, when some options sold at 4290 and others at 4320. But the high of the July option was reached at the end of July, 1920, when July cotton sold at 4375, which was the highest price of any option since the Civil War. After the World War ended and our boys returned to the cotton fields production was increased.

1920-1921 crop, 13,440,000 bales. Then the boll weevil got in its work. And, with adverse weather conditions, this caused the shortest crop in many years.

1921 crop, 7,954,000. This was the first time the crop had been this low since 1895.

1921—March, low, 1210, for October cotton.

1921—June, extreme low, 1130. This short crop was known in September, 1921, and there was a rapid advance in cotton up to around the 21c level in September and October, 1921. The crop was small in 1922, amounting to 9,762,000 bales. In 1923, the crop was still comparatively small—10,130,000 bales. This year there were adverse weather conditions, boll weevil damage and, with the increased demand, there was a wild scramble for cotton and prices advanced rapidly. In fact, one of the fastest advances in history took place from August to November, 1923. October cotton was selling at 2085 in the early part of August, when the Government Report was issued, which was very bullish, and a rapid advance followed. This was one of the most rapid advances in peace-time with very small reaction, winding up in a run-away market in November, 1923.

1923—November 30, Extreme high. July cotton and other options sold at 3690 to 3725 on November 30, then the main trend turned down and prices continued to work lower. Extreme high prices in 1923 again induced farmers to plant large acreage in cotton and increased production.

1924—Crop, 13,628,000 bales.

1925—Crop, 15,603,000 bales.

1926—Crop, 13,628,000 bales.

1927—Crop, 16,104,000 bales.

During 1924 and 1925 the October option made several lows around 2160, with extreme high around 30 cents per pound. In October, 1925, prices broke 2160 and declined fast.

The large crop of 1926 built up a large supply and this caused prices to decline rapidly during the Fall of 1926, reaching extreme low prices in December, 1926, when the October option sold at $12\frac{1}{2}$c per pound.

The 1927 crop proved to be short, due to excessive rains and other damages. This brought about a rapid recovery in prices, and also due to the fact that there was a big demand for cotton in 1926 and 1927. Prices advanced rapidly during 1927, with very small reactions.

1927, the September 6 high for October cotton, 2440. Higher prices caused a larger acreage, but the 1928 crops were smaller and prices reached higher levels in June, the October option selling around 2280. The 1928 crop was 14,555,000 bales; the 1929 crop was 14,718,000 bales. These crops were far in excess of the demand and piled up the surplus on top of the record crop of 1926, causing prices to continue to work lower.

Conditions in the United States from 1929 to 1932 reduced consumption of cotton and the demand increased. 1930 crops were smaller. 13,873,000 bales were more than the mills would take as the world production of cotton was large. The 1931 crop was 16,877,000 bales. This was the fourth largest crop on record. The price of cotton then declined to 5c per pound, the lowest since 1895 and 1898. The July option in 1934 sold at 492, the first time any option had ever sold below 5c per pound on the New York Cotton Exchange.

In March 1933 President Roosevelt took office and the New Deal policy started to reduce production to enhance the price. The policy was put into effect to plow up cotton, kill the hogs and cattle, and a general period of reduction took place.

The 1933 cotton crop was 12,712,000. In February and March cotton was still selling just a little above 5c per pound, and advanced to 12c per pound in July, 1933. This sharp advance was too rapid and was not warranted by business conditions. A sharp decline followed in August, carrying the October option down to 870.

In 1934 the Government Crop Control Plan got well under way and they succeeded in reducing acreage and reducing production. The production of cotton in Brazil had increased and they were able to grow cotton and sell it for 3 to 4c per pound lower than it could be sold in this country. The New Deal was simply ruining the farmers' market for cotton and helping the South American countries.

The 1935 crop was 10,495,000 bales; the 1936 crop was 12,378,000 bales. The fact that prices held at fairly high levels during the New Deal administration induced farmers to plant a heavier crop than in 1937, regardless of what the Government was willing to let them do.

The 1937 crop was 18,412,000 bales, the second largest crop on record, and about the same size as the 1926 crop. This large supply of cotton, with the decreased demand, brought about lower prices. In 1937 the extreme high for October cotton was 14 cents, back to the same level of August, 1934. Stocks broke wide open in 1937 and all commodities followed the decline. This large crop of cotton forced prices lower, regardless of Government control. These low prices helped as much as anything else to bring about a reduction in acreage, because farmers could not make any money selling cotton at these levels.

The 1938 crop was 11,665,000 bales. But, with the large carry-over and the large amount of old cotton in the world supply, prices could not advance much, even on this small crop. The highest price cotton reached during 1938 was 950 in the month of March. At the end of the year October cotton was selling at 725. Then followed several months in narrow range of less than 50 points.

The 1939 crop was 11,516,000 bales. These two small crop years, with the Government buying cotton and holding it, forced prices up. In September, 1939, the October cotton high was 1050. A decline followed, with a November low of 8c. This was the last low level for cotton before it advanced to very much higher levels.

The 1940 crop was 12,287,000 bales. The breaking out of the war in September, 1939, was bullish on cotton. Even though there was not much cotton sold in the foreign countries, the consumption in the United States increased. As the Government permitted more production for war purposes in 1940, there was an increase in the consumption of cotton, with the result that in the Spring of 1941 the price of cotton crossed 10c per pound, the high of 1939. Later advanced rapidly, going above the high of 1933 and 1934, reaching extreme high in September, 1941, most of the options selling around 1850 or higher, the highest they had sold since 1926. These prices were not warranted on supply and demand, but were the result of the Government holding over 10,000,000 bales in storage and refusing to put it on the market.

Under the conditions, with the supply on hand, cotton should not be selling above 10 or 12c per pound. If cotton had to be sold in the world market it could not be sold above this price.

When all of this New Deal business ends, and all of the countries in Europe after the war start producing commodities and everything else, and South America, with low-cost labor, produces cotton at 5c a pound, corn at 20c per bushel, wheat at 40c, then conditions are going to blow up in this country and prices are going to take their natural course, influenced by supply and demand, and go very much lower.

COTTON SWINGS FROM HIGH TO LOW
TIME PERIODS

Year		Price	Advance or Decline	Time Months
1864	Sept. to	$ 1.89		
1865	Apr. to	3600	$1.53	8
1865	Oct.	3990	390	6
1866	Aug.	3280	710	2
1866	Oct.	3710	430	8
1867	Dec.	1760	1950	13
1869	Aug.	3500	1740	20
1871	Apr.	1330	2170	8
No rally over 2 Mo				
Third Small Section				
1871	July	2050	720	3
	Aug.	1690	360	1
1872	June	2750	1060	10
2 Sections or Swings Up				
1872	Sept. Low	1775	975	3
1873	Feb.	2260	485	5
1 Section Up				
1873	Apr.	1800	460	2
	July	2180	380	3
	Nov.	1380	800	3
2 Sections Down				
1874	May	1910	530	6
	Oct.	1440	470	5
1875	Apr.	1770	330	6
	Oct.	1250	520	6
1876	Mar.	1470	220	5
	May	1150	320	2
1877	Jan.	1470	320	8
	Apr.	1090	380	3
	July	1240	150	3
	Aug.	1060	180	1
	Dec.	1230	170	4
1878	Apr.	1080	150	4
	July	1175	95	3
	Dec.	940	235	5
1879	May	1420	480	5
	Aug.	1000	420	3
	Dec.	1490	490	4
1880	Sept.	1050	440	9
	Dec.	1325	275	3
1881	May	1040	295	5
	Aug.	1295	255	3
	Sept.	1160	145	1
	Dec.	1280	120	3

COTTON SWINGS FROM HIGH TO LOW (Continued)
TIME PERIODS

Year		Price	Advance or Decline	Time Months
1882	Feb.	1140	140	2
	Apr.	1240	100	2
1883	July	970	270	3
1884	Apr. & June	1140	170	9 to 11
	Oct.	970	270	6
1885	Feb.	1150	180	4
1886	Feb.	870	280	12
1887	June	1060	190	4
	July, Aug. & Sept.	920	140	2 to 3
	Dec.	1090	170	4
1888	Oct.	920	170	10
	Nov.	1010	90	1
	Dec.	960	50	1
1889	Nov.	1100	140	13
	Dec.	1010	90	1
1890	Mar.	1140	130	3
1891	July	775	365	16
	Sept.	900	125	2
	Nov.	630	270	2
1892	June	810	180	7
	Sept.	710	100	3
	Nov.	1020	310	2
1893	Aug.	715	305	9
	Nov.	865	150	3
1894	Nov.	535	530	12
1895	Feb.	535	——	3
	Oct.	930	395	8
1896	July	620	310	9
	Sept.	865	245	2
1897	Apr.	660	205	7
	Aug.	720	60	4
	Nov.	660	60	3
1898	Jan.	550	110	2
	Apr.	640	190	3
	Nov.	535	105	7
1899	Feb.	635	100	3
	June	570	65	4
1900	Apr.	990	420	10
	May	825	165	1
	July	1020	195	2
	Sept.	880	140	2
	Oct.	1015	135	1

COTTON SWINGS FROM HIGH TO LOW (*Continued*)
TIME PERIODS

Year		Price	Advance or Decline	Time Months
1901	May	750	265	7
	June	900	150	1
	July & Aug.	915	185	2
	Sept.	800	85	2
	Nov.	720	80	2
1902	May	960	240	6
	Sept.	810	150	4
	Oct.	870	60	1
	Nov.	800	70	1
1903	July	920	575	8
	Oct.	1275	455	3
1904	Feb.	1755	835	4
	Mar.	1275	480	1
	Apr.	1560	285	1
	Aug.	980	580	4
	Sept.	1100	220	1
	Dec.	690	410	3
1905	Jan.	685	5	1
	Mar.	800	115	2
	Apr.	705	95	1
	July	1110	405	3
	Aug.	990	120	1
	Sept.	1120	130	1
	Oct.	1000	120	1
	Dec.	1260	260	2
1906	Apr.	1030	230	4
	May	1140	110	1
	Aug.	900	240	3
	Oct.	1160	260	2
1907	Feb.	920	240	4
	July	1250	330	5
	Nov.	1000	250	4
1908	Jan.	1150	150	2
	May	810	340	4
	May	1140	330	1
	Oct.	830	310	5
1909	Jan.	970	140	3
	Mar.	900	70	2
	Dec.	1645	745	9

COTTON SWINGS FROM HIGH TO LOW (*Continued*)
TIME PERIODS

Year			Price	Advance or Decline	Time Months
1910		Jan.	1350	295	1
		Feb.	1495	145	1
		Apr.	1390	105	2
		May	1570	180	1
		June	1410	160	1
		July	1655	245	1
		Sept.	1290	365	2
		Dec.	1540	250	3
1911		Feb.	1370	170	2
		May	1610	240	3
		Dec.	885	725	7
1912		July	1300	415	7
		Oct.	1070	230	3
		Dec.	1300	230	2
1913		Jan.	1160	140	1
		Feb.	1240	80	1
		Apr.	1120	120	2
		Sept.	1385	265	5
1914		Mar.	1150	235	6
		June	1340	190	3
		Dec.	750	590	6
1915		Apr.	1050	300	4
		July	840	210	3
		Oct.	1360	520	4
First Section					
1915		Nov.	1185	175	1
		Dec.	1330	145	1
1916		Feb.	1145	185	2
		June	1350	205	4
		July	1270	80	1
		Nov.	2150	880	4
Second Section					
		Dec.	1650	500	1
1917		Jan.	1910	260	1
		Feb.	1375	535	1
		July	2750	1375	5
Third Section					
		Sept.	2010	740	2
1918		Jan.	3130	1120	4
		Feb.	2880	250	1
		Apr.	3380	500	2
		May	2310	1070	1
		Sept.	3550	1240	4
4th Section					

COTTON SWINGS FROM HIGH TO LOW (*Continued*)
TIME PERIODS

Year		Price	Advance or Decline	Time Months
1919	Jan.	1920	1630	4
	July	3600	1680	6
	Sept.	2850	750	2
	Nov.	3630	780	2
	Dec.	2920	710	1
1920	Jan.	3400	480	1
	Feb.	2950	450	1
5th Section				
	Apr.	4040	1090	2
	Dec.	1350	2690	8
1 Long Section Down				
1921	Jan.	1660	310	1
	Mar.	1120	540	2
2nd Section				
	Apr.	1350	230	1
	May	1050	300	1
3rd Section				
1921	Sept.	2020	970	4
1 Section Up				
May Option				
	Sept. High	2240		
	Nov.	1600	640	2
	Dec.	1860	260	1
1922	Jan.	1580	280	1
	Apr.	2270	690	3
	May	2000	270	1
1923	Mar.	3155	1155	10
2nd Section				
	July	2075	1080	4
	Nov. 30	3725	1650	4
3rd Section—Final Top				
1924	Mar.	2650	1075	4
1st Section Down				
	May	3230	580	2
	July	2330	900	2
	Aug.	2910	580	1
	Sept.	2175	735	1
2nd Section				
	Oct.	2640	465	1

COTTON SWINGS FROM HIGH TO LOW (Continued)
TIME PERIODS

Year		Price	Advance or Decline	Time Months
1925	Jan.	2340	300	2
	Mar.	2625	285	2
	May	2170	455	2
	July	2570	400	2
	Aug.	2200	370	1
	Sept.	2500	300	1
	Oct.	1850	650	1
	Nov.	2040	190	1
	Dec.	1830	210	1
3rd Section				
1926	Jan.	2000	170	1
	Mar.	1830	170	2
	May	1910	80	2
	June	1630	280	1
	Sept.	1865	235	3
	Dec.	1210	655	3
End of 4th Section				
1927	Sept.	2440	1230	9
1928	Feb.	1710	730	5
	June	2288	578	4
	Sept.	1720	568	3
	Oct.	2010	290	1
	Nov.	1800	210	1
1929	Mar.	2070	270	4
	June	1800	270	3
	July	1950	150	1
	Aug.	1785	165	1
	Sept.	1960	175	1
1930	Mar.	1400	560	6
	Apr.	1615	215	1
	Oct.	1000	615	6
	Nov.	1230	230	1
	Dec.	1010	220	1
1931	Mar.	1225	215	3
	June	850	375	3
	July	1078	225	1
	Oct.	540	535	4
	Nov.	780	240	1
	Dec.	680	100	1
1932	Feb.	755	75	2
	June	515	240	4
	Sept.	950	435	3
	Dec.	585	365	3

COTTON SWINGS FROM HIGH TO LOW (Contiuued)
TIME PERIODS

Year		Price	Advance or Decline	Time Months
1933	Jan.	690	105	1
	Feb.	615	75	1
	July	1200	585	5
	Aug.	840	360	1
	Sept.	1040	200	1
	Oct.	860	180	1
1934	Feb.	1290	430	4
	May	1085	205	3
	Aug.	1395	310	3
	Nov.	1170	220	3
1935	Jan.	1270	100	2
	Mar.	1000	270	2
	May	1190	190	2
	Sept.	1030	160	4
	Nov.	1145	115	2
1936	Jan.	985	160	2
	Feb.	1060	75	1
	Mar.	990	70	1
	July	1275	285	4
	Sept.	1130	145	2
	Oct.	1240	110	1
	Nov.	1110	130	1
1937	Apr.	1395	285	5
	Oct.	780	615	6
1938	Mar.	950	170	5
	June	770	180	3
	July	915	145	1
	Dec.	705	210	5
1939	Sept.	1015	310	9
	Nov.	795	220	2
1940	Jan.	1015	220	2
	Feb.	910	105	1
	Apr.	1025	115	2
	May	845	180	1
	June	965	120	1
	July	900	65	1
	Oct.	980	80	3
	Nov.	870	110	1
1941	July 28	1760	890	8
	Aug. 13	1582	178	16 days
	Sept. 12	1846	264	30 days
	Oct. 16	1557	289	34 days

COTTON SEED OIL

Cotton Seed Oil is traded in on the New York Produce Exchange and the New Orleans Cotton Exchange. The contract is for 30,000 pounds. The fluctuation is 1/100 of a cent per pound, making the minimum fluctuation $3.00 per contract. A decline of 100 points or 1c per pound is the loss or gain of $300.00. If you buy a contract of Cotton Seed Oil and it advances 1c per pound, your profit is $300.00, less the commission. The commission for buying or selling Cotton Seed Oil is $15.00 regardless of the price. The margin for buying Cotton Seed Oil is 10% of the price nearest to $100.00.

Seed Oil is derived from seed of Cotton and the Oil is obtained by crushing the seeds. There are many uses for Cotton Seed Oil, the principal use is a substitute for Lard and when Cotton Seed Oil is mixed with Lard it makes a good compound for cooking.

Cotton Seed Oil prices do not run exactly the same as Cotton prices, that is, Highs and Lows are not made in the same month as Cotton as you can see by comparing the chart. The price of Cotton Seed Oil is determined by Supply and Demand. When there is a very large Cotton crop, this means an increased supply of Cotton Seed Oil and lower prices. Cotton Seed Oil prices are influenced by the price of Lard and by Soybean Oil and other competitive oils and fats. When the Cotton crop is very short, this means a short crop of Cotton Seed Oil and higher prices under normal conditions. One reason why Cotton Seed Oil does not move with Cotton is because Cotton will advance on reports of crop damage but Cotton Seed Oil may not show a big advance until it is well known that the Cotton crop is short and therefore the crushings of Cotton Seed Oil will be smaller.

It is the same when there is a very large crop of Cotton. Cotton will decline before it is definitely known how large the crop is. Later when it is an established fact, that the cotton crop is very large, this means that the crushing of cotton seed will be large, producing more Cotton Seed Oil, then the Cotton Seed Oil market starts to discount the large crop which will increase the supply, but as a general rule, the trend of Cotton Seed Oil follows the trend of Cotton, sometimes later and sometimes running ahead of Cotton prices. You can see this by study of the Chart.

SEASONAL CHANGES FROM 1904 TO 1941

During the 27-year period, the yearly Highs and Lows have been made as follows:

JANUARY	Low	7 times
	High	8 "
FEBRUARY	Low	5 "
	High	4 "
MARCH	Low	2 "
	High	3 "
APRIL	Low	3 "
	High	1 "

MAY	Low	2	"
	High	5	"
JUNE	Low	1	"
	High	1	"
JULY	Low	4	"
	High	4	"
AUGUST	Low	6	"
	High	3	"
SEPTEMBER	Low	3	"
	High	3	"
OCTOBER	Low	3	"
	High	4	"
NOVEMBER	Low	3	"
	High	2	"
DECEMBER	Low	6	"
	High	5	"

From this you can see that the greatest number of lows have been made in February, August and December. This is the seasonal time of the year when it is generally known whether the Cotton crop is large or small. It appears that if the year's Cotton crop is large, Cotton Seed Oil is low in August. February is also an important month, being six months from August.

April, September, October and November all have been the same, that is the lows have been made three times during these months.

July—Lows have been made 4 times.

May and June—The least number of Lows have been made.

Only two lows have been made in May and one in June.

When the market runs opposite the seasonal trend and the Cotton crop is short, Cotton Seed Oil makes High levels in December and January following the trend of Cotton.

The Months when the most Highs have been reached are January, May and December. When the crop is large and reports are good during the Summer and early Fall, Cotton Seed Oil declines to discount a large crop. This is why the smallest number of Highs have been reached in June and August. When the trend is down High prices are reached before the summer period and when the trend is up they are reached later than August and September. As you will see only two Highs have been reached in November, this being the time when if there is a large Cotton crop prices are declining.

You will note that April, June and November showed the least number of Highs.

If the market runs against the seasonal trend it will make highs and lows opposite.

HIGH AND LOW PRICES FOR COTTON SEED OIL

1904	December	Low	225	
1919	July	High	2815	½ is 1407
1921	April	Low	575	

NOTE: 1921 September High 1420, making September 1941 High DOUBLE TOP against 1921.

1926	May	High	1675
1932	May	Low	315 cents
1935	February	High	1190
1936	May	Low	865
1937	January	High	1185
1939	August	Low	520
1940	August	Low	530
1941	September	High	1415

NOTE: BOTTOMS was September 1921.

RESISTANCE LEVELS: LOW, 225 TO 2815

The percentages of the resistance Levels are as follows:

12½%	548	62½%	1843
25%	872	66 2/3%	1951
33 1/3%	1088	75%	2167
37½%	1195	87½%	2490
50%	1520	100%	2815

The percentages of 2815, the Highest Selling Price are as follows:

12½%	351	62½%	1758
25%	703	66 2/3%	1876
33 1/3%	938	75%	2109
37½%	1055	87½%	2460
50%	1407	100%	2815

The percentages of 2815 to 315 are as follows:

12½%	627	62½%	1888
25%	940	66 2/3%	1981
33 1/3%	1148	75%	2200
37½%	1152	87½%	2513
50%	1575	100%	2815

The percentages of 1675 to 520 are as follows:

12½%	664	62½%	1241
25%	808	66 2/3%	1284
33 1/3%	902	75%	1385
37½%	952	87½%	1530
50%	1097	100%	1675

Until prices go below these Extreme Low Levels or advance above the Extreme High Levels, these resistance Levels or percentage points will be the ones to watch in the future for TOPS and BOTTOMS or High and Low Levels. Watch the market for any option of Cotton Seed Oil when it advances or declines to these resistance Levels and if it holds for several days or several weeks without declining more than 30 points below these Levels or advancing more than 30 points, above them, you can consider that it is making BOTTOM or TOP and that it is safe to buy or sell protected with Stop Loss Order 30 to 50 points away, depending upon whether the markets are at very

High Levels or Extremely Low Levels. When Cotton Seed Oil is selling above 20c a pound STOPS should be about 50 points above or below these Resistance Levels. When it is selling at 10c a pound or under, STOPS should be about 30 points above or below these Levels.

Always consider how far the market has advanced or declined from any previous TOP or BOTTOM and consider the time period from any previous TOP or BOTTOM.

COTTON SEED OIL, SINGLE, DOUBLE AND TRIPLE TOPS AND BOTTOMS

To help you determine the trend of Cotton Seed Oils in the future, and to know when to buy and sell at important Tops and Bottoms, we are giving examples of Tops and Bottoms in the past.

1904—December Low 225. A single Bottom.

1905—April and September. Double Bottoms, First and Second Higher Bottoms, showing strength and indicating higher prices.

1907—May High. A sharp Single Top.

1907—November Low. A Single Low.

1908—March and August Low. Double Bottoms and Triple Bottoms. Buying level.

1910—August High. Single Sharp Tops.

1911—August and September. Low. Double Bottoms and buying levels.

1913—July High. A Single Sharp Top and lower than August 1910, showing change in main trend.

1914—October Low. Buying level.

1915—August Low. Double Bottom and safer BUYING LEVEL.

1916—March High. A single sharp Top.

1916—July, Low. A single sharp Bottom and BUYING LEVEL.

1919—June and July, Extreme High. A double Top and safe selling Level.

1921—April. A single sharp Bottom. Buying level for a rally.

1922—March and May Highs. Double Tops and SELLING LEVEL.

1922—September Low. Single sharp Bottom.

1923—October High. A single Top, and lower than the High of September 1920.

1924—August High. First lower Top, indicating main trend down.

1924—December High. A second lower Top, showing main trend down.

1925—March High. A third lower top. This was one of the safest places to sell short.

1926—May High. A SINGLE sharp TOP. Has not been higher than that top up to this writing, November 1, 1941.

1926—November low. A SINGLE sharp BOTTOM.

1927—April low. The FIRST HIGHER BOTTOM. Safe to buy for higher prices.

1927—October high. A SINGLE TOP.

1928—May high. A DOUBLE TOP.

1929—February High. A DOUBLE TOP AND SELLING LEVEL, A SHARP DECLINE following.

1932—May extreme low. Note that this extreme low was made seven months before cotton reached extreme low, showing that cotton seed oil and cotton do not always reach extreme lows or highs at the same time.

1932—August. A DOUBLE TOP against November, 1931 top.

1932—December low. A SECONDARY DECLINE and HIGHER BOTTOM than May, 1932, making this a safer buying level, especially as cotton was at the extreme low in this month.

1933—February and March lows. A DOUBLE BOTTOM and A SECOND HIGHER BOTTOM, making this a still safer buying point.

1933—July high. A SINGLE SHARP TOP and under OLD BOTTOMS.

1933—October and December lows. DOUBLE BOTTOMS and higher than 1932 and 1933, making this a safe buying point.

1934—April low. A THIRD HIGHER BOTTOM showing strong uptrend.

1935—February high, 1195. A SINGLE TOP but a DOUBLE TOP against October, 1927.

1936—May low, 865. A SINGLE BOTTOM.

1937—January high, 1185. A DOUBLE TOP AGAINST February, 1936. A safe selling level.

1939—August low, 520.

1940—August low, 535. A DOUBLE BOTTOM one year later and a safe buying level.
Later the main trend turned up but crossing the PREVIOUS TOP at 50% points on the last move down you should have bought more cotton seed oil, as the main trend was upward.

1941—March and April. Prices crossed the TOPS of 1938, 1939 and 1940, showing strong uptrend and safe to buy more.

1941—June, crossed 1935 and 1937 TOPS, showing strong uptrend. The TOP was reached in June and a sharp break followed in the latter part of June and in July. The market had good support and the advance was resumed.

1941—September high, 1415. Note that this was exactly one-half, or 50% of 2815, the extreme high level of July, 1919. This was the highest level since 1926. A sharp decline followed in the month of October, 1941.
Apply all of the rules. Keep up a weekly high and low, monthly high and low and quarterly charts on cotton seed oil and you will be able to determine changes in trend and the proper places to buy and sell.

BUTTER

Butter is traded in on the Chicago Mercantile Exchange and the New York Mercantile Exchange. The contract for the Chicago Mercantile Exchange and the New York Mercantile Exchange is for 19,200 pounds.

Fluctuations are in cents per pound and the price is based on cents per pound. The fluctuations are 5/100 of a cent per pound, so on a contract of 19,200 pounds, 5/100 of a cent gives a minimum fluctuation of $9.60.

The commission for buying and selling butter is $50.00 per contract.

Butter is very profitable to trade in, especially when you catch the trend at the time of the seasonal trend, as it follows the seasonal trend closer than almost any other commodity. War is always bullish on butter, as well as on other commodities and highest prices have always occurred during war periods. Then with high prices, over production is the result and then prices reach very low levels after war or after extreme high prices.

THE HIGH AND LOW PRICES ON SPOT BUTTER AND NOVEMBER AND DECEMBER FUTURES

The most active future options and the best to trade in, are October, November and December. November never runs very long. October is the best to trade in because trading in this option lasts the longest.

1860—HIGH 50c per pound.

1895 and 1899—LOW 20c.

1919—EXTREME HIGH, 73c per pound.

1921—June, LOW 31¼.

1921—July, HIGH 45¼.

1921—December, LOW 34¼.

1923—December, HIGH 50½.

1924—October, LOW 32¼.

1925—September, HIGH 48½c. This was a LOWER TOP than 1923 and a SELLING LEVEL.

1926—April, LOW 40c.

1926—December, HIGH 47¼c. A SECOND LOWER TOP and a SELLING LEVEL.

1927—August, LOW 40½c. A DOUBLE BOTTOM against April, 1926, and a BUYING LEVEL. August was one of the most important months for a change in trend.

1928—December, HIGH 48⅜c. The fourth time around this level and lower than the EXTREME HIGH of December, 1929. Note how often butter makes the change in trend in December. This was the last high from which a fast decline followed.

1933—December, EXTREME LOW 14c.

1936—August, HIGH 36¼c.

1937—May, LOW 29½c.

1937—September and December HIGHS 34½c.

1938—August, LOW 23¼c.

1939—February, LOW 23c.

1939—December, LOW 23c. Three bottoms around the same level. A TRIPLE BOTTOM. This indicated a big advance to follow. All commodities made triple bottoms in 1938, 1939 and 1940 and since that time big advances in all the commodities have followed. Therefore, watch all of these important triple bottoms in the future, or double bottoms, when they occur. Also watch TRIPLE TOPS. Note that in 1923, 1925, 1926 and 1928 triple tops were made and a big decline followed.

1940—December, LOW 34½c.

1941—February, LAST LOW 28½c.

1941—June, HIGH 38¼c.

1941—July, LOW 34½c.

1941—September, HIGH 37c.

1941—October, LOW 32¼c. Note that prices failed to get back to the high of December, 1928—in fact they only advanced slightly higher than August, 1936, and met resistance, making a LOWER TOP in September, 1941.

RESISTANCE LEVELS FOR BUTTER: The most important resistance levels are between the EXTREME HIGHS and EXTREME LOWS. We have given the resistance levels from 69c to 14c and from 50½c to 14c.

The resistance levels could be figured from the LOW of 23c to the high of 38¼, or any other HIGH that may be reached before the low of 23c is broken.

Also, the last resistance level between the last EXTREME LOW and EXTREME HIGH—28½c to 38¼c—is important. This is around 33c and in October, 1941 prices were slightly under this level. Breaking 33c and staying under this price would indicate LOWER. Butter gives all indications of having made TOPS for the present, but should it later cross 38¼c, then the next important points to watch would be around the old bottoms of 40c and then the old tops of 47c to 50c.

SEASONAL TREND—1921 TO 1941: Below we give the months when EXTREME HIGHS and EXTREME LOWS have been reached each year and the number of times LOWS or HIGHS have been reached in each calendar month.

	Lows	Highs		Lows	Highs
January	0	0	July	1	2
February	3	1	August	3	3
March	1	1	September	0	4
April	3	1	October	2	0
May	1	1	November	0	1
June	4	1	December	5	8

From the above you can see that the greatest number of LOWS have been reached in the month of December. The next in importance was June, with four LOWS reached in that month. The next months in importance are February, April and August, three LOWS having been reached in those months. In the months of March, May and July, LOWS were reached only one time.

In the months of January, September and November no LOWS were reached.

The greatest number of HIGHS have been reached in December. Eight times in twenty years HIGHS have been reached in December. The next important months are September and August—with four HIGHS reached in September and three in August. The next important month is July. Two HIGHS were reached in July. In the months of February, March, April, May, June and November, HIGHS were reached only one time. In the months of January and October no HIGHS were recorded.

From the above you can see that when the seasonal demand takes place for the winter season, HIGHS are reached in December and when there is an over-supply, LOWS are reached in December. After the Christmas demand has been filled, LOWS are reached in February and April. When there is very small demand in the month of June, a large number of LOWS have been reached and the next in August. August is almost always an important month for a change in trend.

The demand starts to pick up in August and September and this accounts for the larger number of HIGHS reached during these months.

Butter makes important TOPS and BOTTOMS in the sixth month. It is also important to watch the third or fourth months. But the most important changes occur six and twelve months apart, as you can see by a study of the past record.

After HIGHS are reached in December for two or three years, the trend changes and the next year there is a LOW, which proves that after three HIGHS or three LOWS occur in any one month in three consecutive years, the next year will run opposite.

The more you study past records, the greater will be your accuracy in determining the future trend of butter.

BUTTER — EXAMPLES OF BUYING AND SELLING POINTS AGAINST DOUBLE, TRIPLE BOTTOMS AND TOPS

1921—June, LOW 34¼c. A BUYING LEVEL because 33-1/3% of 69 to 14 is 33⅜c.

1921—July, HIGH 45¼c. A SELLING LEVEL, since 46c is 87½% of 50½ to 14.

1921—December, LOW 34½c. A HIGHER BOTTOM. December is the month for seasonal change, and a BUYING POINT.

1922—June, HIGH 40¾c. This is 75% of 14 to 50½c.

1922—August, LOW 34¾c. A DOUBLE BOTTOM and a RESISTANCE LEVEL. A BUYING LEVEL, because August is a month for a change in trend.

1922—December, HIGH 47½c. A RESISTANCE LEVEL and SELLING LEVEL. A reaction followed.

1923—June, LOW 38½c. A month for a change in trend and 66-2/3% of 14 to 50½c.

1923—December, HIGH 50½c. Fifty is a natural selling level, because 50 is ½ of $1.00, or 50% of the dollar. Later prices broke back under the 50% point between 38½c to 50½c, indicating LOWER.

1924—October, LOW 32¼c. A DOUBLE BOTTOM against 1921 and a BUYING LEVEL. Note that 33-1/3 is one-third of a dollar, an important resistance level.

1925—September, HIGH 48½c. AN OLD TOP LEVEL, a RESISTANCE LEVEL and a SELLING LEVEL. Also because September is a month for seasonal change in trend.

1926—April, HIGH 40c. A RESISTANCE LEVEL because 41⅜ was 75% of 14 to 50½c.

1926—December, HIGH 47½c. A LOWER TOP and SELLING LEVEL because December is the month for a change in trend and the most TOPS come out at this time.

1927—August, LOW 40¼c. A DOUBLE BOTTOM against April, 1926 — again August the month for a change in trend, making this a BUYING LEVEL.

1928—December, HIGH 48½c. A THIRD TOP and a safe SELLING LEVEL — under 50c and December is the month for TOPS and a change in trend. Note from last low of 40¼ to 48½c makes 44¼c, the half way, or 50% point.

1929—February, LOW 43c.

1929—May, HIGH 44½.

1929—July, LOW 43c. A DOUBLE BOTTOM and a BUYING LEVEL.

1929—September, HIGH 44¾c. A SELLING LEVEL because September is the month for a change in trend. Later prices broke the DOUBLE BOTTOM of 43c, indicating LOWER and a decline followed.

1929—December, LOW 33½c. Higher than 1921 and 1924. A RESISTANCE LEVEL because 33⅜ was a resistance point between 14 and 69.

1930—April, HIGH 41½c. Under old bottoms, a RESISTANCE LEVEL and a SELLING LEVEL.

1930—May, LOW 35¼c. Dull and narrow around this low level. A rally followed.

1930—August, HIGH 42c. Under old bottoms and 41½ was a resistance level between 69 to 14. August a month for change in trend. Makes this a SELLING LEVEL. Prices broke back and broke the resistance levels and the bottoms at 35¼c, indicating great weakness and lower prices followed.

1930—December, LOW 25¼c. This was a natural SUPPORT LEVEL and 50% decline from 50½c — and 25c is a natural LEVEL because it is ¼ or 25% of a dollar. Makes this a SAFE BUYING LEVEL.

1931—March, HIGH 32½c. Under old bottoms and a SELLING LEVEL.

1931—May, June and July, LOW 24c. Just under the bottom of December and six months later. Held for three months around this same level, showing good support. June was a month for a change in trend, because it was the sixth month from December.

1931—October, HIGH 30½c. Under the 50% point from 14 to 50½c. A SELLING LEVEL.

1932—June, LOW 16¼c. A resistance level, because 33-1/3% of 50½ was 16⅞. This makes this a BUYING LEVEL.

1932—November, HIGH 24c. Under the old bottoms and as long as it was under ½ of 50½, it was a SELLING LEVEL.

1933—March, LOW 16¾c. A DOUBLE BOTTOM and slightly higher. A BUYING LEVEL for a rally. A rally followed. Prices crossed 24c, the last TOP.

1933—July, HIGH 27⅝c. This was 25% of 69 to 14 and a SELLING LEVEL on a sharp top.

1933—December, FINAL LOW 14c. December was the month for a change in trend and this was running OPPOSITE the seasonal trend. Had declined from the last top of 27⅝ almost 50%. This was a panicky decline and a safe BUYING LEVEL.

1934—August, HIGH 28½c. A DOUBLE TOP against July, 1933. A SELLING LEVEL.

1934—October, LOW 25c. A BUYING LEVEL.

1934—December, HIGH 28½c. A DOUBLE TOP and a SELLING LEVEL. December is a month for change in trend, and one year from the EXTREME LOW.

1935—June and July, LOW 23⅝c. An old bottom level, 25% of 50½ to 14 being 23⅛c.

1935—December, HIGH 33c. Up to the top of March, 1931. A SELLING LEVEL.

1936—March, 25½c. Back to the BUYING LEVEL of 50% of 50½c. A HIGHER BOTTOM made it a safer buy.

1936—August, HIGH 36¼c. This was 62½% of 50½ to 14. August is the month for a change in trend. TIME TO SELL.

1936—October, LOW 30c. A SUPPORT LEVEL, as 31½c was 62½% of 50½c.

1937—February, LOW 29½c. A DOUBLE BOTTOM and a SAFER BUYING LEVEL.

1937—September, to December, SAME HIGH 34½c. A RESISTANCE LEVEL as 37½% of 69 to 14 is 34¼c. December was a month for a change in trend and a month where most tops are made. A DOUBLE TOP level and a place to SELL OUT and GO SHORT.

1938—January, — broke all bottoms and resistance levels, 30 to 29½. Showed extreme weakness and indicated LOWER PRICES.

1938—August, LOW 23c. The same as April, 1930.

1938—November, HIGH 28c. A SELLING LEVEL.

1939—February, LOW 23c. Held in a narrow trading range the balance of the year.

1939—August, LOW 23c. A TRIPLE BOTTOM and a safer BUYING LEVEL.

War broke out in September and the market advanced, crossing the tops at 25c, showing STRONG UPTREND.

1939—September, HIGH 28c. A DOUBLE TOP against November, 1938 and a SELLING LEVEL.

1939—December, LOW 26½c. A HIGHER BOTTOM and a stronger SUPPORT LEVEL.

1940—January, HIGH 28⅛c. A TRIPLE TOP and in a month for a change in trend. A SELLING LEVEL.

1940—June, LOW 25⅞c. A DOUBLE BOTTOM and at the RESISTANCE LEVEL of 33-1/3% of 50½ to 14. Held for three months around this low level, making this a safer BUYING LEVEL.

1940—September — BREAKAWAY POINT. When prices crossed 28c, a series of old tops, this was the BREAKAWAY POINT and a safe place to BUY MORE.

1940—December, HIGH 34½c. An old top of 1937 and a SELLING LEVEL because December is the month for HIGHS and a change in trend.

1941—February, LOW 28¼c. An old top level and a SAFE BUYING LEVEL. The advance resumed and prices gradually worked HIGHER.

1941—June, HIGH 38¼c. Ten cents advance and one year from June, 1940. Indicated a change in trend. This was a RESISTANCE LEVEL from old levels around this point. The last high in September, 1930 was 38½c and 66-2/3% of 50½c to 14c is 38⅜, making this a safe selling level.

1941—July, LOW 34¼c. An old top level and again a BUYING LEVEL.

1941—September, HIGH 37¼c. A SECONDARY RALLY and a LOWER TOP. A SELLING LEVEL, because September is a month for a change in trend.

1941—October, LOW 32¼c. Note last LOW, 28¼, to 38¼, made the 50% point 33¼c. Therefore, this was a SUPPORT LEVEL.

Butter gives indications of having made TOPS and the trend has turned DOWN, but should prices break under 32c, the RESISTANCE POINT, it will then indicate LOWER and should decline back to around the old levels of 28c. The next point is around 25c.

However, later on, if butter should cross 38½c, a DOUBLE TOP, it will indicate resistance levels around 42c and next around 47c to 48c TOP LEVELS.

The next important date for a change in trend is December, 1941. Possibly the change might not come until January. This should be the important point to watch and should the market rally and make TOPS around that time, it will be the time to SELL. On the other hand, should prices decline and make LOW in December or early in January, it will be the time to BUY FOR A RALLY.

Apply all of the rules. Watch resistance points and the time from EXTREME HIGH LEVELS to EXTREME LOW LEVELS and you will be able to determine future trends.

COCOA FUTURES

Cocoa is traded in on the New York Cocoa Exchange. A contract for cocoa is 22,000 pounds. The fluctuations are in cents per pound and the minimum fluctuation is $\frac{1}{8}$ of a cent per pound. This amounts to $27.50 on a contract.

The commission for buying and selling cocoa is $25.00 per contract.

The margin requirements for buying and selling cocoa vary according to the price. If cocoa is selling at around 6c to 8c per pound, the margin is usually $600 to $700 per contract. When cocoa is selling at around 4c per pound, the margin requirements are usually about $400.

Cocoa is grown in many of the South American countries and in Africa and some of the British possessions.

HARVESTING COCOA. Cocoa is harvested in most countries in October to March. In some countries the harvesting does not start until May or July, but in almost all countries the harvesting is over by August or September. A large percentage of the cocoa grown is sold in the United States. The uses for cocoa in the United States have increased from year to year.

SEASONAL CHANGES
SEPTEMBER COCOA FUTURES
1925 to 1941

Below we give the times each month that cocoa has made HIGH and LOW.

	High	Low		High	Low
January	5	1	July	1	2
February	4	0	August	0	2
March	3	1	September	3	2
April	0	2	October	2	1
May	3	3	November	1	2
June	3	2	December	1	2

From the above you will see that the greatest number of LOWS have been reached in May during this period. This is due to the fact that in most countries harvesting is going on by May and receipts and selling pressure increase at this time of year. The next months for LOW are April, June, July, August, September, November and December, when the same number of LOWS have been reached. The smallest number of LOWS has been reached in the months of March and October. No LOWS have been made during any year in the month of February because, as you can see, this is a month for seasonal highs.

The greatest number of HIGHS was reached in January, the next in February and the next in March, May, June and September, in each of these last four months three HIGHS having been reached. The cause of this is that HIGHS are reached just before the crops start to move on the market or at the end of the season before harvesting is started. September is one of the important months for HIGHS and this month is after most of the harvesting is over.

In figuring when the next TOP or BOTTOM will be reached it is always important to consider when the last EXTREME HIGH or EXTREME LOW was reached and the number of months the market has moved up or down. This will help you in determining the change in trend.

RESISTANCE LEVELS

In figuring the resistance levels, we use the EXTREME HIGH in 1919 of 2325 to 1933, April LOW 330.

Another one of the important resistance levels to figure from is 1926, March HIGH 1785, to the EXTREME LOW of 330.

These two prices and the resistance levels between them and the percentage on the high and low price will be all that is needed for a long time to come to figure future resistance levels from.

SEPTEMBER COCOA

YEARS PRICE	1927 March to 1933 April	1927 March to 19—	1937 January to 19—	1937 January to 19—
HIGH LOW	1785 to 335	1785 to 0	1310 to 335	1310 to 0
12½%	516	223	457	164
25%	697	446	579	328
33⅓%	818	595	660	437
37½%	878	669	701	492
50%	1059	892	823	655
62½%	1240	1115	945	819
66⅔%	1301	1190	985	874
75%	1421	1338	1067	983
87½%	1602	1561	1189	1147
100%	1785	1785	1310	1310

EXTREME HIGHS AND LOWS FOR COCOA — cash prices.

1865—HIGH 32c.

1874—LOW 12c.

1879—HIGH 23c.

1890—LOW 13c.

1893—HIGH 16c.

1896—LOW 12c. This was the lowest since Civil War prices. Most all commodities made LOWS between 1894 and 1898.

1900—HIGH 17c.

1910—LOW 11c. This was lower than 1896.

1915—HIGH 1675.

1917—LOW 17c.

1919—HIGH 2325. This was the EXTREME HIGH.

1921—LOW 7c.

1922—HIGH 1050.

1923—LOW 6c.

From 1925 on, we use the September cocoa future contracts for examples and for HIGHS and LOWS.

SEPTEMBER COCOA — 1925 to 1941 — DOUBLE, SINGLE AND TRIPLE TOPS AND BOTTOMS AND RESISTANCE LEVELS

1925—November, LOW 905. A 100% advance on this low level would be 1810.

1926—March, HIGH 1785. Failing to reach the 100% advance from the bottom showed weakness, and made this a SELLING LEVEL. At 1785 the market had made three moves or sections up, and there were three tops around this level, making this a SELLING LEVEL. When prices broke back under 1685, which was $12\frac{1}{2}\%$ of the HIGH and selling price, it indicated lower. The decline continued.

1927—LOW 1290. This was fourteen months from the EXTREME HIGH and our rule says around the fifteenth month to watch for a change in trend.

1928—May, HIGH 1560. Under old tops and bottoms and a SELLING LEVEL. Later it broke one-half of the last move and then broke the EXTREME LOW of 1290, indicating lower prices.

1928—August, LOW 1020. A DOUBLE BOTTOM against October, 1926, and a BUYING LEVEL for a rally.

1928—October, HIGH 1140. A two months' normal rally.

1928—November, LOW 1035. A HIGHER BOTTOM and a DOUBLE BOTTOM. Time to BUY FOR RALLY.

1929—February, HIGH 1210. February is one of the months for a seasonal change in trend. This was a TOP and a SELLING LEVEL.

1929—May, LOW 1030. A TRIPLE BOTTOM. Seasonal changes occur in the month of May.

1929—September, HIGH 1110. A small rally for a long period of time. September is a month for a change in trend. A decline followed and rallies were very small.

1930—September, LOW 525. One year from September, 1929 and 595 was 66-2/3% of 1785. September is a month for a change in trend. Time to BUY FOR A RALLY. A rally followed.

1930—November, HIGH 765. A two months' rally and 140 points advance, which was only normal. The main trend was still down and it was time to SELL OUT and GO SHORT.

1932—May, June and July, LOW 390. This was an important RESISTANCE LEVEL as 446 was 75% decline from 1785. The prices holding for around three months at the same level made it a time to BUY FOR A RALLY.

1932—September, HIGH 510. The same TOP as March. A DOUBLE TOP and SELLING LEVEL.

1933—April, EXTREME LOW 330. Held at this low level for three months. A BUYING LEVEL. From the last high, 510 to 330, the 50% point was 420. The market held in a narrow trading range for quite a few months.

1933—Later in the month of April the advance started and prices crossed 420, indicating HIGHER.

1933—July, HIGH 680. The same top as January, 1931 and note that 660 was the 100% advance on 330, making this a SELLING LEVEL. A fast decline followed.

1933—September, LOW 4c. A SECONDARY DECLINE. The same low as June, 1932 and a SAFER BUYING LEVEL.

1934—February to June, HIGH 6c. A TRIPLE TOP and a SELLING LEVEL.

1934—June to August, LOW 450. From 680 to 330, the 50% point was 505 and 50% advance on 330 was 495. This was six months from February, when a change in trend should occur, according to our rules.

1935—February, HIGH 560. Six months from the last TOP, but a LOWER TOP and at a RESISTANCE LEVEL. Cocoa should have been sold out and sold short at this level.

1935—June, LOW 430. A DOUBLE BOTTOM and a BUYING LEVEL.

1936—HIGH 560. A DOUBLE TOP against February, 1935 and a SELLING LEVEL.

1936—March, LOW 505. Held two months in a dull, narrow range, holding above resistance point from the bottom. It was a BUYING LEVEL for another advance.

1936—May — crossed all tops since June, 1934.

BREAKAWAY POINT

1936—August — crossed 660, a 100% advance on 330, showing strong uptrend. This was the time after the BREAKAWAY POINT to BUY MORE, for the run was on. The prices moved up fast out of the valley of depression, crossing old tops and indicated much higher prices.

1936—September — prices crossed 680, the top of July, 1932, showing very strong uptrend. The market continued to work higher, with very small reactions. When the market gets beyond the BREAKAWAY POINT and in the run, this is where you can make large profits in a short period of time.

1937—January, FINAL HIGH 1310. Under old bottoms of 1928. A 100% advance on 680, the HIGH of July, 1933, would give 1360. A 300% advance on 330, the EXTREME LOW, would give 1320, making this a place to SELL OUT and GO SHORT. January was one of the most important months for HIGHS and a change in trend. The market had advanced for nineteen months and was nine months up since the BREAKAWAY POINT. This was the time to SELL OUT and GO SHORT. The prices broke back under 1188, 12% of the advance, and a signal for a lower price. The 50% point between 1310 and 330 was 840.

1937—February, LOW 940. One month's sharp decline and a SECONDARY RALLY was due. From 1310 to 940, the half-way point was 1125.

1937—March, HIGH 1245. A LOWER TOP and a SELLING LEVEL. When prices broke back under 1215, it was an indication of weakness and lower prices.

1937—May, LOW 695. Down to OLD TOP. A decline of four months and a rally due. May was also an important month for seasonal changes in trend, and one year since the big move started.

1937—August, HIGH 850. A three months' rally and a SELLING LEVEL because 840 was the half-way point between 1310 and 330.

1938—May, LOW 410. A DOUBLE BOTTOM and one year from the low of May, 1937.

1938—September, HIGH 550. The market became very slow and dull at the top and indicated this was the time to SELL. Prices gradually worked lower from this time on.

1939—August, LOW 390. A DOUBLE BOTTOM down to September, 1933 low. September was the important month for a change in trend and during this month the prices crossed the tops of many months past, crossing the tops of 470. Showed strong uptrend.

1939—September, HIGH 670. A DOUBLE TOP as against January, 1938. This was the rush up on the breaking out of war. This double top was a place to SELL OUT LONGS and SELL SHORT. A 100% advance on 330 gave 660 as a RESISTANCE LEVEL.

1939—October and November LOW 490. A 50% advance on 330 gave 495, making this a BUYING LEVEL.

1940—May, HIGH 650. A DOUBLE TOP, slightly lower and a SELLING LEVEL. Also at RESISTANCE LEVEL.

1940—July, LOW 395. A TRIPLE BOTTOM and a SAFER PLACE TO BUY. A slow advance followed. Later when prices crossed

530 which was the 50% point between 670 and 390, this was an indication of higher prices and the market moved up fast.

1941—May, HIGH 810. A 150% advance on 330. This was also a DOUBLE TOP and a SELLING LEVEL.

1941—July, LOW 715. A two months' reaction — a normal reaction and a BUYING LEVEL.

1941—September, HIGH 850. The same level as August, 1937 and a SELLING LEVEL. September is always an important month for a seasonal change in trend. In October a decline followed. At this writing, November 6, 1941, the main trend is up and if prices cross 850 and hold above this level, they will indicate the possibility of the next HIGH around 1310. Breaking back under 780 would indicate LOWER and breaking 650, a 50% decline from 1310, would put cocoa in a weaker position.

Apply all of the rules and you will be able to determine the future trend of cocoa.

COFFEE FUTURES

Coffee is traded in on the New York Coffee and Sugar Exchange. The fluctuations are in cents per pound.

A contract is for 32,500 pounds and fluctuations are in 1/100 of a cent per pound and the minimum fluctuation of 1/100c per pound is $3.25 per contract. In other words, if coffee advances 1c per pound, you would make $325 on a contract. If it declines 1c per pound, you would lose $325.

The commission for buying and selling coffee when it is under 10c per pound is $25.00 per contract. From 10c per pound to 1999 — $30.00 per contract. When coffee is selling above 20c per pound, the commission is $40.00 per contract.

Coffee is grown in many part of the world, but the greatest production is in the South American countries, Brazil being one of the largest coffee producers. United States is the largest consumer of coffee and a very large amount of business is done in coffee on the New York Coffee and Sugar Exchange.

SEASONAL CHANGES IN TREND

Below we give the months of the year when the greatest number of LOWS and HIGHS have been reached.

	Lows	Highs		Lows	Highs
January	2	10	July	6	3
February	0	6	August	3	4
March	6	0	September	2	3
April	5	2	October	4	4
May	3	3	November	3	1
June	4	3	December	4	3

From the above you can see that the greatest number of HIGHS have been reached in January and February — ten times highs were reached in January and six times in February. If we use the months of December, January and February, we get a total of 22 highs out of the past forty years. Therefore, these months are the most important to watch for highs and a change in seasonal trend. The next most important months for highs are August and October, — four highs were reached during these months. Next are May, June, July, September and December. Highs were reached three times during these months. April is next, with two highs and only one high was reached in November. During the month of March, from 1901 to 1941, no highs were reached. This is because the greatest number of highs are reached in January and February next and when March comes along, the trend is down.

The greatest number of lows have occurred in March, and July, with six lows reached in each. Next is April, when five lows were made. Next are June, October and December, when lows were made four times each. Then, May, August and November, when three lows have been made. Next are January and September, with two lows in each month. In February no lows were reached. Thus, you can see that the most important months to watch for lows are March and April and again June and July. Then in the Fall of the year, October, November and December are most important for lows.

Apply all of the rules that we have applied to other commodities, using resistance levels, and the time periods between extreme highs and extreme lows to determine the trend on coffee and the best places to buy and sell. Many opportunities come from time to time to make safe investments in coffee and make large profits. The greatest opportunities come when prices are at extreme high levels, where you can sell short and an investment on the short side is just as safe as an investment on the buying side. When prices reach extreme low levels and the time period is up for a fast move on the UP side, it is a safe investment to buy coffee. A lot of people think that an investment is something where you invest your money and get so much in dividends per year or so much in interest, but it makes no difference where you derive income from or how you derive it, so long as when you buy or sell something or invest your money, you get a return and when you make an investment in coffee at low levels and when the trend is up, you get greater dividends and greater returns than buying stocks for dividends or loaning money at interest. There is no such thing as a sure thing in any commodity market. You have to take some risk. That is why I give you rules for the amount of capital used and how to place STOP LOSS ORDERS for your protection. Losses come in any business. Losses come in buying and selling any commodity, but they are part of the expense of the business. No one can expect to consistently make money in anything all the time. You must take some risk, but when you take a risk, if you limit your losses, your percentage of gain is greater than in any other business.

You must learn to make speculations in commodities an investment business and a real business, and not make gambling out of it. If you learn to use the rules, you can make it a business of investment, and not a gambling proposition.

People who lose money in commodities often blame the Exchange and the market, but there is no one to blame but themselves. You can always make money buying and selling commodities provided you go with the trend and if you cannot learn how to determine the trend, then stay out. In fact, at all times when in doubt, keep out. Only buy or sell when you have good reasons for buying or selling, based on past history and facts that are proven to be reliable.

COFFEE MAY FUTURES RIO, TRADING IN NEW YORK IN CENTS PER POUND

1901—April low 5c Single Bottom. November high 770 Single Top.

1902—April low 480 Double Bottom 1 year from 1901. August, September, October high 600 to 590 Double Tops Selling Level.

1903—April low 465 Single Bottom 1 year from April 1902, change in trend due.

1904—January and February high 850 Single Sharp Top, fast decline followed. March low 520 Single Bottom. April high 620 Single Top, only 1 month rally. May low 530 Double Bottom. December high 820 Double Top, Lower Selling Level.

1905—March and April low 610 Double Bottom Buying Level. December high 820 Double Top 1 year from 1904 Selling Level.

1906—May low 625 Double Bottom, higher Buying Level. August high 800, the 3rd Lower Top Safer Selling Level, August the month for change due in trend.

1907—January low 530 Double Bottom Buying Level, January month change in trend due. March high 670 under old Bottom Selling Level. April, low 530 Double and Triple Bottoms Safer Buying Level. August high 780 Double and Triple Lower Top Selling Level. August month for Tops and change in trend due. December low 555, a higher Bottom and Buying Level, month for change in trend.

1908—February high 620. April low 560, a Double Bottom and higher Buying Level. May high 620 same as February Selling Level.

1908—July low 540 Triple Bottoms Safe Buying Level. October high 650 under old Bottoms Selling Level. November low 560, a Double Bottom.

1909—January low 565, a higher Bottom and safer Buying Level. May high 725 Double Top and Selling Level. October low 510, down to lows of 1901 and 1904, a buying level and October month for lows and change in trend made this a safe Buying Level.

1910—January and February high 715 Double Tops same as 1909, a Selling Level, and January month for Tops and change due in trend. August low 530, a higher Bottom than October 1909 and same lows as 1907, a safe Buying Level, August month for change in trend, an advance followed. Prices crossed 1909 and 1910. Tops showing strong uptrend, later crossed 1904 Tops.

1911—January high 1195, a single sharp Top, a quick decline followed. February low 960, only one month normal reaction. A rally followed. May high 1075, a 50% rally 1185 to 960 made 1075 a Selling Level. July low 685 down to old Tops, a 6 months' decline. Buy for a rally. A rapid advance followed. Prices crossed 810, 25% of 1185 to 685, and later crossed 935, the 50% of 1185 to 685, showing strong uptrend. This was a *Breakaway Point* and Runaway Market and you should buy all the way up.

1912—April high 1405, up 8 months from July 1911. May low 1310, only 1 months' normal reaction, a rally followed. June high 1415, a Double Top and Selling Level, a change due in trend in July, 1 year from last low.

1912—July low 1055, only 1 months' reaction, down to old Tops and Buying Level. October high 1440, the 3rd Top, and October a month for Tops and change in trend due made this a safe Selling Level. Prices were up over 100% from low of July 1911, and fast move up of 3 months from July 1912, also the last extreme low was October 1909 and at end of 3rd year important for a change in trend. This was the place to sell out and sell short.

1912—October, FINAL HIGH, 1440. At this point we use the Resistance Levels from the EXTREME LOW, 365 in April, 1903. From this sharp top in October a fast decline followed.

1912—November, LOW 1180. This was the first sharp decline and 75% of 365 to 1440 was 1171, making this a SUPPORT LEVEL. Also, it was down to the old tops of January, 1911. After the first sharp decline our rule says there is always a SECONDARY RALLY which runs about 50% or more of the decline. From 1180 to 1440 the 50% point was 1310.

1912—December, HIGH 1350. This was a one month's normal rally, and a SELLING LEVEL, because December is important for a change in trend. A fast decline followed.

1913—March, LOW 825. The 50% of 1440 was 720 and 62½% was 9c. Half of these two points would give 810 as a RESISTANCE and SUPPORT LEVEL and 903 was 50% of 1440 to 365. March was a month for seasonal change in trend and April is important because it was six months from the top. The market held in a narrow trading range for two months and then moved upward.

1913—June, HIGH 975. A RESISTANCE LEVEL, because 960 was 66-2/3% of 1440.

1913—July, LOW 9c. A DOUBLE RESISTANCE LEVEL, 9c being 62½% of 1440 and 903 being 50% of 1440 to 365, making this a SAFE BUYING LEVEL on a SECONDARY REACTION. An advance followed and prices crossed the tops of three months around 980, showing strong uptrend.

1913—October, HIGH 1150. October is a month for change in trend because it was one year from the EXTREME HIGH and the last decline from 1440 to 825 gave a 50% point as 1132. The market broke back under this point, indicating a weaker position and lower prices.

1913—December, LOW 910. The third higher bottom and an exact SUPPORT LEVEL, or 50% point. Two months decline, normal, making this a BUYING LEVEL. A rapid advance followed.

1914—January, HIGH 1380. A slightly higher top than December, 1912, but under the top of October, 1912. January is an important month for a TOP and a change in trend — the place to SELL out and GO SHORT. A sharp decline followed.

1914—June, LOW 975. Down to old top levels and a BUYING LEVEL. Also at resistance point.

1914—July, HIGH 1410. Around old top levels. A reaction followed.

1914—August, LOW 1260. An exact SUPPORT LEVEL, 87½% of 1440. A one month's normal reaction. A rally followed.

1914—October, FINAL HIGH 1465. This was a DOUBLE TOP, slightly higher than October, 1912 and two years later, making October important for a change in trend, and a place to SELL OUT AND GO SHORT. A decline followed, prices breaking 50% of the last move up and later breaking other important resistance points, showing strong down trend.

1915—April, LOW 830. A DOUBLE BOTTOM against March, 1913 and a slightly higher bottom. A rally followed.

1915—June, HIGH 975. Under old bottom levels and a SELLING POINT. Note that 960 was 66-2/3% of 1440, making a SELLING LEVEL and one year from the bottom in June, 1914. A change in trend due.

1915—July, LOW 720. This was an exact RESISTANCE LEVEL and a BUYING LEVEL and down to old top levels, — 723 being 33-1/3% of 1440 to 365. A moderate rally followed. Later prices continued down.

1915—December, LOW 580. A slightly higher bottom than the low in 1910 and December a month for a change in trend, and being two years from December, 1913 and one year from December, 1914. Note that 540 was 37½% of 1440. Failing to reach this level showed strength and made this a BUYING POINT in December. A quick, sharp rally followed.

1916—May, HIGH 920. A RESISTANCE LEVEL and SELLING LEVEL. Under old bottoms. This was in the sixth month from the bottom and you should watch for a trend change in June, as the last high was June, 1915. A decline followed.

1916—September, LOW 620. A HIGHER BOTTOM than 1915 and September a month for a change in trend. Note that 633 was 25% of 1440 to 365, making this a SUPPORT LEVEL and a BUYING POINT. The market held in a narrow trading range for several months and then moved up.

1917—January, HIGH 910. At the 50% point between EXTREME HIGH and EXTREME LOW, a lower top, making this a SELLING LEVEL for a reaction.

1917—March, LOW 725. A third higher bottom. Note that 720 is 50% of 1440, making this a safe BUYING LEVEL. A rally followed.

1917—September, HIGH 980. A DOUBLE BOTTOM against June, 1915. September is an important month for tops and changes in trend, which made this a SELLING LEVEL. A decline followed.

1917—December, LOW 825. Down to the old bottoms and a SUPPORT LEVEL. A rally followed.

1918—January, HIGH 910. At old top levels and January important for a change in trend because one year from the TOP of January, 1917. Also at exact Resistance level of 50% point between EXTREME HIGH and EXTREME LOW. A sharp quick decline followed.

1918—February, LOW 950. This was the fourth higher bottom from the EXTREME in December, 1915. BUY FOR A RALLY. A one-month's rally followed.

1918—March, HIGH 880. A second lower top.

1918—April, LOW 810. An old bottom level and higher than February.

1918—June, HIGH 880. A DOUBLE TOP and a third lower top from the Extreme High of September, 1917. June is important for a change in trend. A decline followed.

1918—November, LOW 710. A DOUBLE BOTTOM against March, 1917 low. Note that 720 was 50% of 1440, the extreme high, making this a safe BUYING LEVEL, especially as December was an important month for a change in trend. The advance started and prices crossed old resistance levels, crossing tops around 980, indicating that coffee was in a very strong position and going very much higher because bottoms had all been progressing from the 1915 low, with each bottom higher. Then when the double tops of June, 1915 and September, 1917 were crossed, it was a sure indication for very much higher prices. When prices crossed 1010, which was the 50% point between 1440 and 580, there was a strong indication that prices were going back to 1440 or higher. The market advanced right on through all of the old tops around 1440.

1919—HIGH in January, 16c. This was about 100% advance on the last low when the move started up in December, 1918. A SHARP TOP and in January which is an important month for important tops. A quick reaction followed.

1919—February, LOW 1395. Down to old top levels and a BUYING LEVEL on a one month's reaction. A rapid advance followed.

1919—June, FINAL HIGH 2375. Add 50% to the old top of 1440 gives 2197 as a RESISTANCE POINT. 2375 was an exact natural SELLING POINT, being 125 points under 25c. Prices broke back under resistance levels and declined fast.

1919—December, LAST HIGH 1750. December was the month for a change in trend and a decline followed.

1920—February, LOW 1360. Down to old top levels and eight months from the top and two months' sharp decline from December top makes this a BUYING LEVEL for a rally. A rally followed.

1920—March, HIGH 1535. Then followed a SECONDARY DECLINE.

1920—April, LOW 1425. Down to old top levels and a higher bottom than February indicated support. A rally followed.

1920—May, HIGH 1545. Note that 1485 was 62½% of 2375 and 1584 was 66 2/3% of 2375. This was eleven months from the EXTREME HIGH and June was an important month for a change in trend, being one year from the EXTREME HIGH.

1920—June, — a sharp, fast decline followed — LOW 12c. Down one year from the extreme high and a change in trend due. This was an important BUYING LEVEL because 1188 was 50% of 2375 and holding slightly above this made it even a better BUY. The market moved up rapidly and crossed the important tops and resistance levels.

1920—July, HIGH 2260. This was a SECONDARY RALLY, thirteen months from the EXTREME HIGH. This was the month in 1920 when July cotton was forced up to 4350. From 1920, July, a fast decline followed in all commodities. Coffee broke wide open.

1920—September, LOW 1350. At about the same low level as February, 1920. This was a two months' fast decline and a rally was due.

1920—November, HIGH 1760. Under old bottoms and at the old top of December, 1919, making this a SELLING LEVEL. Also note that 1782 was 75% of 2375. This was only a two months' normal rally in a bear market, and September was a month to watch for a change in trend. The decline continued. Rallies were very small.

1921—March, LOW 510. Back to the old bottom of October, 1909 and a BUYING LEVEL. This was 21 months from the EXTREME HIGH and our rule says to watch for a change in trend in the 21st month. It was eight months from the last EXTREME and four months from November, 1920, making this an important point to BUY.

Cotton and all commodities at this time had experienced a wide open break.

1921—April, 645. This was the first sharp rally and a SECONDARY DECLINE is always due to follow.

1921—May, LOW 560. A SECONDARY DECLINE and third higher bottom. A SAFER BUYING LEVEL. Note that 595 was 25% of 2375 and on the next advance prices crossed this level and gradually worked higher, with never a reaction of more than two or three weeks.

1921—December, HIGH 9c. At old SUPPORT LEVELS AND RESISTANCE LEVELS. A SELLING POINT, as December is a month for a change in trend.

1922—January, LOW 830. A one month's normal reaction and did not break the lows of December. BUY FOR HIGHER PRICES. From 2375 to 5c, the 50% point was 1437. One-third, or 33-1/3% was 1125.

1922—May, HIGH 1050. The market made two months' tops around this level. As this was 14 months from EXTREME LOW, it was time for a change in trend in the 15th month. A decline followed.

1922—October, November and December, LOW 9c. Down to the tops of December, 1921. December is the month for a change in trend. 9c being an exact old support and RESISTANCE LEVEL, and 891 being 37½% of 2375 makes this a SAFE BUYING LEVEL. A rapid advance followed.

1923—February, HIGH 1210. Under the lows of June, 1920 and under bottom levels of former years. At a natural resistance level. Note 1188 was 50% of 2375, making this a SELLING LEVEL. When prices broke back under 1188 they never rallied above it until they went much lower. Nothing but one month's rallies occurred.

1923—July, LOW 680. A higher bottom than the low of June, 1921, where the advance started. 50% added to the low of 510 would give 765 as a natural resistance point. The rally started when prices crossed 765, and never sold back to the lowest.

1923—October and November — both months made LOWS around 760. Then the advance was resumed. Prices crossed the 50% point between 1210 and 680 and also crossed 1188, the 50% point of 2375, showing strong UPTREND.

1924—March, HIGH 1450. An old top level of 1911 to 1913. Note that 1485 was 62½% of 2375 and 1437 was 50% of 2375 to 510, making this a SAFE SELLING LEVEL. March was important for a change in trend, being thirteen months from February, 1923 and exactly three years from the extreme low in 1921 and our rule says at the end of three years an important change usually takes place. A sharp decline followed.

1924—June, LOW 1110. A three months' normal seasonal decline and June an important month for a change in trend, being 11 months from the extreme low of July, 1923, which makes July important for a change in trend also. A rapid advance followed, crossing all important resistance levels and tops.

1924—October, FINAL HIGH 2205. A SECOND LOWER TOP,— the extreme high being June, 1919, the next top July, 1920 — this top October, 1924. This was three months from the extreme high and our rule says to watch for a change in trend every six months in each year. From July, 1923 was 15 months. Our rule says important changes in trend often take place in the fifteenth month. From June, 1924, low of 1110, a 50% advance would give 2220, which was almost the exact high, and our rule says that after four months' sharp advance, it is time to watch for a change in trend and October was an important month for a change in trend. This was the time to SELL OUT all long coffee and go short. A sharp decline followed.

1924—December, LOW 1650. Note that 1584 was 66-2/3% of the extreme high, 2375, making this a BUYING POINT for a rally, as there is always a SECONDARY RALLY after the first sharp decline.

1925—January, HIGH 2070. Note that 87½% of 2375 was 2079, making this a SAFE SELLING LEVEL. January is one of the important months for TOPS and a change in trend.

1925—April, LOW 1750. A three months' decline and at an important RESISTANCE LEVEL. Late in April and the early part of May, quick rally followed.

1925—May, HIGH 20c. Three tops around this level, made it a SELLING LEVEL and a sharp decline followed, breaking badly in the month of May and continuing on down.

1925—July, LOW 1235. Around the old top and bottom levels. A BUYING LEVEL for a rally. Six months down from January high makes this important for a change in trend.

From the low in July, prices moved up rapidly, crossing the first important resistance levels, 25% of 2205 down to 1235. Later prices crossed the 50% point at 1722.

1925—October, HIGH 1725. This was a 50% point and an IMPORTANT SELLING LEVEL. Prices held until the early part of November and then broke fast.

1925—November, LOW 1560. This was an important resistance level because 1584 was 66-2/3% of 2375, making this a BUYING LEVEL for a rally. The market advanced and crossed the 50% level and made three months' tops at 1725.

1926—January, HIGH 1850. This was one year from January, 1925 top and six months from the low in July, 1925, making it important for a change in trend. Also note that the last low in 1923 was made in the month of July, making January and July important points for a change in trend. A 250% advance on the base of 510 is 1785 and 75% of 2375 was 1782 as a resistance level. 62½% of 2210 to 1235 made 1825 an important resistance, or SELLING LEVEL. The market held in a narrow range during the month of

February, LOW 1780—HIGH, 1825. Showing that the market was meeting resistance and making a lower top. Time to sell out all long coffee and then go short.

1926—March — prices broke under the bottom of February — time to SELL MORE. The decline continued.

1926—May, LOW 1475. This was an important resistance level because 1485 was 62½% of 2375. The market was down four months and a rally was due. 50% of the last move from 1235 to 1850 was 1545. When prices crossed this level they were in a stronger position and the advance continued.

1926—August, HIGH 1645. This was a selling level. August was important for a change in trend because over a year had elapsed since the last low in July, 1925 and August is always important for a change in trend. 1584 was an important resistance level, being 66-2/3% of 2375, the extreme high. The trend turned down.

1926—October, LOW 13c. Down to old top levels. A two months' decline and a SECONDARY RALLY due.

1926—November, HIGH 1550. Under old bottoms and about 50% from the last decline. A SELLING LEVEL.

1927—February, LOW 1285. A HIGHER BOTTOM than July, 1925 and down over one year from the last top, January, 1926. A rally due.

1927—March, HIGH 1440. A lower top than January and a SELLING LEVEL. The trend continued DOWN.

1927—May, LOW 11c. A DOUBLE BOTTOM against June, 1924.

1927—July, HIGH 1175. A two months' rally in a bear market. A normal rally. Note 1188 was 50% of 2375, making this a SELLING LEVEL for a reaction, as there is nearly always a SECONDARY REACTION after lows are reached.

1927—August, LOW 1195. A DOUBLE BOTTOM and a TRIPLE BOTTOM against June, 1924. The market was down one year from August, 1926 top and two years from July, 1925, bottom. This was a SAFE BUYING LEVEL, protected with close STOP LOSS ORDERS.

1927—September, — prices crossed the high of July and crossed the 50% point of 2375, putting the market in strong position. No reaction over three to four weeks until

1928—February, HIGH 1550. One year from the low of February, 1927. A SELLING LEVEL for a reaction.

1928—April, LOW 1405. April an important month for bottoms and a change in trend. May important because one year from the last extreme low. This was a two-months normal reaction in a bull market and the UPWARD trend was resumed.

1928—August, HIGH 1595. This was one year from the last low and two years from August high 1926 and August was one of the most important months for high levels, making this a place to sell out and go short. Note this is an important resistance level because 1584 was 66-2/3% of 2375, making this a SELLING LEVEL for a reaction. A decline followed.

1928—December, LOW 1345. December is one of the important months for lows and this was a four months' reaction, one year from the last low, where the market started up, making this important for a change in trend. This was a safe buying level because from the last low at 11c to the high 1595, the 50% point was 1345. The market rallied quickly.

1929—February, HIGH 1665. A DOUBLE TOP against August, 1926, and our rule says that when tops or bottoms come out three years apart, it is important for a change in trend. February was one year from the top of February, 1928 and also two years from the low of February, 1927. February was an important month for a change in trend and being at a double top, time to SELL OUT longs and go short. Then when prices broke back under 1584, which was 66-2/3% of 2375, it would be an indication of LOWER PRICES.

1929—March and April, LOW 1560.

1929—May, LAST HIGH 1640. A LOWER TOP and a SAFER SELLING LEVEL.

1929 was the year of the great panic in stocks — that is, in the Fall of the year. The next option of May coffee made three tops around 1340 to 1350, just under the bottom of December, 1928, making this a SELLING POINT. This was an important 50% point. The market was in a weak position.

1929—July — the break started.

1929—August, LOW 1250.

1929—September — a moderate rally followed to 1290.

1929—October — coffee prices broke wide open, breaking the lows of 1927 and declining fast. Down to old bottom levels and a moderate rally followed.

1929—November, HIGH 9c. This was a one month's rally in a bear market. Note that 37½% of 2375 was 891, making this a SELLING LEVEL.

1929—December, LOW 7c. Down to the old low levels of 1923, making this a double bottom and slightly higher than the low of 1923. A rally followed.

1930—April, HIGH 9c. A double top against November, 1929 and a SELLING LEVEL because April is important for a change in trend as the last high was in May, 1929, also 3 years from the low of May, 1927, which made May important for a change in trend. The trend turned down again. The market was a safe short sale when it broke 50% of the last advance of 200 points or when it broke 8c.

1930—August, LOW 525. Down near the old levels of 1921.

1930—September and early October — rallied to 640. After the early part of October the market declined sharply again.

1930—October, LOW 525. A double bottom against August 1930.

1930—November, HIGH 6c. A weak rally.

1930—December, HIGH 585.

1931—January, HIGH 590. Note that 594 was 25% of 2375, an extreme high, making this a SELLING LEVEL, and the main trend was still DOWN, because the market was making lower tops and lower bottoms and had never crossed the highs of previous months but one time.

1931—April, LOW 435. This was the lowest since 1903. April is important for a change in trend because it was one year from 1930 HIGH and May would be two years from 1929 HIGH, making coffee a BUY FOR A RALLY in the months when many seasonal LOWS have been made. A rally followed.

1931—June, HIGH 690. Under old bottoms. June also important for a change in trend because two years from the last high of May, 1929 and extreme high level in 1919 was reached in the month of June. 9c was 50% of the last high in January, 1926. 7c was under the 50% point of the last high of 1660. The market had failed to advance 100% on the extreme low of April. There always has to be a SECONDARY DECLINE after the first sharp advance, and this rally had lasted two months.

1931—September, LOW 475. A bottom of a SECONDARY DECLINE, which had run three months and a higher bottom, making this a BUYING LEVEL, because September is important for a change in trend. 5c is always an important resistance level, either for tops or bottoms. The advance was resumed.

1932—May, HIGH 685. A DOUBLE TOP against June, 1931 and a SELLING LEVEL, because it was three years from the top in May, 1929 and our rule says important changes in trend often take place at the end of a three year period. Also the bottom of 1927 was made in May and August, making this a five year period from this bottom. The market was up one year from April, 1931, making this the time to SELL OUT and go short.

1932—The early part of September, LOW 530. A higher bottom and at a RESISTANCE POINT. A quick rally followed in the month of September — High 635 — A LOWER TOP. 50% on 440, the extreme low, gives 660 as a resistance level. The main trend continued DOWN.

1933—April, LOW 515. A third higher bottom from 1931 low. April important for a change in trend because two years from April, 1931, and May was important because it was one year from the top of May, 1932 and two years from June high, 1931. Prices started to move UP in June, crossed resistance levels and tops of several months, showing strong UPTREND. Then a rapid advance took place in the month of July.

1933—July, HIGH 8c. A resistance level because 792 was 37½% of 2375 and from the last high in February, 1929, of 1665, the 50% point was 835, making this a SELLING LEVEL. A quick, sharp decline followed.

1933—August, LOW 560.

1933—September, HIGH 650. A rally of around 100 points and a normal rally in one month.

1933—October, LOW 540. This was the third higher bottom since 1931 and October was important for a change in trend because it was three years from the high of October, 1930. Also, the last final high was in October, 1924, nine years previous, which is three times three, making this important. A BUYING LEVEL, protected with STOP LOSS ORDERS under the old bottom of 515. The advance was resumed and, when prices crossed 594, 25% of 2375, it indicated higher prices and later crossed 650, the top of September, 1933, put it in still stronger position.

1934—February, HIGH 890. Just under old top levels of November, 1929, and April, 1930, when tops were made at 9c. Note that 925 was one-half, or 50% of the last high in January, 1926, making this a SELLING LEVEL, protected with STOP LOSS ORDERS just above the old tops of 9c. A REACTION followed.

1934—May, LOW 790. Down to the old top of July, 1933.

1934—June, HIGH 880. A DOUBLE TOP against February and June an important month for a change in trend. SELL OUT and go short.

1934—July, LOW 770. One month's decline, but it broke bottom levels and showed the main trend was DOWN.

1934—August, HIGH 860. A second lower top and safer SELLING LEVEL, because August was one year from August, 1933, and August is important for a change in trend—this being only a normal rally—a safe place to SELL OUT and go short with STOPS above previous tops.
A DECLINE continued, and prices broke under resistance levels, later breaking 50% of the advance from 435 to 9c, which put the market in a very weak position.

1935—LOW 460. Just under the low level of September, 1931, but above the low of April, 1931. This was a point to BUY for a rally.

1935—May, HIGH 560. The market was in a weak position because 25% of 2375 was 594. As long as it remained under 594, it was in a weak position. For three months—May, June and July—tops were just under 560.

1935—December, LOW 475. A higher bottom than April, 1935. December is a month for a change in trend. A rally followed.

1936—January, HIGH 555. A DOUBLE TOP as against May and June, 1935, and January important for a change in trend, because one year from the last high in 1935, when the big break started and, until prices could cross 594, 25% of 2375, it was in a weak position.

1936—July, LOW 425. A new low, breaking all previous bottoms. A moderate rally followed.

1936—August, HIGH 5c. Under old bottoms and a SELLING LEVEL. There were several TOPS around this figure. The DECLINE continued.

1936—October, FINAL LOW 3c per pound for May coffee. October was an important month for a change in trend because the last low in October, 1933, was three years back, making it an important time for a change in trend. Then, going back to the last high in October, 1924, made this important. This was almost a 50% decline from the last high and was 66 2-3% decline from the tops around 9c. Certainly this was low enough. Regardless of how much coffee Brazil burned up, coffee was down to a place where it was a BUY for an investment. Note that there was an exact resistance level here. 25% of 2375 was 297, which means that from the extreme high of 2375 in June, 1919, coffee had declined 87½%. Certainly this was enough discount on anything. From this level we calculate resistance points between the extreme high at 2375 and 3c and also calculate the resistance points, or percentage points, on 3c per pound. 450 is 50% advance, 6c is 100% advance, 750 is 150% advance, 9c is 200% advance, 1050 is 250% and 12c being 300%.

1936—November. Prices advanced and crossed 450, 50% advance on the LOW, and later crossed all of the tops around 5c and then, when prices crossed all of the tops around 560, this was the BREAKAWAY POINT and a SAFER BUY for a rapid advance to follow.

1937—February, HIGH 815. Under a series of old bottoms. Note that 818 was 25% between 2375 and 3c, making this a SELLING LEVEL, and February was important for a top because it was three years from 1934, the last extreme top, and the market had made a fast move up for four months from the October low. This was a SELLING LEVEL, as the market had never had a real SECONDARY REACTION from the low.

1937—April, LOW 645. April is important for a change in trend. This had been a two months' sharp, quick decline and a RALLY was due.

1937—May, HIGH 735. Only a one month's rally and failed to cross the high of the previous month—150% advance on 3c was 750. Failing to reach this level showed it was weak and indicated lower and time to SELL OUT. The decline continued.

1937—November, LOW 4c. Breaking 450, the 50% point on 3c, indicated weakness and November was an important month for a change in trend, because one year from the extreme low and the market was down six months from May, the last high. Prices held in a narrow trading range for many months.

1938—January, HIGH 435.

1938—March, LOW 395. Making a double bottom against November. It was a slow, creeping market, reaching high in
August, HIGH 475. This was just above the 50% advance on 3c and around the TOP of November, 1937. Still meeting selling and a very feeble rally. The main trend turned down again. August was important for a change in trend because so many bottoms and tops come out in this month and the last high was in August, 1934, and there was a low in August, 1935, three years back. The trend turned DOWN and prices worked LOWER.

1939—March, LOW 405. Down to a series of bottoms and a third time at this level. BUY for a rally.

1939—September, HIGH 445. Note that 450 was the 50% advance on 3c. Failing to reach the previous high level indicated weakness and the trend turned DOWN.

1939—October, LOW 345. Only 45 points above the extreme low and coming out in October, three years later, was important for a change in trend.

MAY COFFEE—SANTOS—D CONTRACT

It is important to review the movements of this contract.

1928—May, HIGH 23c.

1929—February, HIGH 2295.

1929—April, HIGH 2280. A third lower top and SELLING LEVEL.

1931—October, LOW 750.

1932—September, LOW 7c.

1933—June, LOW 750. A double bottom and a third higher bottom.

1934—June, HIGH 1170. This was the last extreme high before very much lower prices were made.

1935—May and August, HIGH 730 and 735. The highs and the lows of October, 1931, and August was an important month for a change in trend, and one year from the last high in August, 1934. A double bottom against May and point to BUY for a rally.

1937—February, HIGH 1155.

1937—May, HIGH 1160. Double tops against June, 1934, and three years from these points, according to our rules, made this an important point for a change in trend and a SELLING LEVEL. The trend turned DOWN in June, 1937, and prices declined. It is important to study the low levels of 1937, 1938, 1939 and 1940, because this was a great valley of depression and if you had studied past movements and bottoms and you saw this formation, you would know later there was a chance to make a fortune in a very short period of time.

1937—November, LOW 565.

1938—January, HIGH 6c.

1938—May, LOW 555. A double bottom. May important for a change in trend because the last high was made in May, 1937.

1938—August, HIGH 720. Under a series of old bottoms and a SELLING LEVEL. August important for a change in trend because the last bottom in August, 1935, was three years back and our rule says at the end of three years tops and bottoms come out. A decline followed.

1939—April, LOW 565. A third bottom around this level. A BUYING POINT.

1939—September, HIGH 685. This was the rush UP after the war broke out. When prices failed to reach the high of August, 1938, by 30 points, weakness was indicated, showing the market was not yet ready to advance.

1940—May, LOW 545. Just 10 points under the extreme low of May, 1938, making this important for a change in trend because the last low was April, 1939, and this was the fourth bottom around this level within a period of thirty months. A rally followed.

1940—June, HIGH 645. At the same top of November, 1939, but under the tops of August, October and September, 1938 and 1939. Still not ready to go up. Note that a 50% advance on the low of 545 would give 717. When prices could cross this level and cross 720, the high of August, 1938, it would be an indication of very much HIGHER PRICES.

1940—August, LOW 555. A higher bottom than the previous bottom —five bottoms around this range in a period of four years—and August is a very important month for a change in trend. After holding for many years and making bottoms at these low levels, it was a BUY for an investment.

1940—September. The advance got under way.

1941—January. Prices crossed 717 and crossed 720, being above all tops since the beginning of 1938—a period of four years. This was the BREAKAWAY POINT and a sure indication of very much higher prices—you should have bought coffee and bought all the way up, figuring that prices would probably advance to 1440 or 100% on the last top of 720. The market advanced rapidly and there was no reaction lasting more than a couple of weeks.

1941—September, HIGH 1305. Note that 1337 was 50% between 2375 and 3c and an important RESISTANCE POINT, or SELLING LEVEL, and that 1395 is 62½% between 2050 and 3c. Also, 1325 was 75% between 1665 to 3c. Going back for tops we find that May, 1939, last high of 1345 and from the extreme high of 2375 to 525 the 50% point was 1420. September was important for a change in trend because the last move started in August, 1940, and this was a thirteen months' advance. Also, August, 1938, was high, which was three years back, making this important for a change in trend.

From the extreme low, May, 1940, September was fifteen months. Our rule says to watch for a change in trend in the fifteenth month, which is a year and a quarter, or 125%, taking twelve months as 100%.

Figuring the percentage on the base of 535, 150% gives 1332. All of the indications pointed to the fact that September, 1941, was high and due for a reaction.

After the top in September, 1941, all commodities which had reached tops in September, 1941, had a sharp decline in October and coffee followed this decline.

1941—October LOW 1180. This was down to the old top levels of 1937 and 1934, and 1188 was the important resistance level, or 50% of 2375, the highest selling point.

The next important month to watch for a change in the trend of coffee will be December, 1941, or November, because November will be eighteen months from May, 1940, and four years from November, 1937, low.

The extreme high on Santos coffee, May, was reached in May, 1928. The other highs were in February and April, 1929, and again in May, 1930, the last high was reached, which has not been crossed up to this writing.

In 1942 May, June and August will be important to watch for a change in trend. Should prices advance later and cross 1350, they will indicate higher and the next important level would be around 1485, 62½% of 2375, or 1596, 62½% between 2375 and 300.

It is important to figure resistance levels from the last low at 535 to the high in September, 1941, of 1305. The 50% point is 920. Breaking back under the October low of 1180, the 50% point would be the next important point. Around 1160, the old top levels, is an important level. Breaking under these would indicate lower prices.

Study and apply all of the rules for coffee that we have given for other commodities. Watch the time periods which are most important from any extreme high or low to the next extreme high or low.

Don't overlook the fact that coffee comes remarkably close at the end of every three-year period. Therefore, watch any important top or bottom three years from a previous top and bottom and watch the most important months when most tops and bottoms have been made in order to determine the seasonal change in trend.

When the market is very active, keep up the daily high and low charts, but at all times keep up the weekly high and low charts, and it will pay you to keep up a quarterly high and low chart on coffee, for in this way you will be able to determine when a big advance or big decline is getting under way. Coffee, like many other commodities, remains a long time at low levels, but when it has a fast advance, it makes a sharp top, and many times fails to make a double top, the secondary rally being only about 50% of the first sharp decline. The more you study the action of coffee, the more you will learn about the formation of tops and bottoms.

EGGS

FUTURE PRICES and TRADING RANGE

Eggs are traded in on the Chicago Mercantile Exchange and the New York Mercantile Exchange. The contract of eggs is 12,000 dozen. Eggs are traded in in cents per dozen. The minimum fluctuation is five-hundredths of a cent per dozen and the minimum fluctuation at this rate is $6 on a contract of 12,000 dozen.

The commission on eggs, regardless of price, is $30 per contract for buying and selling.

Eggs are very profitable to trade in, as the fluctuations are wide enough to make considerable profit on the investment. If you buy and sell eggs at the time of seasonal trends, or you determine the change of trend, you can make as much percentage on eggs as on many of the other commodities. The egg futures are governed by supply and demand. During the summer months the hens lay less eggs and the demand is somewhat smaller. During the Fall season the supply of eggs is increased, but the demand during the Fall and Winter season is also increased.

The price of corn and other feed for chickens governs the price of eggs, as cost of production always has something to do with the selling price.

SEASONAL HIGHS AND LOWS FOR EGGS

These prices, or time periods, cover the October and December options of eggs.

Below we give the months when highs and lows have been reached from 1929 to 1941.

	Low	High		Low	High
January	1	2	July	1	1
February	0	0	August	1	0
March	1	1	September	0	3
April	1	0	October	1	0
May	1	1	November	1	3
June	0	0	December	7	2

From the above you can see that the most LOWS have been reached in the month of December and December is an important month for a seasonal change in trend because after the Christmas demand for eggs is filled, there often occurs a change in trend. You will note that the most HIGHS have occurred in September and November. The reason for this is that the hens start laying in the early part of Fall and after this there is a scarcity of eggs and a seasonal change in trend, or TOP often comes out in September. Then again, TOPS are often made in November, when the Christmas demand has been supplied.

You should always watch the months of March and April for a change in trend, then watch August and September, and the next in importance are November and December. Of course, the change in trend may come in the early part of the year — that is, in January. The important thing is to watch the last EXTREME HIGH and EXTREME LOW and watch for important changes four months from any important top and bottom, but the most important time is the sixth or seventh month from any important top or bottom. Three months is also important to watch for a change in trend. The eggs often advance or decline and never react more than about 1c a dozen and often never react more than one month until they reach HIGH, and then, when they are declining, often never rally more than one month, until they reach extreme LOW.

YEARLY HIGH AND LOW PRICES AND SWINGS

These cash prices are based on price in cents per dozen in the markets of Boston and New York.

1858—Average price, 16c per dozen.

1858—Average price, 21c per dozen.

1861—Average price, 14⅝c per dozen. This was the last LOW before high prices during the Civil War.

1865—EXTREME HIGH, 29½c per dozen.

1867—LOW, 27½c per dozen.

1868—AVERAGE HIGH, 32½c per dozen.

1871—LOW, 25c per dozen.

1873 and 1874—28c per dozen.

1878—17c per dozen.

1879—18c per dozen.

1880—14½c per dozen. Down to about the same levels as 1861.

1883—HIGH, 23½c per dozen.

1885 and 1886—LOW, 19¼c per dozen.

1887—HIGH, 21c per dozen. Then came the long swing down and the price of eggs and every other commodity went down.

1896 and 1897—Eggs sold around 12c per dozen. This was the price for fresh eggs in New York. Eggs in these days sold on farms as low as 5c per dozen.

When the long upward swing in commodities started, eggs worked up with other commodities.

1899—HIGH, 20c.

1900 and 1901—Eggs were as low as 12c a dozen again.

1909 and 1910—The peak prices were reached again around 25c per dozen.

1911—Around 20c per dozen.

1919—EXTREME HIGH, 73c a dozen.

1933—December LOW, 13c per dozen.

RESISTANCE LEVELS ON EGGS

We have calculated the resistance levels from 42c, the HIGH in November, 1929, to 13c LOW in December, 1933, and the resistance levels on percentages of 42c.

We have calculated the resistance levels from 73c to 20½c. This was from the 1919 HIGH to the 1921 LOW.

We also have calculated the resistance levels from 73c to 13c, and the percentages on 73c.

These are all of the resistance levels that you will need to locate buying and selling points in the future, or until eggs sell above 42c per dozen, and then you can still use the 73c top and the bottom, or base, of 13c will be good to use until eggs sell below this price.

EXAMPLES OF TRADING IN OCTOBER AND DECEMBER EGGS FUTURE CONTRACTS IN CHICAGO

1929—September, LOW 36½c.

1929—November, HIGH 42c. A 50% advance on 20½c low to 41, making this a SELLING LEVEL.

1929—December, LOW 31½c. Trend down.

1930—September, 29c. Under 50% of 73c, showing a weak position.

1930—December, LOW 13c. A SUPPORT LEVEL because 12½% of $1.00 is always a BUYING LEVEL. Eggs were down to the lowest level since 1901 and 1902. Time to BUY because December was the month for important changes in trend, and when tops and bottoms come out in December it is time to buy or sell.

1931—October and early December, HIGH 20½c. A RESISTANCE LEVEL and a SELLING LEVEL because 13c, the base, with 50% added, gives 19½c.

1931—December, LOW 13¼c. A DOUBLE BOTTOM and one year from the last bottom made this a BUYING LEVEL.

1932—March to June, LOW 15c. A HIGHER BOTTOM and a SAFER BUYING LEVEL. A rally followed.

1932—December, HIGH 28½c. Note RESISTANCE LEVEL, 27½c, is 50% of 42 to 13, and 28 was 25% of 73 to 13, and December is the month for changes in trend, and one year from the previous LOW—TIME TO SELL OUT and GO SHORT.

1933—March, LOW 15c. A DOUBLE BOTTOM against 1932 and a BUYING LEVEL.

1933—July, HIGH 23c. A RESISTANCE LEVEL because 33 1-3% of 42 to 13 is 22⅝. A DECLINE followed.

1933—December, LOW 13c. A third time at this same level. A SAFE BUY for an investment. December is a month for seasonal change in trend and, when prices are low in December, it is the time to BUY. When prices are high in December, it usually is the time to SELL.

1934—February, HIGH 20¾c. An old bottom level and 25% of 42 to 13 is 20¼.

1934—March and May, LOW 17½c. A HIGHER BOTTOM and a RESISTANCE LEVEL at 18¼, which was 25% of 73 and 19½ was 50% advance on 13c.

1934—November, HIGH 23¾c. A DOUBLE TOP and a SELLING LEVEL.

1934—December, LOW 19c. A RESISTANCE LEVEL and again December the month for a change in trend. BUY for a rally.

1935—May, HIGH 26¾c. At the 50% point of 42 to 13c and a SELLING LEVEL. The market was dull and narrow.

1935—June, LOW 24¾c.

1935—September, HIGH 26½c. A DOUBLE TOP and a SELLING LEVEL. Prices then broke four months bottom at 24¾c, showing the trend DOWN and it was a SAFER SHORT SALE. A fast decline followed.

1935—December, LOW 17¾c. A DOUBLE BOTTOM against 1934, and a BUYING LEVEL AGAIN because December was a month for a seasonal change in trend, and it was two years from 1933 LOW and one year from 1934 LOW.

1936—April, BREAKAWAY POINT. At this time prices crossed the tops of three months, showing strong UP TREND. This was the BREAKAWAY POINT and the time to BUY MORE. Crossing 22c showed much higher prices.

1936—July, 27½c. A DOUBLE TOP against May, 1935, and under

the 50% point of 13c to 42c—a SELLING LEVEL for a reaction.

1936—August, LOW 24c. A one month's normal reaction and a resistance level because 24¼ was 62½% of 42c and August was a month for a change in trend. Prices just under 25c made this a BUYING LEVEL.

1936—November, HIGH 30¾c. A RESISTANCE LEVEL because 32½ was 150% advance on 13c, and 31½ was 62½% of 42 to 13c. The market was up eleven months and December was a month for a change in trend. This was a SELLING LEVEL. A fast decline followed in December.

1937—February, LOW 24½c. A DOUBLE BOTTOM and a SUPPORT LEVEL. BUY for a rally.

1937—March, HIGH 26¾c. AN OLD TOP and a SELLING LEVEL.

1937—June, LOW 23c. Held above 22⅝c, or 33 1-3% of 42c to 13c.

1937—July, HIGH 25½c. A second lower top and a SELLING LEVEL.

1937—August, a month for a change in trend.

1937—October, LOW 17c. A RESISTANCE LEVEL because 12½% of 42 to 13 was 16⅝, and 15⅜ was a 50% decline from 30¾ top. Holding above this level showed strength and good BUYING. The market slowly worked higher.

1938—September, HIGH 25⅝c. A DOUBLE TOP against July, 1937, and a SELLING LEVEL. September an important month for a change in trend. An important month for TOPS.

1938—December. Prices broke RESISTANCE LEVELS from the last move and continued on down.

1939—May, LOW 18¼c. A HIGHER BOTTOM, and 18¼c is 25% of 73c.

1939—July, 19½c. A small two months' rally. Under old bottom. A SELLING LEVEL.

1939—August, LOW 16c. Above 50% of 30¾. A rally followed. August is the month for a change in trend.

1939—September, HIGH 18½c. Under old bottoms and a RESISTANCE LEVEL.

1939—October, LOW 16¾c. A HIGHER BOTTOM and a SAFER BUYING LEVEL.

1939—November, HIGH 18½c. A DOUBLE TOP and SELLING LEVEL because tops are often reached in November and a decline followed in December.

1939—December, LOW 13c. Down to old bottoms—A TRIPLE BOTTOM, the same as 1931 and 1933, a BUYING LEVEL, as December is a month for seasonal change in trend and this was a real investment buy because the war was on and war is always bullish on eggs, as well as other commodities.

1940—April, HIGH 19¾c. Under old bottoms and tops and the same level as July, 1939. A SELLING LEVEL for a reaction.

1940—May, 17⅝c LOW.

1940—August, 17⅝c LOW.

1940—October, 17⅝c LOW. A TRIPLE BOTTOM and HIGHER RESISTANCE LEVEL. Time to BUY.

1940—December, HIGH 23½c. The resistance level of 23⅞ was 37½% of 42c to 13c. December was the month for a change in trend.

1941—February, LOW 18⅝c. A HIGHER BOTTOM and a RESISTANCE LEVEL. A BUYING LEVEL.

1941—March. Prices crossed 20½ over two months' tops, and crossed 21c, the 50% point of 42c, indicating strength and higher prices.

1941—September, HIGH 31⅝c. Under the 150% advance on 13c, which was 32½c. September was a month for a change in trend and was seven months from the LOW of February and three years from September, 1938, TOP.

1941—October, LOW 28c. Held above the 50% point of 13 to 42c.

1941—December will be the next important month for a change in trend because it will be two years from December, 1939.
Should prices cross 32½c in the future, the next important level will be 42c, the last old top.
Should prices break back under 27½c, the next support level would be 22c.

Apply all the rules to eggs that we used on the other commodities and you will be able to determine the future trend and buying and selling levels.

HIDES

Hides futures are traded in on the Commodity Exchange, Inc., of New York, and on the Chicago Mercantile Exchange. A contract for hides is 40,000 pounds. Hides are traded in in cents per pound. The minimum fluctuation is one-hundredth of a cent per pound, or $4.00 per contract. Each point representing $4.00 or a 100-point advance or decline, or 1c per pound, gives the profit or loss of $400.

The commission for trading in hides when they are selling under 10c per pound is $30.00. Above 10c per pound it is $40.00. This is on the Commodity Exchange of New York.

On the Chicago Mercantile Exchange there is one commission at any price $30.00 per contract.

The margin requirements for trading in hides vary with the price, running from $300 per contract when prices are low up to $700 to $1,000 when prices are high.

Hides are very profitable to trade in, as you can see by going back over past records and studying the range between extreme high and extreme low. By following the rules and getting in hides when there is an important change in trend, you can make substantial profits on the amount of money invested or the margin put up.

BEST OPTIONS TO TRADE IN. As a rule, the best options in hides to trade in are the June, September and December options. These options as a rule are the most active and have the widest swings.

SEASONAL CHANGES FOR HIDES—1924 TO 1941—SEVENTEEN YEARS

Below we give the number of times LOWS have been reached each month and the number of times HIGHS have been reached.

	Lows	Highs		Lows	Highs
January	0	2	July	1	4
February	3	0	August	5	1
March	4	2	September	0	2
April	1	2	October	0	3
May	0	1	November	2	1
June	2	1	December	0	1

From the above you can see that August is the month when the greatest number of LOWS have been reached. Five times during this period lows were reached. The next important months are February and March—three times lows have been reached in February and four times in March. Therefore, the most important months for you to watch for a change in trend to low prices are February and March, with August the most important.

Two lows have been made in June and November, which make them next in importance. April and July—only one low was reached in each of these months. In January, May, September, October and December, no lows have been made. You will note that the months when no lows have been reached are the months as a rule when HIGHS are reached.

The greatest number of HIGHS was reached in July and October— four highs in July and three in October. The next months in importance are January, March, April and September. In each of these months two highs have been reached. In the month of February, no highs have been reached. You will note that February and March are the months when the most lows are reached. May, August, November and December had only one HIGH each.

You understand, of course, that the market at times runs opposite the seasonal trend, making HIGHS in the months when LOWS are usually made, and then at other times making LOWS in the months when HIGHS are usually made. The best way is to study the EXTREME HIGHS and the EXTREME LOWS and then watch for a change in trend in the sixth or seventh month from any important high and low, and at the end of twelve months, eighteen months, twenty-one months, twenty-four months, and at the end of any even year from any important top and bottom. Normal minor swings run from thirty to sixty days. Many reverse moves will only last thirty to thirty-six days and then the trend will continue in the same direction. It is always important to watch for a SEASONAL CHANGE IN TREND in the third or fourth month. This does not necessarily mean in the seasonal changes of the year like March, June, September and December, but three to four months from any important top and bottom.

SWINGS FROM EXTREME LOW TO EXTREME HIGH
AND FROM EXTREME HIGH TO EXTREME LOW

These important swings give you the most important tops and bottoms to figure time periods from.

1924—April, LOW 9c. November, HIGH 16c.

1925—March, LOW, 13c. July, HIGH 1630.

1926—March, LOW 11c. October, HIGH 15c. December, LOW 1330.

1927—January, HIGH 1450. February, LOW 13c. July, HIGH 24c. August, LOW 20c.

1928—January, HIGH 2550. March, LOW 22c.

April, HIGH 2650. This was the extreme high, from which the main trend turned down. Note that the long swing UP was from April, 1924, to April, 1928, or four years. If you were watching the anniversary date from extreme low to high, you would have been watching for a change in trend in April because, according to the seasonal trend, most HIGHS in the Spring are reached in the months of March and April. You would apply all of the other rules, of course, to show when the main trend turned down. A bear market started.

June, LOW 2240. July, HIGH 25c. October, LOW 1850. November, HIGH 20c.

1929—February, LOW 1350. March, HIGH 19c. May, LOW 14c. August, HIGH 1715. The reaction followed in August. LOW late in the month of August, 16c. October, HIGH 1830. November, LOW 1290.

1930—January, HIGH 1680. February, LOW 1480. March, HIGH 1510. August, LOW 990. October, HIGH 1450.

1931—February, LOW 950. March, HIGH 1340. May, LOW 990. July, HIGH 1210. August, LOW 720. November, HIGH 1070.

1932—June, EXTREME LOW 315. September, HIGH 8c. December, LOW 410.

1933—January, HIGH 710. February, LOW 600. July, HIGH 1490. October, LOW 800.

1934—January, HIGH 1210. March, LOW 1120. April, HIGH 1290. August, LOW 560. September, HIGH 810. October, LOW 635.

1935—January, HIGH 1095. March, LOW 930. May, HIGH 1150. June, LOW 10c. October, LOW 1235. November, LOW 1110.

1936—January, HIGH 1295. March, LOW 12c. April, HIGH 1250. July, LOW 1090. September, HIGH 1210. October, LOW 1140.

1937—March, FINAL HIGH 19c. Note this was under the top of June, 1929, making this a SELLING LEVEL.

June, LOW 1550. July, HIGH 1775. A LOWER TOP and safe selling point. November, LOW 790. December, HIGH 1200.

1938—March, LOW 835. April, HIGH 1010. June, LOW 875. July, HIGH, 1175. September, LOW 1050. October, HIGH 1295. November, LOW 1050.

1939—January, HIGH 1400.   April, LOW 1010.   July, HIGH 1220.
August, LOW 975.   September, HIGH 1500.   November, LOW
1250.

1940—January, HIGH 1585.   This was the LAST EXTREME HIGH.
April, LOW 1370.   May, HIGH 1490.   May, LOW 940.   This
was at the end of May on Hitler's drive against Belgium and
France.   June, HIGH 10c.   August, LOW 780.   November,
HIGH 1350.

1941—February, LOW 1215.   May, HIGH 1570.   July, LOW 1410.
October, HIGH 1495.

In June, 1941, the Government put a ceiling on hides, which virtually
stopped trading.   This accounts for the narrow range from July until
October.   After the war is over, restrictions will be removed and the
HIDES will continue to make the normal range and fluctuation and
offer the usual opportunities for making profits.   Study the resistance
levels, the single, double and triple tops or highs, and watch for the
seasonal change in trend and the time periods between extreme highs
and extreme lows, and you will be able to forecast the trend of hides.

DOUBLE AND TRIPLE TOPS AND BOTTOMS,
RESISTANCE LEVELS AND BUYING AND SELLING POINTS

SEPTEMBER HIDES:

1924—January, HIGH 12c.

1924—April, LOW 9c.   A 25% decline from top.   A BUYING POINT.

1924—November, HIGH 16c.   A 33 1-3% advance on 12c.   A SELL-
ING LEVEL.

1925—March, HIGH 1300.   Held above 12½, the half-way point
between 9c and 16c.   BUY FOR A RALLY.

1925—July, HIGH 1625.   A DOUBLE TOP and SELLING LEVEL.

1926—March, LOW 1100.   Note that 1125 was 25% on 9c.   A BUY-
ING LEVEL.

1926—October, HIGH 15c.   A LOWER TOP and SELLING LEVEL.

1927—February, LOW 13c.   A HIGHER BOTTOM, and above 1262,
one-half of 9c to 1625.   This was a safe BUYING LEVEL.
Later prices crossed 15c, showing a strong uptrend, and when the
prices crossed 1625, the old high, they indicated very much higher.
This was a place to BUY MORE.

1928—April, HIGH 2650.   A FINAL TOP and a SELLING LEVEL.
Note the last low was 13c.   A 100% advance made 2600 a selling
level.

1928—June, LOW 2250.   Higher than March, 1928.   A BUYING
LEVEL, because a SECONDARY RALLY was due after the
first sharp decline.

1928—July, HIGH 2500.   A SECONDARY LOWER TOP and one
year from July, 1927, making this a SELLING LEVEL.   A fast
decline followed and prices broke 2250 and 2200 and the main
trend was down.   The market continued to decline, with only
small rallies.

1929—February, LOW 1350. Two years from February, 1927. The market holding above 1325, a 50% decline from 2650 indicated this as a BUYING POINT for a rally.

1929—March, HIGH 19c. A LOWER TOP and under old bottoms. Eleven months' decline from the top. A change in trend due in April because April was 12 months from FINAL TOP.

1929—May, LOW 1400. A HIGHER BOTTOM and a rally followed.

1929—October, HIGH 1830. A LOWER TOP, under old bottoms and only a year from 1928. A SELLING LEVEL.

1929—November, LOW 1290. A DOUBLE BOTTOM and just under 1325, 50% of 2650. This was a sharp decline and a panicky decline in stocks and everything else occurred at this time, and our rule says to BUY on sharp, panicky declines. A rally followed.

1930—January, HIGH 1680. A SELLING LEVEL, as 1656 was 62½% of 2650. The market broke back 50% of the last move and broke the 50% point of 1325, putting it in a very weak position, and a rapid decline followed.

1930—August, LOW 990. Note that RESISTANCE LEVEL, 998, was 37½% of 2650, making this a BUYING LEVEL.

1930—October, HIGH 1450. Under old bottoms and a SELLING LEVEL. Broke back under 1325 again, the 50% point, and was in a weak position.

1931—February, LOW 950. Note that 950 was 50% of 1900, the last HIGH of March, 1929, making this a BUY FOR A RALLY.

1931—March, HIGH 1340. A short sale, because 1325 was the 50% rally point.

1931—May, LOW 990. A TRIPLE BOTTOM and a HIGHER BOTTOM. BUY FOR A RALLY.

1931—July, HIGH 1310. A two months' normal rally. Sell out and go short.

1931—August, LOW 725. August is a month for a change in the seasonal trend. This was a 50% decline from the last top in October, 1930, high 1480. BUY FOR A RALLY.

1931—November, HIGH 1075. Under old bottoms and a SELLING LEVEL. Later broke all former lows and the bear market continued, with very small rallies from time to time. Remember the rule says that the lower prices get, the smaller the rallies, because people who have been buying and losing money, take their loss, lose hope and courage and refuse to buy—in fact, they sell out. And the bears are encouraged and over-sell the market, and it finally reaches lows where everybody is so bearish a sharp rally takes place.

1932—June, FINAL LOW 315. Note that 331 was 87½% decline from 2650, the EXTREME HIGH, and this was the fourth section of the bear market, fifty months down from the extreme top. A change in trend was due. This was the time to BUY for an investment.

1932—September, HIGH 810. A RESISTANCE LEVEL. 33 1/3% of 1900 to 315 was 843. A SECONDARY RALLY was due after the first sharp advance.

1932—December, LOW 325. A HIGHER BOTTOM and a SECONDARY DECLINE and a SAFER BUYING LEVEL. Later crossed the 50% point of the last move, crossing 810, the September high, which indicated a safe position and the TIME TO BUY MORE.

1933—July, HIGH 1490. A SAFE SHORT SALE because 50% of 2650 to 315 was 1482, and July is a month for a seasonal change in trend.

1933—October, LOW 8c. AN OLD BOTTOM and TOP LEVEL and a DOUBLE BOTTOM. A BUYING LEVEL.

1934—April, HIGH 1280. A RESISTANCE LEVEL, under 1325, the 50% point and 62½% of 1900 to 315. April is the month for seasonal changes, and the EXTREME HIGH was reached in the month of April. The decline started and the market broke under 1120, showing DOWN trend. The prices then worked lower, with very small rallies.

1934—August, LOW 560. Down 66 2-3% from 1490 is 607, and 513 is 87½% of 1900. This was a SAFE BUYING LEVEL, as August is a month for seasonal change in trend.

1936—January, HIGH 1300. A DOUBLE TOP and a SELLING LEVEL. Under the half-way point of 1325.

1936—July, LOW 1090. OLD TOPS and BOTTOMS and a BUYING LEVEL. Also, 1093 was 33 1-3% of 2650 to 315, making this a a strong SUPPORT LEVEL.

Later prices crossed 1300 and crossed 1325, the 50% point, showing strong uptrend, and it was safe to BUY MORE.

1937—March, FINAL HIGH 1900. A DOUBLE TOP against March, 1929, and March is a month for a change in trend. This was the place to sell short, with a STOP LOSS ORDER around 1940.

1937—June, LOW 1540. A DOUBLE BOTTOM against February, 1937. A SECONDARY RALLY DUE, as after the first decline, a secondary rally almost always takes place and then the market is safe for a short sale.

1937—July, HIGH 1770. A TOP of SECONDARY RALLY, and at 62½% of 315 to 2650, making this a safe short sale. Later prices broke the lows of February. The main trend turned down. You should have sold more.

1937—November, LOW 785. At OLD TOPS and BOTTOMS levels. Watch for a seasonal change in trend. There had been a panicky decline in stocks and all commodities, and the market was down four months from July and eight months from the market tops. Time to BUY at the bottom of the panicky decline.

1937—December, HIGH 1200. Under OLD BOTTOMS. A RESISTANCE LEVEL, 37½% of 2650 was 1190, and 62½% of 1900 to 315 was 1187. A SELLING LEVEL because only a one month's rally. A natural rally in a bear market.

1938—March, LOW 835. At 33 1/3% of 1900 to 315, which was 843. A HIGHER BOTTOM and a SECONDARY DECLINE. Held for three months, with slightly higher bottoms. This was a safe place to BUY.

Crossing 10c put the market in a stronger position and later crossed 12c, the place to BUY MORE.

1939—January, HIGH 1400. A RESISTANCE LEVEL. 66 2/3 of 1900 to 315 was 1371. 75% of 1900 was 1425, making this a place to sell out and go short.

1939—April, LOW 1010. OLD TOPS AND BOTTOMS, and April a month for a change in trend. A rally followed.

1939—July, 1220. A RESISTANCE LEVEL, a place to SELL, and a decline followed.

1939—August, LOW 980. A DOUBLE BOTTOM and a RESIST-ANCE LEVEL. A one month's decline and a place to BUY for a rally. In September war broke out and all commodities advanced rapidly.

1939—September, HIGH 1600. The RESISTANCE LEVEL, 1620, was 75% of 1900 to 780, and 1636 was 62½% of 2650. This was a sharp advance and time to SELL OUT and GO SHORT.

1939—November, LOW 1350. Strong, because it held above 1325, 50% of 2650. A rally followed.

1940—January, HIGH 1585. A secondary rally and LOWER TOP. Only a two months' rally and a place to SELL, protected with STOP LOSS ORDERS above the extreme high.

1940—April, LOW 1360. A DOUBLE BOTTOM against November, 1939.

Early in the month the market rallied to 1480. There were three tops around this level, making this a SELLING LEVEL.

1940—May. Hitler started the drive against France and Belgium, and all commodities broke wide open. A panicky decline followed. May, LOW 940. At the 50% point from 1900. A SUPPORT LEVEL for a RALLY.

1940—June, HIGH 1100. One month's rally, with the main trend still down, made this a place to SELL SHORT.

1940—August, LOW 780. A DOUBLE BOTTOM against November, 1937, and a SAFE BUYING LEVEL, with STOP thirty to forty points under. The market was eleven months down from the top and September was the month for a CHANGE IN TREND. An advance followed, and prices crossed resistance levels.

1940—November, HIGH 1350. A SELLING LEVEL because 1325 was 50% of 2650, the most important point.

1941—February, LOW 1210. A SUPPORT LEVEL AND A BUYING POINT.

1941—March, BREAKAWAY POINT. At this time prices crossed five months' tops around 1325, the 50% point of 2650. This was the time to BUY MORE because the main trend was a strong UPWARD trend.

1941—May, HIGH 1570. A TRIPLE TOP and lower. One year from 1940 Low.

1941—July, LOW 1410.

1941—October, HIGH 1495.

The Government put a ceiling on Hide Prices in July and this practically stopped all trading except liquidation of old contracts. However, after the war is over, trading in Hides will continue and there will be opportunities for making profits.

An important RESISTANCE LEVEL to watch will be from the last LOW, 980 to 1600—the 50% point is 1290 and 25% decline is 1420. Breaking this level is an indication of lower prices, and crossing 1620 would be an indication of higher prices.

Follow all rules. Study all important bottoms and tops and consider the time periods between important bottoms and tops and you will be able to determine future buying and selling points for hides.

BLACK PEPPER FUTURES

Black pepper has been traded in in England and other foreign countries for many years, but future trading in black pepper just started in New York a few years ago. Black pepper futures are traded in on the New York Produce Exchange. A contract is for 33,600 pounds. The minimum fluctuation is one-hundredth cent per pound, making a minimum fluctuation on a contract of $3.36. A decline of 1c per pound would mean a loss of $336, or an advance of 1c per pound on a contract would mean a profit of $336, less the commission.

The commission for buying and selling black pepper is $25 per contract as long as the price is under 10c per pound.

The margin requirements run from $250 to $500 per contract, depending upon the price at which black pepper is being traded.

YEARLY HIGH AND LOW PRICES: We are giving some of the important high and low prices.

1895 and 1896—LOW 5c.

1900—HIGH 13½c.

1903—HIGH 15c.

1909—LOW 7½c.
1912—HIGH 12c.

1913—LOW 10c.

1918—HIGH 26½c.

1921—LOW 850.

1928—HIGH 4150. This was the extreme high for black pepper.

1932—LOW 7c.

1933—LOW 6c.

1933—HIGH in July, 10c.

1934—HIGH 14c.

1936—LOW 4¼c.

1937—HIGH 7½c.
1938—LOW 4¼c.
1939—EXTREME LOW, 3c per pound.
1940—LOW 3½c.
1941—HIGH 7½c.

You would figure resistance levels from the **EXTREME HIGH** of
4150 to 3c per pound and figure the percentages on 3c, and the percentages on 4150, the same as we have figured the other Commodities.

If you wished to forecast the future trend of black pepper, you would
look up the months when extreme high and low have been reached, and
find the months when the most seasonal lows and highs have been
reached in the past.   Then keep up some of the active future options.
Apply all of the rules we use on other commodities and you will be
able to determine the trend on black pepper futures.

JULY BLACK PEPPER FUTURES
HIGHS AND LOWS

Trading began in June, 1937.

1937

June, HIGH 680; LOW 630.   September, HIGH 710; LOW 610.
July, HIGH 670; LOW 620.   October, HIGH 605; LOW 510.
August, HIGH 720; LOW 655.   November, HIGH 555; LOW 495.
            December, HIGH 550; LOW 520

1938

January, HIGH 565; LOW 530.   July, HIGH 515; LOW 475.
February, HIGH 675; LOW 565.   August, HIGH 540; LOW 485.
March, HIGH 545; LOW 560.   September, HIGH 525; LOW 485.
April, HIGH 555; LOW 520.   October, HIGH 550; LOW 495.
May, HIGH 540; LOW 505.   November, HIGH 535; LOW 475.
June, HIGH 530; LOW 475.   December, HIGH 490; LOW 440.

1939

January, HIGH 500; LOW 395.   July, HIGH 335; LOW 305.
February, HIGH 425; LOW 385.   August, HIGH 365; LOW 335.
March, HIGH 405; LOW 325.   September, HIGH 480; LOW 380.
April, HIGH 345; LOW 320.   October, HIGH 440; LOW 395.
May, HIGH 345; LOW 295.   November, HIGH 420; LOW 390.
June, HIGH 320; LOW 295.   December, HIGH 455; LOW 425.

1940

-January, HIGH 455; LOW 405.   May, HIGH 415; LOW 325.
February, HIGH 425; LOW 405.   June, HIGH 340; LOW 320.
March, HIGH 420; LOW 390.   July, HIGH 360; LOW 350.
April, HIGH 410; LOW 375.   August, HIGH 395; LOW 375.

1940

September, HIGH 415; LOW 385.   November, HIGH 420; LOW 405.
October, HIGH 425; LOW 405.   December, HIGH 440; LOW 415.

1941

January, HIGH 445; LOW 425.   June, HIGH 605; LOW 500.
February, HIGH 510; LOW 425.   July, HIGH 605; LOW 525.
March, HIGH 695; LOW 505.   August, HIGH 665; LOW 615.
April, HIGH 670; LOW 595.   September, HIGH 675; LOW 600.
May, HIGH 760; LOW 595.   October, HIGH 635; LOW 585.

DECEMBER BLACK PEPPER FUTURES—MONTHLY:

1937

June, HIGH 630; LOW 587.   September, HIGH 675; LOW 575.
July, HIGH 635; LOW 585.   October, HIGH 555; LOW 465.
August, HIGH 690; LOW 625.   November, HIGH 515; LOW 475.
December, HIGH 510; LOW 500.

1938

January, HIGH 560; LOW 555.   July, HIGH 565; LOW 505.
February, HIGH 705; LOW 590.   August, HIGH 495; LOW 450.
March, HIGH 680; LOW 570.   September, HIGH 475; LOW 450.
April, HIGH 605; LOW 545.   October, HIGH 515; LOW 485.
May, HIGH 575; LOW 505.   November, HIGH 495; LOW 445.
June, HIGH 565; LOW 505.   December, HIGH 455; LOW 410.

1939

January, HIGH 525; LOW 410.   July, HIGH 355; LOW 327.
February, HIGH 450; LOW 405.   August, HIGH 340; LOW 302.
March, HIGH 445; LOW 340.   September, HIGH 445; LOW 350.
April, HIGH 370; LOW 340.   October, HIGH 410; LOW 365.
May, HIGH 365; LOW 310.   November, HIGH 385; LOW 345.
June, HIGH 340; LOW 315.   December, HIGH 425; LOW 400.

1940

January, HIGH 465; LOW 425.   July, HIGH 360; LOW 330.
February, HIGH 440; LOW 415.   August, HIGH 365; LOW 350.
March, HIGH 435; LOW 405.   September, HIGH 385; LOW 365.
April, HIGH 420; LOW 400.   October, HIGH 395; LOW 380.
May, HIGH 430; LOW 345.   November, HIGH 390; LOW 380.
June, HIGH 360; LOW 345.   December, HIGH 415; LOW 385.

1941

January, HIGH 465; LOW 445.   March, HIGH 705; LOW 515.
February, HIGH 525; LOW 445.   April, HIGH 685; LOW 615.

1941

May, HIGH 785; LOW 605.   August, HIGH 640; LOW 590.
June, HIGH 640; LOW 515.   September, HIGH 650; LOW 560.
July, HIGH 665; LOW 545.   October, HIGH 610; LOW 555.

POTATOES
IDAHO

Potatoes are traded in on the Chicago Mercantile Exchange. A contract is 36,000 pounds. Potatoes fluctuate in 1/100 cent per bushel. The minimum fluctuation is $3.60 per contract. A decline of 1c per bushel would be $360 loss, or an advance of 1c per bushel would be a profit of $360.

The commission for buying and selling potatoes at any price is $12.50 per contract.

The margin requirements run $250 to $500, depending on the price.

HIGH AND LOW PRICES FOR POTATOES IN NEW YORK, 1914 TO 1941:

1914—LOW 42c.	1928—LOW 80c.
1919—HIGH $3.00 per bushel.	1929—HIGH $2.00.
1920—LOW 90c.	1932—LOW 57c.
1921—HIGH $1.25.	1933—HIGH $1.25.
1922—LOW 85c.	1934—LOW 50c.
1923—HIGH $1.25.	1936—HIGH $1.45.
1924—LOW 70c.	1937—LOW 68c.
1925—HIGH $2.70.	1940—HIGH $1.25.

Future trading in potatoes has not been running very long. Therefore, it is difficult to get records of prices. Below we give high and low on some of the future options:

November option on potatoes: 1941:

June	—HIGH $2.45	September	—HIGH $2.75
	LOW $1.90		LOW $2.15
July	—HIGH $2.20	October	—HIGH $2.39
	LOW $2.05		LOW $2.03
August	—HIGH $2.20	November	—HIGH $2.53.
	LOW $2.02		LOW $2.19.

This includes prices up to November 10, 1941.

January option for 1942 delivery:

September—HIGH $3.75.   October   —HIGH $3.14
              LOW $2.57   LOW $2.60
                       November—HIGH $3.15
                                       LOW $3.01

This includes prices up to November 10, 1941.

From the above you can see that future prices reached the highest of the year 1941 in September, with the price of the November option $2.75 and the price of the January option $3.75 per bushel.

Therefore, if you wanted to figure resistance levels on potatoes, you would figure from the extreme low of 50c in 1934 to the highs of $2.75 and $3.75.

Apply all of the rules that we apply to other commodities in figuring the trend of future options on potatoes. Keep up monthly high and low, weekly high and low charts and, when potatoes are very active keep up the daily high and low chart.

Potato prices are very high at the present time, because war is always bullish on potatoes, as well as on other commodities. The time will come before the war is over, or just after the war is over, when potatoes, like every other commodity, will have a drastic decline, as they had after 1925, and again after extreme high prices were reached in 1929.

Potatoes are harvested in different parts of the country of the United States at different times of the year. The greatest amount of the crop is harvested in the Summer and early Fall. Therefore, in years when the market is running according to the seasonal trend, prices should be low in the Summer or early Fall, when the weight of the crops is on the market, and no doubt many important tops and changes in trend will take place on potatoes in September and October.

Study of past records will show you how the seasonal trend should run.

RUBBER FUTURES

Rubber futures are traded in on the Commodity Exchange in New York and also traded in at London and Singapore. The contract on the Commodity Exchange, Incorporated in New York is 22,400 pounds. The fluctuations are in cents per pound and each fluctuation is one one-hundredths of a cent per pound and on each contract a move of one point, or one one-hundredths of a cent, equals $2.24.

The commission for buying and selling rubber on the commodity exchange in New York is as follows:

$25.00 for the round turn or for buying and selling and closing the transaction. This is when rubber is selling under 10c per pound.

From 10c to 1499, $30.00 for the round turn.

From 15c to 1999, $35.00.

From 20c to 2999, $40.00.

30c and above, $50.00 commission for the round turn.

The margin requirements for buying and selling rubber vary according to the condition of the market. When prices are very low, around 3c to 5c per pound, margin requirements are usually $200 to $300 per contract. Then when prices get above 10c per pound, the margin is usually $750 per contract. Above 15c up to 25c, the margin requirement is $1000 per contract. The margin requirements are changed according to the condition of the market. You can always find out the margin requirements for buying and selling rubber by asking any broker who is a member of the Commodity Exchange.

SWINGS ON RUBBER—1890 To 1941: Rubber prices have had the greatest range of fluctuations of almost any commodity.

1890—September, HIGH 95c. The trend continued down, reaching 65c in 1892 and 1893. Then the trend moved UPWARD.

1898—HIGH, $1.05 per pound.

1899—HIGH, $1.05 per pound.

1900—HIGH, $1.05 per pound.
Then the trend worked down.

1902—LOW, 65c per pound. Back to the same lows of 1892 and 1893. After that, prices continued to work higher each year.

1904—HIGH, $1.25 per pound.

1905—HIGH, $1.35 per pound.

1907—LOW, 90c per pound.

1908—EXTREME LOW, 67c per pound. Then prices worked higher.

1909—HIGH, $1.95 per pound.

1910—April—HIGH $3.05 per pound. This was the EXTREME HIGH in New York for smoked rubber sheets, cash prices. Futures were not traded in at this time. Hardly anyone dared to dream that when rubber was $3.05 per pound, twenty-two years later, or in 1932, rubber would sell at 2⅝c per pound, but it did. Which again proves that when prices get so high that there is a big profit in producing any kind of a commodity, over production takes place, and prices are forced to abnormally low prices.
From the 1910 HIGH, the 1914 LOW was 45c.

1916—HIGH, $1.02 per pound. Then prices worked lower to 1920.

1920—LOW, 15c per pound.

1921—EXTREME LOW, 11¾c per pound. This was the lowest on record up to this time.

1923—HIGH, 32c per pound.

1924—LOW, 15c per pound. A DOUBLE BOTTOM and higher than 1921. A rapid advance followed.

1925—HIGH, $1.25 per pound. Very few people would realize, or believe at that time that seven years later rubber would sell for around 2½c per pound. Yet it did.

1926—FUTURE TRADING in rubber was started on the rubber exchange in New York, which was later consolidated with the commodity exchange in New York, where rubber is now traded.

1926—February HIGH 6450. This is the highest level at which any future contract sold and this price was for the September option.

1926—August, EXTREME LOW, 3670.

1927—March, HIGH 4280.
June, LOW 3380.
November, EXTREME HIGH for the year of 4340.
From this high a rapid decline followed.

1928—April LOW 17c.
May HIGH 2030.
September LOW 1750.

1929—February, last EXTREME HIGH, 2770.
    September, LOW 1930.
    October, HIGH 2350. This is the last time that rubber sold at this high level.

1930—September, LOW 780.
    December, HIGH 1050.

1931—September, LOW 470.

1932—June, EXTREME LOW 265 for the September option.

1933—July, HIGH 1125.
    September, LOW 660.

1934—September, HIGH 1590.

1935—March, LOW 1070.

1936—December, HIGH 2250. This was the highest since October, 1929.

1937—January, LOW 2010.

1937—March, HIGH 2745. This was EXTREME HIGH and prices have not exceeded this high level up to this writing, November 5, 1941.

1938—March, LOW 1050. This was the last time that prices were around the 10c level.

1938—October, HIGH 1750.

1939—January, LOW 15c. This was the last time that the price was 15c

1939—September, HIGH 2390.   1941—May, HIGH 2410.

1940—March, LOW 1750.   June, LOW 2060.

    May, HIGH 2185.   July, HIGH 23c.

    June, LOW 1870.   August, LOW 2225.

RUBBER
SEASONAL CHANGES FROM 1890 TO 1941

Below we give the time each month when extreme HIGH and extreme LOW has been reached during the period of 51 years.

January	LOW	7 times	July	LOW	4 times
	HIGH	6 times		HIGH	1 time
February	LOW	7 times	August	LOW	4 times
	HIGH	9 times		HIGH	1 time
March	LOW	4 times	September	LOW	6 times
	HIGH	3 times		HIGH	3 times
April	LOW	1 time	October	LOW	3 times
	HIGH	6 times		HIGH	3 times
May	LOW	2 times	November	LOW	5 times
	HIGH	5 times		HIGH	3 times
June	LOW	5 times	December	LOW	5 times
	HIGH	3 times		HIGH	9 times

From the above you can see that the greatest number of LOW LEVELS has been reached in January and February and the next number of LOW LEVELS in September,—next in March and June. The smallest number of LOW LEVELS was in April, the next May and the third month for LOW LEVELS was October. November and December had five times each. From this we consider that when the trend is running down and if it is started down in the summer, LOWS can come out anywhere from November to February, but the MOST LOWS come out in January and February. However, September is quite important for a change in trend, as LOWS have come out six times in this month.

The greatest number of HIGHS has occurred in February and December—nine times in each of these months. The next month for highs is January. Therefore, the important months to watch for HIGHS and a change in trend are December, February and January. The next important month is April, when six highs have occurred and next is May, with five highs. September, October and November are all the same—three times each—and June also had three highs. The months when the least number of HIGHS was reached were July and August with one high each. This indicates that the trend had run down into July, August and September, when a great number of LOWS had been made, that the trend does not change around September, and then turns up and HIGHS are made in December, January or February. The smallest number of LOWS was shown in April and the second number of HIGHS in April, which shows that when the trend is running UP, lows are not reached in April, but HIGHS come out in this month, the Spring of the year.

Rubber runs about the same as cotton as far as the number of months up and down before a change takes place. Always watch for a change in trend in the third or fourth month from any important TOP or BOTTOM, especially if there has been a fast advance or decline. The next important point to watch for a change in trend is the sixth or seventh month. Then at the end of one year, or twelve months, fifteen months, eighteen months, twenty-one months, twenty-four months and at the end of any even year from the EXTREME LOW or the EXTREME HIGH.

In checking over the past records of rubber, you will find that in a very bullish uptrend, reaction seldom lasted more than one month and hardly ever more than two months—the same way when the main trend turned down and prices were declining fast,—one month's rally is about all it gets and sometimes two months' rally until the trend has run its course. Rubber moves in sections of from two and four, bull campaigns often not running out until the fourth section. You should always watch the third section for a change. Sometimes an extreme decline will take place and there will only be halting places and rallies of one month and it will run out the extreme decline in practically one section, or three swings.

Always watch the anniversary dates. In other words, if LOWS have been made in June, watch the next June for a change in trend and watch six months, or December, for a change. By checking over past records, you will see how prices have worked out against the important TOPS or BOTTOMS.

Rubber often makes a SHARP TOP and then declines fast. Rubber, like other commodities, has SECONDARY RALLIES and SECOND-

ARY DECLINES and the FINAL TOPS or FINAL BOTTOMS are made. The greatest advances and declines come from DOUBLE and TRIPLE TOPS and BOTTOMS. These should be watched and you should watch the old HIGHS or LOWS for years back in order to determine when these old price levels are reached. Then watch for a change in trend in the months when a seasonal trend is indicated.

RESISTANCE LEVELS: We are giving the resistance levels on rubber from the LOW of June, 1921, LOW 1175, to HIGH 6450 and 6450 to LOW of 265. Also from 4340 to 265 and 2770 to 265, and giving the important percentage points of 6450 to 2770 and the percentage points on the base, or extreme low of 265, and on up. These points are all you need to check against TOPS and BOTTOMS in the future. You can always take the last EXTREME LOW and the last EXTREME HIGH and watch the 50% reaction point and then when important BOTTOMS and TOPS are broken, use the EXTREME HIGH and EXTREME LOW for calculating resistance points. Rubber comes out with EXTREME HIGH and EXTREME LOW against some mathematical point or percentage of some former HIGH or low price.

REVIEW AND EXAMPLES OF SEPTEMBER RUBBER FUTURES

1926—February, HIGH 6450. LAST EXTREME HIGH and the highest price made since trading in rubber futures started on the New York Rubber Exchange. A sharp decline followed.

1926—August, LOW 3670. This was a sharp decline in a short period of time. 3628 was 9/16 of 6450, making this a SUPPORT LEVEL for a rally.

1926—November, HIGH 4420. Note that 4400 was 2/3 of 6450, making this a RESISTANCE LEVEL.

1927—September, LOW 3280. Holding above ½ of 6450, making this a BUYING LEVEL for RALLY.

1927—December, LAST HIGH 4340. A LOWER TOP and a SELLING LEVEL.

1928—February. Prices broke 3225, the 50% point of 6450 and have never sold for 3225 again up to this writing, November 5th, 1941. Breaking this half-way point put the market in a very weak position and a fast decline followed.

1928—February, LOW 1740. A RESISTANCE LEVEL. 75% of 6450 was 1613 and ½ of the BOTTOM at 3280 was 1640. 1732 was 62½% of 2770.

1928—May, HIGH 2030. A one month's rally and a SELLING LEVEL.

1928—September, LOW 1750. A DOUBLE BOTTOM and BUYING LEVEL.

1929—February, LAST HIGH 2770. The same high as April, 1928. A DOUBLE TOP and A SELLING LEVEL. The trend turned down.

1929—April, LOW 2010. An OLD TOP LEVEL. A rally followed.

1929—May, HIGH 2450. A RESISTANCE LEVEL. 87½% of 2770 was 2425 and 250% of 1175 to 6450 was 2493 and 2170 was ½ of 4340. The market broke 2170, again this important half-way point, which indicated much lower prices.

1929—September, LOW 1930. AN OLD BOTTOM LEVEL and a month for seasonal change in trend. A rally followed.

1929—October, HIGH 2250. A LOWER TOP. Later broke all bottoms, breaking 1740, which was a very weak position. After that time, never rallied more than two months.

1930—January, LOW 15.70.

1930—February, HIGH 1785. An OLD BOTTOM and a SELLING LEVEL on a one month's rally. A rapid decline followed.

1930—September, LOW 780. After breaking 1175, the low of 1921, the market declined fast and rallies were very small. Note that 87½% of 6450 was 806, making 780 a BUYING LEVEL for a RALLY.

1930—December, HIGH 1050. A two months' rally and a 250 point rally, which was a normal rally in a bear market. The main trend was still down.

1932—June, EXTREME LOW 265. The fourth section down from 6450 and the lowest price in history. Prices remained dull and narrow and in a narrow range for two months, holding under 320.

1932—August. Prices crossed 320. Note that 397 was 50% advance on 265.

1932—September, HIGH 465. Under old bottoms. The first rally. After the first rally there is always a SECONDARY DECLINE and September was the month for a seasonal change in trend.

1933—February, LOW 3c per pound. A SECONDARY BOTTOM and a HIGHER BOTTOM. A safer place to buy. The market held for two months in a narrow trading range.

1933—April. Prices crossed three months' TOP. This was the time to buy more, and later prices crossed 465, the HIGH of September, 1932, which showed strong uptrend.

THE BREAKAWAY POINT: When prices crossed 480, the runaway move started and this was a safe place to BUY MORE.

1933—July, HIGH 1125. The first section of the bull market. A SELLING LEVEL, because 33 1/3% of 2770 to 265 was 1163 and 250% on 265 was 1125. A sharp decline followed. 1125 to 265 the 50% or half-way point, was 695.

1933—September LOW 650. A BUYING LEVEL. 662 was 150% on 265. This was only a normal two months' decline and a safe BUYING LEVEL.

1934—May, HIGH 1605. Second section of the BULL market. A SELLING LEVEL, as 33-1/3% of 4340 to 265 was 1623.

1934—June, LOW 1280. A seasonal change in trend due in June. Time to buy for a rally.

1934—September, HIGH 1590. A DOUBLE TOP and slightly lower. A SELLING LEVEL.

1935—March, LOW 1065. AN OLD TOP and RESISTANCE LEVEL and A BUYING LEVEL.

1935—June, HIGH 1310. One year from June, 1934, and three years from June, 1932. Time for a change in trend.

1935—September, LOW 1120. A HIGHER BOTTOM, and a BUYING LEVEL. September is one of the important months for a change in trend. An advance followed. Prices crossed the TOP at 1600 and later crossed 50% of 4340 to 265, showing strong uptrend.

1937—March, FINAL HIGH, 2745. A DOUBLE TOP against February, 1925, when the last high was 2770, making this a SAFE SELLING LEVEL, especially as it was the fourth section of the bull market and a rapid advance had taken place the last few weeks. The advance had run from September, 1935, LOW of 1120, with never more than a one month's reaction.

From 2745 a sharp decline followed. The trend turned down and no rally lasted more than one month. Don't overlook the fact that any time the market cannot rally into the second month, it is weak and a short sale on any rally of two to three weeks.

1938—March, LOW 1050. A DOUBLE BOTTOM, an old top level and a BUYING LEVEL, as 300% on 265 was 1060, making this a safe buying level for a rally. The reason for a change in trend here was because it was one year from the extreme high.

1938—November, HIGH 1750. A SELLING LEVEL, as 1788 was 37½% of 265 to 2770 and 1722 was 550% on 265. A decline followed.

1939—January, LOW 15c. A SAFE BUYING LEVEL. At 1517, it was 50% of 265 to 2770. The market held in a long, dull, narrow range for eight months. Finally, when prices crossed eight months' top, a rapid advance followed, running up 8c per pound.

1939—September, HIGH 2390. A SHARP TOP and a SELLING LEVEL.

1939—October, LOW 1730. OLD TOP and BUYING LEVEL.

1939—December, HIGH 1890. A reaction followed and made TRIPLE BOTTOM, around 1760.

1940—April, LAST LOW 1740, from which a rapid advance followed. This was a safe buying level a third time at this low price.

1940—May. The early part of the month the market advanced to 2185. This was a safe SELLING LEVEL, as 2170 was ½ of 4340, being the important 50% point, and the safest place to buy and sell. A fast decline followed. The break was due to the fact that Hitler made the drive against Belgium and France and all commodities had a wide open break.

1940—June, LOW 1850.

1940—August, HIGH 1980. A SELLING LEVEL.

1940—September, LOW 1880. A DOUBLE BOTTOM and a slightly higher bottom and a BUYING LEVEL. Also because 1846 was 66-2/3% of 2770.

1940—November, HIGH 2710. A SELLING LEVEL for reaction.

1941—January, LOW 1880. A TRIPLE BOTTOM. This was a safe place to buy, protected with STOP LOSS ORDER 30 to 50 points under.

1941—May, HIGH 2410. A DOUBLE TOP against September, 1939.
A SELLING LEVEL. Note resistance levels around this price.

1941—June, LOW 2060. A SUPPORT LEVEL as 2078 was 75% of
2770. A rally followed.

1941—July, HIGH 23c. A SELLING LEVEL, as 2302 was ½ of 4340
to 265.

At this time the government put a ceiling on rubber and re-
stricted future trading and future trading has been discontinued
since that time, but later on, or after the war is over, trading in
rubber futures will start again on the commodity exchange. The
range in rubber futures is always quite wide and it is a profitable
commodity to trade in.

Study the past history of rubber. Use all the rules that we
have applied to other commodities and you can make a success
of trading in rubber futures, provided you limit your loss by
using STOP LOSS ORDERS, knowing that you can be wrong
when you enter the market and your protection is a STOP LOSS
ORDER.

SILK FUTURES

Japan controls the silk market of the world and the United States is
the best customer of Japan.

Silk is traded in on the Commodity Exchange, Inc. of New York. A
contract is 1300 pounds and fluctuations are in cents per pound. The
minimum fluctuation is ½c per pound and this amounts to $6.50 on a
contract of 1300 pounds.

The commission for trading in silk when the price is under $1.75 per
pound is $26.00. When the price is $1.75 to $2.24½ per pound, the com-
mission is $29.00 per contract. When the price is $2.25 to $2.74½, the
commission is $32.00 per contract. When the price is $2.75 and over, the
commission is $34.00 per contract.

Silk is also traded in on the Yokohama Exchange, Ltd. in Japan and
in Kobe Exchange, Ltd., in Japan.

At this writing, November 8, 1941, there is no trading in silk futures
on the Commodity Exchange at New York, prices and trading having
been discontinued on account of the war and also because the United
States has stopped buying silk from Japan.

Silk makes a wide range of fluctuation, even in normal times, and is
profitable to trade in. By studying past records and applying all the
rules that we apply to other commodities, you can forecast the trend of
silk as well as any other commodity.

During the world war, silk prices made a very wide range of fluctuation and reached extreme high prices.

1919—December, EXTREME HIGH $17.50 per pound.

1920—LOW, $5.00 per pound. The extreme low price for silk after the
world war was reached in 1933, February and April, LOW $1.10,
but the EXTREME LOW was reached in

1934—August, EXTREME LOW $1.07 per pound.

The first thing to do to determine the trend of silk is to find the time
cycles because time periods are the most important in figuring future
trends.

From 1919, December HIGH to 1933, February and April LOW, the time is thirteen years and two months and thirteen years and four months. Add this time period to the EXTREME LOW to get the most important time period, which is September, 1939 and November, 1939. These were important time periods to watch for Tops.

The next EXTREME HIGH was reached in 1939 in the month of December, HIGH $4.39 per pound. This proves the value of knowing these time periods.

Then, if we take the time periods, that is, the total time period of thirteen years and two months and add it to the LOW, we get February and March, or April, 1946 as another important time.

We use the 12½%, 25%, 50%, 75% and 100% of time periods in figuring future time periods.

Taking the extreme time period from 1919, HIGH to August, 1934, EXTREME LOW, it would be fourteen years and nine months. Adding this time period to August, 1934, or one-half of this time period, we get 1942, the month of January, as being important for a change in trend. You can use other time periods in the same way, or the total time period and the percentage for an important change in trend point.

From 1934, August, LOW to 1939, December, HIGH, the time period was sixty-four months. One-half of this would be 32 months—one-fourth would be 16 months and one-eighth would be 8 months. Adding eight months gives us August, 1940, and there was a LOW and prices started to advance. Adding sixteen months gives April, 1941. Prices started up from January, 1941. Adding one-half of the time period, (thirty-two months) to December, 1939, gives 1942, August, as important to watch for a change in trend.

The minor time periods are the runs from the minor tops and bottoms. 1932, January to June, 5 months,—to 1933, February, 13 months, and April 15 months. Our rule says to watch for a change in trend every twelve months, fifteen, eighteen and twenty-first, twenty-fourth, etc.

1933, February to June, 4 months. Our rule says that fast moves up often come in the eighth and fourth months.

1933, June to August, 1934,—14 months. A change in trend took place in the fifteenth month.

1934, August to November, 1935—15 months. A change in trend took place.

Then to June, 1936—8 months.

Then to January, 1937—7 months.

The rule says to watch for a change in trend in the sixth to seventh months.

January, 1937 to March, 1938—14 months and coming out of the time period for a change in trend.

From March, 1938 to December, 1939—21 months. A final top and important for a change in trend.

Adding 21 months to December, 1939 gives September, 1941. If the exchange had been open and active trading had been going on, no doubt there would have been a change in trend in September, 1941.

From December, 1939, to April, 1940,—was four months, when an important change in trend took place.

To the bottom in August, 1940, was eight months, and the last HIGH, July, 1941, was eleven months.

You can see how these important time periods work out TOPS and BOTTOMS according to our rules for time periods.

SEASONAL CHANGES IN TREND

We have not made a study of records far enough back on silk to give a definite idea of the months when important changes in the seasonal trend take place. But from 1932 to 1941, which is a short time period, the greatest number of LOWS was made in March, April and June. No LOWS were recorded in May, September, October or December.

The greatest number of HIGHS was reached in the month of January —four during this period. The next in importance were February, June, July, August, October, November and December, when one EXTREME HIGH was reached in each. March, April, May, September had no HIGHS reached in these months.

From this record, you would watch for important changes in trend in January,—and in March, April, May and June—but a study of time changes in extreme highs and lows over a long period of time might give different months than these, but this is a period to watch, because it is the times when extreme highs and extreme lows were reached. However, the month of December is quite important, as an EXTREME HIGH was reached in December and trend changes may come often around December and January.

RESISTANCE LEVELS FOR SILK

We have given the resistance levels from the HIGH in 1919 to the LOW in 1920—$17.50 per pound to $5.00 per pound and have calculated the percentage points on $17.50.

From 1934 August, EXTREME LOW of $1.07 to the EXTREME HIGH, December, 1939, of $4.39 have also been calculated.

These will be the most important resistance levels to watch for TOPS and BOTTOMS until prices go above this high price or break under the low price.

We have also calculated for you the percentage of $4.39 per pound and these resistance levels between 439 and 1.07 have been working out quite accurately.

EXAMPLES OF TOPS AND BOTTOMS, MARCH AND SEPTEMBER SILK FUTURES

1932—January, HIGH $1.88 per pound. Under $2.00 was a SELLING LEVEL.

1932—June, LOW $1.15. This was a 93-1/4% decline on $17.50 the Extreme high. Holding above $1.09½, a resistance point, made this a BUYING LEVEL, especially as the market had only had a three months' downward trend, and a change was due.

1932—August, HIGH $1.96. Under $2.00 and still a SELLING LEVEL.

1933—February, March and April, LOW $1.10. A TRIPLE BOTTOM and a BUYING LEVEL. Also, $1.12½ was a resistance level because it was 12½% above $1.00.

1933—June, HIGH $2.25. A SELLING LEVEL because 12½% of $17.50 was $2.19. 100% on $1.10 bottom gave $2.20, making this a selling level. Ten months time from August, 1932, tops.

1933—November and December, LOWS $1.32. Held two months in a narrow trading range. This was the place to BUY FOR A RALLY.

1934—February. HIGH $1.57. From $1.10 LOW to $2.25 HIGH, the 50% point was $1.57½, making this a safe SELLING LEVEL for a reaction.

1934—July, August and September, EXTREME LOW $1.07. Just under 1933 LOWS, making this a DOUBLE BOTTOM. Holding for three months, making LOWS around 107, made this a SAFE PLACE TO BUY. Crossing $1.12½, the 50% point of $2.25 HIGH, indicated higher.

1933—January and February, HIGH $1.43. A three months' rally, indicating TOP and a SELLING LEVEL.

1933—March, LOW $1.25. A natural SUPPORT LEVEL, as it was 25% on $1.00. Held for two months in a normal and narrow range, indicating low and a time to BUY.

1933—July—prices crossed the tops of $1.43, showing a strong UP-TREND. Later crossed $1.61 which is 50% of $2.25 to $1.07, indicating still stronger uptrend.

1935—November, HIGH $2.10. A 100% advance on $1.07 gave $2.14, making this a SELLING LEVEL. A reaction followed.

1936—February. LOW $1.48. Four months down and three years from 1933 LOWS. A change in trend is due.

1936—March, HIGH $1.73. From $1.48 to $2.10 made $1.79 a RESIST-ANCE LEVEL and a SELLING LEVEL while it was under this price.

1936—June, LOW $1.39. This was a RESISTANCE LEVEL because 12½% of 1.07 to 2.25 is $1.35-⅛. Holding above this level showed a strong uptrend. A rally followed.

1936—August, HIGH $1.77. A SELLING LEVEL.

1936—September, LOW $1.55. A one month's reaction and time to BUY. When prices crossed $1.62, which was the 50% point between $1.07 and $2.25, they were in a stronger position.

1936—October—Prices crossed the tops of August and September, showing strong uptrend.

1937—January, HIGH $2.19. A RESISTANCE LEVEL because 12½% of $17.50 the EXTREME HIGH, was $2.19, making this a selling level. Still under the TOP of $2.25 made it a SAFER SELLING LEVEL.

1937—February, LOW $1.79. An old top level. A rally followed.

1937—March, HIGH $2.07. A lower top, a secondary rally and a safer SELLING LEVEL.

1937—June, LOW $1.73. An old top and bottom and a RALLY DUE.

1937—July, HIGH $1.95. Under $2.00—a SECOND LOWER TOP and only a one month's normal rally, which made this a SELLING LEVEL. Later prices broke $1.73, showing the main trend DOWN and indicating extreme weakness. A sharp decline followed.

1937—November, LOW $1.43. An OLD BOTTOM, a top level. BUY FOR A RALLY.

1938—February, HIGH $1.62. A SELLING LEVEL because 50% of $2.25 to $1.07 was $1.61.

1938—March, LOW $1.39. A DOUBLE BOTTOM against June, 1936. A BUYING LEVEL.

1938—June, LAST LOW $1.45. Later crossed the TOPS at $1.62, showing UPTREND.

1938—July, HIGH $1.77. Under old tops. A reaction followed.

1938—August, LOW $1.60. Old tops and RESISTANCE LEVEL. A BUYING LEVEL because the prices held for four months between $1.68 and $1.70.

1939—January—prices crossed $1.78, showing strong UPTREND.

1939—May—prices crossed $2.25, the 1933 HIGH, showing STRONGER UPTREND.

1939—August, HIGH $2.80.

1939—September, LOW $2.16. AN OLD TOP LEVEL and a RESISTANCE LEVEL at $2.19.
War broke out in September, 1939 and war has always been bullish on silk and a rapid ADVANCE followed.

1939—December, FINAL HIGH $4.39 per pound. A SELLING LEVEL because $4.38 was 25% of $17.50, the EXTREME HIGH PRICE.

1940—April, LOW $2.25. The old top of 1933, a buying level, and 50% of 4.39 is $2.19½, making this a SUPPORT and BUYING LEVEL for a rally.

1940—May, HIGH $2.81. A selling level, because $2.75 was 62½% of $4.39.

1940—August, LOW $2.40. OLD TOP LEVEL and $2.33 was 37½% of $1.07 to $4.39.

1940—October, HIGH $2.91. A SELLING LEVEL because 66 2/3% of $4.39 was $2.92 and October was a month for a change in trend.

1941—January, LOW $2.47. A HIGHER BOTTOM. Held for two months in a narrow trading range, making this a BUYING LEVEL for a rally.

1941—February—prices crossed tops of two previous months, the trend was up, and a big move followed.

1941—March, HIGH $2.99. A SELLING LEVEL, just under $3.00, where there is always resistance.

1941—April, LOW $2.76. A BUYING LEVEL because 62½% of $4.39 was $2.75 and 50% of $4.39 to $1.07 made this a BUYING LEVEL for a RALLY.

1941—July, HIGH $3.55. A RESISTANCE LEVEL because 75% of $4.39 to $1.07 is $3.59.

Silk trading was stopped on account of the war and the United States stopped shipments to Japan and forbid Japanese shipping into the United States.

As a rule, silk moves very rapidly from HIGH to LOW after it has reached any EXTREME HIGH or LOW point and moves down more rapidly from HIGHS than it does up from LOWS, but after accumulation takes place and a long time period has elapsed near LOW LEVELS, it advances.

Therefore, it is important to always keep up the weekly high and low price on silk futures, and when it gets very active, keep a daily high and low and depend on the daily high and low to give the first indication of a change in trend. Do not overlook the fact to always use STOP LOSS ORDERS when you buy and sell silk, because the market moves very rapidly and if you get wrong, you could lose money very fast. Therefore, protect your capital by using a STOP LOSS ORDER.

Applying all of the rules that we apply to other commodities, you will be able to forecast the trend in silk.

SUGAR FUTURES

Sugar futures are traded in on the New York coffee and sugar exchange. A contract for sugar is 112,000 pounds and prices are based on cents per pound. The minimum fluctuation is $5.60 per point.

The minimum commission on sugar is $15.00 per hundred for a round turn and the commission is fixed at the rate of one and one-half percent of the value of the initial side traded on. In other words, if you buy sugar first before you sell it, you pay on the value of the buying price. If you sell short, you pay commission based on a percentage of the selling price.

WORLD SUGAR NO. 4: This contract for sugar and price varies from the domestic sugar price. The fluctuations are in 1/200 of a cent per pound. World sugar is just as profitable to trade in as domestic sugar and has quite enough fluctuations to make plenty of profit.

Sugar is very profitable to trade in if you will watch the time when it shows it has finished, either on the UP or DOWN side and then shows a change in trend. By watching resistance levels you will be able to tell when the trend changes and can buy and sell near tops and bottoms.

SUGAR FUTURES—SEASONAL TREND

1915 to 1941

The following are the swings from high to low and low to high.

1915—August, LOW 3c.

1920—May, EXTREME HIGH 2335.

1921—November and December, LOW 235.

1923—April, HIGH 685.

1924—February, LOW 580.

1925—September, LOW 235. A double bottom and BUYING LEVEL.
In fact, this was the THIRD BOTTOM around this same level as
low in 1921 was 235.

1927—January, HIGH 355. The last high in September, 1924, was 365,
making this a lower top, and a SELLING LEVEL.

1932—EXTREME LOW 60/100 of a cent, or just above ½ cent per
pound. The lowest price at which sugar ever sold.

1933—February, LOW 72.

1937—January, HIGH 310.

1938—May, LOW 172.

1939—September, HIGH 295.

1939—October, LOW 175.

1940—June, LOW 172.

1941—September, HIGH 305.

SEASONAL HIGHS AND LOWS

Below we give the number of times that HIGHS and LOWS have
been reached in each month from 1915 to 1941.

January	HIGH 5 times	July	HIGH 1 time
	LOW 7 times		LOW 1 time
February	HIGH 3 times	August	HIGH 2 times
	LOW 3 times		LOW 2 times
March	HIGH 2 times	September	HIGH 4 times
	LOW 0 times		LOW 2 times
April	HIGH 2 times	October	HIGH 0 times
	LOW 0 times		LOW 1 time
May	HIGH 2 times	November	HIGH 1 time
	LOW 3 times		LOW 0 time
June	HIGH 0 times	December	HIGH 4 times
	LOW 6 times		LOW 7 times

From the above you will see that the most HIGHS have been made
in January and December and the next HIGHS in September. September is always a very important month for a change in the seasonal
trend. As a rule, sugar grinding starts in October and the receipts are
heavy from October to February and this is depressing on the market,
especially when there is a large crop.

February is the next month for HIGHS, three being made in this
month. The months of March, April, May and August are the same,
two HIGHS being made in each month.

The months of June and October had no HIGHS reached. The
reason for this is that as a rule the seasonal trend is down during these
months and especially during October to December, as lows are made
during these times instead of highs. Only one time in July and November were HIGHS reached.

You will note that the greatest number of Lows was reached in
December and January—seven in each month, making a total of

fourteen LOWS. This is due to the fact that the receipts of sugar are heavy during these months and a large amount is forced on the market.

June is the next month for LOWS—six having been made in June. Many important changes in trend come out in this month. This is often due to the fact that if the new crop of sugar promises to be very large, there is heavy selling during the summer.

The months of February and May are the next, three lows having been made in these months. The next months in importance are August and September, two LOWS having been made in these months. As a rule, these are the most important months for HIGHS. The months of March, April and November—no LOWS have been made in these months. This is because these months, especially the Spring months, are important for high prices, and in November, if the trend is down, LOWS are not reached in November, but in December and January.

The next months in importance are July and October. Only one LOW has been reached in these months.

By watching the months when EXTREME HIGHS and EXTREME LOWS are reached and then watching the months when the most seasonal highs and lows have been made, you can determine the main trend.

RESISTANCE LEVELS. Below we give resistance levels and percentages of 2325, the HIGH of May, 1920, and percentages from 2325 to 60 the EXTREME LOW, 1932 in the month of June. We also give the resistance levels from 685 to 60. 685 was the HIGH for 1923, April. We give the percentage of 685 to 60 and the percentage of 685. At the present time, these are about all the resistance levels you will need to figure resistance prices and buying and selling prices on sugar. We have given the percentage on 60 up to 420.

	(May, 1920) 2325 to 0	(June, 1932) 2325 to 60	(Apr., 1923) 685 to 60	685 to 0
12½%	290½	283	138	86
25%	285	566	216	171
33 1/3	775	815	268	228
37½%	871	849	294	257
50%	1162½	1192	372	342½
62½%	1452	1475	450	428½
66 2/3%	1550	1570	476	457
75%	1742	1758	528	514
87½%	2082	2041	606	609
100%	2325	2325	685	685

Percentage on 60 up to 420.

(60—EXTREME LOW—June, 1932)

50%	90	350%	270
100%	120	400%	300
150%	150	450%	330
200%	180	500%	360
250%	210	550%	390
300%	240	600%	420

DOUBLE, TRIPLE AND SINGLE BOTTOMS AND TOPS

1915—January, LOW 315.

1915—February, HIGH 430.

1915—August, LOW 3c. This was the EXTREME LOW after the World War started and the price that you can figure percentages on up to the EXTREME TOP. 450 would be 50% advance on 3c and 6c would be 100% advance.

After the double bottoms around 3c, the trend turned up and prices of sugar worked higher, with very small reactions.

1916—January, HIGH 575. Failed to make the 100% advance on the lowest price of 3c. A decline followed.

1916—August, LOW 390.

1916—September, LOW 385.

1917—February, LOW 385. Making a TRIPLE BOTTOM and a BUYING LEVEL. 12½% on 3c gives 375. The fact that the price held at this time ten points above that level indicated strength and higher prices.

1917—April, HIGH 575. A DOUBLE TOP against January, 1916, and a SELLING LEVEL.

The exchange was closed from August 17, 1917, until February 15, 1920, and there are no quotations during this period.

1920—February, LOW 960. Over 300% on the base of 3c and a 50% advance on the tops of 575. There was a great shortage of sugar after the WORLD WAR and prices advanced rapidly.

1920—May, HIGH 2335. This was the EXTREME HIGH. These high prices caused a great increase in production of sugar and a sharp decline followed.

1920—June, LOW 1550.

1920—July, HIGH 1810. This was the last HIGH.

1920—December, LOW 435. Down to old bottom levels. A rally followed.

1921—January, HIGH 510. A LOWER TOP than December.

1921—February, LOW 415. This was three bottoms around the same low level, indicating support and a rally followed.

1921—March, HIGH 580. This was a DOUBLE and TRIPLE TOP and at the same level as January, 1916, and April, 1917, making this a SELLING LEVEL. A sharp decline followed. Rallies were very small.

1921—December, LOW 235. Note that 50% of the last high, 570, was 285.

1922—March, HIGH 285. Up to this important half-way point, the resistance was met and a reaction followed. The market had not yet had a secondary decline which is always natural after extreme lows are reached.

1922—May, LOW 245. This was a SECONDARY RALLY and a SAFER BUYING POINT.

June—prices crossed the tops of six months and crossed the half-way point of 285, indicating higher prices.

Note that when prices were at 235, they were 20% off of the LOW of 3c per pound, the lows made in 1915, and 25% decline would have been 225. Holding above this level indicated strength.

When prices crossed 260 they were in a stronger position. Crossing 360, a 50% advance on 235, indicated higher prices. A rapid advance followed in 1923, with very small reaction.

1923—April, HIGH 685. Note that 660 was 175% advance on the low of 235. At this top of 685, you should figure the percentage between the low of 235 and 685. The trend turned down and a fast decline followed.

1923—June, LOW 460. Note that this was the 50%, or half-way point between 235 and 685, making this a BUYING LEVEL for a rally. A rally followed.

1923—July, HIGH 550. Here the trend again turned down, with later prices breaking under the important half-way point.

1923—November, LOW 405. Note that 175% advance on the extreme low would give 415 as a support level. November was the month to expect a seasonal low. A rally followed.

1924—February, HIGH 585. This was up to OLD TOP LEVELS and a SELLING LEVEL, and prices are opposite the seasonal trend. The advance had run four months and a change in trend was due. A decline followed and prices broke back under the half-way point of 235 and 685, indicating weakness and lower prices. The decline was rapid.

1924—June, LOW 305. Down to old BOTTOM and TOP levels. The market was weak and the main trend was down. Only a moderate rally followed.

1924—September, HIGH 365. September is the important month for a change in trend. Prices broke back under 342, which was one-half of 685, showing weakness and indication of lower prices.

1925—June, LOW 235. Down to OLD BOTTOMS and a BUYING POINT. A rally followed.

1925—July, HIGH 295. Only a one month's rally. The market was dull and narrow during the month of August and then turned down again.

1925—September, LOW 235. A DOUBLE BOTTOM.
October also made the same.

1925—December, HIGH 280. A LOWER TOP and opposite the seasonal trend. The main trend turned down again and prices worked lower.

1926—June, LOW 230. A TRIPLE BOTTOM in 1925 and 1926 and a BUYING LEVEL.

1927—January, HIGH 355. Up to the half way point of 685, a SELLING LEVEL and a DOUBLE TOP against September,

1924.   A decline followed and the rallies were small, not lasting more than six or seven weeks.

1929—June, LOW 165.   This was a new low for sugar futures.   June is a month when BOTTOMS often come out and a rally followed.

1929—September, HIGH 310.   This was under old bottom level and 320 would have been 100% advance on 165.   In October the trend turned down by breaking under three months' bottom, showing a weak position.

1930—July, LOW 120.   This was a 50% decline from 240, A BOTTOM LEVEL.

1930—September and October.   Bottoms around 120.   A rally followed. October, HIGH 172.

1930—December, LOW 125.   A SLIGHTLY HIGHER BOTTOM, but the market was weak and only a small rally followed.

1931—January, HIGH 150.   The trend continued down.

1931—May, LOW 118.   A NEW LOW.   The usual two months' rally in a bear market followed.

1931—July, HIGH 160.

1931—August, HIGH 165.   Under the OLD BOTTOM LEVELS and a LOWER TOP.   Still a short sale and the main trend was down. A long, slow decline followed.

1932—June, FINAL LOW 60.   This was 60/100 of a cent, or just a little above ½c per pound.   Note that the 75% decline from 240 to 60 held for three months, making bottoms around this extremely low figure.

1932—September, HIGH 120.   A 100% advance on 60.   After the first advance from the extreme low levels there is always a SECONDARY RALLY.

1933—February, LOW 72.   This was a SECONDARY RALLY and a HIGHER BOTTOM.   The market held for two months in a range of less than 30 points.   Then the main trend turned up and prices crossed 120.   They were above six months tops and over 100% on the bottom level.

1933—July, HIGH 185.   This was a 200% advance on the LOW LEVEL and up under old bottom levels and around old top levels.   A decline followed.

1933—October, LOW 125.   Holding above the 100% advance on the low level and at a place where there was a series of bottoms.   A BUYING LEVEL.   Prices worked higher.

1934—February, HIGH 172.   A LOWER TOP and a REACTION POINT.

1934—April, LOW 140.   A two months' normal rally and making HIGHER BOTTOM.   Sugar continued to advance, making higher bottoms and higher tops, until

1935—May, HIGH 255.   Note that 240 was a 300% advance on the extreme low.   From this level a decline followed.

1936—Low, 295. A series of OLD TOP LEVELS and holding above 200% on the base indicated higher. The upward swing was resumed.

1936—June, HIGH—with four months' tops around this level of 290. Note that 300 was 400% on the base, or extreme low. A reaction followed.

1936—October, LOW 235. At a natural SUPPORT POINT, 300% on the base. There were TRIPLE BOTTOMS at this level and this was a BUYING LEVEL.

1937—FINAL HIGH, 305. This was an EXACT RESISTANCE LEVEL, being 400% on the EXTREME LOW of 60. This was in January and opposite the seasonal trend, making this a SELLING LEVEL. The main trend turned down and later prices broke the last bottom at 235, showing weakness.

1938—May, LOW 175. This was 200% advance on the base, or extreme low, and was back to the low level of 1934, making a DOUBLE BOTTOM and a SUPPORT LEVEL. Prices held for three months around this low level, giving plenty of chance to buy.

1938—December, HIGH 220. This was opposite the seasonal trend and, before the month was over, prices declined and broke under three months' bottom, indicating lower.
The market was in a narrow, dull trading range during the greater part of 1939.

1939—June, LOW 180. A DOUBLE BOTTOM and a SAFE BUYING LEVEL as the 200% advance point on 60, extreme low. Prices continued dull and narrow until September, 1939, when the war broke out and then prices crossed tops of twelve months and a rapid advance followed.

1939—September, HIGH 295. A DOUBLE TOP against January, 1937, and a SELLING LEVEL, because this was 400% on the base of 60. A rapid decline followed.

1939—October, LOW 175. A TRIPLE BOTTOM and again a BUYING LEVEL. A moderate rally followed.

1940—February, HIGH 205. The market held in a narrow trading range and prices worked lower.

1940—June, FINAL LOW 170. A TRIPLE BOTTOM and still just under the 200% advance on the base, making this a BUYING LEVEL for an investment, as the war was still on and war always is bullish on sugar. Prices gradually worked higher until November, 1940, crossing all tops since November, 1939, indicating higher prices.

1941—The real advance got under way. Prices crossed the 50%, or half-way point, of 3c to 175, and later crossed 240, the 300% on the base, or extreme low price.

1941—September, HIGH 305. This was a TRIPLE TOP against 1937 and 1939, and the 400% advance on the base, making this a NATURAL RESISTANCE LEVEL.

Watch all resistance points, extreme high and low points, double and triple tops, in the future.

Watch the months for seasonal changes in trend and apply all of the rules, and you will be able to determine the trend in sugar and the BUYING and SELLING POINTS.

Keep up the weekly HIGH and LOW charts on the most active option of sugar and this will help you to catch the trend quicker.

Again let me remind you to always use the STOP LOSS ORDER for your protection, because if you interpret the market wrong and the trend changes, the way to protect your capital is to place a STOP LOSS ORDER and take a small loss. Remember that there are always new opportunities for getting in the market and, if you watch and wait, you will find an opportunity to make back the small loss and make it very easily. Large losses are harder to make back and, when you have a large loss, it interferes with your judgment and, after you get out, you may have lost your nerve and are not able to make a trade again when a real opportunity comes.

No matter what commodity you trade in, study that commodity carefully. Go back over its past history and the knowledge of past movements will enable you to determine the correct trend in the future.

WOOL

Wool is traded in on the New York Cotton Exchange by the Wool Associates of the Cotton Exchange.

Wool is also traded in the foreign countries in the Antwerp Wool Market.

Futures are traded in on the New York Cotton Exchange, and the contract is for 5,000 pounds. Fluctuations are in 1/10 of a cent per pound and the minimum fluctuation of 1/10c is $5.00 on each contract.

The commission for buying and selling, regardless of the price, is $30.00 per contract.

Wool is grown in many countries of the world. The United States consumes a large amount of foreign wool and produces a large amount in this country as well. The finest wool comes from Australia and India. Also, very fine wool comes from China.

Wool follows the trend of wheat, cotton and other commodities, and naturally follows the trend of cotton closer than any other commodity. We are giving some swings of high and low prices from 1850 to 1941, to give you an idea of how to figure resistance levels and so that you can see where extreme highs and extreme lows have been made and where double tops have been made and double bottoms made in the past.

If you intend to trade in wool in the future, you should keep up a monthly high and low price of the future option, and also keep up weekly high and low charts. When wool is very active and at high levels, keep a daily high and low chart. Wool moves very fast once a move gets under way. War is always bullish on wool, as you can see by going over past war periods, and you can see that wool has always reached extreme highs during these periods. By studying the months when extreme highs and extreme lows have been reached over a number of years past, you will be able to locate the months when seasonal changes in trend take place.

As a comparison of how close wool runs to the trend of cotton, you will find that wool made high in 1918 and a high at slightly lower level in 1919, and a slightly lower top in 1920.

In 1932, July, wool made an extreme low. Cotton reached bottom in June, 1932.

1933, January and February, wool made a SECONDARY LOW, but higher than the July LOW. At the same time, in February, 1933, cotton made a SECONDARY LOW.

In 1937, wool made HIGH in January and February. Cotton reached high in April.

In 1938 and 1941, cotton made a series of bottoms and low levels, and wool did the same thing.

1938—June, LOW 65c. This was the EXTREME LOW on wool.

1939—April, LOW 69c.

1940—July, LOW 88c. From this you will see that from the low in 1938, wool made higher prices each year and then advanced to the highest level in November and December, 1940, and followed the advance of other commodities in 1941, reaching the highest levels for years.

HIGHS AND LOWS, 1913 TO 1941.

Below we are giving some of the imortant swings in wool to help you to determine resistance levels in the future.

1913—LOW   50c.

1920—HIGH $2.05.

1921—LOW   81c.

1924—HIGH $1.69.

1932—LOW   47½c. Down around the same lows as 1913. A BUYING
                 LEVEL.

1934—HIGH $1.11.

1935—LOW   71c.

1941—HIGH $1.30.

You will find a chart in the back of the book showing the quarterly swings on wool from 1912 to 1941.

"If I can throw a single ray of light
Across the darkened pathway of another;
If I can aid some soul to clearer sight
Of life and duty, and thus bless my brother;
If I can wipe from any human cheek a tear,
I shall not then have lived in vain while here."

CONCLUSION

Fully realizing the fact that the man who serves best, prospers most, and that the man who does the greatest good for others gets the most happiness out of life, I have written this book with the supreme desire to be of benefit to others and to help trade interests, investors, traders, to follow the trend of commodities more successfully and to teach them how to avoid pitfalls, prevent losses and protect their capital. After forty years of experience, in which time everything has happened to me that can happen to a trader in the future, I know that I am competent to offer advice and to give rules that I have found practical in the past.

It is not my object to teach people to go into speculation and reckless gambling, but to give them rules that will make them conservative and teach them how to prevent losses by the use of STOP LOSS ORDERS, and to protect their capital by eliminating the risk and by trading on facts—not guesswork.

To those who read my book and study it, I offer this suggestion. The book was not written just to be read over once and laid aside. The book was written for use and study and to be read over many times. Then the reader should make up charts and study them and watch the market as action develops from extreme highs to extreme lows from time to time. Prove to yourself that these rules work. Remember, there is no short-cut road to success. The man that makes the greatest success does not necessarily have to be the smartest man, but if he is the hardest worker, success will crown his efforts. Do not look for the easy way to make money—take the hard road and the hard way. The hard way is deep study and hard work.

I have done my best to give you the rules that will help you to make a success. It is up to you to learn the rules and follow them.

Never become discouraged. Remember "the time to act is when others show signs of tire. The battle is fought in the home stretch and won twixt the flag and the wire."

I have made a success because I never knew when I was licked—or, if so, I never admitted it to myself. I am thankful to say that my nerve has never failed me. The reason for this is because the nerve was backed by knowledge, which gave me confidnce to try again and win.

W. D. GANN.

NOVEMBER 18, 1941.

PREFACE

Since writing the first edition of HOW TO MAKE PROFITS IN COMMODITIES in 1941, the rules that I gave then have stood the TEST OF TIME and thousands of people who bought my book have made profits. This has resulted in a big demand for an up-to-date revised 1951 edition, which is the reason for publishing a new book containing some new rules and discoveries made since 1941.

The rules which I gave in 1941 and the new rules that I have worked out since are all based on mathematical law. They have always worked in the past and will continue to indicate the trend in the future. These rules determine the time to buy and sell in abnormal or war markets as well as in normal markets.

To be helpful to others is my greatest pleasure. Therefore it is very gratifying to have received so many letters from my readers expressing appreciation of my work. It is my sincere hope that traders and investors will study the rules and apply them and by protecting their capital with stop loss orders will be rewarded with profits.

W. D. GANN

June 6, 1951

FAST MOVES CORRECT POSITION IN SHORT
TIME PERIODS

After markets have been advancing for a long period of time, they become overbought. The public gets loaded up on the long side and shorts after fighting the advance, lose hope and cover. This leaves the market in a weak technical position at high levels, because the market has advanced too fast and made more than a normal gain. A correction or a decline to normal levels naturally follows. This correction could run for several weeks or several months, but when a rapid decline occurs in a comparatively short period of time and the decline in prices amounts to much more than a normal decline; then this fast decline corrects the weak technical position and another advance follows. For example:

MAY SOY BEANS—There was no trading in Soy Beans from January, 1943 to October, 1947, when May Soy Beans made a low of 334, and then advanced to 436¾ on January 15, 1948, which was the highest price that May Beans or any future option had ever sold. This was a rapid above-normal advance of 102¾ cents in 3 months and a correction was overdue. The decline to February 14, 1948 was sharp and swift with low at 320½, a decline of 116¼ cents in 30 days, wiping out more than the gain of 3 months. When declines of this kind occur, there is nearly always a secondary rally and many months may occur before the low level is broken. From February 14, 1948, an advance followed to May 19, 1948, high 325, where the May option ended.

The same rule applies when a market has been declining for a considerable period of time and shorts become overconfident and increase their lines, and at the same time longs lose hope and sell out near low levels. This causes the market to become oversold and the technical position becomes strong instead of weak, which results in a fast advance in a short period of time, bringing the market back to normal levels. For example:

MAY SOY BEANS—November 23, 1948, high 276¾. The decline started and from January 21, 1949, high 247½, the market declined to 201½ on February 9, 1949, a decline of 46 cents in 12 calendar days. This was a real clean-out in a short period of time and a correction was overdue. The first fast advance to February 16 carried prices up to 228½; then there was a secondary reaction to March 22 with a low at 210½. After that the market continued up to the end of the option in May, reaching 243.

By going over charts of past records, you can see how often these sharp advances and sharp declines in a short period of time correct the technical position of the market and a long period of time then occurs before high levels are crossed or low levels are broken.

TIME TURNS TREND

The meaning of a change in trend in variable time periods is that after a prolonged advance when final top is made, there is a reaction or a swing down which may last one, two, three days or more and then a swing up follows, making a lower top; from this top a decline follows, breaking the low levels of the first swing down. This is what I call a TIME TREND TURN, because it is not based on a decline of so many cents per bushel but on a decline of a certain number of days, followed by a rally of a certain number of days, which makes the change in trend. For example:

MAY SOY BEANS—October 28, 1947, low 334. Following that there was no SWING BOTTOM broken until January 15, 1948, high 436¾, followed by a reaction on the same day to 433¼. January 17, high 436¼, a slightly lower top. From this high a fast decline started and when prices broke the low of January 15, it was the first TIME CHANGE IN TREND since the advance started. From that time on no rally lasted more than one day until February 14, when the low was reached at 320½. In cases of this kind where the markets are at dangerously high levels, you should have a stop loss order under the low of January 15 and get out just as soon as this low was broken and sell short and stay short all the way down because there was no indication that bottom was being made until February 14, when a 3-day rally followed to February 17, indicating that the trend was changing.

An exception to the above rule occurs when the market has a sharp advance and makes a single top with no TIME TREND TURN. For example: NOVEMBER SOY BEANS low June 16, 1950, 208; then a higher top on June 24, which was Saturday; then on Monday, June 26, the Korean War broke out. This caused a rapid advance on public buying and short covering. July 26, high 272, up 62⅜ cents from June 24, an abnormal advance in a period of 30 days. The market made a sharp top; declined to 256 on August 2, followed by a one-day rally to August 3, high 261½. After that the first TIME TREND BOTTOM at 256 was broken. In this case, if you had waited until the TIME TREND TURN, the market would be down 16 cents a bushel. This would be too much profit to lose and too long to wait to go short. In cases of this kind, you would apply the rules on GAPS, REVERSE SIGNAL DAYS, RESISTANCE LEVELS, and LIMIT DAYS, which will be given later, which would get you out the following day after the top and put you short.

TIME TURNS TREND AT TOP LEVEL

On February 8, 1951, NOVEMBER SOY BEANS opened at 329 and advanced the same day to 334. Note that the extreme high had been 383 and the extreme low 191¼, making the ¾ point 335, which would be a natural resistance and selling level, where you could have gone short with a stop loss order at 338 or 3c above the resistance level. However, from this top the market had a TIME TREND TURN which gave definite indication that the top had been made. February 10, low 326½; February 13, high 331½; February 15, low 325, which had broken the bottom of February 10, indicating that the minor trend, at least, was turning down. A rally followed to February 19, high 332½, making two tops lower than February 8. When the low of February 15 was broken at 325, this was a definite indication of a TIME TREND TURN and you should have gone short. The decline was rapid, reaching first low on March 15 at 286½; then after a minor rally, the trend continued down.

TIME TURNS TREND AT LOW LEVEL

Example: NOVEMBER SOY BEANS. June 25, 1950, high 230. This was a double top and a selling level because the previous high had occurred at the same level on May 3. Prices declined, making three swings down, reaching low of 208 on June 16, followed by a rally to 215 on June 21; then a secondary decline to 209⅝ on June 24. This was a higher bottom and the war news came on June 26. As soon as prices crossed 216, which was one cent above the high of June 21, this was a TIME TREND TURN, and if you had not already bought, this was an indication to buy to hold for the big advance which followed.

Apply these same rules to any other Grain, Cotton or other Commodity.

NORMAL PRICE MOVES

Prices always move slower at low levels and faster at high levels. It is therefore well to figure what a normal move would be at the different levels.

When Soy Beans or any other Grain is selling at $1.00 per bushel, a normal reaction would be 6¼ cents or 1/16 of $1.00.

When prices are selling around $2.00, a normal move would be 12½ cents per bushel.

When prices are selling around $3.00 per bushel, a normal move would be three times as much as at $1.00 per bushel or 18¾ cents per bushel.

When prices advance or decline more than 18¾ cents, the next point to watch would be 37½ cents advance or decline from the extreme high or low level.

NORMAL TIME MOVES

In a normal market, when prices are advancing slowly and not running up the limit, after prices have moved up several weeks or several months, a normal reaction is 10 to 14 days. When this is exceeded, the next normal reaction is 28 to 30 days. These are important time periods to watch.

Reverse this rule for a bear or declining market, when rallies last 10 to 14 days and sometimes 28 to 30 days.

As a general rule, a move that exceeds 30 days up or down means that the trend is likely to continue on for two months or 60 days.

It is important to remember that the closing price on a daily high and low chart, a weekly high and low chart, or a monthly high and low chart is very important. Example: Suppose prices have been advancing for 14 days and the high is made on the 14th day and prices close near the low of the day, you would then consider that the move was not going to continue upward until prices crossed the high of the 14th day and closed well above it.

TIME PERIODS

You should always figure the time from any top or high level to the next top or high point. Also figure the time from any low level to the next low level. Then figure the time from a low level to a high level and the time from the last high level down to the low level. By doing this, you will know when time periods balance or come out about the same as a previous move. This is BALANCING OF TIME. By knowing these dates and prices, it will help you to determine the duration of the next move. The longer the period of time that elapses before a previous high level is crossed or a previous low level is broken, the greater the advance or decline which follows: For example:

In January, 1925, MAY WHEAT high 205⅞, which was the last high before it declined to 43⅝ on December 26, 1932. This high level of 205⅞ was not crossed until 1947. After such a long period of time, you would figure that Wheat could advance 50% of 205⅞, which would give a high of 308⅝. In November, 1947, and January, 1948, May Wheat advanced to 306⅞, which was the highest level it reached after the war ended in 1945.

Another example: Future trading in NOVEMBER SOY BEANS tarted July 7, 1947, low 265. November 22, high 383, which was the highest price at which this option has sold up to this writing. 1948, June 15, high 347½, which was the first lower top on the big swings. 1950, February 6, low 191¼, extreme low up to this writing. 1951, February 8, high 334. This makes 383, 347½, and 334 the important high levels to figure percentage and resistance levels against the extreme low of 191¼ and any other minor lows. These dates of extreme highs and lows are important for TIME PERIODS, running 6½ to 7 weeks, 13 weeks, 17 weeks, 20 weeks, 26 weeks, 32½ weeks, 35 weeks, 42 to 45 weeks, and 52 weeks. Carry these same

TIME PERIODS throughout future years and watch for changes in trend around these dates. All the ANNIVERSARY DATES or the dates which are one year from any extreme high or low are the most important.

PRICE SWINGS OVERBALANCED

When prices have advanced for a considerable period of time and have made several reverse swings, the first time a reverse swing or reaction exceeds the previous downswing, it is an indication that the trend is changing. But never consider that the trend has definitely changed until the TIME PERIOD has OVERBALANCED. Example: If prices have been advancing for a considerable time and there have been several reactions running 5 to 7 days; then a downswing starts and runs more than 7 days, it is an indication that the trend is changing, at least temporarily. If the price reaction had also overbalanced, then it would be a definite indication of a change in trend, either minor or major.

In a declining market, keep account of all the rallies and how many cents the market has rallied from time to time and also record the time period of each rally; then when low is reached and the advance exceeds the previous or last swing up and the time period is also greater than the previous rallies in a Bear Market, it is an indication that both PRICE and TIME are OVERBALANCED and the trend is changing.

Remember that all rules work best when markets are very active and near extreme high or extreme low levels. Changes in trend which occur between extreme high and low do not mean as much as a reversal when prices are near extreme high or low and are very active. Always use all the rules and not just one or two of them, especially when prices are at extreme high or extreme low levels.

PRICES TO USE FOR TREND INDICATIONS

The extreme low and the extreme high of any Future Commodity Option are the most important prices to figure TREND   ˹ ˢ˰ TIONS and to arrive at Supply and Demand levels and get buying and selling points.

The lowest and highest Cash Price is also good to use as a ba for future indications provided the low for a Cash commodity w ˢ lower than the Future Option ever sold and the highest price higher than any Future Option sold. But the extreme high and low levels of a Future Option are the most important TREND INDICATORS.

The percentage of the extreme high price and the percentage of the extreme low price should be used.

Secondary highs or lower tops and secondary lows or higher

bottoms can also be used but should be considered of secondary importance.

Examples—EXTREME HIGHS AND LOWS

1936, October 5—Future trading started in Soy Beans.

1939, July—May Beans extreme low 67c.

1948, January 15—Extreme high 436¾.

These are the most important prices to use for May Soy Beans. CASH SOY BEANS—1920, February 15, high 405, highest in history up to that time. 1932, December 28, extreme low 44c. You should use the PERCENTAGE of 44c as a basis for resistance levels in Future Options. Divide 44 by 8 gives 5½c. ¼ or 25% is 11c. ⅜ or 37½% is 16½c. 1/2 or 50% is 22c. Add 22c to 44, the base, gives 66c. Note 67c was the lowest price for May Futures in July, 1939. 9 times 44c or a gain of 900% added to 44 gives 440 and the highest for May Futures was 436¾.

MAY SOY BEANS—Low 67c is the base price for future indications. 1941, September 14, high 202. 1942, January high 203. Note that 3 times 67c or an advance of 200% on 67c gives 201, making this a resistance and selling level. Also ½ of 405, Cash Price, gives 202½ as a resistance level.

In 1947, when May Soy Beans were well above 203, the highest price for Futures previous to that time, if you figured an advance of 100% on 203, it would give 406. Note that in 1920 the highest Cash Price was 405. When prices advanced above 405 in 1947, they indicated higher.

In June, 1930, the last high for Cash Beans was 216. When this price was crossed, you would add 100% on 216 or double the price, which would give 432 as a possible final high. The extreme high was 436¾.

By using the percentage of 67c, extreme low of May Futures, we get closest to the final high. 5½ times 67 or 550% gives 368½. Add this to the base of 67c gives 435½, missing the top by 1¼c. This is proof that FUTURE high and low prices are the best to use for trend indications and for buying and selling levels.

Between 67c and 436¾, the important ½ point is 251⅞. From 44c to 436¾, the ½ point is 240⅜. ½ of 436¾ is 218⅜. All of these prices are important when the Future option advances above them or declines below them. Study the charts and see what has happened around these prices in the past.

Example: 1948, October, May Beans declined to 239, just below the ½ point between 44c and 436¾. This was a buying level. Later they crossed 251⅞, which indicated higher and advanced to 276¾ in November, 1948. Later, they broke 251⅞ and 240⅜ and 218⅜, all of which indicated lower. The final low came when prices reached 201½ in February, 1949.

Why did prices get support and make low at 201½ after they had declined from 436¾?

1. This was the top level of 1941-42. My rule says, "Old tops become bottoms and old bottoms become tops."
2. ½ of 405 is 202½. Another reason for support around this level.
3. Most important of all, 3 times 67c, or an advance of 200% on 67c, equals 201, making this a support and buying level.
4. When prices advance to around $1.00, $2.00, and $3.00 a bushel, there is always selling around these even figures. When they decline to around the even figures, there is public buying and support.

From the low of 201½ in 1949, May Soy Beans advanced to 344½ in February, 1951, just before the Government froze prices. Why did May Beans make a high of 344½ before the Government price ceiling was fixed at 333? Because 344⅜ was the ¾ point between 67c and 436¾, making this the next most important selling level after the main ½ point was crossed, again proving the importance of using the extreme low and extreme high prices of Futures.

1950, October 16—May Soy Beans low 232½, which was the last low before the price advanced to 344½. Why was this low of 232½ a support or buying level? The main mathematical reason was that 250% of 67 added to 67 equals 234½, making this a support and buying level when confirmed by other rules.

Remember, ½ of any price or 50% decline or advance is most important. After the low of October 16, 1950, May Soy Beans crossed 240⅜, the ½ point between 44 and 436¾ and next crossed 251⅞, which is the ½ point between 67 and 436¾. Getting above this important ½ point of the range in Future high and low was a strong indication of much higher prices and indicated the possibility of the next strongest resistance level or ¾ point between 67 and 436¾, which was 344⅜. And the extreme high was 344½.

November Soy Beans—Extreme high 383 in November, 1937. Extreme low 191¼ on February 5, 1950. Note that ½ of 383 is 191½, making this a safe buying level with stop loss order at 188. 1951, February 8, high 334. What was the mathematical reason for this top price? From 191¼ to 383, ¾ of the range is 335, making 334 a safe selling level when it was confirmed by other rules as a top, and also by so many time periods of previous tops and bottoms coming out in February. The extreme low on November Beans occurred February 6, 1950, and this secondary high was made February 8, 1951, an Anniversary Date one year from the extreme low, making it important to watch for a change in trend.

Keep up all figures from extreme high and low prices and the dates when extreme highs and lows have been made and apply all the rules which I have given and you will make a success.

IMPORTANT NEWS CAUSES TREND CHANGES

On page 58 you will find information on "Anniversary Dates and Seasonal Changes." These dates are based on the high and low prices in different years, but when war breaks out or some other sudden unexpected news is announced, the last extreme low or the last extreme high price (at the time this news comes out) is very important to carry time periods from and figure resistance levels from.

On December 7, 1941, when the Japs attacked Pearl Harbor, the sudden unexpected news brought price changes, therefore the dates at that time are important. The next most important date was June 26, 1950, when the Korean War started, which was unexpected news that caused a rapid advance in all Grains and most commodities. Therefore the lows of June 24, just previous to this news, are very important for calculating future dates and resistance levels.

NOVEMBER SOY BEANS—June 24, 1950, low 209⅜. July 26 high 272, an advance of 62⅜ cents in approximately 30 days. The low of 209⅝ is important to figure resistance levels from. From July 26 to October 16 prices declined to 226¾, which was ¾ or 75% decline of the range between 209⅝ and 272, making this a natural support and buying level. After October 16, when prices advanced and crossed 249⅜ (the ½ point), it was an indication of higher prices; and later when prices crossed 272, the high of July 26, they indicated higher. If we add the first advance of 62⅜ cents to 272, we get 334⅜ as a balancing point or the point which makes 272 the ½ point between 209⅝ and 334⅜. The extreme high on February 8, 1951, was 334.

After the high of 334, you would figure resistance levels between this high and the extreme low of 191¼, which was recorded February 6, 1950. This extreme low of 191¼ was a 50% decline or ½ the highest price that November Soy Beans ever sold, which gives 262⅝ as the important ½ point of the swing which lasted for one year. The ½ point or 50% between 191¼ and 383 is 287⅛, a support and buying level. On March 15, 1951, November Beans declined to 286½ and rallied from this level to 305½; then the decline was resumed.

For TIME PERIODS you would watch one, two, or three years from June 24 and June 26, 1950, the low just before the Korean War started and the date of the starting of this war.

In 1952 you should watch February 6 to 14, because these are the dates of previous lows and highs. In fact, in any future year watch the market for a change in trend around these dates in February because these are dates for seasonal change in trend, anyway.

SWING TRADING MOST PROFITABLE

Many traders buy right or sell right and then take 7, 10, or 15 cents' profit, getting out of the market just because they have a profit without using any rule, whereas they could have profits of 60 cents to $1.00 per bushel if they followed rules until there was a reverse move in a SWING. It does not pay to try to scalp the market or to trade for short swings.

Examples of SWINGS in JULY SOY BEANS—1950

Feb. 6—Low 219, May 8—High 321, up $1.02 per bushel in 3 months and no SWING BOTTOM was broken during that time and no reaction lasted more than 3 days. The profit on this SWING, trading in 10,000 bushels, would be $10,200.00.

Oct. 16—Low 233½, Feb. 8, 1951—High 334, up $1.10 per bushel. The greatest reaction lasted only 5 days and no SWING BOTTOM was broken. Profits on 10,000 bushels would have been $11,050.00.

If you could have caught 75% of these two SWINGS, the profit would have been $15,936.00. You could have started with a capital of $3,000.00 and would not have had to risk more than $300.00 of your capital. By pyramiding during this period and buying more after you had 20c a bushel profit, your profits would have been well over $40,000.00.

You can go over past records for any period and prove to yourself that SWING TRADING is the most profitable and that it pays to follow rules and not guess.

SWING CHARTS

Swing Charts are very valuable. The best kind to keep for daily moves is a chart which records all reverse moves or reactions that run 2 to 3 days; then after there has been a series of advances or up-swings, the first time prices break below the last SWING BOTTOM on the 2 or 3-day chart, it is indication the trend is changing.

When a market is declining and has run for a considerable length of time, making lower tops and lower bottoms on the 2 or 3-day chart, the first time it crosses the last high on this SWING CHART, it is an indication that the trend is changing and that a further rally will take place.

WEEKLY SWING CHARTS

A Swing Chart which records reverse moves of 7 calendar days or more, is of greater importance for a change in trend than the 2 or 3-day chart. Suppose a market starts to advance and continues to advance for 4 weeks without breaking the low of any previous week; then it reacts 7 days or more, you would move your SWING CHART down to the bottom of the reaction. After it crosses the top of the 4 weeks' upswing, it might continue to move up for 7 or 8 weeks or even 13 or 14 weeks without breaking the low of any previous week; then have a reaction or swing down of 7 days or more, followed by an upswing of 7 days or more; after that, should prices decline and break the low of the previous downswing, it would be an indication that the trend has changed.

Apply this same rule in a declining market. After the last downswing, when the first rally comes and crosses the high of the previous upswing in a Bear Market, it is an indication of a change in trend.

I consider the 7-DAY SWING CHART one of the most valuable trend indicators. You can start counting the time period from any extreme high or extreme low and when the advance or decline runs for 7 calendar days or more, you would move the Swing Chart up or down. Example:

NOVEMBER SOY BEANS—June 16, 1950, low 208. There were 4 upswings to July 26, high 272. None of these reverse moves lasted more than 4 days. Therefore when the first downswing exceeded 4 days, it indicated a reversal or change in trend. The first decline reached 256 on August 2, 1950. This was a decline of 7 days and a decline of 16 cents per bushel. There was only one day rally; then the decline continued to August 15, low 236¼. There was a rally to 254½ on August 29. This was 14 days' advance followed by another decline. The final low of 226½ was reached on October 16. The greatest rally in time from September 25 to October 3, was 8 calendar days, which would move the 7-day Swing Chart up for the first time since the high of August 29. After that the market advanced from October 16 to 23, a period of 7 days, crossing 3 previous tops on the 2-day chart, which were all just below 240. A rapid advance followed with no reaction lasting 7 days until the option expired or reached high at 299 on November 20. These examples prove the value of these SWING CHARTS for long pull trading.

3 RULES FOR DETERMINING EXTREME PRICES

When prices are very active and making a wide range in prices, either in a fast advancing market or a fast declining market, we use the daily high and low chart to determine the first change in trend, using three important rules: REVERSE SIGNAL DAY, GAP DAYS and LIMIT DAYS.

REVERSE SIGNAL DAY

A REVERSE SIGNAL DAY is when the price opens higher than the high of the previous day and advances to a new high for that particular move; then declines and closes near the low of the day, which is an indication of weakness. I call this a REVERSE SIGNAL DAY and indication for a change in trend. If on this same day, it is a GAP DAY and a LIMIT DAY (explained later), it is of greater importance for a change in trend.

A REVERSE SIGNAL DAY in a declining market—After a prolonged decline the end often comes with a wide swing and a sudden sharp decline. The market opens lower than the low of the previous day; declines to a new low level for that particular downswing and later in the day the market rallies and closes near the high of the day day and in some cases above the range of the previous day, this is what I call a REVERSE SIGNAL DAY in a declining market, because the market is weak in the early part of the day, making a new low level, and strong late in the day, closing near the high.

Do not overlook the fact that a change in trend can come on a REVERSE SIGNAL DAY without it being a GAP DAY or a LIMIT DAY, especially when prices have been declining for 7 to 10 days and possibly as much as 14 days without ever crossing the high of the previous day. When a reversal comes and the high of the previous day is exceeded and the market closes above it, it is a REVERSE SIGNAL DAY, indicating a change in trend.

In a fast advancing market when prices have not broken the low of a previous day for a period of 7 to 10 days or a period of 14 days or more, the first day that prices break the low of a previous day and close near the low of the day, it is a REVERSE SIGNAL DAY, regardless of whether it is a GAP or a LIMIT DAY, but it is more important for a change in trend when it is a GAP DAY and a LIMIT DAY.

GAPS AND WHAT THEY INDICATE ON GRAINS

For the benefit of new traders who are not familiar with GAPS, I will explain just what is meant by GAPS in prices. It is the space or area formed when an option of Grain or other commodity opens up one to 3 cents or more overnight or opens down one to 3 cents or more overnight and does not trade in this area during that day. This creates what I call a vacuum or GAP in prices.

GAP ON THE UPSIDE

This is a range where there is no trading between the high of the previous day and the opening on the following day and all of the buying is above the opening of that day. This is what I call a vacuum or GAP ON THE UPSIDE. For instance, if the high on Monday was 124 and the opening the next day, Tuesday, was 127 and it did not sell below 127 all that day, this would leave a GAP from 124 to 127 in which there was no trading. This GAP may not be filled for 3 days,

3 weeks, 3 months, and in some cases GAPS are not filled for several years.

GAP ON THE DOWNSIDE

Suppose Soy Beans, Wheat, Corn or any other Commodity was declining and the price on Wednesday was 154 and the next day, Thursday, the price opened at 150 and continued to decline and during that day did not sell higher than 150, this would leave a range from 154 to 150 or 4 cents a bushel in which there was no trading during the day This is a GAP ON THE DOWNSIDE.

CAUSE OF GAPS

The cause of GAPS is usually due to some sensational or unexpected news which comes overnight. In an advancing market the public rush in to buy and shorts scramble to cover as soon as the news is out. If this happens overnight or over a weekend, then buying orders pile up before the opening of the market, causing the demand to far exceed the supply. Therefore the market is bid up several cents at the opening, leaving a GAP.

In a declining market, traders who have been holding on and hoping for a rally finally lose hope in the last stage and when some unfavorable news comes out, they all try to sell at once and at the same time shorts put out additional lines, causing the market to open several cents lower, leaving a GAP.

GAPS are often important in determining the culmination of a major swing at high levels or at low levels. I am going to give you rules and examples to prove when GAPS are important signals at such culminations.

EXHAUST GAPS ON UPSIDE

After a prolonged advance in a Grain option or any commodity, sometimes there occurs just one day with a GAP, which is often a REVERSE SIGNAL DAY. Many times this occurs near some important $\frac{1}{2}$ point. When a GAP of this kind occurs and the price declines the following day and fills the GAP, it is what I call an EXHAUST GAP. Your stop-loss order at this time should be 1c below the lowest price on the day the GAP is made, or if it is a REVERSE SIGNAL DAY, you can sell out at the opening of the following day or on any small rally. However, as a rule you should place a stop-loss order 1c under the low of the day the GAP was made and then reverse position when the stop is caught.

Example—NOVEMBER SOY BEANS-1950

July 15 High 250½, closed 249.

July 17 Monday, a large accumulation of buying orders came in.

Opening price 254, low 253, high 257½, close 255. This was not a REVERSE SIGNAL DAY but it was a GAP DAY because the lowest price was 2½c above the high of the previous day. Therefore, you would place a stop-loss order at 252, which was 1c under the low of July 17. This would put you out of long Beans and put you short at 252. A sharp decline followed.

July 19 Low 240, which was a buying level because it was at the ½ point of 44c to 436¾.

July 21 High 253, low 249, closed at 253 on the top, leaving a GAP at 247½. Your stop-loss order should be at 246½ or 1c under the low of the GAP DAY.

July 22 Low 248. Did not catch stop-loss order because it did not go 1c below the GAP.

July 25 Low 253½, high 263, closed at 263.

July 26 Prices opened strong at 266, which was 3c above the closing price, leaving a GAP 3c wide. Low 266, high 272, closing price 268. This was a REVERSE SIGNAL DAY and 269⅜ was ½ point between 191¼ and 347½. Here were two reasons why you should sell out November Beans on July 26 and go short because it was a REVERSE SIGNAL DAY and at an important ½ point. Prices had a sensational advance and if you did not sell out, you should raise your stop-loss order to 265, 1c under the low level of July 26 when the GAP was made.

July 27 The GAP was filled. The option closed at 264 and continued down.

EXHAUST GAPS ON DOWNSIDE

When a market has been declining for a considerable period of time and the range of decline is quite large, GAPS are of greater importance. EXHAUST GAPS can occur on the extreme low day, the same as they can occur at an extreme high. This is usually due to a large accumulation of selling orders which causes the market to open off, leaving a GAP, and if it is just one day and the GAP is filled the following day, it is an EXHAUST GAP and a REVERSE SIGNAL DAY and often occurs near an important ½ point. When you are short of the market and such a GAP occurs after a prolonged decline and the volume of sales increases over previous days, you should pull stop-loss orders down 1c above the highest price made on the day the GAP occurred or cover shorts and buy the first time the market goes above the high of the GAP DAY.

Example—NOVEMBER SOY BEANS-1950

Sept. 16 Hight 241½, low 239¼, closed at 240. Note that 240 is an important ½ point. Large buying or selling orders often occur around these important points. The market had declined at this time from the high of 254 and from the extreme of 272.

Sept. 18 High 238, low 233½, closed at 236, leaving a GAP from 238 to 239¼, which was the low of the previous day. This GAP was not filled for some time. Your stop-loss order on short Beans would have been pulled down to 239 or 1c above the high of September 18.

Sept. 25. Prices declined to 231¼, which was the ½ point between 191¼ and 272. This was the natural support and buying level for at least a moderate rally.

Oct. 4 High 239¼, which filled the GAP, and advanced to the low of September 16 but failed to reach the closing price. The reason it failed to go thru this level was because 240⅜ was the important ½ point. Therefore, you could have sold short at this level and placed a stop-loss order at 241⅜.

Oct. 16 Low 226½. This was a REVERSE SIGNAL DAY. Prices declined at the opening only ½c per bushel under the low of September 14; then rallied and closed above the close of September 15 and near the high price of the day. This was a REVERSE SIGNAL DAY and the time to cover shorts and buy even though there was no GAP at this time. If you did not cover shorts, when you observed near the closing of that market day, that it was SIGNAL DAY, you would have placed a stop-loss order at 230¾, 1c above the high of September 16.

NUMBER OF GAPS

The number of GAPS that occur in a major swing or a long campaign are quite important. As a general rule, when 3 to 4 consecutive GAPS have occurred in new high territory in an advancing market or new low ground in a declining market, the price is near a culmination for some kind of a reverse move by the time the third or fourth GAP is made. But often, counting the WITHIN GAPS, there may be as many as 6 to 7 GAPS before a culmination and in extreme cases as many as 10 GAPS may occur. Some of them may be filled with a reaction running 2 to 3 days but quite a few will be left before the market reverses and starts to fill the GAPS.

A good rule to remember is that after an EXHAUST GAP is made at extreme high or extreme low, then a reverse move starts and continues for as much as 3 consecutive days from the high where the GAP was made, it is an indication that the trend is changing, at least temporarily. In a declining market. when an EXHAUST GAP occurs at the bottom of a decline and a rally follows for 3 days, it is a good indication of a change in trend.

ILLUSTRATION—NOVEMBER SOY BEANS-1950

June 24 to 26, GAPS.   This was the war run.

July   3 Gap at new high for the move.

July   5 Gap filled, only one-day decline; then crossed top of July 3 and continued up.

July 17 Gap at new high levels.   High 257½, low 253 that day.   The gap was filled the following day.

July 19 Low 240, down 17½c in 2 days, a move down on 2-day chart, which was a short time period that corrected an overbought market.   240, being an important ½ point, made this a support and buying level.   The fact that this decline of 17½c per bushel was the greatest since June 16 low was a WARNING SIGNAL that top might come in the near future.

July 25 LIMIT DAY, prices up 10c per bushel; closed strong at the high of the day.

July 26 The price was within one cent of the LIMIT DAY.   It was a GAP DAY and the 4th GAP since June 24.   It was also a REVERSE SIGNAL DAY, confirming three rules that this was top after an abnormal swing up lasting 30 days and advancing 64c per bushel.   With these three indications that the market had made top, you should either sell out at the market or place a stop-loss order one cent below the lowest

July 27 The GAP made on July 26 was filled.   You should then be out of the market and go short protecting with a stop-loss order one to two cents above the high of July 26.

INSIDE GAPS

After a market has made top and a reaction follows for several days; then a GAP occurs above the high of the previous day, but on the day the GAP is made, the high is not a new high, this is an INSIDE GAP.   Reverse this in a Bear Market.   INSIDE GAPS are not as important as those which occur at extreme tops and bottoms.

GAPS AT OPENING OF NEW OPTIONS

It often happens that at the end of the May Option or any other option of Grain or other commodity, when the new option for the following year starts, it may open far below the low or far above the high of the previous option.   These GAPS that are left between the high of the previous option and the opening of the new option or between the low of the previous option and the opening of the new option are more important for the long pull than GAPS made on a daily high and low chart or a weekly high and low chart.

When a new option opens above the high of the previous option, leaving a GAP in prices, it is nearly always an indication that prices are going higher before the GAP is filled.

When a new option opens far below the low of the previous option, leaving a GAP in prices, it is likely to decline to a lower level before the GAP is filled.

Example—MAY SOY BEANS

1948 January 15, high 436¾. February 9, extreme low of option occurred at 320½. Then rallied to 425 in May, 1948, which was the end of the option. When the next option for 1949 delivery opened in October, 1948, the price was around 245, which left a GAP below the low of 320½ of the previous option. The 1949 option declined to 239 in October, 1948. This was a support and buying level because it was the main ½ point between 44c, extreme low in December, 1932, and 436¾, extreme high in January, 1948. On November 23, 1948, it made high at 276½, final high for the option. This still left a GAP of 44c from the low of 320½ of the previous option.

1949 The decline continued until February 14, 1949, reaching extreme low at 201½. This was down to the old tops of 1941 and 1942. Also 202½ was ½ of 405, the high of 1920. The 1949 option ended at 241 in May, 1949. The option for 1950 delivery made a low of 220½ in November, 1949, which was a support and buying level because 218⅜ was ½ of 436¾. This option then started to advance.

1950 In March, 1950, it crossed the ½ point at 240 and two tops at 243 and 244, indicating higher prices. In May, 1950 it crossed 276½, the high of November, 1948, moving into the GAP territory. We would then figure that the price could move up and fill the GAP at 320½. It advanced to 323½ on May 8, 1950.

From the low of 1948 to the high of May, 1950 the time was 27 months before the GAP was filled. The fact that the price opened so far below this GAP indicated that it was a Bear Market and that prices would go lower before the GAP was filled.

GAPS AND DAILY LIMITS

At the time of this writing, the LIMIT of fluctuations on Soy Beans in any one day is 10c per bushel, which means that the price can advance or decline 10c from the closing price of the previous day. The LIMIT on Wheat is 8c per bushel each day.

When prices move up the LIMIT in one day, it is the result of increased demand and heavy buying both for long and short accounts.

When prices move down the LIMIT in one day, it is the result of heavy liquidation by the public and further selling by shorts who become overconfident of lower prices. Often when prices move the LIMIT in one day, there is a GAP and when prices are at the extreme, it is often a REVERSE SIGNAL DAY and frequently near some important resistance level.

When markets are very active and prices are moving rapidly, they sometimes go the LIMIT for 3 to 4 consecutive days. In September, 1939, when Hitler started the war, Wheat prices moved up the LIMIT for 4 consecutive days and made top at the opening of the 5th day; then a sharp decline followed. However, under normal conditions, prices seldom go up or down the LIMIT for more than 2 to 3 days. When they go up the LIMIT for 2 consecutive days in an advancing market and close at the extreme high for the day, it is generally safe to sell at the opening the following day and place a stop-loss order 2 to 3c away. In a declining market, when prices go down the LIMIT for 2 consecutive days and close on the extreme low for the day, it is usually safe to buy at the opening the following day and place a stop-loss order 2 to 3c away.

If on the same day that the price goes up the LIMIT and gives a REVERSE SIGNAL, it leaves a GAP above the high of the previous day, it is an indication that it is final high. If on the following day, it starts to decline and fill the GAP left on the day extreme high was reached, it is an indication that the trend has changed and that prices are going lower. These three indications can be confirmed later by OVERBALANCING PRICE REACTION and previous TIME PERIODS. The top can also be confirmed by an important RESISTANCE LEVEL, such as, the ½ point. Reverse this rule in a Bear campaign or declining market.

Example—NOVEMBER SOY BEANS-1950

July 25 Prices advanced the LIMIT and closed at extreme high of the day.

July 26 Opened higher, leaving a GAP and made a REVERSE SIGNAL DAY. This was after an advance of 32c per bushel in 6 market days, and leaving a GAP and also a SIGNAL DAY. The 7 to 10 Day Rule could be applied as well as the Weekly Time Rule, which was 30 days from June 24 low, 60 days from May 25, and 4 months or 1/3 of a year from March 27 high, making this a time to sell out longs and go short because it was an EXHAUST GAP, a REVERSE SIGNAL DAY, and prices had gone up the LIMIT and were at an important ½ POINT.

Oct. 16 Low 226½, a SIGNAL DAY and a day to cover shorts and buy based on the 7 to 10 Day Rule and Resistance Level.

Oct. 18 Opened higher, leaving a small GAP and advanced the LIMIT, closing at the high price of the day, and after this time did not give a signal for lower prices. Reactions were very small.

Oct. 25 Opened sharply higher, leaving a GAP and advanced the LIMIT of 10c per bushel, closing only 1c below the high of the day. This was the second time since October 16 that prices had advanced the LIMIT.

Oct. 27 The advance continued thru October 26 and 27, making new high levels, up within 8c of the high of the life of the option. Still there was no SIGNAL DAY and prices had not broken 1c per bushel below the low of any previous day since the bottom on October 16.

Do not overlook the fact that when a GAP is filled either way, it does not mean that the main trend is changing, but it does mean that the minor trend is reversing and it may later be confirmed that the main trend has changed.

Always watch for GAPS after a prolonged advanced or a prolonged decline and then apply all the rules. Also watch for SIGNAL DAYS and LIMIT DAYS when there has been a prolonged advance or a prolonged decline. Apply the 7 to 10 Day Rule when prices have been advancing and making higher bottoms each day, or when they have been declining and making lower bottoms each day.

LONG TERM INVESTMENTS IN COMMODITIES

People often write me and say, "I would like to trade in Commodity Futures because I know they are very profitable but you cannot carry them for long-term income tax gains the same as you can stocks." Other people think that trading in Future Options is like gambling and that it is dangerous.

Buying and selling Commodity Futures is just as legitimate as investing in Stocks because you are dealing in the necessities of life. You can trade in Commodities for long-term capital gains and save on your taxes. This is the way you do it. Suppose that soon after February 6, 1950, when November Soy Beans was selling at ½ the extreme high price and indicated they should be bought, you would have bought, maybe as late as February 20 after they showed definite uptrend. On July 26, 1950, November Beans made high at 272 and by three rules there was an indication that they should be sold. You had large profits but you would say, "If I sell out before the six months' period, I will have to pay all the profits for taxes." This is what you would do:

At the time November Beans sold at 272, May Beans sold at 279½, you would sell short an equal amount of May Beans and hold your long position in November Beans until the 6 months' period had expired.

The market declined and it would not make any difference where you sold out as you would have your profits equal to a price near the top. If you had sold May Beans short when they were at 275 and later in August when the market was much lower and the 6 months' period was up on the November Beans, you would sell them out and stay short of the May Beans until there was a definite indication that they had reached bottom.

October 16, 1950, or soon after that time, both May and November Beans indicated bottom by all the rules. You would cover your short position in May Beans and buy May Beans for long account. You would have a short-time gain on your short position and if at a later date, you had a short-time loss on something you bought, you could offset it by this short-time profit.

All options of Soy Beans advanced from October 16, 1950 to February, 1951. When the indications were that May Beans were high and it was time to sell, as the Government was freezing prices, you would not have a long-time gain on your May Beans bought in October, 1950. Therefore soon after February 8, 1951, when November Beans indicated top and a selling level (after they had made high at 334), you would sell short November Beans and hold your long position in May Beans until the 6 months' period was out some time in April. By that time you would still be able to sell May Beans at the price fixed by the Government and would have more than 40c profit in the short sale of November Beans. You would remain short of November Beans until they indicated bottom and if the May Option was being traded in, you would cover your short position in November Beans and again buy May Beans.

As a general rule, it pays to buy for long account the May and July options because from the Spring to Summer, the supply of old Beans is getting less. The reason November Beans is the better option to sell short is that the new crop can be delivered in November and prices will be depressed more than the May and July options.

Apply this same rule to any other Grain, Eggs, Cotton or any commodity. In this way you can make long-term gains by following the rules for Swing Trading as outlined.

CONCLUSION

In 1941, when I wrote the first edition of HOW TO MAKE PROFITS IN COMMODITIES, I said that the Soy Bean is King. Previous to that time Cotton had been King, providing the greatest money-making moves of any commodity. During the past ten years Soy Beans have remained on the throne as King of all Commodities as far as wide swings and fluctuations are concerned. They have proved to be more profitable for long pull trading than any other commodity. I am confident that if my readers follow the rules, they will make substantial profits in the years ahead.

Soy Beans have many wide swings in short periods of time because there are so many uses for them. People in trade lines buy and sell Soy Bean Futures. Speculators and investors trade in Soy Beans because the trend is so easy to follow and large profits can be made from small risks provided you use stop-loss orders for protection.

During war periods the demand for Soy Beans increases even more than some other Commodities due to the demand from various sources. After the United States entered the war in 1941 all commodities advanced and made a wide range in price swings. The Government stopped trading in Soy Beans in January, 1943 and trading was not resumed until July, 1947. After that the greatest activity and some of the widest swings in prices occurred from 1947 until 1951. If you will review the Swing Charts on Soy Beans in the back of this book, you will be able to see for yourself the possibilities for profits.

Wheat, Corn, Cotton, Cotton-seed Oil, Eggs, Coffee and Rubber have made wide swings in prices the same as Soy Beans. Eggs have been very profitable to trade in. Cotton-seed Oil proved to be a late mover, advancing to new high levels in 1947-1948, while Cotton made high in 1946. However, Cotton Futures reached extreme high in March, 1951. Some Commodities make new high or new low levels after other Commodities have made tops and started down or have made bottoms and started up.

Coffee made the greatest advance in history during 1950 (see Swing Chart.) Rubber Futures had the greatest advance in 1950 of any time since Future trading started. This was due in part to the outbreak of the Korean War in June, 1950.

The public has become interested in trading in Cotton, Coffee, Cotton-seed Oil, Soy Bean Oil, and Rubber during the past 7 years. They still trade in the old reliable Commoditites, such as, Wheat, Corn, Oats, Rye, and Cotton. These Commoditites still offer many opportunities for profitable swing trading, but it is my opinion that Soy Beans will remain King for a long time to come and offer some unusual money-making opportunities.

KNOWLEDGE BRINGS PROFITS

I strongly urge my readers to keep up charts and study market movements and apply mathematical scientific rules and gain Knowledge of the market before they risk their money. Do not trade on guesswork or gamble on hope. If investors and traders follow my old and new rules, my efforts will not have been in vain and I shall be amply rewarded in being able to help others.

W. D. GANN

June 6, 1951

CHART NO. 1—BUTTER
November and December Swing Chart—1930 to 1941

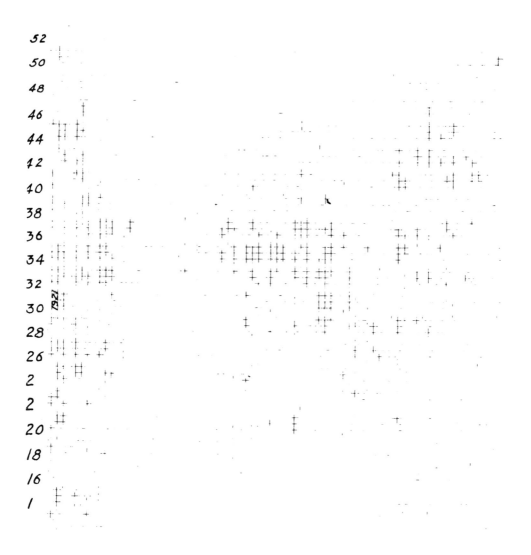

330

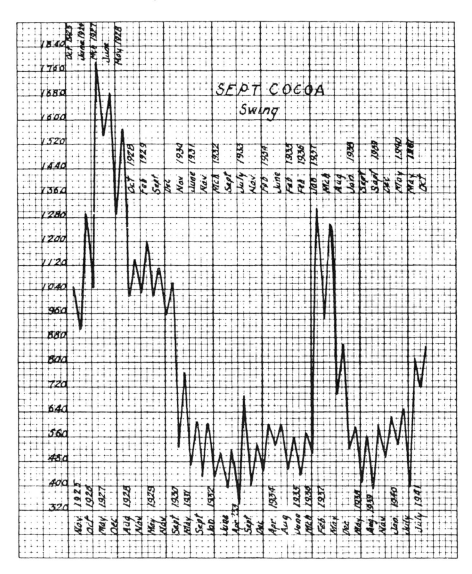

SEPT COCOA
Swing

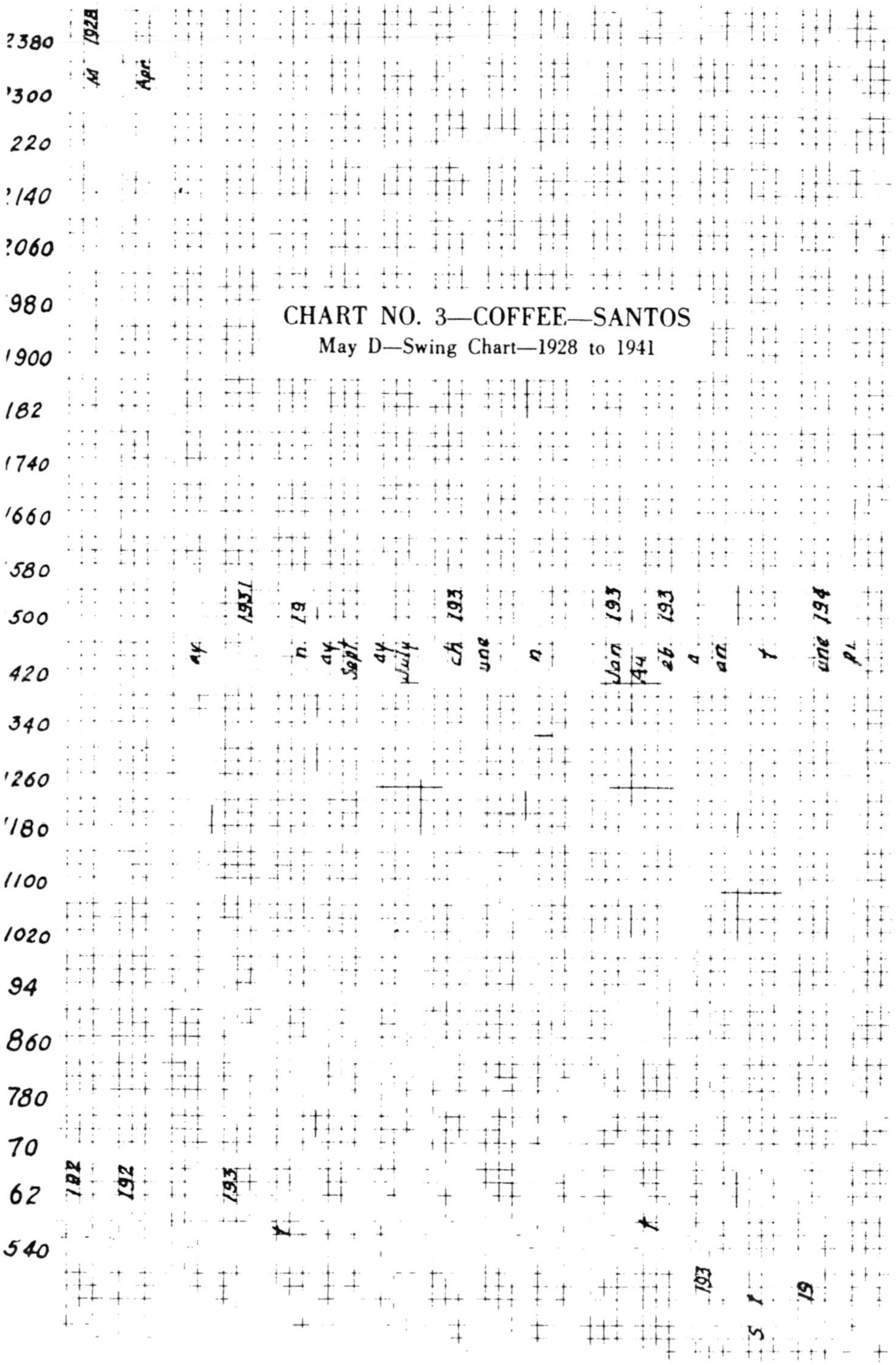

2380
'300
220
?140
?060
980

CHART NO. 3—COFFEE—SANTOS
May D—Swing Chart—1928 to 1941

1900
182
1740
'660
'580
500
420
340
'260
'180
1100
1020
94
860
780
70
62
540

CHART NO. 4—COFFEE—RIO
May—Swing Chart—1901 to 1941

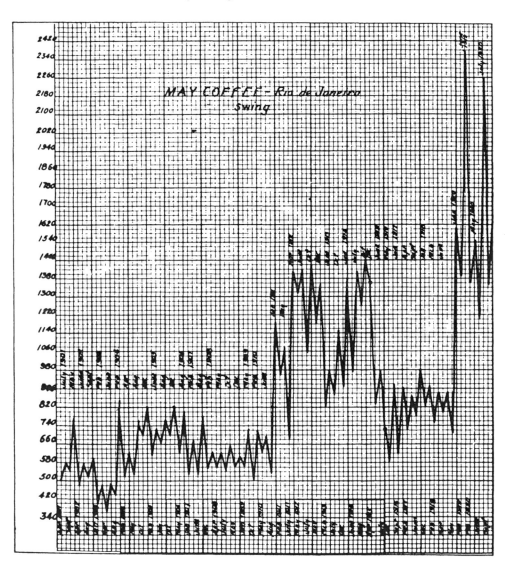

CHART NO. 4—COFFEE—RIO
May—Swing Chart—1901 to 1941

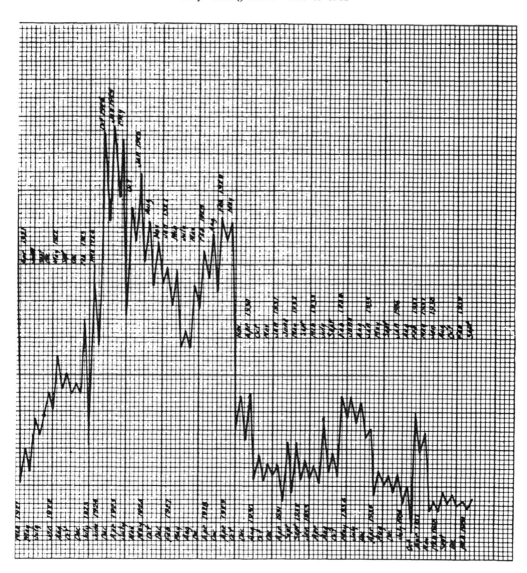

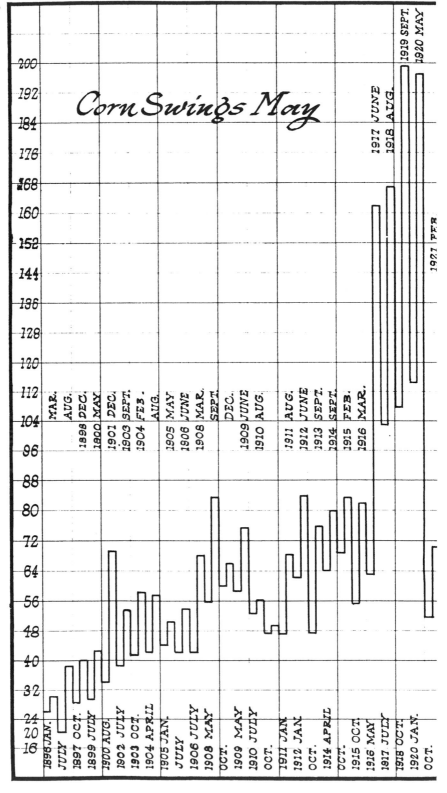

Corn Swings May

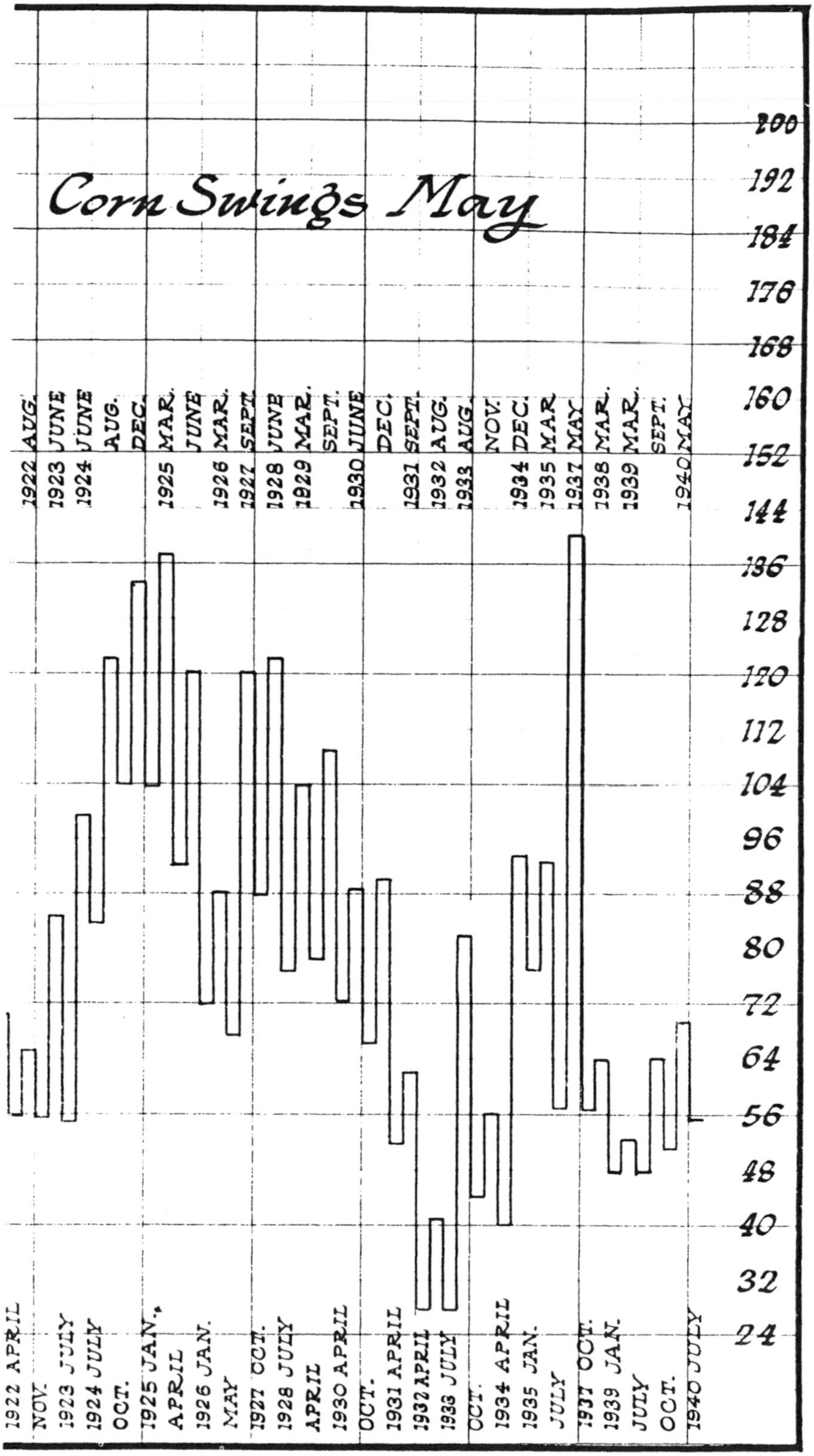
Corn Swings May
200
192
184
176
168
160
152
144
136
128
120
112
104
96
88
80
72
64
56
48
40
32
24
1922 AUG.
1923 JUNE
1924 JUNE
AUG.
DEC.
1925 MAR.
JUNE
1926 MAR.
1927 SEPT.
1928 JUNE
1929 MAR.
SEPT.
1930 JUNE
DEC.
1931 SEPT.
1932 AUG.
1933 AUG.
NOV.
1934 DEC.
1935 MAR.
1937 MAY
1938 MAR.
1939 MAR.
SEPT.
1940 MAY
1922 APRIL
NOV.
1923 JULY
1924 JULY
OCT.
1925 JAN.,
APRIL
1926 JAN.
MAY
1927 OCT.
1928 JULY
APRIL
1930 APRIL
OCT.
1931 APRIL
1932 APRIL
1933 JULY
OCT.
1934 APRIL
1935 JAN.
JULY
1937 OCT.
1939 JAN.
JULY
OCT.
1940 JULY

336

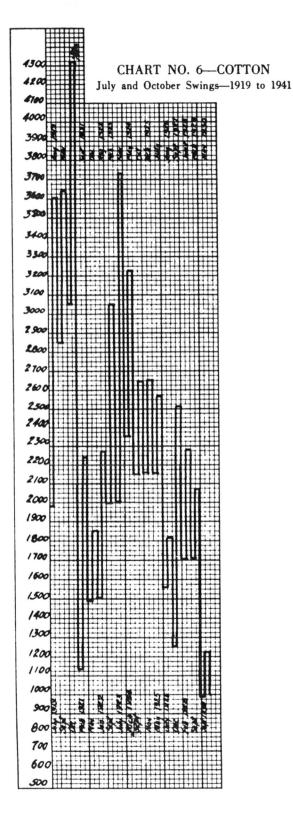

CHART NO. 6—COTTON
July and October Swings—1919 to 1941

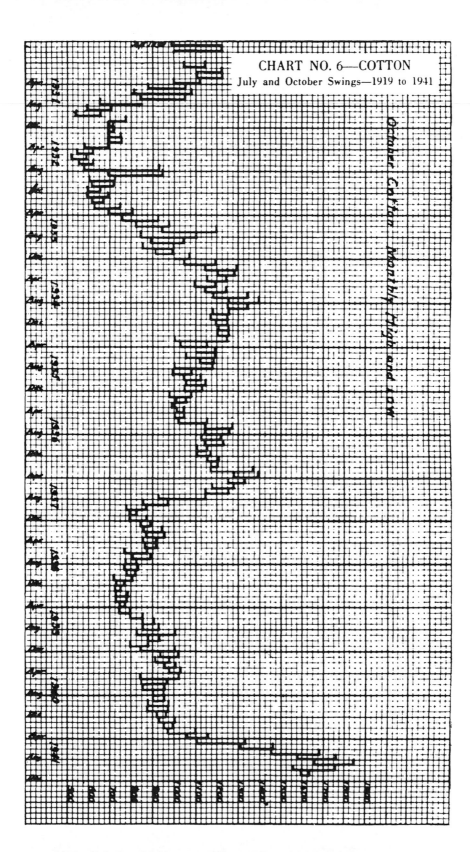

CHART NO. 6—COTTON
July and October Swings—1919 to 1941

October Cotton Monthly High and Low

338

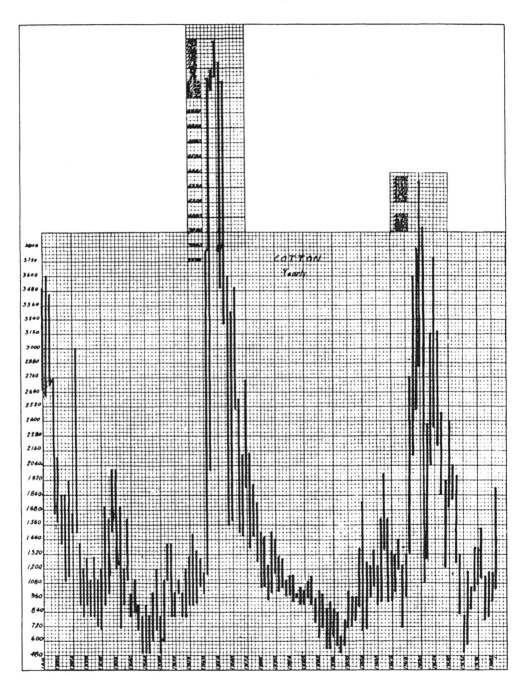

CHART NO. 8—COTTON SEED OIL
May and October Swings—1904 to 1941

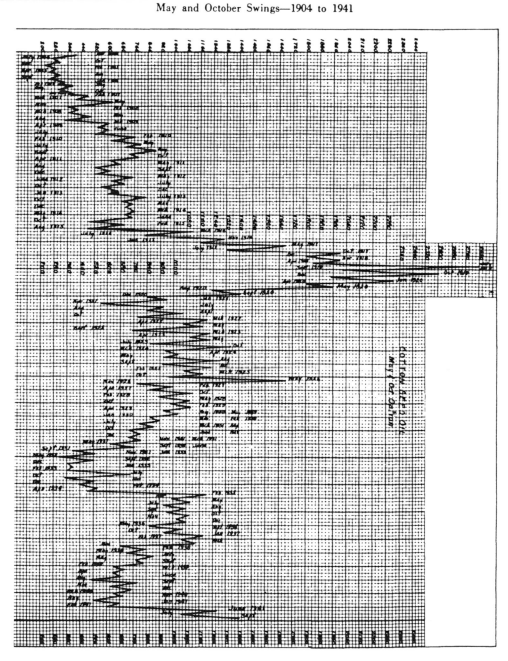

CHART NO. 9—EGGS
October and December Swings—1930 to 1941

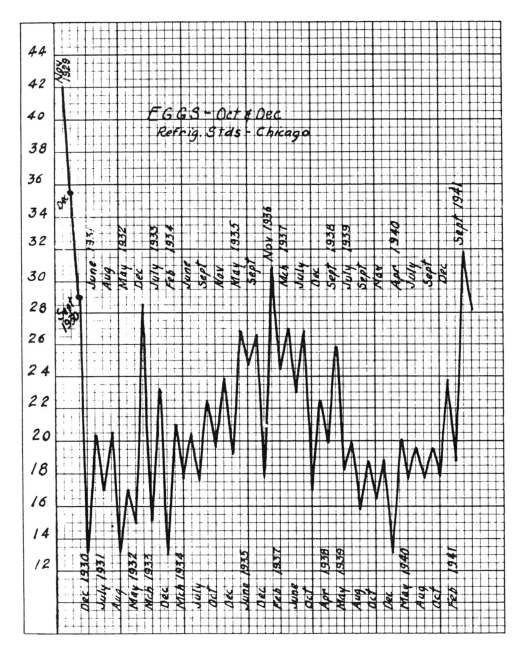

341

CHARTS

CHART NO. 10—HIDES
September and December Swings—1924 to 1941

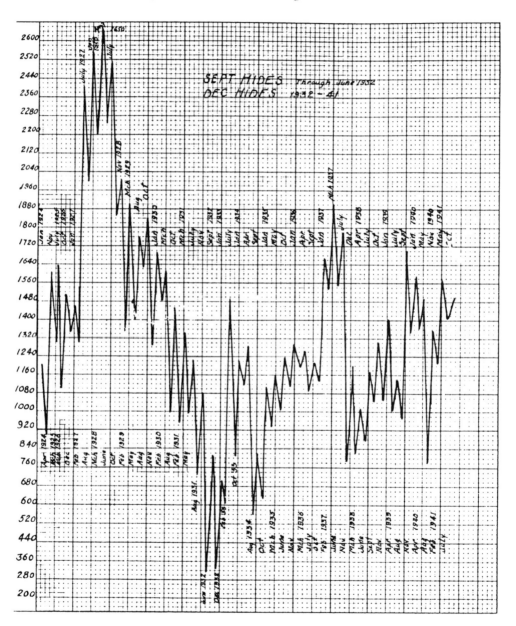

342

CHART NO. 11—HOGS—LIVE
Chicago—Yearly—1898 to 1941

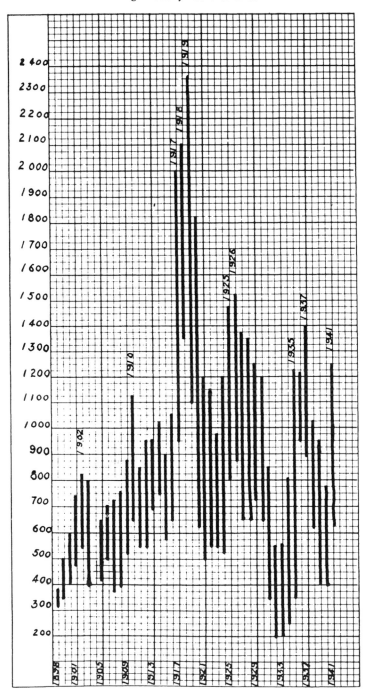

CHART NO. 12—RYE—CASH
May Swings—1914 to 1941

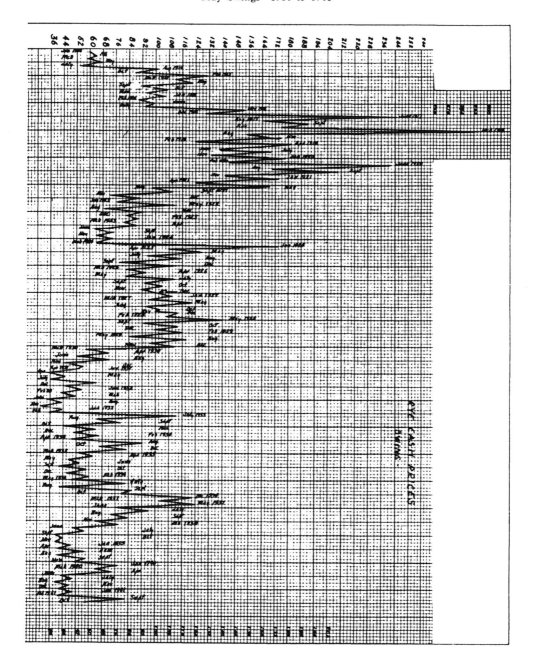

CHART NO. 13—LARD—CASH
May, October and December Swings—1868 to 1941

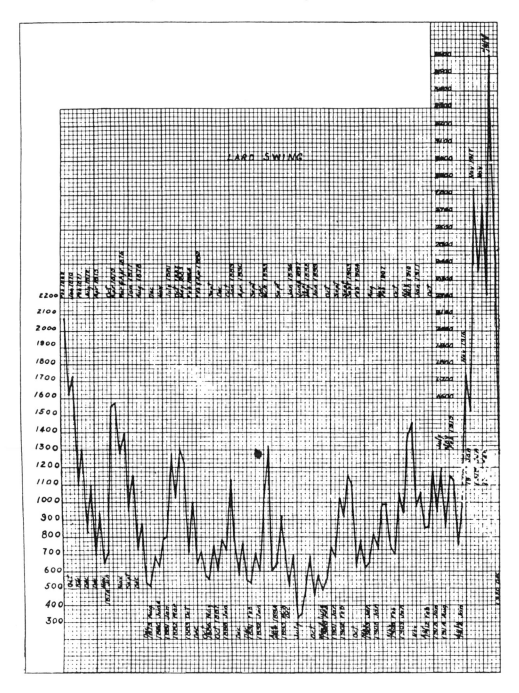

CHART NO. 13—LARD—CASH
May, October and December Swings—1868 to 1941

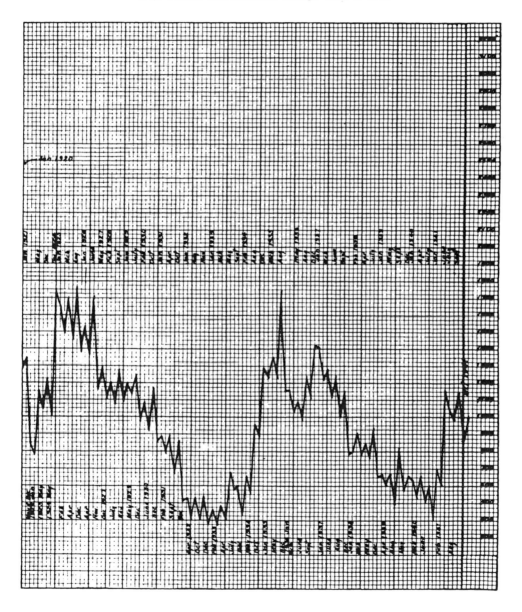

CHART NO. 14—OATS—CASH
May and December Swings—1888 to 1941

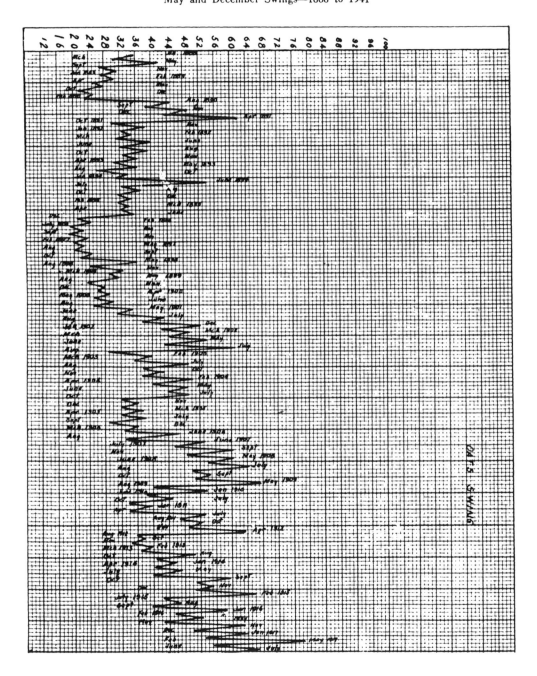

CHART NO. 14—OATS—CASH
May and December Swings—1888 to 1941

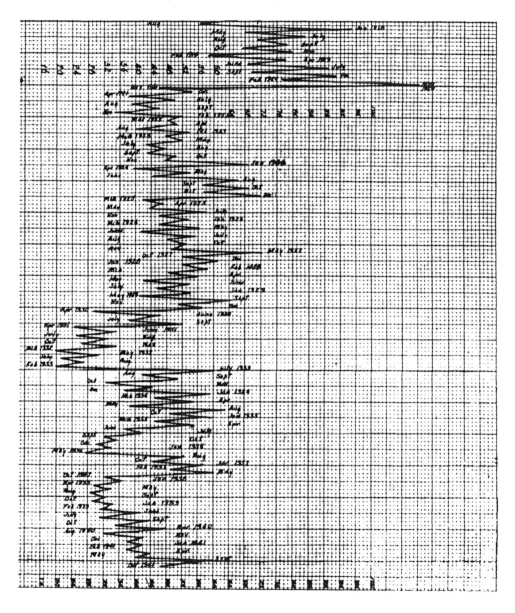

CHART NO. 15—RUBBER
September—Monthly—1928 to 1941

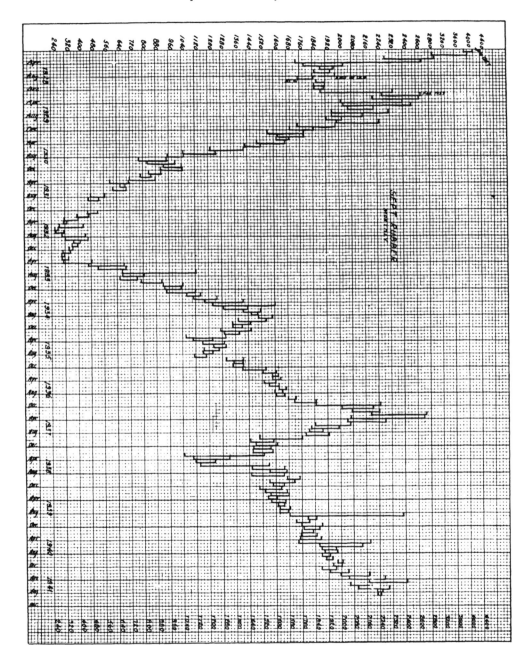

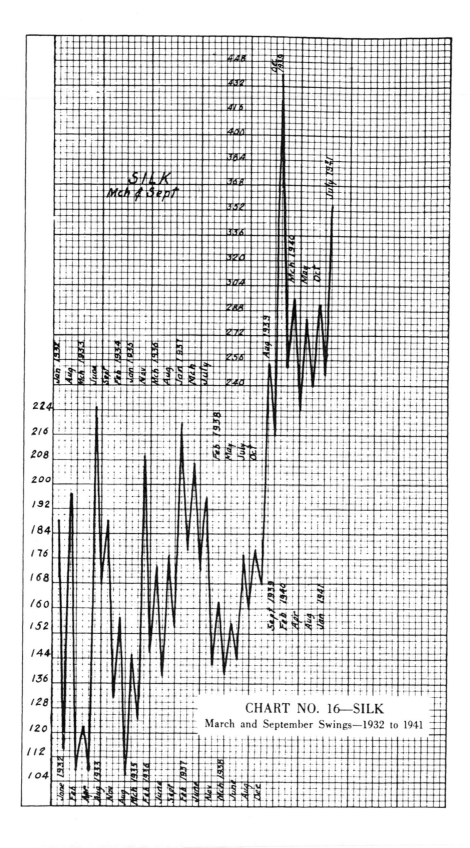

CHART NO. 16—SILK
March and September Swings—1932 to 1941

CHART NO. 17—SOY BEANS
QUARTERLY—1920 to 1941

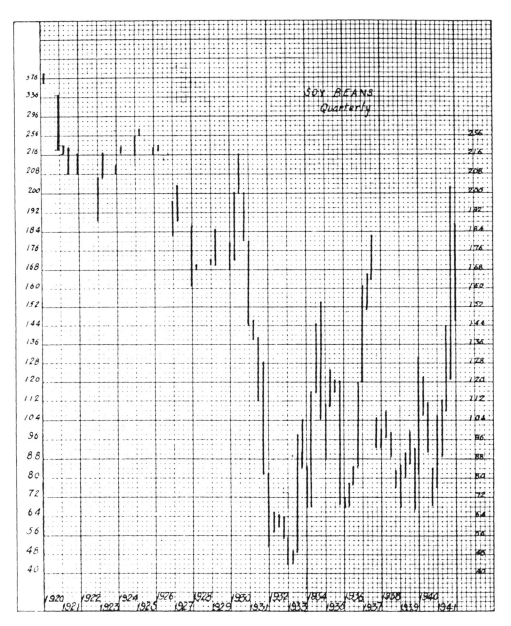

SOY BEANS
Quarterly

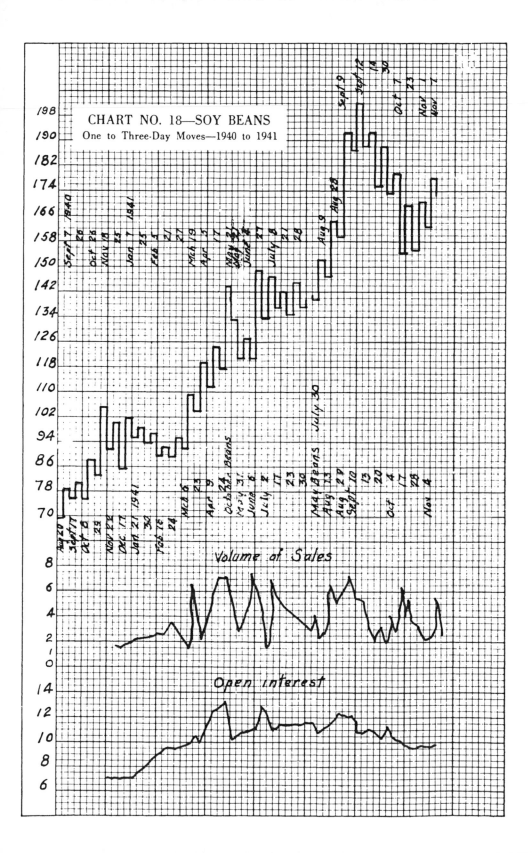

CHART NO. 18—SOY BEANS
One to Three-Day Moves—1940 to 1941

Volume of Sales

Open Interest

CHART NO. 19—SUGAR
July Swing—1915 to 1941

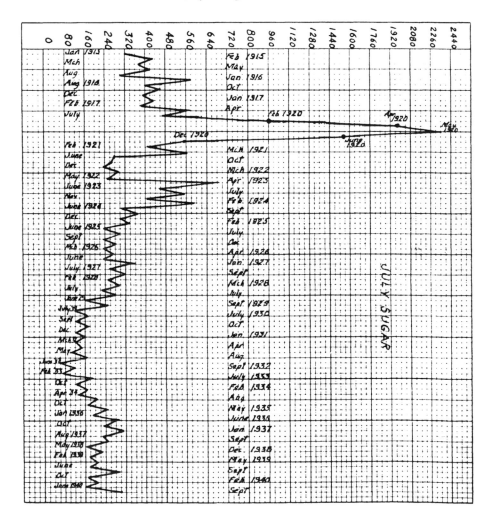

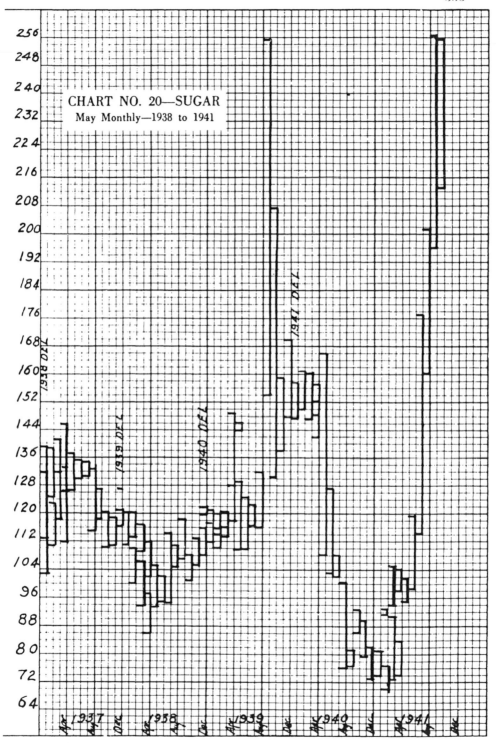

CHART NO. 20—SUGAR
May Monthly—1938 to 1941

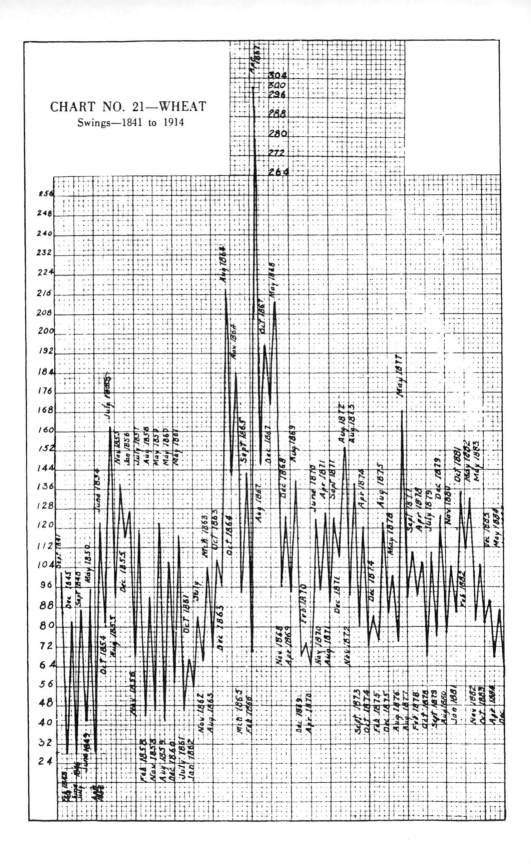

CHART NO. 21—WHEAT
Swings—1841 to 1914

CHART NO. 21—WHEAT
Swings—1841 to 1914

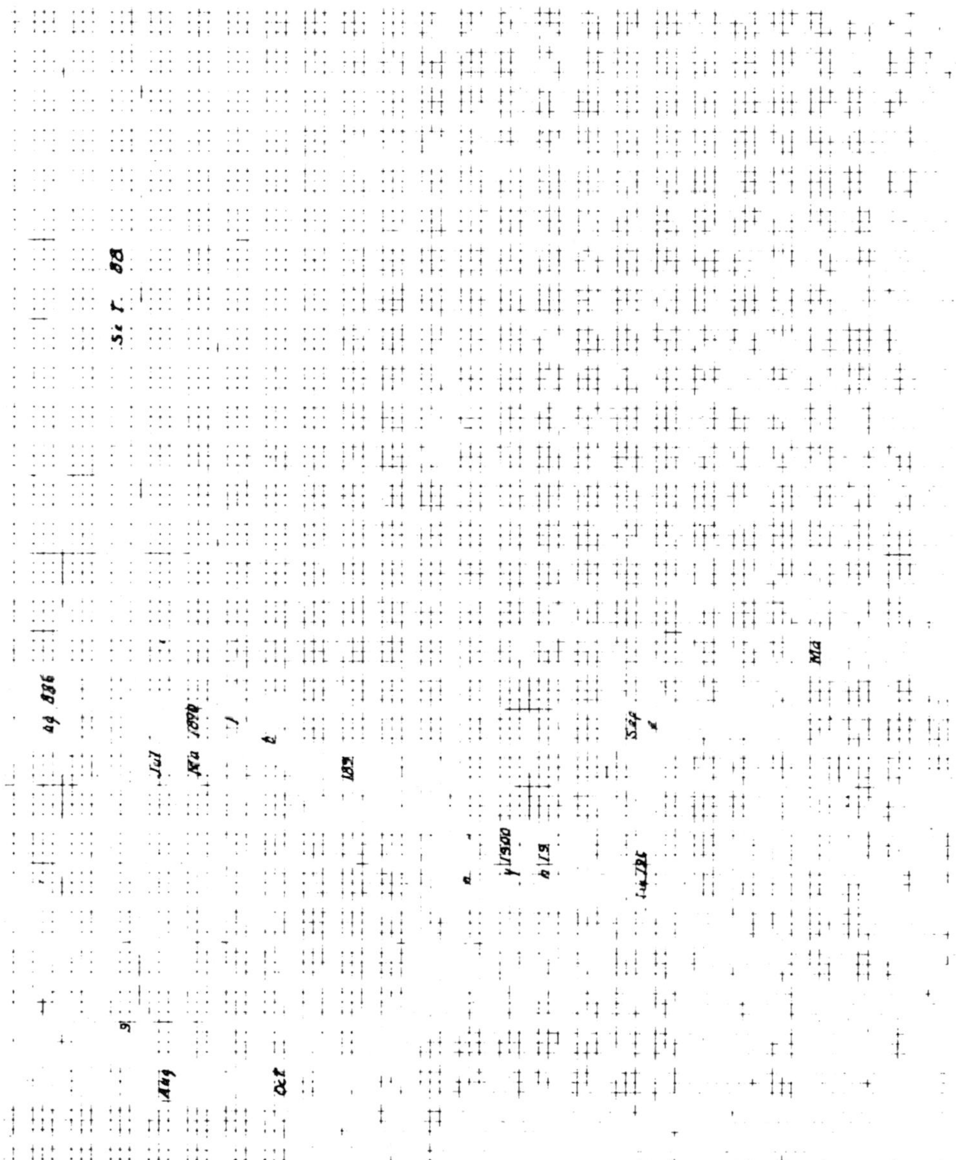

CHART NO. 22—WHEAT
War Swings—1914 to 1941

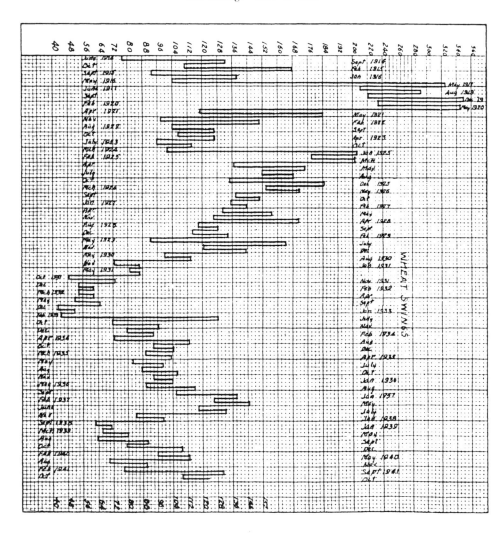

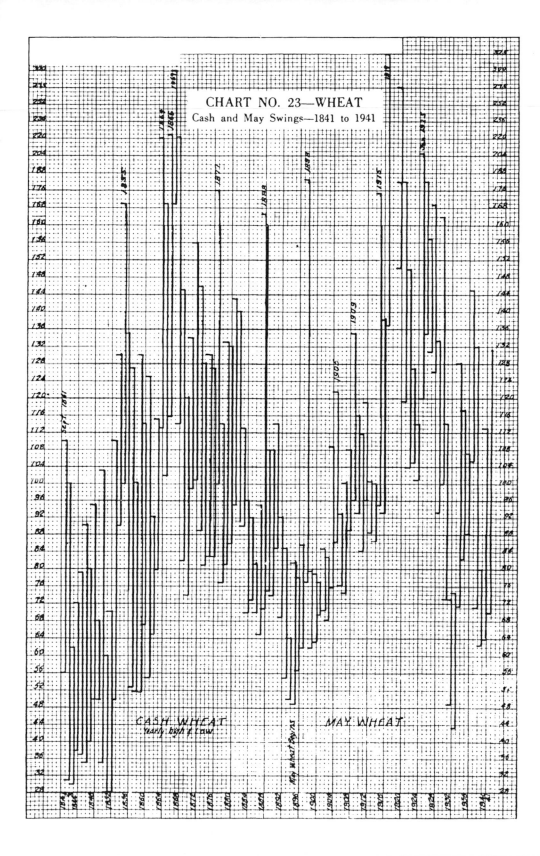

CHART NO. 23—WHEAT
Cash and May Swings—1841 to 1941

CASH WHEAT
Yearly high & low

MAY WHEAT

CHART NO. 24—WOOL
Quarterly—1912 to 1941

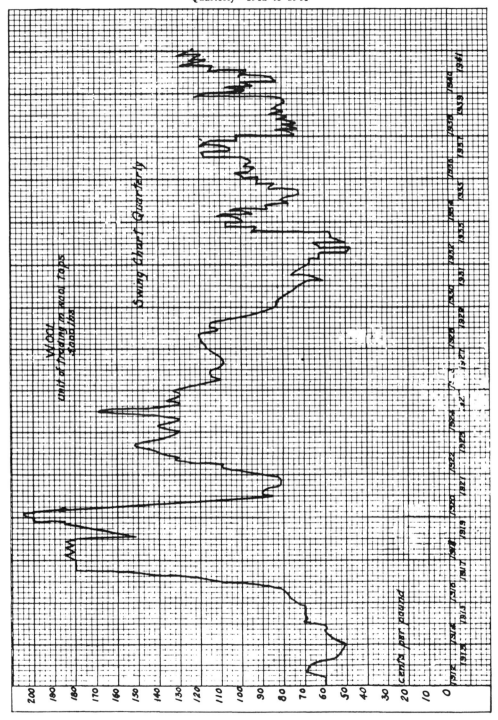

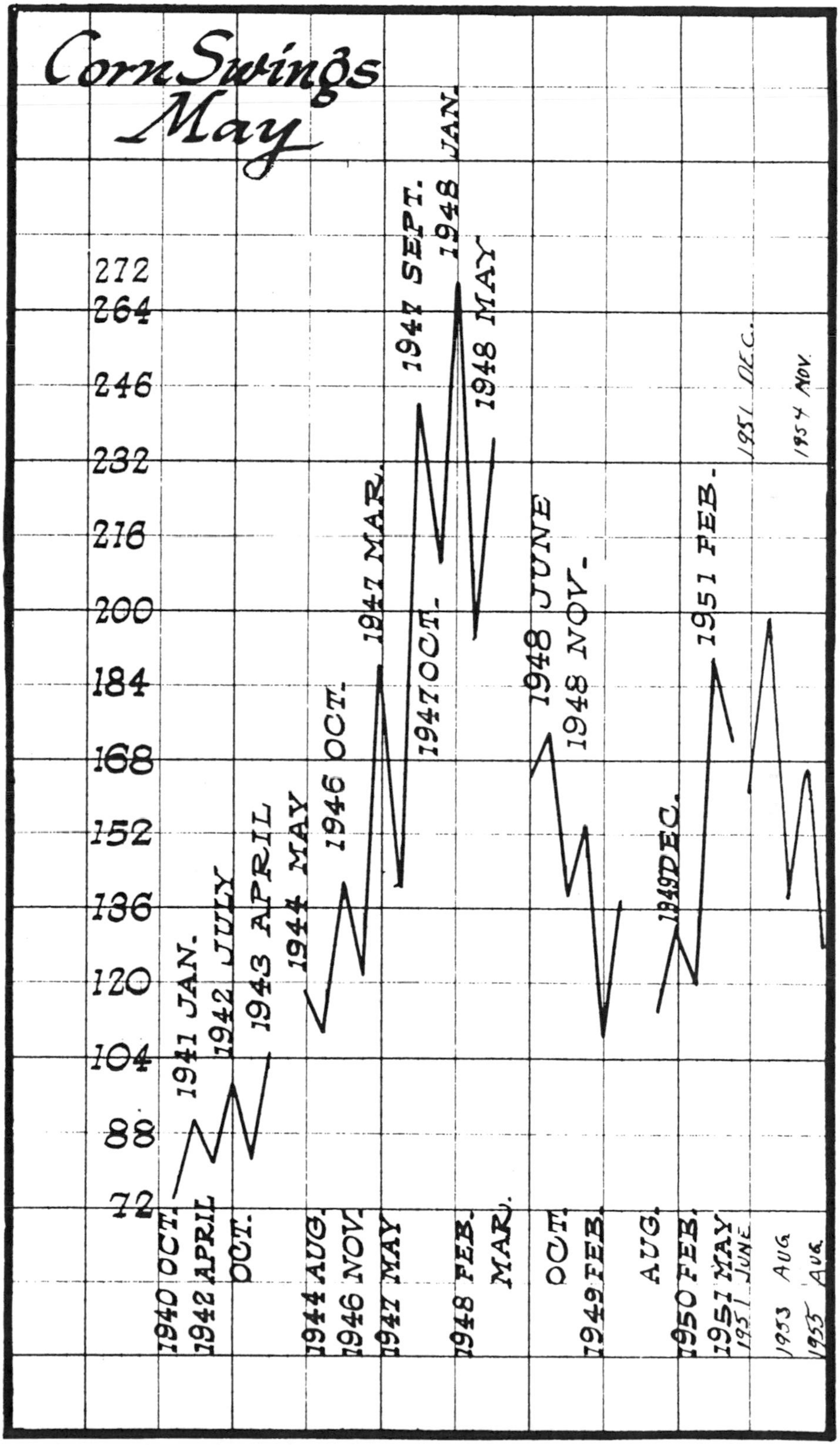

Corn Swings
May

272
264

246

232

216

200

184

168

152

136

120

104

88

72

1947 SEPT.

1948 JAN.

1948 MAY

1947 MAR.

1947 OCT.

1946 OCT.

1944 MAY

1943 APRIL

1942 JULY

1941 JAN.

1948 JUNE

1948 NOV.

1951 FEB.

1949 DEC.

1951 DEC.

1954 NOV.

1940 OCT.
1942 APRIL
OCT.
1944 AUG.
1946 NOV.
1947 MAY
1948 FEB.
MAR.
OCT.
1949 FEB.
AUG.
1950 FEB.
1951 MAY
1951 JUNE
1953 AUG
1955 AUG.

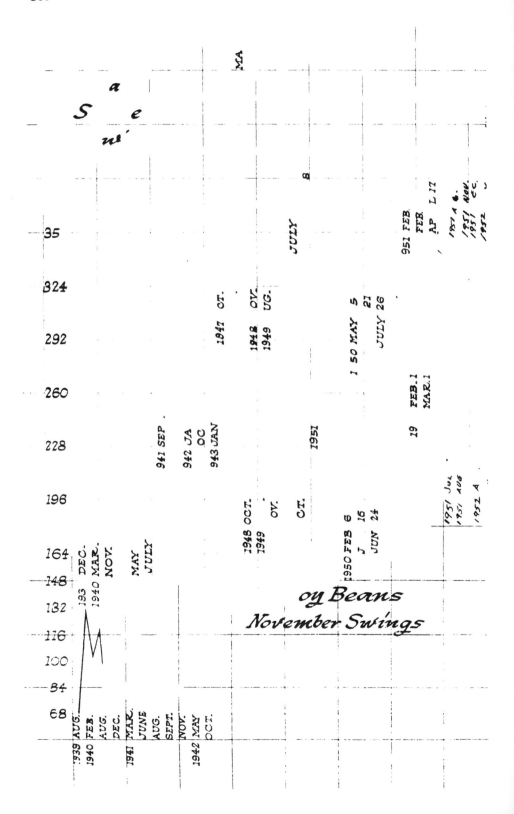

oy Beans
November Swings

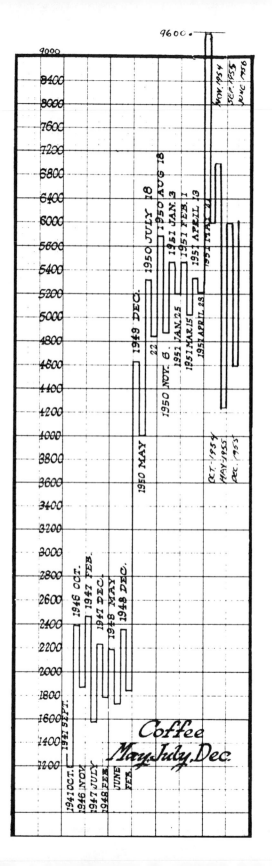

Coffee

May.July.Dec.

362

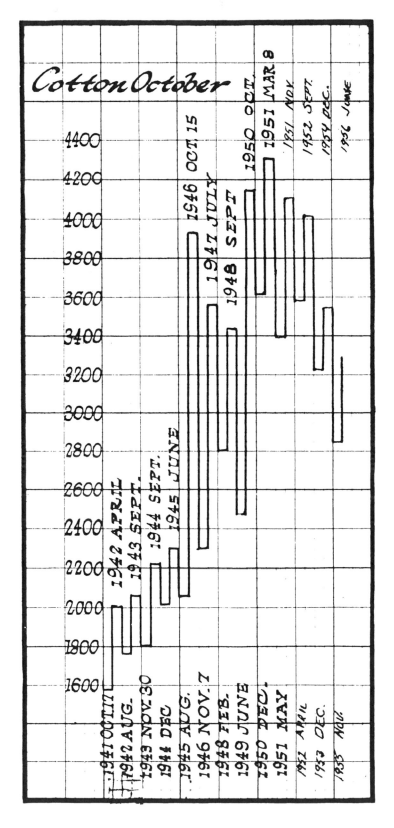

Cotton October

Cotton Seed Oil
July October

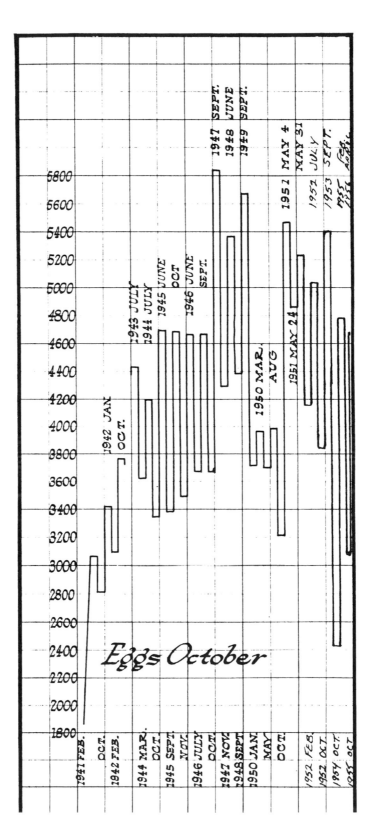

Eggs October

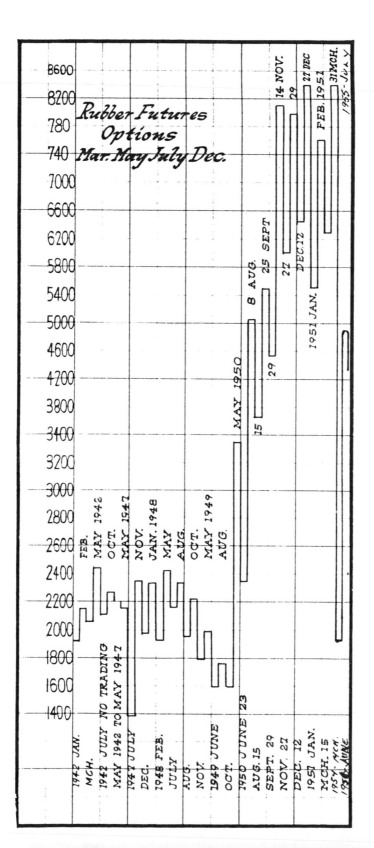

Rubber Futures
Options
Mar. May July Dec.

306

1 47 2

184 J

1 45 AY

19 60 T.

DEC

148 A RIL
194 D
194 M Y

19 OJ LY
51

heat a i s

942 AY
44
945 UG

OV.

BC.

EC
U

949

OCI

953 UG

955 AUG.

APPENDIX

PRICES OF LARD FOR 72 YEARS

Years	Months the lowest prices were reached	Range for the entire year		Months highest prices were reached
		Low	High	
1869	October and November	$16.25	$20.75	February
1870	December	11.00	17.25	January
1871	November and December	8.37½	13.00	February
1872	December	7.00	11.00	July
1873	November	6.50	9.37	April
1874	January	8.20	15.50	October
1875	November	11.80	15.75	April and May
1876	September	9.55	13.85	March and April
1877	December	7.55	11.55	January
1878	December	5.32½	7.80	August
1879	August	5.30	7.75	December
1880	June	6.35	7.85	November
1881	February	9.20	13.00	July
1882	March	10.05	13.10	October
1883	October	7.15	12.10	May
1884	December	6.45	10.00	February
1885	October	5.82½	7.10	February and April
1886	May	5.82½	7.50	September
1887	June and October	6.20	7.92½	December
1888	January	7.25	11.20	October
1889	December	5.75	7.55	January
1890	December	5.50	6.52½	April
1891	February	5.47½	7.05	September
1892	January	6.05	10.60	December
1893	August	6.00	13.20	March
1894	March	6.45	9.05	September
1895	December	5.15	7.17½	March
1896	July	3.05	5.85	January
1897	June	3.42½	4.90	September
1898	January and October	4.62½	6.82½	May
1899	May and June	4.90	5.77½	January
1900	February	5.65	7.40	October
1901	January	6.90	10.25	September
1902	February	9.07½	11.60	September
1903	October	6.20	11.00	September
1904	May	6.15	7.92½	February

PRICE OF LARD FOR 72 YEARS

Years	Months lowest prices were reached	Range for the entire year		Months highest prices were reached
		Low	High	
1905	January	$ 6.55	$ 8.10	August
1906	January	7.32½	9.85	November
1907	November	7.50	9.97½	February
1908	February	6.97½	10.45	October
1909	January	9.40	13.90	November
1910	November	9.70	14.65	March
1911	April	7.70	10.67½	January
1912	February	8.65	11.97½	October
1913	January	9.47½	11.87½	July
1914	August	8.60	11.60	November
1915	July	7.55	11.27½	February
1916	February	9.75	17.45	November
1917	January	15.10	28.20	November
1918	January	23.50	27.30	November
1919	February	22.05	35.85	June
1920	December	12.62½	24.45	January
1921	November and December	8.50	13.30	January
1922	January	8.60	12.37½	November
1923	July	10.27½	14.25	November
1924	May	10.15	17.15	October
1925	April	14.60	17.72½	July
1926	November	11.72½	17.10	June
1927	December	11.10	13.25	September
1928	February	10.82½	12.85	September
1929	December	9.75	12.50	July
1930	December	8.60	11.90	September
1931	December	5.20	9.22½	March
1932	June	3.57½	5.37½	August
1933	February	3.77½	7.90	July
1934	January	5.30	12.97½	December
1935	December	11.55	17.25	August
1936	May and June	9.90	14.15	December
1937	December	7.90	14.10	January
1938	December	6.55	9.30	July
1939	August	5.00	8.25	September
1940	December	4.15	6.55	April
1941	January	6.15	11.65	June

LARD SWINGS — 1910 to 1941

1910	March	1460	1926	January	1537	1935	January	1245
	November	975		April	1370		March	1360
				June	1710		May	1245
1911	January	1060		November	1172		August	1745
	April	850					December	1155
			1927	May	1297			
1912	February	860		December	1110	1936	January	1157
	October	1185					March	1042
			1928	February	1207		May	1097
1913	January	940		July	1083		June	990
	July	1185		September	1285		August	1245
				November	1097		September	1120
1914	August	860	1929	January	1207		December	1415
	November	1150		May	1145			
				July	1250	1937	January	1410
1915	February	1125		December	975		January	1225
	July	760					March	1287
			1930	February	1095		June	1125
1916	January	975		June	927		June	1247
	November	1740		October	1175		August	1000
				December	860		September	1165
1917	January	1525					December	790
	November	2835	1931	January	895			
				February	795	1938	January	810
1918	January	2350		April	895		February	905
	November	2740		September and			March	785
				October	677		April	847
1919	February	2220		October	865		May	770
	June	3600		December	520		July	930
							December	655
1920	January	2475	1932	January	535			
	December	1275		April	420	1939	January	672
				August	537		April	612
1921	January	1340		October	410		May	675
	November and			November	532		August	500
	December	850		December	387		September	825
							November	575
1922	January	790	1933	January	470		December	665
	May	1160		February	377			
				March	487	1940	January	630
1923	March	1235		April	415		March	537
	May	1050		May	680		April	655
	December	1235		July	580		June	507
				September	612		July	612
1924	May	1015		December	445		December	415
	December	1750						
			1934	February	655	1941	January	700
1925	January	1662		May	570		February	617
	February	1495		August	957		June	1155
	March	1707		October	895		July	1035
	April	1460		December	1297		August	990
	August	1772					September	1150
	December	1387					October	875

OATS SWING FROM HIGH TO LOW

Year			Year			Year			Year			Year		
1888	Jan.	31¾	1896	Feb.	20½	1904	July	45	1914	Jan.	41⅜	1921	Sept.	41¾
	Mar.	26¾		July	15		Oct.	28¼		Apr.	36¼		Nov.	30½
	May	37¾		Aug.	18⅙		Nov.	32¼		May	42⅞	1922	Feb.	47⅜
	Sept.	23¼		Sept.	14¾		Dec.	28¼		July	35⅞		Mar.	44¼
	Nov.	27¼		Nov.	19¾	1905	Mar.	33¼		Sept.	54⅞		Apr.	46½
1889	Jan.	23¾	1897	Feb.	15⅝		Apr.	28⅜		Oct.	46½		Aug.	36¼
	Feb.	25¼		May	18¾		July	34¼		Nov.	50⅝	1923	Feb.	49¾
	Apr.	21½		Aug.	16¼		Sept.	25		Dec.	46⅝		Mar.	43¾
	May	23⅝		Sept.	20¾		Dec.	32¼	1915	Feb.	62		May	47¾
	Oct.	17¾		Oct.	17¾	1906	Mar.	28⅞		July	38½		July	38⅞
	Dec.	21¼	1898	May	32		June	42¾		Aug.	42⅞		Aug.	43½
1890	Feb.	19¼		Aug.	20¼		Aug.	29⅛		Sept.	35¼		Sept.	39
	Aug.	40¾	1899	Feb.	28¼	1907	June	49⅜	1916	Jan.	54⅜		Oct.	46⅜
	Sept.	35		Mar.	25¼		July	41⅛		Feb.	41¼		Nov.	43¾
	Nov.	45		May	27½		Sept.	56½		May	48¼	1924	Jan.	64¾
	Dec.	39¾		Aug.	19¼		Nov.	44½		May	38⅜		Apr.	35¾
1891	Apr.	57¾		Nov.	24	1908	May	56½		Nov.	59		May	49⅞
	Oct.	26¼		Dec.	22¼		June	50		Dec.	46		June	40⅜
	Nov.	34	1900	Apr.	25¼		July	60½	1917	Jan.	59½		Aug.	62¾
1892	Jan.	28		May	21¼		Aug.	46		Feb.	49¼		Sept.	53¼
	Feb.	31		June	26¼		Sept.	50¼		May	73½		Oct.	65
	Mar.	27		Aug.	21		Oct.	46¾		June	51¼		Oct.	52⅝
	June	35½	1901	May	31	1909	May	63		July	62⅝		Dec.	67¾
	June	28		June	27		Aug.	36		Aug.	52½	1925	Mar.	38
	Aug.	34¾		July	39	1910	Jan.	49⅜	1918	Jan.	90⅞		Apr.	43
	Oct.	28½		Aug.	33½		June	34½		May	64		May	39¾
	Nov.	32½		Dec.	48⅜		July	41		July	78½		July	54
1893	Apr.	26⅝	1902	Jan.	38⅛		Oct.	29¾		Aug.	66⅞		Nov.	42⅜
	May	32		Mar.	45½	1911	Jan.	35⅜		Sept.	74⅜	1926	Jan.	49¾
	Aug.	22		Mar.	40¼		Apr.	29¾		Oct.	63		Mar.	42
	Oct.	29¼		May	49¼		July	49¼		Nov.	75⅜		May	52¼
1894	Jan.	27		June	39		Aug.	42½	1919	Feb.	54½		June	37½
	June	50		July	56		Oct.	48⅜		Apr.	73¾		July	50⅞
	July	28⅜		Aug.	25		Nov.	45		June	64⅝		Aug.	44¼
	Aug.	33	1903	Feb.	36	1912	Apr.	59		July	84¾	1927	May	68⅛
	Oct.	27½		Mar.	31¼		Aug.	31½		Sept.	65½		Oct.	48
	Dec.	30¼		July	45		Oct.	33¾		Dec.	87		Dec.	57
1895	Feb.	27½		Aug.	33⅝		Nov.	30¼	1920	Feb.	73¼	1928	Jan.	47⅞
	Mar.	30¼		Oct.	38½	1913	Feb.	35⅞		May	108½		Feb.	54⅝
	Apr.	28		Nov.	33¼		Mar.	32⅞		Nov.	42		Mar..	44½
	June	31½	1904	Feb.	46		Aug.	46½		Dec.	50⅜		Apr..	51⅜
	Dec.	16⅞		Apr.	36⅛		Oct.	36¾	1921	Apr.	34½		May	38¼
				May	44¾					July	45⅞		June	49¼
				June	39⅞					Aug.	35⅜		July	41⅜

OATS SWING FROM HIGH TO LOW

Year			Year			Year			Year			Year		
1929	Jan.	50	1932	Mar.	15¾	1934	May	34¾	1936	Aug.	48⅛	1939	June	37
	May	37¼		May	26⅞		Aug.	59⅛		Oct.	40⅜		July	27¼
	Sept.	60¾		July	17½		Oct.	45¼	1937	Jan.	54⅞		Sept.	39⅛
	Nov.	47		Aug.	23½	1935	Jan.	55¾		Feb.	45⅛		Oct.	31⅜
	Dec.	52⅞	1933	Feb.	15⅞		Mar.	41⅜		May	56¼	1940	Apr.	43¼
1930	Apr.	25½		July	56¾		Apr.	51		Oct.	28½		Aug.	28⅝
	June	42⅛		Aug.	38⅛		June	33⅝	1938	Jan.	32¾		Nov.	38
	July	34½		Sept.	46¼		July	37½		Apr.	26		Dec.	34¼
	Sept.	47⅞		Oct.	28⅞		Sept.	28⅛		May	29½	1941	Jan.	37¾
1931	Apr.	20⅞		Nov.	40½		Oct.	31		Aug.	24⅞		Feb.	34
	June	32⅛		Dec.	33¾		Dec.	26½		Sept.	28½		Apr.	40
	July	21⅛	1934	Jan.	55½	1936	Jan.	29⅝		Oct.	25¼		May	36⅜
	Aug.	29		Mar.	41½		May	23¼	1939	Jan.	30½		Sept.	55½
	Oct.	23		Apr.	50⅞					Feb.	27½		Oct.	42⅜
	Nov.	31⅛												

BARLEY NO. 2—WEIGHTED AVERAGE PRICE PER BUSHEL, MINNEAPOLIS—1909-1941

Month	1909	1910	1911	1912	1913	1914	1915	1916	1917	1918	1919	1920
Jan.		0.61	.77	1.05	.49	.52	.68	.70	1.17	1.56	.90	1.52
Feb.		0.60	.74	1.00	.48	.50	.75	.66	1.17	1.88	.87	1.37
Mar.		0.58	.81	.96	.46	.48	.70	.65	1.21	2.12	.93	1.51
Apr.		0.54	.88	1.01	.46	.47	.70	.68	1.36	1.82	1.00	1.60
May		0.54	.75	.99	.50	.48	.70	.70	1.48	1.46	1.13	1.74
June		0.53	.77	.76	.52	.47	.66	.68	1.38	1.23	1.12	1.49
July		0.60	.87	.60	.48	.45	.68	.69	1.49	1.18	1.21	1.16
August	0.45	.61	.85	.46	.58	.59	.59	.81	1.31	1.02	1.33	1.02
Sept.	.48	.63	.94	.49	.61	.58	.48	.81	1.33	.95	1.27	.99
Oct.	.49	.63	.95	.50	.56	.55	.51	1.03	1.28	.91	1.29	.92
Nov.	.52	.66	.98	.47	.53	.59	.56	1.11	1.27	.94	1.33	.82
Dec.	.57	.70	.91	.45	.50	.57	.61	1.07	1.49	.92	1.52	.74

Month	1921	1922	1923	1924						1930	1931	1932
Jan.	.69	.51	.57	.62								.51
Feb.	.65	.56	.60	.68								.52
Mar.	.67	.58	.59	.70								.53
Apr.	.61	.61	.64	.75								.51
May	.59	.62	.61	.70								.44
June	.57	.56	.58	.73								.35
July	.62	.56	.59	.76								.31
Aug.	.58	.49	.56	.80							.45	.31
Sept.	.55	.54	.58	.81							.50	.32
Oct.	.50	.57	.60	.85							.50	.29
Nov.	.54	.60	.61	.81							.51	.31
Dec.	.47	.61	.62	.87							.51	.29

Month	1933	1934	1935	1936	1937	1938	1939	1940	1941			
Jan.	.26	.71	1.18	.69	1.33	.84	.60	.60	.54			
Feb.	.25	.71	1.15	.71	1.37	.84	.55	.57	.50			
Mar.	.30	.70	1.08	.69		.80	.56	.56				
Apr.	.40	.68	1.07	.71		.77	.57	.58				
May	.45	.72	.94	.67	1.28	.78	.56	.57				
June	.43	.85	.82	.70	.91	.61	.60	.51				
July	.64	.91	.65	.92	.78	.54	.47	.51				
Aug.	.58	1.00	.60	1.24	.72	.56	.48	.46				
Sept.	.69	1.16	.69	1.28	.83	.56	.58	.45				
Oct.	.67	1.10	.65	1.32	.79	.54	.55	.50				
Nov.	.63	1.17	.62	1.28	.78	.56	.54	.48				
Dec.	.68	1.20	.66	1.32	.78	.57	.58	.52				

HOG — CORN PRICE RATIO* AT CHICAGO

Month	1931	1932	1933	1934	1935	1936	1937	1938	1939	1940	1941
Jan.	11.8	10.8	13.2	6.9	8.5	16.2	9.1	13.3	14.2	9.0	12.1
Feb.	11.6	11.4	15.0	9.0	9.5	16.9	9.1	14.6	16.2	8.9	12.4
Mar.	12.4	13.0	15.1	8.8	10.3	16.8	8.7	15.8	15.6	8.8	11.6
Apr.	12.5	11.8	10.9	8.1	10.0	16.6	7.4	14.1	14.2	8.7	
May	11.6	10.6	10.7	6.8	10.6	15.2	8.0	14.2	13.0	8.1	
June	11.0	12.0	10.4	7.0	10.9	15.4	9.0	14.9	12.4	7.6	
July	11.1	14.4	7.9	7.0	11.2	11.4	9.8	14.7	12.3	9.1	
Aug.	13.1	13.2	7.8	7.7	13.4	8.9	11.3	14.5	12.3	9.4	
Sept.	12.9	13.3	8.9	8.5	13.2	8.8	10.7	15.8	13.8	10.0	
Oct.	13.4	13.6	11.0	7.2	12.0	9.0	15.2	17.5	14.2	9.7	
Nov.	10.8	13.4	9.1	6.8	15.0	9.1	16.2	16.7	12.0	9.5	
Dec.	11.3	13.2	7.0	6.3	16.2	9.3	14.1	14.2	9.6	10.2	

Ratio computed by dividing average price packer and shipper drove hogs by average price No. 3 yellow corn both at Chicago.

COTTON SPOTS AND JULY OPTION MONTHS OF YEARLY HIGH AND LOW

Year	High	Low	Year	High	Low
1816	May	Nov.	1868	May & July	Jan.
1817	Dec.	Jan.	1869	Aug.	Nov.
1818	Apr. & Oct.	Dec.	1870	Jan.	Oct.
1819	Jan.	June	1871	Dec.	Apr.
1820	July & Aug.	Mar. & Dec.	1872	June	Sept.
1821	Aug. & Dec.	Mar. & Apr.	1873	Jan. & Apr.	Nov.
1822	Apr.	Dec.	1874	May	Dec.
1823	Oct.	Mar.	1875	Feb. & Apr.	Sept. & Oct.
1824	May & June	Mar. & Dec.	1876	Apr.	July
1825	May	Dec.	1877	Jan.	Sept.
1826	Jan.	Dec.	1878	Jan.	Sept.
1827	Mar.	Oct.	1879	Dec.	Dec. & Sept.
1828	May	Jan.	1880	Jan.	Sept.
1829	Oct.	Jan.	1881	Aug.	May
1830	Oct.	Jan.	1882	Dec.	Dec.
1831	Jan.	July	1883	Dec.	July
1832	Nov.	Jan.	1884	Mar.	Oct.
1833	Oct.	Feb.	1885	Feb.	Dec.
1834	Jan.	Nov.	1886	Feb.	Dec.
1835	June	Dec.	1887	June	Aug.
1836	Aug	Jan.	1888	Nov.	Oct.
1837	Jan.	May	1889	Nov.	Jan.
1838	Dec.	Mar. & May	1890	Mar.	Dec.
1839	Apr.	Nov.	1891	Ja	Dec.
1840	Jan.	Apr.	1892	Nov.	Mar.
1841	Jan. & May	Sept. & Nov.	1893	Dec.	Aug.
1842	Mar.	Dec.	1894	Dec.	Oct.
1843	Sept.	Feb.	1895	Sept.	Jan.
1844	Feb.	Dec.	1896	Aug.	June
1845	Sept. & Oct.	Jan.	1897	Aug.	Oct.
1846	Oct.	Jan.	1898	May	Sept.
1847	May	Nov.	1899	Dec.	Jan.
1848	Jan.	Nov.	1900	Sept.	Jan.
1849	Dec.	Jan.	1901	Mar.	May
1850	Oct.	Apr.	1902	June	Jan.
1851	Jan.	Dec.	1903	Dec.	Feb.
1852	Aug.	Jan.	1904	Mar.	Dec.
1853	Apr. & Aug.	Jan.	1905	Dec.	Jan. & Feb.
1854	Mar. & Aug.	Dec.	1906	Mar.	Sept. & Oct.
1855	May	Jan.	1907	Sept.	Jan.
1856	Oct.	Feb.	1908	Mar.	May & Dec.
1857	Sept. & Oct.	Dec.	1909	Dec.	Jan.
1858	Sept. & Oct.	Jan.	1910	Mar.	June
1859	Apr.	Dec.	1911	June	Oct.
1860	Nov.	Dec.	1912	Sept.	Jan.
1861	Dec.	Jan.	1913	Oct.	Aug.
1862	Dec.	Mar. & May	1914	May	Dec.
1863	Oct.	June	1915	Oct.	Dec.
1864	Sept.	Apr.	1916	Nov.	Feb.
1865	Jan.	Apr.	1917	Dec.	Feb.
1866	Jan.	Aug.	1918	Sept.	May
1867	Jan.	Dec.	1919	Nov.	Feb.

MAY AND OCTOBER COTTON FUTURES ON NEW YORK

COTTON EXCHANGE

	Jan.	Feb.	Mar.	Apr.	May	June	July	Aug.	Sept.	Oct.	Nov.	Dec.
1931	1140	1225	1230	1120	1050	1080	1050	850	715	660	775	720
	1040	1100	1110	1000	880	815	840	660	590	540	700	690
1932	720	750	760	695	620	585	625	930	950	725	720	660
	695	690	690	585	540	520	560	580	690	605	615	590
1933	690	670	750	810	930	980	1200	1110	1045	1000	1095	1075
	590	615	630	690	765	825	940	845	890	860	915	1000
1934	1190	1290	1285	1240	1190	1245	1340	1395	1340	1265	1250	1250
	950	1140	1205	1160	1090	1140	1185	1260	1255	1185	1170	1200
1935	1265	1265	1250	1150	1190	1190	1185	1195	1080	1185	1145	1135
	1215	1210	1005	1035	1100	1060	1120	1005	995	1040	1060	1050
1936	1080	1065	1005	1045	1050	1155	1275	1265	1220	1235	1155	1170
	980	1015	990	1015	1005	1020	1140	1145	1130	1140	1110	1110
1937	1215	1210	1370	1395	1335	1280	1260	1140	970	870	825	870
	1155	1175	1170	1280	1255	1180	1140	930	855	780	790	795
1938	890	940	955	915	915	870	885	825	835	820	805	770
	840	865	870	855	865	770	810	775	770	780	720	735
1939	750	785	780	770	795	855	905	925	1005	935	880	1000
	725	725	730	740	745	795	855	855	825	880	795	840
1940	1015	975	1000	1025	1020	965	955	950	955	975	970	960
	935	915	960	975	845	850	855	900	900	875	870	920
1941	1000	990	1095	1155	1330	1460	1680	1765	1846	1755	1634	....
	930	950	970	1060	1100	1310	1450	1575	1655	1557	1596	....

COTTON SPOTS AND JULY OPTION MONTHS OF YEARLY
HIGH AND LOW

Year	High	Low	Year	High	Low
1920	July	Nov.	1931	Mar.	Oct.
1921	Sept.	Mar.	1932	Sept.	June
1922	Dec.	Feb.	1933	July	Feb.
1923	Nov.	July	1934	Aug.	Jan.
1924	Dec.	Sept.	1935	Jan. & Feb.	Mar.
1925	Mar.	Dec.	1936	July	Jan.
1926	Jan.	Dec.	1937	Apr.	Oct.
1927	Sept.	Dec.	1938	Mar.	Dec.
1928	June	Feb.	1939	Sept.	Feb.
1929	Mar.	Sept.	1940	Apr.	May
1930	Apr.	Dec.	1941	Sept.	Jan.

VOLUME OF TRADING IN COTTON FUTURES AT CONTRACT MARKETS, BY MONTHS IN MILLIONS OF BALES

	1928-29	1929-30	1930-31	1931-32	1932-33	1933-34	1934-35	1935-36	1936-37	1937-38	1938-39	1939-40
Aug.	14.6	9.0	7.2	6.0	9.6	7.3	5.5	3.6	3.0	4.6	2.8	3.0
Sept.	14.1	11.4	8.0	7.7	10.2	8.7	5.4	3.4	5.6	5.8	5.0	6.1
Oct.	14.5	11.8	7.5	8.8	5.1	6.1	4.0	4.7	5.1	5.0	3.9	3.7
Nov.	13.3	11.4	6.7	8.3	6.2	6.6	4.5	3.8	4.4	3.6	3.5	4.6
Dec.	9.5	6.0	6.5	4.4	3.5	2.6	2.7	3.2	5.2	3.6	2.8	5.7
Jan.	9.2	6.2	3.7	3.5	2.4	6.9	2.8	4.1	3.6	2.5	2.5	4.0
Feb.	7.5	10.7	5.1	5.3	4.0	8.8	3.1	2.2	2.7	4.2	2.3	2.2
Mar.	12.5	9.6	4.3	4.5	3.1	4.0	5.5	1.9	7.9	3.5	2.9	
Apr.	12.0	7.7	6.6	5.2	7.5	5.7	3.9	2.1	6.0	3.1	2.7	
May	9.9	5.8	5.7	3.6	10.9	3.6	3.8	1.9	2.7	3.2	3.4	
June	8.6	7.4	7.7	4.5	10.8	5.8	3.2	4.0	4.2	4.7	3.3	
July	8.7	4.5	5.5	3.2	14.3	6.3	2.5	4.7	4.0	3.5	3.0	
Total Season	134.4	101.7	74.5	65.0	87.6	72.4	46.9	39.6	54.4	47.3	38.1	

VOLUME OF TRADING IN COTTON FUTURES AT ALL CONTRACT MARKETS
BY MONTHS
In Millions of Bales

	1929-30	1930-31	1931-32	1932-33	1933-34	1934-35	1935-36	1936-37	1937-38	1938-39	1939-40	1940-41
Aug.	9.0	7.2	6.0	9.6	7.3	5.5	3.6	3.0	4.6	2.8	3.0	1.3
Sept.	11.4	8.0	7.7	10.2	8.7	5.4	3.4	5.6	5.8	5.0	6.1	2.2
Oct.	11.8	7.5	8.8	5.1	6.1	4.0	4.7	5.1	5.0	3.9	3.7	2.3
Nov.	11.4	6.7	8.3	6.2	6.6	4.5	3.8	4.4	3.6	3.5	1.6	3.3
Dec.	6.0	6.5	4.4	3.5	2.6	2.7	3.2	5.2	3.6	2.8	5.7	2.0
Jan.	6.2	3.7	3.5	2.4	6.9	2.8	4.1	3.6	2.5	2.5	4.0	2.2
Feb.	10.7	5.1	5.3	4.0	8.8	3.1	2.2	2.7	4.2	2.3	2.2	1.7
Mar.	9.6	4.3	4.5	3.1	4.0	5.5	1.9	7.9	3.5	2.9	2.4	3.9
Apr.	7.7	6.6	5.2	7.5	5.7	3.9	2.1	6.0	3.1	2.7	2.8	
May	5.8	5.7	3.6	10.9	3.6	3.8	1.9	2.7	3.2	3.4	4.3	
June	7.4	7.7	4.5	10.8	5.8	3.2	4.0	4.2	4.7	3.3	2.8	
July	4.5	5.5	3.2	14.3	6.3	2.5	4.7	4.0	3.5	3.0	1.4	
Total Season	101.7	74.5	65.0	87.6	72.4	46.9	39.6	54.4	47.3	38.1	43.0	

Markets are New York Cotton Exchange, New Orleans Cotton Exchange and Chicago Board of Trade.

COTTON SEED OIL PRICES IN NEW YORK SINCE 1875
In cents per Pound.

YEARLY AVERAGE SPOT PRICES OF PRIME SUMMER YELLOW COTTON SEED OIL IN NEW YORK

Year	Price	Year	Price	Year	Price
1875	7.6	1893	6.0	1911	6.3
1876	6.8	1894	4.3	1912	6.3
1877	7.0	1895	3.6	1913	7.3
1878	6.3	1896	3.4	1914	6.7
1879	5.8	1897	3.2	1915	6.8
1880	5.7	1898	3.1	1916	10.6
1881	6.2	1899	3.5	1917	15.6
1882	7.1	1900	4.7	1918	20.1
1883	6.2	1901	4.8	1919	22.4
1884	5.6	1902	4.8	1920	15.4
1885	5.1	1903	5.4	1921	8.0
1886	4.6	1904	4.1	1922	10.2
1887	5.4	1905	3.6	1923	11.3
1888	6.1	1906	5.0	1924	10.9
1889	6.3	1907	6.5	1925	10.8
1890	4.7	1908	5.6	1926	11.9
1891	4.9	1909	5.9	1927	9.7
1892	4.2	1910	8.1	1928	9.9

MONTHLY AVERAGE PRICES OF PRIME SUMMER YELLOW COTTON SEED OIL IN NEW YORK

Month	SPOT PRICE			NEAR FUTURE ON N.Y. PRODUCE EXCHANGE								
	1929	1930	1931	1932	1933	1934	1935	1936	1937	1938	1939	1940	1941[2]
Jan.	10.3	8.5	7.2	4.1	3.6	4.7	10.9	10.1	11.4	7.4	7.1	6.9	6.4
Feb.	10.6	8.5	7.3	4.1	3.5	5.1	11.4	9.7	11.0	7.9	6.7	6.9	6.2
Mar.	10.7	8.4	7.6	4.0	3.7	5.1	10.8	9.4	11.1	8.2	6.9	6.7	7.1
Apr.	10.1	8.8	7.4	3.4	4.0	5.2	10.3	9.4	10.6	8.2	6.6	6.8	8.6
May	9.4	8.8	6.9	3.2	5.0	5.0	10.5	8.8	10.5	8.1	6.6	6.4	
June	9.4	8.5	6.7	3.2	5.6	5.3	10.1	9.1	10.0	8.0	6.5	6.0	
July	9.7	8.0	7.0	3.8	6.4	5.9	9.6	9.8	9.2	8.6	6.1	6.0	
Aug.	9.7	8.3	5.4	4.5	5.2	6.8	9.9	10.1	8.0	8.1	5.5	5.6	
Sept.	9.2	8.2	4.2	4.5	4.7	7.5	10.2	10.2	7.4	7.8	7.1	5.6	
Oct.	9.4	7.6	4.4	4.0	4.2	8.1	10.4	9.9	7.3	7.6	6.8	5.4	
Nov.	9.0	7.6	4.5	3.7	4.5	9.2	10.3	10.0	7.1	7.4	6.5	5.7	
Dec.	8.8	7.3	4.1	3.5	4.3	10.1	10.7	11.0	7.1	7.4	6.9	5.9	
YEARLY AVERAGE	9.7	8.2	6.1	3.8	4.5	6.5	6.5	10.4	9.8	9.2	7.9	6.6	

[1] Prices after Dec. 1931 are for Bleachable Prime Summer Yellow.
[2] Bleachable Prime Summer Yellow, Cash, in Tanks, N.Y.

COTTON SEED OIL SWINGS HIGH TO LOW
MAY AND OCTOBER OPTIONS

Year		
1904	Feb.	410
	July	270
	Oct.	310
	Dec.	225
1905	Feb.	289
	Apr.	255
	Aug.	318
	Sept.	245
1906	Jan.	340
	Feb.	305
	May	390
	Aug.	310
	Dec.	390
1907	Jan.	375
	Feb.	480
	Mar.	415
	May	631
	Nov.	360
1908	Feb.	428
	Mar.	370
	May	500
	Aug.	343
1909	Jan.	608
	Apr.	545
	June	609
	July	530
1910	Feb.	765
	Feb.	620
	May	808
	July	715
	Aug.	890
	Sept.	735
	Oct.	782
1911	Apr.	612
	May	675
	Aug.	525
	Sept.	618
	Dec.	528
1912	May	752
	June	622
	July	700
	Oct.	565
	Dec.	661

Year		
1913	Jan.	610
	July	838
	Oct.	684
	Nov.	749
	Dec.	715
1914	Mar.	760
	May	705
	June	750
	Oct.	495
1915	Feb.	700
	Aug.	485
1916	Mar.	1118
	July	830
	Nov.	1300
1917	Jan.	1170
	May	1680
	July	1322
	Oct.	1999
	Dec.	1800
1918	Apr.	2000
	Apr.	1850
1919	July	2815
	Sept.	2020
	Oct.	2590
	Dec.	1952
1920	Jan.	2318
	Apr.	1810
	May	1950
	Aug.	1240
	Sept.	1418
	Dec.	850
1921	Jan.	955
	Apr.	575
	July	945
	Aug.	840
	Sept.	1052
	Oct.	825
1922	Mar.	1200
	Apr.	1063
	May	1195
	Sept.	750

Year		
1923	Mar.	1225
	Apr.	1110
	May	1230
	July	865
	Oct.	1358
1924	Mar.	952
	Apr.	1035
	May	948
	Aug.	1279
	Sept.	940
	Dec.	1239
1925	Feb.	1075
	Mar.	1178
	Oct.	973
1926	May	1678
	Nov.	803
1927	Feb.	1005
	Apr.	850
	Oct.	1193
1928	Feb.	918
	May	1090
	Oct.	998
1929	Feb.	1103
	Apr.	943
	May	1028
1930	Jan.	863
	Feb.	930
	July	790
	Aug.	885
	Oct.	740
	Nov.	795
	Dec.	738
1931	Mar.	808
	May	625
	June	762
	Sept.	400
	Nov.	538
1932	May	318
	Sept.	525
	Dec.	370

Year		
1933	Jan.	400
	Feb.	372
	July	747
	Oct.	435
	Nov.	542
	Dec.	445
1934	Feb.	555
	Apr.	495
1935	Feb.	1193
	Apr.	1005
	May	1095
	July	943
	Aug.	1089
	Sept.	975
	Oct.	1100
	Nov.	1030
	Dec.	1085
1936	May	865
	Sept.	1067
	Oct.	975
1937	Jan.	1185
	Feb.	1065
	Mar.	1138
	Nov.	693
1938	Feb.	858
	May	725
	July	890
	Aug.	780
	Sept.	827
1939	Feb.	645
	Mar.	735
	Apr.	643
	June	700
	Aug.	520
	Sept.	797
1939	Nov.	635
	Dec.	755
1940	Mar.	645
	Apr.	709
	Aug.	532
1941	Jan.	685
	Feb.	610
	Sept.	1415

ONE HUNDRED AND TEN YEARS OF BUTTER PRICES IN NEW YORK

In Cents per Pound

YEARLY AVERAGE PRICES

Year	Price	Year	Price	Year	Price	Year	Price	Year	Price	Year	Price	Year	Price
1831	13.9	1845	17.7	1859	23.9	1873	35.4	1887	26.7	1901	21.4	1915	29.8
1832	15.2	1846	16.7	1860	21.9	1874	36.2	1888	27.5	1902	24.7	1916	34.0
1833	15.8	1847	20.7	1861	19.4	1875	32.8	1889	24.4	1903	23.4	1917	42.7
1834	14.4	1848	20.1	1862	20.9	1876	31.3	1890	23.7	1904	21.7	1918	51.5
1835	19.2	1849	18.9	1863	28.2	1877	28.5	1891	26.2	1905	24.6	1919	60.7
1836	23.9	1850	19.6	1864	42.7	1878	27.3	1892	26.3	1906	24.6	1920	61.4
1837	21.6	1851	18.4	1865	39.8	1879	24.2	1893	27.1	1907	28.1	1921	43.3
1838	23.4	1852	23.6	1866	42.7	1880	30.5	1894	23.0	1908	27.6	1922	40.7
1839	22.9	1853	23.0	1867	34.8	1881	31.8	1895	21.2	1909	29.9	1923	46.9
1840	17.4	1854	23.0	1868	44.7	1882	35.6	1896	18.5	1910	31.1	1924	42.6
1841	18.6	1855	26.4	1869	43.3	1883	31.2	1897	19.0	1911	27.9	1925	45.3
1842	16.5	1856	25.8	1870	38.1	1884	30.3	1898	19.6	1912	31.6	1926	44.4
1843	13.3	1857	25.7	1871	33.6	1885	26.6	1899	21.3	1913	32.2	1927	47.3
1844	15.2	1858	23.8	1872	32.0	1886	26.8	1900	22.2	1914	29.8	1928	47.4

ONE HUNDRED AND TEN YEARS OF BUTTER PRICES IN NEW YORK

In Cents per Pound

MONTHLY AVERAGE PRICES:

Month	1929	1930	1931	1932	1933	1934	1935	1936	1937	1938	1939	1940	1941
Jan.	47.9	36.6	28.5	23.6	19.8	19.8	34.2	34.6	34.2	33.7	26.3	31.8	30.8
Feb.	49.9	35.7	28.4	22.5	18.6	25.4	36.2	36.9	34.3	31.1	26.2	29.3	30.8
Mar.	48.4	37.3	28.9	22.6	18.2	25.4	31.7	32.2	35.8	30.3	24.3	28.7	31.2
Apr.	45.4	38.5	26.1	20.1	20.7	23.7	34.5	31.0	32.9	27.7	23.2	27.9	
May	43.5	34.8	23.7	18.8	22.5	24.5	27.3	27.5	32.3	26.4	23.6	27.7	
June	43.5	32.9	23.3	17.0	22.8	24.9	24.3	29.7	30.9	25.9	23.9	26.8	
July	42.4	35.3	25.0	18.2	24.5	24.5	23.9	33.6	31.6	26.1	23.6	26.8	
Aug.	43.4	38.9	28.1	20.3	21.3	27.4	25.0	35.6	32.8	26.3	24.2	27.6	
Sept.	46.2	39.8	32.5	20.8	23.6	25.8	26.2	35.0	35.0	26.3	27.5	28.4	
Oct.	45.6	40.0	33.8	20.7	24.0	26.9	28.1	32.9	36.0	26.3	29.0	30.2	
Nov.	42.7	36.1	30.9	23.3	23.6	29.4	32.3	33.6	38.1	27.3	30.4	33.0	
Dec.	41.1	32.2	30.5	24.1	20.1	31.0	34.0	34.2	38.9	28.3	30.2	34.7	
Yrly Average	45.0	36.5	28.3	21.0	21.7	25.7	29.8	33.1	34.4	27.8	26.0	29.5	

NOVEMBER AND DECEMBER BUTTER STORAGE STANDARDS — CHICAGO

SWINGS FROM HIGH TO LOW

Year	Month	Value	Year	Month	Value	Year	Month	Value	Year	Month	Value
1921	July	45¼	1929	Feb.	43	1934	Mar.	25⅞		May	29½
	Aug.	37		May	44⅞		Apr.	23		Sept.	34¾
	Sept.	41½		July	43		June	27		Oct.	32½
	Dec.	34¼		Sept.	44⅞		July	24¼		Dec.	34⅝
1922	June	40¾		Dec.	33⅜		Aug.	28⅜			
	Aug.	34¾	1930	Apr.	41⅝		Oct.	25⅛	1938	Aug.	23¼
	Dec.	47½		May	35¼		Dec.	28½		Nov.	27⅞
1923	June	38¾		Aug.	42⅛				1939	Feb.	23
	Dec.	50½		Dec.	25¼	1935	Mar.	27⅛		Oct.	25
1924	Apr.	38	1931	Mar.	32½		Apr.	29¼		Dec.	23
	June	42⅛		May	23⅞		July	23⅝			
	Oct.	32¼		Oct.	30½		Dec.	32⅞	1940	Jan.	28⅛
1925	Sept.	48½	1932	June	17¼	1936	Mar.	25⅜		June	25⅞
1926	Apr.	40		Aug.	21½		Aug.	36¼		Dec.	34½
	Dec.	47½		Oct.	18½		Oct.	30⅛			
1927	Aug.	40¼		Nov.	24		Dec.	33	1941	Feb.	28¼
	Sept.	44	1933	Mar.	16¾					June	38¼
1928	Feb.	41⅝		July	27¾	1937	Feb.	29¾		July	34¼
	Dec.	48⅜		Dec.	14⅛		Mar.	32¼		Sept.	37⅛

SEPTEMBER COCOA

SWING — HIGH AND LOW

Year	Month		Value	Year	Month		Value	Year	Month		Value
1925	Oct.	High	10 45	1931	May	Low	4.65	1936	Feb.	High	5.60
	Nov.	Low	9.05		June	High	6.15		Mar.	Low	5.05
					Sept.	Low	4.30				
1926	June	High	12.98		Nov.	High	5.98	1937	Jan.	High	13.10
	Oct.	Low	10.42						Feb.	Low	9.40
				1932	Jan.	Low	4.30		Mar.	High	12.50
1927	Mar.	High	17.85		Mar.	High	5.05		May	Low	6.90
	May	Low	15.50		June	Low	3.90		Aug.	High	8.50
	June	High	16.95		Sept.	High	5.10		Dec.	Low	5.20
	Dec.	Low	12.90								
				1933	Apr.	Low	3.35	1938	Jan.	High	6.70
1928	May	High	15.60		July	High	6.80		May	Low	4.10
	Aug.	Low	10.12		Sept.	Low	4.00		Sept.	High	5.55
	Oct.	High	11.42		Nov.	High	5.35	1939	Aug.	Low	3.90
	Nov.	Low	10.30		Dec.	Low	4.50		Sept.	High	6.70
									Nov.	Low	4.90
1929	Feb.	High	12.10						Dec.	High	6.15
	May	Low	10.20	1934	Feb.	High	5.98				
	Sept.	High	11.10		Apr.	Low	5.30	1940	Jan.	Low	5.30
	Nov.	Low	9.58		June	High	5.95		May	High	6.45
	Dec.	High	10.60		Aug.	Low	4.58		July	Low	3.95
								1941	May	High	8.10
1930	Sept.	Low	5.25	1935	Feb.	High	5.58		July	Low	7.15
	Nov.	High	7.65		June	Low	4.30		Oct.	High	8.43

COCOA HIGH AND LOW — 1825 to 1941

AVERAGE YEARLY PRICES

Caracas Cocoa in Philadelphia

Year	Price	Year	Price
1825	26.54	1840	15.75
1826	23.58	1841	16.00
1827	19.67	1842	16.42
1828	21.13	1843	14.25
1829	19.00	1844	15.83
1830	18.79	1845	15.79
1831	16.50	1846	13.50
1832	16.50	1847	13.69
1833	16.50	1848	13.75
1834	16.50	1849	13.75
1835	15.67	1850	13.75
1836	14.44	1851	13.23
1837	15.75	1852	10.70
1838	15.75	1853	10.75
1839	15.75	1854	10.75

Guayaquil Cocoa in Philadelphia

Year	Price	Year	Price	Year	Price
1855	8.71	1870	12.90	1885	16.00
1856	10.06	1871	12.20	1886	14.67
1857	17.15	1872	15.20	1887	13.97
1858	14.54	1873	12.34	1888	13.50
1859	13.42	1874	11.92	1889	1336
1860	13.96	1875	12.48	1890	13.10
1861	12.81	1876	14.21	1891	13.44
1862	14.38	1877	16.09	1892	15.43
1863	19.85	1878	19.52	1893	15.56
1864	29.65	1879	21.40	1894	14.13
1865	32.91	1880	14.13	1895	11.38
1866	22.27	1881	13.73	1896	12.21
1867	18.42	1882	13.20	1897	13.13
1868	14.86	1883	16.23		
1869	14.16	1884	15.82		

Guayaquil Cocoa in London

Year	Price
1898	17.70
1899	15.96
1900	16.82
1901	15.77
1902	1587
1903	16.04
1904	16.44
1905	16.12
1906	16.49
1907*	19.98
1908	13.86
1909	11.90
1910	11.23
1911	11.81
1912	12.47

Accra Cocoa in New York

Year	Price
1913	13.92
1914	12.40
1915	16.68
1916	14.22
1917	11.19
1918	12.87
1919	18.36
1920	13.10
1921	7.29
1922	8.80
1923	7.42
1924	7.51
1925	9.68
1926	11.56
1927	15.70

MONTHLY AVERAGE PRICE OF SPOT COCOA IN NEW YORK — N. Y. COCOA EXCHANGE STANDARD

Month	1928	1929	1930	1931	1932	1933	1934	1935	1936	1937	1938	1939	1940	1941
January	13.53	10.03	9.31	5.96	4.03	3.58	4.60	5.10	5.13	12.15	5.84	4.46	5.58	5.10
February	13.78	10.64	9.23	5.51	4.07	3.40	5.16	5.11	5.29	10.20	5.82	4.47	5.32	5.65
March	13.69	10.56	8.67	5.41	4.44	3.40	5.30	4.92	5.24	11.34	5.73	4.57	5.43	7.16
April	14.10	10.17	8.75	5.44	4.26	3.63	5.15	4.81	5.22	9.87	5.11	4.38	5.91	
May	14.97	10.23	8.20	5.00	4.17	4.20	5.43	4.71	5.41	7.70	4.44	4.37	5.45	
June	14.31	10.51	8.31	5.17	3.99	4.60	5.54	4.60	5.97	7.28	4.57	4.23	4.93	
July	13.33	10.60	8.51	5.45	4.20	4.87	5.06	4.80	6.21	7.81	5.22	4.18	4.58	
August	12.26	10.61	7.68	4.84	4.49	4.72	4.92	4.79	6.43	8.27	5.38	4.19	4.21	
September	11.07	10.79	6.26	4.47	4.63	4.41	4.75	4.95	7.19	7.78	5.14	6.01	4.41	
October	10.63	10.51	6.57	4.35	4.09	3.93	4.50	4.88	8.03	6.18	4.89	5.30	4.43	
November	10.07	9.38	6.28	4.67	3.88	4.33	4.60	4.75	9.19	5.69	4.70	5.17	4.81	
December	10.14	9.13	6.10	3.97	3.71	4.11	4.92	4.93	11.17	5.42	4.52	5.80	5.26	
Average	12.66	10.26	7.82	5.02	4.16	4.10	4.99	4.86	6.71	8.31	5.11	4.76	5.03	

*1907-12, Bahia in New York. Source: University of Pennsylvania, Economist, N. Y. Cocoa Exchange.

COFFEE SWINGS

HIGH AND LOW—RIO DE JANERIO

Future—May and September Options

Year	Month	H/L	Price	Year	Month	H/L	Price	Year	Month	H/L	Price
1901	Apr.	Low	5.00	1912	Apr.	High	14.05	1922	Jan.	High	8.25
	July	High	5.80		May	Low	13.12		May	Low	10.55
	Sept.	Low	5.45		June	High	14.18		Aug.	High	9.15
	Nov.	High	7.70		July	Low	10.53		Sept.	Low	9.80
					Oct.	High	14.40		Oct.	High	8.98
1902	Apr.	Low	4.80		Nov.	Low	11.82		Nov.	Low	9.42
	June	High	5.75		Dec.	High	13.50		Dec.	High	8.98
	Aug.	Low	5.20									
	Sept.	High	5.95	1913	Mar.	Low	8.25	1923	Feb.	High	12.15
					June	High	9.77		July	Low	6.78
1903	Jan.	Low	4.00		July	Low	8.78					
	Feb.	High	4.80		Oct.	High	11.50	1924	Mar.	High	14.53
	Apr.	Low	3.65		Dec.	Low	9.10		June	Low	11.05
	June	High	4.80						Oct.	High	20.30
	Aug.	Low	4.40	1914	Jan.	High	13.80		Dec.	Low	16.50
					June	Low	9.75					
1904	Feb.	High	8.50		July	High	14.10	1925	Jan.	High	20.65
	Mar.	Low	5.20		Aug.	Low	12.62		Apr.	Low	17.52
	Apr.	High	6.20		Oct.	High	14.65		May	High	20.00
	May	Low	5.30		Dec.	Low	13.60		July	Low	12.35
	Aug.	High	7.60						Oct.	High	17.25
	Oct.	Low	7.00	1915	Apr.	High	8.35		Nov.	Low	15.60
	Dec.	High	8.20		June	Low	9.78					
					July	High	7.22	1926	Jan.	High	18.50
1905	Mar.	Low	6.10		Dec.	Low	5.83		May	Low	14.75
	June	High	7.20						Aug.	High	16.48
	July	Low	6.65	1916	May	High	9.20		Oct.	Low	13.75
	Aug.	High	7.60		Sept.	Low	6.20		Nov.	High	15.55
	Oct.	Low	7.00						Dec.	Low	13.80
	Dec.	High	8.20	1917	Jan.	High	9.05					
					Mar.	Low	7.?5	1927	Jan.	High	14.58
1906	May	Low	6.25		Apr.	High	8.oo		Feb.	Low	12.85
	Aug.	High	8.00		June	Low	7.85		Mar.	High	14.38
					Sept.	High	9.80		May	Low	10.98
1907	Jan.	Low	5.30		Dec.	Low	8.25		July	High	11.78
	Mar.	High	6.70						Aug.	Low	10.97
	June	Low	5.30	1918	Jan.	High	9.?0		Nov.	High	13.70
	Aug.	High	7.80		Feb.	Low	7.52		Dec.	Low	12.62
	Dec.	Low	5.55		Mar.	High	8.80					
					Apr.	Low	8.00	1928	Feb.	High	15.15
1908	Feb.	High	6.21		June	High	8.80		Apr.	Low	14.05
	Apr.	Low	5.60		Nov.	Low	7.12		Aug.	High	15.92
	May	High	6.20						Dec.	Low	13.45
	July	Low	5.42	1919	Jan.	High	16.05					
	Oct.	High	6.50		Feb.	Low	13.95	1929	Feb.	High	16.65
	Nov.	Low	5.62		June	High	23.78		Apr.	Low	15.62
	Dec.	High	6.05						May	High	16.40
				1920	Feb.	Low	13.60		Oct.	Low	7.50
1909	Jan.	Low	5.65		May	High	15.45		Nov.	High	9.00
	May	High	7.25		June	Low	12.00		Dec.	Low	7.00
	Oct.	Low	5.05		July	High	22.60					
					Sept.	Low	13.50	1930	Apr.	High	9.00
1910	Feb.	High	7.15		Nov.	High	17.60		Aug.	Low	5.22
	May	Low	6.25						Oct.	High	6.41
	June	High	6.85	1921	Mar.	Low	5.10		Oct.	Low	5.20
	Aug.	Low	5.33		Apr.	High	6.60		Nov.	High	6.00
					May	Low	5.60		Dec.	Low	5.50
1911	Jan.	High	11.87		June	High	8.00					
	Feb.	Low	9.60		July	Low	7.15	1931	Jan.	High	5.92
	May	High	10.75		Sept.	High	8.25		Apr.	Low	4.38
	July	Low	6.85		Dec.	Low	9.03		June	High	6.90
									Sept.	Low	4.75

COFFEE SWINGS (Continued)

HIGH AND LOW—RIO DE JANERIO

Future—May and September Options

1932	May	High	6.85		July	Low	7.70	1937	Feb.	High	8.18
	Sept.	Low	5.30		Aug.	High	8.60		Apr.	Low	6.45
	Sept.	High	6.35		Dec.	Low	7.12		May	High	7.33
1933	Jan.	Low	5.35	1935	Jan.	High	7.50		Nov.	Low	3.98
	Mar.	High	5.87		Apr.	Low	4.62	1938	Jan.	High	4.37
	Apr.	Low	5.12		May	High	5.65		Mar.	Low	3.95
	July	High	8.00		Aug.	Low	5.05		Aug.	High	4.77
	Oct.	Low	5.40		Sept.	High	5.43		Sept.	Low	4.23
1934	Feb.	High	8.90		Dec.	Low	4.75		Oct.	High	4.62
	May	Low	7.95	1936	Jan.	High	5.55		Dec.	Low	4.18
	June	High	8.81		July	Low	4.25	1939	Feb.	High	4.37
					Aug.	High	4.98		Mar.	Low	4.03
					Oct.	Low	3.00		Sept.	High	4.45

MAY COFFEE—SANTOS "D" CONTRACT

SWINGS FROM HIGH TO LOW

1928	Jan.	1922		Sept.	770		Nov.	780
	May	2315		Sept.	940	1936	Jan.	918
	Nov.	1915	1933	Mar.	765		May	792
1929	Feb.	2295		May	860		Aug.	939
	Mar.	2210		June	750		Oct.	855
	Apr.	2280		July	1012	1937	Feb.	1155
	Aug.	1815		Aug.	808		Mar.	1003
	Sept.	1927		Sept.	895		May	1160
	Dec.	965		Oct.	782		Nov.	565
1930	May	1355	1934	Mar.	1130	1938	Jan.	650
	Aug.	835		Apr.	1047		May	555
	Oct.	1045		June	1167		Aug.	718
1931	Feb.	765		July	1025		Sept.	633
	Mar.	883		Aug.	1138		Oct.	705
	Apr.	735		Oct.	1015	1939	Apr.	565
	July	970	1935	Jan.	1062		Sept.	685
	Oct.	705		May	732	1940	May	545
1932	Jan.	858		June	805		June	648
	Mar.	815		Aug.	735		Aug.	555
	May	975		Oct.	832	1941	Sept.	1308

COFFEE NO. 7—CONTRACT PRICES AT NEW YORK

TRADING STARTED MARCH 7, 1882

PRICES IN CENTS PER POUND

1882	Low	5	1903-1904	Low	3½	1923	High	12¾
1884	High	11½	1905	High	9⅜	1924	Low	6¾
1885	Low	6½	1907	Low	5	1925	High	23.30
1887	High	27¼	1908	High	5	1927-1928	Low	10.90
1888-1889	Low	9½	1912	High	15	1929	High	17.35
1890	High	18½	1914	Low	5¼	1931	Low	4.40
1892	Low	10¼	1917	High	9.90	1933	High	9.00
1893-1894	High	17¾	1918	Low	6.60	1935	Low	4.10
1900	Low	4	1919	High	24.60	1936-1937	High	8.75
1901	High	9¼	1921	Low	5	1937-1938	Low	3.60
						1939	High	4.00

COFFEE PRICES FROM 1826-1941
ONE HUNDRED AND FIFTEEN YEARS OF COFFEE PRICES IN NEW YORK
In Cents per Pound

YEARLY AVERAGE SPOT PRICE OF COFFEE IN NEW YORK

Year	*Price*	*Year*	*Price*	*Year*	*Price*	*Year*	*Price*	*Year*	*Price*	*Year*	*Price*	*Year*	*Price*
1826	15	1841	10	1856	10¾	1871	13	1886	14⅝	1901	6½	1916	9⅜
1827	14¼	1842	8⅜	1857	11	1872	16¾	1887	14½	1902	5½	1917	6⅛
1828	12⅞	1843	7¼	1858	10⅜	1873	20¼	1888	14⅞	1903	5⅝	1918	9
1829	12⅜	1844	6½	1859	11¼	1874	20⅞	1889	16¾	1904	7¾	1919	17⅞
1830	11⅛	1845	6¾	1860	12	1875	18⅞	1890	18⅛	1905	8¼	1920	11⅞
1831	11¼	1846	7⅛	1861	13¾	1876	18	1891	15	1906	8	1921	7⅛
1832	12½	1847	7	1862	22	1877	18½	1892	15⅝	1907	6½	1922	10¼
1833	12⅜	1848	6⅛	1863	30⅛	1878	16¼	1893	17⅛	1908	6¼	1923	14¾
1834	11½	1849	6⅞	1864	16¼	1879	14⅞	1894	15⅞	1909	7⅞	1924	21¾
1835	11¾	1850	10⅝	1865	16	1880	15⅛	1895	15⅝	1910	9⅝	1925	24⅝
1836	11½	1851	9	1866	13⅞	1881	6⅞	1896	12⅝	1911	13⅜	1926	22½
1837	10½	1852	8½	1867	12¼	1882	7	1897	7¾	1912	14⅜	1927	18⅛
1838	10½	1853	8¾	1868	10½	1883	9⅜	1898	6¼	1913	10⅞	1928	23½
1839	10¾	1854	10⅛	1869	10½	1884	7½	1899	6⅛	1914	8⅛	1929	22⅜
1840	10⅛	1855	9⅞	1870	11¼	1885	7½	1900	8¼	1915	7½	1930	13

MONTHLY AVERAGE SPOT PRICE OF SANTOS 4's IN NEW YORK

Month	1931	1932	1933	1934	1935	1936	1937	1938	1939	1940	1941
January	9¾	9⅛	9⅞	10¼	11	9	11⅜	8½	7½	7.32	7.69
February	9¼	9	9½	11⅛	10⅛	9½	11¾	7¾	7½	7.38	8.22
March	8½	9	9¼	11½	9¼	9	11¼	7½	7⅜	7.38	9.09
April	8½	9½	8¾	11⅜	8⅝	8¾	11⅛	7¼	7¼	7.16	
May	9	10⅛	9¼	11¼	8⅜	8⅝	11½	7½	7¼	7.00	
June	9½	10⅛	9	11¼	8¼	8¾	11¾	7½	7⅜	7.04	
July	9⅜	10⅝	9¼	10⅝	8⅛	9⅜	11½	7½	7¼	7.13	
August	8¼	12	9	11⅝	8⅛	9¾	11⅜	7¾	7½	6.75	
September	8	15	9⅛	11⅜	8⅝	9⅝	11⅛	7⅝	7¾	6.82	
October	7⅝	12½	8⅞	11¼	8¾	9¾	11⅜	7¾	7⅝	7.00	
November	8⅛	10¾	9	11	8½	10¼	9⅜	8	7⅜	7.03	
December	8⅜	10½	9¼	11	8½	11	8½	7⅝	7¼	7.25	
Yearly Average	8⅝	10⅝	9⅛	11⅛	8⅞	9½	11	7¾	7½	7.10	

EIGHTY-FIVE YEARS OF EGG PRICES

In Cents Per Dozen

YEARLY AVERAGE PRICE OF

Fresh Eggs in Boston

Year	Price	Year	Price	Year	Price	Year	Price
1856	16¾	1868	32⅛	1879	18	1890	18
1857	16⅞	1869	31¼	1880	14⅜	1891	21
1858	16	1870	31¼	1881	22¼	1892	20
1859	20⅞	1871	25	1882	22½	1893	21
1860	17½	1872	26¼	1883	23⅓	1894	17
1861	14⅝	1873	28	1884	22⅞	1895	18
1862	15¾	1874	28	1885	19¼	1896	15
1863	20¾	1875	25¾	1886	19¼	1897	15
1864	26⅛	1876	22⅞	1887	21	1898	16
1865	29⅜	1877	21⅛	1888	20¾	1899	19
1866	28⅜	1878	16⅞	1889	18¾		
1867	27⅜						

Fresh Eggs in New York

Year	Price	Year	Price	Year	Price
1900	17	1910	25	1920	57
1901	18	1911	22	1921	41
1902	22	1912	25	1922	35
1903	21	1913	25	1923	35
1904	23	1914	27	1924	36
1905	22	1915	26	1925	40
1906	21	1916	30	1926	36
1907	21	1917	40	1927	32
1908	22	1918	49	1928	33
1909	25	1919	53	1929	37
				1930	28

EIGHTY-FIVE YEARS OF EGG PRICES

In Cents per Dozen

MONTHLY AVERAGE PRICE OF FRESH FIRSTS IN NEW YORK

Month	1930	1931	1932	1933	1934	1935	1936	1937	1938	1939	1940	1941
January	42.7	23.4	18.8	23.3	22.3	29.8	24.5	24.9	22.4	19.4	21.9	19.4
February	36.5	17.7	16.9	13.5	19.2	30.3	31.0	22.6	18.5	17.7	23.6	17.7
March	25.7	20.9	13.9	13.7	17.7	21.5	21.2	23.4	17.9	17.4	17.8	19.3
April	25.7	18.9	14.2	13.7	16.8	23.9	20.1	22.5	18.1	17.1	17.4	
May	23.6	18.0	14.8	14.2	16.4	25.3	21.5	20.9	20.9	16.4	17.4	
June	23.1	17.0	14.1	13.4	16.1	24.3	22.3	20.5	20.6	16.2	16.6	
July	21.4	19.1	15.1	15.1	16.6	24.3	22.8	21.4	21.4	16.2	16.5	
August	24.5	19.6	17.3	14.2	20.6	25.9	23.6	21.2	22.1	16.3	17.2	
September	25.1	21.1	20.1	18.0	22.1	27.1	24.7	23.1	25.2	19.0	20.8	
October	25.2	23.9	24.0	19.9	23.6	27.0	26.9	23.6	26.6	20.6	22.4	
November	33.5	29.2	30.6	24.1	27.6	29.1	33.3	26.4	29.0	23.7	24.1	
December	27.1	25.6	31.4	20.7	27.3	27.5	31.5	25.4	27.7	20.7	26.4	
Yearly Average	27.8	21.2	19.3	17.0	20.5	26.3	25.3	22.9	22.5	18.4	20.2	

EGGS — WHOLESALE PRICE OF EGGS (Fresh Firsts) AT CHICAGO, BY MONTHS

In Cents per Dozen

Month	1930	1931	1932	1933	1934	1935	1936	1937	1938	1939	1940	1941
January	40.8	21.1	17.5	20.6	20.3	27.5	23.2	23.2	20.9	18.6	20.6	18.4
February	33.4	16.2	14.6	12.9	17.0	27.8	27.5	21.7	16.8	16.4	20.8	16.4
March	24.3	19.2	12.2	12.4	16.6	21.2	19.6	22.6	17.6	16.6	16.4	18.1
April	23.7	17.5	12.5	12.7	15.6	23.0	19.2	21.8	17.6	16.4	16.4	
May	21.4	16.7	12.9	13.2	15.2	24.0	20.2	20.1	19.4	15.8	16.5	
June	22.1	15.9	12.5	12.2	14.7	22.9	21.0	19.1	19.2	15.3	15.6	
July	21.1	17.9	13.8	14.0	15.3	22.9	21.4	20.0	20.2	15.4	15.8	
August	24.9	19.1	17.0	13.7	19.5	24.6	22.6	20.1	21.0	15.3	16.1	
September	25.9	20.0	20.0	17.0	21.3	26.1	24.6	22.2	24.2	18.0	19.1	
October	28.2	24.3	23.7	19.5	23.5	26.8	27.4	22.1	25.1	19.8	22.2	
November	33.7	29.3	29.7	22.6	26.7	29.2	33.5	25.6	27.5	23.2	22.5	
December	26.4	24.8	28.8	19.3	26.2	27.2	29.6	24.3	25.6	19.0	25.2	
Yearly Average	27.2	20.2	17.2	15.8	19.3	25.3	24.2	21.9	21.3	17.5	18.8	

OCTOBER AND DECEMBER EGGS
REFRIGERATOR STANDARDS — CHICAGO
SWINGS FROM HIGH TO LOW

1929	Nov.	41⅞		Dec.	13	1936	Nov.	30¾		Sept.	18⅝
	Dec.	35½	1934	Feb.	20⅞	1937	Feb.	24½		Oct.	16½
1930	Sept.	29		Mar.	17¾		Mar.	26⅞		Nov.	18⅝
1931	June	20¼		June	20⅛		June	23		Dec.	13⅛
	July	17		July	17⅝		July	26¾	1940	Apr.	19⅞
	Aug.	20½		Sept.	22¼		Oct.	17		May	17⅝
	Aug.	13¼		Oct.	19⅝		Dec.	22¼		July	19⅜
1932	May	16⅞		Nov.	23¾	1938	Apr.	19⅞		Aug.	17¾
	May	15		Dec.	19⅛		Sept.	25⅝		Sept.	19⅜
	Dec.	28½	1935	May	26¾	1939	May	18¼		Oct.	23⅝
1933	Mar.	15⅛		June	24¾		July	19¾	1941	Feb.	18¾
	July	23⅛		Sept.	26½		Aug.	15⅞		Sept.	31¾
				Dec.	17¾					Oct.	28⅛

HIDES—AVERAGE PRICES (PACKERS LIGHT NATIVE COWS) IN CHICAGO

In cents per pound

YEARLY AVERAGE PRICES

Year	Price	Year	Price	Year	Price	Year	Price	Year	Price	Year	Price
1893	4.75	1899	11.40	1905	13.10	1911	13.50	1917	25.59	1923	12.94
1894	4.67	1900	10.44	1906	14.84	1912	16.50	1918	22.72	1924	12.29
1895	8.52	1901	10.07	1907	11.71	1913	17.27	1919	39.56	1925	14.62
1896	7.53	1902	10.12	1908	11.04	1914	19.27	1920	29.23	1926	13.08
1897	9.74	1903	9.64	1909	14.83	1915	22.97	1921	11.37	1927	18.71
1898	11.02	1904	10.52	1910	13.04	1916	24.89	1922	15.16	1928	22.63

HIDES—HIGHEST AND LOWEST PRICES OF JUNE HIDE FUTURES ON THE COMMODITY EXCHANGE, BY MONTHS

In cents per pound

Trading During Month of—

	June 1936		June 1937		June 1938		June 1939		June 1940	
	High	Low	High	Low	High	Low	High	Low	High	Low
YEAR PRIOR TO DELIVERY										
June	11.25	10.90	12.81	12.02	17.11	17.11	9.61	L9.40	11.98	11.78
July	11.09L	10.88	12.38	L11.59	H18.38	17.13	11.94	11.25	12.75	11.90
Aug.	11.59	11.40	12.13	11.79	17.95	16.98	12.30	11.80	12.00	10.50
Sept.	11.93	11.65	12.70	12.02	17.30	15.33	12.40	11.73	16.67	11.57
Oct.	H1304	11.86	12.37	12.05	15.73	12.30	H14.46	12.45	16.23	14.20
Nov.	12.06	11.75	13.94	12.35	12.32	8.40	14.13	12.18	14.81	14.17
Dec.	12.29	11.72	15.42	13.47	11.75	9.24	13.46	11.90	15.99	14.82
DELIVERY YEAR										
Jan.	12.50	11.65	16.19	15.04	11.28	8.76	13.50	11.06	15.91	13.78
Feb.	11.90	11.38	15.88	14.80	10.07	8.45	11.99	11.05	14.71	13.81
Mar.	12.05	11.36	H18.34	15.75	9.94	L7.60	12.35	10.55	14.45	13.28
April	12.05	11.12	18.15	16.12	9.58	7.77	11.05	L9.40	14.31	13.13
May	11.51	10.94	16.40	14.85	9.40	8.21	11.20	9.95	14.12	L8.80
June	11.55	11.18	15.57	14.50	9.25	8.30	11.15	10.61	10.35	9.25

1—"New Standard" contract used in August, 1938 and subsequent months.
2—During May, 1936, the June, 1937, delivery sold at 12.70 high and 12.70 low.
H—Highest During Life of Contract.
L—Lowest During Life of Contract.

HIDES—HIGHEST AND LOWEST PRICES OF JUNE HIDES FUTURES ON THE COMMODITY EXCHANGE, BY MONTHS

In cents per pound

TRADING DURING MONTH OF JUNE, 1941.

YEAR PRIOR TO DELIVERY			DELIVERY YEAR		
	High	Low		High	Low
June			January		
July			February	13.63	12.12
August	9.90	8.30	March	13.50	12.02
September	10.71	9.65	April	14.16	13.19
October	12.85	10.50	May	14.28	13.51
November	13.05	11.65	June		
December	12.85	12.20			

SEPTEMBER HIDES—OPTION—SWING—HIGH AND LOW

1924—			
	Jan.	High	12.00
	Apr.	Low	9.00
	Nov.	High	16.00
1925—			
	Mar.	Low	13.00
	July	High	16.25
1926—			
	Mar.	Low	11.00
	Oct.	High	15.00
	Dec.	Low	13.50
1927—			
	Jan.	High	14.50
	Feb.	Low	13.00
	July	High	24.00
	Aug.	Low	20.00
1928—			
	Jan.	High	25.50
	Mar.	Low	22.00
	Apr.	High	26.50
	June	Low	22.50
	July	High	25.00
	Oct.	Low	18.50
	Nov.	High	20.00

1929—			
	Feb.	Low	13.50
	Mar.	High	19.00
	May	Low	14.00
	Aug.	High	17.50
	Aug.	Low	16.25
	Oct.	High	18.30
	Nov.	Low	12.90
1930—			
	Jan.	High	16.80
	Feb.	Low	14.85
	Mar.	High	16.10
	Aug.	Low	9.90
	Oct.	High	14.50
1931—			
	Feb.	Low	9.50
	Mar.	High	13.40
	May	Low	9.90
	July	High	12.10
	Aug.	Low	7.25
	Nov.	High	10.75
1932—			
	June	Low	3.18
	Sept.	High	8.08
	Dec.	Low	4.10

DECEMBER HIDES

1933—			
	Jan.	High	7.10
	Feb.	Low	6.05
	July	High	14.90
	Oct.	Low	8.05
1934—			
	Jan.	High	12.15
	Mar.	Low	11.18
	April	High	12.85
	Aug.	Low	5.60
	Sept.	High	8.10
	Oct.	Low	6.30
1935—			
	Jan.	High	10.95
	Mar.	Low	9.35
	May	High	11.50
	June	Low	10.05
	Oct.	High	12.38
	Nov.	Low	11.10
1936—			
	Jan.	High	12.95
	Mar.	Low	11.95
	April	High	12.70

SEPTEMBER HIDES—OPTION—SWING—HIGH AND LOW

1936—*Continued*			1938—				Sept.	High	17.00
July	Low	10.90	Mar.	Low	8.30		Nov.	Low	13.50
Sept.	High	12.10	April	High	10.10	1940—			
Oct.	Low	11.38	June	Low	8.75		Jan.	High	15.85
			July	High	11.65		April	Low	13.62
1937—			Sept.	Low	10.50		May	High	14.85
			Oct.	High	12.95		Aug.	Low	7.80
Jan.	High	16.62	Nov.	Low	10.50		Nov.	High	13.50
Feb.	Low	15.38	1939—			1941—			
Mar.	High	19.00					Feb.	Low	12.15
June	Low	15.50	Jan.	High	14.00		May	High	15.70
July	High	17.75	April	Low	10.10		July	Low	14.10
Nov.	Low	7.85	July	High	12.20		Oct.	High	14.95
Dec.	High	12.00	Aug.	Low	9.75				

HIGHEST AND LOWEST PRICES OF DECEMBER RUBBER FUTURES ON THE COMMODITY EXCHANGE, BY MONTHS IN CENTS PER POUND

FOR DELIVERY IN

TRADING DURING MONTH OF—

	December 1932		December 1933		December 1934		December 1935		December 1936	
	High	Low	High	Low	High	Low	High	Low	High	Low
Jan.	H5.50	4.90	3.71	3.25	11.39	L9.90	H14.88	13.06	15.68	L14.65
Feb.	4.88	4.20	3.31	L3.12	11.90	11.00	14.20	13.23	16.33	15.55
Mar.	4.24	3.39	3.57	3.15	12.92	11.43	13.27	L10.91	16.43	16.08
April	3.56	3.28	5.30	3.25	14.50	12.13	12.44	11.34	16.50	16.00
May	4.35	2.96	7.25	4.76	16.36	12.59	13.20	11.86	16.17	15.48
June	3.00	L2.78	7.25	5.60	14.76	13.26	13.28	12.53	16.38	15.77
July	3.37	2.89	H11.60	6.95	15.59	14.50	12.85	11.92	16.82	16.35
Aug.	4.80	3.24	8.75	7.34	H16.49	15.00	12.50	11.94	16.55	16.18
Sept.	495	3.42	8.70	6.91	16.28	14.85	12.28	11.30	16.66	16.15
Oct.	3.83	3.92	8.60	6.91	15.04	12.85	13.55	11.81	17.12	16.33
Nov.	3.51	3.18	9.33	7.67	13.72	12.45	13.52	12.82	18.58	17.07
Dec.	3.26	3.13	9.20	8.40	13.12	12.80	13.34	12.83	H22.76	18.43

FOR DELIVERY IN

TRADING DURING MONTH OF—

	December 1937		December 1938		December 1939		December 1940		December 1941	
	High	Low	High	Low	High	Low	High	Low	High	Low
Jan.	22.00	20.44	15.90	14.97	16.30	L15.02	18.45	17.55	18.64	18.60
Feb.	22.44	20.76	16.05	14.82	16.74	15.35	18.10	17.50	20.15	19.42
Mar.	27.43	22.00	15.51	L10.77	16.79	15.75	18.28	17.45	21.59	20.10
April	H27.00	20.75	13.40	11.28	16.19	15.59	18.61	17.32	22.48	20.30
May	22.82	20.60	12.55	11.27	16.65	15.85	H21.15	L16.93		
June	20.80	18.62	15.65	11.51	16.60	16.25	19.90	17.50		
July	20.06	18.35	16.55	14.75	16.99	16.36	19.05	17.76		
Aug.	19.00	18.29	16.90	15.74	16.79	16.18	19.35	18.95		
Sept.	19.55	17.46	16.70	14.60	H22.00	16.50	16.95	18.88		
Oct.	17.76	14.77	H17.33	16.62	20.60	18.68	20.56	19.46		
Nov.	15.33	L14.01	17.20	15.48	20.60	19.80	21.14	20.23		
Dec.	15.60	14.37	16.70	15.75	20.85	19.35	20.92	20.40		

H—Highest During Life of Contract.
L—Lowest During Life of Contract.
1—New Standard Contract.

RUBBER SMOKE SHEETS AND RUBBER FUTURES
1890 TO 1941
YEARLY HIGH AND LOW PRICES

1890—	Low	70c	1899—	Low	90	1908—	Low	67	1917—	Low	45
	High	95		High	105		High	115		High	75
1891—	Low	62	1900—	Low	87	1909—	Low	115	1918—	Low	45
	High	90		High	105		High	195		High	60
1892—	Low	65	1901—	Low	80	1910—	Low	120	1919—	Low	40
	High	80		High	88		High	305		High	50
1893—	Low	65	1902—	Low	65	1911—	Low	90	1920—	Low	15
	High	80		High	80		High	157		High	45
1894—	Low	60	1903—	Low	85	1912—	Low	95	1921—	Low	12
	High	70		High	100		High	105		High	25
1895—	Low	70	1904—	Low	93	1913—	Low	60	1922—	Low	15
	High	75		High	125		High	100		High	22
1896—	Low	70	1905—	Low	110	1914—	Low	45	1923—	Low	20
	High	85		High	135		High	72		High	32
1897—	Low	80	1906—	Low	115	1915—	Low	50	1924—	Low	15
	High	88		High	125		High	72		High	35
1898—	Low	82	1907—	Low	90	1916—	Low	55	1925—	Low	35
	High	105		High	115		High	85		High	120

RUBBER SWINGS FROM HIGH TO LOW
FUTURE SEPTEMBER OPTIONS

1926—			1930—			Aug.	Low	18.10
Feb.	High	64.55	Jan.	Low	15.70	Sept.	High	19.30
Feb.	Low	47.70	Feb.	High	17.90	Nov.	Low	14.50
Mar.	High	53.50	Sept.	Low	7.80	Dec.	High	16.15
June	Low	38.00	Dec.	High	10.50	1938—		
July	High	43.30	1931—			Jan.	Low	14.65
Aug.	Low	36.70	Apr.	Low	6.00	Feb.	High	15.90
Nov.	High	44.20	June	High	7.00	Mar.	Low	10.50
Dec.	Low	39.00	Sept.	Low	4.70	Aug.	High	15.70
1927—			1932—			Sept.	Low	14.50
Jan.	High	42.00	Jan.	High	5.25	Oct.	High	17.50
Feb.	Low	40.20	June	Low	2.65	Nov.	Low	15.60
Mar.	High	42.80	Sept.	High	4.65	Dec.	High	16.50
April	Low	41.50	1933—			1939—		
May	High	42.30	Feb.	Low	3.00	Jan.	Low	15.00
June	Low	33.80	July	High	11.25	Mar.	High	16.80
Aug.	High	36.40	Sept.	Low	6.60	April	Low	15.60
Sept.	Low	32.80	1934—			Sept.	High	23.90
Nov.	High	43.40	May	High	16.05	Nov.	Low	16.30
1928—			June	Low	13.00	Dec.	High	18.80
April	Low	17.40	Sept.	High	15.90	1940—		
May	High	20.30	Dec.	Low	13.50	Mar.	Low	17.55
July	Low	18.50	1935—			April	High	18.80
Aug.	High	19.80	Jan.	High	14.60	May	Low	17.40
Sept.	Low	17.50	Mar.	Low	10.70	May	High	21.85
Oct.	High	19.20	June	High	13.10	June	Low	18.70
Nov.	Low	18.50	Sept.	Low	11.15	Aug.	High	19.80
1929—			1936—			Sept.	Low	18.80
Feb.	High	27.70	April	High	16.40	Nov.	High	20.15
Apr.	Low	20.10	May	Low	15.40	1941—		
May	High	24.50	July	High	16.70	Jan.	Low	18.80
June	Low	20.60	Aug.	Low	16.00	May	High	24.10
July	High	23.10	Dec.	High	22.50	June	Low	20.60
Sept.	Low	19.30	1937—			July	High	23.00
Oct.	High	23.50	Jan.	Low	20.10	Aug.	Low	22.25
			Mar.	High	27.45			

MONTHLY AVERAGE PRICE OF JAPANESE RAW SILK

13-15 DENIER 78% GENERAL EVENNESS—WHITE

MONTH	1927-28	1928-29	1929-30	1930-31	1931-32	1932-33	1933-34	1934-35	1935-36	1936-37	1937-38	1938-39	1939-40	1940-41
July	5.50	4.86	4.93	3.16	2.66	1.30	2.31	1.20½	1.49	1.72	2.02	1.84½	2.68	2.56½
August	5.34	4.88	5.10	3.17	2.63	1.69	1.96	1.19½	1.75	1.80	1.98½	1.75½	2.65½	2.54½
September	5.36	5.04	5.20	2.93	2.57	1.89	1.96	1.18½	1.91	1.72½	1.93	1.78	3.01½	2.57½
October	5.16	5.30	5.10	2.53	2.43	1.75	1.70½	1.23½	2.12	1.78½	1.78	1.87½	3.29	2.72
November	4.98	5.19	4.86	2.53	2.42	1.61	1.54	1.33½	2.13	2.01½	1.69½	1.81½	3.42	2.60
December	4.99	5.24	4.86	2.69	2.18	1.60	1.47½	1.43½	1.99	2.03	1.61½	1.82½	3.93	2.57½
January	5.13	5.17	4.77	2.98	2.06	1.36	1.49½	1.51	1.98	2.12½	1.59½	1.91½	3.73½	2.57½
February	5.30	5.18	4.70	2.87	1.92	1.25	1.61	1.46½	1.80½	2.02½	1.63½	2.10½	3.09½	2.62
March	5.32	5.20	4.68	2.77	1.71	1.25	1.47½	1.38½	1.74	2.07½	1.66	2.25½	2.97½	2.84
April	5.44	5.23	4.51	2.61	1.55	1.40	1.39	1.44	1.73	2.03	1.64	2.42½	2.70½	......
May	5.37	5.07	4.20	2.37	1.33	1.64	1.34	1.46½	1.62	1.91	1.64	2.71	2.79½	......
June	5.03	4.96	3.56	2.40	1.27	2.17	1.25	1.43	1.60½	1.91½	1.63½	2.55½	2.74	......
Average	5.24	5.10	4.69	2.75	2.06.	1.58	1.62½	1.36	1.82	1.93	1.73½	2.07	3.08½	......

SILK PRICES FROM 1840—1941

YEARLY AVERAGE IN DOLLARS PER POUND

ITALIAN RAW SILK IN NEW YORK—JAPANESE RAW SILK, PRINCIPAL GRADE

Year	Price	Year	Price	Year	Price	Year	Price	Year	Price	Year	Price	Year	Price
1840	6.00	1853	7.69	1866	9.12	1879	6.25	1891	4.81	1901-02	3.80	1914-15	3.24
1841	5.44	1854	5.94	1867	9.50	1880	6.00	1892	4.12	1902-03	4.14	1915-16	4.20
1842	5.94	1855	5.81	1868	10.75	1881	6.06	1893	4.93	1903-04	3.93	1916-17	5.09
1843	5.12	1856	7.62	1869	9.12	1882	5.62	1894	4.10	1904-05	3.86	1917-18	6.01
1844	6.25	1857	7.19	1870	8.50	1883	5.37	1895	3.62	1905-06	4.15	1918-19	6.88
1845	6.25	1858	7.06	1871	8.00	1884	5.12	1896	4.11	1906-07	4.90	1919-20	11.22
1846	6.44	1859	8.75	1872	9.19	1885	4.50	1897	3.49	1907-08	4.34	1920-21	5.91
1847	4.69	1860	9.12	1873	8.37	1886	4.62	1898	3.57	1908-09	3.75	1921-22	6.57
1848	4.37	1861	7.50	1874	6.75	1887	4.62	1899	3.97	1909-10	3.51	1922-23	8.23
1849	5.25	1862	6.94	1875	5.87	1888	4.69	1900	4.88	1910-11	3.63	1923-24	7.11
1850	6.75	1863	6.31	1876	7.37	1889	4.62			1911-12	3.42	1924-25	6.07
1851	6.81	1864	7.37	1877	7.31	1890	4.56			1912-13	3.52	1925-26	6.49
1852	6.87	1865	9.00	1878	5.44					1913-14	3.94	1926-27	5.77

MARCH AND SEPTEMBER SILK SWINGS

FROM HIGH TO LOW—1932-1941

Year	Month	Price	Year	Month	Price	Year	Month	Price
1932	Jan.	188	1936	Feb.	147		July	177
	June	115		Mar.	173½		Aug.	160
	Aug.	196		June	139		Oct.	178¾
				Aug.	177		Dec.	168
1933	Feb.	110		Sept.	154½			
	Mar.	122				1939	Aug.	254
	Apr.	110	1937	Jan.	219¾		Sept.	216
	June	225		Feb.	179		Dec.	437½
	Aug.	168		Mar.	206½			
	Sept.	188		June	173	1940	Feb.	252
	Nov.	132		July	195		Mar.	295½
				Nov.	142½		Apr.	224½
1934	Feb.	157					May	281
	Aug.	107					Aug.	239¾
			1938	Feb.	162		Oct.	291½
1935	Jan.	144¾		Mar.	139½			
	Mar.	125		May	155¾	1941	Jan.	247½
	Nov.	209⅞		June	144½		July	355

SUGAR—RAW, PRICES IN NEW YORK FROM 1846-1941

In cents per pound.

Yearly Average Price of "Fair Refining" Duty Paid in New York   Year Average Price of Raw Sugar (96%) Duty Paid in New York

Year	Price	Year	Price	Year	Price	Year	Price	Year	Price	Year	Price	Year	Price
1846	6.70	1858	6.33	1870	9.60	1882	7.25	1894	3.24	1906	3.69	1918	6.45
1847	5.98	1859	6.32	1871	9.11	1883	6.76	1895	3.27	1907	3.76	1919	7.72
1848	3.92	1860	6.48	1872	8.88	1884	5.27	1896	3.62	1908	4.07	1920	12.36
1849	4.59	1861	5.87	1873	7.58	1885	5.02	1897	3.56	1909	4.01	1921	4.76
1850	5.13	1862	8.18	1874	8.25	1886	4.88	1898	4.23	1910	4.19	1922	4.63
1851	4.79	1863	10.60	1875	7.90	1887	4.70	1899	4.42	1911	4.45	1923	7.02
1852	4.36	1864	16.73	1876	8.40	1888	5.05	1900	4.57	1912	4.16	1924	5.96
1853	4.42	1865	13.07	1877	8.78	1889	6.43¹	1901	4.05	1913	3.51	1925	4.33
1854	4.57	1866	10.32	1878	7.22	1890	5.45	1902	3.54	1914	3.81	1926	4.34
1855	5.68	1867	10.94	1879	6.85	1891	3.86	1903	3.72	1915	4.64	1927	4.72
1856	7.88	1868	11.73	1880	7.58	1892	3.31	1904	3.98	1916	5.79	1928	4.23
1857	8.85	1869	11.40	1881	7.62	1893	3.69	1905	4.28	1917	6.23	1929	3.76

MONTHLY AVERAGE PRICE OF RAW SUGAR (96%) DUTY PAID IN NEW YORK

MO.	1930	1931	1932	1933	1934	1935	1936	1937	1938	1939	1940	1941
Jan.	3.70	3.37	3.12	2.72	3.20	2.79	3.27	3.83	3.21	2.78	2.85	2.93
Feb.	3.58	3.31	2.95	2.73	3.32	2.90	3.35	3.55	3.13	2.77	2.83	3.00
Mar.	3.58	3.28	2.76	2.96	3.10	3.03	3.61	3.50	3.05	2.83	2.82	3.30
Apr.	3.43	3.29	2.62	3.14	2.78	3.25	3.81	3.46	2.87	2.92	2.84	3.37
May	3.20	3.18	2.59	3.33	2.78	3.28	3.81	3.40	2.72	2.92	2.79	
June	3.28	3.32	2.72	3.44	2.97	3.32	3.78	3.41	2.69	2.85	2.70	
July	3.27	3.49	3.06	3.56	3.16	3.25	3.71	3.45	2.78	2.89	2.68	
Aug.	3.18	3.46	3.15	3.48	3.29	3.30	3.69	3.55	2.79	2.86	2.64	
Sept.	3.14	3.41	3.16	3.62	2.90	3.50	3.57	3.39	2.98	3.65	2.70	
Oct.	3.28	3.41	3.14	3.33	2.91	3.62	3.39	3.18	3.08	3.44	2.80	
Nov.	3.41	3.35	3.08	3.23	2.87	3.38	3.73	3.32	3.04	2.96	2.88	
Dec.	3.29	3.14	2.83	3.23	2.67	3.13	3.82	3.24	2.88	2.93	2.91	
Average	3.36	3.33	2.93	3.22	3.00	3.23	3.63	3.44	2.94	2.98	2.79	

¹ 96% raw centrifugal 1889-92.

Sugar—Refined—Duty Paid in New York.

HIGH AND LOW PRICES

Prices in cents per pound.

1848—LOW 392.	1930—LOW 314.	1937—January, HIGH 383.
1864—HIGH 1673.	1931—HIGH 349.	1937—October, LOW 318.
1866—LOW 1032.	1931—December, LOW 314.	1938—June, LOW 269.
1868—HIGH 1173.	1932—April, LOW 262.	1939—April-May, HIGH 292.
1892—LOW 331.	1932—August, HIGH 315.	1939—June, LOW 285.
1893—HIGH 369.	1932—December, LOW 282.	1939—September, HIGH 365.
1894—LOW 324.	1933—July, LOW 272.	1939—December, LOW 292.
1900—HIGH 457.	1933—September, HIGH 362.	1940—January, HIGH 285.
1902—LOW 354.	1934—February, HIGH 332.	1940—August, LOW 264.
1911—HIGH 445.	1934—December, LOW 267.	1940—December, HIGH 291.
1913—LOW 351.	1935—October, HIGH 262.	1941—January, LOW 293.
1920—HIGH 1236.	1936—May, HIGH 381.	

JULY SUGAR—SWINGS FROM HIGH TO LOW

Year	Month	Value	Year	Month	Value	Year	Month	Value	Year	Month	Value
1915	Jan.	315	1921	Feb.	415	1927	Jan.	355	1934	Feb.	172
	Feb.	430		Mar.	570		July	258		Apr.	140
	Mar.	370		June	275		Sept.	315		Aug.	205
	May	412		Oct.	265	1928	Feb.	255		Oct.	172
	Aug.	300		Dec.	235		Mar.	295			
1916	Jan.	575	1922	Mar.	288		July	225	1935	May	255
	Aug.	390		May	245		July	279	1936	Jan.	195
	Oct.	450	1923	Apr.	685	1929	June	165		June	290
	Dec.	388		June	458		Sept.	248		Oct.	238
1917	Jan.	432		July	550	1930	July	118	1937	Jan.	308
	Feb.	385		Nov.	403		July	168		Aug.	230
	Apr.	578	1924	Feb.	582		Sept.	122		Sept.	250
	July	465		June	305		Oct.	172	1938	May	172
1918-19—Ex. Closed				Sept.	365		Dec.	122		Dec.	222
on account of war				Dec.	300	1931	Jan.	155	1939	Feb.	185
			1925	Feb.	335		Mar.	128		May	205
1920	Feb.	960		June	235		Apr.	147		June	182
	Apr.	1975		July	298		May	108		Sept.	295
	May	2335		Sept.	238		Aug.	163		Oct.	175
	June	1550		Dec.	280	1932	June	58			
	Dec.	550	1926	Mar.	238		Sept.	120	1940	Feb.	205
				Apr.	265	1933	Feb.	72		June	170
				June	231		July	187		Sept.	303
							Oct.	122			

SUGAR FUTURES ON THE NEW YORK COFFEE & SUGAR EXCHANGE
VOLUME OF TRADING MONTHLY

In Thousands of Long Tons.

Month	1930	1931	1932	1933	1934	1935	1936	1937	1938	1939	1940	1941
January	881	461	291	247	446	600	496	1,040	245	389	526	378
February	910	607	651	467	460	488	192	482	546	503	464	466
March	679	568	672	633	339	504	359	911	438	505	391	779
April	977	644	527	1,019	441	724	224	929	637	465	644	365
May	932	555	318	686	283	583	121	382	351	315	706	
June	874	673	667	747	510	320	146	673	371	391	296	
July	785	497	468	887	243	280	131	515	501	237	307	
August	810	496	459	542	671	260	91	959	483	497	446	
September	554	347	349	244	393	182	206	416	396	810	151	
October	1,167	332	366	540	444	153	181	266	206	623	209	
November	853	426	462	571	306	145	392	223	244	444	226	
December	935	319	291	265	252	146	288	249	388	549	287	
Total Year	10,372	5,916	5,521	6,847	4,789	4,384	2,828	7,047	4,807	5,728	4,653	

WOOL PRICES IN BOSTON FROM 1851-1941

In cents per pound.

YEARLY AVERAGE PRICES OHIO FINE SCOURED FLEECE WOOL				Territory Fine Combing Wools Grades 64's, 70's, 80's Scoured Basis	
Year Price	Year Price	Year Price	Year Price	Year Price	Year Price
1851 85½	1864 177	1877 91	1890 73¼	1903 55	1916 84
1852 81¾	1865 166	1878 74¾	1891 70¾	1904 59	1917 157
1853 107	1866 131¼	1879 71¾	1892 61	1905 72	1918 182
1854 91¼	1867 113¼	1880 102¾	1893 56	1906 71	1919 178
1855 85¾	1868 88¾	1881 95½	1894 44½	1907 70	1920 160
1856 104¾	1869 90½	1882 90½	1895 37¾	1908 60	1921 85
1857 102	1870 89¾	1883 86	1896 39½	1909 70	1922 125
1858 82½	1871 106¾	1884 80½	1897 49½	1910 65	1923 141
1859 109¼	1872 156¾	1885 71¼	1898 61½	1911 57	1924 141
1860 102½	1873 119¾	1886 74	1899 62¼	1912 64	1925 139
1861 82¾	1874 115¼	1887 73¼	1900 56	1913 56	1926 116
1862 93¾	1875 104½	1888 68	1901 47	1914 59	1927 110
1863 151½	1876 87	1889 73½	1902 51	1915 71	1928 116

MONTHLY AVERAGE PRICES TERRITORY FINE COMBING WOOLS—SCOURED BASIS—GRADES 64's, 70's, 80's

Mo.	1929	1930	1931	1932	1933	1934	1935	1936	1937	1938	1939	1940	1941
Jan.	114	82	68	58	44	86	76	88	114	77	73	105	108
Feb.	111	79	66	56	44	87	71	94	114	71	73	99	108
Mar.	108	78	66	54	46	87	66	94	113	68	72	94	109
Apr.	104	76	66	49	48	86	66	89	113	69	69	89	108
May	100	75	64	44	62	85	67	88	105	68	70	89	
June	97	76	62	38	70	84	74	89	102	65	71	90	
July	94	76	62	36	77	84	76	89	102	69	72	88	
Aug.	94	76	64	41	79	76	76	89	102	71	74	89	
Sept.	93	76	62	48	82	76	79	89	98	70	99	92	
Oct.	90	75	59	48	83	76	80	90	92	71	110	105	
Nov.	88	73	59	47	84	76	84	99	86	74	105	109	
Dec.	84	72	59	45	85	76	84	107	81	73	106	109	
Average	98	76	63	47	67	82	75	92	102	70	83	96	

WHEAT CROPS OR PRODUCTION

The production of Wheat increased from 1866 to 1915, when a record crop of over one Billion Bushels was harvested.

1866 Crop 150 Million Bushels

1880 " 500 " " a record to that time.

1881 " 400 " " a shorter Crop.

1882 " 500 " " or slightly over this figure, making 1880-82-84—three years of large Crops to that time.

1885 Crop 350 Million Bushels, a short crop for that time. From 1885 two crops were around 400 Million Bushels, and under 500 Million.

1891 Crop 600 Million Bushels a new record.

1893 " 400 " " the last short crop just under 400 Million.

1894 to 1897 Small crops under 500 Million bushels, but not as low as 400 Million, but more than enough to suppply the demand. Wheat sold at lowest level since the Civil War, reaching extreme low Jan. 1895, when May Wheat sold at 48⅞. After that the long trend was up to 1919-20, when Top prices were reached in the War period.

1898	Crops	675,149,000	a record to date.
1900	"	522,230,000	this was two years smaller crops.
1901	"	748,460,000	a record to date.
1904	"	552,400,000	two years smaller crops.
1906	"	735,261,000	just under the record of 1901.
1907	"	634,687,000	one year smaller crop.
1909	"	737,181,000	one year from low still under 1901 record.
1911	"	621,338,000	two years smaller crops following four years larger crops.
1913	"	763,380,000	a record to date.
1915	"	1,625,801,000	the first crop over one Billion bushels. A record that has not been exceeded to 1941.
1916	"	636,318,000	or smaller.
1917	"	636,655,000	two crops almost the same.
1919	"	968,279,000	two years larger crops and 1919 crops, just under 1915 record.
1921	"	814,905,000	two years smaller crops.
1922	"	867,598,000	one year larger crops.
1923	"	797,281,000	one year smaller.
1924	"	872,673,000	one year larger.
1925	"	676,429,000	one year smaller and the smallest crop since 1916 or 10 years from a record to extreme short Crop. This was smallest since 1916-17.
1928	"	914,876,000	the third year larger but not up to 1919 crop.
1929	"	812,573,000	one year smaller crop.
1931	"	932,000,000	two years large crop the largest since 1919.
1934	"	526,393,000	three years smaller crops and the shortest crop since 1896 and 19 years from the 1915 record to the smallest crop and 15 years from 1919 last record.
1938	"	931,702,000	four years larger crops and almost the same size crop as 1931.
1939	"	751,435,000	one year shorter crop.
1941	"	961,194,000	two years larger crops and up to 1919 crops which were two largest on record.

According to my study of Crop periods and time cycles, crops should be larger up to 1945 and should record low prices, the same as 1841 to 1852 was a period of extreme low prices.

GRAIN CROPS OF THE UNITED STATES

Year	Wheat	Corn	Oats	Rye	Barley	Buckwheat	Potatoes	Hay, tons
1888	415,868,000	1,987,790,000	701,735,000	28,415,000	38,884,000	12,050,000	202,365,000	46,643,000
1889	490,560,000	2,112,892,000	751,515,000	28,420,000	78,333,000	12,110,000	204,990,000	66,830,000
1890	399,262,000	1,489,970,000	523,621,000	25,807,000	67,168,000	12,433,000	148,079,000	60,198,000
1891	611,780,000	2,060,154,000	738,394,000	31,752,000	86,839,000	12,761,000	254,427,000	60,818,000
1892	515,949,000	1,628,464,000	661,035,000	27,979,000	80,097,000	12,143,000	156,655,000	59,824,000
1893	396,132,000	1,619,496,000	638,855,000	26,555,000	69,869,000	12,132,000.	183,034,000	65,766,000
1894	460,267,000	1,212,770,000	662,037,000	26,728,000	61,400,000	12,668,000	170,787,000	54,874,000
1895	467,103,000	2,151,139,000	824,444,000	27,210,000	87,073,000	15,341,000	297,237,000	47,079,000
1896	427,684,000	2,283,875,000	707,346,000	24,369,000	69,695,000	14,090,000	252,235,000	59,282,000
1897	530,149,000	1,902,968,000	698,768,000	27,363,000	65,685,000	14,997,000	164,016,000	60,665,000
1898	675,149,000	1,924,185,000	730,907,000	25,658,000	55,792,000	11,722,000	192,306,000	66,377,000
1899	547,304,000	2,078,144,000	796,178,000	23,962,000	73,382,000	11,094,000	210,927,000	56,656,000
1900	522,230,000	2,105,103,000	809,126,000	23,996,000	58,926,000	9,567,000	228,783,000	50,111,000
1901	748,460,000	1,522,520,000	736,809,000	30,345,000	109,933,000	15,126,000	187,598,000	50,591,000
1902	670,063,000	2,523,648,000	987,843,000	33,631,000	134,954,000	14,530,000	284,633,000	59,858,000
1903	637,822,000	2,214,177,000	784,094,000	29,363,000	131,861,000	14,244,000	247,128,000	61,306,000
1904	552,400,000	2,467,481,000	894,596,000	27,235,000	139,749,000	15,008,000	332,800,000	60,696,000
1905	692,979,000	2,707,994,000	953,216,000	28,486,000	136,651,000	14,535,000	260,741,000	60,532,000
1906	735,261,000	2,927,416,000	964,904,000	33,375,000	178,916,000	14,642,000	308,038,000	57,146,000
1907	634,087,000	2,592,330,000	754,443,000	31,566,000	153,597,000	14,290,000	297,942,000	63,677,000
1908	664,602,000	2,668,651,000	807,156,000	31,851,000	166,756,000	15,874,000	278,985,000	70,798,000
1909	737,189,000	2,772,376,000	1,007,353,000	32,239,000	170,284,000	17,438,000	376,537,000	64,938,000
1910	695,443,000	3,125,713,000	1,126,765,000	33,039,000	162,227,000	17,239,000	338,811,000	60,978,000
1911	621,338,000	2,531,488,000	922,298,000	33,119,000	160,240,000	17,549,000	292,737,000	54,916,000
1912	730,267,000	3,124,746,000	1,418,337,000	35,664,000	223,824,000	19,249,000	420,647,000	72,691,000
1913	763,380,000	2,446,988,000	1,121,768,000	41,381,000	178,189,000	13,833,000	331,525,000	64,116,000
1914	891,017,000	2,672,804,000	1,141,060,000	42,779,000	194,953,000	16,884,000	409,921,000	88,686,000
1915	1,025,801,000	2,994,713,000	1,549,030,000	54,050,000	228,817,000	15,056,000	359,731,000	107,263,000
1916	636,318,000	2,566,927,000	1,251,837,000	48,862,000	182,309,000	11,662,000	286,953,000	110,992,000
1917	636,655,000	3,065,233,000	1,592,740,000	62,933,000	211,759,000	16,022,000	438,618,000	98,439,000

GRAIN CROPS OF THE UNITED STATES (Continued)

Year	Wheat	Corn	Oats	Rye	Barley	Buckwheat	Potatoes	Hay, tons
1918	917,100,000	2,582,814,000	1,538,359,000	89,103,000	256,375,000	16,905,000	397,676,000	91,139,000
1919	968,279,000	2,816,318,000	1,184,030,000	75,542,000	147,608,000	14,295,000	322,867,000	104,760,000
1920	833,027,000	3,208,584,000	1,496,281,000	60,490,000	189,332,000	13,142,000	403,296,000	105,315,000
1921	814,905,000	3,068,569,000	1,078,341,000	61,675,000	154,946,000	14,207,000	361,659,000	97,770,000
1922	867,598,000	2,906,020,000	1,215,803,000	103,362,000	182,068,000	14,564,000	453,396,000	112,013,000
1923	797,281,000	3,053,557,000	1,305,883,000	63,077,000	197,691,000	13,965,000	416,105,000	106,611,000
1924	872,673,000	2,436,513,000	1,541,900,000	63,446,000	187,875,000	15,956,000	454,784,000	112,450,000
1925	676,429,000	2,916,961,000	1,487,550,000	46,456,000	216,554,000	13,994,000	323,465,000	98,141,000
1926	831,040,000	2,692,217,000	1,246,848,000	40,795,000	184,905,000	12,676,000	354,328,000	96,065,000
1927	878,374,000	2,763,093,000	1,182,594,000	58,164,000	255,882,000	15,755,000	402,741,000	123,327,000
1928	914,876,000	2,818,901,000	1,439,407,000	43,366,000	357,487,000	13,148,000	465,350,000	106,226,000
1929	812,573,000	2,535,386,000	1,118,414,000	34,950,000	280,242,000	8,692,000	329,134,000	87,308,000
1930	857,427,000	2,059,641,000	1,276,035,000	45,481,000	303,752,000	6,960,000	333,936,000	74,310,000
1931	932,000,000	2,588,000,000	1,126,913,000	32,290,000	198,543,000	8,890,000	372,994,000	73,708,000
1932	744,000,000	2,906,000,000	1,246,658,000	40,639,000	302,800,060	6,727,000	358,009,000	82,405,000
1933	527,000,000	2,330,000,000	722,485,000	21,184,000	156,104,000	7,844,000	317,143,000	74,485,000
1934	526,393,000	1,478,027,000	542,306,000	16,045,000	118,348,000	9,042,000	385,421,000	57,028,000
1935	623,444,000	2,291,629,000	1,198,668,000	58,587,000	285,774,000	8,332,000	386,380,000	89,742,000
1936	626,766,000	1,507,089,000	785,506,000	25,319,000	147,475,000	6,285,000	331,918,000	70,386,000
1937	875,676,000	2,651,284,000	1,161,612,000	49,830,000	220,327,000	6,764,000	394,139,000	82,617,000
1938	931,702,000	2,562,197,000	1,068,431,000	55,564,000	253,005,000	6,654,000	374,163,000	91,531,000
1939	751,435,000	2,602,133,000	935,942,000	39,149,000	274,767,000	5,669,000	363,159,000	85,124,000
1940	816,698,000	2,449,200,000	1,235,628,000	40,601,000	309,235,000	6,350,000	397,722,000	95,156,000
1941	961,194,000	2,625,502,000	1,138,843,000	46,462,000	(1941 Crops Estimated			

SOY BEANS TOTAL PRODUCTION IN U. S.

	Production	Acreage Harvested		Production	Acreage Harvested
1924	4,947,000	448,000	1933	13,147,000	997,000
1925	4,875.000	415,000	1934	23,095,000	1,539,000
1926	5,239,000	466,000	1935	44,378,000	2,697,000
1927	6,938,000	568,000	1936	29,983,000	2,132,000
1928	7,880,000	579,000	1937	45,272,000	2,549,000
1929	9,398,000	708,000	1938	62,729,000	3,105,000
1930	13,471,000	1,008,000	1939	91,272,000	4,417,000
1931	16,733,000	1,104,000	1940	79,837,000	4,961,000
1932	14,975,000	977,000	1941	111,000,000	Estimated

CORN CROPS

1867 crop	750,000,000	Bushels	—This was the last time that a crop this small was produced.
1870-1872	1,000,000,000	"	—The first time a crop of over 1 billion was produced.
1874	825,000,000	"	—Two years smaller crop.
1880	1,700,000,000	"	—A record to date. 6 years larger crops.
1881	1,200,000,000	"	—I year shorter crop.
1885	1,900,000,000	"	—4 years larger crops. A record to date.
1887	1,445,000,000	"	—2 years shorter crops.
1889	2,100,000,000	"	—2 years larger, the 1st crop over 2 billion bushels.
1890	1,500,000,000	"	—1 year smaller crop.
1891	2,000,000,000	"	—1 year larger crop and 2nd largest on record.
1894	1,200,000,000	"	—3 years shorter crops. This was last crop this small..
1896	2,300,000,000	"	—2 years larger crops and a record to date.
1901	1,522,520,000	"	—5 years shorter crops.
1902	1,523,648,000	"	—6 years shorter crop and the last small crop.
1904	2,467,481,000	"	—2 years larger crop. A record to date.
1906	2,927,416,000	"	—5 years larger crops. A record to date
1907	2,592,330,000	"	—1 year smaller crop.
1910	3,125,713,000	"	—3 years larger crops. The first crop over 3 billion.
1911	2,531,488,000	"	—1 year smaller crop.
1912	3,124,746,000	"	—1 year larger crop, and the 2nd crop over 3 billion.
1913	2,446,988,000	"	—1 year smaller crop.
1920	3,208,584,000	"	—7 years from last short, and a record crop.
1921	3,068,569,000	"	—1 years smaller crop, but 2 years over 3 billion.
1922	2,906,020,000	"	—1 year smaller, but still a large crop.
1923	3,053,557,000	"	—1 year larger crop, and 4 years averaging over 3 billion. A record.
1924	2,436,513,000	"	—1 year smaller crop.
1925	2,916,961,000	"	—1 year larger crop.
1930	2,059,641,000	"	—5 years smaller crops and the lowest since 1902.
1932	2,906,000,000	"	—2 years larger crop.
1934	1,478,000,000	"	—2 smaller crops, and smaller than 1901 and 1902. This extremely short crop reduced the supply and laid the foundation for higher prices for several years to follow.

CORN CROPS (*Continued*)

1935	2,291,629,000	"	—1 year larger crop.
1936	1,507,089,000	"	—1 year smaller, and one almost as low as 1934 crop. 2 very short crops in 3 years was very bullish, as prices advanced rapidly in 1936-37, corn prices going higher than wheat.
1937	2,651,284,000	"	—1 year larger crop and enough to start a big decline in corn prices.
1938	2,562,197,000	"	—1 year smaller crop, but not much below 1937 crop.
1939	2,602,133,000	"	—1 year larger crop, but 5 years from extreme low crop in 1934.
1940	2,449,200,000	"	—1 year smaller crop, but still more than enough to supply the demand.
1941	2,625,502,000	"	—Estimated by Government Sept. 10th. This is one year larger crop but will be largest crop since 1936. Plenty of corn to cause lower prices.

The record crops were 1910, 1912 and 1920, and 1942 to 1944 the record should be broken or at least years of larger crops and lower prices. The increased demand and many new uses for Soy Beans may cause a larger acreage to be planted in Soy Beans, which may cause some reduction in corn acreage. Farmers will plant more of any crops that they can get the most money for.

A study of crop records in connection with price and time charts will help you to forecast the trend of corn and other commodities.

TOTAL PRODUCTION OF HOGS IN UNITED STATES

In Thousands

Year	Total	Year	Total	Year	Total	Year	Total
1926	75,444	1930	74,135	1934	56,766	1938	71,101
1927	81,246	1931	83,176	1935	55,086	1939	85,894
1928	78,682	1932	82,525	1936	64,917	1940	76,976
1929	76,125	1933	84,200	1937	61,907		

UNITED STATES PIG CROP STATISTICS BY SEASONS AND REGIONS

In Thousands

Year	Spring Pig Crop		Fall Pig Crop		Eastern Corn Belt	Western Corn Belt	Total Corn Belt	Other States	Total United States
	Sows Farrowed	Pigs Saved	Sows Farrowed	Pigs Saved					
1926	9,048	50,579	4,330	24,865	18,428	38,704	57,132	18,312	75,444
1927	9,754	54,502	4,609	26,744	20,015	40,236	60,251	20,995	81,246
1928	9,301	52,390	4,429	26,292	18,974	40,382	59,356	19,326	78,682
1929	8,854	50,179	4,264	25,646	18,247	40,229	58,476	17,649	76,125
1930	8,278	49,332	4,073	24,803	17,881	40,025	57,906	16,229	74,135
1931	8,969	53,984	4,797	29,192	19,886	44,651	64,537	18,639	83,176
1932	8,810	51,031	5,179	31,494	21,836	39,487	61,323	21,202	82,525
1933	9,122	53,460	5,207	30,740	23,022	40,670	63,692	20,508	84,200
1934	6,825	39,698	2,936	17,068	15,445	25,025	40,470	16,296	56,766
1935	5,394	32,438	3,758	22,648	15,442	22,646	38,088	16,998	55,086
1936	6,920	41,234	3,857	23,683	18,081	26,376	44,457	20,460	64,917
1937	6,175	38,476	3,757	23,431	17,860	23,581	41,441	20,466	61,907
1938	6,827	43,450	4,372	27,651	20,106	27,366	47,972	23,129	71,101
1939	8,695	53,207	5,192	32,687	23,725	35,593	59,318	26,576	85,894
1940	8,057	48,389	4,504	28,587	23,190	32,112	55,302	21,674	76,976
1941	6,938*	....	....	....	....	....	....	....	....

*Indicated to farrow from Breeding Intentions Report.

WORLD PRODUCTION OF COMMERCIAL COTTON
INCLUDING UNITED STATES and ALL FOREIGN COUNTRIES

In Thousands of Bales

Season	World Total	Season	World Total	Season	World Total
1921-22	15,173	1928-29	25,802	1935-36	26,320
1922-23	18,451	1929-30	26,251	1936-37	30,796
1923-24	19,090	1930-31	25,376	1937-38	36,784
1924-25	24,094	1931-32	26,479	1938-39	27,407
1925-26	26,743	1932-33	23,461	1930-40	27,450
1926-27	27,930	1933-34	26,066	1940-41	29,421
1927-28	23,343	1934-35	23,050		

COTTON PRICES, CROPS, EXPORTS ACREAGE
IN UNITED STATES

	High Price	Low Price	Crop Bales	Exports From U. S. Bales	Acreage
1888-89	11-1/16	9⅛	6,935,000	4,709,000	19,362,000
1889-90	12-5/16	9¾	7,314,000	4,996,000	20,172,000
1890-91	10-9/16	7⅜	8,655,000	5,783,000	20,809,000
1891-92	8-3/16	6¼	9,038,000	5,868,000	20,714,000
1892-93	9-9/16	6⅝	6,717,000	4,410 000	18,067,000
1893-94	8⅛	6-7/16	7,550,000	5,360,000	19,684,000
1894-95	7¾	5⅛	10,025,000	7,281,000	21,454,000
1895-96	8-5/16	6-11/16	7,157,000	4,751,000	18,882,000
1896-97	8½	6-11/16	8,758,000	5,971,000	23,273,000
1897-98	7½	5⅝	11,200,000	7,700,000	24,319,000
1898-99	673	۵96	11,274,000	8,007,000	24,967,000
1899-1900	10	676	9,439,000	6,542,000	25,035,000
1900-1901	1060	79ι	10,383,000	7,176,000	27,532,000
1901-02	967	735	9,675,000	7,247,000	27,950,000
1902-03	1375	787	10,784,000	7,281,000	27,874,000
1903-04	1724	901	10,015,000	6,575,000	28,907,000
1904-05	1115	639	13,697,000	9,539,000	31,730,000
1905-06	1201	860	11,346,000	7,296,000	26,117,000
1906-07	1210	858	13,540,000	8,708,000	31,374,000
1907-08	1205	833	11,678,000	7,435,000	31,311,000
1908-09	938	835	12,920,000	....	32,081,000
1909-10	1615	1243	10,005,000	8,578,000	32,444,000
1910-11	1505	1125	11,609,000	6,263,000	31,918,000
1911-12	1299	876	15,693,000	8,068,000	33,418,000
1912-13	1318	1000	13,703,000	11,070,000	36,045,000
1913-14	1445	1198	14,156,000	8,725,000	34,766,000
1914-15	1038	715	16,135,000	9,165,000	37,089,000
1915-16	1338	968	11,191,000	8,426,000	37,406,000
1916-17	2765	1336	11,450,000	5,956,000	31,412,000
1917-18	3600	2120	11,302,000	5,947,000	34,985,000
1918-19	3820	2500	12,041,000	4,529,000	33,841,000
1919-20	4375	2845	11,421,000	5,296,000	36,008,000
1920-21	4000	1085	13,440,000	5,409,000	33,566,000
1921-22	2375	1280	7,954,000	6,542,000	30,509,000
1922-23	3130	2035	10,124,000	5,066,000	33,036,000
1923-24	3765	2350	10,330,000	5,803,000	37,123,000
1924-25	3150	2205	14,006,000	8,064,000	40,115,000
1925-26	2423	1805	16,181,000	4,444,639	45,945,000
1926-27	1920	1215	18,162,000	11,222,000	46,053,000
1927-28	2390	1700	12,957,000	7,836,000	47,207,000
1928-29	2165	1765	14,555,000	8,053,000	40,138,000
1929-30	1955	1245	14,716,000	6,669,000	45,326,000
1930-31	1315	825	13,873,000	6,820,000	41,189,000
1931-32	815	500	16,877,000	8,754,000	40,693,000
1932-33	1175	570	12,961,000	8,426,000	36,542,000
1933-34	1045	865	12,712,000	4,089,000	30,144,000
1934-35	1380	1015	9,576,000	4,816,000	26,987,000
1935-36	1365	1065	10,495,000	6,040,000	27,335,000
1936-37	1525	1118	12,375,000	5,511,000	30,054,000
1937-38	1135	771	18,412,000	5,672,000	34,001,000
1938-39	1002	788	11,665,000	3,353,000	24,248,000
1939-40	1166	882	11,516,000	6,447,000	23,805,000
1940-41	1041	968	12,287,000	607,000	24,078,000
1941-42			11,061,000		

COTTONSEED PRODUCTION AND DISPOSITION
IN THE UNITED STATES
In Thousands of Short Tons

July 31 to Aug. 1	Ex- changed for Meal	Sold or for Sale	Total	As Percent- age of Production	Total	As Percent- age of Production
1921-22	336	2.559	2,895	82.1	3,008	85.3
1922-23	310	2,907	3,217	74.3	3,242	74.9
1923-24	259	3,019	3,278	72.8	3,308	73.5
1924-25	294	4,293	4,587	75.8	4,605	76.1
1925-26	351	5,164	5,515	77.1	5,558	77.7
1926-27	412	5,952	6,364	79.7	6,306	78.9
1927-28	322	4,264	4,586	79.6	4.654	80.8
1928-29	329	4,755	5,084	79.0	5,061	78.6
1929-30	317	4.705	5,022	76.2	5,016	76.1
1930-31	490	4,204	4,694	75.8	4,715	76.2
1931-32	859	4,761	5,620	73.9	5,328	70.1
1932-33	596	3,947	4,543	78.5	4,621	79.9
1933-34	385	3,774	4,159	71.6	4,157	71.6
1934-35	208	3,210	3,418	79.8	3,550	82.9
1935-36	316	3,434	3,750	79.3	3.818	80.7
1936-37	294	4,225	4.519	81.9	4,498	81.6
1937-38	655	5,966	6,621	78.6	6,326	75.1
1938-39	447	3,700	4,147	78.1	4.471	84.2
1939-40	....	....	....	......		.....

UNITED STATES PRODUCTION OF CRUDE
COTTONSEED OIL, BY MONTHS
In Millions of Pounds

Mo.	1930-31	1931-32	1932-33	1933-34	1934-35	1935-36	1936-37	1937-38	1938-39	1939-40	1940-41
Aug.	49	17	46	72	59	43	30	53	68	45	23
Sept.	170	136	173	159	134	130	177	231	179	162	111
Oct.	285	271	218	200	184	227	224	288	205	220	225
Nov.	238	271	209	182	165	191	203	274	195	202	205
Dec.	202	224	150	137	129	156	198	246	162	160	174
Jan.	182	134	136	145	124	136	173	222	145	166	179
Feb.	124	171	137	136	108	107	130	198	118	139	148
Mar.	90	168	116	112	34	82	100	176	129	98	123
Apr.	52	113	81	60	43	43	59	110	85	62	
May	28	68	73	38	33	24	34	69	68	36	
June	14	40	57	30	23	14	24	54	33	19	
July	7	29	50	31	21	11	13	45	24	14	
Total Sea- son	1,442	1,694	1,446	1,303	1,109	1,164	1,364	1,966	1,409	1,324	

COTTONSEED PRODUCTION AND DISPOSITION
IN THE UNITED STATES

In Thousands of Short Tons

Aug. 1st to July 31st	Production	Retained on Farms Used for Seed Following Year	Fed or used for Fertilizer	Total
1921-22	3,528	500	133	633
1922-23	4,330	568	545	1,113
1923-24	4,503	619	606	1,225
1924-25	6,050	700	763	1,463
1925-26	7,150	703	932	1,635
1926-27	7,989	604	1,021	1,652
1927-28	5,758	677	495	1,172
1928-29	6,435	684	667	1,351
1929-30	6,590	670	898	1,568
1930-31	6,191	607	890	1,497
1931-32	7,604	572	1,412	1,984
1932-33	5,784	622	619	1,241
1933-34	5,806	432	1,215	1,647
1934-35	4,282	437	427	864
1935-36	4,729	481	498	979
1936-37	5,511	542	450	992
1937-38	8,426	424	1,381	1,805
1938-39	5,310	389	662	1,163
1939-40	5,239	402	698	1,100
1940-41	5,645			

UNITED STATES PRODUCTION OF REFINED COTTONSEED OIL, BY MONTHS

In Millions of Pounds

Month	1930-31	1931-32	1932-33	1933-34	1934-35	1935-36	1936-37	1937-38	1938-39	1939-40	1940-41
Aug.	27.1	12.0	39.8	57.4	50.1	38.2	20.5	28.1	53.4	54.7	32.4
Sept.	103.5	64.0	79.7	78.3	79.5	74.3	95.2	127.3	94.9	93.9	46.2
Oct.	231.4	206.6	170.0	157.8	155.0	164.5	178.6	213.5	159.9	163.3	134.4
Nov.	213.9	227.6	183.3	152.2	149.7	173.0	182.4	214.1	161.9	163.1	158.4
Dec.	190.4	226.0	133.1	120.7	132.3	139.3	184.2	218.7	144.7	157.2	168.5
Jan.	149.9	155.5	112.9	110.0	111.9	127.4	153.0	192.2	139.4	140.4	179.9
Feb.	131.5	161.6	112.2	134.3	103.0	112.4	142.8	195.4	113.4	126.2	145.1
Mar.	116.6	136.3	108.8	127.4	97.2	86.3	133.5	192.1	132.0	114.7	123.8
Apr.	75.8	112.1	98.3	94.5	73.4	65.2	92.2	128.8	98.8	97.3	
May	36.8	90.3	108.2	65.8	52.0	41.2	55.1	107.9	82.0	79.5	
June	30.4	70.9	69.6	54.6	37.1	40.4	46.2	80.3	78.7	51.1	
July	16.0	47.8	58.0	43.5	26.1	29.6	26.5	53.9	41.5	49.5	
Season Total	1,323.3	1,513.2	1273.9	1,196.5	1,067.3	1,091.8	1,310.2	1,752.3	1,297.7	1,288.9	
Season Total in thousands of barrels	2,308	3,783	3,185	2,991	2,668	2,729	3,275	4,381	324.4	322.0	

COFFEE PRODUCTION, BY SELECTED COUNTRIES

In Thousands of Bags of 132 Pounds

Year[1]	Brazil	Colombia	Salvador	Guatemala	Mexico	Costa Rica	Venezuela	Nicaragua	Other Americas	European Colonies	Total World
1881	5,568	100	110	300	70	280	680	70	783	2,454	10,415
1885	5,773	120	225	277	80	160	665	75	978	1,569	9,922
1890	5,576	150	250	300	100	180	620	72	980	1,169	9,397
1895	5,990	250	100	650	400	180	700	70	815	1,265	10,420
1900	11,314	250	300	575	350	300	800	140	570	963	15,562
1905	10,844	500	520	550	350	295	740	160	487	628	15,074
1910	10,848	500	475	560	320	207	650	150	693	627	15,030
1915	15,960	750	450	680	300	180	1,000	150	758	1,076	21,304
1920	14,496	1,700	450	690	300	117	1,045	180	735	1,208	20,921
1925	15,460	1,918	832	750	402	307	902	295	972	2,179	24,017
1926	15,848	2,438	590	717	346	270	923	163	876	1,994	24,165
1927	27,122	2,529	603	686	534	314	760	300	920	2,426	36,194
1928	13,621	2,608	885	702	527	328	900	240	726	3,088	23,625
1929	28,228	3,060	730	754	498	392	1,072	368	866	2,361	38,379
1930	16,552	3,017	977	960	512	384	1,000	295	735	2,338	26,770
1931	27,933	3,015	911	610	455	308	934	270	787	2,361	37,584
1932	16,500	3,348	661	775	334	380	750	135	1,105	3,372	27,400
1933	29,610	3,464	936	598	688	463	569	200	877	2,579	40,004
1934	17,366	3,330	850	800	650	450	800	220	771	2,725	27,932
1935	20,803	3,824	807	901	528	365	850	225	1,154	3,559	33,016
1936	25,614	4,135	975	750	714	465	1,100	200	1,249	4,086	39,308
1937	22,630	4,135	756	740	585	550	1,000	232	1,345	4,133	36,152
1938	23,113	4,250	740	900	450	340	500	200	1,180	4,050	35,943
1939	21,861	4,200	900	925	1,100	425	1,000	260	1,260	4,230	36,161
1940	20,850	4,300	750	795	950	400	600	150	——	——	——
1941[2]	12,000										

[1] Calendar year shown, or crop year beginning July 1st of year shown.
[2] Estimated.

HIDES — WETTINGS (Hides* Put into Tanning Process) FOR ALL CATTLE HIDE LEATHERS

MONTHLY

In Thousands of Hides

Month	1931	1932	1933	1934	1935	1936	1937	1938	1939	1940	1941
January	1,206	1,228	1,353	1,732	1,940	2,009	2,086	1,478	1,851	1,996	2,201
February	1,194	1,166	1,259	1,712	1,738	1,944	1,985	1,411	1,570	1,791	2,051
March	1,304	1,381	1,204	1,716	1,773	1,862	2,223	1,465	1,887	1,597	2,115
April	1,377	1,177	1,178	1,641	1,702	1,804	2,089	1,389	1,620	1,520	
May	1,309	1,050	1,429	1,637	1,830	1,709	1,933	1,457	1,777	1,704	
June	1,483	1,092	1,596	1,592	1,667	1,739	1,869	1,458	1,711	1,485	
July	1,439	1,022	1,612	1,531	1,792	1,899	1,767	1,470	1,677	1,638	
August	1,580	1,157	1,711	1,651	1,850	1,834	1,813	1,802	1,954	1,829	
September	1,368	1,343	1,559	1,462	1,779	1,848	1,678	1,755	1,736	1,720	
October	1,372	1,444	1,486	1,733	2,069	2,152	1,538	1,762	1,908	2,060	
November	1,213	1,411	1,478	1,755	1,911	2,020	1,345	1,837	1,900	1,989	
December	1,196	1,190	1,567	1,732	1,945	2,068	1,400	1,903	1,824	2,015	
Total	16,041	14,661	17,432	19,914	21,996	22,888	21,726	19,187	21,715	21,353	

*Cattle hides and kips.

ACREAGE, PRODUCTION AND FOREIGN TRADE OF POTATOES IN THE UNITED STATES

| | Acreage Harvested | Average Yield Per Acre | Production | AVERAGE PRICE PER BUSHEL | | Farm Value | FOREIGN TRADE JUNE-JULY | | Merchantable Stocks December 31st |
| | | | | Farm Price | Wholesale at New York | | Domestic Exports | Imports | |
	1,000 Acres	Bushels	1,000 Bushels	Cents per Bushel	Cents per Bushel	1,000 Dollars	1,000 Bushels	1,000 Bushels	Million Bushels
1911	3,532	85.7	302,713	94.6	106	286,281	1,237	13,735	
1912	3,505	115.9	406,215	56.6	62	229,890	2,028	337	
1913	3,477	95.6	332,447	67.8	78	225,386	1,794	3,646	
1914	3,417	107.8	368,249	56.2	47	207,030	3,135	271	
1915	3,433	98.1	336,760	67.4	103	227,076	4,018	210	
1916	3,274	82.6	270,388	149.7	238	404,848	2,489	3,079	
1917	3,801	104.9	398,653	127.9	129	509,728	3,453	1,180	
1918	3,597	96.2	346,114	118.8	127	411,235	3,689	3,534	
1919	3,300	90.1	297,341	190.9	284	567,742	3,723	6,941	70.0
1920	3,301	111.8	368,904	132.8	99	489,783	4,803	3,423	112.0
1921	3,598	90.4	325,312	112.8	118	366,978	2,327	2,110	88.4
1922	3,901	106.5	415,373	68.5	91	284,527	2,980	572	136.7
1923	3,378	108.5	366,356	91.4	109	334,821	3,075	564	109.5
1924	3,106	123.7	384,166	71.2	79	273,443	3,653	478	120.4
1925	2,810	105.5	296,466	165.8	249	491,482	1,824	5,420	66.3
1926	2,811	114.4	321,607	136.1	170	437,851	2,092	6,349	80.4
1927	3,182	116.2	369,644	108.5	140	400,996	2,424	3,803	104.1
1928	3,499	122.1	427,249	57.1	87	244,048	3,165	2,698	130.0
1929	3,019	110.0	332,204	131.8	180	438,006	2,386	6,006	82.9
1930	3,103	109.8	340,572	91.9	118	313,072	1,548	5,729	88.4
1931	3,467	110.8	384,125	46.3	65	177,912	816	1,493	108.2
1932	3,549	106.1	376,425	39.2	64	147,496	973	440	109.3
1933	3,412	100.3	342,306	82.1	118	281,178	721	2,102	98.4
1934	3,597	112.9	406,105	44.8	57	181,748	1,218	535	3.7
1935	3,541	109.1	386,380	59.7	106	230,809	1,790	864	106.1
1936	3,063	108.4	331,918	114.0	137	378,387	1,315	1,384	85.4
1937	3,185	124.1	395,294	52.8	75	208,785	2,079	683	113.2
1938	3,023	123.8	374,163	55.8	88	208,835	2,703	1,014	103.6
1939	3,018	120.3	363,159	69.3	115	250,199	2,746	1,732	103.3
1940	3,053	130.3	397,722						

Printed in the United States
149981LV00006B/1/P